WRITING
FOR A READER

WRITING
FOR A READER

Robert M. Brown

LITTLE, BROWN AND COMPANY
BOSTON   TORONTO

Library of Congress Cataloging-in-Publication Data

Brown, Robert M., 1946-
  Writing for a reader.

  Includes index.
    1. English language—Rhetoric. 2. College readers.
  I. Title.
  PE1408.B858 1987 808'.0427 86-21154
  ISBN 0–316–10994–0

Library of Congress Catalog
  Card No. 86–21154

ISBN 0-316-10994-0

10 9 8 7 6 5 4 3 2 1

MV

Published simultaneously in Canada
by Little, Brown & Company (Canada) Limited

Printed in the United States of America

Acknowledgments

Page 12 "Onomastics, You and Me Is Quits" by Joseph Epstein. Reprinted from *The American Scholar*, Volume 50, Number 1, Winter 1980/81. Copyright © 1980 by the author. By permission of the publisher.

Page 16 Reprinted by permission of Farrar, Straus & Giroux, Inc.: "The First Girl at Second Base" from *The Possible She* by Susan Jacoby. Copyright © 1973, 1974, 1976, 1977, 1978, 1979 by Susan Jacoby.

Page 67 From *The Presidential Papers* by Norman Mailer. Copyright © 1960, 1961, 1962 by Norman Mailer. Copyright © 1963 by Norman Mailer. Reprinted by permission of the author and the author's agents, Scott Meredith Literary Agency, Inc., 845 Third Avenue, New York, New York 10022.

Page 74 From *Shooting an Elephant and Other Essays* by George Orwell. Reprinted by permission of Harcourt Brace Jovanovich, Inc., the Estate of the late Sonia Brownell Orwell, and Martin Secker and Warburg, Ltd.

Page 75 Reprinted by permission of Hill and Wang, a division of Farrar, Straus & Giroux, Inc.: "Salvation" from *The Big Sea* by Langston Hughes. Copyright © 1940 by Langston Hughes. Copyright renewed © 1968 by Arna Bontemps and George Houston Bass.

Page 78 From *The Snow Leopard* by Peter Matthiessen. Copyright © 1978 by Peter Matthiessen. Reprinted by permission of Viking Penguin, Inc.

Page 80 From *Confessions of a Knife* by Richard Selzer. Copyright © 1979 by David Golman and Janet Selzer, Trustees. Reprinted by permission of Simon & Schuster, Inc.

Page 85 "The Car" from *Blood and Grits* by Harry Crews. Copyright © 1975 by Harry Crews. Reprinted by permission of Harper & Row, Publishers, Inc.

Page 90 From *The Duke of Deception: Memories of My Father*, by Geoffrey Wolff. Copyright © 1979 by Geoffrey Wolff. Reprinted by permission of Random House, Inc.

Page 92 © 1957 *Saturday Review* magazine. Reprinted by permission.

Page 95 From *Shooting an Elephant and Other Essays* by George Orwell, copyright 1950 by Sonia Brownell Orwell; renewed 1978 by Sonia Pitt-Rivers. Reprinted by permission of Harcourt Brace Jovanovich, Inc., and Martin Secker and Warburg, Ltd.

Page 99 From pp. 55–56 of "The Fixed" in *A Pilgrim at Tinker Creek* by Annie Dillard. Copyright © 1974 by Annie Dillard. Reprinted by permission of Harper & Row, Publishers, Inc.

Page 100 "On Hating Piano Lessons" from *Peripheral Vision* by Phyllis Theroux. Copyright © 1982 by Phyllis Theroux. By permission of William Morrow & Company.

Page 102 Reprinted from *Short Work of It* by Mark Harris by permission of the University

(continued on page 780)

Preface

When I was a novice writing instructor, full of fire and optimism, and constantly searching for ways to improve my students' writing, I made an interesting discovery: To teach is to learn. The years of teaching that followed were years of learning about the process of writing—from scholars of rhetoric, from my own mistakes, but most of all from my students. Then, with slightly less fire and perhaps with measured optimism, I became an administrator and learned even more about the process of writing, this time from graduate assistants who were supposed to be learning from me. Now I should like to share with other students and instructors those concepts and strategies that others, over the years, patiently helped me to understand.

Writing for a Reader is a compilation of ideas from classical rhetoric, insights from modern rhetoric, and practical tips from the classroom that I, teaching assistants, and our students have found useful. In that the book includes numerous readings and covers invention, argument, style, modes of discourse, research, and grammar, it is intended to be a comprehensive textbook.

The book seeks to improve writing by providing students with inventional methods, by analyzing different rhetorical strategies, and by increasing their awareness of audience. Emphasized throughout is the principle that the cognitive process is inseparable from the composing process and that the best way to cultivate writing skills is to help students discover and then critically examine their beliefs. The reciprocity between thinking and writing is indisputable: On the one hand, clear thinking is necessary for producing lucid and intelligent writing, and on the other hand the act of writing forces us to examine our current beliefs and generate new ideas. To help students formulate an appropriate rhetorical stance and select effective arguments and evidence, I stress that writing is intended for a reader, whom the writer must accommodate and convince.

Accompanying these underlying principles are several assumptions on which the text is based. One assumption is that students learn to write more effectively by understanding the *why* as well as the *how* of various rhetorical techniques. Another is that the students who populate this course are from all disciplines but have similar needs; this text is geared toward all first-year college students of average and above average writing skills. Other assumptions are that the best writing originates in a *need* to express oneself, that a good thesis requires the writer to take an intellectual risk, that dullness is an unpardonable vice in prose, that the writer should develop his or her personality in an essay, and that writing is hard work for everyone.

Throughout this book I have tried to exemplify the philosophy that teaching at its best is a kind of prompting, and accordingly my approach is characterized by flexible prescription. Those instructors who prefer proscriptive rules and set formulas will be disappointed with my approach, for I believe that rhetoric is more than a matter of rules—it requires judgment as well as correctness. I realize, however, that many students welcome some prescription and direction, and therefore I have offered practical advice where needed and, on occasion, friendly warnings.

Mostly I try to show options—different ways of seeing and saying. My goal is to increase writers' awareness of stylistic and rhetorical options by showing that a variety of approaches is available. Even more important, I try to describe the effects of each option and give the rationale for choosing one option over others so that students will develop the skills and judgment needed to make effective rhetorical choices. The best option in a particular writing situation, I stress, is determined by subject, audience, and purpose.

My approach combines the new emphasis on process and the traditional emphasis on product, and the design of the book reflects this union. Unit I explores the writing process: Chapter 1 explains the qualities of good writing by examining several student drafts and showing how an awareness of audience influences rhetorical decisions. Drawing upon recent research and on the composing procedures of professional writers, Chapter 2 analyzes the steps of the writing process and offers two models for generating ideas and for writing: the prewrite/write method and the freewriting method. Unit I is devoted solely to the process of writing, and units II, III, and IV continue that exploration by analyzing how to proceed in specific rhetorical situations.

Units II, III, and IV are arranged in an order of increasing complexity, from personal experience (II) to critical analysis (III) to persuasion (IV). The sequential movement from perceptual to conceptual modes and from interpretation to evaluation seems logical for both teaching and learning.

Most chapters in units II (Experiential Writing) and III (Modes of Exposition) follow a similar pattern. Each chapter first establishes the reasons for studying a particular mode, and current examples are given to demonstrate its relevance. Next come (a) a specific application of invention, (b) an analysis of a principle using draft essays and professional essays as examples, (c) a division of the mode into two or three subtypes, (d) an explanation of how to proceed in writing this type of essay, (e) various structures available and the appropriate times to use each, (f) potential pitfalls to avoid, (g) revision activities, (h) a summary called "Advice, Reminders, and Warnings," and (i) additional readings at the end of the chapter. The emphasis is on *showing* and *doing* instead of merely telling students about rhetorical principles. Inserted throughout each chapter are various exercises that require students to participate by applying the principles they are learning.

One of the distinguishing features of the book is the extensive and realistic treatment of argument and persuasion in Unit IV. I have devoted four lengthy chapters to argument and have tried to demonstrate in a pragmatic and uncomplicated way how students can apply the principles in their own writing. The chapter on logic, for example, not only thoroughly explains the principles of induction and deduction, but also shows students how to use a major premise to establish common ground with readers, how to move from evidence to inference, and how to translate facts to fit an audience. Chapter 12, "Psychological Strategies," explores ways of reaching and moving readers by presenting a good ethos, appealing to standard motivators, using emotional appeals, and adapting one's argument to readers. It also discusses the ethics of using these hidden persuaders. Chapter 13 is devoted entirely to structural strategies in argument. First, the classical structure is explained, analyzed, and used as an inventional pattern; then alternative structures are presented and related to the reader's attitude toward the writer's thesis. The emphasis remains throughout on the students' writing: When should they open with their thesis, and when should the thesis be delayed? Where should they put their strongest evidence? What arguments should they refute? Why should they sometimes concede points? How do they conclude an argument? The final argument chapter, proposal writing, demonstrates how to use problem-solving as an inventional device, how to anticipate objections to a proposal, and how to refute alternative proposals. Step-by-step instructions and three annotated student proposals provide students with direction in this assignment.

Although the current order reflects a definite pedagogical scheme, the book is broad enough and flexible enough to allow for variation of emphases. I recommend including chapters 1 and 2 in any scheme, but instructors may elect to emphasize certain chapters in a unit and omit others. For example, a plan that includes chapters 1, 2, 3, 5, 6, 9, and 10 would enable instructors to move more quickly into argument and would still introduce students to basic principles of audience, structure, purpose and so forth. For courses of two semesters or quarters, the first course might cover chapters 1 through 8 and Appendix I on style; the second course could begin with chapters 9 and 10, which have an argumentative edge, then cover the four chapters on argument, and integrate the research paper into those assignments.

The text includes over 50 full essays and many shorter readings, a sufficient number to preclude using an essay anthology. The selections were chosen for their excellence, appropriateness as illustrations, and diversity of style and subject. Most of the professional samples are contemporary, though examples by Swift, Fielding, Lincoln and others are included, and student essays are interspersed to show that amateur writers can also produce quality prose. Because students in most writing courses come from natural and social sciences as well as arts and humanities, the essay selections are interdisciplinary; such varied subjects as astrophysics, ballet, marsupials, nuclear winter, brain surgery, boxing, glaciers, piano lessons, and paleoanthropology are represented. In addition to acquainting students with the qualities of excellent prose and provocative theses, the readings serve as concrete illustrations of principles and strategies and demonstrate how and why the writers have made various stylistic and rhetorical choices. To increase students' *active reading*, I have composed pre-reading and post-reading questions for essays and have annotated numerous essays.

Our task as writing instructors is to teach students not only to express their ideas clearly and convincingly, but also to generate new ideas, critically analyze their beliefs and evidence, and intelligently select among options. It has been my experience that students produce what is expected of them, and therefore we should demand that they meet the intellectual challenge of realistic writing assignments. This text, whose ultimate goal is to give students the confidence and skills to approach any writing task, shows ways of meeting that challenge. It urges, and I hope requires, students to sharpen their thinking as the means of improving their writing.

Acknowledgments

Although only one name appears on the title page, this book had many contributors, and I should like to acknowledge those who helped me convert two decades of notes scribbled to myself into a more coherent and unified structure.

Thanks first go to the many students who, while striding through my class on their way to what they called the real world, paused to show me better ways of teaching, participated in my research projects, and modified some of my assumptions about writing. I had the privilege of learning also from dozens of teaching assistants, whose innovations, questions, and enthusiasm provided a constant source of enlightenment and inspiration.

Special thanks go to Robert Coogan of the University of Maryland, who introduced me to classical rhetoric and served as a model teacher, administrator, and human being.

I am indebted as well to theorists whose ideas influenced this book: Plato, Aristotle, Quintilian, Richard Whately, George Campbell, Hugh Blair, William Cairns, Wayne C. Booth, Kenneth Burke, Francis Christensen, Edward P. J. Corbett, Frank D'Angelo, Peter Elbow, Janet Emig, Linda Flower, Robert Gorrell, James Kinneavy, Richard Larson, James Moffett, Richard Ohmann, Frank O'Hare, Richard Young, and Robert Zoellner.

To colleagues around the country who reviewed the manuscript at various stages, I owe tremendous thanks: Richard Beal; William Connelly, Middle Tennessee State University; A. Harris Fairbanks, University of Connecticut; Nancy W. Johnson, Northern Virginia Community College; Russell Larson, Eastern Michigan University; William Lutz, Rutgers University; Leah Masiello; Nancy I. Sommers, Rutgers University; Edward M. Uehling, Valparaiso University; and especially Judith Stanford, Merrimack College. By challenging my opinions, these reviewers often made me rethink my approach, and by offering suggestions on style and format, they vastly improved the text and made it more teachable. The faults that remain in the book are due to my stubbornness and not to their oversight.

Several publishing persons deserve mention for their diligence and discriminating judgment. Paul O'Connell encouraged me to write this book, gave me a contract, and offered sound advice when I needed it. Dean Ragland at Cobb/Dunlop Publisher Services supervised the design of the book, kept the production rolling, and tolerated my disregard for deadlines. Cynthia Chapin, my book editor at Little, Brown, coordinated all aspects of the project with grace and competence.

A few personal thanks are also called for: to my parents, without whose sympathetic murmurs and rustic retreat I would have dropped the project on several occasions; to Shirley Strum Kenny, for giving me my first administrative job in writing even though I was young, half-learned, and audacious; to Charles Mish, for being Charles Mish; and to Sharon Storm-Brown, who endured my monomania, handled the tedious task of obtaining reprint permissions, and rescued my spirit by frequently enticing me away from the desk.

Contents

I

THE WRITING PROCESS

In Unit I we will examine what holds a reader's attention, how we can encourage the reader to accept our ideas, and how different writers compose. The questions we will explore are basic to all types of writing: What do we want to say, how should we say it, to whom do we want to say it, how can we interest readers and gain their approval, how do we start to write, and what method do we use to draft? After discussing these basic questions in Unit I, we will move on to other units that address specific writing assignments, such as how to narrate a story, how to give directions, how to write a proposal, how to write a research paper, and so on. Since all of these assignments require that we address basic questions of subject, audience, and purpose, these are the concerns that will be discussed first.

CHAPTER 1

*Considering
the Reader's
Perspective*

What "Writing for a Reader" Means

Writing for a reader means (1) that writing is other-oriented and (2) that we must therefore keep in mind the reader's needs and attitudes when we write if we are to retain that reader. To say that writing is other-oriented means, of course, that we direct our writing to other persons, not to ourselves. All of our efforts—our thinking, evidence, and clever phrases—are aimed at the persons on the other side of the page. Although this fact seems obvious, inexperienced writers often forget that they are writing for someone else and that this other person is their ultimate judge, since the reader decides whether an essay is successful or not. Remembering as we write that our essays are intended for a reader will improve our writing perhaps more than any other principle of writing.

Consider the following letter, which first-year college student Hanya C. wrote and intended to send to the campus newspaper.

The students on this campus are about the most selfish, shallow people I've ever been around. They have no social conscience whatsoever. They're a bunch of spoiled brats who spend their time loafing around, going to fraternity parties, drinking beer, and being loud and obnoxious. The thought never occurs to them to help anyone else. There are lots of ways students can contribute to persons less fortunate than themselves, but do the students on this campus donate even an hour a week of their time to help others? Of course not. They're too lazy. Blind children can remain illiterate, and people with prostheses don't concern them. The Student Center for Community Action needs volunteers to staff various positions. Try being a human being. Help someone else. Call 399-4343.

Is this letter to the editor likely to draw volunteers from the student population? Based on this appeal, would you call the number and volunteer your time? I certainly wouldn't. For one thing, the writer has insulted her readers by calling them selfish, shallow, spoiled, loud, and obnoxious brats. Instead of creating an atmosphere that encourages her readers to act as she wishes, she has damaged her cause by being rude and sounding self-righteous. Another problem is that she hasn't given her fellow students specific information about the activities for which they would be volunteering. Mentioning particular activities would not only clarify what the volunteers would be doing, but also help them to understand the need for their volunteering. For example, had Hanya listed such duties as driving a van for senior citizens once a week, helping to organize a baseball team for underprivileged youths, staffing a hotline, and reading to the blind, our social consciences would be stimulated, and we would be more inclined to offer our assistance.

A third problem is that in the one place where she is specific—the reference to blind children and to people with prostheses—the connection isn't clear. What is the connection between students being lazy and blind children remaining illiterate? A writer who keeps readers in mind will explain such connections so that readers can follow the thoughts. Hanya, however, has omitted important information: Two of the services that the Student Center for Community Action provides are reading aloud to blind students and helping people who have new artificial limbs. Still another way that she hasn't considered readers is that she uses a word that many of her fellow students may not be familiar with: *prostheses* (artificial limbs). To ensure that readers understand our message, we must use language that we think they will know.

Hanya committed two other errors: She failed to consider and understand her fellow students' situation, and she failed to open the letter on a point of agreement. Even though Hanya is a student herself, she demonstrates little understanding of the demands on students' time. Instead of analyzing the reasons that students don't volunteer, she assumes that they are all uncaring loafers who do nothing but "party." If she wants her peers to look favorably on her request, she must demonstrate that she understands their position. The reason that students don't normally do volunteer work is that they aren't aware of the possibilities or they don't have the time. In the first instance, Hanya's task is to inform them of those possibilities; in the second instance, her task is to demonstrate her understanding of the demands on their time and to convince them that they can nevertheless afford to donate a brief amount of time each week.

Because Hanya has a negative view of her fellow students as a result of not having seriously considered their situation, she opens the letter in a hostile manner. Instead, she should realize that she and they probably have similar duties and values, and she should try to build a relationship based on that foundation of similarity. A good strategy in persuasive writing is to open an essay with a statement of agreement—that is, pointing out what we and our readers have in common and can agree upon—in order to establish a rapport with readers. Once readers recognize that we are allies rather than foes, they are more inclined to listen to our propositions. Here is Hanya's revised letter:

Most of us feel that because of our busy schedules we don't have time to do volunteer work, even though we might like to help others. We have essays to write, books to read, and exams to study for, and on top of that many of us hold part-time jobs. But surely all of us can spare just one hour a week to help persons less fortunate than ourselves. There are lots of ways we could make life easier for others in our community. We could take hot meals to the elderly, read aloud to the blind, staff a hotline, drive a shuttle van for senior citizens, deliver library books to invalids, organize a baseball league for underprivileged youngsters, or help patients with new artificial limbs. Helping someone else will make you feel great. I know because I donate a couple of hours a week and it absolutely cheers me. Why don't you call the Student Center for Community Action at 399-4343 and say "I want to donate an hour a week?"

Would you be more likely to volunteer an hour a week after reading this letter in your campus newspaper? Why, or why not?

Like Hanya, we sometimes forget that we are dependent on readers for our existence as writers; without readers, no communication takes place. As the essayist E. B. White once said, "a person engaged in the flimsy business of expressing himself on paper is dependent on the large principle of being heard." We want to be heard—why else do we write?— and therefore we need readers, since without them we are simply carrying on conversations with ourselves. A writer without a reader is like an actor performing *Hamlet* without an audience, or a chef preparing an elaborate dinner without anyone to taste it. An unread essay is a meaningless creation, similar to an unmailed letter: It just sits there, having no effect on anyone. Yet our intention is usually to effect a change in readers, whether that change is in their knowledge, perception, beliefs, or behavior; that is, our intention may be to introduce readers to new ideas, to help them see something in a new way, to persuade them to accept an idea, or to convince them to act in a certain way. Although our ultimate goal is to effect some type of change, we aren't likely to achieve that goal if no one is listening. Having a reader, therefore, is essential if we are to share our ideas; without readers, those ideas die within us, and the death of an idea is no small loss.

Strategies for Wooing the Reader

Since our existence as writers depends on our having readers, we should do our best to create in readers a desire to read and accept our ideas. If we want other persons to take time from their busy schedules to read what we have to say, we must somehow entice them. The strategies for wooing readers are similar to those of courting a lover, although the goals, naturally, are a little different. Our first move to seduce readers is to put on our best behavior in order to make a good impression. To some extent, readers judge our ideas by judging us. If we appear intelligent, knowledgeable, and ethical, they are more likely to accept our ideas than if we appear uninformed, egoistical, and devious. It's just human nature. The first step in getting readers to accept our ideas is to get them to accept us. We want to show them, therefore, that we are morally trustworthy (humane, fair, truthful, well-intentioned, and honest) as well as intellectually trustworthy (perceptive, logical, well-read, pragmatic, discerning, and informed on the particular subject we're writing about). Once we have gained their trust, selling them our ideas is much easier.

In addition to presenting ourselves in a favorable light, we want to create an atmosphere that is conducive to forming a good relationship between our readers and us. Writing is a social act—that is, writers and readers participate in an interdependent relationship, with one talking and the other listening—and therefore it is subject to social graces such as respect, courtesy, and cordiality. As in any social relationship, our readers expect us to be polite and to treat them and their ideas with respect. If we don't show basic good manners, they stop reading.

Another way of encouraging readers to accept our ideas is by understanding their situation and needs, showing that our essay is relevant to their situation, and addressesing their needs. This means that we must first analyze our audience to determine what their needs and beliefs are. The next step is to tailor our argument to their specific needs. Readers want to know why they should endorse our ideas, how they will be affected, and what they have to gain from our essay. Before they will endorse an idea, most readers must feel not only that the idea is good in general, but also that it will benefit them in some specific way. To foster this sense of gain, we should communicate to readers where their interests and ours coincide on this issue. If readers feel that we are looking out for their best interest, they will be less prone to doubt our views and will more readily listen to them. If, on the other hand, we disregard their beliefs and values, they will very likely set us aside and, in essence, end our existence as writers.

Now let's consider another piece of student writing to see if the writer, Neal, has followed these principles. His topic is gun control, and he has very strong feelings on the subject.

People who believe that handguns should be abolished are unthinking and un-American. They simply don't understand the issue and what is at stake. They have no respect for the U. S. Constitution and would trample on the Bill of Rights, which guarantees "the right to keep and bear arms." Banning any kind of handgun would just be the first step to outlawing all firearms. We need guns to protect ourselves and our homes, especially in this era of high crime. The gun abolishers are a bunch of misguided zealots. They don't realize that when guns are outlawed, only outlaws will have guns. Gun control would invite criminals to loot, mug, rape, and kill. Gun control advocates would take away Americans' basic right of self-defense. And that's why I oppose gun control.

The paragraph is no doubt an accurate statement of Neal's beliefs, but is it a good way to win converts to his point of view? Who would you think are his intended readers? If you favored gun control or were undecided on this issue, would you be persuaded to change your mind because of this argument? Has Neal wooed his readers in any way? Has he established a good relationship with them? Has he served his cause well? Probably not. In fact, he has inadvertently done several things to anger readers and to increase their opposition to his point of view. Instead of treating them with respect, he has called them uncomplimentary names; instead of treating their ideas with respect, he has distorted those ideas; and instead of offering a logical argument filled with specific facts and fresh arguments, he has resorted to slogans, generalities, and worn-out arguments.

Like many fledgling writers, Neal has forgotten that he is writing for other people, whose esteem and trust he must earn before they will give him their full attention and seriously consider his point of view. Being read is a privilege that writers must earn.

APPLICATION

Rewrite Neal's argument in such a way that you gain readers' trust, show respect for their views and concerns, and convince them that your argument is sound. Assume that your readers are middle-class suburbanites who are undecided on the issue but are leaning in favor of gun control.

Reasons for Writing

There's a joke about an 8-year-old boy who had not spoken a word in his whole life. Understandably, his parents were perplexed over the child's muteness and took him to a series of psychiatrists, none of whom could discover any reason for his silence. Then one morning at breakfast the child casually announced, "The eggs are cold." The whole family dropped their forks and jaws in astonishment. At last the mother managed to compose herself sufficiently to ask the obvious question: "If you can talk, why haven't you said anything before?" "Up till now," the child replied, "everything has been okay."

The point is, we must have a reason to say something—or to write something. But one of the greatest weaknesses in student writing is lack of purpose because the writer has no strong attachment to an idea and no commitment to a point of view.

Writing must come from a need to express a relevant and innovative thought. We must feel a need to explore a problem, to clarify our thinking, to propose a solution, or to share our perceptions with others. We write to enlarge other human beings' understanding and perspective by lending to them our point of view and reasoning. As Norman Mailer once put it when asked whether he feels any obligation to his readers: "Yes. I have a consciousness now which I think is of use to them. I've got to be able to get it out and do it well, to transmit it in such a way that their experience can rise to a higher level." Writing should raise consciousness and should nurture and stimulate readers. At the same time, of course, writing can serve our own ends. Selfishly, we write to spread our beliefs and to influence readers by having them see the world as we see it. Especially in a society where freedom of expression allows all to voice their ideas, those who have a greater ability to convince others of their ideas will have a greater influence on society. We write, therefore, because we want readers to accept our ideas and to think and act in a certain way, either for the public good, our private gain, or both.

There are three basic purposes for writing: to entertain, to inform, and to persuade. The three purposes are not, of course, mutually exclusive, and the best writing accomplishes all three in some degree. For example, humorists such as Art Buchwald have as their main goal to poke fun at political figures and ideas, but they simultaneously instruct us about current events and indirectly persuade us to accept a certain view of them. Likewise, an effective argument often provides considerable information as it unfolds, and it may also entertain the reader in the process; entertainment doesn't necessarily mean drama or humor, since ideas themselves and a lively style can be highly entertaining. Finally, an expository article, whose function is purely to explain something, should inform in an entertaining manner; such an article also is indirectly argumentative because it tries to convince readers to accept our facts as truthful and to accept our interpretation of those facts. For example, our purpose might be to show readers that their information is incorrect or incomplete, in which case we are also attempting to persuade them that their perception is incorrect and that, based on the new information we provide, they should adopt our view of the issue.

To be truly informative, a writer must offer knowledge that readers do not already have. Beginning writers, however, frequently present common knowledge or simply state the obvious. Because readers don't want to read about what they already know, we should avoid material our audience probably already knows unless we can present it in a fresh way or give it a new perspective. New information, however, need not necessarily be scientific or impersonal; we can inform through our own experience and perspective. For example, if you once worked in a chicken-processing plant, visited Tibet, or skydived—anything outside of common experience—relating that experience would be considered informative.

Engaging the Reader's Interest

As readers, what we demand of an article or book above all else is that it be interesting; otherwise, we quit reading. But as writers, we seldom give much consideration to how interesting our prose is. We pay great attention to grammar, organization, accuracy of facts, and word choice, but we fail to realize that unless our writing holds sufficient interest it will not hold a reader—and therefore all the effort spent on grammar, organization, and so forth is for naught. "The first principle of aesthetics," John Cheever said, "is either interest or suspense. You can't expect to communicate with anyone if you're a bore." Since interest is what attracts readers and what keeps them turning the page, the primary question is: How can we make our writing interesting? To answer this question, perhaps we should look at it from the other side: When we read, what do we look for in an article? What keeps our attention?

Rather than originating in a single element, interest results from several things: an intriguing subject, a lively style and tone, convincing evidence that starts readers thinking, and a provocative and challenging thesis.

An Inviting Subject

Most of us are attracted first by the subject matter of an essay. The subjects that usually entice readers are current events, controversial topics (if they haven't been discussed to death), and anything that is curious or out of the ordinary. Which of the following topics would you find alluring enough to read about?

1. My favorite restaurant
2. The hazards of smoking
3. College athletes' special privileges
4. The Number One bass fisherwoman in the United States
5. The effects of airline deregulation

6. Human cloning—can it be done?
7. The dangers of nuclear power plants
8. Advantages of a small college versus a large one
9. The uses of lasers

A couple of these—topics 2 and 7—have been explored almost to the point of exhaustion, and therefore it would be difficult for a writer to state anything new about them. Overexposure diminishes a reader's curiosity from the very outset. It would also be difficult to say anything new about topics 3 and 8 because everyone on campus already knows what the writer would probably say. An individual reader's taste and inclination would determine the appeal of the other topics, though topic 5 sounds a little dull unless you travel frequently or work in the airline industry. I would most likely read topic 4 because it suggests a departure from the usual, but of the other topics I would probably read the first few paragraphs to see whether the writer could interest me. Although we should be able to make almost any subject interesting, the less tempting the subject inherently is, the harder we will have to work to make it worth reading. Starting with a subject that has an inherently high level of interest certainly makes the writer's job easier, but I've read delightful essays on tennis shoes and boring ones on sex. It takes more than a marketable subject to ensure interest.

A Lively Style

Having a lively style can help to retain a reader's interest even when the subject isn't fresh or unusual. Using strong verbs, crisp diction, figurative language, and emphatic sentence structure (these are discussed in Chapters 16 and 17) helps to hold the pleased attention of a reader. But making our prose energetic and vigorous is not simply a duty to readers; it's also a source of pleasure for ourselves because we derive a certain pride in creating a spirited piece of writing. As Robert Frost said, "All the fun's in how you say a thing." Part of the way we say a thing is the tone or attitude we take toward our subject, and since we can assume any attitude we wish, our tone can be critical, frivolous, angry, buoyant, ironic, or humble. We can create interest in a potentially dull topic by infusing it with wit or by taking an unexpected tone—for example, treating a serious topic whimsically. Notice how the writer of the following passage takes a common topic—people's names—and makes it interesting primarily through the style:

Show me a man or woman entirely happy with his or her name and I'll show you a somehow defective human being. Our name is another of those decisive items in life that we have not been called in to decide upon, another card dealt us while we were away from the table, along with the quality of our intelligence, our physique, the geographical and social location of our birth. However suitable it may appear to others, one's own name almost always seems rather a poor fit to oneself. But there it is, like a shoe that either pinches or flops loosely over the heel, and such as it is we are compelled to wear it through life. Names not our own generally seem more appropriate to us. For myself, had I been given a choice in my own name, I think I might have been content with Julian Havilan, or Jean-Louis Beaumarchais, though in earlier years the name Blackie Thurston had a certain ineffable allure for me.

—From Aristides (pseudonym),
"Onomastics, You and Me Is Quits," *American Scholar*

Convincing Evidence

The primary purpose of presenting evidence, of course, is to prove our point. By offering facts, examples, quotations, observations, and other types of evidence (Chapter 11 includes a detailed discussion of evidence), we establish the truthfulness of our assertions, and the more evidence we muster, the stronger case we make for our thesis. But the amount of evidence we offer is not the only consideration; the freshness of the evidence and its relevance to our particular audience are also important. We have to find evidence that our readers haven't heard before and then translate it into terms that are meaningful to our readers.

The value of evidence must be judged by the effect it has on readers. Some facts lack impact because they are general and dull or because they have not been made relevant to readers. Other facts cause readers to sit up and pay attention because we have made them relevant, specific, and dramatic. Obviously, we want to use the dramatic type. Here is a mundane fact: American high school students watch an average of 17 hours of television a week. Now here is that same information translated into a dramatic fact: By the time American students graduate from high school, they have watched an average of 13,000 hours of television, compared with 11,000 hours of being in the classroom. Other examples:

> General fact: The 55-mile-per-hour speed limit that was imposed in 1975 has saved lives and gasoline.

> Specific fact: The 55-mile-per-hour speed limit has saved approximately 9,000,000 gallons of gasoline a day and 7,000 lives a year, according to the National Safety Council.

> Mundane fact: Fewer American families today can afford to buy homes than they could several decades ago.

> Arresting fact: "In 1950, seven out of ten American families had sufficient income to purchase a medium-sized house. By November 1978, seven in ten did not." (from James Dale Davidson)

Obvious fact: Because wildlife draws tourists to Africa, wildlife parks in Africa can be a source of revenue for African nations.

Convincing fact: Because of tourism, wildlife parks in Africa bring in a hundred times more money per acre than a farm or ranch could on that same land.

Most people find the dramatic fact interesting because they have inquiring minds that welcome new knowledge, and this kind of evidence satisfies their curiosity. Readers will find interesting any evidence that translates a generalization into understandable terms, that tailors facts to the readers' situation, that corrects a common misperception, or that provokes them to thought. At the same time that we are using evidence to convince readers of the soundness of our thesis, we should be stimulating them intellectually and thereby entertaining them.

Another important function of evidence is to demonstrate that we are knowledgeable about an issue. Evidence lends us credibility. Whenever we pull a fact out of our hat, we implicitly communicate to readers that we have a thorough command of the subject. When readers think that we know what we're writing about, they tend to trust us; and when they trust us, they accept our thesis more readily.

APPLICATION

How might you translate these general facts into dramatic facts for the audience indicated?

Example: Each year thousands of Americans are killed with handguns.

Audience: black Americans

Task: Find out the specific death rate by handguns for blacks, and if possible narrow the sample to the group that would have the highest death rate by handguns. (Chapter 15 lists various reference works where you can find such statistics.)

[Dramatic fact: Murder by handguns is the leading cause of death among black males between the ages of 16 and 25.]

1. The debt problems of Third World countries such as Brazil, Mexico, Venezuela, Chile, and Nigeria affect Americans because those nations now import fewer American products.

   Audience: U.S. farmers

   Task:

2. The Florida Everglades is shrinking each year.

   Audience: environmentalists

   Task:

3. Many college students now have computers to help in their studies.

   Audience: your parents

   Task:

A Provocative Thesis

Perhaps the best way to achieve a high level of interest in an essay is to start with a provocative thesis. (The thesis is the central proposition that we set out to prove.) Instead of examining the concept of thesis from our point of view as writers, we might gain more insight by looking at it from the readers' viewpoint: What is it that readers demand in a thesis? What engages their interest?

Most readers want an innovative, bold thesis that stimulates, challenges, and educates them. They want their imaginations sparked and their intellects stirred. They want to read ideas they haven't considered before, and they usually want ideas that relate to them in some way.

A good thesis grabs readers by the shoulders, gives them a quick shake, and jostles their brains out of complacency and passivity. By disturbing their mental calm, it forces readers to react, ask questions, and perhaps even take issue with the thesis. It should cause them to question their beliefs, see the subject in a different light, or rethink the issue. Consider, for example, the thesis statements below and determine what makes them provocative or what makes you want to read the essays that would develop from these ideas:

> Ideals inhibit thinking.
> Most people make too few mistakes in their lives.
> The majority of Americans are too patriotic.
> Students planning to enter medical school should major in the humanities and minor in science.

These thesis statements pique our interest because we want to know why the writers hold their views and we want to hear their explanations. A provocative thesis makes readers ask "why?" or "how?" How do ideals inhibit thinking? Why should people make more mistakes in their lives? How can people be too patriotic? Why should premed students major in philosophy or literature instead of in biology or zoology?

Once we recognize what readers expect in a thesis, we will be less likely to settle for mundane theses that state the obvious and the accepted. Most of us come up with mundane theses because we don't think about a reader's need for freshness, or we don't explore the subject sufficiently, or we don't stretch ourselves intellectually. It takes a bold and energetic mind to formulate an exciting and novel thesis, but if you didn't have that kind of mind you wouldn't be in college.

Now that we have analyzed the general qualities of a good essay, we need to examine the process by which we discover and develop a provocative thesis. How do we find a subject that will interest our readers as well as us? How do we generate a tough, thoughtful thesis? Where do we get fresh, convincing evidence to prove our thesis? And how do we compose? These are the questions we will address in Chapter 2, "Exploring How Writers Compose."

Exercises

1. Write a short paper analyzing your own writing ability. Specifically, address these questions:
   A. What are your strengths and weaknesses as a writer?
   B. Why do you think you write excellently, competently, adequately, or badly?
   C. What would you like to accomplish in this course?

2. Find an effective editorial in a newspaper or a news magazine (such as *Time* or *Newsweek*), analyze it, and bring it to class. Be ready to discuss these questions:
   A. What is the thesis, and is that thesis provocative?
   B. Is the evidence new and interesting, and are individual facts dramatic?
   C. Does the editorial inform while it is trying to persuade?
   D. Is the argument convincing?
   E. In what ways has the writer taken into consideration his or her readers?
   F. Is the style lively or dull?
   G. Does the writer seem knowledgeable, ethical, and intelligent?

3. Apply the principles discussed in Chapter 1 to the following essay. You may wish to use these questions as a guide:
   A. What is the writer's intent in this essay? Does the essay entertain, inform, persuade, or achieve a combination of these? Explain.
   B. What is the thesis? Does it cause you to think? Is it challenging in any way? Has the writer convinced you of the truthfulness of her thesis?
   C. If you find the essay interesting, what in it holds your interest—the style, facts, subject, or thesis? Elaborate on your answer. If you do not find the essay interesting, why not?

D. Does Jacoby seem to be a reasonable, intelligent, and likable writer? How would you describe her based on what she says and how she says it? Support your description with examples from her essay.

E. How does she infuse human warmth into the essay to keep it from being a cold, impersonal discussion?

THE FIRST GIRL AT SECOND BASE

Susan Jacoby

Between the ages of seven and ten, I spent a good deal of time dreaming of the day I   1
would follow in the footsteps of my hero, Jacob Nelson (Nellie) Fox, and play second base for the Chicago White Sox. The crowd would roar as I stepped up to the plate in the bottom of the ninth with two out, runners on second and third, and the Sox trailing by one run. The roar would turn to whoops of joy as I, like the ever-reliable Nellie, punched a game-winning hit through the infield.

In endless conversations between innings at Comiskey Park, I badgered my   2
grandfather about my desire to break the sex barrier in major league baseball. Nellie was small for a ballplayer—the sportscasters called him "Little Nell"—and it was quite possible that I might grow up to be as tall as he was. If Jackie Robinson (another of my heroes) could become the first Negro in the big leagues, there was no reason why Susan Jacoby could not become the first girl on the diamond. No reason at all, my grandfather agreed. He was too softhearted to point out the facts of life to a granddaughter he had helped turn into a baseball nut.

Not all of my childhood heroes were sports figures, but they all had one thing in   3
common: They were men. The most important nonsportsman in my pantheon was Franklin D. Roosevelt, who captured my imagination not because of anything he had done as President but because he had overcome polio. I associated heroism not only with courage but with the sort of courage that is expressed in a visible, physical way. I had never heard of any woman who embodied my notions of what a hero did and was.

When I questioned my women friends about their childhood heroes, an ex-   4
traordinary number insisted they never had any. Of those who did remember, all but one acknowledged that their heroes had been men. It turned out that the exception— a woman who said Margaret Sanger had been her hero—was speaking from a newly acquired feminist consciousness rather than from any true memory of childhood.

When I asked men the same question, nearly all of them immediately produced   5
long lists of heroes. All-male lists. Not a single man grew up with a woman for a hero. In fact, it seems that Eleanor Roosevelt was the only public woman (apart from movie stars) whose achievements impinged upon the consciousness of boys who were growing up in the 1930's, 40's, and 50's.

Growing up in a culture with male criteria for heroism undoubtedly exerts its   6
influence on a boy's image of women. For a girl, though, the matter is more personal and more crucial: Her image of herself is at stake. Hero worship confined to the opposite sex—a phenomenon that seems to have been almost universal among

women of my generation and almost nonexistent among men—poses a psychological problem on at least two levels.

On the surface level—the rational one—the problem is obvious and solvable.   7
Reggie Jackson, who brought on a bad relapse of my baseball hero worship by hitting three home runs in the final game of this year's World Series, is just my age. I was not at all surprised to read in the sports pages that Jackie Robinson had been Reggie's hero as well as mine. The difference between us, of course, is that Reggie Jackson could grow up to play his hero's game.

The feminist movement has a sensible answer to the predicament of a girl who,   8
having been born the wrong sex, can never grow up to be like her hero. Feminists say: "Give us our rightful place in the history books, establish equal opportunity for women now, and soon we'll have our share of heroes." Fair enough. A girl who dreams of achievement in sports or politics or law or medicine certainly has more women to emulate today than girls did when I was growing up.

The sensible feminist solution would be enough if a hero were only an object of   9
emulation. The true function of the hero, however, lies in the realm of imagination. Most boys, after all, are no more likely to grow up to be Jackie Robinson than I was. Heroes give a child access to what the novelist Cynthia Ozick calls "the grand as if." When a young girl dreams of heroes, she dreams as if she were free: Limitations of height or weight or sex or race become irrelevant. A hero represents not so much a specific achievement as a whole range of human possibilities, an awe-inspiring glimpse of perfection.

On this level of awe and myth, it is difficult to develop a feminist alternative to   10
the cultural values that have made both men and women regard heroism as a male characteristic. Heroism has almost always been linked with physical prowess and strength: Moral and physical courage are inseparable in most heroic sagas. This ideal of the hero places women at a disadvantage, because most societies have imposed severe restraints on public displays of female strength. Even today, when many of those restraints have crumbled, women are still at a disadvantage if the traditional concept of the hero is upheld. There is no getting around the fact that most men are stronger than most women.

Many adults talk about the need to smash traditional notions of heroism by   11
stressing the moral rather than the physical aspects of courage. It sounds like a good idea, but I suspect these adults haven't been talking to many kids. In a sampling of my favorite ten-to-twelve-year-old girls, I elicited the name of just one woman hero: Billie Jean King. One of the girls expressed regret that her hero had trounced the aging Bobby Riggs rather than a man her own age. Two girls said their hero was the great Brazilian soccer player Pelé, and two others, to my delight, mentioned Reggie Jackson. (I admit I spoke to the girls just a few days after the dramatic ending of the World Series.) One eleven-year-old said her ambition was to become a pilot. . . . So much for adult notions of dispensing with physical daring and achievement as standards of heroism.

There are people who think the end of the traditional hero would produce more   12
realistic men and women. I doubt it. I still remember the pure joy I took in my

baseball-playing fantasies. Doing well under extreme pressure was an important element in my fantasies, and that ideal is certainly suitable for any "realistic" adult. To dream as if you were free is a moving and beautiful experience—so beautiful that many adults feel obliged to forget it. I wish some of those dreams had come to me in the form of my own as well as of the opposite sex. Things ought to have changed by now, but it seems that barriers to women are more formidable in the world of heroes than in union hiring halls or executive suites.

—From *The Possible She*

CHAPTER 2

Exploring How Writers Compose

This chapter explores ways that writers write: how we come up with ideas and evidence, how we start writing, and how we proceed from idea to essay. Most of us have a set way of writing that we use without conscious thought and without considering its effectiveness. This chapter encourages you to examine your own writing process and shows you an alternative way of proceeding. While there is no one standardized procedure that everyone should follow, we *can* analyze the process we use and, if necessary, alter it to improve the final product.

Improving a process is usually the way of improving a product. If you were a potter and your urns turned out ill-formed or crumbly, you probably would scrutinize your throwing or firing techniques to determine a better method. When your pottery falls to pieces, you say "I must have done something wrong"; but when your essay doesn't turn out well, you tend to say "I can't write." Both tasks, however, result from a process and constitute learned skills. Many of us may find writing frustrating because the steps we go through are inefficient, or because the method we use isn't appropriate for a particular assignment.

Using the following questions as guidelines, examine your own writing process:

Where do I primarily find my ideas for a paper—from memory, research, casual reading, conversations, or class discussions?

How do I start writing? Do I jot down notes and outline my thoughts, or do I launch into the first draft without preliminary activities?

If I outline, do I outline before I start to write, after I have written part of a draft, or after I have completed the final draft?

What do I usually write first—the introduction, a portion of the body, or the conclusion?

Do I write nonstop, or do I stop and revise as I go along?

Do I usually start with a thesis, or does one evolve as I write?

Do I usually stick with my original thesis, or does it often change during drafts?

Once I have a first draft, do I revise it, or do I write a totally new second draft?

What do I usually change from one draft to another—the order of paragraphs, the sentence structure, the word choice, the examples, or the main idea?

Do I find that in general I add or delete material while revising?

Do I work better under pressure from a deadline or without time constrictions?

Where do I write best—at my desk, on the sofa, or in bed?

Do I compose in longhand, or do I use a typewriter or word processor?

When do I write best—morning, afternoon, or evening?

Under what conditions do I write best—in silence, while watching television, or while listening to radio?

What is my biggest problem in writing—getting started, finding a thesis, finding evidence, organizing, or revising? What solutions have I tried to overcome this problem?

What kind of writing do I like best—descriptions, stories, arguments, or explanations? Why? What kind of writing do I like least, and why?

Do I use the same process for all writing projects, or do I use one process for a certain type of assignment and another for a different type?

APPLICATION

Write a one-page description of your writing process. You may find that with certain writing tasks you use one process and with other tasks you follow another procedure. If that is the case, specify what kind of assignment goes with each procedure and explain how the procedures differ.

Although there are many variations in the ways people write, the majority of writers seem to use two basic patterns. The first pattern, which most of us were taught to use, might be called the "prewrite/write method" because before we begin actual writing, we do a series of important prewriting activities such as generating ideas, formulating a solid thesis, generating support for that thesis, and then organizing the material. The other pattern is called "freewriting" because instead of thinking through the thesis and organization before writing, we just write nonstop until we discover what we want to say and how we want to organize it.

We will explore both models to discover the merits of each and to decide when each seems appropriate. In addition to helping us locate and overcome any problems in our writing process, an analysis of the way we write should take some of the mystery out of the writing process and therefore decrease our anxiety about writing.

The Prewrite/Write Method

The traditional way of looking at writing has been to see it as a linear process (that is, proceeding along a straight line) that has three stages:

prewriting	writing	revising

According to this method of writing, before we begin the first draft we engage in several activities, including exploring a subject, formulating and testing a thesis, gathering evidence, and outlining the essay. The topic, thesis, and structure are sharply focused in this first stage. The second stage is drafting the essay. The third is revising the logic, organization, and style. Roughly, the steps are *think*, *write*, and *revise*.

Although this approach works well for some writers, many who use it have difficulty because they slight the first stage. We have to remember that generating ideas is an essential first step in the writing process, since writing is as concerned with generating ideas as with presenting them. Even if we already have a thesis—usually our reason for writing in the first place is to express a strong opinion—we need a method of generating evidence to support that thesis. When we have not decided on a thesis or when we must find both a topic and a thesis, a formal system of generating ideas is indispensable.

Invention: Using Journalistic Questions

The student complaint that I have heard most often over 15 years of teaching has been "I don't have anything to say." The complaint always surprises me because I know that every student has had insightful experiences, has struggled with ethical dilemmas, has formed opinions about diverse subjects, and has laughed at the absurdities of modern life. Simply from having lived to adulthood in the twentieth century and from having thought about themselves and the world around them, students have plenty to write about.

I finally realized that the complaint "I don't have anything to say" was actually another kind of complaint: "I don't know how to retrieve and then focus my thoughts." My students admitted that they didn't know how to judge which of their experiences would be interesting, or how to make an apparently common subject into something worth reading. Although they felt alone in this respect, their difficulty in coming up with a subject and thesis is typical of most writers' experience. In fact, the problem of discovering what to say causes even veteran writers to pull their hair, gnash their teeth, and stare at the blank paper. Most of us sit around waiting for a thesis to fall out of the sky into our lap, preferably a clearly focused and already substantiated thesis, or waiting to be moved by some unknown force called "inspiration," though the force is seldom with us. We wait and wait, until we have cultivated a good case of writer's block.

Fortunately, there are methods to help us overcome writer's block and explore subjects. Called "methods of invention" because they help us generate or invent ideas, they are systematic procedures designed to jostle memory, to retrieve stored thoughts and knowledge, to stimulate our rational faculties, and to lubricate our imaginations—in other words, to open the faucets of our minds and let ideas flow.

Although the process of generating ideas is not completely understood, and although it is neither mechanical nor totally rational, we can nevertheless aid the process by using an inventional system. The brain is like a gigantic computer that sorts and files information in clusters, and just as we can retrieve information from a computer by giving it certain commands, we can retrieve information from the brain. But an inventional method is not simply a means of retrieving information; it is also a means of stimulating thinking that leads to new knowledge. When we retrieve stored information, that information sparks new ideas, leads to new paths of inquiry, and ultimately helps us to see the subject in a new way.

One inventional method that has proved useful and easy for writers is the journalistic method of asking six types of questions: who, what, when, where, how, and why. Journalists have traditionally relied upon this approach to ensure that they are covering all the details of a news story, and because of its practicality and simplicity other writers over the years have borrowed the method.

The philosophy behind this approach is that writers are first of all inquirers and that the first step in writing should be formulating the right questions about a subject. Often, our reason for writing is to explore a question that intrigues or haunts us: What causes glaciers to advance and then retreat? How do artificial hearts function? Why do female human beings, alone among primates, have hymens? What would the United States do if the Russians invaded another adjacent state, such as Iran, as they invaded Afghanistan? At the outset of the writing process we feel a need to analyze a situation, to explain our feelings about a topic, to comprehend the motivation or behavior of others, to explore an inconsistency, or simply to satisfy our curiosity about the nature of the subject. The journalistic method of inquiry allows us to analyze a subject or an issue in a systematic way.

Although we may decide not to include in our essay all the information we generate from the journalistic questions, such information will help us to understand the total issue and to form an intelligent thesis; then we can select from the body of information those facts that substantiate our thesis. The journalistic method is so flexible it can be used to dissect any conceivable subject, and it is comprehensive because we can formulate one round of questions after another until we completely understand a subject. As an example, let's apply these questions to a specific subject: a terrorist hijacking of a commercial airline and the ensuing rescue of the passengers. Through a systematic probing using the six key questions, we should be able to cover all angles of the hijacking and rescue so that we could then write on some aspect of the subject.

Questions About Our Subject

WHO: the individuals, organizations, and nations involved. Try to look at the question of "who" from all perspectives, examining those parties indirectly affected as well as those directly affected.

Who were the hijackers (nationality, number, names, experience, affiliation)?

Who was the leader of the hijackers?

Who planned the piracy?

Who supported the hijackers?

Who trained the terrorists?

Who helped the terrorists get through airport security?

Who were the passengers (nationalities, number, prominent names)?

Who were the airline personnel on board (number, captain's name, previous experience with hijackers)?

Who gave permission for the plane to take off for a different country after it was hijacked?

Who organized the rescue team?

Who were the members of the rescue team (nationality, number,
  leader)?
Who plotted the rescue?
Who opposed/supported a rescue attempt?
Who was the official representing American interests?
Who were the main negotiators?
Who decided to send in the counterterrorist team?
Who was killed?

WHAT: events and effects. In addition to looking at what happened,
examine the consequences of the event on the various parties identified in "who."

What did the terrorists hope to achieve?
What airplane was hijacked?
What, if anything, was unique about this hijacking?
What is the relationship between this hijacking and previous
  ones?
What is the United States policy in such situations?
What were the terms of the negotiations?
What were the alternatives to a rescue attempt?
What should have been done?
What, if anything, went wrong with the rescue?
What political factors influenced the way the negotiations and
  rescue were handled?
What did the United States do to facilitate the release of its
  citizens?
What happened to the terrorists?
What will be the immediate political consequences of this hijack-
  ing on the concerned nations?
What will be the long-term political effects?
What will be the economic effects, if any?
What are the lasting psychological effects of being a hostage in
  these situations?
What is the psychological profile of the typical terrorist?
What does the world community plan to do about terrorism?
What is the history of terrorism?
What is the history of the terrorist organization that carried out
  the hijacking?
What does terrorism in general say about the world of today?

WHEN: time—past, present, and future. Ask questions not only about
the present occurrence, but also about the background and probable
future occurrences.

When did the hijacking occur, and is this a significant date, such
  as the anniversary of another event?

When did the counterterrorist team arrive?
When did the rescue occur, and how long did the siege last?
When are the surviving terrorists scheduled for trial?
When was this terrorist organization formed?

WHERE: place. Questions of place should be as specific as possible; that is, ask not only about the country in which the hijacking occurred, but also about the actual position of the main players at key moments.

Where did the hijacking occur?
Where was the plane coming from and going to?
Where did the terrorists plan to take the plane?
Where did they plan to hide after the mission?
Where did they board the plane?
Where were they trained?
Where did the negotiations occur?
Where have other piracies occurred?
Where in the plane were the hijackers when the rescue team stormed the plane?
Where are the terrorists now?
Where were the American passengers taken after the rescue?
Where is the most likely place in the world for planes to be hijacked?

HOW: procedure. Ask questions that will get a detailed description of the steps of the hijacking.

How did the terrorists smuggle weapons aboard the plane?
How did they overpower the crew?
How did they treat the hostages?
How did they demonstrate the seriousness of their threats?
How do terrorists justify killing to call attention to their own unjust treatment?
How was the counterterrorist team transported to the scene?
How did the counterterrorist team get aboard the plane?
How did the rescuers overpower the hijackers?
How was this operation similar to or different from previous hijackings and rescues?
How should rescues ideally be conducted?
How should one negotiate with terrorists?
How can hijackings be averted in the future?

WHY: causes. Try to explore the psychological, social, political, and economic causes.

Why did the terrorists strike?
Why did they select this particular flight?

Why did they feel that their people had been unjustly treated?
Why is there a continued state of undeclared war between the
   nations involved?
Why did negotiations break down?
Why did the terrorists murder selected passengers?
Why did they allow certain passengers to go free?
Why didn't the terrorists carry out their threats?
Why were the terrorists allowed to take the plane to another
   country?
Why did the second country allow the plane to land?
Why weren't the terrorists' demands met?
Why did the responsible official give the order to storm the plane?
Why was the rescue successful?
Why do people resort to terrorism?

Each new topic, of course, invites its own particular questions, but
the approach remains the same: who, what, when, where, how, and why.

The journalistic approach requires not only common sense and an
inquisitive intellect, but also diligence. Asking a few obvious questions is
easy, but we can't settle for the superficial and the obvious. We have to
ask detailed questions that probe all areas of an event, issue, or object
because the more questions we ask, the more we learn about the topic.
Also, the answer to one question helps to form another question. Instead
of quitting when we have the answers to our first round of questions, we
must use those answers to spark more questions until we have no more
questions. By asking questions, follow-up questions, and more follow-up
questions, we eventually narrow the topic to a manageable size and find a
portion of the topic that intensely engages our attention. The first round
of answers is usually asked just to explore the subject generally and to
inform ourselves of its nature; the follow-up questions are the ones that
lead us to a thesis. But the method works only if we are absolutely
relentless in our quest for answers and for more questions. It takes an
imaginative thinker and an untiring inquirer to chase after answers and
to keep probing a subject.

APPLICATION

Using the journalistic method, make an extensive list of first-round questions to
guide yourself in exploring one of the following subjects:

1. movies made from novels
2. congresswomen
3. the decline of labor unions
4. Bruce Springsteen
5. flamenco dancing

6. hang gliding
7. guide dogs
8. black holes
9. endangered United States birds
10. black television sitcoms

Questions About Our Readers

In addition to asking questions about the subject, we should also ask a few about our intended audience. By learning about our readers' beliefs, values, and interests, we generate approaches to our material and discover ways of interesting readers in our thesis. Reader analysis is especially useful in forming argumentative essays, where we need to know how to appeal to readers' sense of fairness and also know what objections they may have to our proposition. For example, if we were arguing that *Math 220* should be required for all science majors, we would have to know who our audience was, whether they favored or opposed our proposal, and why they held that opinion. If our readers were college administrators, who would probably favor the idea, we would use a line of argument and a set of appeals different from those we would use if our readers were classmates, who might view this new course requirement as just another obstacle to graduating. Even in essays that are not primarily argumentative, we need to know something about our audience in order to gauge how much background information to present and how sophisticated our discussion should be. If readers already know a great deal about the subject, we can quickly summarize the background material and go on to the body of the essay, but if they have hardly heard of the topic, we must carefully inform them about it in a lengthy background section.

Here are some basic questions to ask in order to discover the nature of our audience:

Who are my intended readers?
What are their characteristics: level of education, social class, political philosophy, age range, profession?
What is their attitude toward my thesis: for, against, or indifferent?
What reasons do they have for opposing my thesis?
What misperceptions or misinformation do the readers hold that I must correct?
What values do my readers and I have in common that I can build upon?
How can I overcome their indifference and woo their interest?
How much background do they have on the subject?

There are also several important questions regarding what we want readers to do as a result of reading our essay. Most writing has as its goal some kind of change on the readers' part: a change in knowledge, perception, belief, or action. Are we trying to create an opinion in readers who at present have no opinion on the subject? Are we trying to reinforce an opinion they already hold? Are we trying to change an existing opinion? Or are we trying to get them to act on an opinion? These are somewhat different tasks and therefore may require different strategies. Whatever our goal—to make readers aware of a situation, instill in them a conviction about a situation, urge them to act on a situation, or all three (awareness-conviction-action)—we must know who our readers are and how to motivate them to change.

Questions About Ourselves

The same method that we use to explore a subject and an audience can be used with ourselves to discover how we feel about a topic. To formulate a thesis on a subject, we have to bring to a conscious level our total response to a subject, and we can do this with systematic introspection and self-questioning.

> How do I feel about the subject? Am I indifferent, angered, amused, skeptical, astonished, or supportive?
>
> Why do I react the way I do toward the subject?
>
> What is my motivation for wanting to write on this subject?
>
> How does the subject fit into my value system?
>
> How does the subject affect me, my family, or my friends?
>
> When have I experienced or when will I experience this subject?
>
> Where can I find more information about this subject?

In summary, the journalistic questions are a method of tapping a valuable source: ourselves. We can use this method to explore a subject, analyze our readers, and discover our attitude toward that subject. By using these questions to activate our intellects and focus our attention on a particular subject, we will discover that we have much more to say about a subject than we had thought at first. Each of us is a storehouse of experiences, visual images, stories, facts, fears, wit, love, imperfections, opinions, and insights, all of which can be called to a conscious level for use in writing. These questions help us to discover not only what we know about a subject, but also what we don't know about it so that we may fill in any gaps in our knowledge. If we keep asking questions, we will forge ahead to new knowledge and make new discoveries—fulfilling the ultimate goal of an inventional method.

Generating a Provocative Thesis

Our journalistic method of inquiry will probably yield two types of opinions: conventional ones, which are inoffensive, respectable, and widely held; and unconventional ones, which are unorthodox, controversial, and original. While there is nothing wrong with holding conventional opinions, our readers probably hold the same opinions. The unconventional opinion is the kind that will interest and challenge readers, so for writing, the unconventional idea is preferable.

Taking Intellectual Risks

Each of us harbors combative, unpopular, scrappy ideas, and the goal of an inventional system is to locate these maverick ideas. After we have discovered one, however, we are sometimes reluctant to state and defend it because we don't want to be considered different. But taking intellectual risks is the obligation of a writer. Rather than suppress these products of independent and original thinking, we should examine them closely, substantiate them, and then share them with readers.

The world would be a much different place if original thinkers had suppressed their controversial ideas. For example, the philosopher Democritus in the fifth century B.C. advanced the "absurd" idea that everything was composed of minute invisible particles—called atoms. In 1492, a daring Italian postulated that the world was round, and he presented so persuasive an argument that the king and queen of Spain funded his trip to the Bahamas. In the sixteenth century, despite theological opposition, Copernicus offered the astounding thesis that the sun, not the earth, is the center of our planetary system. In the nineteenth century, after accumulating and analyzing data on nature, Charles Darwin offered his highly controversial theory of evolution, and then Freud offered an equally controversial theory of human psychology. At the start of the twentieth century, the free-spirited Isadora Duncan rebelled against ballet, took off her shoes, and created modern dance, while Pablo Picasso was challenging traditional art and developing cubism. In 1927 a Belgian astronomer proposed the bizarre idea that the universe was once a cosmic egg that exploded, resulting in a "Big Bang" and the formation of galaxies. More recently, imaginative thinkers have given us the theories of plate tectonics and black holes.

These thinkers weren't afraid of taking intellectual risks; instead, they observed, analyzed, questioned, and then formulated a thesis and backed it up with logic and evidence. Knowledge of the subject through observations and questioning is essential, but a good thesis requires combining that knowledge with creative, unconventional thinking.

APPLICATION

Name two discoveries or theories in your major field of study that required the inventor to go against traditional wisdom, and explain why his or her thinking was considered controversial or unorthodox.

Naturally, no one expects first-year college students to formulate such extraordinary theories as those above, but it's not too much to expect fresh and provocative ideas that engage a reader's intellect and imagination. The British writer J. B. Priestley said that his intention in essays is "to provoke thought and discussion, chiefly by their refusal to treat routine topics in a routine fashion." That should be our intention as well.

Generating a fresh and provocative thesis usually requires (1) refusing to accept traditional ways of viewing a subject and (2) going out on a limb. (This doesn't mean, however, that we should adopt a position simply because it is controversial, or that we should offer a provocative thesis that we can't defend with sound evidence.) Here are a few examples of the kinds of unconventional opinions that make good theses. Notice that each goes against traditional thinking, stimulates us to rethink an issue, and makes us want to read on to discover why the writers think as they do and how they can defend their propositions.

> "Solar energy is potentially the most polluting and ecologically threatening form of commercial power being proposed in the world today." (From "There Goes the Sun," Donald C. Winston)

> General Custer's men were not slaughtered by the Indians as is commonly thought; Custer's men, who were mainly inexperienced recruits, panicked and committed mass suicide. (From *Keep the Last Bullet for Yourself,* Thomas B. Marquis)

> All illicit drugs—including heroin, LSD, and cocaine—should be legalized, taxed, and regulated for quality because, as is, the laws infringe on an individual's right of choice, artificially drive up the price, invite organized crime, and make quality control impossible. (From "The Ethics of Addiction," Thomas S. Szasz)

> "If we were not provided with the knack of being wrong, we could never get anything useful done" since mistakes often result in new ideas and solutions. This capacity for daily mistakes "is a uniquely human gift, perhaps even stipulated in our genetic instructions." (From "To Err Is Human," Lewis Thomas)

> "I define as most seriously overpopulated that nation whose people by virtue of their numbers and activities are most rapidly decreasing the ability of the land to support human life. With our large population, our affluence and our technological monstrosities the United States wins first place by a substantial margin." (From "Overpopulated America," Wayne H. Davis)

APPLICATION

Find two interesting theses in magazines or newspaper editorials, write them down, and bring them to class with the title of the article and the name of the publication.

Looking at the Usual in a New Way

As these writers have done, we must learn to question conventional ways of seeing a subject and not allow traditional modes of thinking to obscure our vision. After we have retrieved all the information we have on a subject, we need to ask two more questions:

> What have been the traditional ways of viewing this subject?
> What are alternative ways of viewing it?

Creative thinking is often nothing more than looking at the routine or usual in a new way, which means making associations between ideas that traditionally haven't gone together. In other words, what we call *originality* often is simply the combination of two or more old facts in a new way. Such insights occur because the brain has somehow scrambled ideas, broken down an old perception, and forged a new relationship between two bits of information. The question is, how can we encourage the mind to alter its usual patterns and to connect ideas in unprecedented patterns?

Put simply, how can we increase our creative thinking and generate a fresh thesis? First, we must resolve not to settle for an obvious, safe, mediocre thesis. Once we recognize the characteristics of a good thesis and are determined not to accept anything less, we are well on the way to generating a good thesis. Second, we must continue to use our inventional method. It is intended not only to jostle our memories and call up our current opinions, but also to break through accustomed patterns of thought that hinder fresh perception. An inventional method can help us to see new relationships among ideas, to shift our perspective, and to propose a thesis that runs counter to conventional ones. Third, we can cultivate a mind-set that is at once skeptical and open. Although we must be skeptical of conventional thinking, we must also be open to seemingly offbeat views and not censor new ideas before we have had a chance to explore them.

Most geniuses responsible for the major mutations in the history of thought seem to have certain features in common; on the one hand scepticism . . . in their attitude towards traditional ideas, axioms and dogmas, towards everything that is taken for granted; on the other hand, an open-mindedness that verges on naive credulity towards new concepts which seem to hold out some promise to their instinctive gropings. Out of this combination results that crucial capacity of perceiving a familiar object, situation, problem, or collection of data, in a sudden new light or new context. . . .

This act of wrenching away an object or concept from its habitual associative context and seeing it in a new context is an essential part of the creative process. It is an act both of destruction and of creation, for it demands the breaking up of a mental habit, the melting down . . . of the frozen structure of accepted theory, to enable the new fusion to take place. This perhaps explains the strange combination of scepticism and credulity in the creative genius. Every creative act—in science, art or religion—involves . . . a new innocence of perception liberated from the cataract of accepted beliefs.

—Arthur Koestler

In addition to using our inventional system and keeping an open mind, we can try several techniques to help us look at situations in a new way. In order to look at regular things in an irregular way, we can consciously tumble our thought patterns by changing our mind-set in various ways.

1. *Brainstorming.* This technique requires the aid of a couple of friends, for brainstorming is a group activity. Each member of the group spontaneously contributes ideas on a given subject, the goal being to come up with as many unrestricted views of a subject as possible. Even ideas that at first may seem far-out or unfeasible must be explored; no idea can be rejected until it has been explored thoroughly and its merits investigated. Members of the group ask each other questions, respond to objections, offer statements and counterstatements, and generally engage in a free-spirited dialogue. They might even divide into two sides and have one side defend an idea while the other side attacks it; then they can trade places. The technique depends primarily on the group's ability not to censor any idea before exploring it.

APPLICATION

Divide the class into groups of four and try brainstorming to generate a good thesis on one of these subjects: world hunger, overcrowded prisons, or marriage.

2. *Tape-recording.* If we are unable to assemble a group for brainstorming, we can attempt the same kind of activity by ourselves. With the same goal as in brainstorming, the technique is to turn on a tape recorder and carry on self-discussions focused on a particular subject. As in brainstorming, we try to generate as many ideas as possible, regardless of how unorthodox they sound at first. Then we carry on arguments with ourselves, first taking one side of the argument and then the other. When we have finished, we play back the tape, take notes, and evaluate the ideas that we have produced.

3. *Self-doubting.* Good writers challenge their own beliefs—not only to determine whether they are worth defending, but also to see if there is a fresher way of viewing the subject. Most of us tend to accept our own

petrified opinions as principles; we are too satisfied with those opinions to examine them critically. As John F. Kennedy told the students at Yale, "Too often we . . . enjoy the comfort of opinion without the discomfort of thought." Usually we're too busy defending our opinions to test them, but if we want to be sure that they are sound, we must cultivate a healthy skepticism toward our own ideas. "To believe with certainty," an old saying goes, "you must begin by doubting." Instead of setting out to prove our thesis, therefore, we should set out to disprove it; if it holds up under that kind of attack, it probably will hold up against our readers' reservations and objections. Since we usually already know the strengths of our thesis, we need to explore its weaknesses. Furthermore, in order to know whether we are supporting the best possible thesis, we should seriously consider rival theses, which we usually dismiss categorically. Only after we have explored the merits of our thesis and of rival theses should we advance our proposition for readers.

4. *Reverse thinking.* If we take the view opposite to the one we now hold and try to defend that opposite view, we may open up an entirely new perspective. We should try to reject all of our assumptions and try to think of the assumptions underlying the opposite view.

5. *Changing positions.* Another technique is to imagine how the issue looks from different persons' positions, from different geographical places, from different political stances, from different social and economic positions, and from different psychological states. We tend to see things only from the point of view that we have been programmed to see them. Like sand crabs, we are afraid to venture very far out of our shells, and if we do go out, we quickly scamper home, backwards. We should try to move around a subject as if it were a physical object, looking at it first from one angle, then from another. Just as observing a building from a different physical position gives us a different conception of that building, observing a subject or situation from different mental places gives us different perspectives.

Sometimes after a long period of intensive thinking on a subject, after racking the brain until we're mentally exhausted, it helps to take a break and do something else, especially physical exercise. Often I chop wood, even though there's enough wood cut for two winters and there's a chain saw right next to the ax. I used to think that this was an avoidance activity, but instead of procrastinating I was shifting thinking modes and giving the unconscious mind a chance to take over. During this period of apparent not-thinking, the unconscious mind continues to mull over the subject without the supervision of the conscious mind; the brain is in a search mode, keeping all circuits open and running while I go about my mindless business. Suddenly it sees a combination of data that the conscious mind had seen separately but had not seen in the right combination. A light switches on telling us that the unconscious mind has hit upon something it considers remarkable, and it shoves that idea into our consciousness. I drop the ax and run back to the desk to evaluate this new idea: Does it hold up under the light of reason? Such breakthroughs seem to occur only if the conscious mind has prepared for them by accumulating and contemplating evidence and options so that the unconscious mind can use the material to reach its sudden insight.

Through a combination of asking journalistic questions, using techniques like brainstorming and reverse thinking, and allowing an incubation period for the unconscious mind to work, we will eventually generate a thesis that is original and challenging.

APPLICATION

1. Which of these theses do you consider fresh and provocative (not necessarily ones you agree with)? Which ones would hold your interest in an essay? Why?

   A. The pursuit of happiness seldom leads to happiness.

   B. Men need liberating even more than women.

   C. Cat lovers are usually better marriage partners than dog lovers, who tend to be emotionally dependent people, demanding constant reinforcement and unquestioning affection.

   D. America should import all of its oil and reserve its own oil supplies for that time in the near future when world oil supplies are depleted.

   E. A person should get his or her first marriage out of the way as soon as possible.

   F. State lotteries, which are nothing more than government-run gambling, should be abolished because lotteries give lower odds than other forms of gambling.

2. What evidence could you generate to support the following thesis statements?

   A. Having a great enemy provides one with a sustaining motivation, much like having a great love.

   B. Most people prefer to be deceived.

   C. There are significant disadvantages to going to college.

   D. History does not teach humankind to learn from its mistakes.

   E. Psychology interprets most human behavior in a negative manner.

   F. Since the United States cannot police the entire world, we should abandon our European allies and concentrate on saving the Western hemisphere from communism.

3. On a subject of your choice, generate a controversial thesis that you could substantiate. To arrive at a thesis that contradicts conventional wisdom, you will probably have to explore the subject using the journalistic questions.
    If you prefer, you may use one of these subjects:

television	aerobics classes	computers
travel	greeting cards	college
neighbors	writing courses	Nicaragua

Structuring and Outlining

After formulating the thesis and asking the appropriate questions to discover convincing evidence, we usually direct our attention to organizing the material in some logical way. Our goal is to arrange it into some form that allows readers to distinguish main ideas from secondary ideas and to follow our meaning. "The recognition of structure gives the mind its ability to find meaning," said Susanne Langer. Structure to some extent determines meaning—that is, the way that we organize our thoughts and evidence affects the way readers understand those thoughts. Structure contributes to meaning because structure largely determines emphasis. Since different structures produce different emphases and communicate different meanings, we must be conscious of the effect each structure will produce. Any material can be organized in several different ways, and each structure is appropriate for a particular purpose.

Our first step in organizing material is to group bits of material together according to their similarities; by doing this, we will have a manageable number of groups instead of a multitude of separate items. Then we label each group to identify it. For our terrorist hijacking example, our groups might be labeled "previous hijackings," "history of the terrorist organization," "problems with the rescue mission," and so forth. Classifying the material (i.e., grouping and labeling) is a way of putting it into blocks so that we can then arrange the blocks in a coherent and logical way. This classifying phase is a preliminary activity to structuring the material in essay form. For now, we are simply trying to put notes and examples into piles and then label the various categories.

The next step is to decide in what order to put the groups. What should come first, what should come second, third, fourth, and last, and where should the thesis statement be placed? A good technique for doing this is to put each classification on a 3-by-5 inch index card and lay all the cards out on a table. That way we can switch the cards around, see the various possibilities, and often discover new relationships among the cards. Physically arranging the cards helps us to explore ways of organizing the material that we may not have considered.

Various types of organization (such as chronological, comparing/contrasting, eliminating alternatives, climatic, and so forth) are discussed at length in the following chapters, and therefore we will reserve our investigation of those structures for later. What I want to emphasize about structure at this point is that (1) rather than imposing an ordering principle on material, we seek to discover the natural ways of ordering that the material itself suggests; (2) of the several structures that the material may suggest, we must select the most appropriate to our audience, purpose, and thesis; and (3) we actually start considering structure during the invention stage.

Although we may not be conscious of doing so, we are discovering the available structures within the material while we are asking our journalistic questions. We begin to see the various ways to organize ideas—how one idea relates to another and how one thought logically comes after another—at the same time we are generating those ideas. The more we investigate the subject, the more we perceive the inherent patterns in the material itself, and we select the structure that best serves our purpose, accommodates our readers, and advances our thesis.

To help in this structuring phase, many writers find outlining useful. Most of my students, however, seem to regard outlines in the way children view spinach: good for them, but odious. If required to hand in an outline with a paper, most students write it after they've finished the paper, which is like an architect drawing up blueprints after having built a house. I use outlines on many writing tasks, and I do so not because I'm energetic but because I'm lazy, and outlines save me time as well as improve my product.

An outline can be as sketchy or as detailed as we like, depending on our need and our composing method. Some people are impatient about outlining and are so eager to start composing that they simply jot down a few major headings, arrange them in a tentative way, and then start drafting. This kind of quick, broad outline is especially good for in-class essays, exams, and other writing tasks performed under time pressure. Other people treat the outline almost as a preliminary draft of the essay, including an introductory paragraph, topic sentences, lists of examples, and a conclusion. For example, I know a report writer who spends 4 or 5 days writing a detailed and lengthy outline for a report chapter. He uses the outline to think carefully through the substantiation and the structure, and he revises the outline as often as necessary. Instead of writing several drafts of the chapter, he writes several versions of the outline; therefore, when he does start to compose, he completes the first draft and polishes it in only a day or so.

Outlines have several advantages. First and most obvious, they force us to think about structure so that when we begin to write we will have a workable plan for proceeding. We can sort out main ideas from supporting ideas and, by their placement in the outline, show their relationships, and assign appropriate emphasis to each. In this prewriting stage, we can carefully examine our ideas, move them around, and try different types of organization. An outline is like a skeleton in which it's easy to see how the bones connect; but once we flesh it out with examples, analogies, and details, it's more difficult to see the structure. Outlines therefore allow us, when we begin to compose, to concentrate on smaller units— paragraphs, sentences, and words. A second advantage of outlining is that it gives us a sense of getting started, which often is the most ornery part of writing. Although the movement from outline to prose is not as mechanical as painting by numbers, an outline will give us something to face the blank page with so that we and it don't just stare at one another.

APPLICATION

Write a one-page outline on one of these thesis statements or on one of your own choosing. To generate evidence, ask who, what, when, where, why, and how. Specify who your readers are and what the purpose of your essay will be.

Sample thesis statements:
1. The renewed interest in turning fiction into film is disproving the adage that good literature makes bad movies.
2. Black television situational comedies fall into [2, 3, 4] categories.
3. Bruce Springsteen is to the 1980s what Bob Dylan was to the 1960s.
4. The knowledge most worth having is. . . .

Sample outline:

Thesis statement: The United States should close its European military bases and concentrate instead on protecting the Western hemisphere.

I. The United States can no longer police the entire world.
   A. There are too many areas of conflict to police, and we will needlessly get involved in another war.
   B. Other countries are becoming strong enough militarily to defend themselves.
   (Cite examples of countries that now have nuclear weapons.)
   C. The United States cannot afford the financial burden.
      1. International defense costs billions of dollars.
      2. The United States needs to reduce its huge budget deficit, especially its military costs.

II. The United States should withdraw its troops from Europe and close its military bases there.
   A. Europe can defend itself.
      1. If the United States weren't there to defend them, they would be forced to defend themselves.

    2. The United States should supply Europe with missiles for defense.

B. The populations of several European nations object to a United States presence in their countries anyway.

(Give examples of protests in Germany, Spain, France, and Italy.)

C. European allies in NATO don't pay their share in their own defense.

(Cite statistics on how much more the United States pays per capita than other nations in NATO.)

D. The likelihood of a conflict with Russia is greater if our troops are on that continent.

E. Overseas bases are expensive to maintain.

F. Overseas troops and bases are easy targets for terrorists.

(Give examples of terrorist acts against United States military personnel in Europe.)

III. We should concentrate on protecting the Western hemisphere by making it economically strong and politically democratic.

A. Mexico, Central America, and even South America are our neighbors; therefore, we have more interest in their well-being.

B. The regions are ripe for communist takeover.

    1. Economically, several countries (such as Brazil, Mexico, and Argentina) are nearly bankrupt.

        a. Their international debts are more than they can pay.

        b. Unemployment is high.

        c. Inflation is high.

    2. Mass poverty, economic chaos, and political instability are the ingredients of communist revolution.

C. There are already communist regimes in Cuba and Central America.

D. The United States and the southern nations are economic complements.

    1. Unlike Europe, which has depleted its natural resources, Central and South America are rich in petroleum, ores, and lumber.

    2. Unlike Europe, which is our competitor, Central and South America import our manufactured products.

E. Rather than trying to dominate these nations, the United States should strive to bolster their economies.

F. Rather than try to police all places inadequately, we should protect one hemisphere well.

    I add to an outline even after I start composing. I keep the outline at my right elbow to use as a notepad as well as a guide. As ideas occur to me, I insert them under the appropriate heading in the outline because I find that if I don't write down a good thought, I forget it later. I constantly revise the outline and flesh it out, jotting down ideas under various headings, crossing out headings that no longer seem relevant, and inserting examples and subheadings. Before I start drafting a section of the essay, I usually mutter to myself "What points do I want to make here?" and quickly write them down on the outline, then consider what order they should come in; sometimes I flesh out each point with a couple of secondary ideas and examples. A working outline, then, is not a rigid structure but rather a flexible and expandable tool that should not intimidate us.

In addition to using an initial outline that becomes a notepad during drafting, I find that outlining after a rough draft sometimes helps me to see if I have written what I intended to write. Occasionally I also include a finished outline with a paper to serve as a guide for readers, much like a table of contents in a book.

Writing the First Draft

A major problem many writers have is overcoming the blank page. The dread of beginning afflicts seasoned professionals as well as novices; even a writer as accomplished as John Steinbeck admitted, "I suffer as always from the fear of putting down the first line." Let's face it: The blank page can be intimidating.

CLASS DISCUSSION

Why do you have trouble writing the first sentence? Enumerate the reasons that contribute to writer's block.

Overcoming the Blank Page

To overcome the blank page, we can try several things. As mentioned earlier, an outline helps immensely because it already lists the ideas, contains support for those ideas, and shows a suggested order. Second, we can begin by writing the easiest section of the outline. There's no rule that we have to write an essay in the order that it will be read. Since some sections of an essay are more difficult than others, I start with the one that I am most interested in, most comfortable with, and most knowledgeable about. Once started, the rest of the paper expands from there.

Third, we should consider the conditions under which we write best and should try to make our environment as conducive to writing as possible. The conditions under which writers work vary from individual to individual: Some writers need peace and quiet, while others prefer background noise; some write best in the evening, some in the early morning, others in the dead of night. We would expect that most writers compose sitting at a desk, but some very famous writers (Ernest Hemingway, Thomas Wolfe, and Virginia Woolf) wrote standing up, and some other well-known authors (Truman Capote and Mark Twain) did most of their writing in bed. The point is that we should think about the time, place, and conditions for doing our best work and try to achieve the right circumstances.

CLASS DISCUSSION

Because almost everyone has difficulty with starting, some writers try warm-up exercises, such as making a journal entry, composing a letter, or writing a short narrative. Thornton Wilder, for instance, took long walks that allowed his mind to relax before starting to write; Hemingway and Steinbeck ceremoniously sharpened pencils as a gearing-up activity; and Willa Cather read a biblical passage for its rhythm. My own ritual is to put on a low-volume jazz recording, pop a piece of sugarless bubblegum into my mouth, and, depending on my mood, either attack a yellow pad with a blue felt pen or bang away at the keyboard of my word processor. Do you have any such relaxing activities, warm-up exercises, or priming activities? What are they, and why do they seem to help?

One helpful technique is to try composing on a computer or word processor, which more and more writers are using these days. I find the monitor much less intimidating than the blank page, perhaps because the words seem less permanent, and therefore I am less hesitant to try out sentences. If the sentences aren't particularly good, I can hit the delete function and try again, but at least I've gotten over the hurdle of beginning and the juices are flowing. Computers are useful throughout the composing and revising stages because we can insert, delete, and transfer material almost effortlessly.

Perhaps what would help most toward getting started would be a change in attitude. We ought to view the blank page not as an obstacle but as an opportunity. It is an invitation to express whatever we wish and therefore should be approached with a sense of exhilaration instead of a sense of dread. As John Updike put it, "An absolute freedom exists on the blank page, so let's use it."

Generating Ideas as We Write

In this prewrite/write model, composing the first draft is usually a somewhat controlled process. That is, rather than relying on spontaneous thoughts, we follow the ideas that we have generated and outlined in previous stages. Most writers who use this model try not to deviate too far from the early game plan—after all, that plan was reached after much careful thought, and what good is it if we don't use it? If outlines are not used judiciously, however, they can restrict our creativity by keeping us from exploring alternative ways of seeing, thinking, and organizing as we compose.

A major disadvantage of the prewrite/write model can be that when composing the first draft we confine our thoughts to those in the outline. We shouldn't assume that composing means simply filling in the outline with paragraphs and sentences; composing is much more than finding words to communicate the ideas in the outline. If our thoughts start to take us into an area not on the outline, we must not prematurely cut off those explorations. An outline is intended as a tentative guide, not as a barrier, and therefore we should not view it as an inflexible structure.

I advocate "working" outlines, similar to itineraries for trips. We wouldn't start off on a European vacation without some general plan—landing in London, taking a boat to Belgium, then getting a train to Paris and staying three nights, and so forth. With writing, the journey is mental, and outlines are our maps in that they tell us where we are headed. Working outlines, like itineraries, are subject to change; we're certainly not obligated to adhere to them if we change our minds and want to go off in a different direction, any more than we should feel obligated to visit Yugoslavia simply because it is on our tentative travel plans.

Nor should we be inflexible about our thesis. We will probably make discoveries about our topic while we are composing, and if we believe that new evidence casts some doubt on our original thesis, we should modify the thesis or change it completely. Most of us tend to feel an allegiance to a thesis, and therefore when we discover new facts that don't support that thesis, we tend to throw out the facts rather than the thesis, or bend the facts to suit the thesis. By doing this we are no longer advancing a truth—we're simply trying to advance our own biases. Naturally, we should have a strong conviction about our thesis, but we can't afford to be blinded by it. We have to maintain a sense of fairness, a desire for truth, and a touch of skepticism.

We might assume that if we have used an inventional system to explore a subject, we will have already considered all the relevant facts, and therefore the possibility of new ideas or evidence popping up during the composing stage would be small. But composing is an inventional method itself, as we will discuss in detail when we come to the next section on "freewriting." When we compose, one thought unexpectedly generates another, and we discover new avenues of reason and new facts that were lodged in the backs of our minds and that didn't come forward during the formal process of invention with journalistic questions. We must be careful not to suppress this natural invention that occurs when we compose. The challenge we face in the composing stage, then, is how to use the ideas we have previously generated and the outline we have constructed without allowing those ideas and that outline to impede the associative nature of composing.

At this point I should insert a qualification about the model of the writing process that we have been exploring. Although for purposes of analysis I have divided the writing process into three distinct stages—prewrite, write, revise—that view of writing is not entirely accurate. Rather than being a strictly linear process (a series of stages along a straight line, each of which must be completed before the next is tackled), writing is more of a recursive process (the stages occur again and again). For example, we don't invent only in the first stage; we go back to invention throughout the writing process. We are generating ideas not only during the formal process of asking journalistic questions, but also when we are outlining, when we are composing, and even when we are revising. We are constantly seeing old ideas in a new light, seeing new ways of arranging material, seeing new objections our readers will have to our thesis, seeing new examples, and seeing holes in our logic. Whenever we react to one idea and that reaction generates a second idea, we are inventing, and that process happens any time that we are working on the product. Likewise, as we revise we often return to the composing mode, and revision and composing become intermingled. Nevertheless, certain activities predominantly occur in one phase or another, and therefore our three-phase view is not entirely a distortion.

Dividing an Essay into Sections

What follows is a method of composing that works for me and for many of my students. Very simply, the method is to divide the essay into small sections and work on one section at a time. This "divide-and-conquer" strategy lends itself to composing with the aid of an outline because an outline has already partitioned off the subject into manageable units of thought. Each major division of an outline marks off one step in the development of the thesis, and each of these steps translates into a group of paragraphs.

My preference is to work on relatively short sections, usually of one to one and a half pages, which I find to be long enough to encompass a secondary idea but short enough to write the entire piece in one sitting. I use the outline as a springboard from which to dive into a section, but when I'm submerged in the section I pretty much disregard the outline and write quickly. I often write this draft on a typewriter or word processor because I can type more quickly than write longhand, and once the words and ideas start flowing, I don't want to lose the momentum due to slow writing. I triple-space so that later, when I go back over the spat-out ideas and view them with a tranquil eye, I can expand ideas and insert whatever material I have forgotten from the outline. But it's important not to consult the outline while composing because it will interfere with invention.

At this point in the composing stage, I also begin to reconsider how this section fits into the whole essay, for as the section develops it may place itself into a new position within the larger scheme. Although my main concern at this time is the internal structure of this small section, my mind periodically shifts to the larger structure when my brain has some insight that insists on being heard. I also find that while I am fiddling with one section, my brain is already thinking ahead to another section. To keep from losing those advance thoughts, I jot them down on the outline, and at some point, if the calling is strong enough, I may even drop one section and begin to work on the new one. Many times during writing I realize that material in one section belongs in another, so I move it. Occasionally, as I work on first one section and then another, I see a new relationship between the sections or a different order for them. When this happens I disregard their organization in the outline and put them together in various new arrangements. This shifting of focus from one section to another and from small structure to large structure is natural, and I don't try to fight it; the brain seems inclined to turn its attention from one thing to another and to work alternately on the large and the small. Working on one part often helps me to see another part better, and working on the whole often helps me to see the individual parts in a more focused way.

When I have written all of the individual sections, I rethink the order in which they should be placed. Sometimes I actually sit down in the middle of my living room with the sections spread over the floor and physically move them around to see how various arrangements look. After considering all the options I can think of, I evaluate those options and select the one that seems most natural, that suits my purpose, and that is appropriate to my audience. I consider this first draft completed when the structure seems logical, when the material is blocked off into unified paragraphs (that is, the information in each paragraph deals with only one subtopic), and, most important, when the thesis is clear and well substantiated. Other qualities—such as proper word choice, effective sentence structure, tone, and coherence (tying the sentences together so that they flow smoothly)—are reserved for the next draft because I consider those revising activities. At this point I have a fairly quick draft with lots of insertions, deletions, and marginal notes, but it's solid enough in terms of thought and organization.

Revising

Since the principles and techniques of revising are discussed in the following chapters, I will devote this space to dispelling some of the common misconceptions about revision and to offer some general suggestions concerning revision. The first misconception is that revision is conducted simply at the level of words and sentences; we tend to think of revision exclusively as searching for the right word or the best sentence structure, or getting the commas and apostrophes in the right places. To equate revision with sentence editing, however, is to take a very narrow view of revision. Sentence editing is certainly one part of revision, and it is the one part that we usually do; as a matter of fact, sometimes we play with words so long that we bruise them. In the process, however, we tend to neglect other considerations that are equally important.

Revision consists of three basic parts: evaluating logic (which includes evidence), organization (of individual paragraphs and of the essay as a whole), and style (sentences and words). The revision stage is not only a time when we pay closer attention to word choice, sentence structure, paragraph form, and organization; it is also a time when we reconsider our thinking, for rethinking is a vital part of revision. To revise means "to look again," and that means looking again at the thesis and logic. The revision stage should be a time for retesting our assumptions, modifying our thesis if necessary, ensuring that we have proved our assertions, and making certain that we have achieved the proper emphasis among ideas.

Another popular misconception is that revision is a kind of remedial work that only weak writers must do. Inexperienced writers in particular feel that if their first draft is a mess and they have to rewrite very much, they must be poor writers. They assume that their first draft is supposed to be nearly perfect, and when it isn't, they assume that revision is their punishment. The truth is that everyone's first draft is an eyesore. James Thurber, for instance, complained that "the first or second draft of everything I write reads as if it was turned out by a charwoman." Not until the sixth or seventh draft, he said, did a piece turn out decently. Other veteran writers say essentially the same thing.

To write adequately one must know, above all, how bad are one's first drafts. They are bad because the need to combine composition with thought, both in their own way taxing, leads initially to a questionable, even execrable result. With each revision the task eases, the product improves. Eventually there can be clarity and perhaps even grace. . . . My commitment is to not fewer than five revisions; this, I trust sprightly, document has had six.

—John Kenneth Galbraith

I have never thought of myself as a good writer. Anyone who wants reassurance of that should read one of my first drafts. But I'm one of the world's great re-writers.

—James Michener

We need to change our attitude about revision. Many developing writers consider revision to be drudgery, but experienced writers have learned that it can be the most rewarding phase of the writing process. It is during revision that we take a rough stone, cut it down, and polish it until it becomes a fine jewel.

> Revision is one of the true pleasures of writing.
>
> —Bernard Malamud

> I am strongly in favor of intelligent, even fastidious revision, which is, or certainly should be, an art in itself.
>
> —Joyce Carol Oates

Another misconception is that revision is simply moving around existing material. Revision usually entails invention of new material as well as modifying and rearranging existing material. The revising stage should be a continuation of the discovery and composing stages. When we reinvestigate a subject, we usually add new material and write new sentences and paragraphs—that is, we compose. Furthermore, when we make a change in the existing material, that change generates other changes, and what started out as revision turns into invention. Some writers say that half of all writing is actually rewriting.

> All my thoughts are second thoughts.
>
> —Aldous Huxley

> For me, it's mostly a question of rewriting.
>
> —James Thurber

I find it interesting that beginning writers, whose products probably need more work, seem to revise less than veteran writers. Inexperienced writers tend to stick to their initial drafts more closely, make fewer changes, and make smaller changes. Experienced writers understand that first drafts are exploratory expeditions that will need considerable reworking. Because composing is often a hurried activity, it is not supposed to be perfect; revising is a more leisurely activity during which we reread our prose slowly, examining carefully what we have captured on the page and mentally comparing it to what we intended to say.

To help us in this careful examination, we can try several practical activities. First, we can type the draft after we have made the first round of revisions; when material is typed we can see our work more objectively. Second, we can outline the draft. An outline at this point is not so much a guide as a reviewing tool for reconsidering the logic and structure and for evaluating the effectiveness of topic sentences. Third, we can enlist a friend to read the draft. I suggest that you set up a buddy system whereby you agree to read a classmate's papers and he or she reads yours. The reason for this is that we often have difficulty catching weaknesses in our own writing, but a "cold" reader isn't hampered by our subjectivity. Classmates may not always be able to articulate precisely what is wrong with a draft, but they can usually tell when something needs reworking. And fourth, we can leave the paper for a day or two, if time allows. A period away from a paper often helps us to see it more objectively and gives us a better perspective on the issue.

A recurring question that students have about revision is "How many revisions should I do, and how do I know when the paper is good enough?" Clearly, there is no definitive standard for the number of drafts we should do.

> I always write three drafts, but you have to leave it eventually. There comes a point when you say, "That's it, I can't do anything more."
>
> —Harold Pinter

> In my own case I usually write to a point where the work is getting worse rather than better.
>
> —John Dos Passos

Rather than setting a prescribed number of revisions, we know when we have reached the end when our draft matches the essay that we have formed in our minds. We have an image of what the finished essay should look like, even though we may not be conscious of that image. In fact, the whole writing process is guided by an internal perception or an intuitive knowledge of what the essay should say and look like. As we compose and revise, we are attempting to achieve the unstated ideal that we have set up, and we are unconsciously comparing our draft to a sense of what is right. Although we may not consciously know what the ideal is, we know what it isn't, and we keep revising because we don't feel that what we currently have is right. When the outward essay that we read finally corresponds to the inner essay that we have envisioned, we have accomplished our goal.

And finally, let's listen to what a few veterans have to say about the art of revision:

> *Interviewer:* Do you rewrite?
> *Frank O'Connor:* Endlessly, endlessly, endlessly.

Interviewer: What do you do exactly?

Robert Graves: Revise the manuscript till I can't read it any longer, then get somebody to type it. Then I revise the typing. Then it's retyped again. Then there's a third typing, which is the final one. Nothing should then remain that offends the eye.

> The rhythm of writing, revising, writing, revising, etc., seems to suit me. I am inclined to think that as I grow older I will come to be infatuated with the art of revision.
>
> —Joyce Carol Oates

> I've worked out my own way to revise, which is almost like somebody that sews at home because I use the rug or the bed or the dining room table and lay pages out where I can see something as a whole and objectively. It's the same feeling as seeing something in the typewriter instead of in your handwriting. It makes it objective, then you can judge it.
>
> —Eudora Welty

This, then, is the way the prewrite/write/revise method operates. Most writers find this method especially useful for long writing projects and for research projects. Next we will consider another model for generating ideas and composing—freewriting.

The Freewriting Model

Although most writers use the prewrite/write model of writing, the freewriting model is sometimes more effective, and therefore I'd like to introduce you to it and encourage you to try it. As the name implies, freewriting is writing that is spontaneous and undirected. Instead of using a formal method of invention—thinking through our thesis deliberately and then outlining our ideas—we simply write in nonstop stretches until we discover a subject that interests us, a thesis about that subject, and evidence to support that thesis. Whereas the traditional method of writing is to think and then write, the freewriting method is to write and then think about what we have written, and then write again. In freewriting, we begin writing before we know our meaning, and the meaning gradually emerges as we compose. This writing model has best been described by Peter Elbow in *Writing Without Teachers,* and the following discussion borrows heavily from Professor Elbow's analysis and commentary.

Writing as a Process of Discovery

The philosophy of freewriting is that writing is itself a process of discovery and an act of invention. Writing is more than a process of recording what we think; it is an associative process whereby one idea sparks another so that ideas come to us as we are composing. Writing stimulates the connecting process that goes on among pieces of information in the brain. By giving free rein to the mind and allowing it the freedom to work by association, we will make new and interesting connections and will spontaneously generate new ideas.

Instead of starting out already knowing what our message is, writing that message in one draft, and then revising it numerous times, freewriting requires that we write several different versions and discover meaning as we proceed through the versions. The meaning develops through stages so that only near the end will we know what our thesis is. According to this model, writing is as much an activity for developing ideas as it is for imparting ideas. "Writing," Professor Elbow says, "is a way to end up thinking something you couldn't have started out thinking." We start out thinking one thing, and by writing we end up thinking something new and engaging.

Freewriting is to the writing process what vagabond sailing is to navigation. We're adrift in a schooner on an open sea, we're the pilot, and we have no designated port in mind. We're ready to explore whatever territory we encounter, and we sail not by a compass or rules but by the wind of our minds. Freewriting is like a type of sailing that carries us where we would not otherwise go. If the mind blows in one direction, we sail with it; if the mind changes direction, we sail in the new direction. The only rule is that we keep sailing, traipsing from one mental seascape to another. Eventually we will hit upon a consistent wind and will sail for a particular port. After we discover our thesis, our sailing is more focused, our destination becomes clear, and we arrive at that destination.

Freewriting Sessions

To learn to compose easily and to stop ourselves from criticizing our work prematurely, Professor Elbow recommends that we do a 10-minute freewriting exercise every other day. During these freewriting sessions, we must write unceasingly, uncritically, and intensely. We should write at a nearly frenzied pace, almost without time for thought. We write as quickly as possible to keep the association of ideas flowing. We have to become maniacs for a short time and write and write and write. Not only do we not edit, we don't read back over what we've written yet and, most important, we don't stop writing. Even if the mind seems to go blank and we can't think of anything to say, we write "I can't think of anything to write." We record thoughts without regard to their pertinence or sequence. Whatever thought the brain produces goes onto paper, for freewriting is exactly that: thinking on paper. Because it is undirected and spontaneous writing, freewriting is an almost subconscious activity in which our thoughts pour out unfiltered. Our minds are sprinting, and our pens are trying to keep up.

To give you an example of freewriting, here is a 10-minute sample that I did recently:

Now I am going to write for 10 mins., nonstop, writing whatever crosses my mind, even if I have nothing bright to say at first, usually something pops into the old brain, nonstop, just keep the left hand moving. Being left-handed can be somewhat of a disadvantage because many things are built just for right handers, even butter knives and rifles, for a higher price you can get a left-handed version. Economic discrimination against southpaws. Billy the Kid was left-handed, who else, Leonardo da Vinci, Gerry Ford, Whitey Ford, all lefties. Baseball, I miss playing the no longer #1 American sport. Little league. Once when I was pitching, my best friend, a kid named Dave, got a hit off of me and he was on first base and as I was winding up to throw he called out "Hey Bobby" and I stopped the windup and the ump called a balk and Dave advanced to 2nd base & I was embarrassed and angered and felt betrayed. A strong image. Eidetic, is that the word. Betrayal is perhaps the most despicable and hurtful vice there is, and unlike other hurts like, well, I can't think of an example, but unlike the examples I can't think of, betrayal has to be done intentionally, consciously, or it isn't betrayal if it isn't intentional, just as suicide has to be intentional, there's no such thing as an accidental suicide, is there?

A neighbor's son called his sister long distance and chatted for a while and then hung up and killed himself. What accounts for such—time's up.

This is a typical example of freewriting. The beginnings of these sessions are usually sluggish, as we wait for a subject to emerge—left-handedness—and then that subject suggests another one—baseball—and then the mention of suicide leads to still another subject, as I rambled from one idea to another. The point is that I wrote whatever came into my mind, not worrying about logic, transitions, punctuation, grammar, or anything.

Separating Composing and Editing

"The main thing about freewriting," Professor Elbow says, "is that it is *nonediting*." Most of us try to edit at the same time that we are composing, and when we do that, our writing suffers because editing (1) slows down the thinking process and (2) censors ideas. Editing is a halting process: It slows down the generation of ideas in order to correct thinking and language. If we slow down when composing, the association of ideas that is essential for discovering new ideas breaks down. Instead of one idea leading to another, we stop to reconsider and revise the first idea and its wording. We lose the momentum that comes with rapid thinking, and the creative juices evaporate. While we compose, the biggest obstacle is considering how something should be said. The other problem with editing while composing is that we censor ideas instead of exploring them. Premature editing cuts off ideas that, if followed for a way, might turn into a provocative thesis. Our tendency is to judge ideas rather than explore them. Before we write down an idea, we usually evaluate it to see whether it is relevant or good. But how do we know what is relevant at that point, and how do we know whether an idea is good if we don't explore it? Relevancy and goodness are qualities to be determined later, not as we are composing.

Think of it this way: We have within us a composing faculty and an editing faculty. They are like two gremlins that reside in the brain. One is a composer who lives in the right side of the brain; the other is an editor who lives in the left side. The composer is imaginative, unruly, spontaneous, intuitive, quick, and flowing. The editor is logical, correct, reflective, analytical, slow, and halting. One is inventive; the other, judgmental. One is rambling; the other, structured. One is free; the other, disciplined. What the composing gremlin produces in a frenzy, the editing gremlin evaluates in cool contemplation, discarding what is not satisfactory and improving what is satisfactory.

To be good writers, we need to have both types of gremlins, the creative composer and the critical editor, because each performs a vital function. The purpose of the composer is to generate thoughts; the purpose of the editor is to clarify those thoughts. Although these two are great collaborators, they fight like demons when they try to work at the same time because they work at different paces, so we have to keep them separated. The problem is that the editorial gremlin insists on barging in while the composing gremlin is trying to do its job. The overly eager editor brings out rules of grammar and logic, demanding that each word be exactly right, each sentence be ideally formed, and each paragraph be completely unified—in short, demanding perfection, which is its goal. When the editor is on the loose, it can cause writer's block by demanding perfection in whatever we write down; we are too intimidated to write down anything because we know that nothing will ever come out fully perfect.

Unfortunately, the editorial gremlin in most of us is considerably more muscular than its composing counterpart. Unless it is caged, it will all but destroy the composing gremlin. Freewriting is one way of caging the little devil, since freewriting requires that we compose now and edit later. There is, of course, a time to unleash the editor, but letting it out prematurely will interfere with our composing and thinking.

APPLICATION

Take a minute to relax. Think of something soothing so that you approach this writing task with a clear mind and have a positive attitude. Now take out a pen and notepad and freewrite for 10 minutes. Write nonstop, keeping the editorial gremlin securely caged.

Practicing these short freewriting sessions will help to prepare us for the longer freewriting sessions necessary for writing a full essay.

Four Steps of Freewriting

Professor Elbow's method for writing an essay consists of four steps. The first step is to write nonstop for 45 minutes. The purpose of this first step is to explore whatever subjects and ideas enter our consciousness, and the only rules are that we keep writing and that we not censor thoughts. After the 45 minutes of writing, we analyze the freewriting to see if a central idea is trying to emerge. We sum up that idea, however vague it is, in one sentence. This summing-up procedure is important because if we omit it, we will just keep writing and rambling with no progress. Step two is to write for another 45 minutes nonstop, but this time we start with the assertion that emerged from step one, and instead of undirected freewriting, we focus on that assertion. Although the writing in step two is focused, it shouldn't be so rigidly controlled that we don't allow for any interesting digressions that occur. After this second 45-minute writing session, we take another 15 minutes to read over the material, underline interesting thoughts and phrases, and then summarize the central idea in a single sentence. By this point the central idea should be increasingly focused. Step three is to write nonstop for 45 minutes more, deliberately directing our focus on the central thought, and follow up with 15 minutes of analysis and revision. By this point we should have a thesis, which we write out, making certain that it is argumentative and fresh. Now that we have found our message, we are able to find the appropriate words to convey that message. Step four is to write in the traditional method: We think about what we want to say, draft an outline, and then write the final version, which we edit and polish.

A basic difference between the prewrite/write model and the freewriting model is that with the former we start with our meaning and then write, whereas with the latter we write to find our meaning. In the traditional way of writing, we start with a thesis, and although we may shift the emphasis of our meaning and change the structure, we keep basically the same message. Even if we write two drafts, they tend to say the same thing in slightly different ways. With the freewriting model, the message evolves through a series of freewriting versions, and each version may reflect a real change in thinking. "Meaning is not what you start out with," Professor Elbow states, "but what you end up with."

An idea must sprout and grow on paper until it reaches maturity. Professor Elbow suggests that an idea evolves through versions of writing just as a human being grows through stages of development from infancy, childhood, and adolescence to adulthood and maturity. Trying to make our first version our final version, he contends, is like trying to skip childhood and adolescence: We will end up with an immature idea. The first version must be used simply as a stepping stone to move to another stage of development.

Freewriting is a means of examining what we currently think and then going beyond that. Because the first ideas we write are usually obvious and mediocre, we must go past those and through the inevitable rubble in order to reach better ideas. Even putting down those first ideas is difficult because they are usually quite bad, but we must push them as far as possible since they usually lead to something better. Initially, we must "accept bad writing in order to end up with something better in the end," Elbow says. By pursuing a train of thought to its end and by keeping the mind open to digressions, "You make yourself available to something better than what you'd be stuck with if you'd actually succeeded in making your meaning clear at the start." We should not merely allow for digressions, but actually encourage them and follow them to see where they lead. A digression that looks like a dirt path leading nowhere could turn out to be a yellow-brick road leading to a new and interesting idea.

The "zip-through" freewriting method has several advantages. First, freewriting helps us to get beyond the first page and to overcome writer's block. Since we don't have to know what our message is, and since we don't have to write perfect prose, we tend not to be intimidated by starting. Many of my students who used to have difficulty writing and who experienced torturous periods of sitting at their desks not-writing and lip-biting have learned to be more relaxed about writing and to turn out prose more easily. Second, because freewriting is nonstop writing, we don't lose thoughts as we sometimes do when we compose slowly and try to perfect as we go along. Third, not only do we not forget thoughts, but we actually generate new thoughts. Freewriting promotes a creative flow and fosters new ideas. Because we don't censor ideas before having a chance to explore them, we can pursue ideas until they amount to something. Because freewriting allows for wandering and digressing, we can readily explore the gypsy avenues that often lead to provocative theses. When we finish a 45-minute freewriting session, we will be surprised to find that we have said more than we seemed to know when we started to write. Our ideas are better and we have stated them more freshly. Finally, freewriting separates the editing gremlin from the composing gremlin so that we don't try to edit while composing.

Despite these benefits, most students find freewriting difficult at first because it is so different from the way they learned to compose. The traditional model is to think and then write, but freewriting requires writing first and thinking later. Anything that is different seems unnatural and difficult initially, but if given a chance, freewriting works. We must have the courage to try a new way of doing an old activity, and freewriting takes a good deal of courage. For one thing, freewriting means accepting bad writing at first, and bad writing is something we're not used to accepting. We must tolerate wretched sentences, wrong words, inapt examples, and even mediocre ideas, realizing that the mediocre ideas will eventually lead to better ideas and that the sentences and words and examples will be perfected later. For another thing, freewriting means that we let chaos reign for a while. Freewriting is ungoverned, undisciplined, and chaotic, and therefore we have to be willing to be out of control in order to freewrite. After years of having written by the rules, we now are asked to disregard them. It's like having learned all the rules about driving, having learned to drive, and having been a good driver for years—and now all of a sudden we're told to ignore stop signs and speed limits, drive like crazy, run red lights, cut across lanes, pass on the right shoulder, and in general be a maniac behind the wheel. After writing by the rules for so long, it's difficult to become a transgressor.

The other reason that students are hesitant to try freewriting is that it seems to them inefficient and wasteful. It seems to take more time than the old way, and much of the writing is just thrown away. In fact, it takes no more time to produce a final draft with freewriting than it does the other way. A three-page essay may take an average of 4 to 6 hours for invention, outlining, drafting, and revising. In the same 4 hours, we can freewrite and analyze three versions (45 minutes each, with 15 minute analyses) and then compose the final version. Nor is freewriting wasteful; although much of what we produce we leave behind, we are simply getting rid of the bad ideas and moving on to better ones.

The ultimate test of any process is the quality of the product, and freewriting frequently produces a better short essay than the traditional method—and produces it more quickly and less painfully.

Combining Freewriting and Prewriting

Which writing method we use may depend on many factors: whether the task has to be completed within an hour (an exam) or over a weekend; how long the paper will be; whether we plan to incorporate research material; whether the topic is dictated to us or self-initiated; whether the writing is goal-oriented or simply personal reflection; whether we already have a thesis or must develop one; and what our mental inclination is at the time. For some projects, one method seems to work better, for other projects, the other method. And sometimes the brain just seems to be in one mode more than another, and I for one try not to oppose the brain's inclinations.

Neither the traditional method nor freewriting is perfect for all writing tasks. The prewrite/write method tends to interfere with the associative nature of composing; the freewriting method is not practical for papers that are long, that must be written quickly in one draft, that require research, or that are written from notes. Whereas the prewrite/write method may not allow enough associative thinking, freewriting may emphasize it at the expense of reflective thinking. Many writers find that instead of spending only 15 minutes on analysis, they need to get away from the task altogether for a while in order to get a better perspective on it and to let the mind reflect on the thesis.

The best advice is to use whichever method works better for you. Having talked with students about their writing processes, compared the processes of weak writers and excellent writers, and read what professional writers say about their processes, I have come to these conclusions:

1. Some good writers and weak writers use one approach; some good writers and weak writers use the other.
2. Some writers use both approaches, depending on the task.
3. Requiring writers to conform to one writing approach or the other seldom achieves the desired goal. The individual's psychological make-up determines as much as anything which approach he or she uses.
4. We must each use whichever process or combination of processes works best for us.

The two processes of writing—the methodical and the associative—need not cancel out each other. In fact, they can be viewed as complementary, and we can combine them to generate focused freewriting in the traditional model. For example, when writing a paper that seems too long for freewriting, we can use the journalistic questions to generate a subject and thesis, and we can divide the paper into smaller units (outline it) according to the traditional method of writing; then, when it comes to writing the blocked-off sections, we can use focused freewriting for each unit, composing and revising one section at a time. By freewriting the individual sections of a longer project, we can promote further discovery during composing, allow digressions, encourage necessary modifications of the thesis, and keep the imagination from being strictly controlled by the outline.

Another combination that many writers use when they already have a good thesis is to think about it for a long time without using a formal inventional method and without outlining. Angus Wilson calls this "the gestatory period before I start to write." The embryo of an idea grows within us, incubates, and then, when it is ready for delivery, we sit down and freewrite, starting perhaps with step two of Professor Elbow's plan.

We should become familiar with and be able to use both processes, not only because it's good to know an alternative to our current approach, but also because different tasks seem better suited to different approaches. When one approach doesn't work for us on a project, we should be able to switch to the other or to try a combination of the two. By combining them, we overcome the limitations of each, though there will still be times when freewriting by itself seems preferable. We need to adapt each process to suit our own personality and needs.

Conclusion

Not everyone writes in the same way, just as not everyone thinks alike or laughs alike. Some writers are perfectionists whose editorial gremlins won't let them write a sloppy first draft. Other writers cage their editorial gremlins and freewrite page after page nonstop. What works well for one writer may not work at all for another. Not only do we differ in our methods of writing, but also each of us may have a different method for different types of writing tasks, as noted earlier. So, what's the right answer?

There's an old Texas saying that goes: "I can tell you how to mount a horse, but I can't tell you how not to mount a horse." The same philosophy applies to writing. I have suggested some ways of writing that are known to work, but there are many ways to do it, and so long as they get the job done, that's what counts.

We will end by listening again to what some veterans say.

> I don't write drafts. I do page one many, many times and move on to page two. I pile up sheet after sheet, each in its final state.
>
> —Anthony Burgess

> I go through the first time in a very slapdash way, . . . and if I get into some nonsense or digressions, I write it through to the end and come out on the

other side. I'm not at all perfectionist at first. I do all the polishing in the last draft.

—Christopher Isherwood

Writing has got to be an act of discovery.

—Edward Albee

I think it out and then write it sentence by sentence—no first draft.

—Dorothy Parker

My ideal way . . . is to write the whole first draft through in one sitting, then work as long as it takes on revisions, and then write the final version all in one, so that in the end the whole thing amounts to one long sustained effort.

—Eudora Welty

I seem to have some neurotic need to perfect each paragraph—each sentence, even—as I go along.

—William Styron

Things come to me in driblets, and when the driblets come I have to work hard to make them into something coherent.

—Aldous Huxley

I just sit at a typewriter and curse a bit.

—P. G. Wodehouse

I suppose half of writing is overcoming the revulsion you feel when you sit down to it.

—Flannery O'Connor

I never quite know when I'm not writing. Sometimes my wife comes up to me at a dinner party and says, "Dammit, Thurber, stop writing." She usually catches me in the middle of a paragraph.

—James Thurber

Writing anything at all is a hell of a chore for me, closely related to acid indigestion.

—E. B. White

I always write my last line, my last paragraph, my last page first.

—Katherine Anne Porter

The art of writing has for backbone some fierce attachment to an idea.

—Virginia Woolf

The tools I need for my trade are paper, tobacco, food, and a little whiskey.

—William Faulkner

Eventually everyone learns his or her own best way.

—Bernard Malamud

II

EXPERIENTIAL WRITING

Experiential writing draws from the writer's own experiences and observations rather than from formal learning and research. The two types of experiential writing we will explore are narration and character description—how to tell a story and how to describe a person. These two chapters will reintroduce you to some basic principles of writing, encourage you to use your imagination, and prepare you for the more objective types of writing that follow.

We begin with experiential writing because most students find writing about their own experiences and perceptions to be less complicated than other kinds of writing. This is not to say that experiential writing isn't challenging, for it is. But when we write about our own perceptions, we are beginning where our expertise lies.

CHAPTER 3

Narration

Narration is the telling of a story. Most people associate narrative prose with fiction, such as fairy tales, short stories, and novels, and certainly these are narrative forms, but much nonfiction is also narrative, including biographies, histories, news articles, and many essays. In fact, the leading essayists today rely heavily on narration because they realize that story-telling is an effective vehicle for conveying a message. Of the various types of nonfiction narration—historical, reportorial, and personal—this chapter studies mainly personal narration, which relates our own experience.

Studying personal narration teaches us to explore our experiences and to seek the meaning of them; as Socrates said, "The unexamined life is not worth living." Studying narration also teaches us how to present our experiences in such a way that readers can mentally participate in and understand them. In addition, this chapter seeks to teach you how to select relevant details, how to arrange material chronologically, and how to use personal experience as evidence in arguments.

Personal narration offers many advantages. First, because it uses our own experience, it requires no research. Second, it has a natural structure; all narration follows a chronological (time) order. Third, everyone likes a good tale. The 4-year-old who pleads for a story at bedtime will retain a similar enjoyment of narration as an adult. Using narration to get a point across is effective because it ensures a certain amount of interest and reader involvement, for narration has more human warmth than nonnarrative essays. Fourth, because narration is entertaining, it makes readers more receptive to our ideas. With other prose forms, the writer sometimes appears to be lecturing readers, which can put them off. Finally, narration is versatile: It can be used not only to relate personal experience, but also to inform and to persuade.

Motives for Narrating

All of us have felt the need to narrate to others experiences that have had an impact on our character and may even have changed our lives in some way. Does this tendency show mere egocentricity? There may be an element of self-centeredness in recounting parts of our lives, but there are also other motives. Our desire to narrate a personal experience derives from an urge to share a part of ourselves with another person. Narration is a way of reaching out and giving an intimate part of ourselves to readers. When we re-create a personal incident, we invite readers to participate in the action and to feel the rare emotion that we originally felt. This imaginative reliving of another person's experience is called *vicarious experience.* Through vicarious experience, readers not only understand the narrator better, they also more fully understand the human condition because they have felt what it is like to be in another person's position and feel that person's emotions. In addition to sharing an emotion with readers, we communicate an insight into human existence when we narrate a personal experience, and therefore we are imparting knowledge and extending understanding.

Just as we learn from our own experiences, others can also learn from our experiences, and therefore one reason to pass along our experiences is to enlighten others. Realizing that considerable knowledge can be gained from analyzing experience, we invite readers to profit from our lessons. In this case, our reason for narrating is unselfish sharing and instruction.

Finally, we narrate to entertain people, and this too is a noble motive.

Invention

Before we go in search of experiences to relate, we need to determine what kinds of experiences make good narratives, for sometimes we have the makings of a good narrative but are not aware of the experience's potential. Most narratives concern incidents that significantly affected us: first encounters, turning points, emotional crises, crucial decisions, and important discoveries about ourselves and our world. An incident may have affected our attitude toward a certain subject, helped to form our character, or given us a valuable insight into human nature.

Personal narration presents the *meaning* of an incident; the reason behind a narrative essay is not so much the event itself as its significance. We interpret the action in a certain way and articulate what the event means to us. Usually the "point" of a narrative is the insight the narrator gained and shares with the readers. This is not to say that all narratives must contain a moral, such as "You can fool too many of the people too much of the time." Some narratives do not contain a message per se; they exist solely for the rare emotion they evoke (for example, the narrative on page 78) or for their entertainment value. In addition to being enjoyable reading, however, most narrative essays are didactic (instructive). They communicate a lesson, an insight, or a message.

The subject of a narrative doesn't have to be monumental or sensational. Sometimes we pass right over experiences that might provide good narrative material because we assume that narratives should be about life-shattering incidents. Instead of looking for incidents worthy of front-page news, we need to think smaller and to look for meaning even in apparently mundane experiences. The essay by Harry Crews on page 85 concerns cars, and the one by Phyllis Theroux on page 100 is on piano lessons.

Many personal narratives relate childhood experiences because incidents that occurred in our early years often helped to form our values and character. Those early experiences seem to take on added significance, and their images tend to glow more dominantly than later images in our memories. Important childhood experiences tend to stay with us for years, and therefore when we probe our memories for significant tales, those formative memories often stand out as being striking and exceptional. But whether the experience is early or late, we should be able to call up and examine those incidents that have affected our lives.

Some writers have no trouble coming up with a story to relate because they have retained vivid memories of their experiences and have contemplated the meaning of those experiences. Other writers do not have ready-made narratives on hand, and therefore they must search for experiences that will interest readers and will illustrate a point or convey a special feeling. We have all retained memories of such experiences, but they are buried and must be retrieved and examined. To help in this retrieval process, we can use the journalistic questions. The following are some initial questions to help you discover a topic, but once you have generated a topic, you will have to ask another series of questions to generate the details of that incident.

What is my most vivid memory of when I was:

5 years old	6 years old	7 years old
8 years old	9 years old	10 years old

How did I first learn about:

perseverance	the law	boundaries
sibling rivalry	hell	cooperation
the meaning of freedom	moral fortitude	racism

How did I learn to:

> overcome shyness
> control my humor, impatience, arrogance
> stop cheating, telling white lies

When was the first time I:

> rejected my parents' values
> stood up for a minority opinion that I held
> realized that America is imperfect
> realized that my mother or father is imperfect
> realized that I have a talent for _____
> realized that being different is all right
> admitted to myself that I lacked courage
> realized that my image of myself didn't correspond to others'
>   image of me
> realized that there are different kinds of victory
> learned to respect an opponent
> realized that neutrality on an issue is safe but not always desir-
>   able
> realized that threats, to be effective, must be carried out
> came to grips with the fact that I don't like one of the members
>   of my family
> defied an authority figure

What was my first encounter with:

blindness	tobacco	death
mental retardation	compromise	guns

What is my most vivid memory of:

rebellion	ridicule	excess
departing	punishment	loyalty
getting caught	shame	deception

What is my most vivid memory from:

sports	night	travel
summer	work	school

Where was I most happy, most sad, most alienated, most frightened?

What is my most vivid memory of my:

sister	brother	mother
father	grandfather	grandmother
best friend	rival	cousin

Why is _____ important to me?

What was my biggest:

ethical decision	boast	fear
lie	joke	hurdle

What have I witnessed (something that happened to someone else) that affected me significantly?

What experience illustrated for me an adage that I had often heard but had never completely understood, such as:

Oppression causes rebellion.
An oak is not felled with one stroke.
If you don't scale the mountain, you can't view the plain.
Mistakes are often the best teachers.
Deceit invites deceit, and trust begets trust.
A little learning is a dangerous thing.
Revenge becomes its own executioner.
Stolen fruit is best.
Success is the child of audacity.

Selecting Details

Any incident is filled with multiple actions, but we cannot possibly include all of them in a narrative because there are simply too many. Furthermore, we would not want to include them all because some are not relevant to the dramatic and emotional movement of the narrative. Our task is to select those actions, great and small, that contribute to a reader's understanding of the experience. We must omit any details that do not enhance our meaning, for we don't want to obscure the action with a mass of irrelevant details. In effect, we impose our perception onto an event and give the event meaning, and we do this by selecting and emphasizing details that we deem significant.

We choose details that are (1) informative, (2) vivid, and (3) revealing. *Informative* details impart necessary actions that allow readers to follow the sequence of events. For example:

At 12:10 P.M., the man turned right at the corner and walked toward a parked car. A woman was getting out of the car.

The purpose of this material is simply to inform readers of the time, place, and people involved in the action.

The purpose of *vivid* details is to give a clear picture of the action and to allow readers to see the events:

> The woman pushed a coin into the parking meter, and when the meter failed to register the time, she gave it a hard blow with the heel of her hand, like a karate instructor punching an inattentive pupil in the forehead. The meter wobbled and vibrated and returned to attention, now showing the allotted time. When she heard the man's footsteps, she turned and ran toward him in that quick, tiny-step gait that woman in high heels and tight skirts have mastered.

Because the actions are described in such a way as to produce a clear mental image, readers can visualize the woman hitting the meter and running toward the man—almost as if they were there watching her. Vivid details create realism in a narrative and convey a keen picture of the action.

Revealing details are often small details that convey an insight about the motivation of a person or about the meaning of an experience. For instance, in the following account of the man and woman meeting, what can we infer from the seemingly insignificant actions of the two people?

> The man looked up and down the street cautiously, then took her in his arms. While his arms were around her, he furtively looked at his watch, and she rubbed off her lipstick on a tissue.

The man looking up and down the street suggests that he doesn't want anyone to see them embrace; his looking at his watch perhaps suggests that they don't have much time together; her rubbing off her lipstick perhaps means that they intend to kiss, and she doesn't want to leave lipstick on him. If we add up all of these suggestions, what conclusion do we draw? Do the man and woman seem married—to each other? Could this be a lunchtime affair between a married woman and her lover, or a married man and his lover? Revealing details are ones that suggest something more than they actually state. Through implication, they communicate qualities and intentions beyond what the words say.

The following narrative by Norman Mailer recounts a tragic boxing match between Benny Paret and Emile Griffith. Your task is not only to pick out the various types of details Mailer uses, but also to explain why he emphasizes certain actions and compresses or ignore others.

THE DEATH OF BENNY PARET

Paret was a Cuban, a proud club fighter who had become welterweight champion because of his unusual ability to take a punch. His style of fighting was to take three punches to the head in order to give back two. At the end of ten rounds, he would still be bouncing, his opponent would have a headache. But in the last two years, over the fifteen-round fights, he had started to take some bad maulings.

This fight had its turns. Griffith won most of the early rounds, but Paret knocked Griffith down in the sixth. Griffith had trouble getting up, but made it, came alive and was dominating Paret again before the round was over. Then Paret began to wilt. In the middle of the eighth round, after a clubbing punch had turned his back to Griffith, Paret walked three disgusted steps away, showing his hindquarters. For a champion, he took much too long to turn back around. It was the first hint of weakness Paret had ever shown, and it must have inspired a particular shame, because he fought the rest of the fight as if he were seeking to demonstrate that he could take more punishment than any man alive. In the twelfth, Griffith caught him. Paret got trapped in a corner. Trying to duck away, his left arm and his head became tangled on the wrong side of the top rope. Griffith was in like a cat ready to rip the life out of a huge boxed rat. He hit him eighteen right hands in a row, an act which took perhaps three or four seconds, Griffith making a pent-up whimpering sound all the while he attacked, the right hand whipping like a piston rod which has broken through the crankcase, or like a baseball bat demolishing a pumpkin. I was sitting in the second row of that corner—they were not ten feet away from me, and like everyone else, I was hypnotized. I had never seen one man hit another so hard and so many times. Over the referee's face came a look of woe as if some spasm had passed its way through him, and then he leaped on Griffith to pull him away. It was the act of a brave man. Griffith was uncontrollable. His trainer leaped into the ring, his manager, his cut man, there were four people holding Griffith, but he was off on an orgy, he had left the Garden, he was back on a hoodlum's street. If he had been able to break loose from his handlers and the referee, he would have jumped Paret to the floor and whaled on him there.

And Paret? Paret died on his feet. As he took those eighteen punches something happened to everyone who was in psychic range of the event. Some part of his death reached out to us. One felt it hover in the air. He was still standing in the ropes, trapped as he had been before, he gave some little half-smile of regret, as if he were saying, "I didn't know I was going to die just yet," and then, his head leaning back but still erect, his death came to breathe about him. He began to pass away. As he passed, so his limbs descended beneath him, and he sank slowly to the floor. He went down more slowly than any fighter had ever gone down, he went down like a large ship which turns on end and slides second by second into its grave. As he went down, the sound of Griffith's punches echoed in the mind like a heavy ax in the distance chopping into a wet log.

—From "The Eleventh Presidential Paper" in *The Presidential Papers*

This is an effective narrative for many reasons: The subject is life and death; the action is physical, even gladiatorial; the sentence structure reflects the action; and the author has a keen understanding of the action and its significance. But a major reason for its success is the choice of details.

Mailer includes only those details that contribute to the clarity, impact, and meaning of the action. There is not a single irrelevant detail.

In his first paragraph, for example, we get a summary of Paret's boxing style and character, and there is an ominous foreshadowing in the last sentence, "bad maulings" being a preparation for the bad mauling ahead. Although the introduction is brief, it tells us all we need in order to understand what follows. Because Mailer is anxious to get to the narrative, he includes only the information essential to understanding the action.

In the second paragraph, Mailer opens with a generalization—"This fight had its turns"—that allows him to summarize nonessential action. He compresses the time and skips over the early rounds because, in his perception of the fight, they are unimportant. A detailed, blow-by-blow account of the early action would contribute little and would bog down the narrative. We are not baffled about what happened in the first through fifth rounds; we know all we need to: Griffith dominated. Mailer keeps the narrative compact and moving. He focuses on the sixth round because he sees it as the first turning point: Although Paret knocked Griffith down, Griffith came back strongly and "Paret began to wilt." In three sentences Mailer has escorted us through six rounds, yet we don't feel confused by the compression. Although he completely skips the seventh round, we don't wonder what happened in that round; we assume that nothing of importance occurred.

After devoting only half a sentence to the first five rounds, Mailer allocates four sentences to a hardly noticeable occurrence in the eighth round: Griffith hits Paret so hard that the blow spins Paret around, and Paret walks away three steps. Why does Mailer focus our attention on this incident, which most sportswriters at ringside would have overlooked? He does so because he sees great significance in the incident; to him, it is a revealing detail. He interprets the walking away as an act of weakness and as a sign of despair and temporary surrender. Mailer surmises that Paret realizes the significance of his turning away, and Mailer speculates as to the champ's psychological reaction: Ashamed of himself, Paret tries to prove his manhood and his champion spirit by not turning away from the grueling beating. The minor action of walking away becomes a psychological motivation.

The next action that the narrator focuses on is the major action, the fatal beating in the twelfth round. The ninth, tenth, and eleventh rounds are skipped because they contain no individually significant incidents, though Mailer has indicated that Paret is taking a pounding. In the twelfth round Mailer describes in detail Paret's entrapment and Griffith's wild frenzy. To communicate the chaos in the ring, Mailer intentionally abandons proper punctuation and writes in a confused style.

At this point, the focus shifts from Griffith to others—to the referee, to the spectators, and to Mailer himself. Mailer chooses to include others' reactions to demonstrate their shock at Griffith's bloodthirsty rampage and to build suspense over what happens to Paret. Time stands still for a moment.

"And Paret? Paret died on his feet." The conclusion focuses on Paret's dying and on its effect on the audience.

In our own narratives, we must, like Mailer, select details that enhance our interpretation of the action. Mailer has selected and ordered the material according to his perception and in doing so has given meaning to the material. He has given us actions that reveal psychological motives and has substantiated his interpretation by emphasizing certain actions over others. The details he has chosen are not necessarily those another writer would have selected, since another writer might have a different emphasis, a different perception, and a different purpose.

The next piece is an early draft of a student essay, and although it contains the kernel of an interesting and poignant tale, the narrator needs to revise the piece. If a fellow student handed this essay to you for comment, which details would you suggest omitting, and which expanding? Why?

When I was young I lived on a farm and had all kinds of summer projects. I raised rabbits and poulets and grew a garden for money. One of my projects when I was ten was growing watermelons. My father, who encouraged me and occasionally lent a hand, plowed up 5 acres, and I planted the seeds in late April. I fertilized and hoed and prayed for rain, and by the middle of July I had melons galore. The price was holding up, and I was taking a pickup load every week to the market. I even won third place at the watermelon contest with my 37-pound entry. Up to that point it was a glorious summer.

Then something started eating the melons. It couldn't have been the cows because the patch was fenced. From the way the melons were eaten, I knew it was raccoons. They make a hole in a melon, stick their paws into the melon, and clean it out. Every morning I found 2 or 3 melons with holes the size of half-dollars in them, empty inside. I was madder than a wet goat. I asked my father what I could do to stop the coons from devouring my profits, and he outlined several options—chaining a watchdog in the patch, hanging lanterns around it, or buying traps. I thought traps sounded reasonable and adventuresome so he drove me to town and while he bought groceries I went to the hardware store and asked Mr. Kanichas, the owner, to show me some coon traps. He had two types. One was a steel spring-trap that caught the animal by the leg; the other was a cage that had a door which locked when the animal entered. Because the leg trap was half the price of the other, I bought it, though Mr. Kanichas pressured me to buy the other one. While at the hardware store I picked up some special seeds my mother had ordered and talked to Mr. Kanichas about trapping coons. He said he too used to trap them when he was a boy and said he even caught a coyote once.

I took the trap home and set it, jaws open and ready to bite, next to the biggest melon in the patch. I chained the trap to a heavy log so a coon couldn't escape with my new trap. Nothing happened for two nights, but the third night I trapped one that got away, leaving its foot in the trap. Determined to catch a whole coon, I reset the trap and put it next to another melon. That night I caught another one, and as it saw me approaching it too tried frantically to gnaw off its paw. It was terrified. I felt sorry for it and tried to let it loose but couldn't get close to it. So I had to shoot it.

I had never stopped to think what it would be like for the animal I would catch. And I could not understand why anything so inhumane as steel-jawed traps was legal. I threw the trap away.

There are several problems with this narration. First, it is not properly proportioned; the introduction is much too lengthy, and the penultimate (next to last) paragraph needs expanding. Second, irrelevant material slows down the narration and interferes with the focus of the story. For example, paragraph 1 can be condensed considerably by omitting the extraneous "projects" and the father's role, maybe also the prize. The second sentence of paragraph 2 contributes nothing, nor do the facts that the father bought groceries, that there were seeds to be picked up, or that Mr. Kanichas trapped coons as a boy. A third weakness is that paragraph 3 *tells* about instead of *showing* the coon's terror and the narrator's reaction. The third paragraph, which is the heart of the story, is mere summary. The writer needs to re-create the emotions of that moment and make the action real and immediate. To achieve this, the narrator must develop more fully the incident in paragraph 3, describing in detail the "leaving its foot in the trap," "It was terrified," and "I felt sorry for it." Here is the revision, several drafts later.

The summer I was ten I planted 5 acres of our family farm in watermelons. Because the patch was my first major farming project, I was determined to make a success of it, and therefore I fertilized and hoed and prayed for rain all summer. My work and prayers having paid off, by July I had enough of a harvest to take a pickup load to market every Saturday.

Introduction states time, place, significance of project, early success

Then the raids began. Every night, marauders invaded the patch and ate two or more choice melons. From the footprints and the method of eating (a small hole through which little paws scooped out juicy chunks), I knew who the bandits were— raccoons. Because I was only ten and lacked any perspective on the situation, I saw the problem of the coons as a personal battle. They were out to destroy my pride and to ruin me financially. When I asked my father how I could stop their plundering, he outlined several options: chaining a watchdog in the patch, hanging lanterns around it, or buying traps.

Narrator's viewpoint

Such words as "marauders," "raids," "plundering," and "bandits" (raccoons have masked faces) used to convey pillage

Narrator makes
choice

"Traps!" I said. The idea of becoming a trapper appealed to me because it conjured up images of Davy Crockett in a coonskin cap. Vowing to win the battle against the varmints, I went to town for supplies.

"Ya got any coon traps?" I asked the owner of the hardware store.

He showed me two types, one being a steel-jawed spring trap that catches the animal by the leg, the other a cage with a door that locks after the animal enters.

Use of dialogue for flavor and variety

"This 'un here," he explained, pointing at the cage, "doesn't hurt the animal. You can release it unharmed and still be certain that it won't return to your patch because it's been scared so bad. This other'un here is effective but makes the animal suffer terribly, and you've then got to kill it."

"How much?" I asked in my deepest, business-like voice.

"The cage is $12.95, the jaws $5.95."

Narrator makes moral decision

Thinking that he was using the lecture on pain as an angle for a sales pitch—I wasn't stupid, even if I was only ten—I bought the jaw trap. Besides, I *wanted* the masked devils to suffer. Hadn't they already cost me over $20 in melons?

Details to show (1) the trap's malicious power and (2) the narrator's moral deficiency

I practiced setting the trap all day. It was so strong that I had to stand on the clamps to pry the jaws open; after hooking the spring under the disc, I slowly stepped off the clamps. Then I took a stick and hit the disc—WHAMP!—the jaws with their ragged steel teeth snapping together on the stick. I was actually a little afraid of the darn thing because it was so ferocious. I was satisfied, at least, that a coon couldn't escape from it.

I placed the trap next to the biggest melon in the patch and chained the trap to a heavy log. The first night the coons raided but ate other melons. "Clever devils," I thought. The second night they didn't come. "Probably full from last night," I grumbled. But the third night I trapped one, evidently a big one. Attempting to escape, it had pulled the trap and the anchoring log halfway

First real action

across the patch but couldn't pull it through the fence. Thwarted in its escape, probably exhausted from tugging the log, and no doubt panicky as dawn neared, the animal did the only thing it could to save its life: it gnawed off its paw. When I found the trap, a tiny, bloody paw was all that was in it.

Considers the coon's reaction

Visual image conveyed

Looking back on the incident, I am appalled by my reaction as I stood over the sacrificed paw. Instead of realizing my cruelty in choosing the bone-crushing jaw-trap, and instead of considering the pain and the courage of the coon, I was angry that it had escaped.

Significance of the first action: narrator is *not* changed

One-sentence paragraph to emphasize the narrator's moral starkness

I reset the trap.

That night an old boar coon stepped into the trap. As with the previous animal, he had begun dragging away the trap and anchor, but he had not reached the fence when I walked out, gun in hand, to check the trap that morning. When he saw me coming, he tugged harder and harder across the field, like a horse pulling a heavy wagon. He made it to the fence, but the log again became lodged in the wire.

Beginning of second action

Simile to convey image

As I approached the ensnared animal, he was frantically gnawing on the offending paw. He looked up at me. His eyes were black holes of terror. Strings of his own flesh were in his teeth. Paralyzed with fear, he stared straight into my eyes for a full minute, both of us breathing heavily. In that long exchange, I suddenly felt what the coon felt—the pain, the desperation, the terror.

Beginning of moral recognition

Emotional climax of the narrative

Suddenly he began jerking at the trap and log with all his strength, the fence squeaking and stretching with every heave. I tried to grab the trap and open the jaws to free the coon, but he was too frantic to let me near him. So I stood and watched guiltily as he pulled and pulled against the fence until I couldn't stand it any longer. I knew even as I fired the rifle that the coon would live long in my memory. He collapsed, quivered, died.

Completion of action

I threw the trap into the creek. I wanted to throw all the traps in the world into the creek.

Action indicative of moral acknowledgment

Even though we know what happens from having read the first version, this revision still holds our attention. The omission of some details and the inclusion of others make all the difference in the world. The revision makes the moral decision more apparent and makes the emotion and the moral recognition at the end more real. Furthermore, the essay is a persuasive statement against steel-jawed traps as well as an important personal experience for the narrator. The essay is in many ways more persuasive than a logical analysis of animal trapping. By *seeing* what happened and by emotionally experiencing the incident, readers have a strong feeling against traps. It is like seeing a photograph of one of those adorable baby seals, all white and furry, about to get its head clubbed in by a furrier. We don't care about the economics of the situation; our emotional reaction overrides all arguments.

Thesis Statement

A narrator communicates the point of a story indirectly, by the selection of details and the tone, and directly, by explicit statement of the thesis. Unless we are certain that our point is inescapable, it is a good idea to state the thesis straightforwardly. Spelling out the thesis precludes a reader's asking at the end, "So what?" or "What's the point?"

For the sake of emphasis, the thesis statement usually comes either at the beginning or the end of the essay. If it comes at the beginning, it should be brief and should prepare the reader for the story that follows. For example, the opening sentence of Richard Wright's "The Ethics of Jim Crow" succinctly provides the general significance of the essay: "My first lesson in how to live as a Negro came when I was quite small." If the thesis statement comes at the conclusion, as in Mark Harris' " 'The Merry Widow Waltz' in Colors" on page 102, it may be expanded to several sentences because readers wish to hear the significance of the story they have just read. Where we place the thesis depends on whether our emphasis is on suspense or enlightenment.

A dual thesis statement is what many writers find effective. In that case, the opening of the narrative hints at the thesis, just enough to entice the reader, but the full statement of the thesis is saved till later. George Orwell, for instance, states in the third paragraph of "Shooting an Elephant":

> One day something happened which in a roundabout way was enlightening. It was a tiny incident in itself, but it gave me a better glimpse than I had had before of the real nature of imperialism—the real motives for which despotic governments act.

This partial thesis does not tell us what the "real nature" is. Orwell merely stakes out the boundaries of the discussion and makes us curious, then fully develops the thesis later in the essay.

APPLICATION

The following piece, taken from Langston Hughes' autobiography, concerns the writer's pretended religious conversion at a small-town revival.

1. What is the purpose of the first paragraph?
2. Why is the description of "seeing the light" in paragraph 2 important to the rest of the story?
3. How does Hughes build up anticipation in his readers?
4. Why does he include details about the preacher's sermon and the old people? Are those details relevant to his story? Why, or why not?

5. Why is the other boy, Westley, important to the tale?
6. Why does Hughes include dialogue?
7. Since the purpose of a religious revival is to save souls, what is the irony of Hughes' final conviction? (*Situational irony* means that the result of a series of events is opposite to the intended outcome.)
8. Where is the significance of the narrative stated? Why does Hughes place the thesis there instead of elsewhere?

SALVATION

I was saved from sin when I was going on thirteen. But not really saved. It happened   1
like this. There was a big revival at my Auntie Reed's church. Every night for weeks there had been much preaching, singing, praying, and shouting, and some very hardened sinners had been brought to Christ, and the membership of the church had grown by leaps and bounds. Then just before the revival ended, they held a special meeting for children, "to bring the young lambs to the fold." My aunt spoke of it for days ahead. That night I was escorted to the front row and placed on the mourners' bench with all the other young sinners, who had not yet been brought to Jesus.

My aunt told me that when you were saved you saw a light, and something   2
happened to you inside! And Jesus came into your life! And God was with you from then on! She said you could see and hear and feel Jesus in your soul. I believed her. I have heard a great many old people say the same thing and it seemed to me they ought to know. So I sat there calmly in the hot, crowded church, waiting for Jesus to come to me.

The preacher preached a wonderful rhythmical sermon, all moans and shouts   3
and lonely cries and dire pictures of hell, and then he sang a song about the ninety and nine safe in the fold, but one little lamb was left out in the cold. Then he said: "Won't you come? Won't you come to Jesus? Young lambs, won't you come?" And he held out his arms to all us young sinners there on the mourners' bench. And the little girls cried. And some of them jumped up and went to Jesus right away. But most of us just sat there.

A great many old people came and knelt around us and prayed, old women with   4
jet-black faces and braided hair, old men with work-gnarled hands. And the church sang a song about the lower lights are burning, some poor sinners to be saved. And the whole building rocked with prayer and song.

Still I kept waiting to *see* Jesus.   5

Finally all the young people had gone to the altar and were saved, but one boy   6
and me. He was a rounder's son named Westley. Westley and I were surrounded by sisters and deacons praying. It was very hot in the church, and getting late now. Finally Westley said to me in a whisper: "God damn! I'm tired o' sitting here. Let's get up and be saved." So he got up and was saved.

Then I was left all alone on the mourners' bench. My aunt came and knelt at my   7
knees and cried, while prayers and songs swirled all around me in the little church. The whole congregation prayed for me alone, in a mighty wail of moans and voices.

And I kept waiting serenely for Jesus, waiting, and waiting—but he didn't come. I wanted to see him, but nothing happened to me. Nothing! I wanted something to happen to me, but nothing happened.

I heard the songs and the minister saying: "Why don't you come? My dear child, why don't you come to Jesus? Jesus is waiting for you. He wants you. Why don't you come? Sister Reed, what is this child's name?"   8

"Langston," my aunt sobbed.   9

"Langston, why don't you come? Why don't you come and be saved? Oh, Lamb of God! Why don't you come?"   10

Now it was really getting late. I began to be ashamed of myself, holding everything up so long. I began to wonder what God thought about Westley, who certainly hadn't seen Jesus either, but who was now sitting proudly on the platform, swinging his knickerbockered legs and grinning down at me, surrounded by deacons and old women on their knees praying. God had not struck Westley dead for taking his name in vain or for lying in the temple. So I decided that maybe to save further trouble, I'd better lie, too, and say that Jesus had come, and get up and be saved.   11

So I got up.   12

Suddenly the whole room broke into a sea of shouting, as they saw me rise. Waves of rejoicing swept the place. Women leaped in the air. My aunt threw her arms around me. The minister took me by the hand and led me to the platform.   13

When things quieted down, in a hushed silence, punctuated by a few ecstatic "Amens," all the new young lambs were blessed in the name of God. Then joyous singing filled the room.   14

That night, for the last time in my life but one—for I was a big boy twelve years old—I cried. I cried, in bed alone, and couldn't stop. I buried my head under the quilts, but my aunt heard me. She woke up and told my uncle I was crying because the Holy Ghost had come into my life, and because I had seen Jesus. But I was really crying because I couldn't bear to tell her that I had lied, that I had deceived everybody in the church, that I hadn't seen Jesus, and that now I didn't believe there was a Jesus any more, since he didn't come to help me.   15

—From *The Big Sea*

Beginning, Middle, and End

A narrative must be complete within itself and must stand as a distinct entity. To be whole, therefore, it should have a beginning, a middle, and an end, and each stage in the narrative has a particular function. A typical beginning, for instance, indicates the time and place, sets the tone, introduces the characters, and suggests a potential conflict or change of fortune. Beginnings often are descriptive or explanatory rather than narrative; they explain the situation and prepare for the telling of the tale.

The middle is the rise and fall of the conflict. Early in this stage, while the conflict develops and the relationships among the characters are revealed, the action may be slow, but then events occur that increase tension, the pace quickens, and the narrative moves inevitably toward a crisis. All the while, the reader is becoming involved in the action and is identifying with the narrator. Eventually, the turn of events precipitates a crucial action or climax, and finally the conflict is resolved, one way or another.

Immediately after the climax and resolution comes the conclusion to the essay. The end of a narrative is not simply the completion of the action; it is the narrator's perception of the story's significance. Often, the end of a narrative essay is a statement of the narrator's revelation or new awareness, which was evoked by the chain of events. The conclusion typically is the thesis statement, or the "point" of the story.

Chronological Order

A distinguishing feature of narration is its use of chronological order, which means that the material is arranged according to a time sequence. Time is the easiest principle for ordering materials because we simply record events in the order that they occurred. Likewise, chronological order is easy for readers to follow because they are accustomed to perceiving actions in sequences.

We perceive our whole lives chronologically. For example, if you were asked to write a brief biography of Abraham Lincoln, where would you start, where would you end, and how would you arrange the material in between? No doubt you would start with his birth in a log cabin in 1809 and follow with his growing up in Indiana and Illinois. In his early twenties he took a series of jobs as store clerk, postmaster, and surveyor. In 1834 he was elected to the Illinois General Assembly, 2 years later he received his law license, and in 1842 he married Mary Todd. He won a seat in Congress in 1847 but failed to be reelected and returned to his law practice for several years. In 1856 he helped to form the Illinois division of the new Republican party and gained national attention for his opposition to slavery. Although he lost to Stephen Douglas a bid for the United States Senate in 1858, 2 years later he was elected the sixteenth president of the United States. Within weeks the Civil War began, and Lincoln spent his entire term of office trying to unify the republic. Shortly after Lee's surrender in 1865, Lincoln was assassinated.

Consider two things about this biographical sketch: First, it uses a straight chronological order and therefore is easy to follow; and second, it directs and orients the reader by providing dates and mentioning time spans. The sketch not only records the major events in Lincoln's life in the order of their occurrence, but also tells readers when those events occurred in relation to one another. These references to time help readers understand the progression of Lincoln's life and help them get from one sentence to the next. Each sentence contains some mention of time: 1809, early twenties, 1834, 2 years later, 1842, 1847, several years, 1856, 2 years later, 1858, within weeks, term of office, after surrender in 1865.

A personal narrative is arranged in the same way and relies on similar references to time. We put the events in their order of occurrence: first this, then that, next this, and so forth until the story is completed. And we use the terminology of time to unite our thoughts and to help readers make the necessary connections. References to time include

then	while	meanwhile
next	soon	at the same time
when	later	simultaneously
now	since	in the interim
momentarily	suddenly	before long
earlier	prior to	immediately
hitherto	already	after
afterward	concurrently	without delay
previously	recently	subsequently
henceforth	until	thereafter

periods of time: minute, hour, day, week, month, year, 1946, decade, the 1970s, century, seasons

APPLICATION

In the following excerpt, Peter Mathiessen recounts a touching episode about his relationship with his dying wife, D.

1. What time references does he use to help readers grasp the chronology of the events?
2. In addition to the direct references to time, the writer has indicated relative time through his verb tenses. Most of the story is in simple past tense— *discovered, was, came, made*—but in several places Mathiessen uses other tenses to indicate prior or future action. Point out those instances and explain the necessity of using these other tenses.
3. Why does the piece carry such a strong emotional impact? Describe the effect the narrative has on you.

In the dark winter afternoon, in the old quarter of Geneva, we discovered a most beautiful bowl in a shop window, seven elegant thin black fishes in calligraphic design on old white and pale blue; the bowl, fired at Istafahan in the thirteenth century, seemed to float in the hands like an old leaf. But it was too expensive, and I found her something else. Next morning, her plane left an hour before mine [she went to

America, he to Italy], and in this interim, carried away by the drama of our parting, I telephoned the antique shop and arranged to buy the Istafahan bowl, which was eventually sent on to Italy to be carried home. The delicate thing was a symbol of a new beginning, and I meant to surprise D with it on her birthday, but when that day came we quarreled, and the bowl, put away for a better occasion, was forgotten altogether as the marriage came apart. No parting was quite final, each wild reconciliation was followed by new crisis; an exhausted decision to divorce was made on a late summer's morning just five months before her death. That decision was firm, we made it calmly and were both relieved. The very next day, acting on an imperious inner command, I made a commitment to D, this time for good. She understood; sipping coffee in the sun, she merely nodded.

In the autumn, D [began] to suffer from obscure pains that the doctors could not identify; she grew thin, wide-eyed, very beautiful. She came home from the hospital in early December, when no clues to her pain were found, but two weeks later metastatic cancer was discovered, and she entered another hospital just before Christmas. She was frightened and depressed, and wished desperately to know that the love I felt for her was not just pity, that it had been there in some measure all along. I remembered the Istafahan bowl.

On Christmas Eve, I had gone home to patch together some sort of Christmas for the children, but I forgot to bring the bowl back to New York. Had I given it to her earlier, she would have understood just what it meant; but by January, D was in such pain and so heavily sedated that any sort of present seemed forlorn. She scarcely knew friends who came to visit: what could she make of a bowl she had seen just once, on another continent, a year before? I had missed a precious chance, and I remember that as I propped her up in bed, coaxing her to concentrate, then opened up the box and placed the bowl in her hands, my heart was pounding. I could scarcely bear to watch how D stared at the bowl, grimacing in the effort to fight off the pain, the drugs, the consuming cancer in her brain. But when I prepared to take it back, she pressed it to her heart, lay back like a child, eyes shining, and in a whisper got one word out: "Swit-zerland!"

—From *The Snow Leopard*

Flashbacks

Stories are not always written in strict chronological order. In addition to straight chronology, narrators often use what is called *flashback*—an interruption in the story in order to relate an event that happened earlier. We flash from the present to the past, stopping the current action to insert a scene from the past. Instead of proceeding according to straight chronological order:

beginning → middle → end

the story jumps back in time, and then picks up the present again:

beginning → stop return to present → end

flashback

There are two types of flashbacks. One gives readers information from the past that is necessary to understand the story. We reach a point in our tale where we deem it necessary to relate a prior event that has a bearing on the story; we therefore insert a flashback. For example, in relating a battle between Grant and Lee, a historian might stop the narration before a cavalry charge to summarize an account of a previous battle between Grant and Lee in which Grant used his cavalry in a certain manuever; Lee, remembering Grant's characteristic tactic, anticipates the move and counters with his own cavalry. The flashback to the previous battle helps readers understand the current battle.

The other type of flashback, instead of providing factual information, provides emotional information. We come to a point in the story that suddenly reminds us of a similar incident or image in the past, and our minds race back to that previous event. The flashback seems spontaneous, and it is tied to the present story thematically; that is, both flashback and story have a common theme, such as loyalty or perversity. Because the flashback relates emotions concerning a previous incident, it helps to explain the motivation or reaction in the current situation. This type of flashback helps to develop the emotional impact of a story.

In either type of flashback, the incident must be relevant to the current story and must contribute to it in a factual or emotional way. Also, we must use transitional phrases to signal when the flashback begins (for example, "four years earlier") and ends so that readers will not become disoriented by the shifts in time. Flashbacks should be used sparingly because they alter the way readers usually perceive action, but there are times when they can be highly effective.

The following essay provides a good example of how to use a flashback effectively. The writer, a surgeon named Richard Selzer, relates his encounters with a professional wrestler, the first encounter when Selzer was a child, the next encounter being nearly 40 years later, and the third encounter 2 years after that. The essay, however, does not proceed according to straight chronology; it opens in one time period, shifts to the earlier one, and concludes with the latest period. How does Selzer effect these shifts without confusing his readers? What is the purpose of the flashback?

THE MASKED MARVEL'S LAST TOEHOLD

MORNING ROUNDS

On the fifth floor of the hospital, in the west wing, I know that a man is sitting up in his bed, waiting for me. Elihu Koontz is seventy-five, and he is diabetic. It is two weeks since I amputated his left leg just below the knee. I walk down the corridor, but I do not go straight into his room. Instead, I pause in the doorway. He is not yet aware of my presence, but gazes down at the place in the bed where his leg used to be, and where now there is the collapsed leg of his pajamas. He is totally absorbed, like an athlete appraising the details of his body. What is he thinking, I wonder. Is he dreaming the outline of his toes. Does he see there his foot's incandescent ghost? Could he be angry? Feel that I have taken from him something for which he yearns now with all his heart? Has he forgotten so soon the pain? It was a pain so great as to set him apart from all other men, in a red-hot place where he had no kith or kin. What of those black gorilla toes and the soupy mess that was his heel? I watch him from the doorway. It is a kind of spying, I know.

Save for a white fringe open at the front, Elihu Koontz is bald. The hair has grown too long and is wilted. He wears it as one would wear a day-old laurel wreath. He is naked to the waist, so that I can see his breasts. They are the breasts of Buddha, inverted triangles from which the nipples swing, dark as garnets.

I have seen enough. I step into the room, and he sees that I am there.

"How did the night go, Elihu?"

He looks at me for a long moment. "Shut the door," he says.

I do, and move to the side of the bed. He takes my left hand in both of his, gazes at it, turns it over, then back, fondling, at last holding it up to his cheek. I do not withdraw from this loving. After a while he relinquishes my hand, and looks up at me.

"How is the pain?" I ask.

He does not answer, but continues to look at me in silence. I know at once that he has made a decision.

"Ever hear of The Masked Marvel?" He says this in a low voice, almost a whisper.

"What?"

"The Masked Marvel," he says. "You never heard of him?"

"No."

He clucks his tongue. He is exasperated.

All at once there is a recollection. It is dim, distant, but coming near.

"Do you mean the wrestler?"

Eagerly, he nods, and the breasts bob. How gnomish he looks, oval as the huge helpless egg of some outlandish lizard. He has very long arms, which, now and then, he unfurls to reach for things—a carafe of water, a get-well card. He gazes up at me, urging. He *wants* me to remember.

"Well . . . yes," I say. I am straining backward in time. "I saw him wrestle in Toronto long ago."

"Ha!" He smiles. "You saw *me.*" And his index finger, held rigid and upright, bounces in the air.

The man has said something shocking, unacceptable. It must be challenged.

"You?" I am trying to smile.

Again that jab of the finger. "You saw *me.*"

"No," I say. But even then, something about Elihu Koontz, those prolonged arms, the shape of his head, the sudden agility with which he leans from his bed to get a large brown envelope from his nightstand, something is forcing me toward a memory. He rummages through his papers, old newspaper clippings, photographs, and I remember . . .

It is almost forty years ago. I am ten years old. I have been sent to Toronto to spend the summer with relatives. Uncle Max has bought two tickets to the wrestling match. He is taking me that night.

"He isn't allowed," says Aunt Sarah to me. Uncle Max has angina.

"He gets too excited," she says.

"I wish you wouldn't go, Max," she says.

"You mind your own business," he says.

And we go. Out into the warm Canadian evening. I am not only abroad, I am abroad in the *evening!* I have never been taken out in the evening. I am terribly excited. The trolleys, the lights, the horns. It is a bazaar. At the Maple Leaf Gardens, we sit high and near the center. The vast arena is dark except for the brilliance of the ring at the bottom.

It begins.

The wrestlers circle. They grapple. They are all haunch and paunch. I am shocked by their ugliness, but I do not show it. Uncle Max is exhilarated. He leans forward, his eyes unblinking, on his face a look of enormous happiness. One after the other, a pair of wrestlers enter the ring. The two men join, twist, jerk, tug, bend, yank, and throw. Then they leave and are replaced by another pair. At last it is the main event. "The Angel vs. The Masked Marvel."

On the cover of the program notes, there is a picture of The Angel hanging from the limb of a tree, a noose of thick rope around his neck. The Angel hangs just so for an hour every day, it is explained, to strengthen his neck. The Masked Marvel's trademark is a black stocking cap with holes for the eyes and mouth. He is never seen without it, states the program. No one knows who The Masked Marvel really is!

"Good," says Uncle Max. "Now you'll see something." He is fidgeting, waiting for them to appear. They come down separate aisles, climb into the ring from opposite sides. I have never seen anything like them. It is The Angel's neck that first captures the eye. The shaved nape rises in twin columns to puff into the white hood of a sloped and bosselated skull that is too small. As though, strangled by the sinews of that neck, the skull had long since withered and shrunk. The thing about The Angel is the absence of any mystery in his body. It is simply *there.* A monosyllabic announcement. A grunt. One looks and knows everything at once, the fat thighs, the gigantic buttocks, the great spine from which hang knotted ropes and pale aprons of beef. And that prehistoric head. He is all of a single hideous piece, The Angel is. No detachables.

The Masked Marvel seems dwarfish. His fingers dangle kneeward. His short legs are slightly bowed as if under the weight of the cask they are forced to heft about. He has breasts that swing when he moves! I have never seen such breasts on a man before.

There is a sudden ungraceful movement, and they close upon one another. The

Angel stoops and hugs The Marvel about the waist, locking his hands behind The Marvel's back. Now he straightens and lifts The Marvel as though he were uprooting a tree. Thus he holds him, then stoops again, thrusts one hand through The Marvel's crotch, and with the other grabs him by the neck. He rears and . . . The Marvel is aloft! For a long moment, The Angel stands as though deciding where to make the toss. Then throws. Was that board or bone that splintered there? Again and again, The Angel hurls himself upon the body of The Masked Marvel.

Now The Angel rises over the fallen Marvel, picks up one foot in both of his hands, and twists the toes downward. It is far beyond the tensile strength of mere ligament, mere cartilage. The Masked Marvel does not hide his agony, but pounds and slaps the floor with his hand, now and then reaching up toward The Angel in an attitude of supplication. I have never seen such suffering. And all the while his black mask rolls from side to side, the mouth pulled to a tight slit through which issues an endless hiss that I can hear from where I sit. All at once, I hear a shouting close by.

"Break it off! Tear off a leg and throw it up here!"

It is Uncle Max. Even in the darkness I can see that he is gray. A band of sweat stands upon his upper lip. He is on his feet now, panting, one fist pressed at his chest, the other raised warlike toward the ring. For the first time I begin to think that something terrible might happen here. Aunt Sarah was right.

"Sit down, Uncle Max," I say. "Take a pill, please."

He reaches for the pillbox, gropes, and swallows without taking his gaze from the wrestlers. I wait for him to sit down.

"That's not fair," I say, "twisting his toes like that."

"It's the toehold," he explains.

"But it's not *fair*," I say again. The whole of the evil is laid open for me to perceive. I am trembling.

And now The Angel does something unspeakable. Holding the foot of The Marvel at full twist with one hand, he bends and grasps the mask where it clings to the back of The Marvel's head. And he pulls. He is going to strip it off! Lay bare an ultimate carnal mystery! Suddenly it is beyond mere physical violence. Now I am on my feet, shouting into the Maple Leaf Gardens.

"Watch out," I scream. "Stop him. Please, somebody, stop him."

Next to me, Uncle Max is chuckling.

Yet The Masked Marvel hears me, I know it. And rallies from his bed of pain. Thrusting with his free heel, he strikes The Angel at the back of the knee. The Angel falls. The Masked Marvel is on top of him, pinning his shoulders to the mat. One! Two! Three! And it is over. Uncle Max is strangely still. I am gasping for breath. All this I remember as I stand at the bedside of Elihu Koontz.

Once again, I am in the operating room. It is two years since I amputated the left leg of Elihu Koontz. Now it is his right leg which is gangrenous. I have already scrubbed. I stand to one side wearing my gown and gloves. And . . . *I am masked.* Upon the table lies Elihu Koontz, pinned in a fierce white light. Spinal anesthesia has been administered. One of his arms is taped to a board placed at a right angle to his body. Into this arm, a needle has been placed. Fluid drips here from a bottle overhead. With his other hand, Elihu Koontz beats feebly at the side of the operating table. His head rolls from side to side. His mouth is pulled into weeping. It seems to me that I have never seen such misery.

An orderly stands at the foot of the table, holding Elihu Koontz's leg aloft by the toes so that the intern can scrub the limb with antiseptic solutions. The intern paints the foot, ankle, leg, and thigh, both front and back, three times. From a corner of the room where I wait, I look down as from an amphitheater. Then I think of Uncle Max yelling, "Tear off a leg. Throw it up here." And I think that forty years later I am making the catch.

"It's not fair," I say aloud. But no one hears me. I step forward to break The Masked Marvel's last toehold.

—From *Confessions of a Knife*

1. What is the thematic connection between the first section and the flashback?

2. Why does Selzer use present tense in all three sections? What other possibilities of verb tense were available to him, and what effect, if any, would they have had on the story's impact?

3. In the first section, readers view Selzer as simply a sympathetic surgeon who has amputated a patient's leg. How does the flashback alter his role and our perception of him?

4. What words in the opening of the third section tie that section to the flashback?

Episodic Action

Instead of being one prolonged story, a narrative can be several episodes, all somehow related. One type of episodic narrative deals with two or more actions that occur at the same time, concern the same subject, and merge to produce a climax. Take the Watergate scandal, for example, during which various actions occurred simultaneously in different places: the reporters, Woodward and Bernstein, were investigating leads from informants; the presidential aide John Dean was testifying before a Congressional committee on possible cover-up activities by the White House; Judge Sirica was ruling on the White House tapes; and Mr. Nixon was conferring with his accomplices—all at the same time. How can we organize these multiple actions so that readers can distinguish the lines of action and yet retain their simultaneity? We have two possibilities. We can narrate one line of action from beginning to end, then pick up a second line and go from start to finish, and then a third. Alternatively, we can divide the actions into short time segments, narrating a portion of each action in each time segment. For instance, we might mark off the Watergate affair in weeks during the summer of 1974 and report the multiple events that occurred simultaneously each week.

Another kind of multiple-action narrative recounts a series of episodes that are not simultaneous but that concern one theme. In the following essay, for example, the author tells several brief stories concerning cars he has owned. Although the stories are arranged chronologically—first car, second car, and so forth—the essay is not a prolonged story but a sequence of short tales, all unified by a common subject and theme.

THE CAR

Harry Crews

The other day there arrived in the mail a clipping sent by a friend of mine. It had been cut from a Long Beach, California, newspaper and dealt with a young man who had eluded police for fifty-five minutes while he raced over freeways and through city streets at speeds up to 130 miles per hour. During the entire time he ripped his clothes off and threw them out of the window bit by bit. It finally took twenty-five patrol cars and a helicopter to catch him. When they did, he said that God had given him the car and that he had "found God." *[Humorous current event used to introduce subject of cars]*

I don't want to hit too hard on a young man who obviously has his own troubles, maybe even a little sick with it all, but when I read that he had found God in the car, my response was: *So say we all.* We have found God in cars, or if not the true God, one so satisfying, so powerful and awe-inspiring that the distinction is too fine to matter. Except perhaps ultimately, but pray we must not think too much on that. *[Initial thesis stated]*

The operative word in all this is *we.* It will not do for me to maintain that I have been above it all, that somehow I've managed to remain aloof from the national love affair with cars. It is true that I got a late start. I did not learn to drive until I was twenty-one; my brother was twenty-five before he learned. The reason is simple enough: in Bacon County, Georgia, where I grew up, many families had nothing with a motor in it. Ours was one such family. But starting as late as I did, I still had my share, and I've remembered them all, the cars I've owned. I remember them in just the concrete specific way you remember anything that changed your life. Especially I remember the early ones. *[Narrator includes himself in the car infatuation and shifts discussion to his experiences]* *[Inserts autobiographical information and location]* *[The last sentence of paragraph 3 sets up discussion to follow about his first three cars]*

The first car I ever owned was a 1938 Ford coupe. It had no low gear and the door on the passenger side wouldn't open. I eventually put a low gear in it, but I never did get the door to work. One hot summer night on a clay road a young lady whom I'll never forget had herself braced and ready with one foot on the rearview mirror and her other foot on the wing vent. In the first few lovely frantic moments, she pushed out the wing vent, broke off the rearview mirror, and left her little footprints all over the ceiling. The memory of it was so affecting that I could never bring myself to repair the vent or replace the head liner she had walked all over upside down.

Tells why the car was memorable; establishes connection between car and romance

Eight months later I lost the car on a rain-slick road between Folkston, Georgia, and Waycross. I'd just stopped to buy a stalk of bananas (to a boy raised in the hookworm and rickets belt of the South, bananas will always remain an incredibly exotic fruit, causing him to buy whole stalks at a time), and back on the road again I was only going about fifty in a misting rain when I looked over to say something to my buddy, whose nickname was Bonehead and who was half-drunk in the seat beside me. For some reason I'll never understand, I felt the back end of the car get loose and start to come up on us in the other lane. Not having driven very long, I overcorrected and stepped on the brake. We turned over four times. Bonehead flew out of the car and shot down a muddy ditch about forty yards before he stopped, sober and unhurt. I ended up under the front seat, thinking I was covered with gouts of blood. As it turned out, I didn't have much wrong with me and what I was covered with was gouts of mashed banana.

"Eight months later"—reference to passage of time

Topic sentence gives the main idea

Remainder of paragraph gives details of how the car was lost; action is described in chronological order

The second car I had was a 1940 Buick, square, impossibly heavy, built like a Sherman tank, but it had a '52 engine in it. Even though it took about 10 miles to get her open full bore, she'd do over 100 miles an hour on flat ground. It was so big inside that in an emergency it could sleep six. I tended to live in that Buick for almost a year, and no telling how long I would have kept it if a boy who was not a friend of mine and who owned an International Harvester pickup truck hadn't said in mixed company that he could make the run from New Lacy in Coffee County, Georgia, to Jacksonville, Florida, quicker than I could. He lost the bet, but I wrung the speedometer off the Buick, and also—since the run was made on a blistering day in July—melted four inner tubes, causing them to fuse with the tires, which were already slick when the run started. Four new tires and tubes cost more money than I had or expected to have

"The second car"—announces change of subject

Feminine pronoun used for the car

The details of the run are omitted; only the outcome—"He lost the bet"—and the effects are reported; why not include details and action?

Why is the phrase "in mixed company" important?

anytime soon, so I sadly put that old honey up on blocks until I could sell it to a boy who lived up toward Macon.

After the Buick, I owned a 1953 Mercury with three-inch lowering blocks, fender skirts, twin aerials, and custom upholstering made of rolled Naugahyde. Staring into the bathroom mirror for long periods of time, I practiced expressions to drive it with. It was that kind of car. It looked mean, and it was mean. Consequently, it had to be handled with a certain style. One-handing it through a ninety-degree turn on city streets in a power slide where you were in danger of losing your ass as well as the car, you were obligated to have your left arm hanging half out the window and a very *bored* expression on your face. That kind of thing.

Those were the sweetest cars I was ever to know because they were my first. I remember them like people—like long-ago lovers—their idiosyncrasies, what they liked and what they didn't. With my hands deep in crankcases, I was initiated into their warm, greasy mysteries. Nothing in the world was more satisfying than winching the front end up under the shade of a chinaberry tree and sliding under the chassis on a burlap sack with a few tools to see if the car would not yield to me and my expert ways.

The only thing that approached working on a car was talking about one. We'd stand about for hours . . . spitting, telling stories about how it had been somewhere, sometime, with the car we were driving. It gave our lives a little focus and our talk a little credibility, if only because we could point to the evidence.

"But hell, don't it rain in with that wing vent broke out like that?"

"Don't mean nothing to me. Soon's Shirley kicked it out, I known I was in love. I ain't about to put it back."

Usually we met to talk at night behind the A & W Root Beer stand, the air heavy with the smell of grease and just a hint of burned French fries and burned hamburgers and burned hotdogs. It remains one of the most sensuous, erotic smells in my memory because through it . . . walked the sweetest, softest short-skirted carhops in the world. I knew what it was to stand for hours with my buddies, leaning nonchalant as hell on a fender, pretending not to look at the carhops, and saying things like: "This little baby don't look like much, but she'll git rubber in three gears." And when I said it, it was somehow my own body I was talking about. It was *my* speed and *my* strength that got rubber in three gears. In the mystery of that love affair, the car and I merged.

Margin notes:

"After the Buick"—transitional phrase used to usher readers into the third car

"Like long-ago lovers"—theme reinforced

First sentence of new paragraph provides transition from previous paragraph and announces new subject: talking about cars

Key term "talk" is repeated for transition, but focus shifts to place: A & W stand

Why does the writer use this sexist language? Is he intentionally portraying himself as immature? If so, why?

"that old honey" —Refers to the car with affection

Is the slang that is used throughout the essay appropriate to the subject and to the audience? (It was originally published in *Esquire*.)

Dialogue for change of pace and for humor

"senuous, erotic"—Continued association of cars and sex

But like many another love affair, it has soured considerably. Maybe it would have been different if I had known cars sooner. I was already out of the Marine Corps and twenty-two years old before I could stand behind the A & W Root Beer and lean on the fender of a 1938 coupe. That seems pretty old to me to be talking about getting rubber in three gears, and I'm certain it is *very* old to feel your own muscle tingle and flush with blood when you say it. As is obvious, I was what used to be charitably called a late bloomer. But at some point I did become just perceptive enough to recognize bullshit when I was neck deep in it.

The 1953 Mercury was responsible for my ultimate disenchantment with cars. I had already bored and stroked the engine and contrived to place a six-speaker sound system in it when I finally started to paint it. I spent the better half of a year painting that car. A friend of mine owned a body shop, and he let me use the shop on weekends. I sanded the Mercury down to raw metal, primed it, and painted it. Then I painted it again. And again. And then again. I went a little nuts, as I am prone to do, because I'm the kind of guy who if he can't have too much of a thing doesn't want any at all. So one day I came out of the house (I was in college then) and saw it, the '53 Mercury, the car upon which I had heaped more attention and time and love than I had ever given a human being. It sat at the curb, its black surface a shimmering of the air, like hundreds of mirrors turned to catch the sun. It had twenty-seven coats of paint, each coat laboriously hand-rubbed. It seemed to glow, not with reflected light, but with some internal light of its own.

I stood staring, and it turned into one of those great scary rare moments when you are privileged to see into your own predicament. Clearly, there were two ways I could go. I could sell the car, or I could keep on painting it for the rest of my life. If 27 coats of paint, why not 127? The moment was brief and I understand it better now than I did then, but I did realize, if imperfectly, that something was dreadfully wrong, that the car owned me much more than I would ever own the car, no matter how long I kept it. The next day I drove to Jacksonville and left the Mercury on a used-car lot. It was an easy thing to do.

Since that day, I've never confused myself with a car, a confusion common everywhere about us—or so it seems to me. I have a car now, but I use it like a beast, the way I've used all cars since the Mercury, like a beast unlovely and unlikable but

---

Marginal notes:

What is the purpose of this admission of his past immaturity?

The idea of "disenchantment" ties this paragraph to "soured" in previous paragraph

Inkling of realization that bestowing such love on an inanimate object is absurd

Narrator's sudden awareness allowed him to sever the relationship

Repetition of "love affair," but a change of attitude is indicated: "soured"

Reintroduces previous subject—1953 Mercury—but this time to explain its role in end of the love affair

Change in choice of words: the car is no longer a lover but a "beast"

By referring to events shared earlier with readers, narrator allows readers to participate in his nostalgia

necessary. True as all that is, though, God knows I'm in the car's debt for that blistering winning July run to Jacksonville, and for the pushed-out wing vent, and, finally, for that greasy air heavy with the odor of burned meat and potatoes there behind the A & W Root Beer. I'll never smell anything that good again.

—From *Blood and Grits*

Point of View

Point of view refers to the writer's relation to and involvement in the action of the narrative. In the preceding essay by Crews, for instance, the writer is the center of the story, and he used the first-person pronoun *I*. We therefore refer to this as the first-person point of view. Another point of view—third-person—is also possible in nonfiction narrative, and it is designated by the pronouns *he, she,* or *they.* The short example on page 67 of the man and woman meeting on the street is told from the third-person point of view.

First Person

First-person point of view invites introspection and reflection and is therefore more appropriate for personal narrative, in which the purpose is usually to reveal an insight that the writer gains from an experience. The "I" point of view allows us to communicate our personal reactions to experience and to give meaning to that experience. With first person, we can relate not only what we see, but also what we feel; this perception and this intimacy are the major advantages of first-person narration.

There are two types of first-person narratives, depending on our involvement in the action: In one we are the main participants, and in the other we are mainly observers. The first type is autobiographical, meaning that we narrate a story about ourselves. It is a "this happened to me" account, in which we are the center of the action, as in the earlier examples by Hughes, Selzer, and Crews, who relate what happens to them, how they feel about it, and what effect their experiences have had on them.

Although in most first-person narratives we are the center of the action, we can also be outside or on the periphery of the action. In the account of the Paret-Griffith fight, for example, Mailer sits at ringside, an observer who also gives his reaction to the bout. With this kind of first-person point of view, the writer witnesses, records, and reacts to the events. In the following example, Geoffrey Wolff relates an incident from his childhood, but another boy, Marion, is the main actor; the young Wolff is for the most part an observer.

1. What is the narrator's role in the Marion episode? Is he simply part of the collective group?
2. What is the advantage of using first-person point of view in this piece?
3. Is there a point to the episode, or is it recounted purely for entertainment?
4. What references to time does the narrator include to orient readers?

MARION FLIES

Marion entered Miss Champion's fifth-grade a month late. We gave him a rough time, because of his name, because he was a new boy, and because his father drove a Studebaker, which our fathers said looked like it was going when it was coming. Marion came to our class Halloween party got up as Superboy. What a costume his mother had put together, and hang the cost! Blue velvet tights under crimson shorts cinched with a sun-gold belt. The cape was silk, he said, probably rayon, and in place of a regulation chest insignia—red *S* on a velvet field—Marion showed a lightning bolt.

This gear raised Marion in our esteem, and he must have enjoyed the sensation, for he wore the costume to school the following day, and the day after that. Miss Champion suggested that he might retire it for a year, but he said he couldn't, that this was what he wore, it was what Superboy son of Superman wore, that he was Superboy and it was what he wore.

Even Miss Champion laughed at the idea, Superman in a Studebaker. But Marion held to his claim, even placing in evidence his dad's thick glasses, a point of similarity with Clark Kent's. We were not persuaded, and it went hard with Marion. And then he offered to demonstrate his powers. He would fly. He would not, he said, fly far, because he wished only to prove a small point. He would fly the following afternoon, while his mother was elsewhere playing bridge. He would launch himself from the roof of his house, beside the public library.

The next afternoon we assembled in his front yard. From the refuge of his attic Marion watched us gather, like a lynch mob. We felt foolish and put-upon, and I was surprised to see Marion crawl through a dormer window and climb to the peak of his roof, almost three stories above us. He inched along the roof to its edge. The wind tugged his wonderful cape, and the sun hit its violent colors—royal blue, crimson, gold—and it was almost possible to believe. Marion, patient but condescending, looked down and asked *us:* "Are you ready?" The girls especially seemed to stir and blush, and one of them called out, "Fly, Marion," and he did. Off the roof, and the cape spread, and he hit the frozen lawn, and gasped and rolled to his stomach. Someone fetched the librarian, and she sent for Dr. Von Glaun, and he shooed us all home and set Marion's leg.

The next week Superboy came to school in civvies and on crutches, and until his father and mother took him away in a new Hudson Hornet to another school in another town, no one teased him. He had said he would fly, and to our satisfaction he had flown.

—From *The Duke of Deception*

If Wolff had taken himself out of this narrative—deleted the references to himself and changed the *we* and *I* to *they*—he would have been using the third-person perspective.

Third Person

In third-person narration, we are invisible; that is, the person telling the story is not identified but is like a camera, selectively recording what it sees and what it considers to be relevant. Participants in the action are referred to by the pronouns *he, she,* or *they,* but we do not refer to ourselves. We assume the role of a disembodied intelligence viewing the action from an elevated and informed position. Unlike fiction, however, in which the third-person point of view allows us to read the characters' minds, nonfiction obviously precludes us from entering other persons' thoughts, though the third-person narrator can see all actions. Although third person lacks the intimacy, introspection, and involvement of first person, it permits a panoramic view not afforded to first person, which limits an account to a single person's vision. Because of its detachment and objectivity, third person is used in writing history, biography, news reports, and accounts of events we have not witnessed firsthand.

Narration for Expository and Argumentative Purposes

In addition to conveying and sharing a personal experience, narration can be a means of clarifying or illustrating an idea. It can also be a formidable tool for persuading because it appeals directly to the emotions.

Although we have been considering only essays that are totally narrative, essays can be a combination of narration and exposition. Within a larger nonnarrative structure, narration can be one of several ways of developing an idea; in the midst of an expository essay, a one- or two-paragraph narrative changes the pace of the essay, increases reader interest, and adds a more personal element. An anecdote (brief narrative) can act as evidence to illustrate a generalization in the same way that facts do. For example, an essay arguing for improved facilities in juvenile detention centers might primarily consist of causes, statistics, quotations, logic, effects, and proposals, but it might also include a story of a 12-year-old boy's terror and mistreatment in a detention center. That narrative very likely would have more impact than all the facts and statistics the writer could recite.

Narration is a particularly effective way to open an argumentative essay because it engages readers' attention immediately and gives us a concrete example from which to launch an argument. In moving from narrative to argument, the essay also moves from experience to analysis and from emotion to intellect.

In the following essay, Norman Cousins' intent and emphasis are expository (that is, the essay intends to explain), but the introductory three-paragraph narrative is as essential to the essay as the final five paragraphs of exposition. In what ways does the narrative section differ from the other section? Why does the narrative make an effective opening to an essay concerning the effects of violence on individuals today? Would the narrative have been as effective if it had come in the middle or at the end of the essay?

THE DESENSITIZATION OF TWENTIETH-CENTURY MAN

It happened at the Stamford, Connecticut, railroad station. It was Sunday evening, at about 10 P.M. Some two dozen persons, among them several young men in uniform, were waiting for the express to New York.   1

The door to the waiting room flew open. A woman, shrieking hysterically, burst into the room. She was pursued by a man just a few steps behind her. The woman screamed that the man was trying to kill her and cried out for the people to save her. I was standing nearest the door. The woman grabbed me, still shrieking. I tried to protect her behind me. The man tried to sweep me aside to get at her. He rushed at me, caught the woman's wrist with one hand, tore her loose and pulled her through the doorway. The woman fell to the ground and was dragged by the wrist just outside the waiting room. I tried to free her wrist. The man broke off, grabbed the woman's pocketbook, and fled on foot.   2

We carried the woman inside the waiting room, sat her down, then telephoned the police. The woman's eye was badly cut; she was moaning. I looked around the room. Except for three or four persons who now came up to her, the people in the room seemed unconcerned. The young men in uniform were still standing in the same place, chatting among themselves as before. I am not sure which was greater, the shock of the attack that had just occurred or the shock caused by the apparent detachment and unconcern of the other people, especially the men in uniform.   3

The next morning I read in the newspaper of another attack. This one was carried out in broad daylight on a young boy by a gang of teen-agers. Here, too, a number of people stood around and watched.   4

It would be possible, I suppose, to take the view that these are isolated 5 instances, and that it would be a serious error to read into these cases anything beyond the fact that the bystanders were probably paralyzed by the suddenness of the violence. Yet I am not so sure. I am not sure that these instances may not actually be the product of something far deeper. What is happening, I believe, is that the natural reactions of the individual against violence are being blunted. The individual is being desensitized by living history. He is developing new reflexes and new responses that tend to slow up the moral imagination and relieve him of essential indignation over impersonal hurt. He is becoming casual about brutality. He makes his adjustments to the commonplace, and nothing is more commonplace in our age than the ease with which life can be smashed or shattered. The range of the violence sweeps from the personal to the impersonal, from the amusements of the crowd to the policies of nations. It is in the air, quite literally. It has lost the sting of surprise. We have made our peace with violence.

No idea could be more untrue than that there is no connection between what is 6 happening in the world and in the behavior of the individual. Society does not exist apart from the individual. It transfers its apprehensions or its hopes, its fatigue or its vitality, its ennui or its dreams, its sickness or its spirituality to the people who are part of it. Can the individual be expected to retain the purity of his responses, particularly a sensitivity to the fragility of life, when society itself seems to measure its worth in terms of its ability to create and possess instruments of violence that could expunge civilization as easily as it once took to destroy a village? Does it have no effect on an individual to live in an age that has already known two world wars; that has seen hundreds of cities ripped apart by dynamite tumbling down from the heavens; that has witnessed whole nations stolen or destroyed; that has seen millions of people exterminated in gas chambers or other mass means; that has seen governments compete with one another to make weapons which, even in the testing, have put death into the air?

To repeat, the causative range is all the way from petty amusements to the 7 proclamations of nations. We are horrified that teen-age boys should make or steal lethal weapons and then proceed to use them on living creatures; but where is the sense of horror or outrage at the cheapness of human life that is exploited throughout the day or night on television? It is almost impossible to see television for fifteen minutes without seeing people beaten or shot or punched or kicked or jabbed. It is also almost impossible to pick up a newspaper without finding someone in a position of power, here or elsewhere, threatening to use nuclear explosives unless someone else becomes more sensible.

The young killers don't read the newspapers, true. They don't have to. If they 8 read at all, they read the picture-story pulps that dispense brutality as casually as a vending machine its peanuts. In any case, the heart of the matter is that the young killers do not live in the world of their own. They belong to the larger world. They may magnify and intensify the imperfections of the larger world but they do not invent them.

The desensitization of twentieth-century man is more than a danger to the 9 common safety. It represents the loss or impairment of the noblest faculty of human life—the ability to be aware both of suffering and beauty; the ability to share sorrow and create hope; the ability to think and respond beyond one's wants. There are some things we have no right ever to get used to. One of these most certainly is brutality. The other is the irrational. Both brutality and the irrational have now come together and are moving toward a dominant pattern. If the pattern is to be resisted and changed, a special effort must be made. A very special effort.

—From *Saturday Review*, May 16, 1957

1. Is the pace of paragraph 2 slower than, quicker than, or the same as the other paragraphs?

2. Are the sentences in paragraph 2 shorter, longer, or about the same as those in other paragraphs?

3. Define these words from paragraphs 6 and 7: *ennui, expunge, causative.*

4. What does Cousins mean by "a sensitivity to the fragility of life?"

   Instead of using an introductory narrative section as a means of leading into the expository body of an essay, we can make the entire essay narrative and have it serve as an argument. The earlier narrative of the trapped coon, for instance, not only relates a compelling personal experience, but also serves as a convincing statement against using steel traps; on one level it is a story about a boy's moral development, but on another level it is an editorial in narrative form. The idea and the narrative are one.
   Whereas exposition and argument deal with ideas, personal narration deals primarily with emotions. In argument, which engages readers' intellect, judgment is dominant. In narrative, which engages readers' emotions, sympathy is dominant. Narration goes straight to our sense of humanity, and that is why narrative is such a powerful persuasive tool.
   For example, a logical, factual argument against capital punishment would not be as effective as the following narrative on the subject because capital punishment is a moral and emotional issue. "A Hanging" simultaneously presents the author's revelation about capital punishment and, because readers experience the story from his point of view, they too *feel* that it is morally wrong. As you read this George Orwell essay, bear in mind these questions:

   1. The writer encounters a potential problem because the climax of the narrative occurs near the middle. What is the climax, and how does Orwell keep the essay from losing its interest and effect after the climax?

2. Two narrators actually seem to relate this story, one the young Orwell who experiences the event, the other an older Orwell. What benefits does the writer gain by this dual recounting?

3. Why might Orwell's style here be characterized as journalistic? Is this style appropriate for the content?

4. Orwell's eye for detail, his ability to characterize with seemingly insignificant details, his recognition of the dramatic importance of minor incidents—these talents account for much of the effectiveness of his essay. Give examples of these qualities in his descriptions of persons, incidents, and setting.

A HANGING

It was in Burma, a sodden morning of the rains. A sickly light, like yellow tinfoil, was 1
slanting over the high walls into the jail yard. We were waiting outside the condemned cells, a row of sheds fronted with double bars, like small animal cages. Each cell measured about ten feet by ten and was quite bare within except for a plank bed and a pot for drinking water. In some of them brown silent men were squatting at the inner bars, with their blankets draped round them. These were the condemned men, due to be hanged within the next week or two.

One prisoner had been brought out of his cell. He was a Hindu, a puny wisp of a 2
man, with a shaven head and vague liquid eyes. He had a thick, sprouting moustache, absurdly too big for his body, rather like the moustache of a comic man on the films. Six tall Indian warders were guarding him and getting him ready for the gallows. Two of them stood by with rifles and fixed bayonets, while the others handcuffed him, passed a chain through his handcuffs and fixed it to their belts, and lashed his arms tight to his sides. They crowded very close about him, with their hands always on him in a careful, caressing grip, as though all the while feeling him to make sure he was there. It was like men handling a fish which is still alive and may jump back into the water. But he stood quite unresisting, yielding his arms limply to the ropes, as though he hardly noticed what was happening.

Eight o'clock struck and a bugle call, desolately thin in the wet air, floated from 3
the distant barracks. The superintendent of the jail, who was standing apart from the rest of us, moodily prodding the gravel with his stick, raised his head at the sound. He was an army doctor, with a grey toothbrush moustache and a gruff voice. "For God's sake hurry up, Francis," he said irritably. "The man ought to have been dead by this time. Aren't you ready yet?"

Francis, the head jailer, a fat Dravidian in a white drill suit and gold spectacles, 4
waved his black hand. "Yes sir, yes sir," he bubbled. "All iss satisfactorily prepared. The hangman iss waiting. We shall proceed."

"Well, quick march, then. The prisoners can't get their breakfast till this job's 5
over."

We set out for the gallows. Two warders marched on either side of the prisoner, 6 with their rifles at the slope; two others marched close against him, gripping him by the arm and shoulder, as though at once pushing and supporting him. The rest of us, magistrates and the like, followed behind. Suddenly, when we had gone ten yards, the procession stopped short without any order or warning. A dreadful thing had happened—a dog, come goodness knows whence, had appeared in the yard. It came bounding among us with a loud volley of barks and leapt round us wagging its whole body, wild with glee at finding so many human beings together. It was a large woolly dog, half Airedale, half pariah. For a moment it pranced round us, and then, before anyone could stop it, it had made a dash for the prisoner and, jumping up, tried to lick his face. Everyone stood aghast, too taken aback even to grab at the dog.

"Who let that bloody brute in here?" said the superintendent angrily. "Catch it,   7
someone!"

A warder, detached from the escort, charged clumsily after the dog, but it   8
danced and gambolled just out of his reach, taking everything as part of the game. A young Eurasian jailer picked up a handful of gravel and tried to stone the dog away, but it dodged the stones and came after us again. Its yaps echoed from the jail walls. The prisoner, in the grasp of the two warders, looked on incuriously, as though this was another formality of the hanging. It was several minutes before someone managed to catch the dog. Then we put my handkerchief through its collar and moved off once more, with the dog still straining and whimpering.

It was about forty yards to the gallows. I watched the bare brown back of the   9
prisoner marching in front of me. He walked clumsily with his bound arms, but quite steadily, with that bobbing gait of the Indian who never straightens his knees. At each step his muscles slid neatly into place, the lock of hair on his scalp danced up and down, his feet printed themselves on the wet gravel. And once, in spite of the men who gripped him by each shoulder, he stepped slightly aside to avoid a puddle on the path.

It is curious, but till that moment I had never realized what it means to destroy a   10
healthy, conscious man. When I saw the prisoner step aside to avoid the puddle I saw the mystery, the unspeakable wrongness, of cutting a life short when it is in full tide. This man was not dying, he was alive just as we are alive. All the organs of his body were working—bowels digesting food, skin renewing itself, nails growing, tissues forming—all toiling away in solemn foolery. His nails would still be growing when he stood on the drop, when he was falling through the air with a tenth-of-a-second to live. His eyes saw the yellow gravel and the grey walls, and his brain still remembered, foresaw, reasoned—reasoned even about puddles. He and we were a party of men walking together, seeing, hearing, feeling, understanding the same world; and in two minutes, with a sudden snap, one of us would be gone—one mind less, one world less.

The gallows stood in a small yard, separate from the main grounds of the   11
prison, and overgrown with tall prickly weeds. It was a brick erection like three sides of a shed, with planking on top, and above that two beams and a crossbar with the rope dangling. The hangman, a grey-haired convict in the white uniform of the prison, was waiting beside his machine. He greeted us with a servile crouch as we entered. At a

word from Francis the two warders, gripping the prisoner more closely than ever, half led half pushed him to the gallows and helped him clumsily up the ladder. Then the hangman climbed up and fixed the rope round the prisoner's neck.

We stood waiting, five yards away. The warders had formed in a rough circle round the gallows. And then, when the noose was fixed, the prisoner began crying out to his god. It was a high, reiterated cry of "Ram! Ram! Ram! Ram!" not urgent and fearful like a prayer or cry for help, but steady, rhythmical, almost like the tolling of a bell. The dog answered the sound with a whine. The hangman, still standing on the gallows, produced a small cotton bag like a flour bag and drew it down over the prisoner's face. But the sound, muffled by the cloth, still persisted, over and over again: "Ram! Ram! Ram! Ram! Ram!" 12

The hangman climbed down and stood ready, holding the lever. Minutes seemed to pass. The steady, muffled crying from the prisoner went on and on, "Ram! Ram! Ram!" never faltering for an instant. The superintendent, his head on his chest, was slowly poking the ground with his stick; perhaps he was counting the cries, allowing the prisoner a fixed number—fifty, perhaps, or a hundred. Everyone had changed color. The Indians had gone grey like bad coffee, and one or two of the bayonets were wavering. We looked at the lashed, hooded man on the drop, and listened to his cries—each cry another second of life; the same thought was in all our minds: oh, kill him quickly, get it over, stop that abominable noise! 13

Suddenly the superintendent made up his mind. Throwing up his head he made a swift motion with his stick. "Chalo!" he shouted almost fiercely. 14

There was a clanking noise, and then dead silence. The prisoner had vanished, and the rope was twisting on itself. I let go of the dog, and it galloped immediately to the back of the gallows; but when it got there it stopped short, barked, and then retreated into a corner of the yard, where it stood among the weeds, looking timorously out at us. We went round the gallows to inspect the prisoner's body. He was dangling with his toes pointed straight downwards, very slowly revolving, as dead as a stone. 15

The superintendent reached out with his stick and poked the bare brown body; it oscillated slightly. "*He's* all right," said the superintendent. He backed out from under the gallows, and blew out a deep breath. The moody look had gone out of his face quite suddenly. He glanced at his wrist-watch. "Eight minutes past eight. Well, that's all for this morning, thank God." 16

The warders unfixed bayonets and marched away. The dog, sobered and conscious of having misbehaved itself, slipped after them. We walked out of the gallows yard, past the condemned cells with their waiting prisoners, into the big central yard of the prison. The convicts, under the command of warders armed with lathis, were already receiving their breakfast. They squatted in long rows, each man holding a tin pannikin, while two warders with buckets marched round ladling out rice; it seemed quite a homely, jolly scene after the hanging. An enormous relief had come upon us now that the job was done. One felt an impulse to sing, to break into a run, to snigger. All at once everyone began chattering gaily. 17

The Eurasian boy walking beside me nodded towards the way we had come, 18 with a knowing smile: "Do you know sir, our friend (he meant the dead man) when he heard his appeal had been dismissed, he pissed on the floor of his cell. From fright. Kindly take one of my cigarettes, sir. Do you not admire my new silver case, sir? From the boxwalah, two rupees eight annas. Classy European style."

Several people laughed—at what, nobody seemed certain.   19

Francis was walking by the superintendent, talking garrulously: "Well, sir, all   20
hass passed off with the utmost satisfactoriness. It was all finished—flick! like that. It iss not always so—oah, no! I have known cases where the doctor wass obliged to go beneath the gallows and pull the prissoner's legs to ensure decease. Most disagree-able!"   •

"Wriggling about, eh? That's bad," said the superintendent.   21

"Ach, sir, it iss worse when they become refractory! One man, I recall, clung to   22
the bars of hiss cage when we went to take him out. You will scarcely credit, sir, that it took six warders to dislodge him, three pulling at each leg. We reasoned with him. 'My dear fellow,' we said, 'think of all the pain and trouble you are causing to us!' But no, he would not listen! Ach, he wass very troublesome!"

I found that I was laughing quite loudly. Everyone was laughing. Even the   23
superintendent grinned in a tolerant way. "You'd better all come out and have a drink," he said quite genially. "I've got a bottle of whiskey in the car. We could do with it."

We went through the big double gates of the prison into the road. "Pulling at his   24
legs!" exclaimed a Burmese magistrate suddenly, and burst into a loud chuckling. We all began laughing again. At that moment Francis' anecdote seemed extraordinarily funny. We all had a drink together, native and European alike, quite amicably. The dead man was a hundred yards away.

—From *Shooting an Elephant and Other Essays*

Advice, Warnings, Reminders

1. Narrative essays don't have to contain a moral or a lesson, but they should illuminate a meaning, which can be an insight or a discovery. Narration weaves character, action, setting, and society into a meaningful pattern, and the interaction of those elements produces conflict, climax, and resolution, resulting in a change in belief, in understanding, or in circumstance.

2. Because a narrative is supposed to *reveal* a meaning, the action should speak for itself as much as possible. Although you may wish to state your thesis explicitly at the end of the story, too much commentary in the body of the narrative interferes with the action and slows the pace. Granted, there are times when you must interpret an action, as Mailer does in explaining the significance of Paret's turning his back in the fight, but such commentary should be brief and infrequent.

3. Remember that it is the telling as much as the tale that makes for a good narrative. "The soundest fact may fail or prevail in the style of its telling. . . ." (Ursula LeGuin).

4. Consider using dialogue to give flavor and to reveal characterization, but use it sparingly since it can shift the focus from the action.

5. Most narratives are in past tense, but you may use present tense to convey a sense of immediacy and realism.

6. Ask yourself these questions:

    What is the main point of the narrative?

    Will readers get the point, or do I need to spell it out? In other words, should the thesis be implicit or explicit?

    Why should anyone read this story?

    Is it believable?

    Can readers identify with the experience?

    Have I made clear the time sequences and the relationships among characters?

    Are the details I've selected vivid, relevant, and revealing?

Exercises

1. The following narrative is from a longer nonnarrative discussion of praying mantises. Is there a moral to this piece? If so, what is it? If not, what is the purpose of the paragraph? What makes the anecdote dramatic and striking?

Newly hatched mantises . . . eat small creatures like aphids and each other. When I was in elementary school, one of the teachers brought in a mantis egg case in a Mason jar. I watched the newly hatched mantises emerge and shed their skins; they were spidery and translucent, all over joints. They trailed from the egg case to the base of the Mason jar in a living bridge that looked like Arabic calligraphy, some baffling text from the Koran inscribed down the air by a fine hand. Over a period of several hours, during which time the teacher never summoned the nerve or the sense to release them, they ate each other until only two were left. Tiny legs were still kicking from the mouths of both. The two survivors grappled and sawed in the Mason jar; finally both died of injuries. I felt as though I myself should swallow the corpses, shutting my eyes and washing them down like jagged pills, so all that life wouldn't be lost.

—From Annie Dillard, *A Pilgrim at Tinker Creek*

2. Analyze the following narrative. What, if anything, is wrong with it, and what would it take to improve it?

I was driving down the freeway the other night around 10:30 when all of a sudden a VW bug about 200 yards ahead began to swerve wildly and then skidded sideways and turned upside down and slid on its top a good hundred feet before finally plunging into the bar ditch and stopping. I sped to the scene, slammed on my brakes, jumped out my car, and ran to the wrecked auto with its wheels still spinning, like a turtle on its back struggling to turn back over.

As I jerked open the driver's door, I couldn't tell how many people were in the car or if anyone was hurt or even alive. All I could see was a tangle of motionless arms and legs; no one moaned or cried or made any predictable sound. "Is anyone hurt badly?" I asked. The teenage driver belched. A girl in the backseat giggled. And then they all started laughing hysterically.

3. Write a short, logical, factual argument for or against an issue. Then, on the same subject write a narrative that serves as an argument itself. Finally, combine the two.

4. All of us know someone who is a boring story teller. To help yourself avoid making the same mistakes, make a list of all the errors this person commits when relating a story.

Additional Readings

ON HATING PIANO LESSONS

Phyllis Theroux

When I was growing up, I conceived of children as being of two kinds: those who took 1
lessons and those who did not. I was the second kind, although I sometimes accompanied my horseback-riding, accordion-playing, baton-twirling friends to their classes and, by osmosis, learned a few things that enabled me to fake an expertise in a crowd. But with one exception I was self-taught, flinging my arms and legs around the living room doing badly executed *tours jetés* to Gilbert and Sullivan records, which allowed me to assume all the parts and, on one occasion, to break my ankle. I did, however, take piano lessons.

Once I discovered the sound that three fingers simultaneously placed on the 2
right keys could produce, I longed so loudly and consistently for piano lessons that my mother began to think maybe I was a genius and she did not want to go to her grave thinking I had become a short-order cook for want of an option. Options, in the long run, are what lessons are all about.

Now I am a parent. I think about giving my children options and lessons, 3 although children don't understand that their once-a-week session with Madame Faustini at the keyboard cancels out their mother's once-a-month visit to "The Magic Scissors." But haircuts play second fiddle to Beethoven if I am financially solvent, and this year my ten-year-old daughter is taking piano lessons—under duress.

My daughter does not like piano lessons. They are too hard. Her teacher, a wild   4
and dedicated woman who drives around in a yellow convertible and annually volunteers to sit on the "Dunk-'Em" chair at the school bazaar, understands about ten-year-old girls who would rather be talking on the telephone, and she always tries to give her pieces to learn that are on the jazzy side. But my daughter, though dutiful, has not been won over by this enlightened approach. Furthermore, she claims, her heart lies with gymnastics, a message I bought last year, along with a leotard which now lies neglected in her bottom bureau drawer.

When she was halfway through gymnastics, her heart began to rove down the   5
hall toward a tap-dancing class that sounded a lot better to her ears. I canceled gymnastics and enrolled her in tap, wanting to stake this small developing plant, my daughter, with the kinds of support that would strengthen and develop her soul.

Unfortunately, her soul turned out to be a shifting, shiftless creature, and her   6
interest in tap dancing waned after the sixth lesson. Suddenly, she saw pottery (which happened to have a class in the same building) as the wave of her future. But tiring of always chasing cultural advantages that were in another room, I decided that what my daughter wanted was immaterial. I wanted her to take piano lessons.

At the beginning, all was well. But when she had gone through the honeymoon   7
period of her first few lessons and realized there was more to it than pasting gold stars in new music books, gymnastics began to appeal to her anew. This time, however, I looked her straight in the eye and said, unflinchingly, "This year it's piano lessons. In fact, next year it's piano lessons, too, unless I can't afford them." It seemed important to let her know that there was no way out.

My daughter thinks I am cruel, that I don't understand her, that I am trying to   8
force her to be something she is not. My daughter is right. I want her, when she is thirty-five or sixty and feeling temporarily low on being, to be able to converse with Mozart, call up Clementi, or have a romp with Rodgers and Hammerstein at *will,* which is what lessons of any kind develop the capacity to use.

This is a difficult wish to communicate to a child who looks at me with "don't   9
make me do it" eyes when I drop her off for a lesson where she must spend another hour forcing her mind and fingers up and down the G and treble clefs. But I have hardened myself to her accusatory looks, and while my daughter has her reasons for complaint, my old heart has its reasons for making her suffer which her heart, being young, cannot fully understand.

There will come a time, I think, as I watch you trudge up the steps to your   10
teacher's house, when your heart will be empty. There will come a time when words, no matter how many or how eloquent, will do you no good at all. There will come a time when no one thing or person can adequately express the soul inside you that needs to be articulated. And then, my gymnastic, tap-dancing daughter, if I have been sufficiently "cruel" to you, you will have music.

But Time divides us at this moment. There are some things one cannot explain   11
to a ten-year-old girl who is only in Book One of piano and life. I must adjust myself to
being the mean parent who doesn't understand, and perhaps I don't. Perhaps my
daughter *is* a gymnast, or a tap dancer, or the world's number one potter who, when
she is grown, will rightly accuse me of having thrown her on the wrong wheel. But in
the meantime, in-between time, she is taking piano lessons.

—From *Peripheral Visions*

1. What is the thesis, and where is it stated?

2. The first two paragraphs are about Theroux's own childhood experiences.
   What does this material add to the essay?

3. Is the chronology straightforward? Paragraphs 3 and 4 have the daughter taking
   piano lesson; in paragraphs 5 and 6 she took gymnastics, tap, and pottery. Were
   these lessons before piano, or did she stop and then resume piano lessons? Is
   the order in which the lessons occurred clear? If so, how has Theroux indicated
   the chronology? If not, what is confusing?

4. Define or identify these terms or names:
   osmosis (paragraph 1)   Rodgers and Hammerstein (paragraph 8)
   tours jetés (paragraph 1)   Clementi (paragraph 8)
   financially solvent (paragraph 3) clefts (paragraph 9)
   duress (paragraph 3)

5. Why does she give details about Madame Faustini in paragraph 4?

6. In what way does paragraph 10 differ from the others? Why do you think
   Theroux decided to make that change?

7. Theroux is an excellent stylist who expresses her thoughts with freshness and
   wit. Give examples of these qualities.

"THE MERRY WIDOW WALTZ" IN COLORS

Mark Harris

At table one evening a summer ago at the MacDowell Colony in New Hampshire, I   1
inquired of a group of musicians whether any had ever heard of Compinsky. Several
had. He was, they said, a concert artist on the West Coast, where he played in a string
ensemble which bore (they believed) his name. They generally agreed that he was a
superior craftsman. Whether he was still a teacher of music, they did not know.

He was my teacher when I was ten, and he was the last of a succession of five   2
or six men engaged in that capacity, one of whom, as I recall, was deaf, and another
of whom habitually stood me before a tripod in his front room, indicated what music I
was to play, tuned my fiddle, and then retired to another part of the house.

It was my understanding, at the time, that after exposure for a certain period to   3
knowledgeable persons, I would master the violin, and that this would happen automatically (as it seemed to be happening to other boys), without my having any real
interest in the violin, or any aptitude for it, and surely without my having any love for it.
I detested it. I detested the case I carried it in, and these emotions I transferred to the
men who tried to teach me. Many years would pass before I could stand without
resentment in the presence of a musician, or before I could respect, if not love, his art.

Since the time process reportedly involved Practice At Home, I practiced at   4
home for the required period each day, my eye always upon the clock. Unable to read
notes, I drew my bow across the strings while fingering them, causing sounds to
emanate. That these sounds were not music did not awaken my parents to the futility
of their persistence in sending me to music teachers, or even, as was so much more
to be expected in those depression days, to the waste of their money. Their faith in
men and time was unwavering, and at last they sent me to Compinsky, whose method
was the most modern, whose fee was moderate, and who, if speech and bearing were
true signs, was the man most likely, if any man could, to cause to flower within me
seeds of musical genius. There was no doubt that I contained genius, if not by
heredity (for no near relation of mine could play, sing, or intelligently listen), then by
analogy: I could, after all, compose verse, I was swift at arithmetic, I laughed at
advanced jokes on the radio, and I could thread film on a motion-picture projector.

The arrangement with Compinsky, because of certain unique ways in which it   5
differed from the arrangements with all the other men, delighted me. I was to place
myself before him four days a week, Monday through Thursday, at half-past two. But
there would be no Practice At Home, and, further, the daily lesson was not to be
undergone in the loneliness and isolation of a private home but in the company of a
group. I did not always manage well with other children, but I liked to be with them. We
were to congregate in the band room of the William Wilson, Jr., Junior High School in
Mount Vernon, now called the Martin H. Traphagen School in honor of the gentleman
who was its principal at that time and whom I feared above either God or my father.
Under the Compinsky method other odiums were abolished. Since he supplied
instruments (they were of a special sort), there was no necessity to carry a violin case
anywhere; indeed, the necessity to own a violin was eliminated, since he did not
believe in Practice At Home and since the notion that anyone might play a violin in a
spare hour, except by decree, did not then fall within the reach of my imagination.

A bonus to all this was, of course, inherent in the fact of one's being dismissed   6
from class at half-past two on four days a week. This immensely shortened the
afternoon session, which otherwise would have extended infinitely to three-fifteen. At
half-past two, then, four days a week, musicians—as my teacher called them—were
excused. Upon this word I hastened from the room, though the fact of my usually
being first from the classroom in no way assured my being first to the band room. I
stopped to drink. I banged my way through the swinging double doors of the boys'
room. With more great noise I emerged. I drank, and I then proceeded into the fresh
air, the entrance to the band room being happily reachable only by a route which
carried me through the out-of-doors and past, and just below, the windows of the

classroom from which, in the name of music, I had escaped. Near the band room my bicycle, with all the rest, stood in its stall, and occasionally I sounded my horn, thus advising my classmates above, who would know whose horn it was and who had sounded it, that I was free and they were not. This behavior was several times described to me by Mr. Traphagen, our principal, as an abuse of privilege. It now occurs to me that in view of my repeated abuses of privilege I could not have feared him as terribly as I thought I did. In any case, I soon turned up in the band room where, from among a large assortment, I chose the smallest available violin. Violins wearied my left arm, and they continued to do so despite the Compinsky method, which was designed to reduce or wholly eliminate so many of the physical hazards.

Under the Compinsky method, students sat on a long bench (or perhaps on   7
chairs) fronted by a horizontal length of lumber supported by uprights. Hooks were drilled into the lumber at intervals, and over these hooks we looped a wire affixed to the scrolls of our fiddles. It was then possible to struggle with at least some small hope of victory against the natural tendency of the violin to point itself floorward. It was even possible, when Compinsky was not looking, to allow the left arm to dangle.

As gravity was defeated, so also was the greatest obstacle of all: under the   8
Compinsky method I could read music, for upon a board elevated before us scores were available, not in the orthodox black-and-white but in color, painted there by Compinsky himself, and very gay, like the wallpaper at home. Notes had colors, and these colors identically corresponded to colors painted upon notches carved into the finger boards of our violins. If I knew which string to play on, as I usually did, it was then required of me only that I place a finger upon the designated color and draw my bow: the desired music would produce itself, as upon a player piano or phonograph. Science operated in conjunction with Time, and it was not to be doubted, after the five or six false starts under the five or six old-fashioned men, that my genius would blossom. A boy who could thread a motion-picture projector could match colors. I was adept. Moreover, it was fun. We played many songs, but the one I best remember was the "Merry Widow Waltz," which to this day I do not hear without responding inwardly, "red-green or-rr-ange, red-green or-rr-ange," and so forth. A waltz is not a piece of music but a series of colors.

The violin now became a game, and because I was quick at the game I liked it. I   9
cultivated an affection for the physical instrument, its smell, its shape, and for the creak of tuning pegs in their sockets. I endlessly adjusted these pegs, blandly undoing the work of tuning which Compinsky accomplished sometime before half-past two, and I doubted, when he pleaded with me to desist, that there was, in the first place, any such thing as a violin's being "in tune" or "out of tune." The E string, tight or loose, had for me an unvarying sound, higher than A, which was higher than D, which was higher than G. It was sufficient that these strings bore a comparative relationship to one another, and any greater discrimination than this was a pretense, a manufactured complication. I liked to resinate my bow; I liked the smell of the rosin and the pleasant identification I then could have with baseball players, who used rosin and who were the figures of earth with whom I most wished to be identified.

Compinsky's system was better suited to my day's program than those of the   10
other men, but I attached no credit to him for his system. For one thing, I could not fully

respect or honor him since he was not a regular teacher on the regular payroll: He was paid by the head, and since his livelihood partially depended upon my continued attendance I was entitled to certain liberties. It was, for example, my privilege to ignore his hands, which he waved before us. This was another pretense, the idea of music being to match colored notes, not to be bound by a tempo. He was a small man, whose hair was gray and who surprised me by his energy, for I thought him very old. He was perhaps forty. He spoke with a foreign accent (Hungarian, I think), and this meant that my feeling toward him had to be ambivalent. It would, for this reason, have been ambivalent even if he had been on the regular payroll. I respected his wisdom and learning, for all foreigners were wise and learned, but it was my patriotic duty to show him less respect and obedience than I showed a birthright American. He had no right to discipline me or to tamper with my morality, as Martin H. Traphagen had, so that coming late to lessons or dangling my arm at my side were my prerogatives as one who spoke with no accent and had had the good sense, to begin with, to be born in so American a place as Mount Vernon, New York. Unquestionably I was cruel to him, not so much by the performance of disruptive acts or deeds as by my habit of fastening upon him a perpetual scowl registering sentiment to the effect that I thought him a manufacturer of complexity, an alien person defective in spirit, that I thought music a humbug, and that ten thousand musicians were not pure enough to touch the letters of the cap of John J. McGraw.

11   Could the Compinsky method make a musician of a child? This was the pragmatic question apparently asked by school authorities, by parents, and perhaps by competing teachers of music who resented the Compinsky monopoly at our school.

12   One thing should be said at the outset. The Compinsky method did not forever paralyze a child's musical development. If this has a negative sound, it is due largely to the absence of data. All that is known is that one of the youngsters who read color-scores with me now plays in the St. Louis Symphony Orchestra; another, according to a Mount Vernon *Daily Argus* of recent date, is "slated" to offer a recital at Carnegie Hall and has been "widely hailed" by "critics."

13   But parents and school authorities could not wait a generation for an answer to their question. As often happens in a community where democracy is better understood than art, it was decided to put the matter to a vote. A concert would be offered, and parents and school officials would judge.

14   I knew nothing of the controversy. Parents and teachers were periodically embattled between and among themselves on a wide variety of issues, and my mother talked about them on the telephone. But I could have not been less interested, and so it was that on the night of the concert I but vaguely sensed that this was somehow to be a test of the Compinsky method. Had I been more aware of the crisis I might have exerted myself more cleverly (though perhaps with a poorer result) than I did, for I was of a naturally sympathetic nature, and these sympathies would have extended to him, even though he was a Hungarian, by virtue of the fact that he stood alone against my natural enemies. His bread and butter and his pride were at stake, and I knew something about both, especially pride, living, as I did, in a predominantly Yankee neighborhood in the year 1932—so triumphant a year for the Yankees and so

dismal a one for the Giants that McGraw quit baseball in mid-season. I may not, day by day, have been cordial, but in a moment of crisis—had I *known* the crisis—I would somehow have risen to the occasion.

Compinsky, the artist reduced in a depression time to teaching the likes of me, 15 stood before us that night in a tuxedo, and this I remember along with a mild sensation of panic when I discovered the black and absolute nakedness of the upper saddles and finger boards of the violins upon which we were to play. I then saw that we were to read from ordinary black-and-white scores placed on individual tripods. I could not read this despicable foreign language, and if I could have read it I would not have known how to finger it. It was a camouflage.

But the group did well. Many of them no doubt practiced at home in excess of 16 the Compinsky minimum. I do not recall what was played, but it was played acceptably. I myself did not play, though I swept my arm upward when others did, and downward when theirs came down, conforming to the direction of the majority. When they pizzicatoed, I assumed the poses and imitated the gestures of one who was pizzicatoing, and when they stopped, I stopped.

The audience applauded, and Compinsky turned to it and spoke briefly, con- 17 cluding with the announcement that I would now perform a solo.

It seems to me unlikely that I had not been told of this in advance. It simply had 18 made no impression upon me. I had no fear of crowds or assemblages of any kind, and it would have made little difference to me whether I was matching colors in the band room or before a sizable gathering. But at some time between the time I was told and the time I was called upon, the decision was made to set black-and-white scores before us. Surely he knew that I was not only not a genius but was, musically speaking, absolutely illiterate and figuratively deaf. Or else he had not meant to call upon me, but on someone else, and then, having spoken my name, could not, in courtesy to my parents, who were present, if not to me, who deserved none, retract.

The soundest hypothesis is that it was deliberate on his part, that he well 19 understood my nature, knew that I had the courage of ignorance and shamelessness; if I was his least promising student I was also his bravest, and to this audience trained more in democracy than in art my confident energy would appear to be virtuosity.

I strode to the front of the stage. Since I could not read music I was frank 20 enough not to take any with me, but I remember Compinsky's setting it before me and breathing a few words which I did not hear but which I understood to be a phrase of encouragement. I needed no encouragement. I waved with my bow to my mother and father, grinned and played. I did not turn a page. I played fragments of melodies as I remembered them from the gay, hand-painted scores, usually the first few bars—for these I knew by memory—of the most familiar waltzes, the strains beyond which nobody whistles.

But as I played I knew for the first time that this was not music. I did not know the 21 word "transitions," but as I leaped from melody to melody their absence offended even me, and as I played I was gripped by a long-enduring guilt, for in these intense moments I realized the enormity of what was taking place: A man's livelihood was in the balance, and his pride. It was I, not he, who was a pretender; I had known this all along, and I did not so much mind the truth of it as I lamented its exposure, and I resolved, while playing, never to touch a violin again. This resolution I faithfully kept.

When my arm wearied I stopped. The applause I received was distinctly greater   22
in volume than that awarded to the group when we had played en masse, and the confusion this generated within me exceeds in vividness all the other vivid memories of that evening. Had all values been inverted, all moral law revoked? Was bad good, and fakery to be applauded? Only in my daydreams was such emancipation conceivable, as when, for example, with the first stirrings of physical passion, I fancied that a law had been passed enforcing universal nakedness.

Perhaps I *was* a genius! Compinsky, arising from the piano stool, smiled a smile   23
at me which clearly told me that his admiration for me was limitless. *You are a genius,* said his smile. Was he, too, deceived? Was I the only person in the hall in possession of the truth? He bade the audience good evening, and then he led us in a recessional.

Not long afterward, Compinsky and the Compinsky method ceased to prevail in   24
the band room of William Wilson, Jr., Junior High School, and though I was at first assailed by a sense of guilt, I came in time to see that there was no causal relationship between my violin solo and his subsequent departure. This guilt, lightly lingering even twenty years after, was put to its final rest at the MacDowell Colony where I heard that Compinsky, secure in his reputation, is on the West Coast. And over the years I have retranslated his smile: *I know, and you have just begun to suspect, that democrats often love us for the wrong reasons.*

—From *Short Work of It*

1. Are the stages of the essay marked off by young Harris' attitudes toward the violin? Explain. Describe the changes in his attitude and point out where those changes occur.

2. Why does Harris give details about his earlier music teachers? Is that information relevant to the essay? Why, or why not?

3. What are the advantages of using first-person point of view in this piece? Support your answer with references to the essay.

4. Describe the tone of the essay. How does the tone contribute to Harris' meaning?

5. Point out the ways that Harris ties together his paragraphs. How does he achieve transition, for example, between paragraphs 5 and 6? Between 7 and 8? Between 15 and 16? Between 17 and 18? Are there places where the transition needs to be strengthened? Explain.

6. Compare the scenes of sudden awareness in the essays by Hughes, Crews, and Harris. What, if anything, do they have in common?

CHAPTER 4

Character Sketch

Descriptions can be of persons, places, or things, of course, but this chapter will be limited to descriptions of persons since most students find such descriptions more interesting and challenging than other types. Our goal is to describe a person so clearly that readers will be able to see the outer person and to understand the inner person. The precise skills to be learned in this chapter will be how to formulate and focus a generalization and how to support that generalization with interesting details. The chapter will also reintroduce you to some familiar but perhaps forgotten concepts, such as topic sentences, paragraph arrangements, similes, and metaphors.

Imagine that you're at a party and you meet someone for the first time. You introduce yourselves, make small talk, and begin to size up each other. Almost automatically you record the other person's height, build, posture, facial expression, smile, shape of nose, color of eyes, mode of dress, hair color and style, and so on. All of us make this quick scan of a stranger. We're seldom satisfied, however, with knowing only a person's looks. We begin with physical appearance because it is obvious and visible, but we want to move from the physical to the psychological, which is more interesting and rewarding. We want to find out what makes people "tick," what their likes and dislikes are, what their values are, and, above all, what's unique about them.

When we set out to describe persons, we seek to capture what is unique about them. Just as no two people in the world have identical fingerprints, no two people have the same personality and looks. Our goal as writers is to depict the essence of their characters and to make them as unique as their fingerprints. Yet capturing someone's essence on paper is a difficult task: People are complex creatures, full of quirks and twitches, emotions and beliefs, pasts, imaginations, neuroses, expectations, and hundreds of other characteristics. What we must do, therefore, is to observe our subject carefully, choose one major trait to portray, select details that contribute to that trait, and then organize the details in such a way that readers can visualize the person.

In the following example, how does Truman Capote capture his subject, Dick Hickok? What major trait or traits is Capote describing about this man? Point out details that allow us to see Dick, and other details that give us a sense of his character.

Dick stripped to his briefs was not quite the same as Dick fully clothed. In the latter state, he seemed a flimsy dingy-blond youth of medium height, fleshless and perhaps sunken-chested; disrobing revealed that he was nothing of the sort, but, rather, an athlete constructed on a welterweight scale. The tattooed face of a cat, blue and grinning, covered his right hand; on one shoulder a blue rose blossomed. More markings, self-designed and self-executed, ornamented his arms and torso: the head of a dragon with a human skull between its open jaws; bosomy nudes; a gremlin brandishing a pitchfork; the word PEACE accompanied by a cross radiating, in the form of crude strokes, rays of holy light; and two sentimental concoctions—one a bouquet of flowers dedicated to MOTHER-DAD, the other a heart that celebrated the romance of DICK and CAROL. . . .

But neither Dick's physique nor the inky gallery adorning it made as remarkable an impression as his face, which seemed composed of mismatching parts. It was as though his head had been halved like an apple, then put together a fraction off center. Something of the kind had happened; the imperfectly aligned features were the outcome of a car collision in 1950—an accident that left his long-jawed and narrow face tilted, the left side rather lower than the right, with the results that the lips were slightly aslant, the nose askew, and his eyes not only situated at uneven levels but of uneven size, the left eye being truly serpentine, with a venomous, sickly-blue squint that although it was involuntarily acquired, seemed nevertheless to warn of bitter sediment at the bottom of his nature.

—From *In Cold Blood*

1. What is the effect of describing the numerous tattoos?
2. How do the sentences in the second paragraph, which focuses on Dick's face, support the idea of "mismatching parts"?
3. Can you speculate on Dick's "nature," which Capote refers to at the end? What adjective in the description contributes to our impression of him? (Would you be surprised to learn that Dick Hickok was at the time on death row, awaiting execution for murdering an entire family?)

Invention: Generating a Dominant Impression

Writing a character description is similar to taking a photograph of someone: We have to place the subject in the correct setting, highlight the characteristics we wish to emphasize, zoom in, and focus. And as with a camera, we try to capture a pose that reveals a specific mood or quality—friendliness, cynicism, grumpiness. For practical and artistic reasons, we have to limit the topic not simply to one person but to one attitude or pose. Choosing a person to write about shouldn't be difficult since each of us knows many people. The best advice is to choose someone whom we know well and whom we find interesting and some-what unusual. Deciding which attitude or trait to emphasize, however, is more difficult because we want to describe not just any trait, but a trait that will help to explain the whole person to our readers.

After choosing a person to describe, we must list our impressions of that person. An impression is a generalization that we have formed from watching and listening to him or her, and we will no doubt have count-less impressions of someone whom we know well. Perhaps the quickest way to recall those stored impressions is to freewrite for 20 minutes nonstop. Freewriting will help us to remember the person's moods, gestures, eccentricities, activities, emotional patterns, physical characteristics, clothes, motivating forces, effect on others, and so forth. At the end of this focused freewriting, we will have generated numerous impressions, which we can then list and evaluate. Here is a sample list of impressions we might generate about a hypothetical friend, Phil:

1. Phil is exceptionally intelligent.
2. In general, he seems happy.
3. He is almost handsome.
4. He is sloppy.
5. He is generous with his time and money and emotions.
6. He is disorganized.
7. He is an odd combination of the traditional and the unorthodox.
8. He dresses rather strangely.
9. He can be sulky at times.
10. He likes to argue and can argue either side of an issue.

Now we must decide on which impression to use, focus it, and find details to support it. Which of these ten impressions has potential for being developed into an interesting character sketch? We could no doubt develop any one of them into a full character sketch, but some of them would probably be more interesting than others. As with any thesis, a good dominant impression suggests something unusual or un-conventional, and it invites further explanation. Items 1, 2, and 5 would have to be developed in creative ways to hold readers' attention because the impressions themselves lack sufficient interest. Items 4, 6, 8, 9, and 10 allow for more interesting possibilities; item 8, for instance, makes readers want to know what is meant by "strangely." Items 3 and 7 seem to offer the most promise because each one arouses readers' interest by hinting at a contradiction that needs further explanation. The "almost" in item 3 is what makes the assertion interesting; if we had written "Phil is handsome," there would be little unusual about it. The "almost" requires explanation and allows for details that illustrate an in-between look: Some features contribute to handsomeness, but others prevent its completion. Likewise, the "odd combination" in item 7 allows for a balancing of features, but at present the generalization is too broad. It needs to be focused and applied to one area of Phil's life, such as his behavior, academic goals, or family life. In fact, each of the ten im-pressions needs to be limited to a specific time, place, and activity in order to be manageable.

APPLICATION

Choose a friend who would make a good subject to describe and ask yourself two questions about that person: "What is unique about him or her, and what are my major impressions of this friend?" These two questions will help you focus on the person's essential nature and should help you generate a long list of impressions. After thinking about these questions for a few minutes, write nonstop for 20 minutes about the person. Then read through the freewriting and evaluate the impressions to see which ones would make interesting theses. Select the best one, write it out in one sentence, and hand it in.

An alternative is to freewrite for 10 minutes about the person's attributes; then freewrite for the next 10 minutes about the person's faults. This approach should give you a balanced picture of the person.

Invention: Generating Different Kinds of Details

Let's say that your main impression of a particular man is that under a thin layer of modesty, he is actually conceited. Ask yourself: How do I know that? What gestures and actions, what language, what interaction with others tell me that? Think back over your dealings with this man, visualize him in your mind, and recall why you think his modesty is false and why you consider him to be stuck-up. To generate support for your dominant impression, freewrite for another 20 minutes, this time listing specific details about this man, focusing as much as possible on the dominant impression. Alternatively, you may wish to use the journalistic questions to generate details. Then read through your list of details, select those that contribute to the dominant impression, and add others to the list. No doubt you'll have some details that are so striking or witty that you'll want to include them even though they don't directly contribute to the dominant image. Don't include them. You want to convey a single personality trait, and therefore every detail must contribute to that one characteristic.

There are different kinds of physical details: those that describe only one feature, those that suggest the person's total look, and those that imply the person's psychological nature. The first type includes individual details that are striking but are isolated because they don't suggest a general impression. Such details are of interest solely because they help us to see one part of a person. For example, in describing a man's physical features, Joyce Cary comments on the "monkey fur on the back of his hands." That's an exceptionally visual detail, but it doesn't say much about his overall appearance, unless we're to assume that he resembles a monkey in general. Similarly, by concentrating on a boy's forelock, John Irving in *The World According to Garp* gives us an immediate and striking picture of what it's like to look into the boy's face, but the image suggests little of his general physical appearance and nothing of his moral character:

Hathaway was an ever-pleasant, slow-thinking boy with a slack, hairless face and a forward-falling flop of reddish blond hair, which partially hid one of his pale eyes. He had a habit of tipping his head back, perhaps so that he could see out from under his hair, and for this reason, and the fact that he was tall, everyone who looked at Hathaway looked up his wide nostrils.

The next type of physical detail is more efficient because it communicates more than itself. It is a detail that indicates what the whole physical person is like; it is a part that suggests the whole. We should be alive to these subtle but significant details with which a perceptive reader can construct the whole person. Such details can catch the essence of the total person, in the same way that an individual molecule reveals the total structure of a substance, or that a sliver of ore tells a mineralogist the composition of a rock. This is communication through small, pertinent, judiciously selected details. For example, in order to capture the sense of an old man's shrinking away, which is his dominant physical characteristic, Larry McMurtry *(In a Narrow Grave)* focuses on the old-timer's coat: "Jesse was in his nineties, and had sunk a little farther into his Mackinaw in the five years since I had last seen him." The old man has been wearing the same Mackinaw coat for years, but because old people shrink from year to year, getting shorter and losing weight, the coat now is far too big for him. He seems to have "sunk a little farther into his Mackinaw." That one detail captures the old man's total appearance.

A writer can, therefore, give an image of a person with only a few details. Notice, for instance, how John Gardner *(Nickel Mountain)* is able to communicate a general impression of sloppiness by mentioning only the position of a man's head and tie: "Simon looked up, his head far forward, like a buzzard's, his tie hanging outside the front of his suit-coat." The tie outside the coat tells us that the man looks uncomfortable in a suit and looks sloppy in general, though Gardner doesn't explicitly say this. And the sagging head tells us that his posture is drooping; Gardner uses a simile (a comparison that uses *like* or *as*) to help with the image—the head is "far forward, like a buzzard's."

Similes are efficient as well as effective because by comparing our subject to some other object, we transfer certain attributes—for example, a buzzard's stance—from that object to our subject. (See pages 615–622 for a more detailed discussion of similes.) Examine the following similes and notice how the comparison succinctly achieves the visual effect in each instance:

> She was extended full length at her end of the divan, completely motionless, and with her chin raised a little, as if she were balancing something on it which was quite likely to fall.
>
> —F. Scott Fitzgerald, *The Great Gatsby*

> . . . his lips stretched back from his teeth like a skier on a tight turn.
>
> —John Updike, *A Month of Sundays*

> . . . her eyes flicked up and down, scanning for foolishness like radar.
>
> —Mary Gordon, *Final Payments*

> . . . his gums were destitute of teeth, his nose sharp and drooping, his chin peaked and prominent, so that, when he humped [chewed] or spoke, they approached one another like a pair of nutcrackers.
>
> —Tobias Smollett, *Roderick Random*

APPLICATION

At an early stage in your writing process, try to compose a dozen or so striking similes about your subject. For practice, complete the following similes, being careful to make the comparisons as visual and original as possible:

eyes like _____   hair like _____
voice like _____   skin like _____
walks like _____   smiles like _____
talks like _____   spends money like _____
built like _____   handles a cue stick like _____

Close observation, judiciously selected details, effective similes, and careful word choice help readers to see the physical characteristics being described, and that is one goal of personal description.

An equally important goal is to reveal the person's character; in writing as in life, we find the inner person more fascinating than the outer person. Usually, however, we must use the physical as a means of getting at the psychological; in order to visualize the whole human being we need a body and a face to put the personality into. Therefore, we sometimes can use a third kind of physical detail that accomplishes both goals—showing the physical and revealing the psychological. This type of detail gives readers an insight into the subject's true nature. The physical reinforces the psychological, so by showing one, we imply the other. Often we can find a hint of people's true nature in their physical representation—eyes, posture, clothes, expression. From physical features we unconsciously make inferences and draw conclusions about an individual's personality since we communicate physically as well as verbally. For example, "body language"—the way someone sits, stands, walks, gestures—tells a great deal about that person's self-image. The angle of the body, the intensity of the eyes, the shape of the mouth, the tilt of the chin—these movements and looks can be external signs of attitudes and moods. I focus first on a person's eyes and by studying them try to judge general intelligence; then I observe the way the lips are held to see if they indicate irony, anger, geniality, nervousness, or something else. Other external characteristics may reflect internal qualities; the way people dress, for example, or their possessions can tell us about their values and self-image. Does she write with a gold fountain pen, or doodle with a red felt-tip? Does he carry a slender, gold-plated cigarette lighter, or a clear one with a fishing lure suspended in butane? What kinds of magazines are on their living room table—*The New Yorker*, or *National Lampoon?* Does she smoke regular or "designer" cigarettes?

Notice in the following example how C. S. Lewis captures a

woman's character by briefly describing physical features and then focusing on her cigarette:

Despite a bust that would have done credit to a Victorian barmaid, she was rather thickly built than fat and her iron-grey hair was cropped short. Her face was square, stern, and pale, and her voice deep. A smudge of lipstick laid on with violent inattention to the real shape of her mouth was her only concession to fashion and she rolled or chewed a long black cheroot, unlit, between her teeth. As she talked, she had a habit of removing this, staring intently at the mixture of lipstick and saliva on its mangled end, and then replacing it more firmly than before. She sat down immediately in a chair close to where Mark was standing, flung her right leg over one of the arms, and fixed him with a gaze of cold intimacy.

—From *That Hideous Strength*

Such attention to revealing details allows us to sum up personalities in prose. We get to know a person by adding up all of the clues—physical, verbal, emotional, and psychological. On first meeting someone, we usually progress from the physical to the intellectual to the emotional; we note looks, then listen to opinions and ideas, and finally we're allowed a glimpse at emotions. All along we're perceptively picking up clues. This same mental process of examining features is duplicated in writing a character sketch so that our reader gets to know our subject because we leave clues as to the identity.

In the next example, observe the levels of detail that the writer uses to show the total person: Some details are isolated but interesting, some convey the general physical appearance, and others provide insight into character. Here, Herman Melville intends for the grotesque scar to reflect Captain Ahab's scarred nature.

There seemed no sign of common bodily illness about him, nor of the recovery from any. He looked like a man cut away from the stake, when the fire has overrunningly wasted all the limbs without consuming them, or taking away one particle from their compacted aged robustness. His whole high, broad form, seemed made of solid bronze, and shaped in an unalterable mould, like Cellini's cast Perseus. Threading its way out from among his grey hairs, and continuing right down one side of his tawny scorched face and neck, till it disappeared in his clothing, you saw a slender rod-like mark, lividly whitish. It resembled that perpendicular seam sometimes made in the straight, lofty trunk of a great tree, when the upper lightning tearingly darts down the bark from the top to bottom, ere running off into the soil, leaving the tree still greenly alive, but branded.

—From *Moby Dick*

APPLICATION

Go back over your list of physical details and select those that reveal inner qualities. If you do not have any such details in your list, reapply the journalistic questions to your subject and generate more details.

Developing Topic Sentences

A dominant impression is necessary whether the character description is several pages in length or only one paragraph. For the paragraph, the dominant quality acts as the topic sentence, which is the main idea of the paragraph. The topic sentence contains two parts: the subject (what the paragraph is about) and the controlling idea (what we say about the subject). A good topic sentence (1) engages readers' attention by being interesting and fresh and (2) serves as the generalization that holds the rest of the paragraph together by providing a focus.

Here is a typical topic sentence: Because Tom is indifferent to public opinion, his behavior is frequently outrageous. The subject is "his behavior," and the controlling idea is "frequently outrageous." Our duty is to prove that Tom's behavior is frequently outrageous by providing examples for readers:

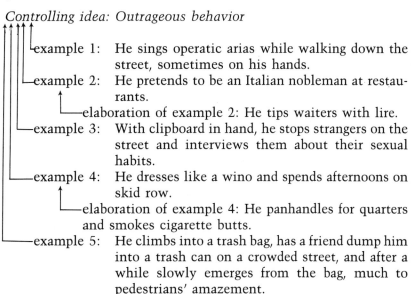

Controlling idea: Outrageous behavior

example 1:   He sings operatic arias while walking down the street, sometimes on his hands.

example 2:   He pretends to be an Italian nobleman at restaurants.
    elaboration of example 2: He tips waiters with lire.

example 3:   With clipboard in hand, he stops strangers on the street and interviews them about their sexual habits.

example 4:   He dresses like a wino and spends afternoons on skid row.
    elaboration of example 4: He panhandles for quarters and smokes cigarette butts.

example 5:   He climbs into a trash bag, has a friend dump him into a trash can on a crowded street, and after a while slowly emerges from the bag, much to pedestrians' amazement.

Notice that each sentence contributes to and explains the controlling idea. (Topic sentences and other elements of paragraphing are discussed in detail in Chapter 18.)

APPLICATION

Evaluate the following topic sentences to determine whether they are specific and engaging. Rewrite the ones that need improvement.

1. My Uncle Homer loves his little ailments.
2. Terry's country humor keeps the office in stitches.
3. Jane is very friendly.
4. James is beginning to show the pressure from med school.
5. Some children can be spoiled yet polite; Milligan is not one of those children.
6. That Karen took assertiveness training is immediately evident when you meet her.
7. Although Oliver claims to value friendship above all else, his actions suggest that he cares little for lasting relationships.
8. Denny is obsessed with his moustache.

Placement of the Topic Sentence

In descriptive paragraphs, as in other types, the topic sentence can come either at the beginning of the paragraph or at the end. Placing the topic sentence at the opening immediately informs readers of the person's nature, and the rest of the paragraph proves that statement. By giving readers an overview before they read the details, this approach acts as a service to the reader. It tells, and then shows; it states the generalization, and then gives life and credibility to it. The other method presents the specific details and then gives the generalization—the dominant impression—at the conclusion. With the topic sentence at the end of the paragraph, readers discover as they read; with the topic sentence first, the writer tells what the impression is and then confirms it. Placing the topic sentence last allows us to lead readers through the details before they see what those details add up to; therefore, it allows readers the satisfaction of discovering the conclusion for themselves. Where we place the topic sentence in a descriptive paragraph depends, therefore, on whether we want readers to discover our meaning as they read or to be told at the outset how to interpret subsequent details.

Occasionally, rather than explicitly articulating the dominant impression, we may wish to omit the topic sentence and allow our readers to draw the conclusion on their own. Descriptive writing is one of the few types of writing in which we can afford to be implicit rather than explicit. In fact, sometimes it's preferable to omit the topic sentence in descriptive and narrative writing. This is not to say that clarity isn't important in these types of writing, but the clarity should be in the image or the tale itself.

Ideally, we should do such a fine job of showing our characters that it is unnecessary to tell about them or to state explicitly what we think of them. We should be able to communicate our attitude without direct commentary and without editorial interjections. Readers should see the characters clearly, but not necessarily be told what to think of them, except through tone and style. Readers should be able to draw the conclusion that we intend. However, if we are afraid that, after showing the characters to the best of our ability, readers may miss what we intend, we should by all means be explicit and insert a topic sentence. If, on the other hand, we're confident that our dominant impression is evident without resorting to explicit telling, we can leave out the topic sentence. Readers have seen the characters, so *telling* readers about the characters is almost repetitive. Besides, readers don't like to be told the obvious; we must allow them to use their critical skills and perception to reach the conclusion.

If our topic sentence simply labels the details with an adjective, we can omit it; if it's particularly ingenious or witty, we might want to open with it. In either case, we should write out the topic sentence and then decide whether to use or omit it.

As you read the following example by John Updike, notice that he avoids telling us the dominant impression that he wants to convey, preferring instead to rely on word choice to communicate the essence of the girl being described. Updike wants to capture that awkward transitional stage between childhood and womanhood when a girl is neither child nor woman. How is the writer able to communicate his dominant impression without explicitly stating it in a topic sentence? What clues does he give readers so that they can reach the right impression of her? What words in the description associate Mary with childhood, and what words, especially ones of a slightly sexual nature, relate her to womanhood?

In the middle of the classroom Mary Landis stood up, a Monitor badge pinned to her belt. She wore a lavender sweater with the sleeves pushed up to expose her forearms, a delicately cheap effect. Wild stories were told about her; perhaps it was merely his knowledge of these that put the hardness in her face. Her eyes in their shape seemed braced for squinting and their green was frosted. Her freckles had faded. She stood a second, eclipsed at the thighs by Jack Stephens' shoulders, looking back at the room with a stiff glance, as if she had seen the same faces too many times before. Her habit of perfect posture emphasized the angularity she had grown into; there was a nervous edge, a boxiness in her bones, that must have been waiting all along under the childish fat. . . . Her brown skirt was snug and straight; she had less hips than bosom, and thin, athletic legs. Her pronged chest poised, she sauntered up the aisle and encountered a leg thrown in her path. She stared down until it withdrew; she was used to such attentions.

—From "A Sense of Shelter"

Narrative Description

To be implicit, we must show the persons instead of simply telling about them. One of the best ways of showing people is placing them in a setting and letting them present themselves, as Updike does to some extent with his description. Since we intend to give a sense of the characters' presence, we can use narration to give life and animation to them. It's like Pinocchio coming to life: We could describe Pinocchio sitting still, with his freckles, protruding nose, Italian hat, and striped suspenders, but the description would be as lifeless as Pinocchio before his transformation. Actions define and reveal personalities much better than still descriptions. To add life to a description, we can construct an environment that is typical for the person we are describing. Then we put the person into that environment and have him or her react to a dramatic situation. The scene doesn't have to be high drama in the sense of a catastrophic event or a physical conflict, but it should contain a blend of action, emotional content, and personality. Once we decide on a dramatic scene, we need to describe how the person responds to the situation and to other people in the scene, how the person talks, and how he or she moves and gestures. This type of dramatic scene also allows us to insert physical descriptions as we are showing the person in action; that is, we can insert at appropriate places descriptions of the person's clothes, body, face, and so on.

A brief dramatic incident or scene is convincing to readers because they see the person in action. It's almost as if they are there watching the event we're describing; the scene is immediate and realistic because the person comes to life in front of their eyes, and seeing is believing. As we create the person in action, we can duplicate in our readers those feelings that we have toward the person, rather than just telling what our feelings are. This is what student Judi George does in the following description of her father. What is Judi's attitude toward her father? What is the dominant impression communicated by this narrative description? Is there any physical description inserted in the narrative? Does Judi let her father's actions speak for themselves, or does she tell us what to think of him?

When the pipe under the kitchen sink sprang a leak, my father was on the scene in a flash. Immediately he ordered everyone and everything out of the kitchen so he could inspect the disaster site. With a serious look on his face, and with his sleeves rolled up, he prodded and poked beneath the sink for half an hour. Deciding a new pipe was needed, he made a detailed list of items for me to buy at the hardware store. Before I was allowed to leave, though, he insisted that I read the list aloud so he was sure that I understood exactly what he wanted.

By the time I returned home, Dad was in his work uniform: a pair of orange tennis shoes, a green pair of too-short trousers, a linty red banlon shirt, and a dirty baseball cap. Without a word, he took the bag from my arms; already he was in a world of his own. During the three hours he labored on that pipe there was no communicating with him. Anyone who tried to speak with him more than once was profusely chastised. Tools and rulers and tubes of caulking lay scattered around him. Measuring and remeasuring, analyzing and computing, he put the new pipe on only to take it off and begin again. It wasn't that he didn't put the pipe on correctly the first five times—he just wanted to make sure.

Finally the task was done, but in no way was it forgotten. The entire following week he checked the pipe as soon as he got home from work. Each afternoon he made a beeline from the front door to the kitchen sink, and each afternoon he walked proudly away mumbling, "O.K., that'll do, that'll do."

Judi could have simply told us "My father loves to fix things around the house, and we all let him think he's terrific for doing it," but by showing him in action, she is better able to communicate what her father is like and what her feelings are for him. Clearly, here is a man who enjoys a mechanical difficulty, who takes his job as seriously as a surgeon and becomes totally engrossed in it, and who takes pride in his ability. Here also is a daughter who finds her father's antics mildly amusing, who tolerates his awarding too much importance to the task, and who looks on him with affection. The description is not only convincing, but also touching and entertaining.

APPLICATION

1. Analyze the following narrative portrayal by first-year college student Debbie Schwartz.
   A. What adjectives would you use to describe Mrs. Engle, the high school teacher being described?
   B. Does the writer give an explicit opinion of Mrs. Engle? If not, how do we know that the writer considers Mrs. Engle to be an uninspiring teacher?
   C. What details or phrases can you point to that contribute to the dominant impression?
   D. Do you find the description convincing? If so, why? If not, why not?

Mrs. Engle stood before the class ready to engage in another lesson. Unconsciously her hand floated to the back of her head, misplacing the few strands of hair still left in order. She steadied her glasses on her face as best she could, and then proceeded to interest the class in a discussion of Aldous Huxley's *Brave New World*. The apple-red line around her mouth moved in rhythm to a voice that was barely audible, like the static on a P.A. system. Midway through her introduction she arranged herself a seat on the edge of her desk and leaned back. Several sheets of paper and master dittoes slid off the other side. She rose and shuffled toward the blackboard, prepared to outline the entire sequence of story events. Perceiving a bit of laughter and commotion in one corner of the room, she glanced nervously in the direction of the sound, but her view was blocked by the outer edge of her glasses' frame. Nevertheless, she continued her explanation, shifting her gaze to the board directly in front of her. While feverishly elaborating on the text, she scribbled notes in yellow chalk, but the incessant clatter of her gold charm bracelet, overloaded with momentos from brief summer excursions, muffled her commentary. A few students finished their reading of the novel, undaunted by any disturbance; others distractedly drummed their fingers on their desk tops. The teacher worked on unblinkingly.

2. Briefly describe someone doing one of these activities:
   A. smoking a cigar in a crowded restaurant
   B. eating breakfast at an all-night diner
   C. riding a crowded bus or subway with an armful of packages
   D. taking an exam on the first warm day of spring
   E. waiting in a dentist's office

Organizing a Character Sketch

The narrative approach is necessarily chronological, but chronological order is only one of several ways of organizing a character description. Descriptions that are primarily of a person's physical appearance, for example, invite a spatial organization (*spatial* means according to space or direction); that is, we start describing at one physical point and move in one direction—upward, downward, across. A description might start at the head and go down to the feet, or it might start at the neck and go up to the forehead, describing the chin, mouth, nose, eyes, and so on as it progresses. What is the movement from the first paragraph to the second in Capote's description on page 110?

Another method of arranging the accumulated details and of conveying a particular impression is to use an extended comparison. In the following example, James Agee uses a comparison to describe the comedian Buster Keaton, whose movements, Agee suggests, are like those of a machine. Notice, however, that Agee doesn't come out and say "Keaton is funny because he acts like a machine"; he doesn't have to say that because he communicates the impression indirectly by using words that refer to mechanical objects. What specific words communicate this dominant impression?

His short-legged body was all sudden, machinelike angles, governed by a daft aplomb. When he swept a semaphore-like arm to point, you could almost hear the electrical impulse in the signal block. When he ran from a cop his transitions from accelerating walk to easy jogtrot to brisk canter to headlong gallop to flogged-piston spring—always floating, above this frenzy, the untroubled, untouchable face—were as distinct and as soberly in order as an automatic gearshift.

—From *Agee on Film*

The implied comparison (called a metaphor, which is a comparison that doesn't use *like* or *as*) helps us to recall the image of Buster Keaton in his silent film days, forever running from the Keystone Cops in his stiff, rapid style.

APPLICATION

The following description by first-year student Terry Thomas uses metaphor to capture the movements of a group of girls on a boardwalk.

1. What is the metaphor upon which the description is based? That is, what is Terry implicitly comparing the actions of the girls to?
2. What words convey the metaphor and help to establish the dominant impression?
3. How effective is this metaphor for portraying the girls' performance?

Their manners changed as they saw our group of males. The girl leading the pack altered her stride to a more to-and-fro motion, and the others instantly picked up the cue, syncopating into a symphony of swing. The leader's jaw stopped mashing her gum, and she fussed with her too-blonde hair, making me wonder how much of the rest of her was real. The unharnessed curves of her body left little to the imagination, however, as they vibrated in counterpoint variations on the lively theme. The other girls knew better than to blatantly upstage the soloist, but at the same time strove to ensure that their own virtuosity would not be missed, all the while effecting an aura of carefully contrived unselfconsciousness. The music became more intense as the two groups neared each other, until all felt the pounding in their ears—the urgency of summer night music. Then the leader, fickle as a flute, discovered something more interesting in the distance. But the piece was well conducted, and as she passed, we all turned to watch the fade-out.

Another organizational pattern open to us is to move from physical description to psychological description. In the first part of our sketch we can describe the outer person, and in the second part, the inner person. We can either contrast the outer person to the inner, or show that they complement each other, as Henry Fielding does in the following description. The woman being described, Mrs. Slipslop, has an inner character that is as ugly as her external appearance. Fielding begins by describing her somewhat gross physical features and then paints an equally unappealing picture of her moral character.

She was a maiden gentlewoman of about forty-five years of age, who having made a small slip in her youth, had continued a good maid ever since. She was not at this time remarkably handsome; being very short, and rather too corpulent in body, and somewhat red, with the addition of pimples in the face. Her nose was likewise rather too large, and her eyes too little; nor did she resemble a cow so much in her breath, as in two brown globes which she carried before her; one of her legs was also a little shorter than the other, which occasioned her to limp as she walked. This fair creature had long cast the eyes of affection on Joseph, in which she had not met with quite so good success as she probably wished, though, besides the allurements of her native charms, she had given him tea, sweetmeats [candy], wine, and many other delicacies, of which, by keeping the keys, she had the absolute command. Joseph, however, had not returned the least gratitude to all these favours, not even so much as a kiss; though I would not insinuate she was so easily to be satisfied; for surely then he would have been highly blameable. The truth is, she was arrived at an age when she thought she might indulge herself in any liberties with a man, without the danger of bringing a third person into the world to betray them. She imagined that by so long a self-denial she had not only made amends for the small slip of her youth above hinted at, but had likewise laid up a quantity of merit to excuse any future failings. In a word, she resolved to give a loose to her amorous inclinations, and to pay off the debt of pleasure which she found she owed herself, as fast as possible.

—From *Joseph Andrews*

1. Fielding's tone in places is ironic; that is, he occasionally says one thing but means something else. For example, when he refers to her as "this fair creature," he expects his readers to realize that he is jesting. Find another example of his use of irony in the portrait.

2. Explain Mrs. Slipslop's moral arithmetic in the final three sentences.

There are many other ways of arranging descriptive material, and each is appropriate in certain circumstances, depending on our purpose, readers, and subject. For instance, we might arrange characteristics in an order of increasing importance, starting with the least significant details and leading to the most significant ones. Or we might begin with the obvious characteristics and then shift to more subtle ones that a casual observer might not notice. Another way of structuring details might be to proceed from a series of minor characteristics to an inclusive major trait; for example, we might describe a person's behavior (such as loudness, boastfulness, and other devices to attract attention) and then classify the behavior under a larger trait (such as a hidden inferiority complex). Another type of organization is to progress from anecdote to explanation; in the first part of the description we would give an account of a person in a mistake or blunder, and in the second part explain how this is indicative of his or her whole personality.

Advice, Warnings, Reminders

1. A good character sketch requires more than a series of good details about a person. We must also communicate a unified image. When we look into a person's face, we see not simply the individual parts—two eyes, a nose, a jawline, a mouth, a chin—but a whole face, and we get a definite impression from that face. Likewise, when we write a character sketch, our readers should see not isolated details but a cluster of details that projects a single impression.

2. We must learn to mold our evidence to fit the dominant impression. If we have a detail that we feel is vital to the understanding of a character and yet the detail doesn't quite conform to the dominant impression, perhaps we can mold the detail to fit. For instance, we might be writing about an Americanized German woman who has three children. If our dominant impression is that her ethnic background is important to her, we wouldn't devote much space to discussing her relationship with her children because it wouldn't contribute to the dominant impression. However, we might point out that she sends her children back to Germany every summer so that they also will have a sense of their ethnic heritage. That is what is meant by molding evidence to fit the dominant impression.

3. Since not all details are equally helpful in animating a subject, we should try to use those that reveal more than the surface statement. A revealing detail isn't that your psychology professor likes lemon pie, but that he or she reads Fabulous Furry Freak Brothers comic books. What does the following two-sentence description tell us about the people involved: the wife (who is the speaker), the mistress (who is being described), and the husband?

> "She's perfect for him. She has enormous breasts; she's smart enough to laugh at his jokes but not smart enough to make her own."
>
> —Mary Gordon, *Final Payments*

4. There are two ways of getting across our opinion of a person: One is direct commentary and editorial statements; the other is more indirect, whereby

we let our choice of words, selection of details, and tone reveal our attitude. One way states, and the other implies. The second method is usually preferable.

5. Verbs should carry a description. For example, instead of writing "The woman walked down the ramp," we should tell how she walked: *marched, strolled, waddled, staggered, strutted, sauntered, traipsed.* Each of these verbs communicates a particular movement and feeling.

6. A tendency exists in description to put an adjective in front of almost every noun: a *strong* jaw, *piercing* eyes, a *hawkish* nose, *ruddy* cheeks. Adjectives should be used sparingly, and when we do use them, we should make them unpredictable ones. Here is another example from Mary Gordon: "My life had the balletic attraction of routine." The word "balletic" is a fresh adjective that effectively expresses the appeal of repetition since ballet dancers practice their movements over and over.

7. Nouns should be specific in descriptions—not just a bird, but a goldenfinch or a vesper sparrow; not a car, but a '53 Chevy coupe or a 1986 Jaguar XJS; not simply a Christian, but specifically a Southern Baptist or a Disciple of Christ.

8. A temptation in character sketches is to conclude with a surprise ending that reverses the person's character. For example, students often portray a grumpy person but then end by saying that the person actually has a heart of gold. After having carefully created a personality, the writers contradict their portrait in the last sentence by introducing an opposite trait. A reversal of this type is unbelievable and unconvincing, and readers often feel tricked by it. It is therefore best to resist the surprise ending.

Exercises

1. In a few sentences, show one of these moods in a specific person:

   dejection   craftiness
   determination   elegance
   sullenness   modesty

2. As a class exercise, compose paragraphs to accompany these topic sentences. Either the entire class can contribute details and then arrange them into a paragraph on the blackboard, or the class can divide into three groups and each group can develop a different topic sentence.
   a. Professor ——————— relies on dramatics for classroom effect.
   b. One look at Rodney Dangerfield's face and you know why he can't get any respect.

c. The first day of English class, Steve spends the entire hour trying to look cool.

> For this last topic sentence, for example, every support sentence in the paragraph must develop the controlling idea "trying to look cool." One person might contribute this as the next sentence: "He strolls into the room, sprawls into a chair, throws his right leg over the arm, puts his left leg over the back of the chair in front, puffs on a Lucky Strike, flicks the ashes on the floor, and leisurely surveys the women." Everyone contributes details and molds them until you have completely conveyed the dominant impression.

3. To describe a person about whom you have mixed feelings, make two lists, one of positive and one of negative characteristics. Then compose a topic sentence that reflects a dominant impression of ambivalence.

4. Describe yourself in one word, and then develop that idea in a paragraph.

5. The following is a list of impressions and details that you might make into a short character sketch. Which sentences would make good impressions (generalizations) and which would make good details to support the impressions? Which details go with which impressions? In what order would you arrange the details under each impression? Which details don't seem to fit?

   A. Jeremy works at Cross Creek golf course on weekends as a caddy.
   B. His hair is shaved in front.
   C. He always looks as if he just woke up.
   D. His money goes to buying hard-rock albums and traveling to golf courses around the country.
   E. He wears patent leather shoes that are candy-apple red.
   F. He smokes an African clay pipe.
   G. In back his hair is long and blue.
   H. His eyes are usually half open.
   I. He owns a pet tarantula named Louisa.
   J. He lives with his aunt and mother.
   K. Jeremy doesn't fit into any academic department on campus, or in any category for that matter.
   L. His favorite beers are Dinklelakker and Tsing Tao.
   M. The college at first refused to approve his unique major, but Jeremy kept bugging his advisor until she finally agreed to support it.
   N. The only things he eats are scrambled eggs, peanut butter, fruit, white chocolate, and fish—that's it.
   O. His hair is seldom combed; he calls it the "sweet neglect" look.
   P. His favorite rock groups are Twisted Sister, ZZ Top, and Mr. Mister.

Q. Jeremy plays golf, but he doesn't play well enough to be on the college golf team.

R. He is 5 feet 11 inches tall.

S. His favorite movies are *Dune* and *My Darling Clementine.*

T. Because Jeremy wants to design golf courses for a living, he created his own major: golf course architecture.

U. He usually wears baggy black slacks with pleats and cuffs and yellow suspenders.

V. The golfers call his hair just plain weird.

W. His major is a mixture of horticulture, physical education, and architecture.

X. He reads lots of science fiction and a few spy books.

Y. He doesn't fit the mold of the typical golfer, who dresses in polyester slacks and cardigan sweaters.

Z. He has three girlfriends.

Additional Readings

---

1. The usual way of describing people is to describe their physical characteristics, as Capote, Melville, and Updike do in earlier examples. Here are two variations on that practice.

LANCELOT

Walker Percy

As I stepped into the parlor with its smell of lemon wax and damp horsehair, I stopped and shut my eyes a moment to get used to the darkness. Then as I crossed the room to the sliding doors, something moved in the corner of my eye. It was a man at the far end of the room. He was watching me. He did not look familiar. There was something wary and poised about the way he stood, shoulders angled, knees slightly bent as if he were prepared for anything. He was mostly silhouette but white on black like a reversed negative. His arms were long, one hanging lower and lemur-like from dropped shoulder. His head was cocked, turned enough so I could see the curve at the back. There was a sense about him of a vulnerability guarded against, an overcome gawkiness, a conquered frailty. Seeing such a man one thought first: Big-headed smart-boy type; then thought again: But he's big too. If he hadn't developed his body, worked out, he'd have a frail neck, two tendons, and a hollow between, balancing that big head. He looked like a long-distance runner who has conquered polio. He looked like a smart sissy rich boy who has devoted his life to getting over it.

Then I realized it was myself reflected in the dim pier mirror.

—From *Lancelot*

A. We don't realize that this is a self-description until the final sentence. What is the effect of placing that sentence at the end instead of opening the description with it?

B. What is the dominant impression? Is it stated explicitly?

C. What does Percy rely on most to convey his description? Does he favor comparisons? Does he rely most on verbs, nouns, or adjectives, or on none more than others? Substantiate your answer.

IGNATIUS J. REILLY

John Kennedy Toole

A green hunting cap squeezed the top of the fleshy balloon of a head. The green earflaps, full of large ears and uncut hair and the fine bristles that grew in the ears themselves, stuck out on either side like turn signals indicating two directions at once. Full, pursed lips protruded beneath the bushy black moustache and, at their corners, sank into little folds filled with disapproval and potato chip crumbs. In the shadow under the green visor of the cap Ignatius J. Reilly's supercilious blue and yellow eyes looked down upon the other people waiting under the clock at the D. H. Holmes department store, studying the crowd of people for signs of bad taste in dress. Several of the outfits, Ignatius noticed, were new enough and expensive enough to be properly considered offenses against taste and decency. Possession of anything new or expensive only reflected a person's lack of theology and geometry; it could even cast doubts upon one's soul.

Ignatius himself was dressed comfortably and sensibly. The hunting cap prevented head colds. The voluminous tweed trousers were durable and permitted unusually free locomotion. Their pleats and nooks contained pockets of warm, stale air that soothed Ignatius. The plaid flannel shirt made a jacket unnecessary while the muffler guarded exposed Reilly skin between earflap and collar. The outfit was acceptable by any theological and geometrical standards, however abstruse, and suggested a rich inner life.

Shifting from one hip to the other in his lumbering, elephantine fashion, Ignatius sent waves of flesh rippling beneath the tweed and flannel, waves that broke upon buttons and seams. Thus rearranged, he contemplated the long while that he had been waiting for his mother.

—From *A Confederacy of Dunces*

A. What is the tone of this piece? Does the author seem to agree with Ignatius' views, or is he making fun of them? Substantiate your answer.

B. Instead of beginning with a generalization, the writer relies on small details in the first three sentences to capture the image of Ignatius J. Reilly. Which details are especially revealing?

C. What adjectives would you use to describe Ignatius, and what details in the description suggest those adjectives?

2. The three paragraphs below illustrate the diverse ways we can approach character description. In addition to the obvious approach of focusing on physical characteristics, we can focus on one habit or concern, on one typical activity, or on the person's typical environment.

THE COOK

John Cheever

The cook we had that year was a Polish woman named Anna Ostrovick, a summer cook. She was first-rate—a big, fat, hearty, industrious woman who took her work seriously. She liked to cook and to have the food she cooked appreciated and eaten, and whenever we saw her, she always urged us to eat. She cooked hot bread—crescents and brioches—for breakfast two or three times a week, and she would bring these into the dining room herself and say, "Eat, eat, eat!" When the maid took the serving dishes back into the pantry, we could sometimes hear Anna, who was standing there, say "Good! They eat." She fed the garbage man, the milkman, and the gardener. "Eat!" she told them. "Eat, eat!" On Thursday afternoons, she went to the movies with the maid, but she didn't enjoy the movies, because the actors were all so thin. She would sit in the dark theatre for an hour and a half watching the screen anxiously for the appearance of someone who had enjoyed his food. Bette Davis merely left with Anna the impression of a woman who has not eaten well. "They are all so skinny," she would say when she left the movies. In the evenings, after she had gorged all of us, and washed the pots and pans, she would collect the table scraps and go out to feed the creation. We had a few chickens that year, and although they would have roosted by then, she would dump food into their troughs and urge the sleeping fowl to eat. She fed the songbirds in the orchard and the chipmunks in the yard. Her appearance at the edge of the garden and her urgent voice—we could hear her calling "Eat, eat, eat"—had become, like the sunset gun at the boat club and the passage of light from Cape Heron, attached to that hour. "Eat, eat, eat," we could hear Anna say. "Eat, eat . . ." Then it would be dark.

From "Goodbye My Brother," *The Stories of John Cheever*

A. Does the paragraph have a topic sentence? If so, where is it located?

B. Are the sentences arranged in any kind of order? If so, describe the order. If not, explain the effect of not having an order.

C. Of the various ways to achieve coherence within a paragraph (order, repetition of key terms, use of transitional markers), which does Cheever rely on most? Explain with examples.

A FAMILY PORTRAIT

Preparing to go to church is a chaotic ritual at the Beaver farmhouse. Eighty-year-old A. W., finally used to indoor plumbing, shaves in the bathroom instead of at the backporch washstand; the first family member fully dressed, he prowls the house, tapping his Stetson against his leg, nervous that they will be late. Knowing that he's entering feminine territory, he peers into the bedroom, timidity personified. Donda, his wife, tries to tell him something but, frustrated by his deafness, she gives up and motions for him to put on his hearing aid. Although he realizes she's addressing him, he can't distinguish her words from the sounds of Turks, so he responds by sticking out his chin and tightening his lips, a reply everyone recognizes as "I didn't hear you, but it doesn't matter." He exits. Donda is standing, knees bent, in front of the dresser mirror brushing her hair, not having learned to sit and brush. Virgie, their city-daughter, applying mascara and giving Donda occasional advice about which way to wear her hair, though nothing helps, talks in monotone about the kids and grandkids, mostly anecdotes. A. W. returns: "Where's Ed?" "ED!" Virgie yells in the other direction, "are you still in the bathtub?" Ed hears his wife but doesn't answer; he and A. W. are a lot alike in some ways. "He's in the bathtub still" Virgie tells her father, who doesn't hear, and raises his eyebrows to let her know. Donda, by this time sufficiently piqued at his not putting on his hearing aid, points toward the bathroom and spews out squeakily "He's-in-the-tub" and then mutters "I don't know why on earth that man insists on asking questions but refuses to put on his hearing aid." No one is listening to her. Ed, not raised to fear women's provinces, comes into the room in his shorts. "For God's sake, Honey," Virgie complains, "hurry up." "What did you bring for me to wear?" She has laid all his clothes out in front of him, as for a child. A. W. is out under the oak tree, whistling "Rock of Ages," Baptist syle.

A. Does the paragraph develop the controlling idea "chaotic ritual?" If you think it does not, create a more appropriate controlling idea for the paragraph.

B. The paragraph hints at a problem in communication among these four people. Give examples of this problem and explain how those recurring references help to characterize the people.

C. Who is the central character, and how does he or she contribute to the narrative?

GRANDMA

Jayne O'Donnell, (student)

Upon the mantel sits a haphazard arrangement of porcelain saints, each donning a layer of dust like a veil. Filling the house are bric-a-bracs, seemingly meaningless, but without a moment's hesitation Grandma will reel off an explanation of something's significance—be it a going-out-of-business sale at a curios shop or a memento from an excursion into New York. Gaudy Christmas bulbs decorating the staircase incessantly flicker despite Christmas' passing nearly two months ago. A stout poodle sprawls over a worn velvet ottoman although his presence can be just as easily detected with a mere whiff. Still attired in his matching cherry red cap and coat from his morning walk, the snowy gray poodle resembles an old usher at a movie theatre taking a nap at intermission. Dishes of chocolates and various other confections collect dust on each table in the living area, placed conveniently to accommodate unexpected visitors that Grandma always strives to make feel welcome.

A. The real subject—Grandma—isn't even present. Still, Jayne could have explained how each item in the house reflects her grandmother's personality, but she refrains from such interpretation. What adjectives would you apply to the grandmother, and why would you choose those particular adjectives?

B. Does the description create a unique individual, or does it rely on common generalities about elderly ladies?

C. Of the many details the writer could have selected, why do you think she focuses on "the snowy gray poodle?"

3. The next three examples rely on a mixture of dialogue, physical description, and anecdote.

LIBIDINS

Agnes de Mille

"Ah-ha!" said a voice in the corner. A large-domed, bald, egg-shaped gentleman by name David Libidins had seated himself behind me. "A young lady who knows her mind. This I like. This I like verrry much." And he went into a mouthful of Russian which sounded like hot chocolate and whipped cream mixed with teeth. Libidins was business manager and comptroller [of the Ballet Russe de Monte Carlo]. He was enormous. He was male. Part llama, part bull. He was also very smart. Every so often he giggled with a high piercing Russian male giggle that boded no good for someone. At the moment he told me he was writing his memoirs and submitting them not to an editor as one might suppose but to his lawyers, and he was right to do this. It is virtually impossible, he told me, to write three consecutive sentences about the Ballet Russe without infuriating colleagues.

—From *Dance to the Piper*

A. Does the paragraph present a unified image of this man, or do we just get a series of unrelated characteristics? Does it have a dominant impression?

B. Most descriptions rely on the eyes, but this one relies as much on the ears. Give examples.

WILL HONEYCOMB

Richard Steele

But that our society may not appear a set of humorists, unacquainted with the gallantries and pleasures of the age, we have amongst us the gallant Will Honeycomb; a gentleman who, according to his years, should be in the decline of his life; but having ever been very careful of his person, and always had a very easy fortune, time has made but a very little impression, either by wrinkles on his forehead, or traces on his brain. His person is well turned, and of a good height. He is very ready at that sort of discourse with which men usually entertain women. He has all his life dressed very well, and remembers habits as others do men. He can smile when one speaks to him, and laughs easily. He knows the history of every mode, and can inform you from which of the French King's wenches, our wives and daughters had this manner of curling their hair, that way of placing their hoods; whose frailty was covered by such a sort of petticoat, and whose vanity to show her foot made that part of the dress so short in such a year. In a word, all his conversation and knowledge has been in the female world. As other men of this age will take notice to you what such a minister said upon such and such an occasion, he will tell you, when the Duke of Monmouth danced at court, such a woman was then smitten, another was taken with him at the head of his troop in the park. In all these important relations, he has ever about the same time received a kind glance, or a blow of a fan from some celebrated beauty, mother of the present Lord Such-a-one. If you speak of a young commoner that said a lively thing in the house, he starts up, "He has good blood in his vein; Tom Mirable begot him; the rogue cheated me in that affair; that young fellow's mother used me more like a dog than any woman I ever made advances to." This way of talking of his very much enlivens the conversation amongst us of a more sedate turn;

and I find there is not one of the company, but myself, who rarely speaks at all, but speaks of him as that sort of man, who is usually called a well-bred fine gentleman. To conclude his character, where women are not concerned, he is an honest, worthy man.

—From *The Spectator*

A. Unlike the other examples in this chapter, which are modern, this selection is from an early eighteenth-century magazine. How does the style differ from modern prose?

B. Will Honeycomb is a character type: the old dandy or ladies' man. What does Steele think of this type of person? Refer to the text to support your view.

THE TATTOOIST

Alistair Cooke

The last American of my half-dozen—and I put him last because it would be impossible to talk about anybody else after him—was a tattooist in San Diego, California. A sleek, foxy-looking little man in his early fifties with a bow tie, an Adolphe Menjou mustache, and his shirt-sleeves rolled high, his arms blue with writhing snakes, cooch dancers, patterns of lacework, and assorted nicknames. The moment I asked him to open up about his work, he adopted the manner of the government people in charge of defense in the last war. Deliberate, but not so that you could get a word in. Defiant, lest you dared to think that anyone in America was in a better position to feel the people's pulse. He announced, choosing his words with great weight, that "no trade or business in these United States is a better barometer, you might say," of the American mood and economy. In the first war, he said, "sailors used to come in here and ask for hearts, and their girl's names. No more," he said. "It's a very different picture. Now they seem to want their mothers, just the word 'Mother.' " He sighed. Tattooing, it seemed, wasn't what it used to be in the good old days of private enterprise. "I mean from the medical angle. I never had a customer yet get blood-poisoning. But in the last twenty years the doctors start hornin' in and settin' up what they call standards. Tattooing today's what you might call a scientific, surgical operation. Sterile needles and all that stuff. That sorta thing makes you pretty leery. They don't encourage tattooing on some parts of the body no more. I have to take it easy. Girls used to come in here, they didn't give a damn what you tattooed on 'em or where. They just want it to hurt, get it? Most guys who get tattooed do it on a dare, just to show they're tough. Sure it hurts. That's the psychology of it. If it didn't hurt, I'd a been outa business thirty-five years ago. But don't forget there are ethics in this game. I don't want to harm nobody. I charge five dollars a square inch for the forearm, ten dollars on the upper arm. I wouldn't touch a chest for fifty bucks."

I asked him what was the weirdest assignment he'd ever had. He looked me over and shut the door and lit a cigarette. He had obviously told this many times before, but he had to set the stage.

"Well, a woman about two years ago was sick some place up north, Los Angeles—Glendale, I guess. But I mean sick. Had some sort of stomach trouble. And seems the doctor wanted to operate. Well, this guy—a brother—phones here around one in the morning. Wanted to know how much I'd charge to get the way out to Glendale and tattoo her stomach. Now, I mean, I told him that was a tough thing to figure. You see, somebody asks a price on a job and you gotta know where it's gonna be. When I was young at this game I used to quote 'em so much a square inch, thinkin' it'd be a forearm or lower leg or some place where the skin's thin and tight. Hell, if you fix the price, then you have to go to work on a flabby leg. By the time you stretched it so's you can keep the needle goin' smooth, you'd cover an acre. So I figured she was a middle-aged dame and anyway I didn't wanna drive a hundred some odd miles out there. So I says a hundred and twenty bucks. Okay, says the guy, and charge the cab. Honest.

"So I collect the dyes and needles and stuff and I'm on my way. I get out there—to this house, I mean—and go up to the bedroom. It was like a morgue in there. Dark and everythin' and this dame lyin' across the bed screamin' about bein' cut up. Seems she was goin' in the hospital the next day for you know what they call it—observation? She was scared they'd operate on her, and me not get there. Well, I took one look at her and, brother, I gypped myself on the deal. She was enormous. It took me three hours. She'd a been a whole lot more comfortable havin' the operation. I sure was glad to get outa that place. How's that?—what did I write? I wrote what she told me, sort of a note to the surgeon. Clear across her middle. 'Do not violate this Body.' "

—From *One Man's America*

A. Why does Cooke rely almost totally on the tattooist's dialogue to describe the man?

B. How does the tattooist's narrative in the last two paragraphs hold readers' attention?

THE OLD LADY

Sharon R. Curtin

She lives in my neighborhood, a holdover from the days when this block was filled   1 with rooming houses occupied by old people living on welfare. In the last few years, families bought the old town houses, hired decorators and rebuilt the buildings; now tourists walk through the area to see what elegant old New York City once looked like. The old lady treats tourist and resident both with noble hostility and grand contempt.

    She hates kids. And can move surprisingly fast on her little gray legs (looking, in   2 fact, like a stick figure drawn by a sick and hungry child) whenever any child tries to play anywhere on the block. She lives in a corner building and let any unsuspecting youngster bounce a ball, take a piece of chalk out of their pocket, unwind a jumprope, strap on a pair of skates, and she will jump out, shaking her cane and muttering obscenities. Nobody taunts or teases her, either; I think children respect her un-compromising hate of childhood. The lady doesn't mess around. Arms crossed, eyes flickering right and left like those of a wise old snake, she protects her corner from fun and games and laughter.

A real old bitch, she is, hating herself and the world with intensity. I am 3 sometimes tempted to cross the street rather than walk in front of her building, feeling haunted by half-remembered fairy tales. I have tried to talk to her, feeling full of goodwill and noble intentions, and quite sure she will simply have to recognize my charming interest in her. She is quite immune and unimpressed by any approach known to man and regards me with the same air one might view the approach of a thief. She is tiny, stringy, tough; in two years, I've yet to hear her say a pleasant word. Winter and summer she hangs about in front of her building, waiting for something, someone to offend her.

She has one beauty: She is, bar none, the finest shoplifter I have ever seen.   4

One afternoon, in search of some kind of shampoo I had become convinced 5 would save me from a fate worse than death, I was canvassing the local drugstores. Since our neighborhood still preserves some of the qualities of old New York, almost every other block has a little drugstore full of treasures dating back twenty years. Finally, I had to go further from home to one of the large chain stores on Sixth Avenue. I had been conscious that the neighborhood viper was hovering about on the edge of my vision in several of the stores, but it wasn't until I reached Sixth Avenue that I began to wonder what she was doing. Was she following me? Would she think I was following her and call a cop? It became difficult to maintain my poise when every time I turned around I caught myself staring into her hard, shifty little eyes. Her eyes had the quality of being deep in color yet suggesting that nothing existed but the hard shiny surface you could see. Looking into those eyes convinced me that living that long could do nothing but pare you down to the smooth hard exterior, destroying all the soft, secret, inner things and leaving a thin shell to walk around as if it were alive.

In the fifth store I finally found my shampoo. The old lady was still there, moving 6 quickly from one area of the store to another, eyes darting around, muttering to herself, her cane knocking down occasional displays and thudding against unwary shins. She left a trail of confused, irritated shoppers in every aisle. Salesladies rushed to soothe customers, tapping their heads and pointing in the direction of the old lady, making it clear to everyone that she was crazy, pitiful, senile. No one offered to wait on the old lady. It was apparent that people in the store were accustomed to her careening around and disrupting the smooth wheels of commerce. I began to feel a little sorry for the old bitch myself, in spite of the fact I knew she was very capable of taking care of herself. I began to follow her around, with some vague idea of making sure she found her way home.

She moved into another store, a large crowded discount drugstore. Several 7 burly security guards stood around, hired by the manager to discourage the light-fingered. Knocking a large and elaborately arranged display of aerosol cans of deodorant down in front of one of the men, and moving on muttering, muttering, head swinging from side to side, eyes flashing, a quick turn—and the other man is on his knees picking up gift-packaged, three-in-one, special-today bath powder, cologne, hair spray. Quicker than the tongue of a fly-hungry frog, her old hand flashes out and things disappear from the counter into her pocket. Seconds later another crash, and a startled customer is standing in the middle of various kinds of denture cleaner while the clerk tries to balance a threatened rack of hair grooming aids. Flick, scoop, and another section of the counter glows smooth glass instead of packaged cologne. The clerk turns, eyes sliding across the glass, missing something but not being sure what, hesitates, glances around, and finally moves to rescue the customer. Meanwhile, my old lady had moved on down the aisle and is glaring at a display of cheap toys for children. The clerk apologizes to the customer, moves her finger in a quick circle at her forehead and points at the old lady. Crazy, the gesture says. Poor crazy old goose, she doesn't know what she is doing. Heads shaking, customer and clerk move toward the shining, clean counter top.

The poor crazy old goose moved on through three more large stores, using the   8
same technique. The response in each place was the same, heads shaking in false pity, tongues clicking soundlessly behind pursed lips. The world just didn't appreciate her artistry. In a few hours she had collected enough to change the way she was walking. The booty pulled her shapeless dress even closer to the tops of her high-laced shoes and she leaned more heavily upon her cane. But her eyes kept moving, and her hand flicking out from under her sweater until the profits of every drugstore in the West Village were considerably reduced. I became exhausted just watching. Finally she turned toward home, and her protected corner. Weighed down with the afternoon's welfare supplement, the old lady came sailing down the street, listing a bit to port because of poor loading. What the old pirate was going to do with all that junk was beyond me. She could have opened her own store with just that afternoon's work. She was obviously tired, yet I didn't dare offer to help. Excuse me, lady, can I carry your stolen goods to the local fence? Let me tell you, I think your method is one hell of a good way to supplement social security, and keep yourself in shape besides. Anyone who could move that fast had no trouble with arthritis; and anyone who could steal in front of television cameras, one-way mirrors, extra security guards, and locked cabinets was obviously not senile.

The next day the fastest hands in town were back on the corner, keeping our   9
block free from the sound of children laughing.

—From *Nobody Ever Died of Old Age*

A. Despite Curtin's avowed dislike of the old lady, the writer seems to have a certain respect or admiration for her. Give examples to substantiate this view.

B. What is the purpose of the first three paragraphs? How does the description in those paragraphs contribute, if at all, to the rest of the character sketch?

C. Why does paragraph 4 come as something of a surprise? Why does Curtin use the word *beautiful*? Do you think that it would have been more effective to omit the announcement of the old lady's kleptomania and simply show her shoplifting? Why, or why not?

D. This character sketch is longer than the others you have examined. How does Curtin keep it from becoming tedious?

E. What is the effect of changing from past tense to present tense in paragraph 7? Were you aware of the shift when you first read the piece?

F. Rather than giving a complete physical description of the old lady in one place, Curtin sprinkles descriptive bits throughout. Why does she do this? Give examples of the inserted descriptions.

Suggested Writing Assignments

1. Describe your family or close friends in a typical activity, similar to "A Family Portrait."
2. Convey as fully as possible someone's personality by showing how he or she acts in a particular situation—for example, in conference with a lab instructor or trying to squirm out of an embarrassing situation.
3. Portray one of your instructors in the classroom, the way Debbie Schwartz does with "Mrs. Engle."
4. Describe an occupational or personality type, for instance a flirt, a cop, a politician, an intern, a gambler, a carnival barker, a rock singer, a beauty contestant, a grocery checker, a short-order cook, a trucker, or a drill instructor, as Steele does in "Will Honeycomb."
5. Imply a person's character, tastes, and values by describing his or her residence and possessions (without the person being there), as Jayne O'Donnell does in "Grandma."
6. Describe a person by using his or her own words to convey values, social class, and attitudes, as Cooke is able to do in "The Tattooist."

III

MODES OF
EXPOSITION

Exposition is writing that explains. Our purpose in expository writing is to impart information, to clarify an idea, to analyze a situation, to summarize details, to provide directions, or to offer an insight. Since there are several types of explanations, there are several types of expository essays, and each chapter in Unit III investigates one mode or type of expository essay. In Chapter 5, we will examine definition, in Chapter 6 comparison/contrast, in Chapter 7 classification/division, in Chapter 8 process description, in Chapter 9 causal analysis, and in Chapter 10 consequential analysis. We will discuss reasons for using a mode and times that it seems appropriate, explore the principles of each mode, use invention to develop ideas, outline various ways of organizing the material, examine essays that illustrate those organizations and principles, and discuss helpful hints to use and pitfalls to avoid when writing. Although these modes are primarily for expository writing, most of them can also be used in argumentative writing. Where applicable, therefore, we will explore how they can be used in argument, and those discussions will prepare us for Unit IV, which deals with argument and persuasion.

CHAPTER 5

Definition

Chapter 5 discusses what types of terms we need to define for readers and how to define those terms. After opening with several examples of terms that need defining or redefining, the chapter shows how to define increasingly complex concepts. Some terms are simple enough to be defined in a phrase or sentence (an *emu*, for example, is a large flightless bird that is found in Australia and is related to the slightly larger ostrich), but other terms are too complicated to be explained adequately in one or two sentences. Words whose meanings are abstract or personal, such as *excellence* or *heroism*, require elaborate clarification through examples, comparisons, descriptions, and anecdotes. By the end of the chapter we will be examining how to develop an entire essay using definition.

Reasons for Studying Definition

One reason we study definition is to learn how to explain unfamiliar terms so that our readers will be able to follow our discussion. Definitions clarify our meaning and therefore improve communication. An even more significant reason to study definition is that definition is central to many social, moral, and legal issues. Before we can intelligently discuss issues such as pornography, abortion, chemical warfare, and insanity pleas, we have to set forth definitions and explain what the terms mean and do not mean. Often the issue *is* definition. For example, if we were to argue that the New York subway vigilante who shot four young men in 1985 was justified in his action, our entire argument would revolve around the definitions of self-defense and justifiable homicide. As the following illustrations demonstrate, definition can be an important and consequential matter.

What is justifiable homicide? "Self-defense," you might answer; "if someone is trying to kill you, you have the legal right to kill that person."

But the question is more complex than it seems at first because the term *self-defense* requires a precise definition. If the definition is too narrow, it inhibits our right to protect ourselves; if it is too broad, it permits unnecessary killing. Consider this situation: If a person has no weapon but is much bigger than you and you think that his or her intent is murderous, do you have the right to use a weapon on that person, even a gun? Or can you respond only with the kind of force that you are threatened with? Consider a different situation: What if you awake at 3:00 A.M. and hear a burglar, possibly armed, stalking through your home. For the safety of your family, can you legally kill the intruder? Is defending someone else, for instance your mother or little brother, regarded as justifiable homicide? How about defense of property? Protecting property might simultaneously involve defending oneself, as in the case of a mugger who might take both your money and your life. Alternatively, if two muggers hold you up and don't harm you, can you legally shoot them in the back as they walk away counting your money? Definition, as you can see, is not a simple matter; sometimes it is a matter of life and death.

Even the words *life* and *death* themselves, which in the past seemed the most absolute of terms, require redefining. Until recently death was synonymous with heart stoppage, but we must currently consider technological advances that allow the body to continue functioning. Does life depend on any biological signs operating, such as tissues still growing or organs working, or only on the brain's functioning? The issue has become legal as well as medical and has led to a distinction between "biological death" and "clinical death." The American Bar Association has accepted the definition of death as that state wherein the brain ceases functioning, but even this concept of "brain death" may be an oversimplification because the brain dysfunction might not be irreversible or the brain might be only partially dead. If the section of the brain that controls breathing and heartbeat is functioning but that portion concerning thinking is dead, is the person dead or alive? Can a person be pronounced clinically dead if the brain shows any sign of an electrical impulse? Perhaps we have to specify not just brain death but neocortical death—the state when the neocortex ceases functioning. Now we can turn the question around: not when does life end, but when does it begin? That is the central question concerning abortion.

Not only increasing technology, but also changing morality creates a need for redefinition. An example of terms changing with time is the Bill of Rights clause that states, "No cruel or unusual punishment shall be inflicted." What was acceptable punishment in the eighteenth century, however, is thought of today as barbarous: branding, lashing, pillorying, ear-cropping. Originally the clause referred to excessive punishment (for instance, cutting off a thief's hand for stealing a loaf of bread) and to certain methods of capital punishment (such as disembowelment and boiling in oil). But because the idea of what is "cruel or unusual" is imprecise, it must, according to former Chief Justice Earl Warren, "draw its meaning from evolving standards of decency." Since the eighteenth century, the trend in punishment has been toward moderation; today's prisoners, while still denied basic freedoms, have many rights and are treated much more humanely than in the past. Recently, American society has been questioning the constitutionality of capital punishment in any form. Do we equate severity with cruelty? Is the death penalty excessive for any crime: espionage, kidnapping, rape, murder? Even though the concept of "cruel or unusual" originally did not refer to capital punishment per se, that does not mean it cannot apply now, for the definition is relative and changing.

Another example of changing social values that affect definition is the word *pornography*. In the past, the United States government banned such classics as *Ulysses* and *Lady Chatterly's Lover*, but now those novels are not only sold in drugstores but even taught in colleges. Were they pornographic then but not now? While the material in those books has not changed, the nation's morality has, and as the nation's morality has shifted, so has the definition of pornography.[1] Over the years the Supreme Court has attempted, with limited success, to define precisely what constitutes pornography. Justice Brennan, for instance, declared that "Obscene material is material which deals with sex in a manner appealing to prurient interest," but this is imprecise because *prurient* is as evasive a term as *pornographic*. More recently the Court ruled that the definition varies with location as well as with time, so that currently the definition is interpreted by local standards. In essence, the Court has stated that pornography is whatever offends the community conscience. *Playboy*, therefore, might be banned in one community but sold at the neighborhood grocery store in another.

In each of these instances, definition is the key to issues of profound concern to our society. As an essential tool of clarification, definition is a method of discourse shared by scientists, legislators, and philosophers.

Terms to Define

We need to define not only words that our readers may not have encountered before—those are often the easy ones—but also terms whose complexity can cause misunderstanding. One group of terms, like those we

---

[1]This brings up the question of who determines the "true" definition. Even in the 1920s, these books had many defenders, but the government declared that they were obscene, and the majority of Americans seemed to agree with the decision at that time.

just examined, are abstractions that require redefining from time to time because their meanings depend on contemporary morality.

Another group of abstractions, such as *love* and *freedom,* needs to be brought down to a personal level for a more exact and vivid meaning. Within the limits of accepted meaning, we make a word more tangible and specific by infusing it with our personal insights and examples. Our attempt is to contribute to a fuller understanding of the term by giving our personal criteria. Take the word *friend,* for example; what are your criteria for calling someone a friend? In Joseph Heller's *Good as Gold,* a Jewish character who had lived in Nazi Germany defines it very simply:

> He has only one test of a friend now, he told me. "Would he hide me?" is the question he asks. It's pretty much my test of a friend, too, when I come down to it. Ralph, if Hitler returns, would you hide me?

Another example of a personal definition comes from the scientist Carl Sagan, who is often asked after lectures to popular audiences whether he believes in God.

Because the word "God" means many things to many people, I frequently reply by asking what the questioner means by "God." To my surprise, this response is often considered puzzling or unexpected: "Oh, you know, *God.* Everyone knows who God is." Or "Well, kind of a force that is stronger than we are and that exists everywhere in the universe." There are a number of such forces. One of them is called gravity, but it is not often identified with God. And not everyone does know what is meant by "God." The concept covers a wide range of ideas. Some people think of God as an outsized, light-skinned male with a long white beard, sitting on a throne somewhere up there in the sky, busily tallying the fall of every sparrow. Others—for example, Baruch Spinoza and Albert Einstein—considered God to be essentially the sum total of the physical laws which describe the universe. I do not know of any compelling evidence for anthropomorphic patriachs controlling human destiny from some hidden celestial vantage point, but it would be madness to deny the existence of physical laws. Whether we believe in God depends very much on what we mean by God.

—From *Broca's Brain*

Discoveries in science and other fields produce a third group of terms requiring definition: concepts that explain new theories and procedures. Because of the proliferation of new knowledge in all disciplines, keeping up with discoveries and their accompanying vocabulary becomes increasingly difficult for the average person. Yet we need to understand the expanding scientific principles, not only because they are interesting, but also because they directly affect our lives. When we fail to understand properly the forces that influence our lives, we relinquish the privilege of controlling those forces.

Another group of new words needing explanation is slang—unconventional terminology invented for a particular time and by a particular social group. Such idioms, which are either coined words or extended meanings of established words, evolve as an attempt to discover more colorful expressions, and then they usually fall into disuse after a time. For example, the 1950s produced such words as *fuzz* (policeman), *passion pit* (drive-in movie), *dig* (understand), *cool*, and *hip*; the 1960s brought *sit-in*, *pig* (policeman), *heavy*, *right on*, *freaked out*, *groovy*, and *hassle*; and the 1970s gave us *hype*, *bag lady*, *male chauvinist pig*, *touchie-feelie* and *bad* (good). Because slang pops up quickly and usually has a broad range of meaning, it is useful to pin down a precise meaning for outsiders' understanding.

A final group of words are those whose connotations (the associations that words convey) need amending. Perhaps their meanings have taken on negative nuances and the writer feels the meanings need rescuing; conversely, they may be words being popularly used in a positive manner, though they represent negative characteristics to the writer. The writer's goal is to rectify the mistaken usage by changing the word's meaning for better or for worse, an example being the attempt to reclaim from disparagement the term *elitist* on page 166.

Whatever the purpose for defining, the length of the definition can vary from a single word to an entire book, depending on the complexity of the term and its centrality to the discussion. A definition can be either incidental to a discourse or absolutely essential to it; often the definition will be an essential *section* of a lengthy paper. The degree to which the definition is the focus of the paper will, of course, determine the proportion allotted to explaining the term.

Brief Definitions

When we use a word that our readers may not know, we must provide a short definition as a matter of courtesy as well as of comprehension. Scattered throughout an essay as needed, these definitions are integrated into the discussion to avoid losing or confusing readers, especially if we plan to use a term several times. This type of quick rendering ensures effective communication without giving the definition undue emphasis and without disrupting the train of thought. The inserted definition can be one word, one phrase, or one clause.

The shortest and simplest kind of definition is a synonym. Occasionally these one-word equivalents serve the purpose sufficiently. For instance:

> Take a wooden dowel, or peg, and insert it into the hole.
> Male ballet stars have a certain panache (flamboyance).
> Howard Hughes was one of America's most famous recluses, or hermits.

The problem with synonyms is that few words that have similar denotations (the explicit meanings of words) will also have identical connotations. The dictionary might tell us that *statesman* and *politician* are synonyms, but the words have different associations. Likewise, we think of a recluse as being a little different from a hermit. Even when a one-word definition is a true synonym for a term we want to explain, it is useless if it is equally unknown to the reader. To give *amulet* as a synonym for *talisman*, for instance, or *frith* for *estuary*, or *recondite* for *esoteric* doesn't aid the reader. Obviously, the synonym must be more familiar than the term being defined. For example, defining the technical term *pelage* with the more common term *fur* does aid the reader.

APPLICATION

Give a synonym for these words and then articulate the differences in connotation, if any:

wish	spasm	lissome
annoy	opposite	ridicule
idea	expect	resolute
fault	intricate	reply

When a synonym is not available or is not adequate, we can insert a brief phrase into the sentence to explain a term's meaning. Again, the advantages are reader convenience and assured communication. For example: "Flextime—the policy of allowing employees to set their own working hours within given limits—is being adopted more frequently in order to boost employee morale and productivity." In another case, if we plan to use the word *doppelgänger* several times in a paper, we might offer a brief explanation the first time it appears: "Jones believed that his doppelgänger, a German term denoting a person's spiritual double or counterpart, resided in the attic." In the example below, the writer plans to use the term *transhumance* repeatedly in an article and therefore takes the time to explain it the first time it is mentioned, which allows him to use it freely thereafter:

> Transhumance, the seasonal trek of livestock and herders between the valley floor and high pastures, has occurred throughout the Scandinavian

mountains, across the Alps, along the Eurasian mountain system through the Himalayas, and on into the inner mountains of China.

—Robert E. Rhoades, *Natural History*, Jan. 1979

Notice how two other writers provide necessary information in the form of inserted definitions:

Although the lines of descent are not entirely clear, the wolf began to develop as a specialized genus of cursorial, or hunt-by-chasing, carnivore in the Paleocene, some 60 million years ago.

—Barry H. Lopez, *Of Wolves and Men*

He was holding a parang, the type of machete Indonesians employ for gardening and disemboweling.

—S. J. Perelman, *Eastward Ha!*

These interposed phrases achieve the intended purpose of defining the term while remaining subordinate to the main idea of the sentence. Handling them in this manner makes a smoother passage than stopping the discourse to devote a full sentence for quick clarification. In addition to achieving the proper emphasis, these inserted definitions make for a more sophisticated prose style. Compare, for instance, these two sentences and decide which is more readable:

My uncle's Model A had a tonneau. A tonneau is an enclosed rear compartment for passengers.

My uncle's Model A had a tonneau—an enclosed rear compartment for passengers.

Formal Definitions

Formal definitions, those found in the dictionary, follow a particular pattern: the word is placed in a class and then distinguished from all other terms in the same class. For example, a *fawn* is a deer less than 1 year old; the class is deer, and the distinguishing feature (called the differentia) is that it is less than 1 year old. When someone asks what a dilettante is or a merganser or an oligarchy, we usually respond with a formal definition—class and differentia.

Term	*Class*	*Differentia*
A farrier is	a person	who shoes horses.

To use a synonym—a farrier is a blacksmith—would be misleading because a blacksmith performs many duties other than shoeing horses; a farrier is a specialist.

Leukemia is   a disease   that attacks the blood.

Although this information is correct, it is not a good definition because it does not differentiate leukemia from other blood diseases. The partial definition above equally describes polycythemia, anemia, leukocytosis, mononucleosis, and leukopenia. Let's try again.

Leukemia is   a disease   of the white blood cells.

This is better but it is still incomplete because mononucleosis, leukocytosis, and leukopenia also are white blood cell disorders.

Leukemia is   a blood cancer   characterized by excessive production of white blood cells, resulting in anemia, in enlarged spleen and lymph glands, and usually in death.

This third attempt meets the requirements: It places the term in the smallest class possible and distinguishes it from all others in the class.

APPLICATION

1. Of the following definitions, only two are acceptable. Which are they? Describe what is unacceptable about the others, and then rewrite them.

A firman is   an edict   issued by an Oriental sovereign.

An arboretum is   a place   where trees and shrubs are grown.

Kinesiology is   the study   of human motion by examining how muscles work.

Imprest is   something   advanced to someone on governmental business.

Hypergamy occurs   when   a female marries above her social class.

A stalagmite is   a mineral formation   in a cavern caused by the dripping of a limestone solution.

2. Define these words by putting each into a class and distinguishing it from all others in that class.

Term	Class	Differentia
magnetism		
claustrophobia		
mule		
accordion		
hula		
creek		
tiara		

Definition Paragraphs

Sometimes a concept is too complex and important to a discussion for a brief definition to suffice; in this case a more extensive explanation is required. Occasionally we may deem it necessary to devote an entire paragraph, or even several paragraphs within a lengthy paper, to defining a term that is essential to the basis of a discourse.

A definition paragraph is especially useful as an introduction, where we stipulate at the beginning of a paper how we plan to use our major term. Giving the meaning of our basic concept is an essential preliminary step for any sophisticated discourse because we and the readers must agree on a meaning before we can possibly lead them through the matrix of ideas dependent on that meaning. Quite simply, before we can get readers to agree with our point of view on an issue, we must make certain that we and they are using the key term in the same way. Once we have reached that understanding of terms, we are ready to reach other understandings. Definition, Plato recommended over 2,000 years ago, is the logical starting point of a discussion:

There is only one way . . . to begin deliberations auspiciously: one must first understand what the deliberations are about or the whole matter will fail of its purpose. Most people are unaware that they do not know the true nature of the things they discuss; but since they assume that they do know, no basic agreement is reached before they begin their discussion. So, as the inquiry proceeds, the result is what one might expect: they can neither remain consistent nor agree with one another. . . . Let us agree on a definition.

Usually the term defined in the introductory paragraph is the term that the whole essay will discuss. For instance, in a paper on the growing distrust of discretionary authority in American society, we might begin with a definition of discretionary authority and cite examples to clarify the concept; the remainder of the paper might go into the causes for the distrust and perhaps the effects in areas such as the judicial and educational systems.

Defining the subject of the essay is not the only form of introductory definition paragraph. A writer can also open the discourse with a term that is directly related to the essay's subject and that serves as a general introduction to the subject. For instance, in a book entitled *Andrew Carnegie and the Rise of Big Business,* the author opens the first chapter with a definition of the American dream because he feels that the concept captures the spirit of his subject and therefore acts as an apt introduction:

Nothing has characterized America more than the "American dream"—the belief that anyone can rise above his origins, however humble, and through hard work, honesty, and thrift achieve positions of power and influence, even the presidency of the United States. The dream evolved logically from the aspirations of the early settlers. Whether they came seeking freedom from established churches or liberation from the social and economic strictures of postfeudal European societies, the restless, ambitious people who populated the New World found in its natural wealth, gentle climate, and seemingly endless land an arena in which to strive for their goals. In colonial America ex-convicts sometimes did become successful businessmen. By the time the republic achieved its independence from Great Britain, the once faint hope that poor men might find a better life in America had been a viable tradition for a hundred and fifty years.

—Harold C. Livesay

APPLICATION

Give your own definition of the American dream and explain what you are doing or plan to do to achieve that dream. Or, if you believe that the American dream is false, contrast your view to the definition of the American dream as it is understood by most people, and explain why you do not feel that working toward that dream is a worthwhile ambition.

Another type of definition paragraph occurs in the body of the essay and usually is offered as evidence in an argument. The purpose of the definition is not simply to clarify a term, but to use the clarification to substantiate a point in the argument. If the clarification is fairly involved, it may require a series of paragraphs to make the point, as in the following passage from *Keep the Last Bullet for Yourself.* Arguing that Custer's men panicked and committed mass suicide at the Little Bighorn, the author uses contrasting definitions of *buffalo gun* to prove his point that, contrary to prevailing opinion, the Indians did not have long-barrelled .50-caliber buffalo guns that would have enabled them to pick off the soldiers from a distance. The writer argues that the cavalry's superiority in weapons should have guaranteed their survival, as it had with previous troops, despite incredible odds. His argument hinges on a confusion in definitions.

It is not probable that any Indian had any one of the very heavy rifles known among white men as the buffalo gun. It is possible that one or more of these guns had been taken from the Custer men or had been obtained at some earlier time. But such guns were not desired by Indians. The gun itself was too heavy to suit the Indian style of hunting, and its ammunition was too expensive. The claim that various Indians in the encirclement about Reno Hill had such rifles is supposed to have been corroborated by statements of the Indians themselves. Different Indians have told interviewers that they had "buffalo guns." But such statements have to be interpreted in accord with Indian meaning, and their conception of a buffalo gun was different from the white man's.

The white buffalo hunter rode out and located a herd. Then he dismounted and crept toward the animals. Commonly, he got down prone on the ground. Taking careful aim, he shot a buffalo. The herd was startled, but the man could not be seen, so they did not run away. They merely milled around in the same vicinity. The hunter took aim again and dropped another buffalo. The animals continued to mill around. The hunter shot one after another, usually for some time. In this way, white hunters regularly made a big killing, often almost cleaning up a small herd. In order that the hunter might keep himself as far as possible out of the sight and scent of the herd, and so that he might send killing bullets across the long intervening distance, he used the heaviest and hardest shooting rifle he could obtain. Since he commonly shot from a prone position, the weight of such a gun was not too great an inconvenience.

Those various unusually heavy rifles were what white men had in mind when they spoke of buffalo guns. The Indian idea of a buffalo gun was of one that was unusually light in weight. This was because the Indian way of hunting buffalo was quite different from the white man's way.

The Indian buffalo hunter rode his pony right into the herd. As the herd set off running, the Indian guided his pony to follow a certain animal. Riding up from behind and to the side of the big game animal, the Indian sent an arrow or a bullet into its chest. He repeated this action until the buffalo began to stumble and to bleed at the nostrils. Then the hunter left the animal to fall and die slowly, while he centered his attention upon another one, which he dealt with in like manner. When he was using a gun instead of his bow and arrows, the Indian hunter wanted a lightweight gun that could be carried conveniently while he was bareback on his running pony. If it was a gun he could fire one-handed, it was even better. The old cap-and-ball revolvers were well suited to this way of killing buffalo. The shortest and lightest rifles could be used. But, in order to improve the firearm for shooting into the vital parts of a running buffalo, the Indian sawed off the rifle barrel to shorter length, and sometimes he sawed off the butt. That was the perfect buffalo gun of the Indian. That was what the Indian had in mind when he told the untutored interviewer that he had "a buffalo gun" for fighting the Seventh Cavalry soldiers. It is possible, too, that he had in mind some other light-weight rifle or a cap-and-ball revolver.

—Thomas B. Marquis

1. What is the purpose of the first paragraph? What does paragraph 2 do? What is the function of the third paragraph? To which other paragraph is paragraph 4 contrasted?

2. Is Marquis' argument convincing? Why, or why not?

3. Write a short argument using definition to disprove a conventional view, as Marquis has done above.

Definition Essays

Instead of being supporting material, definition can be the entire focus of an essay. When we feel that a term, perhaps an abstraction such as *beauty* or a scientific term such as *genetic determinism* or *chemosynthesis*, is important enough to require a thorough explanation, we can devote a whole essay to definition. Take the concept of cryonics, for instance. We have a dozen questions about it that are not answered by the skeletal definition of "the process of freezing people for future life." We want to know whether it is feasible, whether experiments have been done, what leading scientists say about it, and what the procedure is. Definitions are useful in business and government, also. For example, the United States Congress held hearings recently and issued a formal report on the definition of *farm* because the term was being used too broadly. The result was a redefinition that properly distinguished among types of farms, including part-time, primary, and business-associated, so that the Census Bureau and the Department of Agriculture could determine policy based on more precise economic and statistical information.

As often as not, extended definitions are not mere expository clarifications but are vehicles for persuasion. In such cases, the word being defined is the issue being argued, and the definition is the basis of the argument. For example, consumer advocates argue that oil company profits are excessive and should be regulated; the companies, of course, argue otherwise. Because *excessive* is a relative term, both groups base their arguments on the definition of the word. Similarly, an attorney might use a definition of *negligence* to demonstrate that his or her client is not responsible for an accident. Ford Motor Company, which was tried for reckless homicide in 1980, argued that it was not negligent in fire deaths resulting from the design of Pinto gas tanks. The company contended that it was not negligent because the car met federal safety standards; the prosecution, however, argued that Ford was negligent because it knew that the cars would explode in rear-end collisions, and that the company consciously chose profit over human life. The whole argument rested on definition, with each side defining the term in favor of its particular standpoint.

Methods of Developing Definitions

Various ways of developing a definition are available, and although we probably would not use all of them in one essay, very likely we would use more than one. Usually we use one basic method with other supporting methods to develop individual paragraphs. The particular method that we select depends on the word and our purpose. A few of the more common patterns follow.

Comparison/Contrast

We can define something by comparing it figuratively or literally to something else. Sir Thomas Overbury used metaphor, for example, when he wrote: "A fine gentleman is the cinnamon tree, whose bark is more worth than his body." Frank Lloyd Wright defined television as "chewing gum for the eyes." Abraham Lincoln, addressing a Baltimore audience during the Civil War, used analogy to help clarify and enliven the meaning of *liberty:*

The world has never had a good definition of the word liberty, and the American people, just now, are much in want of one. We all declare for liberty; but in using the same word we do not all mean the same thing. With some the word liberty may mean for each man to do as he pleases with himself, and the product of his labor; while with others the same word may mean for some men to do as they please with other men, and the product of other men's labor. Here are two, not only different, but incompatible things, called by the same name, liberty. And it follows that each of the things is, by the respective parties, called by two different and incompatible names—liberty and tyranny.

The shepherd drives the wolf from the sheep's throat, for which the sheep thanks the shepherd as his liberator, while the wolf denounces him for the same act, as the destroyer of liberty, especially as the sheep was a black one. Plainly, the sheep and the wolf are not agreed upon a definition of the word liberty; and precisely the same difference prevails to-day among us human creatures, even in the North, and all professing to love liberty. Hence we behold the process by which thousands are daily passing from under the yoke of bondage hailed by some as the advance of liberty, and bewailed by others as the destruction of liberty.

In a more literal comparison, I. A. Richards defines *thesaurus* by contrasting it to *dictionary*. A thesaurus, he explains,

is the opposite of a dictionary. You turn to a dictionary when you have a word but are not sure enough what it means—how it has been used and what it may be expected to do. You turn to the *Thesaurus* when you have your meaning already but don't yet have the word. It may be on the tip of your tongue, or in the back of your mind or the hollow of your thought, but what it is you don't yet know. It is like the missing piece of a puzzle. You know well enough that the other words you try out won't do. They are not the right shape. They say too much or too little. They haven't the punch or have too much. They are too flat or too showy, too kind or too cruel. But the word which just fills the bill won't come, so you reach for the *Thesaurus.*

Description

When asked what an ibex is, or a yoyo or a coyote, we rely on description of shape, size, color, prominent characteristics. The description can be objective:

A coyote is a wild dog smaller than a wolf, about 3 feet long including a 15-inch tail, about 2 feet tall at the shoulder, weighing approximately 30 pounds, its reddish gray pelt being bushy.

A description can also be more opinionated:

The cayote is a long, slim, sick and sorry-looking skeleton, with a gray wolf-skin stretched over it, a tolerably bushy tail that forever sags down with a despairing expression of forsakenness and misery, a furtive and evil eye, and a long, sharp face, with slightly lifted lip and exposed teeth.

—Mark Twain

APPLICATION

Write an objective description of an animal or object and then follow that with an opinionated description. Possible subjects might be a Jeep, a Clydesdale horse, a dentist's chair, a palm tree, a mockingbird, a corn popper, a catfish, or a deep-sea diving suit.

Etymology

Tracing a word's etymology (origin and development) often is revealing because the current meaning reflects earlier denotations; today's connotations sometimes can be explained logically in terms of previous meanings. Consider a few examples to see how etymology can be enlightening:

> *Windfall*, meaning today "good fortune," results from a medieval English law stating that timber on estates belonging to the king could not be chopped down; however, trees blown down by the wind could be used for firewood and building. Hence, any unexpected piece of good luck came to be called a windfall.

> *Hybrid* comes from the Latin *hybrida*, referring to the offspring of a wild boar and a domestic sow.

> *Sabotage* has as its origin the French *sabot*—wooden shoe—the connection being that French factory workers protested their dismal working conditions by throwing their wooden shoes into the machinery, causing extensive damage.

> *Amateur* grows out of the Latin *amator*, lover, adapted by the French to mean a lover of art or sport, eventually becoming one who dabbles or plays without real training.

> *Assassin* originated during the Crusades. In eleventh-century Persia a secret band of fanatical *hashshashin*, Arabic for hashish-eaters, were sent out by their chieftain to murder public officials and Christian leaders; thus fortified on hashish, the crazed *hashshashin* would dispatch his victim. The crusaders misunderstood the term to be *assassin*, and assumed it referred to a hired killer.

> *Sophomore* stems from two Greek roots: *sophos*, meaning wise, and *moros*, meaning foolish. A sophomore, therefore, is a wise fool because a second-year student has some learning but thinks he knows everything.

A word's etymology, therefore, can explain a great deal both for us and our reader. Check the *Oxford English Dictionary (OED)* and read the history of your term; xerox the *OED* commentary for your word. Later, if you feel that it is relevant to your paper, include the commentary. Some etymologies, however, add nothing to the reader's understanding of the term; don't include these in your discussion simply because you researched them.

APPLICATION

Check the *OED* to clarify the contemporary meanings of the following words by finding their original meanings.

cunning	boor	sinister	enthrall
kleptomania	pedagogue	doll	cad
livery	hymen	Levant	energy
customer	prevent	catastrophe	drab
toilet	glamour	handkerchief	villain

Exemplification

Furnishing typical examples helps the reader more readily to understand a concept because it makes the class more tangible. But a writer shouldn't rely exclusively on exemplification for defining because examples are too specific to communicate a term's full character. Instead, this technique should be used as an auxiliary method of developing a word.

An earlier America seemed to have many eccentrics, such as Johnny Appleseed and Thoreau, both of whom heard "a different drummer." The Boston Brahmins produced Eleonora Sears, a ferocious walker who once hiked 110 miles nonstop. Mrs. Isabella Gardner shocked Beacon Hill by practicing Buddhism, drinking beer and strolling down Tremont Street with a lion. Until he died in 1955, "Silver Dollar" Jim West was Houston's favorite millionaire. He owned 30 cars, lived in a $500,000 castle, often wore a pistol and a diamond-studded Texas Ranger badge. He lugged his own butter to expensive restaurants and carried up to 80 silver dollars for tips.

—From "The Sad State of Eccentricity," *Time*, March 14, 1969

Negation

Telling what something is not may seem pointless because it insufficiently narrows the meaning, but in fact negation can be an excellent way to open an essay if our intention is to correct a common misconception about our term. Starting out by defusing the erroneous notion quickly eliminates the misunderstanding and prepares the way for our explanation of what the term really means.

> The American prong-horned antelope is not really an antelope despite popular opinion. Nor is it a deer, for it has horns instead of antlers. Rather, the prong-horn is. . . .

> The U.S. General Accounting Office is not, despite its name, a mere accounting office. GAO has little to do with ledgers, receipts, balances, and bookkeeping procedures these days. It has evolved as the investigative arm

of Congress, and its functions are to seek out and eliminate examples of waste, inefficiency, and mismanagement in all areas of government.

Often our whole purpose for writing a definition essay is to show that our subject is not what people commonly think it is. Since our intention is to correct a misperception, we start by telling what it is not (which is what people think that it is) and then go on to explain what it actually is. For example:

> Geisha girls are not masseuses or bar girls or prostitutes. Although they are professionals who entertain men, geishas are intelligent and elegant hostesses who are accomplished singers, dancers, musicians, and above all clever conversationalists. *Geisha* literally means "art-person," and geishas. . . .

APPLICATION

Generate a topic that the public generally misunderstands, and write an opening paragraph for an essay on that topic. Then outline the body of the essay and write a conclusion.

Organizing a Definition Essay

Regardless of which methods we use to develop our definition, most definition essays follow a conventional pattern. We establish the need for a definition, usually in the opening two paragraphs, and also establish the term's relevance and significance. An extension of this is to show the inadequacy of current or traditional definitions and perhaps discuss problems inherent in defining the word. The main body of the essay, however, is our definition: our departure or refinement, our reasons and examples. In short, we present, explain, and defend our definition using a combination of methods, as the student writer of the following essay has done.

CHOPPER

Laurence Burley (first-year student)

Opens with popular definition
Contends that definition is inadequate
Presents connotative definition that sets up key ideas to be developed

Most people think that a chopper is simply a souped-up motorcycle. But this definition doesn't do justice to the chopper because it is more than just a motorcycle. It is a symbol that is shot through with images of freedom and individualism on the one hand, and violence and power on the other.

Paragraph 2 is definition by description to give readers a mental picture of the subject

Details are arranged spatially, starting at front of bike and moving to rear

Diction reinforces theme of violence and power: "hungry-looking machine," "big chopper engine," "temperamental monster," "tremendous power," "World War I machine guns," "high-powered explosions"

Develops the first image mentioned in paragraph 1

Repeats key terms ("image," "freedom," "individualism") from paragraph 1 to tie the parts of the essay together

Develops paragraph only briefly; focus of essay not intended to be on Easy Rider image

Develops second image mentioned in paragraph 1

Explains historical source of image

Achieves transition from paragraph 4 to paragraph 5 with "appealing" and "appeal"

Uses comparison to convey idea

Introduces sexual associations

States connotation of the term

Places topic sentence at end of paragraph

Illustrates the antisocial image alluded to in previous paragraph

The chopper is a special kind of motorcycle. It is a long, low, hungry-looking machine with high handlebars on top of an extended chrome fork. The front wheel is incredibly thin, little more than a bicycle wheel and seemingly too delicate to support such a big machine. Directly in back of the handlebars is a work of art—the gas tank. It has been covered with a dozen coats of special flame-paint and then buffed and polished until it fairly glows in the dark. In back of the tank is the seat, just a tiny leather pad sunk deep within the engine. The big chopper engine—a temperamental monster coming from a standard Harley 74, the biggest motorcycle engine made—puts forth tremendous power. When the engine is let out, it produces a sort of pounding thunder much like the staccato sounds of World War I machine guns. The engine rests beside the large rear wheel, which is the exact opposite of the front wheel, for it is a hard, thick, deeply grooved mass of rubber that looks like something off a truck. The wheel is flanked on either side by flashy silver tailpipes that belch black exhaust, the only indication of the high-powered explosions occurring within the engine.

One image that the chopper evokes is that of the "Easy Rider." This image espouses an easy-going individualism, living for the open road and the pure joy of riding a chopper on a mountain highway. Easy Rider is a knight in search of experience, a contemporary cowboy drifter who lives from moment to moment. His bike is not so much a symbol of power as an expression of individuality. Easy Rider is in search of peace and love and freedom.

But the chopper also evokes a different kind of image, that of violence. The violent mystique surrounding the bike is mainly due to its long association with groups like the Hell's Angels, Satan's Slaves, and other motorcycle gangs, and the violence connected with such groups has carried over into the image of the chopper. This violence, coursing through the mechanical beat of every chopper, is appealing: It is a force that attracts and holds.

The basic appeal of the chopper lies in its power and danger. Big choppers have the same attraction as Ferraris and .44 Magnum revolvers. They are a challenge to a man's skill and machismo. They are a sexual symbol, an extension of the body, a rumbling force between the legs. Because such blatant sexuality, violence, and power offend the average American, the chopper has negative connotations; it has become a symbol of "what is wrong with the country." The chopper challenges the social order in its rejection of apple pie, mom, and middle America. It is the essence of antisocial behavior.

The whole mystique of the chopper is exemplified in a poster I have seen many times in the rip-off stores down at the beach. It's a poster that fourteen-year-old boys stop and stare at and eventually buy. It shows a dusty, booted, leather-jacketed male astride a chop-

Drives home antisocial theme
with obscene gesture

per, riding across the mud flats out West. The sun is intense, and his eyes are hidden behind mirrored aviation sunglasses. He is giving the camera the finger.

Advice, Warnings, Reminders

1. Choose a word that will have some significance to your audience and that needs clarifying because it is vague or misused. The best definitions are those of concepts that are important to society and that are central to controversial issues.

2. Consult standard reference works such as the *OED, American Heritage Dictionary, Oxford Dictionary of Quotations, Roget's International Thesaurus, Encyclopaedia Britannica,* and, if appropriate, specialized dictionaries in slang, medicine, social sciences, and so forth. Discover the etymology of the word: where it came from, what it originally meant, and what changes it underwent. What connections exist between its past and current meanings? Find out what other persons think on the subject and integrate that with what you think. Call on your reading over the past few years and

3. Have a firm understanding of your purpose. Are you trying simply to clarify the term for the sake of improved communication, or are you using the definition as an indirect means of arguing? Your purpose may be both: to clarify and then to persuade. Lack of purpose is the main weakness in most student definition papers. What is your thesis?

4. Know your audience. What misconceptions do they have about the term? What is their level of sophistication and their knowledge about the concept you are discussing? If the concept is social, political, or religious, is your audience hostile or sympathetic? Do you have to overcome any barriers?

5. Don't open with "According to Webster's Collegiate Dictionary. . . ." Also, too many definition papers begin with a question: "What is the PLO?" Try a different ploy. An excellent way of opening is to cite a contemporary event that exemplifies the meaning. Beginning with a quoted definition (if it is not too familiar) is effective because it gives you a point of departure for your discussion. If you agree with the tone and meaning of the quotation, you can use it as a kernel and expand it. If you disagree with it, use the quotation as a means of refuting the opposition, and then present your definition. Here are some examples of quotations that make good introductions:

"An ambassador," Sir Henry Wotton said, "is an honest man sent to lie abroad for the good of his country."

Ambrose Bierce once observed that a corporation is "an ingenious device for obtaining individual profit without individual responsibility."

"Arrogance is contempt for everything but oneself," Theophrastus wrote in the fourth century.

"Conscience is the inner voice which warns us," said H. L. Mencken, "that someone may be looking."

Exercises

1. Evaluate these definitions to determine whether they are complete and unambiguous. Place the appropriate number in the blank:
   1. if the term is not placed into a class
   2. if the class is too small or too large
   3. if the differentia fails to distinguish the term
   4. if the definition is clear and complete

   A. _____ Existentialism is a type of pessimistic philosophy.

   B. _____ A mill is where you grind grain.

   C. _____ A grimace is a distorted facial expression.

   D. _____ An autobiography is a written account of a person's life.

   E. _____ A peccary, standing about 18 inches tall, has thick bristly skin, a dreadful smell, a quarrelsome disposition, and sharp tusks.

   F. _____ A dormitory is a building where people live and sleep.

   G. _____ "Marriage is that relation between man and woman in which the independence is equal, the dependence is mutual, and the obligation is reciprocal." (Louis Anspacher)

   H. _____ Oats are "A grain, which in England is generally given to horses, but in Scotland supports the people." (Samuel Johnson)

   I. _____ "I think an optimist is just someone who isn't paying attention." (Dick Lord)

   J. _____ "Adultery is the application of democracy to love." (H. L. Mencken)

   K. _____ Home is "the place where, when you have to go there, they have to take you in." (Robert Frost)

   L. _____ Childhood is "The period of human life intermediate between the idiocy of infancy and the folly of youth—two removes from the sin of manhood and three from the remorse of old age." (Ambrose Bierce)

2. Each person in the class should take one of the following words and, without consulting a dictionary, compose a formal definition and write it on the board for commentary.

ledge	mythology	modesty	rehearsal
wharf	jetlag	propeller	snuff
album	key	vitamin	candle
corn	lattice	glacier	soup
impression	dot	memento	emissary
investment	risk	gnat	petroleum

3. In one paragraph, distinguish between two words that are so similar that they are often used interchangeably but that in fact are subtly different in meaning. For example, many people, assuming that the terms are synonymous, refer to a wine's fragrance as either *bouquet* or *aroma*, when actually *aroma* is the smell of the grape and *bouquet* is the smell produced by the oxidizing process in fermentation. Pick a pair and distinguish:

individuality—individualism   dilemma—predicament
autobiography—memoir   freedom—liberty
morality—ethics   sensuality—sexuality

4. You are chosen by your college to contribute a one-paragraph definition of your field of study for a pamphlet to be distributed at freshman orientation. Because course catalogs also are distributed at the orientation, you should not outline or describe the various courses within the major. You might, for instance, begin with a formal definition and then give the essential function of your field, but whatever your approach, do not make your paragraph a simple job description.

5. Read an article in *Scientific American, Natural History,* or *The New England Journal of Medicine* and study the techniques that the writer uses to define terms that readers will not likely understand.

Suggested Writing Assignments

These suggested topics for definition essays encourage you to draw on your knowledge from your own discipline. Remember, however, that the best topics are those that start with a purpose, so you should come up with your own topic if possible.

1. Define a scientific concept—such as black holes, antimatter, the greenhouse effect, fiber optics, or DNA—in terms understandable to an intelligent lay reader. Analogies are especially helpful in such explanations.

2. Choose a term from economics and explain it in terms that average news-

paper readers will be able to apply when they read the term in the business/ finance section of the paper. You might define *cartel, the Common Market, trade deficit, the Laffer Curve, mutual funds, commodities markets, holding companies, futures,* or *securities.*

3. By describing its reasons for emergence, its methodology, and its borrowings from related disciplines, define a new discipline, such as sociobiology, gerontology, archaeoastronomy, ice dancing, or agribusiness.

4. Define a popular contemporary word or slang expression—such as psychologize, telegenic, klutz, charisma, macho, or camp—so that even your grandparents will understand it.

5. Explain what some quality or movement means to you personally—for example sisterhood, privacy, decadence, Zionism, cheating, friendship, left-handedness, cowardice, honor, idealism, civil disobedience, or imagination.

6. Define a term that typifies the political climate today, such as *atomic diplomacy* or *terrorism,* or a political term that is used vaguely, such as *Third World.*

7. Define an American activity or popular art form that itself defines a subculture of society: rodeo, punk rock, jogging, Tex-Mex music, jazz, gambling.

8. Use a definition to argue against a traditionally positive attribute—progress, maturity, conscience, patience, pragmatism, coolness, commiseration—by showing that the characteristics of the concept are actually negative. Or define a conventionally negative attribute in positive terms—naiveté, cunning, anxiety, rashness, mediocrity, bureaucrat, arrogance, cynic.

9. Define a consumer product in terms of its larger sociological value, account for its popularity, and speculate on what an attraction to such a product says about society: calculators/minicomputers, briefcases, water beds, beer, jeans.

Additional Readings

The following dialogue from *One Flew Over the Cuckoo's Nest* takes place in a mental institution. The first speaker, Harding, has been institutionalized for years and therefore understands the specialized language of the place. He defines *shock treatment* for a new patient, McMurphy, who has been uncooperative and antagonistic toward the staff.

"And, my friend, if you *continue* to demonstrate such hostile tendencies, such as telling people to go to hell, you get lined up to go to the Shock Shop, perhaps even on to greater things, an operation, an—"

"Damn it, Harding, I told you I'm not up on this talk."

"The Shock Shop, Mr. McMurphy, is jargon for the EST machine, the Electro Shock Therapy. A device that might be said to do the work of the sleeping pill, the electric chair, *and* the torture rack. It's a clever little procedure, simple, quick, nearly painless it happens so fast, but no one ever wants another one. Ever."

"What's this thing do?"

"You are strapped to a table, shaped, ironically, like a cross, with a crown of electric sparks in place of thorns. You are touched on each side of the head with wires. Zap! Five cents' worth of electricity through the brain and you are jointly administered therapy and a punishment for your hostile go-to-hell behavior, on top of being put out of everyone's way for six hours to three days, depending on the individual."

—Ken Kesey

1. What is jargon, and why is it used? When should jargon not be used?

2. Is the definition of electroshock therapy totally literal?

3. Following Harding's technique, briefly define a term such as lobotomy, chiropractic adjustment, face-lift, chemotherapy, or inoculation.

The following excerpt is taken from the *Amnesty International Report on Torture.* Amnesty International is a nonpolitical organization that monitors human rights throughout the world and issues reports evaluating each country's record on human rights. Before the organization can determine whether torture is occurring in a country, it must have a good definition of what torture is, and therefore the report opens with its own definition.

TORTURE

Amnesty International

Everyone has an idea of what torture is; yet no one has produced a definition which covers every possible case. There is good reason why the concept of torture resists precise and scientific definition; it describes human behaviour, and each human being is unique, with his own pain threshold, his own psychological make-up, his own cultural conditioning. Furthermore, torture is a concept involving degree on a continuum ranging from discomfort to ill treatment to intolerable pain and death, and a definition must resort in part to qualitative terms which are both relative and subjective. Despite these difficulties it is important to try to be as precise as possible in order to eliminate ambiguity, especially in that 'grey area' in which the modern state and modern technology are anxious to operate. Also, torture, like other words, has an evaluative as well as descriptive content. Given that the word 'torture' conveys an idea repugnant to humanity, there is a strong tendency by torturers to call it by another name, such as 'interrogation in depth' or 'civic therapy' and a tendency of victims to use the word too broadly.

There are certain essential elements which give torture its particular meaning 2
and which should be incorporated in any comprehensive definition. In the first place the nature of torture assumes the *involvement of at least two persons,* the torturer and the victim, and it carries the further implication that the victim is under the physical control of the torturer. The second element is the basic one of the *infliction of acute pain and suffering.* It is the means used by the torturer on the victim and the element that distinguishes him from the interrogator. Pain is a subjective concept, internally felt, but is no less real for being subjective. Definitions that would limit torture to physical assaults on the body exclude 'mental' and 'psychological' torture which undeniably causes acute pain and suffering, and must be incorporated in any definition. The concept of torture does imply a strong degree of suffering which is 'severe' or 'acute'. One blow is considered by most to be 'ill-treatment' rather than 'torture', while continued beatings over 48 hours would be 'torture'. Intensity and degree are factors to be considered in judging degrees.

Thirdly, there is implicit in the notion of torture the effort by the torturer, through 3
the infliction of pain, to make the victim submit, to 'break him'. The *breaking of the victim's will* is intended to destroy his humanity, and the reaction to the horror of this finds expression in various human rights instruments in such phrases as 'respect for the inherent dignity of the human person'.

Finally, torture implies a *systematic activity with a rational purpose.* The unwit- 4
ting, and thus accidental, infliction of pain, is not torture. Torture is the deliberate infliction of pain, and it cannot occur without the specific intent of the torturer. Inherent in this element of purpose are the goals or motives for employing torture, and while torture can be used for a variety of purposes, it is most generally used to obtain confessions or information, for punishment, and for the intimidation of the victim and third persons. The first two motives relate directly to the victim, while the purpose of intimidation, in wide use today as a political weapon, is intended to be a deterrent to others as well as the victim.

The definition of torture adopted here is: 'Torture is the systematic and de- 5
liberate infliction of acute pain in any form by one person on another, or on a third person, in order to accomplish the purpose of the former against the will of the latter.'

The question arises whether or not what constitutes torture is culturally de- 6
termined and can vary from culture to culture. On this issue the distinction may usefully be made between 'physical' and 'mental' torture. The physiology of the

human nervous system is the same for all human beings regardless of race, climate or culture. In general the effect of physical torture such as beating, electro-shock, near-drowning, sleep deprivation and drugs will be the same on any human system. Although cultural conditioning can have remarkable effects on resistance to pain, as for example in the case of religious firewalkers, the result of the infliction of pain against the victim's will would seem to be universal at the physiological level. Mental or psychological torture, on the other hand, can be different, for it usually depends on the value system of the victim for its effect. Some values, such as the protection of children, might be universal for reasons deeper than culture, but values like religion are culturally determined. To make a Moslem fall to his knees and kiss the cross can be a humiliation and torture for him, while the same act for a Christian would not be. What is universal is the prohibition of torture; the means of infliction of pain might vary from culture to culture, the prohibition of torture is universal.

1. The first sentence of this essay states that there is not currently an acceptable definition of *torture*. What other two assertions does the rest of the paragraph make? Does this paragraph serve as an effective introduction to an essay that intends to define *torture*?

2. Paragraph 2 introduces the distinction between physical and psychological torture, but that distinction is not developed until paragraph 6—after the formal definition is given. Why is the discussion postponed? Has the writer included psychological torture in the formal definition in paragraph 5?

3. Why does the writer wait until paragraph 5 to present the formal definition? Could you make a case for placing it earlier?

4. One of the difficulties in defining such a concept as torture or pornography is that the terms used to define it may also be subjective. Does the adjective *acute* present such a problem in the definition here?

5. How do paragraphs 2, 3, and 4 relate to paragraph 5?

6. Although the essay is fairly general, it does occasionally use examples to clarify its statements. Give several instances.

7. The intent of the essay is to establish a legal definition of torture in order to determine which cases constitute torture and which do not. Does the essay contain legal jargon or sound like a legal document? Substantiate your answer.

THE BADGE OF 'ELITISM'

John Bunzel

When I was president of a state university in California from 1970 to 1978, I was often   1
called an "elitist" (among many other things) by certain students and faculty members

who felt they were taking one of their best shots by invoking the term that has become a favorite expression of scorn and censure. Those who have embraced uncritically the pieties of the new populist morality regard "elitist" as one of the dirtiest of dirty words.

I do not, provided it is clear how it is being used and by whom. I confess I would be terribly disappointed if some people I know didn't consider me an elitist. For example, I regard the label as almost a badge of honor when it is used by people who like to celebrate the ordinary disguised as democracy. I say this as a Democrat, a lifelong supporter of the civil-rights and labor movements, a believer in women's rights and someone addicted to the freedoms of the First Amendment. I also believe that all men are born equal, although the tough job (as the wag said) is to outgrow it.

It is a matter of standards and values. Thus I am an elitist if what is meant and understood is that I recognize there are differences in individual talent and capacity. Further, it is silly to pretend that anyone who acknowledges these differences is somehow an "anti-democrat." And it is just as foolish to claim that anyone who recognizes there are different physical and behavioral traits among various groups is a racist. Properly used, the term "racism" means discrimination against individuals or groups because of their background or membership in one race or another. When an individual is denied equal opportunity in education or employment, or any of the rights of citizenship in a democracy on the basis of color or national origin—that is racism. It is morally wrong and socially pernicious. But one can oppose racism without believing that people are equal in abilities. Put another way, there is a world of difference between "discriminatory practices" and "discriminating standards."

EXCELLENCE AND MEDIOCRITY: The trouble is that many people have simplistic notions about democracy. They assume that the existence of any differences constitutes prima facie evidence of inequality—and since in a democracy "all men are created equal," these differences are presumed to be a self-evident indictment of democracy. I even know some faculty members who cheat their students by failing to distinguish between excellence and mediocrity and insist on their right to award only A's and B's. Presumably, they are practicing "democracy" in the classroom.

Or take another variation on the same theme. It is unarguable that everyone has a right to his or her own opinion. But the right to express it does not make that opinion as good as anyone else's. It may be wrong or ignorant or both. Besides, some place along the line we all should be taught the necessity and value of seeking out facts that are "inconvenient" for our own opinions and ideas. Certainly in a college or university the student also has a right to be told that knowledge is better than ignorance and that his opinion may just be downright dumb. I remember it hurt the first time I was made to understand that intelligence is better than stupidity and that I should stop trying to prove otherwise.

I know of no system of government more tolerable or desirable than a political democracy, especially where the conditions for its successful operation exist. But I do not believe that all of these conditions necessary for democracy exist, or should exist, in a college or university. An academic community is not a natural or egalitarian democracy because the relationship between students and faculty is not completely or inherently equal. If the university were to follow the democratic principle of treating students and faculty alike on a one-person, one-vote basis, the students would have a greater voice in determining who should be hired and what should be studied. I am an elitist if that means I believe any self-respecting university cannot permit questions of scholarship and learning to be resolved by popular vote. Nor am I persuaded that the applause meter will produce high academic standards.

I have heard it said that if students majoring in English voted to remove   7
Shakespeare from the curriculum because he is no longer relevant (I wish "relevant" could be struck from the English language), the faculty should concur. There is a lot wrong with that view. Putting Shakespeare to a vote indicates confusion not only about democracy but about the ballot box. Asking students to vote on something they have not thought seriously about is to equate ignorance with knowledge and the inexperience of youthful judgment with the experience of professional and cultivated taste. As Daniel Bell has pointed out, there can never be complete democratization in the entire range of human activities—and we should count our blessings. It makes no sense to insist on a "democracy of judgment."

I am an elitist regarding other concerns too. As an educator I am unhappy about   8
the rise of vulgarity disguised as freedom. I refer here to intellectual and esthetic vulgarity, to aggressive coarseness in speech and manners, to contempt for grammar and indifference to logic, to sloganeering as a substitute for thought, to hatred of culture, antipathy to history and release into fashionable nihilism. All of these are too often paraded as the sweet, necessary and inevitable fruits of liberty, but more accurately they represent a betrayal of freedom and the life of the mind, both of which are essential to the very idea of a university.

INDIVIDUAL MERIT: It is worth remembering that Thomas Jefferson believed in a   9
"natural aristocracy among men." He also thought that education should encourage and cultivate leaders of "virtue and talents" (as opposed to a privileged class based on birth and wealth) so that the best from all walks of life could serve the nation. He would agree that while we may seek the "highest mean level in the world," the pace of progress is set "not by the mean but by the best." In today's terms, Jefferson believed in equality of opportunity based on personal effort, but not in an equality of results. He had sufficient insight to realize that equality does not imply an identity of reward for effort. He would have dissented vigorously from any suggestion that individual merit should be sacrificed for a quota system or its functional equivalent. Respecting too much the dignity of the person, he would never have viewed the world as a series of numbers or statistics.

Good God. Jefferson, a democrat, was an elitist.   10

—From *Newsweek*, Oct. 1, 1979

1. What are the usual connotations of the word *elitist*?

2. Why does Bunzel open the essay by stating that he was president of a university? What else does he tell us about himself? What is his purpose in relating this information?

3. By what we say and how we say it, we project an image of ourselves (called an ethos) and readers form an opinion of our character, values, and intelligence. What kind of ethos (implied moral character) does Bunzel project? Does he sound like a hothead, a patriot, a snob, a dictator, a wise guy? Does he sound intelligent, friendly, dignified, modest, articulate, humble, condescending, aloof? What adjectives would you use to describe him, and why? Be able to substantiate your views with references to his essay.

4. Why does he discuss racism in paragraph 3?

5. How does Bunzel portray those who believe other than as he does? Give examples.

6. Why does he discuss Thomas Jefferson's beliefs in the next to the last paragraph?

7. Does Bunzel ever define *elitist*? What is an elitist according to Bunzel?

THE LAST COWBOY

Jane Kramer

The first American cowboy was probably a rustler—one of the men from Stephen Austin's Texas colony who rode south into the Nueces Valley in the eighteen-twenties and stole longhorns from Mexican rancheros' herds. It took the rest of the century and the imagination of Easterners to produce a proper cowboy—a cowboy whom children could idolize, and grown men, chafing at their own domesticated competence, hold as a model of some profoundly masculine truth. The proper cowboy had less to do with any Austin colonist than with Owen Wister's Virginian,[1] riding west onto the vast liminal stage of the American plains to shoot straight, with a noble and virtuous heart, and kill his villain. The proper cowboy was a fiction appropriate to a frontier so wild and inhospitable that most Easterners regarded it as a landscape of Manichaean possibilities.[2] He became for those Easterners the frontier's custodian. They made him Rousseau's Émile[3] with a six-gun. They turned man-in-nature into a myth of natural man, and added natural justice to ease the menace of a place that lay beyond

[1] Owen Wister was the novelist who wrote *The Virginian;* Kramer is suggesting that the image of the "proper cowboy" was formed more from fiction than from reality.

[2] *Manichaean* refers to a believer in a religious sect founded by the Persian prophet Mani in the third century A.D.; since Manichaeans believed in a world composed of two opposing principles (good and evil), Kramer is saying that to Easterners the West seemed a land where the distinction between good and evil were clear and absolute.

[3] Jean Jacques Rousseau (1712–1778) was a French philosopher and writer whose novel *Émile* espoused, through its hero, the dignity and wisdom of the "natural man."

their hegemony[4] and their institutions. They saw to it that he was born good, and that if he died violently, he died wise and defiant and uncorrupted. They set him against outlaws and spoilers, card sharks and Comanches. Their fears became his own sworn enemies. When the myth demanded that they meet—the Virginian paying his duty call on his bride's New England family—he showed them up, with his solemn, masculine behavior, as weak men and petty moralists. And the weak men and petty moralists were reassured.

The West, of course, had other, older heroes. By the cowboy's time, Western   2 folklore was already full of trappers and explorers and pioneering farmers, but they had carried some psychic legacy of the East with them in their canoes and wagons, and the cowboy had not. The trappers who crossed the timberline into the North American wilderness were, in fact, Yankee woodsmen, crowded out of home and pushing west toward a lost privacy that had more to do with Eastern forests than with Western plains. The farmers who followed them were immigrants, mostly, bringing to their homestead claims a romantic European dream of rural life. The historian Henry Nash Smith once said that their vision was the vision of the garden plot. It was a vision refreshed by the prospect of an extraordinarily spacious continent, but it was rooted in Europe just the same. The trouble they had with the cowboys and cattlemen who tried to stop them always involved much more than rights-of-way and fences; it had to do with different notions of what the West meant. The farming settlers of our folklore, rattling across the prairie in Conestoga wagons with their hearty, bonneted wives and broods of children, their chests of pots and pans and quilts, their plows and oxen, shared a republican dream of modest property and the rules and rhythms of domestic law. But the cowboy carried no baggage. Like the frontier, he had no past and no history. He dropped into the country's fantasies mysterious and alone, the way the Virginian arrived one day in his Wyoming town—by right, and not for any reason that he cared to give. With his gun and his horse and his open range, he followed the rules and rhythms of unwritten law and took counsel from his own conscience. He stood for the kind of imperial vision that staked out cattle kingdoms and for the kind of sweeping, solitary power that vigilantes and guardian angels have.

People looked west in the nineteenth century and were inspired to the most   3 jingoistic rhetoric.[5] They talked about manifest destiny and the restless eagle of expansion, and took their images from politicians like the Mississippi Democrat who, eying independent Texas, once demanded, "Who will desire to check the young eagle of America, now refixing her gaze upon our former limits, and repluming her pinions for her returning flight?" Those images suited a people determined to expand across the continent and profit from it. And the cowboy, decked out in his qualities like a knight of their frontier, represented something original and indigenous—something, to their satisfaction, necessarily American. He gave the field of their expansion a kind of

[4]Hegemony: dominating influence.

[5]Jingoistic rhetoric: remarks that are extremely nationalistic, especially talk of going to war or seizing lands.

mythic geography. They, in turn, gave him extravagant prerogatives, which they later claimed for themselves. A cowboy shook hands where ordinary men signed contracts. A cowboy drew his gun where ordinary men went home. A cowboy took the land for his cattle where ordinary men applied for deeds at the local courthouse. A cowboy claimed the right-of-way where ordinary men built fences and paid tolls.

There was not much room in the cowboy myth for the real cowboys of the nineteenth century—range bums and drifters and failed outlaws, freed slaves and impoverished half-breeds, ruined farmers from the Reconstruction South and the tough, wild boys from all over who were the frontier's dropouts, boys who had no appetite for the ties of land or family, who could make a four-month cattle drive across a thousand miles and not be missed by anyone. But eventually the myth, with its code and its solemn rhetoric, caught up with most of them, and if it left them still outside the law, at least it took the edge off their frightful lawlessness and made a virtue of their old failures. Henry Blanton's grandfather Abel was one of the ruined farmers.[6] The Blantons had lost their five slaves to the Thirteenth Amendment and their Georgia hog farm to carpetbaggers, and Abel, at sixteen, had left for Texas, hired out as a trail hand, and, after ten years in a bedroll, as he liked to say, collected a mail-order bride at the Amarillo depot. It was 1892. Owen Wister's cowboy had settled down to a sober prosperity and was on his way to becoming "an important man, with a strong grip on many various enterprises, and able to give his wife all and more than she asked or desired." And Amarillo was a boom town, with two railroads crossing, a drygoods store, and a street of whorehouses. Ranchers around the town had abandoned cattle drives to graze their herds at home in fenced pastures and ship them, fat, by rail to the Illinois and Missouri auctions. Bankers and brokers from London and Edinburgh had bought up Panhandle land, and they were turning cattle kingdoms into cattle companies. The business of running cattle had become big business by the time Abel Blanton brought a bride out to Texas. But there were still ranchers around who paid part of a cowboy's wages in calves or let a favorite hand claim mavericks. Cowboys, with luck, could run a few steers on their ranchers' land along with the ranch cattle, put the profit from those steers toward a couple of sections, and talk about becoming ranchers themselves. Few of them succeeded—only enough to make a man like Henry Blanton bitter that his grandfather had not. The West that Henry mourned belonged to the Western movie, where the land and the cattle went to their proper guardians and brought a fortune in respect and power. It was a West where the best cowboy got to shoot the meanest outlaw, woo the prettiest schoolteacher, bed her briefly to produce sons, and then ignore her for the finer company of other cowboys—a West as sentimental and as brutal as the people who made a virtue of that curious combination of qualities and called it the American experience.

—From *The Last Cowboy*

[6]Henry Blanton, a Texas cowboy, is the central character in the book from which this excerpt is taken.

1. The essay is developed mainly by comparison and contrast. What is being compared in paragraph 1? What is being compared in paragraph 2? Although paragraph 3 relies less on comparison and contrast, it reverts to that technique in its last four sentences. What do those four sentences have in common? Where in paragraph 4 is comparison used? Why does Kramer use comparison and contrast so heavily in developing her topic?

2. Some of the vocabulary and sentence structure in this essay are rather sophisticated, especially for the topic. Examples of this diction include *domesticated competence, liminal stage, Manichaean possibilities, hegemony,* and *psychic legacy.* Most essays about cowboys tend to use the leathery language of the West—colloquial, earthy, and dry-humored. For example, where she used *villain,* another writer might have used *desperado.* Why does she use a somewhat elevated style for a common subject? This essay was originally published in *The New Yorker.* How would you describe that magazine and its readers?

3. Using "The Last Cowboy" as a model, write an essay defining another romanticized topic from American history and explain how and why the myth evolved. Potential subjects might be George Washington, the Apache Indian, the suffragette, the pirate, the madam, the gangster.

CHAPTER 6

Comparison and Contrast

I came to England when I was twelve, and when I landed I could speak, rather badly, two words of English which I had learnt on the channel boat. I did not read English at all easily for two or three years after. The first writers in whom I was able to distinguish what my patient schoolmasters called style were, I remember, Macaulay and Joseph Conrad. I do not remember now whether at that time I was also able to distinguish between their styles. I read greedily, with excitement, with affection, with a perpetual sense of discovering a new and, I slowly realised, a great literature. But I was handicapped then, and I have been ever since, by the disorderly way in which I fell upon my masterpieces: Dickens cheek by jowl with Aphra Behn and Bernard Shaw, and elsewhere leaving tracts of neglected literature by the century. To this day I have not read the Waverley novels, and in consequence I have remained rather insensitive to historical romance, particularly if much of the conversation is in dialect.

I make these confessions because they seem to me to bear on many stories besides my own. The difficulties which I had are not mine alone, and they are not in any special way literary difficulties. On the contrary, what now strikes me about them is their likeness to the trouble which other people have with science. At bottom my difficulties in facing a strange literature are precisely the difficulties which all intelligent people today have in trying to make some order out of modern science.

—From J. Bronowski, *The Common Sense of Science*

There is a natural tendency to view one experience in terms of another, as Bronowski has done in this example. By comparing his own literary difficulties to the difficulties others have with science, he effectively expresses the frustration that many of us feel with science: It's like learning a new language. Bronowski concretely illustrates our difficulty by relating it to his own feeling of helplessness, and he implicitly offers us hope that, like him, we can learn to translate science into comprehensible terms.

Comparative thinking[1] means placing two experiences, ideas, or

[1]Strictly speaking, to compare means to discover similarities, and to contrast means to discover differences. But the two processes are interrelated so closely that we seldom do one without the other, and therefore for our purposes we will consider them as a single process. Some essays, as we will see, stress differences, some stress similarities, but they use both comparison and contrast to some degree.

objects side by side and noting their likenesses and differences. We use this thought pattern so naturally that we often don't realize we are using it. For example, I recently overheard two cattlemen discussing whether it is better to breed their heifers as yearlings or as 2-year-olds. They considered the question in terms of the cow's health, calf weight, cost, and profit, and after half an hour of debate decided that breeding earlier is better. They would not have labelled their thinking as comparison/contrast, but it was precisely that.

We employ comparative thinking hourly—which fast food joint to eat at, MacDonald's or Burger King; which movie to see, a comedy or a drama; and which candidate to vote for—and we base our actions on this comparative thinking—we eat a Big Mac, see *Out of Africa,* and vote for the incumbent. How many decisions have you made today unconsciously based on comparisons? You may also regularly encounter comparative thinking in your studies: In history you might compare the Korean and Vietnam Wars; in political science, socialism and capitalism; in psychology, Freud's and Jung's theories on dreams; and in astronomy, the atmosphere of the Saturnian moon Titan and the atmosphere of the earth 3 billion years ago.

Comparative thinking not only is utilitarian, but also can be creative. In fact, some psychologists suggest that the ability to discern hidden differences amid superficial similarities, or similarities amid differences, is a primary mark of creativity and intelligence. In science, Darwin's investigation into the differences among butterflies led him to the theory of evolution. In literature, our most vivid perceptions take the form of comparisons that we call similes and metaphors. Far from being a dull and mechanical exercise, comparison/contrast is a vital way of perceiving and expressing the world.

Comparative thinking, then, can be a way of learning in general and an inventional device for the writer, who can, by comparing X and Y, generate ideas about both subjects that might not occur when each is considered individually. Comparison/contrast is a way of analyzing and understanding the relationship of one thing to another in a world where things often take meaning only in relation to other things. Sometimes we can discover a subject's essence only by comparing it to another subject. Furthermore, juxtaposing two ideas (placing them side by side) encourages us to see their relative merits and helps us to judge which is superior.

Perception becomes structure in comparison/contrast. We examine two topics, see similarities and differences, and then structure our essay based on those similarities and differences. Although comparison/contrast is a convenient and useful structure, we should remember that there must first be a reason for comparing.

Reasons for Comparing and Contrasting

A comparative essay, like any other, must begin with an intelligent purpose and seek to discover and advance a worthwhile, provocative thesis. We could compare oranges and basketballs and come up with similarities and differences, but because there would be no point to the exercise, it would not be a serious intellectual endeavor. Writers turn to comparison/contrast in order to clarify, to argue, or even to describe. Listed below are some of the reasons a writer might use a comparison/contrast pattern.

1. To Evaluate

Our most frequent use of comparative thinking is to determine the better of two things. When required to decide between two options, we analyze the options to discover the advantages and disadvantages of each, we weigh their relative merits, and then we select one over the other. We make such evaluations constantly: which toothpaste to buy, which college to attend, which football team to bet on, whether to work flextime or regular time, whether to marry or just live together. Like many of our selections in life, these entail comparing and contrasting in order to determine a preference.

Weighing the relative merits and making a comparative evaluation require keen judgment. People too often make incorrect choices because they have not carefully analyzed the options or have not given proper emphasis to important items. Although X may have three advantages to Y's one advantage, Y may be preferable because that one advantage, such as safety, is the most important criterion.

When evaluating, we focus on differences between the two subjects because it is differences, not similarities, that distinguish the two and aid in decision making. As you probably have noticed in previous evaluations, the fewer differences there are between two options, the more difficult it is to reach a decision. For example, when neither presidential candidate is perceived as being a strong leader (or if both are strong), the public has great difficulty deciding which to support.

A variation of the comparative evaluation is the real-versus-ideal contrast. In this case, we contrast an existing system to an ideal system to expose the deficiencies of the present system. We can also hold up one existing system as a model and contrast it with another system to show the latter's weaknesses; the purpose of the contrast is not only to expose the latter's deficiencies, but also to offer the former as the solution to the problem at hand. For instance, advocates of television reform compare the American broadcasting system to the British system and point out the numerous advantages of the latter in order to suggest that American television adopt some of the British features. In the following example, the chairman of the National Commission on Social Security contrasts the American approach to old age with the Chinese approach.

1. What is the writer's purpose in using comparison/contrast? Is the essay purely expository (explanatory, informational), or is it argumentative? What is the thesis, and where is it stated, if at all?
2. The first part of the essay focuses on the Chinese system. Where does the contrast to the American system begin?
3. How does the writer keep the discussion from being abstract and general?
4. Is the essay purely logical, or is there an appeal to emotions also?
5. Outline the essay to discover what kind of structure the writer uses.

RESTORED TREASURE

Milton Gwirtzman

In his family's tiny, three-room apartment in the Tianshan Workers Residential Area in Shanghai, Yang Liche sips tea with me and talks of his plans for the future. Yang is 29, the eldest of three children, and works as a telegraph operator for the Yangtze River Shipping Authority. "Next month I am getting married," he says. "The room over there will belong to us. Of course, my mother will move in with us for the rest of her days."   1

The "of course"—the casual acceptance of what to many Americans would seem an impossible burden—explains why, despite their spartan standard of living, old people in China seem secure, almost serene, compared with their contemporaries in the United States. The Chinese have traditionally looked to the family for the things that matter most in life, and the Communist regime has not tried to change that pattern. Filial devotion is the most admired of virtues, old age the most respected stage of life. Yang quotes a Chinese saying: "If you have an old person at home, it is as if you have restored a piece of treasure."   2

Prominently framed on the wall is his mother's Certificate of Honorable Retirement from the factory where she worked as a seamstress. She receives a small pension, $30 a month, which is pooled with the wages of her three children to keep the family going. To collect it, she must return each month to her old factory, giving her a chance to keep up ties with her old friends. She and the other 2,300 retired residents of Tianshan keep busy caring for the children of working parents, helping their grandchildren with schoolwork, answering the telephones that serve the area, dispensing family-planning information. Occasionally, they pick up posters and march through the streets to the crash of cymbals, exhorting the younger people to keep the neighborhood clean.   3

LIFE SUPPORT

Although Shanghai is one of the five largest cities in the world, it has just one home for   4
the aged. Older people in China don't need Golden Age clubs or retirement communities. They have the most important life-support system of all: active, dignified
work in an atmosphere of close family life and community respect.

In America we have chosen a different path. We glorify the "nuclear family":   5
father, mother and a sufficiently small number of children so as not to interfere with
the life-styles, careers or vacations of the parents. Major Federal programs help as
many nuclear families as possible live in homes of their own—$70 billion in home-loan
guarantees, $20 billion a year in tax deductions for mortgage-interest payments,
thousands of miles of highways reaching into the suburbs. Children leave home as
soon as they can, often before marriage, in search of privacy and independence from
their parents. To large numbers of small children, a grandparent is a remote voice on
the other end of a telephone line—fun to visit occasionally but scarcely an important
part of their lives.

As generations drift apart physically, they begin to see each other as economic   6
adversaries. Young executives grumble at the recent increase in the mandatory
retirement age to 70. Forget what it does for an old person's mental health and
self-respect—it might hold back younger ones' advance up the corporate ladder.
Younger workers balk at the prospect of paying higher social-security taxes so that
retirement benefits can keep up with inflation. Roll back those taxes now, they tell
their congressmen, not realizing that to do so could set a precedent for how they will
be treated when they reach retirement.

I do not mean to belittle the genuine love people have for their parents, or the   7
fruitful companionship that exists between generations in many families, especially
when the young and the old live in the same community. Most Americans are willing to
dig down deep into their financial resources so that aged parents can stay at home
rather than be sent to institutions. But money cannot replace physical presence. I do
not believe that older people remain alone out of preference. They do so out of
neglect, or pride, or a desire not to be a "burden" on the children they made and
reared, and to whom they gave so much of their lives. The direction of our society
continues to be toward greater isolation of old people. They must be satisfied with the
pictures, rather than the presence, of their children and grandchildren. When very old,
they sit by their apartment windows and watch us speed by on the expressways below
on our way to bigger kicks than they can give us.

We would do well to consider some of the real advantages of the Chinese   8
approach to old age. Older people need to be needed. Like the rest of us, they need a
sense of purpose in life, and this is best attained through work and through strong
family ties. Americans are living longer and staying healthier than they once did. Many
of those reaching retirement age are perfectly able to go into business for themselves,
working out of their homes, or to volunteer in a significant way in their community.

SOMETHING DIFFERENT

True, most people can't wait to retire from the hard, dull jobs they have held all their   9
lives. But this doesn't mean they do not want to do something different—such as

teach children to read, free teachers from administrative chores so they can teach, or follow up on patients discharged from hospitals and mental institutions. They could keep very busy filling out the forms small-business men get from government regulatory agencies. At least one member of Congress, Michael Barnes of Maryland, uses senior volunteers in his office. More of this would provide a useful balance to the 17,000-member Congressional-staff Establishment, which seems to be made up mostly of people in their 20s.

Older people have more than just experience to offer. They have ideas, commitment and skills. Even more could qualify for work if colleges opened their doors to the old, as they have in recent years to minority youth. The thought of their partial re-entry into the labor force should be viewed not as competition with the young but as a source of economic strength. And we can surely help our own parents find something to do, if they wish to.   10

We have many things the Chinese envy. They want our technology and are willing to pay with their friendship. They may be desperately poor by Western standards, but they seem to be protected from the loneliness, insecurity and loss of self-respect that plague old age. And as there is none among us who will not have to face these adversaries sooner or later, we might do well to emulate, in our family lives and public policies, the spirit of generational sharing that shone so strongly in that small apartment I visited in Shanghai.   11

—From *Newsweek*, Sept. 10, 1979

2. To Explain the Unfamiliar

If our goal is to inform readers about something that is new to them, we can explain it by comparing and contrasting it to something they already know. We can explain the unfamiliar in terms of the familiar, the new in terms of the old. For example, the way that the British Parliament operates might be explained by pointing out similarities to and differences from the American Congress; the juvenile judicial procedure might be contrasted to the adult judicial procedure, or the military judicial system to the civil. Relating one system to another through comparison/contrast draws on readers' current knowledge and gives them a reference point from which to start constructing an understanding of a new system.

In any comparative essay, but especially when we are using the familiar to define the unfamiliar, one subject may receive much more attention and space than the other. We need only mention the familiar and then spend our time explaining how and in what areas the new subject is like and unlike it.

3. To Establish Distinction

Sometimes the public may confuse two closely related things, and our job is to show that the two are not identical. We point out hidden but substantial differences where only similarities are apparent, and in doing so provide readers with a new perception and a more complete understanding of the subjects. We wish to distinguish one system from another by contrasting them, thereby restoring each subject's individuality. Consider these examples of pairs that, although so similar that they are commonly confused, are essentially different:

> Political scientists complain that Americans confuse socialism and communism; therefore, political theorists contrast the two in order to highlight the unique features of each and to clarify their separateness.

> Conservationists try to educate hunters to distinguish between the snow goose and the endangered whooping crane. In flight the two species resemble each other in form and in color, but whooping cranes are longer (the goose is 19 inches, the crane 45) and have wider wing spreads (59 inches versus 90). Each year hunters mistakenly shoot the nearly extinct whooping cranes because they think they are shooting snow geese. The same is true with antlered female animals: Hunters must learn to discriminate at a distance between the female pronghorn antelope, caribou, Rocky Mountain sheep, and Dall sheep, and their male counterparts.

> Robert Frost and Carl Sandburg have become so closely associated in the popular mind that distinctions are blurred. Professor Mark Harris suggests that "this loving national lumping-together does a gross injustice to each man. Though each is venerable, each is gray, and each has written poetry upward of a half-century, each is enormously different from the other." Harris sets out to delineate their uniqueness in an essay entitled "Old Enough to Know, Young Enough to Care."

> In political primaries, campaigners for the same nomination within the same party have difficulty distinguishing themselves from other candidates. Because they are in the same party, their views are usually similar, but each candidate must convince the public that his or her views are different from fellow candidates and better than theirs.

> As we saw in Chapter 5, a writer might wish to define a word by contrasting it to a similar term in order to clear up a misunderstanding—for instance, with *aroma* and *bouquet*.

> If a person or movement is trying to divorce itself from a negative association, the contrasting approach proves effective. For instance, if a political candidate is endorsed by the John Birch Society, the candidate may feel that the public will assume that

his or her views are therefore identical to those of the Birch Society. To dissociate him- or herself from the extremist group, the candidate might point to significant differences between his or her stand and that of the Birchers.

Establishing differences may sometimes be an intermediate step; that is, the difference is not an end in itself but is information needed for another purpose. A union leader, for instance, might compare the wage scale of his or her members to that of other trades; if there is a difference—and the other unions are receiving higher wages—those figures become a means of bargaining with management.

Contrast can be used effectively as the basis for argument. In the essay on page 190, Margaret Mead argues that in relation to former times of downright fear, our age of anxiety is actually an improvement and a sign of humankind's progress. Another example of contrast to substantiate a thesis is the argument for gun control; advocates of gun control contrast the high murder rate by handguns in America to the lower rates in countries that have gun control and suggest that we should abolish handguns.

4. To Establish Similarity

Establishing similarity is the reverse of the preceding purpose. The writer's purpose here is to show underlying similarities amid superficial differences. If readers do not perceive the common traits between two subjects, the writer's job is to prove their mutuality.

5. To Reach a Compromise

When our purpose is to resolve a conflict between two opposing stands, we first compare the two views to establish their similarities and then contrast the two views to determine where they differ. This is essentially what negotiators do: establish points of agreement, then address and try to resolve differences by taking parts of each view and requiring each side to compromise. The key to any compromise is to make each side feel that it has gained as much as and has not relinquished any more than the other side. Each side must be able to preserve its dignity and self-respect.

A comparative essay should fulfill one of these five purposes. The failure of many comparative papers is that they are *about* two subjects but prove nothing. They lack theses. Another danger is getting caught up in the comparison and forgetting the thesis. We must not become so involved in pointing out similarities and differences that we lose sight of our purpose and thesis.

Comparison/Contrast Structures

A comparative essay is one of the easiest to organize because there are three basic structures, and each structure is fairly mechanical. (In fact, a major weakness of most comparison/contrast essays is that they are too mechanically structured.) Each structure has its advantages, and we must select the one that is most advantageous to our subject and purpose.

Whole-to-Whole

In this structure we discuss one subject in the first part of the essay and the other subject in the second part; sometimes we conclude with a discussion of the similarities and differences.

Discussion of one subject	*X*	*X*	*X*	*X*	*X*	*X*	*X*
	X	*X*	*X*	*X*	*X*	*X*	*X*
Discussion of second subject	*Y*	*Y*	*Y*	*Y*	*Y*	*Y*	*Y*
	Y	*Y*	*Y*	*Y*	*Y*	*Y*	*Y*
Conclusion compares and contrasts the two subjects	Similarities, differences						

This structure works well (1) when we want the emphasis on the subjects themselves more than on the comparison, or (2) when readers are unfamiliar with the subjects. Before readers can understand a comparison of two unknowns, they must first be informed about those subjects. Contrasting specialized subjects—for example, the two procedures for inspecting grain weighing—will be futile unless we first educate readers about the two procedures. The whole-to-whole structure has the advantage of discussing one subject at a time, but readers must wait until the end of the essay for explicitly comparative statements. In emphasizing the subjects, this approach de-emphasizes the comparison. The potential problem, therefore, is that the essay can become two little essays, one on *X*, one on *Y*, with the two being only loosely related. The subjects are separated so widely that the comparative intent is lessened and the focus is diminished.

The whole-to-whole structure works best for short essays, in which the subjects cannot be too far apart. In a short essay, we can keep the comparison alive by constantly referring to the other subject and by using parallel constructions.

As you read the following essay by E. B. White, ask yourself these questions: Why does he use a whole-to-whole structure? How does he keep the comparison alive? If his purpose in contrasting city and country schooling is to express a preference, how does he communicate that preference?

EDUCATION

I have an increasing admiration for the teacher in the country school where we have a third-grade scholar in attendance. She not only undertakes to instruct her charges in all the subjects of the first three grades, but she manages to function quietly and effectively as a guardian of their health, their clothes, their habits, their mothers, and their snowball engagements. She has been doing this sort of Augean task for twenty years, and is both kind and wise. She cooks for the children on the stove that heats the room, and she can cool their passions or warm their soup with equal competence. She conceives their costumes, cleans up their messes, and shares their confidences. My boy already regards his teacher as his great friend, and I think tells her a great deal more than he tells us. 1

The shift from city school to country school was something we worried about quietly all last summer. I have always rather favored public school over private school, if only because in public school you meet a greater variety of children. This bias of mine, I suspect, is partly an attempt to justify my own past (I never knew anything but public schools) and partly an involuntary defense against getting kicked in the shins by a young ceramist on his way to the kiln. My wife was unacquainted with public schools, never having been exposed (in her early life) to anything more public than the washroom of Miss Winsor's. Regardless of our backgrounds, we both knew that the change in schools was something that concerned not us but the scholar himself. We hoped it would work out all right. In New York our son went to a medium-priced private institution with semi-progressive ideas of education, and modern plumbing. He learned fast, kept well, and we were satisfied. It was an electric, colorful, regimented existence with moments of pleasurable pause and giddy incident. The day the Christmas angel fainted and had to be carried out by one of the Wise Men was educational in the highest sense of the term. Our scholar gave imitations of it around the house for weeks afterwards, and I doubt if it ever goes completely out of his mind. 2

His days were rich in formal experience. Wearing overalls and an old sweater (the accepted uniform of the private seminary), he sallied forth at morn accompanied by a nurse or a parent and walked (or was pulled) two blocks to a corner where the school bus made a flag stop. This flashy vehicle was as punctual as death: seeing us waiting at the cold curb, it would sweep to a halt, open its mouth, suck the boy in, and spring away with an angry growl. It was a good deal like a train picking up a bag of mail. At school the scholar was worked on for six or seven hours by half a dozen teachers and a nurse, and was revived on orange juice in midmorning. In a cinder court he played games supervised by an athletic instructor, and in a cafeteria he ate lunch worked out by a dietitian. He soon learned to read with gratifying facility and 3 discernment and to make Indian weapons of a semi-deadly nature. Whenever one of his classmates fell low of a fever the news was put on the wires and there were breathless phone calls to physicians, discussing periods of incubation and allied magic.

In the country all one can say is that the situation is different, and somehow   4
more casual. Dressed in corduroys, sweatshirt, and short rubber boots, and carrying a tin dinner-pail, our scholar departs at crack of dawn for the village school, two and a half miles down the road, next to the cemetery. When the road is open and the car will start, he makes the journey by motor, courtesy of his old man. When the snow is deep or the motor is dead or both, he makes it on hoof. In the afternoons he walks or hitches all or part of the way home in fair weather, gets transported in foul. The schoolhouse is a two-room frame building, bungalow type, shingles stained a burnt brown with weather-resistant stain. It has a chemical toilet in the basement and two teachers above stairs. One takes the first three grades, the other the fourth, fifth, and sixth. They have little or no time for individual instruction, and no time at all for the esoteric. They teach what they know themselves, just as fast and as hard as they can manage. The pupils sit still at their desks in class, and do their milling around outdoors during recess.

There is no supervised play. They play cops and robbers (only they call it "Jail")   5
and throw things at one another—snowballs in winter, rose hips in fall. It seems to satisfy them. They also construct darts, pinwheels, and "pick-up sticks" (jackstraws), and the school itself does a brisk trade in penny candy, which is for sale right in the classroom and which contains "surprises." The most highly prized surprise is a fake cigarette, made of cardboard, fiendishly lifelike.

The memory of how apprehensive we were at the beginning is still strong. The   6
boy was nervous about the change too. The tension, on that first fair morning in September when we drove him to school, almost blew the windows out of the sedan. And when later we picked him up on the road, wandering along with his little blue lunch-pail, and got his laconic report "All right" in answer to our inquiry about how the day had gone, our relief was vast. Now, after almost a year of it, the only difference we can discover in the two school experiences is that in the country he sleeps better at night—and *that* probably is more the air than the education. When grilled on the subject of school-in-country *vs.* school-in-city, he replied that the chief difference is that the day seems to go so much quicker in the country. "Just like lightning," he reported.

—From *One Man's Meat*

Point-by-Point

Instead of devoting half of the essay to *X*, the other half to *Y*, a point-by-point structure alternates between *X* and *Y*. Rather than discussing each subject in its entirety, a point-by-point organization considers one element or criterion at a time, applies that criterion to *X* and then to *Y*, and then picks up another criterion.

Criterion 1	*X* *Y*
Criterion 2	*X* *Y*
Criterion 3	*X* *Y*
Criterion 4	*X* *Y*
Criterion 5	*X* *Y*

If we were to restructure White's essay to conform to a point-by-point pattern, it might look something like this:

	I. Introduction
(Criterion 1)	II. Dress
	A. City: uniform of overalls and sweater
	B. Country: more casual—corduroys, sweatshirt
(Criterion 2)	III. Transportation
	A. City: by bus
	B. Country: by car or foot
(Criterion 3)	IV. Teachers
	A. City: six teachers per grade and a nurse
	B. Country: two teachers for six grades
(Criterion 4)	V. Athletics
	A. City: athletic instructor in cinder court
	B. Country: unsupervised games outdoors
(Criterion 5)	VI. Food
	A. City: orange juice at midmorning, dietitian's lunch
	B. Country: tin dinner-pail lunch and candy, food cooked by teacher

This structure stresses the individual aspects—the dress, transportation, etc.—instead of the general subjects of city and country schools, which are subordinated under the major headings.

The advantage of the point-by-point structure is that the comparison is drawn immediately. We have the two subjects side by side so that readers can compare them with regard to one criterion. The comparison is emphatic and inescapable. Another advantage is that this structure breaks the subjects into manageable units, each criterion usually being a paragraph. The major disadvantage of the point-by-point organization is that it can become a see-saw, back-and-forth pattern that becomes monotonous and induces seasickness.

The point-by-point comparison is most appropriate when we have several major criteria, we wish to emphasize those criteria, and our purpose is to determine the superiority of one subject over another. For example, if we were considering buying a new sports car, and we had narrowed the selection to a Mazda RX7 or a Toyota MR-2, our next step would be to evaluate the two in terms of price, size, gas mileage, and safety. Our outline would resemble this:

    I. Price
       A. Mazda _____
       B. Toyota _____
   II. Size and design
       A. Mazda _____
       B. Toyota _____
  III. Gas mileage and horsepower
       A. Mazda _____
       B. Toyota _____
  IV. Safety
       A. Mazda _____
       B. Toyota _____
   V. Conclusion: We should buy _____.

This outline reflects our usual thinking in evaluative comparisons: We select several criteria, apply those criteria one at a time to both subjects, and finally reach a conclusion.

The point-by-point pattern can be illustrated in miniature by this excerpt comparing W. C. Fields and Charlie Chaplin:

Chaplin is innocent or naive, oppressed and downhearted, pathetic and threadbare, and yet deft, quick to escape from the tyrant and the cop, and to make the most of the worst; and he is profoundly silent. Fields is an out-and-out scoundrel with no reservations—he frankly hates children most of all—and he is overwhelmingly articulate, not to say verbose (redundant is one of his favorite words), in the best tradition of that key character in American life and humor, the suave and fluent swindler. Where Charlie skids around the corner rapidly enough to escape the falling lamp post or to make the cop the victim of his own cruel night stick, Fields envelops every situation of superior force in elaborate schemes, alarming and mystifying reformulations, beautifully self-righteous attitudes, and a sophisticated cynicism about everyone, including himself—which is very different from Chaplin's melancholy, pathos, and hurried evasions but which is at the same time a response to the very same world and social set-up. Chaplin makes desperate and downcast efforts to behave with decorum, although the ceiling is falling down or the law is after him. Fields, faced with a bank examiner who will discover a robbery in which he is involved, lures this official gentleman to a bar and orders a drink for him, instructing the bartender by asking him if he has seen his friend Michael Finn lately. The two comic strategies are recognizable and pervasive: you can respond to a threat by being crushed or by being a crook, by running or by making a speech, by pleading or by bluffing, by making faces or by becoming as oratorical as a barker.

—From Delmore Schwartz, "The Genius of W. C. Fields,"
Selected Essays of Delmore Schwartz

Notice how the focus shifts back and forth from Chaplin to Fields as the author considers their screen personalities and comic strategies: sentence 1 on Chaplin, sentence 2 on Fields, 3 on both, 4 on Chaplin, 5 on Fields, and so forth.

Within the point-by-point structure, several internal options are available at the paragraph level. As in the paragraph above, we can alternate sentences: *X, Y, X, Y, X, Y.* Alternatively, we can devote the first half of the paragraph to one subject and the second half to the other subject: *X, X, X, X, Y, Y, Y, Y.* We can also have pairs of paragraphs, devoting one paragraph to *X,* the next to *Y,* both paragraphs dealing with the same criterion. All three options have a common alternating pattern, but the alternating occurs at different levels. The alternating sentence pattern—*X, Y, X, Y, X, Y*—has a ping-pong effect if carried on very long, and the rapid shifting back and forth can confuse readers, who may have difficulty remembering which trait goes with which subject. Here are diagrams of the three alternating patterns:

Alternating sentences	Half-paragraphs	Alternating paragraphs
criterion 1 — X, Y, X, Y, X, Y	criterion 1 — X, X, X, Y, Y, Y	criterion 1 — X, X, X, X, X, X
criterion 2 — X, Y, X, Y, X, Y	criterion 2 — X, X, X, Y, Y, Y	criterion 1 — Y, Y, Y, Y, Y, Y

A quick way to discover and organize your thoughts for a comparative essay, especially for an examination or an in-class essay, is to construct a chart with three columns. Suppose that in a history exam you are required to compare and contrast the Boer War and the Vietnam War. In the top row, place in the middle and righthand boxes the subjects being compared. In the vertical boxes at the left, insert the criteria you plan to apply, starting in the second box. In this case, you might analyze the two wars in terms of the nations involved, causes of the wars, difficulties encountered by the larger nations in each situation, the outcomes, and the consequences. Your chart would look like this:

	Boer War	Vietnam War
nations		
causes		
difficulties		
outcomes		
consequences		

Then all you have to do is fill in the chart, noting similarities and differences as you proceed. By using this chart, you can organize either whole-to-whole or point-by-point, and you can do so quickly and easily. The chart serves as a fast outline that allows you to generate ideas and forces you to organize them. To develop an essay from this box outline, make each criterion a paragraph, provide an introduction, and reach a conclusion.

Similarities/Differences, or Differences/Similarities

This third structure is often overlooked, but there are occasions when our purpose is to prove that similarities or differences do in fact exist, and on those occasions this structure is appropriate.

To show differences:

I. Similarities briefly noted
II. Differences enumerated
   and developed
   A.
   B.
   C.
   D.

To show similarities:

I. Differences briefly noted
II. Similarities enumerated
   and developed
   A.
   B.
   C.
   D.

If our purpose is to demonstrate that differences exist between very similar subjects, we would briefly discuss the similarites and then launch into a detailed discussion of differences. We compare, then contrast. If our purpose is to demonstrate that, despite superficial differences, there are strong similarities between *X* and *Y*, we mention those differences but dwell on the similarities. In this case, we contrast, then compare. Whichever we are trying to prove, differences or similarities, comes second. This structure is also appropriate when either similarities or differences are far more important or interesting.

Mixed Structure

Comparison/contrast structure need not be, and usually is not, a rigid and perfectly balanced pattern. More likely, comparative essays use a combination of organizational patterns. An essay might use whole-to-whole in the first part to acquaint readers with the subjects, then shift to a closer structure, such as alternating paragraphs, and even use alternating sentences occasionally.

Writers typically mix comparative structures because (1) they wish to avoid the monotony of a repetitive pattern; (2) tight, rigid structures tend to be mechanical and restrictive; and (3) some points of comparison require more explanation and development than others. Obviously, we must achieve a sense of order to focus the material and to help readers follow the comparison, but one pattern does not have to be adhered to rigidly.

Many students get the mistaken impression that a comparative essay should be little more than a skeleton and that the structure is the most important part of the essay. That is why so many student essays of comparison are sterile and mechanical: The bare bones of a structure are all that exist. Remember that comparison/contrast is a way of seeing, of evaluating, and of reaching conclusions. Don't let structure dominate your purpose, ideas, and personality. Don't start with a structure as if it were a bottle that you're looking for words to pour into. Like all patterns of organization, comparison becomes interesting and engaging as illustrative details amplify the structural skeleton.

Examining a few comparative essays by professional writers will show that these writers do not let structure dominate their ideas or inhibit their personalities, yet they organize their materials in a clear, comparative manner. Within basic patterns they find room for anecdotes, examples, descriptions, and irony, and they fully develop their theses in lively prose.

In the following essay, for example, Margaret Mead uses a whole-to-whole structure because she is not interested in making a point-by-point comparison. In fact, the comparative intent in the essay is secondary; she wishes to make only enough of a contrast to illustrate her thesis. Therefore, she opens with a comparison that readers are to store in the back of their minds, and then she forsakes the explicit comparison.

ONE VOTE FOR THIS AGE OF ANXIETY

When critics wish to repudiate the world in which we live today, one of their familiar 1
ways of doing it is to castigate modern man because anxiety is his chief problem. This, they say, in W. H. Auden's phrase, is the age of anxiety. This is what we have arrived at with it, our vaunted progress, our great technological advances, our great wealth—everyone goes about with a burden of anxiety so enormous that, in the end, our stomachs and our arteries and our skins express the tension under which we live. Americans who have lived in Europe come back to comment on our favorite farewell which, instead of the old goodbye (God be with you), is now "Take it easy," each American admonishing the other not to break down from the tension and strain of modern life.

Whenever an age is characterized by a phrase, it is presumably in contrast to 2
other ages. If we are the age of anxiety, what were other ages? And here the critics and carpers do a very amusing thing. First, they give us lists of the opposites of anxiety: security, trust, self-confidence, self-direction. Then without much further discussion, they let us assume that other ages, other periods of history, were somehow the ages of trust or confident direction.

The savage who, on his South Sea island, simply sat and let bread fruit fall into 3
his lap, the simple peasant, at one with the fields he ploughed and the beasts he tended, the craftsman busy with his tools and lost in the fulfillment of the instinct of workmanship—these are the counter-images conjured up by descriptions of the strain under which men live today. But no one who lived in those days has returned to testify how paradisaical they really were.

Certainly if we observe and question the savages or simple peasants in the 4
world today, we find something quite different. The untouched savage in the middle of New Guinea isn't anxious; he is seriously and continually *frightened*—of black magic, of enemies with spears who may kill him or his wives and children at any moment, while they stoop to drink from a spring, or climb a palm tree for a coconut. He goes warily, day and night, taut and fearful.

As for the peasant populations of a great part of the world, they aren't so much 5
anxious as hungry. They aren't anxious about whether they will get a salary raise, or which of the three colleges of their choice they will be admitted to, or whether to buy a Ford or Cadillac, or whether the kind of TV set they want is too expensive. They are hungry, cold and, in many parts of the world, they dread that local warfare, bandits, political coups may endanger their homes, their meager livelihoods and their lives. But surely they are not anxious.

For anxiety, as we have come to use it to describe our characteristic state of   6
mind, can be contrasted with the active fear of hunger, loss, violence and death.
Anxiety is the appropriate emotion when the immediate personal terror—of a volcano,
an arrow, the sorcerer's spell, a stab in the back and other calamities, all directed
against one's self—disappears.

This is not to say that there isn't plenty to worry about in our world of today. The   7
explosion of a bomb in the streets of a city whose name no one had ever heard before
may set in motion forces which end up ruining one's carefully planned education in
law school, half a world away. But there is still not the personal, immediate, active
sense of impending disaster that the savage knows. There is rather the vague
anxiety, the sense that the future is unmanageable.

The kind of world that produces anxiety is actually a world of relative safety, a   8
world in which no one feels that he himself is facing sudden death. Possibly sudden
death may strike a certain number of unidentified other people—but not him. The
anxiety exists as an uneasy state of mind, in which one has a feeling that something
unspecified and undeterminable may go wrong. If the world seems to be going well,
this produces anxiety—for good times may end. If the world is going badly—it may get
worse. Anxiety tends to be without locus; the anxious person doesn't know whether to
blame himself or other people. He isn't sure whether it is . . . the Administration or a
change in climate or the atom bomb that is to blame for this undefined sense of
unease.

It is clear that we have developed a society which depends on having the *right*   9
amount of anxiety to make it work. Psychiatrists have been heard to say, "He didn't
have enough anxiety to get well," indicating that, while we agree that too much anxiety
is inimical to mental health, we have come to rely on anxiety to push and prod us into
seeing a doctor about a symptom which may indicate cancer, into checking up on that
old life insurance policy which may have out-of-date clauses in it, into having a
conference with Billy's teacher even though his report card looks all right.

People who are anxious enough keep their car insurance up, have the brakes   10
checked, don't take a second drink when they have to drive, are careful where they go
and with whom they drive on holidays. People who are too anxious either refuse to
go into cars at all—and so complicate the ordinary course of life—or drive so
tensely and overcautiously that they help cause accidents. People who aren't anxious
enough take chance after chance, which increases the terrible death toll of the
roads.

On balance, our age of anxiety represents a large advance over savage and   11
peasant cultures. Out of a productive system of technology drawing upon enormous
resources, we have created a nation in which anxiety has replaced terror and despair,
for all except the severely disturbed. The specter of hunger means something only to
those Americans who can identify themselves with the millions of hungry people on
other continents. The specter of terror may still be roused in some by a knock at the
door in a few parts of the South, or in those who have just escaped from a totalitarian
regime or who have kin still behind the Curtains.

But in this twilight world which is neither at peace nor at war, and where there is 12 insurance against certain immediate, down-right, personal disasters, for most Americans there remains only anxiety over what may happen, might happen, could happen.

This is the world out of which grows the hope, for the first time in history, of a 13 society where there will be freedom from want and freedom from fear. Our very anxiety is born of our knowledge of what is now possible for each and for all. The number of people who consult psychiatrists today is not, as is sometimes felt, a symptom of increasing mental ill health, but rather the precursor of a world in which the hope of genuine mental health will be open to everyone, a world in which no individual feels that he needs be hopelessly brokenhearted, a failure, a menace to others or a traitor to himself.

But if, then, our anxieties are actually signs of hope, why is there such a voice 14 of discontent abroad in the land? I think this comes perhaps because our anxiety exists without an accompanying recognition of the tragedy which will always be inherent in human life, however well we build our world. We may banish hunger, and fear of sorcery, violence or secret police; we may bring up children who have learned to trust life and who have the spontaneity and curiosity necessary to devise ways of making trips to the moon; we cannot—as we have tried to do—banish death itself.

Americans who stem from generations which left their old people behind and 15 never closed their parents' eyelids in death, and who have experienced the additional distance from death provided by two world wars fought far from our shores are today pushing away from them both a recognition of death and a recognition of the tremendous significance—for the future—of the way we live our lives. Acceptance of the inevitability of death, which, when faced, can give dignity to life, and acceptance of our inescapable role in the modern world, might transmute our anxiety about making the right choices, taking the right precautions, and the right risks into the sterner stuff of responsibility, which ennobles the whole face rather than furrowing the forehead with the little anxious wrinkles of worry.

Worry in an empty context means that men die daily little deaths. But good 16 anxiety—not about the things that were left undone long ago, that return to haunt and harry men's minds, but active, vivid anxiety about what must be done and that quickly—binds men to life with an intense concern.

This is still a world in which too many of the wrong things happen somewhere. 17 But this is a world in which we now have the means to make a great many more of the right things happen everywhere. For Americans, the generalization which a Swedish social scientist made about our attitudes on race relations is true in many other fields: anticipated change which we feel is right and necessary but difficult makes us unduly anxious and apprehensive, but such change, once consummated, brings a glow of relief. We are still a people who—in the literal sense—believe in making good.

—From *The New York Times Magazine,* May 20, 1956

1. Define these words from Mead's essay:

repudiate (paragraph 1)	locus (paragraph 8)
castigate (paragraph 1)	inimical (paragraph 9)
admonishing (paragraph 1)	precursor (paragraph 13)
carpers (paragraph 2)	transmute (paragraph 15)
paradisaical (paragraph 2)	harry (paragraph 16)
coups (paragraph 5)	consummated (paragraph 17)

Does the vocabulary seem appropriate for the intended audience (readers of *The New York Times*)?

2. What is the purpose of paragraphs 1 and 2?

3. Where is the thesis explicitly stated? Why do you suppose that it is positioned where it is?

4. Which paragraphs are devoted to the savage/peasant view? Why does Mead spend so little time discussing this subject?

5. Where does the comparison between uncivilized and modern peoples end? What is the purpose of the remainder of the essay?

APPLICATION

Mead says that "Whenever an age is characterized by a phrase, it is presumably in contrast to other ages." The same might be said of decades. What is a characteristic phrase of the 1980s, and to what phrase of a previous decade might it be contrasted? Generate a thesis that captures your perception of the decades and then construct a comparison chart like the one on page 188 to generate ideas for that thesis.

In the following comparison of the American Northeast and West, the author, an Easterner, confesses his preference for the vitality and democracy of the American West. (The article was originally published in *The Washington Post.*)

1. What structure does he use?
2. Why does the essay disproportionately discuss the West and all but ignore the East? Does this fact interfere with the comparative intent?
3. Is the author holding up Western values as a model for Easterners to adopt? Is his thesis that the East should again "look to the West for inspiration?"
4. Does he apply the same criteria to both subjects? What are the criteria he employs?

5. Within the comparative pattern, point out instances of anecdote, description, exemplification, and definition.
6. Is the writer simply offering old stereotypes, or does he contribute some fresh insights on this subject?

BEYOND THE ALLEGHENIES, AMERICA STILL HOPES

Henry Fairlie

Whenever I go west of the Alleghenies for a while, I feel refreshed almost on my first   1
morning, as if there the real life of America is still coursing. I look back at this
Northeast that boasts so much of itself, and in comparison it seems forlorn and
nail-biting and fretful.

It used to be only a cliché to say this, but now its truth has the force of   2
revelation. What was said some 60 years ago by Randolph Bourne, the American
critic who died so tragically young, seems more clear and urgent even than when he
wrote it: "No Easterner can pass very far beyond the Alleghenies without feeling that
American civilization is here found in the full tide of believing in itself;" in the East "no
one really believes that anything startling will be done to bring about a new heaven
and a new earth;" "Hope has not vanished from the East, but it has long since ceased
to be our daily diet."

If we no longer believe that this full tide is still flowing, is it not because the East   3
has ceased to look to the West? The only real work of Boston and New York and
Washington, after all, is to draw a map of America from which most of America is
eliminated.

The annual migration of our eastern intellectuals is about to begin. And where   4
do they go? They go to Martha's Vineyard and the Hamptons and Cape Cod.
Squeezed for the rest of the year into this narrow corridor of the Northeast, they now
squeeze themselves for the summer into even narrower corners of it. Having talked to
each other for the past ten months, they now pack their bags, and flock to where they
may still talk to each other.

Then they come back again, to redraw their baleful maps, refreshed by their   5
own dejection. Yet it is not very long since the East was willing to look to the West for
inspiration, when it responded eagerly to the flowering of new life in the Great Valley.

It is zest and brawn that I find in the West, and it should at once be clear that I   6
am not talking of California, for these are hardly the words that it pricks in one's mind.
Nothing was more invigorating on a recent visit to Texas than to find that the Texan's
mild amusement at California has hardened into contempt. He feels that he has no
more in common with it than with Florida. An oil man in Houston, still with something
of the wildcatter in him, said dismissively to me: "Florida is where the old go to
die—yes? Well, California is where the young go to die."

THE ZEST OF THE WEST
West of the Alleghenies, then, but east of the Sierra Nevada. And how does one   7
encounter its zest? First, in its hospitableness. There is no other hospitality like it

in the world. It is as if every table has been laid in the expectation that a stranger will pass through town. And not only for the stranger, but for the neighbor as well.

I do not know the origins of the phrase—so felicitous and so American—to "visit with" instead of to "visit." But it is only in the West that I hear it, or from Westerners transplanted to the East. A friend in Colorado who was trying to explain it to me said: "You can visit with someone with whom you just stop to chat on the street." It is a concept that alters the way in which a neighbor may just drop in. Not only does a place seem always to be laid, but the time seems always to be made available. Yet these are people busy with making and producing. 8

But this hospitableness tells of something else. There were no servants in the West, as it grew, in the sense that there were in the East and in Europe. Hired hands and hired help, of course, but no idea of the servant. There was no work that only the servant was able to do. That is why the millionaire and even the multimillionaire in the West is as likely as not to be found in the kitchen: not peering at a few pebbles of charcoal on a grill, but moving quite naturally among all the modern gadgets, drinking and talking as he whips something up or takes it suddenly into his head to roast a whole ox. 9

There is democracy in this; and there is zest in it. Everyone is able to take part in every activity. The open-plan house is quite natural to the West. Everything that makes the liveliness of a home is there done in front of one. 10

Then there is the land. To believe that the land is the source of virtue and strength in a people is now regarded as sentimental. Yet close one's eyes as one leaves the West, and one sees these people in their great land. Talk of Texas to those who do not know it, and they think only of its oil. But leave to Texas all its oil, all its refining, all the petrochemical industries built on them, and Texas would die without its agriculture. 11

No Texan ever forgets it. But then neither does anyone in Chicago. Walk down Michigan Avenue in Chicago, and still you feel the prairie at your back. Stand in the now cosmopolitan heart of Houston, and someone will soon remind you that Texas is wheat; that it is cotton and rice and sorghum and cattle; that it is tomatoes and peanuts and even goats. Name whatever grows from the earth, and Texas (of course) has it! 12

THE PRESENCE OF LAND

This presence of the land in the West is quite different from that of the countryside in the East. The industrial towns of New England seem disfigurements of the countryside; but the huge new cities of the West seem to rise out of the plains. As one drives toward them, what is more, that is in fact what they do. 13

W. H. Auden once said that the last time that the town and the countryside were in a harmonious relationship with each other was in the 18th century. But he was thinking, of course, of Europe, and he might have been thinking of Europe's extension in New England. When one gets into the West, the metropolis falls into place, against the vastness of the Great Valley; and since the Westerner thinks nothing of getting into his car and driving 200 miles to go to a cocktail party or a drive-in movie, the 14 hugeness of the prairie with all its changes of seasons is at least as accessible to him as the fenced-off countryside of New England.

When the presence of the land is so strong, work is something that is meant to produce. Out in the West, they still produce. One of the reasons why wealth in the West is less offensive than it is in the East is that it at least comes from producing and making. All that Boston and New York and Washington make are images of the rest of the Americans who are making things. Wealth here is paper; out there it is products.   15

It is typical that Houston in recent years should have had a chic restaurant for the young with the name of "Daddy's Money." There is still in that the edge of contempt for a younger generation that will not go out and make its own way in the world by itself making and producing. The West should tighten its laws of inheritance.   16

There is still the space to make—but time also is different. It is unnerving to look at the holes of the worked-out mines in the sides of the Rockies, and realize that it was only yesterday that men and women clawed and grubbed in them with their hands. It is awesome to stand in the emptiness of the great railroad station at Cheyenne, and realize that its whole legendary story took place in little more than a lifetime. It is strange to sit with an international oil banker in Texas, and realize that the memory of the republic is still actual to him.   17

This time-scale is now as lost to the East as it is to Europe. It is so compressed and, for that reason, still so open. The West is still making. That is why its deserted towns and villages tell so much. They grew and boomed and died, all in so short a span, and there has not been the time, perhaps there will never be, to clean them up or trick them out with boutiques. The history of the West does not need to be preserved, because its history is still in the process of decay and growth. The West is for this reason strangely a place of ruins among the new.   18

I sometimes have the feeling that the East is now closing down America, that it is putting up the shutters, to share the fear and failure that live at the heart of the Old World. It is true that much of the new in the West is ramshackle and tawdry, especially in the smaller towns that still spring up, but one turns back to Randolph Bourne as he wrote of the West: "It is a litter of aspiring order, a chaos which the people are insensitive to because they are living in the light of a hopeful future." So it once was of Venice or Amsterdam as they grew. . . .   19

So it still is west of the Alleghenies. . . . And few things seem more important to me than that Texas, with its zest and brawn, thrusts not east and west, but north and then out into the Great Valley, into the prairie where time and space are different.   20

—From *The Washington Post*, May 27, 1979

Achieving Coherence

Achieving coherence means connecting all the sentences in a paragraph so that readers can easily move from one sentence to another and can comprehend the relationships among sentences. The first step in achieving coherence is to arrange the sentences in a logical structure, such as the structures we have just examined. Other ways of achieving coherence are repeating key terms from one sentence to the next, using transitional words, and using parallel constructions. In this next paragraph, which compares Fred Astaire and Gene Kelly, the various coherence devices are marked so that you can see how the writer skillfully leads readers from sentence to sentence. The two main subjects, Astaire and Kelly, and the words that refer to them directly are capitalized; other key terms are circled; transitional words are boxed; and parallel constructions are in boldface.

The figure of FRED ASTAIRE **implies that** dance is the perfect form, the articulation of motion that allows the self the most freedom at the same time that it includes the most energy. **The figure of** GENE KELLY **implies that** the true end of dance is to destroy excess and attack the pretensions of all forms in order to achieve some new synthesis. KELLY the sailor teaching Jerry the Mouse to dance in *Anchors Aweigh* (George Sidney, 1945) stands next to Bill Robinson teaching Shirley Temple to dance in *The Little Colonel* (David Butler, 1935). ASTAIRE may move dance away from the more formal orders of the ballet, but KELLY emphasizes its appeal to the somewhat recalcitrant, not quite socialized part of the self, where the emotions are hidden. ASTAIRE and KELLY are part of the same continuum of themes and motifs in musicals (an interesting study could be done of the interaction of THEIR images in the 1940s and 1950s). There are many contrasts that can be made between the way THEY use dance and the way THEY appear in THEIR films, but the basic fact of THEIR continuity should be remembered. The question of personal energy, which I have characterized as the musical's basic theme, once again appears centrally. The social world against which ASTAIRE defined HIMSELF in the 1930s no longer had the same attraction to movie audiences in the 1940s; it was a hangover from the early days of film and THEIR simultaneous fascination with 1920s high life and the higher seriousness of theater, in a double effort both to imitate and to mock. ASTAIRE is the consummate theatrical dancer, while KELLY is more interested in the life outside the proscenium. The energy that ASTAIRE defines within a theatrical and socially formal framework KELLY takes outside, into a world somewhat more "real" (that is, similar to the world of the audience) and therefore more recalcitrant. KELLY's whole presence is therefore more rugged and less ethereal than ASTAIRE's. Both ASTAIRE and KELLY resemble Buster Keaton, THEIR prime ancestor in dancing's paean to the freedom and confinement of the body. **But ASTAIRE is the spiritual Keaton while KELLY is the combative, energetic Keaton** compounded with the glee of Douglas Fairbanks. KELLY has more obvious physical presence than ASTAIRE, who hides HIS well-trained body in clothes that give the impression HE has nothing so disruptive as muscles, so that the form of HIS dancing is even more an ideal and a mystery. ASTAIRE **often wears suits and tuxedos, while KELLY generally wears open-collared shirts, slacks, white socks, and loafers**—a studied picture of informality as opposed to ASTAIRE's generally more formal dress. ASTAIRE wears the purified Art Deco makeup of the 1930s, but KELLY keeps the scar on HIS cheek visible—an emblem of the interplay between formal style and disruptive realism in HIS definition of the movie musical.

—From Leo Braudy, *The World in a Frame*

What becomes apparent when the paragraph is annotated is that the author has taken pains to tie his sentences together. What he has done at the paragraph level is equally applicable to an essay as a whole. Here are the techniques that he uses to achieve coherence:

1. Paragraph Structure

The closely knit alternating pattern with sentences keeps the comparison alive and binds the sentences together.

2. Repetition of Key Terms

In addition to repeating Astaire's and Kelly's names and using pronouns and pronominal adjectives *(they, their, his, he),* the author repeats words such as *dance/dancer/dancing, form, energy, formal, freedom, recalcitrant, musicals/movies/films, continuum/continuity, social/socialized/ society, theater/theatrical, presence, Keaton, real/realism.* When he repeats one of these terms from a previous sentence, the author effectively links those sentences with a verbal tie. Almost every sentence verbally refers to earlier sentences and therefore connects itself to them, the whole paragraph being woven together by verbal threads.

3. Transitional Markers

In addition to repeating key terms, the author has used transitional markers to tell readers whether a new sentence is going to express a contrast or a comparison. Using transitional markers is especially necessary in comparison/contrast essays because the focus constantly shifts from one subject to the other, and the markers alert readers to the next direction that will be taken. The transitional markers announce differences or similarities and usually appear either at the opening or in the middle of the sentence. In the Astaire/Kelly paragraph, we encounter not only such terms as *both, but, while,* and *as opposed to,* but also such words as *same, contrast, more,* and *less,* which express comparativeness. Here is a list of other transitional words appropriate in comparative essays:

similar, similarly	by contrast
like	opposite, oppositely
likewise	dissimilar
compared with	conversely
resembling	contrarily
parallel to	on the other hand
correspond to	unlike
comparably	antithetically
identically	although
by the same token	however, whereas

There is an intimacy between subjects in comparison/contrast essays; the subjects derive their significance only in relation to one another. Either subject, *X* or *Y*, by itself lacks full meaning in a comparison; neither is complete without the other. That is another reason we need transitional markers: to connect the two subjects, to show their relationship, and to keep the intimacy going.

4. *Parallelism*

The intimate relationship between *X* and *Y* can be shown by placing similar ideas in similar constructions—in parallel constructions. Comparison/contrast invites parallelism because parallelism usually deals with two structures, and comparison/contrast usually deals with two subjects; the form is natural for the content. In the Astaire/Kelly comparison, for instance, the first two sentences are partially parallel:

> The figure of Fred Astaire implies that dance is. . . .
> The figure of Gene Kelly implies that the true end of dance is. . . .

When opposing ideas are placed in parallel constructions, the result is called antithesis:

> But Astaire is the spiritual Keaton
> while Kelly is the combative, energetic Keaton. . . .

In this case, *spiritual* is the opposite of *combative, energetic*; the sentence is structurally balanced to emphasize the opposition.

> Astaire often wears suits and tuxedos,
> while Kelly generally wears open-collared shirts, slacks. . . .

Again, the opposite natures are placed in parallel forms for emphasis.

Parallelism can occur between paragraphs as well as between sentences. Here is an example in which the writer plans to draw major similarities between the Emancipation Proclamation and the 1954 desegregation ruling. He begins with two parallel paragraphs in which he lets the similarity of construction imply the likenesses between the two laws.

> On January 1, 1863, Abraham Lincoln issued the Emancipation Proclamation, the nation's first civil rights law. Like most of its successors, the order ending slavery in the states and territories of the Confederacy was highly controversial. Its legality was questioned, its wisdom challenged, but even critics acknowledged that Lincoln's action had enormous political importance. Blacks, whether bondsmen or freedmen, ignored its limitations. They viewed the Proclamation as proof that the country's whites at last were acknowledging what they as blacks had always known: that slavery was a moral evil and a legal abomination. Acting on that proof, many blacks proceeded to free themselves.
>
> On May 17, 1954, the Supreme Court ruled in *Brown* v. *Board of Education* that state-mandated segregation in the public schools violated

the Constitution. The decision was controversial. Its legality was questioned, its wisdom challenged, but few doubted the political importance of the Court's pronouncement. Blacks, having suffered under the restraints and limitations of Jim Crow laws for three-quarters of a century, hailed the decision as proof that the nation's whites were ready to acknowledge what blacks had always known: that segregation was a moral evil and a legal abomination. Acting on that proof, the civil rights movement was born.

> —From Derrick Bell, "Integration Can Be Unequal, Too,"
> *The Nation*, July 7, 1979

On a larger scale, parallelism can help to tie together the two halves of an essay structured whole-to-whole. By arranging the materials under *X* and under *Y* in the same order, we can call readers' attention to similarities:

    I. Solar energy
       A. Cost
       B. Feasibility
       C. Safety
   II. Nuclear energy
       A. Cost
       B. Feasibility
       C. Safety

The parallel order helps to connect the separate halves of the essay.

Topic Sentences

As in any paragraph, the topic sentence of a comparison/contrast paragraph serves to focus and tie together the other sentences. The topic sentence in a comparison/contrast paragraph almost always is the first sentence, and its function is to state a criterion and to declare whether the subjects are similar or dissimilar in regard to that criterion. Here are some sample topic sentences taken from the book *Roosevelt and Churchill, 1939–1941* by Joseph P. Lash:

> Both Churchill and Roosevelt understood that information was not only essential to wise judgment, but conferred authority on its possessor.

> The administrative methods of Roosevelt and Churchill were unorthodox, sometimes untidy.

> For Roosevelt, public speaking was a skill, one he had mastered in order to get men to do his bidding; for Churchill, it was a compulsive manifestation of personality.

For Churchill, literary composition, whether in speech or essay form, was a necessity of the spirit; for Roosevelt, it was a burden.

The contrasting attitudes of Roosevelt and Churchill toward the working class and the trade unions showed Roosevelt's openness and Churchill's resistance to social change.

Both Churchill and Roosevelt were endowed with magnetic personalities that drew people to them, the prime minister's authority being fed by inner fires of imagination, instinct, and intuition, and the president's by a superb sensitivity to men and their dreams.

Spontaneity characterized Churchill's approach to men and events, self-control Roosevelt's.

There is a tendency in comparison/contrast paragraphs to compose "say-nothing" topic sentences: "Although *X* and *Y* are alike, they also have differences." The topic sentences quoted above demonstrate that intelligent, informative topic sentences are possible.

Analogy

Usually we compare and contrast items in the same class, for example the Oilers and the Steelers (professional football teams), democracy and communism (political systems), Gary Hart and Mario Cuomo (political figures). An analogy, however, is a limited comparison of two items in different classes. Here are some common analogies: life is like a game; life is like the seasons of a year; war is like a chess game; the heart is like a pump; the brain is like a computer; society is like a living organism. An analogy asserts that two essentially different and unrelated things are similar in one or two significant respects. Although they are dissimilar in all other ways, the subjects (*X* and *Y*) share some essential property, such as structure, function, or behavior, and the analogy concentrates on that resemblance in order to illustrate or clarify an idea.

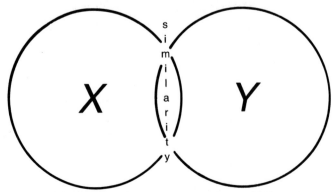

Analogies can be excellent rhetorical devices for explaining difficult concepts. They can clarify complex ideas by likening them to ideas that are common and less complicated. Because they promote understanding of complex concepts, they are often used to explain scientific principles. Analogous thinking, in fact, has led to many scientific discoveries—for example, Newton's thinking about the falling apple and coming up with the theory of universal gravitation. In the following example the writer explains the earth's atmosphere by likening it to a window:

> The atmosphere of Earth acts like any window in serving two very important functions. It lets light in and it permits us to look out. It also serves as a shield to keep out dangerous or uncomfortable things. A normal glazed window lets us keep our houses warm by keeping out cold air, and it prevents rain, dirt and unwelcome insects and animals from coming in. . . . Earth's atmospheric window also helps to keep our planet at a comfortable temperature by holding back radiated heat and protecting us from dangerous levels of ultraviolet light.
>
> —From Lester del Rey, *The Mysterious Sky*

Notice that the writer first announces the comparison and then explains the less familiar concept (atmosphere) in terms of the more familiar one (window). We are able to grasp the idea because the writer has translated it into commonplace experience. The analogy has the advantage of brevity as well as clarity; the author can omit lengthy explanations of principles and theories by transferring the properties of the familiar to the unfamiliar. In addition, the analogy makes a principle concrete and visual.

APPLICATION

1. The following is another example of using an analogy to make a complex principle understandable to average readers.
   A. Why does the writer fully explain ocean waves before explaining his real subject, light waves?
   B. Where does he introduce the comparison?
   C. Is it confusing not to announce the analogy immediately?
   D. Is the comparison between ocean waves and light waves made generally or is it made point by point?
   E. Why does the writer drop the analogy in paragraph 4?
   F. Why is this explanation easier to understand than most scientific explanations, which tend to be complex, long, and difficult to follow?

WHY THE SKY LOOKS BLUE

Sir James Jeans

Imagine that we stand on an ordinary seaside pier, and watch the waves rolling in and   1
striking against the iron columns of the pier. Large waves pay very little attention to
the columns—they divide right and left and reunite after passing each column, much
as a regiment of soldiers would if a tree stood in their road; it is almost as though the
columns had not been there. But the short waves and ripples find the columns of the
pier a much more formidable obstacle. When the short waves impinge on the columns, they are reflected back and spread as new ripples in all directions. To use the
technical term, they are "scattered." The obstacle provided by the iron columns hardly
affects the long waves at all, but scatters the short ripples.

We have been watching a sort of working model of the way in which sunlight   2
struggles through the earth's atmosphere. Between us on earth and outer space the
atmosphere interposes innumerable obstacles in the form of molecules of air, tiny
droplets of water, and small particles of dust. These are represented by the columns
of the pier.

The waves of the sea represent the sunlight. We know that sunlight is a blend of   3
many colors—as we can prove for ourselves by passing it through a prism, or even
through a jug of water, or as nature demonstrates to us when she passes it through
the raindrops of a summer shower and produces a rainbow. We also know that light
consists of waves, and that the different colors of light are produced by waves of
different lengths, red light by long waves and blue light by short waves. The mixture of
waves which constitutes sunlight has to struggle past the columns of the pier. And
these obstacles treat the light waves much as the columns of the pier treat the
sea-waves. The long waves which constitute red light are hardly affected but the short
waves which constitute blue light are scattered in all directions.

Thus the different constituents of sunlight are treated in different ways as they   4
struggle through the earth's atmosphere. A wave of blue light may be scattered by a
dust particle, and turned out of its course. After a time a second dust particle again
turns it out of its course, and so on, until finally it enters our eyes by a path as zigzag
as that of a flash of lightning. Consequently the blue waves of the sunlight enter our
eyes from all directions. And that is why the sky looks blue.

—From *The Stars in Their Courses*

2. Explain one of the following concepts by use of analogy. For example, a
   volcano is like a tea kettle; when the tea kettle is heated, the water boils and
   turns into steam; the steam must have an outlet, which is the spout release;
   when the water boils, the kettle whistles. Likewise, when steam builds up in
   a volcano, it must have a release valve; if enough pressure builds up, the
   volcano, like the kettle, blows its stack.

radar	neutron bomb	genes
meditation	nuclear fallout	camera

False Analogy

Although analogies can be helpful in explaining new or complex ideas, we should be aware that uncritical use or acceptance of analogies can be dangerous. If they are pushed beyond the valid similarities between the two subjects, the analogies lose their usefulness. For example, the common analogy of society being like a living organism serves to illustrate the way society works—each part of society has special functions, as does each part of an organism (even to the point of referring to the "head" of a government), all the parts work toward a unified goal, and so forth. Thinkers in previous ages, however, took the analogy to extremes. Francis Bacon, for one, argued that just as a body needs exercise, so does a society, and that war being a form of national exercise, war is good because it keeps the nation healthy. The analogy has been pushed beyond its logical limits and has become a *false analogy*. A false analogy asserts that a similarity exists where none does—for instance, a mind is like a knife; it becomes dull with constant use. That is a false analogy because minds usually become sharper with use. Just because a comparison is valid in one respect does not mean it will be valid in every respect, and a writer who forces a comparison further than its legitimate similarities commits an error in thinking and misleads readers. Some writers get carried away with the ingenuity of their analogies and forget that they are valid only to a certain point.

Analogies must be used with particular care in arguments, where they are of limited value. They are more useful for explaining than for proving. Although analogies are vivid rhetorical figures, they make weak evidence, and conclusions drawn from analogies are often suspect. In argument, analogy helps at best to eliminate doubt. It does not so much offer infallible evidence as it offers parallel logic that seems valid, but the validity of analogical reasoning depends on the extent and the substantiveness of the similarities. The rhetorical value of analogy is that it convinces through cleverness, as with this excerpt of a speech on slavery, delivered by Lincoln:

> If I saw a venomous snake crawling in the road, any man would say I might seize the nearest stick and kill it; but if I found that snake in bed with my children, that would be another question. I might hurt the children more than the snake, and it might bite them. Much more, if I found it in bed with my neighbor's children, and I had bound myself by a solemn compact not to meddle with his children under any circumstances, it would become me to let that particular mode of getting rid of the gentleman alone. But if there was a bed newly made up, to which the children were to be taken, and it was proposed to take a batch of young snakes and put them there with them, I take it no man would say there was any question how I ought to decide.

That is just the case. The new territories are the newly made bed to which our children are to go, and it lies with the nation to say whether they shall have snakes mixed up with them or not. It does not seem as if there could be much hesitation what our policy should be.

Lincoln has cleverly associated slavery with a venomous snake that is in the bed of children. He has set forth a hypothetical situation about snakes and children and then asserted "That is just the case" within the nation.

That analogous thinking can be dangerous is illustrated by the famous "domino theory." This theory, which has been the basis of American foreign policy in Central America and Asia for the past 30 years, asserts that countries are like dominoes standing on end; if one of those nations falls to the communists, the rest will also fall, just as when one domino falls it knocks down the rest.

APPLICATION

Judge the validity of these arguments based on analogy. If the analogies are false, explain why.

1. If we allow wars between nations, we should allow dueling between individuals because it is the same principle on a smaller scale.

2. A company that manufactures the same product today that it did in 1920 would not survive; Ford, for example, has changed and improved its cars. But universities are using the same old methods and teaching the same authors—Plato, Chaucer, Shakespeare, Newton, and Milton. Universities should keep up with the times.

3. Having former railroad executives serve on the government's regulatory railroad commission because they have experience in transportation is like putting former convicts in charge of the police department because they have experience in crime. The point is, it's the wrong kind of experience.

4. I oppose banking deregulation because it will lead to the demise of the small savings and loan companies and small banks. What will happen is that a few large banks, such as Chase Manhattan and Citibank, will open branch offices in every state and drive out the small, locally owned establishments. Just look at how few independent corner grocery stores are left after such chain stores as A&P, Safeway, and 7-11 took over.

5. Every civilization follows the life cycle of a living organism. A nation is born, it develops and gains strength the way a youth does, it matures and gains stability, the set patterns of middle age emerge, and it begins to decline, the infirmities of old age set in, and it dies from disease and weakness.

6. Political progressives from FDR to LBJ maintained that a government is like a parent. Just as parents have a duty to take care of their children, the government has a duty to take care of its citizens who are dependent on it. Therefore, the government must take care of those who cannot take care of themselves: the aged, the unemployed, the ill, and the poor.

7. "Experience seems to be like the shining of a bright lantern. It suddenly makes clear in the mind what was already there, perhaps, but dim." (Walter de la Mare)

8. "In the autumn and winter, water begins to freeze into ice. When the warm breezes of spring come, the rigidity is dissolved, and the elements that have been dispersed in ice floes are reunited. It is the same with the minds of the people. Through hardness and selfishness the heart grows rigid, and this rigidity leads to separation from all others. Egotism and cupidity isolate men. Therefore the hearts of men must be seized by a devout emotion. They must be shaken by a religious awe in face of eternity—stirred with an intuition of the One Creator of all living beings, and united through the strong feeling of fellowship experienced in the ritual of divine worship." (*The I Ching*, Wilhelm/Paynes translation)

9. If a person were explaining to your children how to make nitroglycerine with their basement chemistry set, you would throw the person out of your house. Likewise, if a person preaches a political doctrine that is intended to destroy the nation—communism, nazism, racial hatred—we should have the right to throw the person out of the country.

10. When you pay $400 for a refrigerator and it breaks down, you go back to Sears and demand service—and get it. What happens when you pay $400 in city taxes and you call up your councilman about a pot hole in your street? You get to keep the pot hole.

11. "Yes, anyone can 'take' a picture—as virtually anyone can type. He who types doesn't necessarily write, however, and he who photographs isn't necessarily creating art." (Douglas Davis, in *Newsweek*)

12. A person's looks are to his or her essence what a bottle is to fine wine. It's what's inside that matters, not the container.

13. "Taking your kids to the movies is an interesting experience. First you look in the paper to see what's being offered, then you pick the one that's least harmful. It's a little like voting." (Robert Orden, in *Parade*)

14. "Free will and determinism, I was told, are like a game of cards. The hand that is dealt you represents determinism. The way you play your hand represents free will." (Norman Cousins, "A Game of Cards")

Exercises

1. What purpose might you have for comparing these pairs?

   the oboe and the English horn
   the Japanese economy and the United States economy
   beagles and dachshunds
   Puerto Rico and Hawaii
   Soviet naval strength and United States naval strength

2. Analyze these two paragraphs from film director Peter Bogdanovich's essay "On Sex and Violence in the Movies." What is being contrasted, what is his purpose, and what is the organization?

The only way I've ever really felt sex scenes work in a picture is when they are treated for comedy, or when the sexuality is implied or veiled. That's one of the main reasons I actually think we've managed to become less erotic and less artistic the more of sex we've shown over the years. Way back in the heavily Code-supervised Forties, you never doubted for a moment that Bogart and Bacall had slept together in *To Have and Have Not*—I mean, it was clear in the movie when the event had taken place, and we didn't need to see it. In fact, we didn't want to. Of course, there were stupidities imposed on filmmakers then—no double beds, for instance, and the length of kisses was timed—but did it matter finally? There was a shorthand at work, and I don't mean panning over to the fireplace—it was more inventive than that. See Hitchcock's *Notorious* again sometime—it is quite apparent to anyone except a child (no ratings necessary) when Grant and Bergman have slept together and when she has gone off and slept with Claude Rains. Luckily, again, we didn't have to see it, as has become obligatory these days; the dramatic point was made with the action offscreen, since the fact, not the act, was important. Today, we're redundantly spelling everything out, leaving little to the imagination, and less to the human spirit.

The good directors also had something else beside the Code or ratings to guide them—they had taste. Not being shown what the child murderer (Peter Lorre) does to his poor victims in Fritz Lang's *M* is far more effective than the slow-motion pyrotechnics of Mr. Peckinpah's type of violence; so much more horrifying, too, since our imagination, with some skillful assistance, can conjure up unspeakable and unspecific terrors no camera can equal. The blood and gore of the Peckinpah school only manage to reaffirm the skills of the makeup and special-effects departments, forcing us either to look away from the screen in disgust or to wonder clinically how some particular bit of exploding flesh or decapitation was achieved. In either case the spell is broken.

3. What criteria would you use to evaluate these subjects?

   the Dallas Cowboys and the Washington Redskins
   soybean patties and ground beef patties

Republicans and Democrats
two newspapers in your area
similar Xerox and Savin photocopiers

4. Develop a thesis concerning one of these pairs of subjects and briefly outline the essay that would follow. Then develop a second thesis and an outline that would use a different structure.

Blacks on television in the 1970s and 1980s
isometrics versus motion exercise
high schools in the United States and in England
United States relations with Taiwan and with Israel

Suggested Writing Assignments

1. Within your field of study, compare and contrast two schools of thought or two practioners' different methods, but narrow the discussion to one specific area. For example, if psychology is the field, don't attempt to contrast topics as broad as behavioralism and psychoanalysis; instead, limit the essay to one aspect on which the two schools differ. If your field is history, contrast traditional historians' views with revisionists' views not simply on American history in general, but, for instance, on one event, issue, or president.

2. Argue the superiority of one product over another, one proposal over another, one candidate over another, or one method over another.

3. Contrast your current attitude to your previous attitude on a subject about which you have changed your mind over the years: religion, abortion, your parents or siblings, marriage, an ethnic group, television, politics.

4. Contrast the past and present nature of a subject: the changing role of the press, from objective reporting to adversarial investigation; dating in the past and today; Christmas today and when you were 10 years old.

5. Contrast your expectation about an experience to the experience itself—for instance, college as you anticipated it and the reality.

6. Contrast any real situation to the ideal situation, or contrast an organization's present goals, character, and methods to its original goals, spirit, and methods, thereby exposing a discrepancy.

7. Compare the prose styles of two writers in this book, such as Phyllis Theroux and Mark Harris, Norman Cousins and J. B. Priestley, Susan Jacoby and Ellen Goodman, or Rachel Carson and Lewis Thomas.

8. Compare a collegiate to a professional sport (football, boxing, wrestling), or students in the sciences to students in the humanities, or two teachers who exemplify different teaching styles.

9. Compare your mother's and your father's (1) family, (2) life philosophy, (3) mode of discipline, or (4) influence on your life.

10. Compare two movies on similar subjects, for instance *Rocky* and *Raging Bull,* or any two horror flicks, two Westerns, two spy thrillers, two sci-fi movies, two comedies, two musicals—in terms of theme, characterization, camera technique, plot, direction, and acting.

11. Compare a novel and a film adaptation of it—for example *Tom Jones, David Copperfield, For Whom the Bell Tolls, One Flew Over the Cuckoo's Nest.*

12. Compare two versions of the same movie—*King Kong* (1933, 1976), *Heaven Can Wait, The Big Sleep, The Body Snatchers, Dr. Jekyll and Mr. Hyde* (3 versions), *The Three Musketeers,* or *The Champ.* Your thesis might be an evaluation—for instance, "Despite a cast of well-known performers, the 1966 remake of *Stagecoach* failed to capture the rugged innocence of the 1939 John Ford original."

Additional Readings

O ROTTEN GOTHAM—SLIDING DOWN INTO THE BEHAVIORAL SINK

Tom Wolfe

I just spent two days with Edward T. Hall, an anthropologist, watching thousands of   1
my fellow New Yorkers short-circuiting themselves into hot little twitching death balls
with jolts of their own adrenalin. Dr. Hall says it is overcrowding that does it. Overcrowding gets the adrenalin going, and the adrenalin gets them queer, autistic,
sadistic, barren, batty, sloppy, hot-in-the-pants, chancred-on-the-flankers, leering,
puling, numb—the usual in New York, in other words, and God knows what else. Dr.
Hall has the theory that overcrowding has already thrown New York into a state of
behavioral sink. Behavioral sink is a term from ethology, which is the study of how

animals relate to their environment. Among animals, the sink winds up with a "population collapse" or "massive die-off." O rotten Gotham.

It got to be easy to look at New Yorkers as animals, especially looking down from some place like a balcony at Grand Central at the rush hour Friday afternoon. The floor was filled with the poor white humans, running around, dodging, blinking their eyes, making a sound like a pen full of starlings or rats or something.

"Listen to them skid," says Dr. Hall.

He was right. The poor old etiolate animals were out there skidding on their rubber soles. You could hear it once he pointed it out. They stop short to keep from hitting somebody or because they are disoriented and they suddenly stop and look around, and they skid on their rubber-soled shoes, and a screech goes up. They pour out onto the floor down the escalators from the Pan-Am Building, from 42nd Street, from Lexington Avenue, up out of subways, down into subways, railroad trains, up into helicopters—

"You can also hear the helicopters all the way down here," says Dr. Hall. The sound of the helicopters using the roof of the Pan-Am Building nearly fifty stories up beats right through. "If it weren't for this ceiling"—he is referring to the very high ceiling in Grand Central—"this place would be unbearable with this kind of crowding. And yet they'll probably never 'waste' space like this again."

They screech! And the adrenal glands in all those poor white animals enlarge, micrometer by micrometer, to the size of cantaloupes. Dr. Hall pulls a Minox camera out of a holster he has on his belt and starts shooting away at the human scurry. The Sink!

Dr. Hall has the Minox up to his eye—he is a slender man, calm, 52 years old, young-looking, an anthropologist who has worked with Navajos, Hopis, Spanish-Americans, Negroes, Trukese. He was the most important anthropologist in the government during the crucial years of the foreign aid program, the 1950's. He directed both the Point Four training program and the Human Relations Area Files. He wrote *The Silent Language* and *The Hidden Dimension,* two books that are picking up the kind of "underground" following his friend Marshall McLuhan started picking up about five years ago. He teaches at the Illinois Institute of Technology, lives with his wife, Mildred, in a high-ceilinged town house on one of the last great residential streets in downtown Chicago, Astor Street; he has a grown son and daughter, loves good food, good wine, the relaxed, civilized life—but comes to New York with a Minox at his eye to record!—perfect—The Sink.

We really got down in there by walking down into the Lexington Avenue line subway stop under Grand Central. We inhaled those nice big fluffy fumes of human sweat, urine, effluvia, and sebaceous secretions. One old female human was already stroked out on the upper level, on a stretcher, with two policemen standing by. The other humans barely looked at her. They rushed into line. They bellied each other, haunch to paunch, down the stairs. Human heads shone through the gratings. The species North European tried to create bubbles of space around themselves, about a foot and a half in diameter—

"See, he's reacting against the line," says Dr. Hall.

—but the species Mediterranean presses on in. The hell with bubbles of space.   10
The species North European resents that, this male human behind him presses forward toward the booth . . . *breathing* on him, he's disgusted, he pulls out of the line entirely, the species Mediterranean resents him for resenting it, and neither of them realizes what the hell they are getting irritable about exactly. And in all of them the old adrenals grow another micrometer.

Dr. Hall whips out the Minox. Too perfect! The bottom of The Sink.   11

It is the sheer overcrowding, such as occurs in the business sections of   12
Manhattan five days a week and in Harlem, Bedford-Stuyvesant, southeast Bronx every day—sheer overcrowding is converting New Yorkers into animals in a sink pen. Dr. Hall's argument runs as follows: all animals, including birds, seem to have a built-in, inherited requirement to have a certain amount of territory, space, to lead their lives in. Even if they have all the food they need, and there are no predatory animals threatening them, they cannot tolerate crowding beyond a certain point. No more than two hundred wild Norway rats can survive on a quarter acre of ground, for example, even when they are given all the food they can eat. They just die off.

But why? To find out, ethologists have run experiments on all sorts of animals,   13
from stickleback crabs to Sika deer. In one major experiment, an ethologist named John Calhoun put some domesticated white Norway rats in a pen with four sections to it, connected by ramps. Calhoun knew from previous experiments that the rats tend to split up into groups of ten to twelve and that the pen, therefore, would hold forty to forty-eight rats comfortably, assuming they formed four equal groups. He allowed them to reproduce until there were eighty rats, balanced between male and female, but did not let it get any more crowded. He kept them supplied with plenty of food, water, and nesting materials. In other words, all their more obvious needs were taken care of. A less obvious need—space—was not. To the human eye, the pen did not even look especially crowded. But to the rats, it was crowded beyond endurance.

The entire colony was soon plunged into a profound behavioral sink. "The sink,"   14
said Calhoun, "is the outcome of any behavioral process that collects animals together in unusually great numbers. The unhealthy connotations of the term are not accidental: a behavioral sink does act to aggravate all forms of pathology that can be found within a group."

For a start, long before the rat population reached eighty, a status hierarchy had   15
developed in the pen. Two dominant male rats took over the two end sections, acquired harems of eight to ten females each, and forced the rest of the rats into the two middle pens. All the overcrowding took place in the middle pens. That was where the "sink" hit. The aristocrat rats at the end grew bigger, sleeker, healthier, and more secure the whole time.

In The Sink, meanwhile, nest building, courting, sex behavior, reproduction,   16
social organization, health—all of it went to pieces. Normally, Norway rats have a mating ritual in which the male chases the female, the female ducks down into a burrow and sticks her head up to watch the male. He performs a little dance outside the burrow, then she comes out, and he mounts her, usually for a few seconds. When The Sink set in, however, no more than three males—the dominant males in the

middle sections—kept up the old customs. The rest tried everything from satyrism to homosexuality or else gave up on sex altogether. Some of the subordinate males spent all their time chasing females. Three or four might chase one female at the same time, and instead of stopping at the burrow entrance for the ritual, they would charge right in. Once mounted, they would hold on for minutes instead of the usual seconds.

Homosexuality rose sharply. So did bisexuality. Some males would mount anything—males, females, babies, senescent rats, anything. Still other males dropped sexual activity altogether, wouldn't fight and, in fact, would hardly move except when the other rats slept. Occasionally a female from the aristocrat rats' harems would come over the ramps and into the middle sections to sample life in The Sink. When she had had enough, she would run back up the ramp. Sink males would give chase up to the top of the ramp, which is to say, to the very edge of the aristocratic preserve. But one glance from one of the king rats would stop them cold and they would return to The Sink. 17

The slumming females from the harems had their adventures and then returned to a placid, healthy life. Females in The Sink, however, were ravaged, physically and psychologically. Pregnant rats had trouble continuing pregnancy. The rate of miscarriages increased significantly, and females started dying from tumors and other disorders of the mammary glands, sex organs, uterus, ovaries, and Fallopian tubes. Typically, their kidneys, livers, and adrenals were also enlarged or diseased or showed other signs associated with stress. 18

Child-rearing became totally disorganized. The females lost the interest or the stamina to build nests and did not keep them up if they did build them. In the general filth and confusion, they would not put themselves out to save offspring they were momentarily separated from. Frantic, even sadistic competition among the males was going on all around them and rendering their lives chaotic. The males began unprovoked and senseless assaults upon one another, often in the form of tail-biting. Ordinarily, rats will suppress this kind of behavior when it crops up. In The Sink, male rats gave up all policing and just looked out for themselves. The "pecking order" among males in The Sink was never stable. Normally, male rats set up a three-class structure. Under the pressure of overcrowding, however, they broke up into all sorts of unstable subclasses, cliques, packs—and constantly pushed, probed, explored, tested one another's power. Anyone was fair game, except for the aristocrats in the end pens. 19

Calhoun kept the population down to eighty, so that the next stage, "population collapse" or "massive die-off," did not occur. But the autopsies showed that the pattern—as in the diseases among the female rats—was already there. 20

The classic study of die-off was John J. Christian's study of Sika deer on James Island in the Chesapeake Bay, west of Cambridge, Maryland. Four or five of the deer had been released on the island, which was 280 acres and uninhabited, in 1916. By 1955 they had bred freely into a herd of 280 to 300. The population density was only about one deer per acre at this point, but Christian knew that this was already too high for the Sikas' inborn space requirements, and something would give before long. For 21 two years the number of deer remained 280 to 300. But suddenly, in 1958, over half the deer died; 161 carcasses were recovered. In 1959 more deer died and the population steadied at about 80.

In two years, two-thirds of the herd had died. Why? It was not starvation. In fact, all the deer collected were in excellent condition, with well-developed muscles, shining coats, and fat deposits between the muscles. In practically all the deer, however, the adrenal glands had enlarged by 50 percent. Christian concluded that the die-off was due to "shock following severe metabolic disturbance, probably as a result of prolonged adrenocortical hyperactivity. . . . There was no evidence of infection, starvation, or other obvious cause to explain the mass mortality." In other words, the constant stress of overpopulation, plus the normal stress of the cold of the winter, had kept the adrenalin flowing so constantly in the deer that their systems were depleted of blood sugar and they died of shock.

22

Well, the white humans are still skidding and darting across the floor of Grand Central. Dr. Hall listens a moment longer to the skidding and the darting noises, and then says, "You know, I've been on commuter trains here after everyone has been through one of these rushes, and I'll tell you, there is enough acid flowing in the stomachs in every car to dissolve the rails underneath."

23

Just a little invisible acid bath for the linings to round off the day. The ulcers the acids cause, of course, are the one disease people have already been taught to associate with the stress of city life. But overcrowding, as Dr. Hall sees it, raises a lot more hell with the body than just ulcers. In everyday life in New York—just the usual, getting to work, working in massively congested areas like 42nd Street between Fifth Avenue and Lexington, especially now that the Pan-Am Building is set in there, working in cubicles such as those in the editorial offices at Time-Life, Inc., which Dr. Hall cites as typical of New York's poor handling of space, working in cubicles with low ceilings and, often, no access to a window, while construction crews all over Manhattan drive everybody up the Masonite wall with air-pressure generators with noises up to the boil-a-brain decibel level, then rushing to get home, piling into subways and trains, fighting for time and for space, the usual day in New York—the whole now-normal thing keeps shooting jolts of adrenalin into the body, breaking down the body's defenses and winding up with the work-a-daddy human animal stroked out at the breakfast table with his head apoplexed like a cauliflower out of his $6.95 semi-spread Pima-cotton shirt, and nosed over into a plate of No-Kloresto egg substitute, signing off with the black thrombosis, cancer, kidney, liver, or stomach failure, and the adrenals ooze to a halt, the size of eggplants in July.

24

One of the people whose work Dr. Hall is interested in on this score is René Dubos at the Rockefeller Institute. Dubos's work indicates that specific organisms, such as the tuberculosis bacillus or a pneumonia virus, can seldom be considered "the cause" of a disease. The germ or virus, apparently, has to work in combination with other things that have already broken the body down in some way—such as the old adrenal hyperactivity. Dr. Hall would like to see some autopsy studies made to record the size of adrenal glands in New York, especially of people crowded into

25

slums and people who go through the full rush-hour-work-rush-hour cycle every day. He is afraid that until there is some clinical, statistical data on how overcrowding actually ravages the human body, no one will be willing to do anything about it. Even in so obvious a thing as air pollution, the pattern is familiar. Until people can actually see the smoke or smell the sulphur or feel the sting in their eyes, politicians will not get excited about it, even though it is well known that many of the lethal substances polluting the air are invisible and odorless. For one thing, most politicians are like the aristocrat rats. They are insulated from The Sink by practically sultanic buffers— limousines, chauffeurs, secretaries, aides-de-camp, doormen, shuttered houses, high-floor apartments. They almost never ride subways, fight rush hours, much less live in the slums or work in the Pan-Am Building.

—From *The Pump House Gang*

1. What is Wolfe's purpose in this essay? Is the analogy between the rats and human beings an end in itself, or is Wolfe using the comparison to clarify something? What is his thesis?

2. Why does he discuss New Yorkers, then rats and deer, and then back to New Yorkers in the final paragraphs of the excerpt? Does splitting the discussion of New Yorkers add to the effect, or is the separation confusing? Why?

3. Approached another way, the ideas and material in this essay could be dry and dull because the essay draws on research studies for theory and substantiation. But Wolfe's essay is anything but dull. How does he incorporate research findings into the essay without making the essay sound stodgy?

4. What is the dominant impression that Wolfe creates of New Yorkers when he describes them?

5. Wolfe's razzle-dazzle style of writing may seem at first undisciplined, but if you examine those instances where his prose seems most unorthodox, you will discover that his sentences are simply reflecting the scene he is describing. His form reflects the content. Give two examples where Wolfe's sentence structure reflects the content.

6. How do paragraphs 2–6 and 8–10 prepare readers to view New Yorkers as animals?

7. The second sentence of the essay states "it is overcrowding that does it," but Wolfe postpones the theory of overcrowding until paragraph 12. Why does he wait until then to present the theory?

8. To understand fully the structure of the essay, outline it. Is the comparison whole-to-whole or point-by-point? Is the comparison between rats and New Yorkers in paragraphs 15–19 explicit or implicit? Explain.

PILGRIMS, SAINTS AND SPACEMEN

Freeman Dyson

Governor William Bradford of the Plymouth Colony, President Brigham Young of the   1
Church of Jesus Christ of Latter-day Saints, and my friend Professor Gerard O'Neill of
the Princeton University physics department have much in common. Each of the three
is a man of vision. Each believes passionately in the ability of ordinary men and
women to go out into the wilderness and build there a society better than the one they
left behind. Each has written a book to record for posterity his vision and his struggles.
Each has his feet firmly on the ground in the real world of politics and finance. Each is
acutely aware of the importance of dollars and cents, or pounds and shillings, in
making his dreams come true.

The human and economic problems that the space colonists of tomorrow will   2
face are not essentially different from the problems faced by Bradford in 1620 and by
Young in 1847. Unfortunately, the extravagant style and exorbitant costs of the Apollo
expeditions to the moon have created in the minds of the public the impression that
any human activities in space must necessarily cost tens of billions of dollars. I believe
this impression to be fundamentally mistaken. If we reject the style of Apollo and
follow the style of the *Mayflower* and the Mormons, we shall find the costs of space
colonization coming down to a reasonable level. By a reasonable level of costs I mean
a sum of money comparable to the sums which the Pilgrims and the Mormons
successfully raised.

I conclude from the evidence of the 1626 settlement that £3600 is a safe upper   3
limit to the original cost of renting and provisioning the *Mayflower*. [Other] evidence
implies a lower limit of £1500. I shall adopt £2500 as my estimate of the cost of the
expedition in 1620 pounds. This figure can hardly be wrong by a factor of two either
way. The payload of the *Mayflower* is stated explicitly by Bradford. It was 180
tons.

The actual numbers that crossed the plains with Young were: 1,891 souls, 623   4
wagons, 131 horses, 44 mules, 2,012 oxen, 983 cows, 334 loose cattle, 654 sheep,
237 pigs, 904 chickens.

So we can estimate the total payload of Young's expedition to be 3,500 tons,   5
mainly consisting of animals on the hoof, and the total cost to be $150,000 in 1847
dollars.

My next problem is to convert the 1620 and 1847 cost figures into their modern   6
equivalents. A good source of information about the history of wages and prices in
England is the work of Ernest Phelps Brown and Sheila Hopkins, published in two
articles in the journal *Economica* and reprinted in a series called *Essays in Economic
History,* put out by the Economic History Society. According to Phelps Brown and
Hopkins, the wages of workers in the building trade in 1620 were in the range from 8
to 12 pence per day. In 1847 the range was from 33 to 49 pence. For the modern
equivalent of these numbers I take the minimum rate of $9.63 per hour imposed by
building trade union contracts in New York in 1975. The exchange rates on the basis
of wages are then:

£1 (1620) equals $2500 (1975)

$1 (1847) equals $100 (1975)

These are very approximate numbers. A rough check on the numbers for 1620 is provided by the fact that each Planter received a credit of £10 for going to Plymouth and working for the community for seven years without wages.

The estimated total costs in 1975 dollars are then 6 million for the *Mayflower*   7 and 15 million for the Mormons. On this basis I have drawn up the first two columns of Table I. The point I am trying to emphasize with these numbers is that both the *Mayflower* and Mormon expeditions were extremely expensive operations. In their time, each of them stretched the limits of what a group of private people without governmental support could accomplish.

The numbers in the bottom row of Table I give an estimate of the number of   8 years an average wage earner would have had to save his entire income to pay the passage for his family. Although the average Mormon family was twice as large as the average *Mayflower* family, the cost in man-years per family was three times as large for the *Mayflower* as it was for the Mormons. This difference had a decisive effect on the financing of the colonies. An average person, with single-minded dedication to a cause and with a little help from his friends, can save two or three times his annual income. An average person with a family to feed, no matter how dedicated he may be, cannot save seven times his income. So the Mormons were able to pay their way, while the Planters on the *Mayflower* were forced to borrow heavily from the Adventurers and to run up debts which took twenty-two years to pay off. Somewhere between two and seven man-years per family comes the breaking point, beyond which simple do-it-yourself financing by ordinary people becomes impossible.

TABLE I   Comparison of Four Expeditions

Expedition	Mayflower	Mormons	Island One L5 Colony	Homesteading the Asteroids
Date	1620	1847	1990+	2000+
Number of People	103	1891	10000	23
Payload (tons)	180	3500	3.6M	50
Payload (tons) per person	1.8	2	360	2
Cost (1975 dollars)	$6M	$15M	$96000M	$1M
Cost per pound (1975 dollars)	$15	$2	$13	$10
Cost in man-years per family	7.5	2.5	1500	6

Cost exchange rates based on building trade wages. M means millions.

I said nothing yet about the last two columns in my table. These represent two   9 contrasting styles of space colonization, both taken from O'Neill's book,* with some changes for which I am responsible. Column 3 comes from O'Neill's Chapter 8, which he entitles "The First New World," describing space colonization organized by the American government in the official NASA style. Column 4 comes from O'Neill's Chapter 11, with the title "Homesteading the Asteroids," in which he describes space colonization done in the *Mayflower* style by a bunch of enthusiastic amateurs.

The cost of the "Island One" project is $96 billion. Many people, myself in- 10
cluded, feel that $96 billion is a preposterously large amount of money to spend on any single enterprise. But still we have to take this number seriously. It was arrived at by a group of competent engineers and accountants familiar with the ways of the government and the aerospace industry. It is probably the most accurate of all the cost estimates that I have included in Table I. For this $96 billion you can buy a great deal of hardware. You can buy a complete floating city to house and support ten thousand people with all modern conveniences at the magic point L5, which is just as far from the earth and from the moon as these bodies are from each other. You can buy enough synthetic farmland to make a closed ecological system which supplies the colonists with food and water and air. You can buy a spaceborne factory in which the colonists manufacture solar power stations to transmit huge amounts of energy in the form of microwave beams to receivers on the earth. All these things may one day come to pass. It may well be true, as O'Neill claims, that the investment of $96 billion will be repaid in twenty-four years out of the profits accruing from the sale of electric-ity. If the debt could be paid off in twenty-four years, that would be almost as quick as the *Mayflower* Planters could do it. But there is one inescapable difference between Island One and the *Mayflower*. The bottom row of Table I shows that the Island One colonist would have to work for 1500 years to pay his family's share of the costs. This means that Island One cannot by any stretch of the imagination be considered as a private adventure. It must inevitably be a government project, with bureaucratic management, with national prestige at stake, and with occupational health and safety regulations rigidly enforced. As soon as our government takes responsibility for such a project, any serious risk of failure or of loss of life becomes politically unacceptable. The costs of Island One become high for the same reason that the costs of the Apollo expeditions were high. The government can afford to waste money but it cannot afford to be responsible for a disaster.

After this brief visit to the superhygienic welfare state at Island One, let us go on 11
to the last column of Table I. The last column describes O'Neill's vision of a group of young pioneers who save enough money to move out on their own from the L5 colony into the wilderness of the asteroid belt. They are going on a one-way trip at their own risk. The cost estimates here describe hopes rather than facts. Nobody can possibly know today whether it will be feasible for a group of twenty-three private people to equip such an expedition at a total cost of a million dollars. Anybody who is pro-fessionally qualified to estimate costs will say that this figure is absurdly low. I do not believe that it is absurdly low. It is no accident that the per capita cost estimates for the

*Gerard O'Neill, *The High Frontier: Human Colonies in Space*.

asteroid colony turn out to be similar to those of the *Mayflower*. This is the maximum level of costs at which the space beyond the earth will give back to mankind the open frontier that we no longer possess on this planet.

According to the third and fourth columns of Table I, the cost per pound of the 12 asteroid expedition is not significantly less than that of Island One. The big differences between the two expeditions lie in the number of people and in the weight carried per person. The feasibility of cheap space colonization in the style of the asteroid expedition depends upon one crucial question. Can a family, bringing a total weight of only two tons per person, arrive at an asteroid, build themselves a home and a greenhouse, plant seeds and raise crops in the soil as they find it, and survive? This is what the *Mayflower* and Mormon colonists did, and it is what the space colonists must do if they are to be truly free and independent.

No space probe has yet visited an asteroid. No scientific instruments have even 13 been flown by an asteroid to give us a closer look at it. We are still as ignorant of the topography and chemistry of the asteroids as we were ignorant of the topography of Mars before the Mariner and Viking missions. Until some of the asteroids have been surveyed with unmanned instruments, it is pointless to try to foresee in detail the problems that colonists would face in making themselves at home there. Cost estimates for farming on an asteroid are meaningless until we know whether the soil is soft enough to be dug without using dynamite. Instead of speculating about the mechanics of space colonization in an unknown environment, I will only mention some institutional reasons why it may not be absurd to imagine a reduction in costs by a factor of 100,000 from the $96 billion of Island One to the $1 million of the asteroid colony. First we save a factor of four hundred by reducing the number of people from ten thousand to twenty-three. That leaves a factor of 250 still to be found. We may hope to save a factor of ten by accepting risks and hardships that no government would impose upon its employees and another factor of five by eliminating trade union rules and bureaucratic management. The last factor of five will be harder to find. It might come from new technology, or more probably from salvaging and reusing equipment left over from earlier government projects. There are already today several hundred derelict spacecraft in orbit around the earth, besides a number on the moon, waiting for our asteroid pioneers to collect and refurbish them.

The Island One and the asteroid homesteading expeditions are extreme cases. 14 I chose them to illustrate high and low estimates of the costs of colonization. The true costs, when colonization begins, will probably lie somewhere in between. In so difficult and long-range a venture, there is room for a mixture of styles. Governmental, industrial and private operations must all go forward, learning and borrowing from one another, before we shall find out how to establish colonies safely and cheaply. The private adventurers will need all the help they can get from governmental and commercial experience. In this connection, it is worth remembering that 128 years passed between the voyages of Columbus and the *Mayflower*. In those 128 years, the kings and queens and princes of Spain and Portugal, England and Holland, were building the ships and establishing the commercial infrastructure that would make the *Mayflower* possible.

O'Neill and I have a dream, that one day there will be a free expansion of small   15
groups of private citizens all over the solar system and beyond. Perhaps it is an idle
dream. It is a question of dollars and cents, as Bradford and Young well knew. We
shall never find out what is possible until we try it.

—Abridged from *Disturbing the Universe*

1. How convincing is Dyson's argument by comparison? Why are you convinced
   or unconvinced?

2. What are the weaknesses in the argument?

3. Dyson admits that there are some weaknesses in his argument. Why does he
   concede those points, and what is the effect of his concessions?

4. Why did he select the *Mayflower* and the Mormons for the comparison to
   space colonization?

5. Most comparison essays treat two subjects; this one compares three. What
   type of structure does the writer use to discuss three subjects?

CHAPTER 7

Classification and Division

Classification and division are patterns of thinking that we rely on daily to sort information; they are especially useful in this era when the problem is not a lack of information but an excess of information—statistics, theories, facts. Whenever we encounter a large body of information, our first impulse is to sort it into groups so that we can more easily deal with it. Look in the telephone Yellow Pages and you will find everything classified and subclassified under headings from A to Z; such codifying is what classification and division are all about. Libraries, faced with the problem of categorizing hundreds of thousands of books, *classify* them according to types and then *divide* those types into smaller categories; for example, one type is "literature," and under that category are subclassifications "fiction," "non-fiction," "poetry," and "drama," all of which can again be subdivided.

You frequently encounter classification and division in your coursework. In psychology, for instance, neuroses are divided into such types as anxieties, phobias, and depressive reactions; history is divided into such periods as the Renaissance and the Enlightenment; philosophy is divided into such parts as aesthetics, ethics, and metaphysics; and anthropology divides humankind into races. Our minds are trained to see the world in terms of categories as well as in terms of individual items, and classification and division are techniques we use to order things in a systematic way.

Although classification and division are so closely related that we seldom separate them in thinking and writing, they are actually two different processes, much as comparison and contrast are complementary but separate processes. The main distinction is direction: With classification, we start with many individual items and move upward in generality; with division, we start with a general topic and become more specific.

Classifying

Classification is useful when we encounter such a multitude of items that they are collectively overwhelming and confusing. To *classify* means to place items into groups or categories, and therefore classification is a means of imposing order by sorting innumerable individual items into a manageable number of groups or types. Besides being an aid to organization, classification is a way of seeing how items are related, for classification is a matter of seeing similarities.

To classify, we must first find similarities among the items and, on the basis of those common characteristics, place the items into categories. After we have grouped the items according to common properties, we give names or labels to the classes. For example, if you were asked to write a brochure on your college for prospective students, and you wanted to discuss all of the features of your college, how would you go about the task? First, you might list all of the features (that is, you would *divide* the college into its parts): the location, social activities, faculty, academic departments, library facilities, types of classes offered, advising services, sports, dormitory life, off-campus housing services, loans, cultural events, parking/commuting, grants, campus police, tuition, Greek organizations, scholarships, rules and policies, student government, degrees offered, internships, and so on. Then you would need to arrange these parts into some kind of order, and most likely you would try to classify the parts. What classifications would you use? Would the headings "Social," "Academic," "Financial," and "Physical" cover all the parts? Such classifications would help you to organize the brochure and would help readers get an overview of what your college has to offer.

For another example, how would you classify the presidents of the United States—men as diverse as Washington, Jackson, Cleveland, Hayes, Taft, Coolidge, Buchanan, Reagan, Madison, Grant, Nixon, Kennedy, and Polk? What classes could you invent? There are many possibilities for grouping the presidents—for example, on the basis of their popularity, their ability, or their political philosophy. Here are several possible classes:

idealists, pragmatists
strong, average, weak
elitists, egalitarians
parliamentarians, autocrats
militarists, pacificists
conservatives, liberals, middle-of-the-roaders
leaders, followers, administrators

Once we have decided on our basis of classifying and on the headings, we must sort the presidents accordingly. In doing so, we will probably discover that subclasses are necessary:

I. Leaders
   A. Creating popular opinion: Lincoln, Franklin D. Roosevelt, Kennedy, Reagan
   B. Dominating Congress: Washington, Jackson, Polk, Theodore Roosevelt, Wilson, Lyndon Johnson
II. Followers
   A. Following popular opinion: McKinley, Tyler
   B. Following cabinet advice or party policy: Grant, Eisenhower
III. Administrators
   A. Supervising competently: Cleveland, Taft, Truman
   B. Supervising incompetently: Harding, Pierce

Our classes help readers to comprehend three groups instead of forty-odd individuals, and in this way classification and division are a service.

When we classify, we impose our perception onto a subject and impose order on a complex subject, at once giving insight and clarity. Another writer might perceive the subject differently and would therefore offer a different—and perhaps equally valid—way of classifying it. For example, another writer might classify American presidents as problem-solvers and problem-makers, which differs significantly from our way of seeing the topic. The wonderful thing about classification is that it encourages each of us to look at a subject in our own individual way.

APPLICATION

Classify these items in at least three different ways:

1. Clint Eastwood	Sean Penn	Jeff Bridges
Matt Dillon	Robert Redford	Sylvester Stallone
Mel Gibson	Michael Douglas	Billy Dee Williams
Robert De Niro	Sam Shepard	Jack Nicholson
Timothy Hutton	Keith Carradine	Paul Newman

2. *Redbook*	*Esquire*	*Atlantic Monthly*
Newsweek	*Vogue*	*GQ*
Ms	*American West*	*Car and Driver*
Ebony	*Money*	*McCall's*
Business Week	*Reader's Digest*	*Fortune*
Good Housekeeping	*Field & Stream*	*Gourmet*
Sports Illustrated	*Psychology Today*	*National Geographic*

Some ways of classifying a subject are more insightful than others and therefore more readily engage readers' imaginations. Classification essays can be rather dry, mainly because the way the writers look at the subject is superficial and obvious. Such essays fail to capture readers' attention because they lack originality and they simply enumerate classes without seeking the meaning of the classes. Read through the following student example and decide whether it has a provocative thesis and an engaging style.

There are four kinds of satchels for carrying personal possessions. The first is a pack that is durable and easy to carry. Hiking packs are often made of nylon and have aluminum supports and a waistband to take some of the weight off of the shoulders. Because these packs hold up to 75 pounds, they are becoming increasingly popular as a type of luggage on vacations since they are much easier to carry than suitcases. Smaller packs made of canvass are popular for local travel, for example when bicycling to campus with one's books and notebooks.

A second type of satchel is a briefcase. Although briefcases have the advantage of being strong, especially the ones with wood frames that are covered with vinyl, they don't hold enough for most students, and, besides, the image fits businessmen and lawyers more than students. In fact, the word *briefcase* comes from the word *brief,* meaning a lawyer's summary.

A third type of satchel is a shopping bag. You see people in shopping malls carrying new purchases in bags marked with the store's name—Sears, Lord & Taylor, Saks. But you also see a very different person with shopping bags filled with personal items: bag ladies. Social outcasts, homeless street roamers, these elderly women carry all of their belongings in double shopping bags as they pick through garbage cans for clothing and even for food. Some of them get enough social security for food but not enough for lodging, so they are forced to live on the street and sleep on park benches. You see them shuffling along urban streets in the midst of hurrying crowds.

The last type of satchel is a leather or cloth pouch that is slung over the shoulder. This type resembles a mail pouch but is much more fashionable. If the satchel is made of cloth, it usually bears the name of a famous designer like Gucci. Although pouches are spacious and can hold almost as much as a pack, most people carry them for decoration rather than for utility. In their pouches they carry a tennis racket, a copy of *The New Yorker*, and mouthwash.

Of course, not everyone carries a satchel. Some people carry nothing on their backs or in their hands. These happy-go-lucky people have escaped both poverty and responsibility.

No doubt about it, the essay effectively classifies satchels, but it doesn't have a thesis that engages our imaginations, and it doesn't tell us anything that we don't already know. It does, however, have potential. Notice, for instance, that the emphasis in the essay begins to shift during the middle from satchels to the people who carry satchels, and the more interesting part is the second half. The human element interests us more than bags. Perhaps the writer could focus on the carriers and develop a thesis concerning the relationship of the bags and the people who carry them. What does a certain type of satchel tell us about its owner? That there are four types of satchels seems true, but it might also be true that there are four types of people. The writer could classify satchels as a means of classifying people and could formulate a thesis, which the original essay lacked. Altering the tone from total seriousness might also be worth considering. Here is the revision:

Psychologists have long sought ways of classifying people—by dominant trait, by phobias, by anatomical build, by fixations, by degree of extroversion—but none of the classifications succeeds in capturing the essence of personalities or in covering all types. After prolonged observation and reflection, I have come upon a solution that is so simple that greater minds, intent on compartmentalizing the world, have over-looked: People can be judged by the satchels they carry. There are four types of satchels and four corresponding personality types (those persons who do not carry satchels, of course, have no personality). The satchels differ in size, material, appear-ance, and function; the people differ in appearance, values, and attitudes.

First, and most indicative of poor psychological adjustment, are briefcases. People who carry these are aggressive; they're out to conquer the world. They are always in a hurry, running after taxis and after clients and after lunch to pressing appointments. Although their professions vary from lawyers and businesspersons to bureaucrats, briefcase carriers wear a common uniform (suit-and-tie required of women as well as men), and they clutch the handle of the briefcase as if the only map to the world is within (some briefcases even have combination locks). The briefcases are of two types: the large, usually box-framed vinyl variety, and the thinner, more chic leather type. The former is carried by salesmen—their cases filled with product evaluations, catalogs, and Dale Carnegie books—and by junior executives—their cases filled with second-draft reports, digital calculators, and micro-mini tape record-ers. Senior executives carry caribou-hide briefcases that are elegantly slim to indicate that their work is done by underlyings; senior execs' briefcases are more for display than for utility.

Also for show are pouches, specifically those designer bags made of leather (imported, of course, from Brazil or Italy or Spain and as soft as unborn elk skin) or of cloth with a foreign designer's name ostentatiously imprinted on it—Gucci, Pierre Cardin, Dior, Yves Saint Laurent. Both types broadcast high fashion and wealth. People carrying pouches are seen in European capitals, Manhattan (East Side, between 51st and 79th), and occasionally in Boston, but they are never seen on the street before noon. Svelte, tanned as their leather bags, wearing Calvin Klein baggy pants and French T-shirts, they always seem to be browsing, not walking. Their common characteristic is their chin: it is lifted upward ever so slightly. Their pouches contain an appointment book, which they use as a diary, a copy of *The New Yorker*, and mouth freshener.

In startling contrast to the pouch people are the bag ladies, those homeless, elderly women who live on urban streets, clutching a reinforced shopping bag in each hand as though their whole lives were in those bags, which is true. The bags are paper, as frail as their owners, as worn and ragged. Dressed in several layers of discarded clothes, the bag ladies shuffle instead of walk, for they have no destination and are in no hurry to get there. Bulging from their bags are broken umbrellas, extra scarves, a blanket, cans of sardines, a swallow of Thunderbird wine, and some newspapers, not for reading, for insulation. As a bag lady peers into a trash can for "recyclable" goods, as she terms them, a pouch lady is peering into the window at Bloomingdale's. They see one another and stare disdainfully at one another's lives. Then their stares are directed at another satchel carrier who is strolling down the avenue: a backpacker.

Backpackers, oblivious to fashion and unconcerned with finances, are usually young persons in unironed shirts and faded jeans—Levis, not Sassons. Inside their canvass or nylon packs one finds vegetarian sandwiches, a granola bar, a leaky pen, a book on South Africa, some crumpled notes, and Wallace Stevens' poetry. In contrast to the manicured casualness of the pouch people, the backpackers' casualness is the product of true neglect. Their appearance conveys a value system which suggests that external matters are superficial and unimportant.

Unconsciously through the satchels we tote we all communicate our personalities on the street to anyone who cares to notice. And now that I have become conscious of this fact, I realize that my personality is schizoid—some days I carry a pack, some days a leather bag from Brazil, and when I feel particularly aggressive and career-oriented, I have been known even to carry a briefcase.

Although this revision has some problems such as the inconsistent tone and the excessive parenthetical remarks, it is nevertheless a refreshing piece that is far superior to the original and is evidence that classification papers need not be lifeless.

Dividing

Division is the opposite of classification; instead of grouping together individual items into larger categories, we start with a broad subject and divide it into its component parts. Whereas we classify on the basis of similarities, we divide on the basis of differences. We reduce a general topic into distinct parts to make the subject easier for us to manage and for our readers to understand. For example, the United States military can be broken down into its three branches—Army, Navy, Air Force—and each of those can be subdivided into smaller units. The United States government is also divided into three branches—judicial, legislative, and executive—and each of those can be subdivided—for instance, the legislative into the House and the Senate, the Senate into its various committees, and so forth. The broad subject of dance is divided into jazz, ballet, modern, ethnic, and social. And biologists divide every living organism into smaller and smaller categories:

Kingdom: Animalia
Phylum: Chordata
Class: Mammalia
Order: Primates
Family: Hominidae
Genus: *Homo*
Species: *Homo sapiens*

Diagraming a broad subject that is dissected into parts helps us to visualize the process of division:

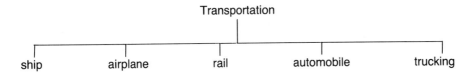

Any of these divisions can be redivided into still smaller units:

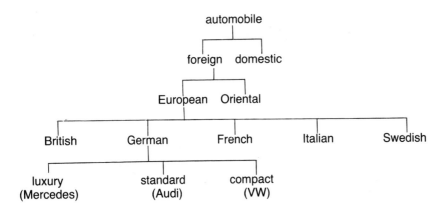

This is an easy example because the divisions are already formed, but where no standard divisions have been formulated, the process of division becomes a matter of personal perception and ingenuity. Mark Twain, for instance, divided funny stories into three types: "The humorous story is American, the comic story is English, the witty story is French." After outlining his categories, Twain gave the characteristics of each and provided examples.

APPLICATION

How would you divide these topics into types:

video games
bumper stickers
liars
curiosity

Uses of Classification and Division

Classification and division serve two basic functions: organizing material, and clarifying relationships. They express relationships of similarity or difference and of generality or specificity: Items within the same class are similar, and items within different classes are, of course, different; likewise, classes above are more general, those below are more specific, and those parallel are equivalent. In the diagram above, for instance, *European* is more general than *Italian,* is more specific than *foreign,* and is equivalent to *Oriental.*

Classification and division may be used at any point in the writing process, from invention to revision, but they are particularly useful in the first stages of thinking and writing.

1. For Invention

Dividing a topic into parts is a way of investigating a broad topic, of generating ideas about it, and of limiting the topic. Let's say, for example, that we want to write about the auto industry. Such an enormous subject requires that we break it into smaller units: safety, history or future of the industry, individual manufacturers (GM, Ford, AMC, Chrysler), labor (United Auto Workers), sales, finances, pollution, technology and engineering. If we subdivided these components into more and more specific areas, we would discover manageable, provocative topics: the ramifications of guaranteed federal loans to Chrysler, projected changes in auto safety for the next decade, problems with gasohol engines, governmental policies that hurt the auto industry, and so forth. We can take almost any unwieldy topic and divide and subdivide it until we arrive at a limited topic and a thesis that we can develop within the confines of the essay form.

APPLICATION

Take one of these topics and keep dividing it until you narrow it sufficiently and generate an intelligent thesis about it:

justice   education
oil   jobs
burials   fruit

2. For Preliminary Organization

The most common use of classification and division is for the initial sorting of material after we have gathered information on the topic. Whereas invention mostly entails division, sorting is primarily a classifying procedure. It is the first step in organizing our material, especially for reports and research projects for which we have accumulated mounds of notes.

Even if our ultimate purpose is not to identify types or classes, we often start with classification and division because they help us to unscramble and then to analyze a subject. Our final paper may reflect another pattern of writing, but by dividing and classifying the subject early in the composing process, we are better able to see other patterns and to see other approaches to the subject. Classification and division, then, are ways of initially imposing order on various types of essays.

By using classification and division early to sort and arrange notes, we can get a handle on the material and see the large parts instead of many isolated and supportive details. In this sense, classification and division are essentially forms of outlining. In an outline, we group similar ideas under one heading and other ideas that are related under another heading until we have our ideas in groups; then we can begin dealing with them as generalizations and can see relationships within and among headings.

3. As a Means to an End

An essay whose emphasis, for example, is causation, may nonetheless be organized according to classification and division. In discussing the causes of pollution, we might for the sake of clarity group those causes into classes: industrial, agricultural, residential, and automotive. The thesis and focus of the essay are the causes of pollution; we use classification merely as a structure and as a means to an end.

For example, if you were writing a report on the effects of marijuana, and your major findings were the following eleven topic sentences, could you classify these statements into two or three categories?

1. Marijuana has been found to be therapeutic in treating glaucoma and has other potential uses in medicine.

2. Some users of marijuana find that they build up a tolerance to the drug, but others report that frequent use makes it easier to get "high" on less marijuana.

3. Although police suggest that marijuana is a major cause of crime among youths, there is little evidence to suggest that this is true.

4. Like tobacco, marijuana contains carcinogens and can lead to lung damage if inhaled.

5. Like alcohol, marijuana temporarily interferes with the user's motor skills.

6. Over the past decade, marijuana use has declined among teenagers.

7. Marijuana is not addictive, nor does it lead to the use of hard drugs such as heroin.

8. Continuing studies on possible chromosome breakage and brain damage due to extended use of marijuana have been conflicting, but the majority suggest some neurological damage.

9. Decriminalization of marijuana is losing support in many states.

10. Whereas marijuana causes sexual dysfunction with some persons, it acts as a sexual stimulant with others.

11. In terms of national sales, marijuana is still one of the top ten big businesses in the United States, but the government is collecting no taxes on this commodity.

To organize these eleven paragraphs, we might group them into categories such as "medical" and "social" concerns, or we could classify them into "known effects" and "unknown effects," or into "psychological," "physiological," and "political" concerns. Which option we use depends on our way of viewing the subject and on our purpose and audience.

Consider how we might organize a paper on the effects of the 1986 fall of the Marcos dictatorship in the Philippines. After generating ideas on the topic, we might have dozens of effects—so many in fact that we would need some way of arranging them. Probably we would group them into major classes, and although our emphasis would be on effects, the effects would be arranged according to classification and division:

I. Effects on the Philippines
   A. Political
   B. Economic
   C. Military
   D. Social
II. Effects on the United States
   A. Political
   B. Military
III. Effects on other Asian nations

In a discussion so complex that readers need to have it divided into parts for ease of comprehension, classification and division are a means of achieving that clarity. For instance, to help readers easily understand the complicated process of listening to music, the composer Aaron Copland divides his discussion of listening to music into parts:

We all listen to music according to our separate capacities. But, for the sake of analysis, the whole listening process may become clearer if we break it up into its component parts, so to speak. In a certain sense we all listen to music on three separate planes. For lack of a better terminology, one might name these: (1) the sensuous plane, (2) the expressive plane, (3) the sheerly musical plane. The only advantage to be gained from mechanically splitting up the listening process into these hypothetical planes is the clearer view to be had of the way in which we listen.

—From *What to Listen for in Music*

4. For Offering an Original Perception

Sometimes our purpose in writing a classification/division paper is to offer a fresh view of the classes within a subject. In such cases, the naming of the classes is important because the names attract the reader's attention and reflect our perception. For example, in the following excerpt males are divided into two classes:

A psychologist friend in southern California has cleared the matter up, as far as he is concerned, by dividing the world's males into "Samurai" and "Wimps." The definitions came to him one day at the zoo while he was watching the baboons. He noticed that the females were busy doing all sorts of things: poking mysterious objects into their mouths, grooming each other, just sitting round, scratching, or whatever. Infants were tumbling about and chasing each other, and big males sat here and there or walked about on all fours, casting quick glances left and right. But in the midst of it all, not far from my friend, sat an enormous male, clearly the largest male in the troop. My friend noticed that the others approached the big male hesitantly and with great care, if they approached him at all, and that often two obsequious females would groom him at once. But the big male seemed to ignore it all and just sat there, like a great Buddha. My friend stood entranced by the whole scene until he was jarred to reality by the fact that the big male had turned and was looking at *him!* He reflexively gulped and looked away. In a flash he recovered himself. What is this?! He was a PhD, a psychologist at an excellent academic institution, a man of many publications, well-respected, formidable in seminars—and he had just been intimidated by a *baboon!* He decided then and there that the baboon was a Samurai and he was a Wimp. The baboon was "greater," even though he did not even have a book review to his credit.

When he told me the story, we had great fun defining the qualities of Samurai and Wimps. Samurai, we said, walked the earth with presence and abandon, took it stoically on the chin, gave as good as they got, could not be intimidated, were powerful and unafraid, and did everything with great authority (we took this last point to some rather indelicate ends). Wimps, on the other hand, were home on time, hoped not to offend anyone—particularly their wives—walked society's chalklines, and generally behaved like the men in TV commercials who are so concerned with clean collars, sparkling dishes, and the state of their cat's appetite.

But, we had to admit, not everyone fell neatly into one classification or the other. Because we were forced to admit independent variables and intermediates, we realized that we had actually constructed a graded barometer of manliness. Perhaps old Ted was afraid of his wife, but he was also a breathtaking stunt pilot. So old Ted wasn't entirely a Wimp. In spite of such problems, we sought to place each of our friends into his proper position on the Samurai Scale.

—From Robert A. Wallace, *The Genesis Factor*

These paragraphs combine classification/division with narration, definition, and comparison/contrast in order to flesh out the two classes.

1. What is the purpose of the long first paragraph?

2. Paragraph 2 contains two rather lengthy sentences, yet they are easy to read. How has Wallace achieved clarity in such long sentences?

3. What is the purpose of the last paragraph?

4. Point out the transitional markers that the writer uses to help readers move from one sentence to the next.

5. Wallace has defined the terms "Samurai" and "Wimps" only briefly. Is further development needed, or do you understand totally what the two classes of men are like? Explain.

5. For Argumentation

As with any mode of writing, classification and division can be used to argue a point. Our intent may be to persuade readers that the current system of classifying is wrong or distorted; for instance, we might wish to argue that although the government recognizes only two classes of small businesses, there are actually four, and that the misclassification discriminates against two types. Another intent might be to convince readers that one class is better than the others, as J. B. Priestley does in this essay:

WRONG ISM

J. B. Priestley

There are three isms that we ought to consider very carefully—regionalism, nationalism, internationalism. Of these three the one there is most fuss about, the one that starts men shouting and marching and shooting, the one that seems to have all the depth and thrust and fire, is of course nationalism. Nine people out of ten, I fancy, would say that of this trio it is the one that really counts, the big boss. Regionalism and internationalism, they would add, are comparatively small, shadowy, rather cranky. And I believe all this to be quite wrong. Like many another big boss, nationalism is largely bogus. It is like a bunch of flowers made of plastics.   1

The real flowers belong to regionalism. The mass of people everywhere may never have used the term. They are probably regionalists without knowing it. Because they have been brought up in a certain part of the world, they have formed perhaps quite unconsciously a deep attachment to its landscape and speech, its traditional customs, its food and drink, its songs and jokes. (There are of course always the rebels, often intellectuals and writers, but they are not the mass of people.) They are rooted in their region. Indeed, without this attachment a man can have no roots.   2

So much of people's lives, from earliest childhood onwards, is deeply intertwined with the common life of the region, they cannot help feeling strongly about it. A threat to it is a knife pointing at the heart. How can life ever be the same if bullying strangers come to change everything? The form and colour, the very taste and smell of dear familiar things will be different, alien, life-destroying. It would be better to die fighting. And it is precisely this, the nourishing life of the region, for which common men have so often fought and died.   3

This attachment to the region exists on a level far deeper than that of any political hocus-pocus. When a man says "my country" with real feeling, he is thinking about his region, all that has made up his life, and not about that political entity, the nation. There can be some confusion here simply because some countries are so small—and ours[1] is one of them—and so old, again like ours, that much of what is national is also regional. Down the centuries, the nation, itself so comparatively small, has been able to attach to itself the feeling really created by the region. (Even so there is something left over, as most people in Yorkshire or Devon, for example, would tell you.) This probably explains the fervent patriotism developed early in small countries.   4

[1]Priestley is British.

The English were announcing that they were English in the Middle Ages, before nationalism had arrived elsewhere.

If we deduct from nationalism all that it has borrowed or stolen from regionalism, what remains is mostly rubbish. The nation, as distinct from the region, is largely the creation of power-men and political manipulators. Almost all nationalist movements are led by ambitious frustrated men determined to hold office. I am not blaming them. I would do the same if I were in their place and wanted power so badly. But nearly always they make use of the rich warm regional feeling, the emotional dynamo of the movement, while being almost untouched by it themselves. This is because they are not as a rule deeply loyal to any region themselves. Ambition and a love of power can eat like acid into the tissues of regional loyalty. It is hard, if not impossible, to retain a natural piety and yet be for ever playing both ends against the middle.

Being itself a power structure, devised by men of power, the nation tends to think and act in terms of power. What would benefit the real life of the region, where men, women and children actually live, is soon sacrificed for the power and prestige of the nation. (And the personal vanity of presidents and ministers themselves, which historians too often disregard.) Among the new nations of our time innumerable peasants and labourers must have found themselves being cut down from five square meals a week to three in order to provide unnecessary airlines, military forces that can only be used against them and nobody else, great conference halls and official yachts and the rest. The last traces of imperialism and colonialism may have to be removed from Asia and Africa, where men can no longer endure being condemned to a permanent inferiority by the colour of their skins; but even so, the modern world, the real world of our time, does not want and would be far better without more and more nations, busy creating for themselves the very paraphernalia that western Europe is now trying to abolish. You are compelled to answer more questions when trying to spend half a day in Cambodia than you are now travelling from the Hook of Holland to Syracuse.

This brings me to internationalism. I dislike this term, which I used only to complete the isms. It suggests financiers and dubious promoters living nowhere but in luxury hotels; a shallow world of entrepreneurs and impresarios. (Was it Sacha Guitry who said that impresarios were men who spoke many languages but all with a foreign accent?) The internationalism I have in mind here is best described as world civilisation. It is life considered on a global scale. Most of our communications and transport already exist on this high wide level. So do many other things from medicine to meteorology. Our astronomers and physicists (except where they have allowed themselves to be hush-hushed) work here. The UN special agencies, about which we hear far too little, have contributed more and more to this world civilisation. All the arts, when they are arts and not chunks of nationalist propaganda, naturally take their place in it. And it grows, widens, deepens, in spite of the fact that for every dollar, ruble, pound or franc spent in explaining and praising it, a thousand are spent by the nations explaining and praising themselves.

This world civilisation and regionalism can get along together, especially if we keep ourselves sharply aware of their quite different but equally important values and rewards. A man can make his contribution to world civilisation and yet remain strongly regional in feeling: I know several men of this sort. There is of course the danger—it is with us now—of the global style flattening out the regional, taking local form, colour, flavour, away for ever, disinheriting future generations, threatening them with sensuous poverty and a huge boredom. But to understand and appreciate regionalism is to be on guard against this danger. And we must therefore make a clear distinction between regionalism and nationalism.

It is nationalism that tries to check the growth of world civilisation. And nationalism, when taken on a global scale, is more aggressive and demanding now than it has ever been before. This in the giant powers is largely disguised by the endless fuss in public about rival ideologies, now a largely unreal quarrel. What is intensely real is the glaring nationalism. Even the desire to police the world is nationalistic in origin. (Only the world can police the world.) Moreover, the nation-states of today are for the most part far narrower in their outlook, far more inclined to allow prejudice against the foreigner to impoverish their own style of living, than the old imperial states were. It should be part of world civilisation that men with particular skills, perhaps the product of the very regionalism they are rebelling against, should be able to move easily from country to country, to exercise those skills, in anything from teaching the violin to running a new type of factory to managing an old hotel. But nationalism, especially of the newer sort, would rather see everything done badly than allow a few nonnationals to get to work. And people face a barrage of passports, visas, immigration controls, labour permits; and in this respect are worse off than they were in 1900. But even so, in spite of all that nationalism can do—so long as it keeps its nuclear bombs to itself—the internationalism I have in mind, slowly creating a world civilisation, cannot be checked. 9

Nevertheless, we are still backing the wrong ism. Almost all our money goes on the middle one, nationalism, the rotten meat between the two healthy slices of bread. We need regionalism to give us roots and that very depth of feeling which nationalism unjustly and greedily claims for itself. We need internationalism to save the world and to broaden and heighten our civilisation. While regional man enriches the lives that international man is already working to keep secure and healthy, national man, drunk with power, demands our loyalty, money and applause, and poisons the very air with his dangerous nonsense. 10

—From *Essays of Five Decades*

1. In general, is Priestley's argument convincing? If so, what specifically convinced you? If not, why not?

2. Most arguments rely on facts and examples to substantiate the assertions. Has he offered evidence to substantiate his assertions? If so, give examples.

3. Does his argument that the nation is led by power-hungry individuals and therefore the nation is power-hungry seem logical? Are there ideals that transcend regionalism and are of a truly national nature?

4. Would you characterize Priestley's diction as formal, informal, or mixed? Substantiate your answer with examples.

5. What purposes does paragraph 1 achieve?

6. Why does he discuss regionalism first, nationalism next, and internationalism last? Why not arrange them differently?

7. How does he achieve transition between paragraphs 1 and 2? Between 2 and 3? Between 5 and 6? Between 7 and 8?

Principles of Classification and Division

When classifying and dividing a topic, we are mainly concerned with being clear and complete—that is, we want readers to understand what criterion we use to divide and classify and what our classes are, and we want those classes to cover all the items.

We can classify a topic in many ways, depending on our purpose. For example, we can classify automobiles according to their safety, cost, design, or size; we can classify literature by genre, historical period, style, or subject matter; and we can classify people by height, sex, race, income, profession, or region. Purpose will dictate the criterion. But whatever our purpose, we must have a natural, consistent, and intelligent basis for dividing and classifying, and we must indicate for our readers why we are classifying the topic in that way.

We should have one criterion and stick to it. For example, if we are classifying Western films, and our criterion is degree of violence, we should not switch in the middle of the paper and classify Western films in terms of budget or actors or settings. Our classes might be minimal violence, moderate violence, and excessive violence; under each heading we could discuss the characteristics of each type, give examples in films, cite directors who use violence, and distinguish each type from the other two classes.

APPLICATION

Here are some topics and the criteria that might be used to classify and divide them; for each subject, come up with a different criterion of your own:

Subject	*Criterion*
murders	motive
television comedies	type of humor
national news magazines	degree of objectivity in reporting
cities	cost of living
prehistoric humans	tools used
cigarette brands	level of tar and nicotine

Our classes should be distinct and should therefore not overlap. In other words, one item should not be able to fit into two classes. Dividing students into science majors, arts majors, social science majors, foreign students, and humanities majors is confusing because the categories overlap: Foreign students also fit one of the majors. Likewise, classifying employees in a company into laborers, technicians, executives, secretaries, and women violates the separateness of the categories because women can belong in any of the other categories.

Another principle is that the classes must be comprehensive; every item being classified must fall into one class or another. Classifying music, for instance, into classical, rock, and folk is an incomplete classification since it omits country, jazz, and pop. Occasionally we discover that a few individual items fall into no class, and they have little in common with each other so they do not form a class by themselves. In such cases, we can make an additional category for them labelled "Miscellaneous," but we should do this only as a last resort.

In addition to being aware of the logical principles involved in classifying and dividing, we should also be aware that classifications sometimes change. As we learn more about the world and about our own species, old classifications sometimes become obsolete. In the second century A.D., for example, the famed physiologist Galen classified human personalities according to the predominance of a bodily fluid—blood, phlegm, yellow bile, black bile—so that a person having too much blood was classified as sanguine; too much yellow bile, choleric; phlegm, phlegmatic; and black bile, melancholic. After the fluids theory was disproved, personalities were classified according to body types—ectomorphic, mesomorphic, and endomorphic—each body type indicating certain psychological characteristics; now even that classification is obsolete. Similarly, the old system of classifying living things into plants and animals is gradually being replaced by a five-kingdom classification: (1) bacteria and viruses, (2) protozoa and algae, (3) fungi, (4) plants, and (5) animals. The problem with the old system was that the criteria caused overlapping. Plants were defined as being immobile and containing chlorophyll, but some algae, which are mobile, contain chlorophyll. The classes were not separate and distinct. A third example is the division of humankind into three races—Caucasian, Mongoloid, and Negroid. This division is based on skin color alone and disregards other genetic characteristics. Where do American Indians, Australian aborigines, or Polynesians fit into these divisions? Today, therefore, anthropologists use additional racial criteria, such as blood components, amino acid excretion, tooth shape and size, skeletal characteristics, urine analysis, color perception, and even texture of ear wax. Based on these criteria, nine genetic races can be distinguished instead of the previous three.

Organizing a Classification and Division Essay

Organizing a classification and division essay should pose little difficulty because each class is a block of one or more paragraphs. Our essay will usually take this form:

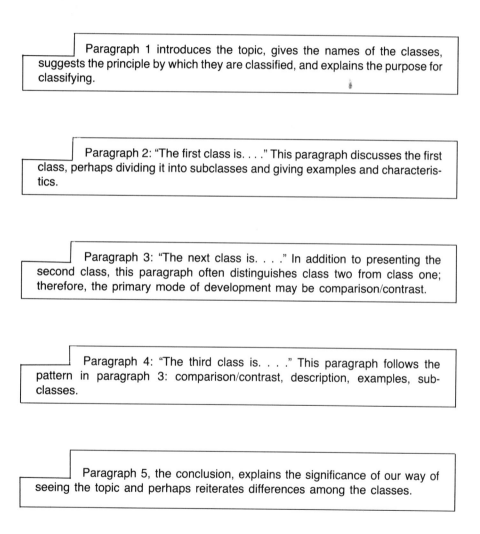

Paragraph 1 introduces the topic, gives the names of the classes, suggests the principle by which they are classified, and explains the purpose for classifying.

Paragraph 2: "The first class is. . . ." This paragraph discusses the first class, perhaps dividing it into subclasses and giving examples and characteristics.

Paragraph 3: "The next class is. . . ." In addition to presenting the second class, this paragraph often distinguishes class two from class one; therefore, the primary mode of development may be comparison/contrast.

Paragraph 4: "The third class is. . . ." This paragraph follows the pattern in paragraph 3: comparison/contrast, description, examples, subclasses.

Paragraph 5, the conclusion, explains the significance of our way of seeing the topic and perhaps reiterates differences among the classes.

Of course, more than one paragraph may be devoted to each class, with subclasses deserving separate development, but the basic structure is the same. The typical structure is enumerative—one, two, three, four—as in this excerpt from "A Few Kind Words for Superstition":

Few people will admit to being superstitious; it implies naïveté or ignorance. But I live in the middle of a large university, and I see superstition in its four manifestations, alive and flourishing among people who are indisputably rational and learned.

You did not know that superstition takes four forms? Theologians assure us that it does. First is what they call Vain Observances, such as not walking under a ladder, and that kind of thing. Yet I saw a deeply learned professor of anthropology, who had spilled some salt, throwing a pinch of it over his left shoulder; when I asked him why, he replied, with a wink, that it was "to hit the Devil in the eye." I did not question him further about his belief in the Devil: but I noticed that he did not smile until I asked him what he was doing.

The second form is Divination, or consulting oracles. Another learned professor I know, who would scorn to settle a problem by tossing a coin (which is a humble appeal to Fate to declare itself), told me quite seriously that he had resolved a matter related to university affairs by consulting the *I Ching*. And why not? There are thousands of people on this continent who appeal to the I Ching, and their general level of education seems to absolve them of superstition. Almost, but not quite. The I Ching, to the embarrassment of rationalists, often gives excellent advice.

The third form is Idolatry, and universities can show plenty of that. If you have ever supervised a large examination room, you know how many jujus, lucky coins and other bringers of luck are placed on the desks of the candidates. Modest idolatry, but what else can you call it?

The fourth form is Improper Worship of the True God. A while ago, I learned that every day, for several days, a $2 bill . . . had been tucked under a candlestick on the altar of a college chapel. Investigation revealed that an engineering student, worried about a girl, thought that bribery of the Deity might help. When I talked with him, he did not think he was pricing God cheap, because he could afford no more. A reasonable argument, but perhaps God was proud that week, for the scientific oracle went against him.

—From Robertson Davies, *Newsweek*, Nov. 20, 1978

Each paragraph presents a superstition, labels it, and develops it with anecdote, example, and description. Does it matter which superstition comes first, which second, third, and so forth?

Usually we arrange the classes according to importance, from least to most significant. For example, in the following excerpt, Samuel Johnson warns of three types of persons who are jealous of others' accomplishments, and he arranges them from least to most dangerous. (Johnson's eighteenth-century essay uses such formal diction that many words may not be familiar to you; perhaps you should read it with a dictionary at your side.)

ROARERS, WHISPERERS, AND MODERATORS

<table>
<tr>
<td>

Sets the stage: the person of distinction versus envious cowards who attack without cause

</td>
<td>

When any man has endeavoured to deserve distinction, he will be surprised to hear himself censured where he could not expect to have been named; he will find the utmost acrimony of malice among those whom he never could have offended. . . .

</td>
<td>1</td>
</tr>
<tr>
<td>

Comparison: just as we can classify stinging insects, we can classify slanderers, who are also pests

Labels the classes and gives the order in which they will be presented

The first type: Roarer

</td>
<td>

As the industry of observation has divided the most miscellaneous and confused assemblages into proper classes, and ranged the insects of the summer, that torment us with their drones or stings, by their several tribes; the persecutors of merit, notwithstanding their numbers, may be likewise commodiously distinguished into Roarers, Whisperers, and Moderators.

</td>
<td>2</td>
</tr>
<tr>
<td>

Characterized as loud but not dangerous

Development by description

Roarer's method of spreading vile rumors is described

Examples of the Roarer's abusive attacks

Effect of Roarer's malice: little, if any, harm

</td>
<td>

The Roarer is an enemy rather terrible than dangerous. He has no other qualification for a champion of controversy than a hardened front and strong voice. Having seldom so much desire to confute as to silence, he depends rather upon vociferation than argument, and has very little care to adjust one part of his accusation to another, to preserve decency in his language, or probability in his narratives. He has always a store of reproachful epithets and contemptuous appellations, ready to be produced as occasion may require, which by constant use he pours out with resistless volubility. If the wealth of a trader is mentioned, he without hesitation devotes him to bankruptcy; if the beauty and elegance of a lady be commended, he wonders how the town can fall in love with rustick deformity; if a new performance of genius happens to be celebrated, he pronounces the writer a hopeless ideot, without knowledge of books or life, and without the understanding by which it must be acquired. His exaggerations are generally without effect upon those whom he compels to hear them; and though it will sometimes happen that the timorous are awed by his violence, and the credulous mistake his confidence for knowledge, yet the opinions which he endeavours to suppress soon recover their former strength, as the trees that bend to the tempest erect themselves again when its force is past.

</td>
<td>3</td>
</tr>
<tr>
<td>

Concludes with simile

The second type: Whisperer

Characterized as "more dangerous"

Whisperer's method is described

</td>
<td>

The Whisperer is more dangerous. He easily gains attention by a soft address, and excites curiosity by an air of importance. As secrets are not to be made cheap by promiscuous publication, he calls a select audience about him, and gratifies their vanity with an appearance of trust by communicating his intelligence in a low voice. Of the trader he can tell that though he seems to manage an extensive commerce, and talks in high terms of the funds, yet his wealth is not equal to his reputation;

</td>
<td>4</td>
</tr>
</table>

Same examples are used as in previous paragraph, but applying Whisperer's technique

he has lately suffered much by an expensive project, and had a greater share than is acknowledged in the rich ship that perished by the storm. Of the beauty he has little to say, but that they who see her in a morning do not discover all these graces which are admired in the park. Of the writer he affirms with great certainty, that though the excellence of the work be incontestable, he can claim but a small part of the reputation; that he owed most of the images and sentiments to a secret friend; and that the accuracy and equality of the stile was produced by the successive correction of the chief criticks of the age.

As every one is pleased with imagining that he knows   5
something not yet commonly divulged, secret history easily gains credit; but it is for the most part believed only while it circulates in whispers, and when once it is openly told, is openly confuted.

Effect of Whisperer's malice: temporary harm

The third type: Moderator

Characterized as "most pernicious"

The most pernicious enemy is the man of Moderation.   6
Without interest in the question, or any motive but honest curiosity, this impartial and zealous enquirer after truth, is ready to hear either side, and always disposed to kind interpretations and favourable opinions. He has heard the trader's affairs reported with great variation, and after a diligent comparison of the evidence, concludes it probable that the splendid superstructure of business being originally built upon a narrow basis, has lately been found to totter; but between dilatory payment and bankruptcy there is a great distance; many merchants have supported themselves by expedients for a time, without any final injury to their creditors; and what is lost by one adventure may be recovered by another. He believes that a young lady pleased with admiration, and desirous to make perfect what is already excellent, may heighten her charms by artificial improvements, but surely most of her beauties must be genuine, and who can say that he is wholly what he endeavours to appear? The author he knows to be a man of diligence, who perhaps does not sparkle with the fire of *Homer,* but has the judgment to discover his own deficiencies, and to supply them by the help of others; and in his opinion modesty is a quality so amiable and rare, that it ought to find a patron wherever it appears, and may justly be preferred by the publick suffrage to petulant wit and ostentatious literature.

Moderator's method is described

Same examples as in other two paragraphs, but applying Moderator's technique

Effect of Moderator's malice: convincing and lasting harm

He who thus discovers failings with unwillingness, and   7
extenuates the faults which cannot be denied, puts an end at once to doubt or vindication; his hearers repose upon his candour and veracity, and admit the charge without allowing the excuse.

The reason for the slanderers' malice: envy

Such are the arts by which the envious, the idle, the   8
peevish, and the thoughtless, obstruct that worth which they
cannot equal, and by artifices thus easy, sordid, and detestable,
is industry defeated, beauty blasted, and genius depressed.

—From *The Rambler*, No. 144

1. Why does Johnson use a similar structure in describing each slanderer, and why does he use the same examples of the trader, beauty, and writer? Does this parallel development become monotonous, or does it contribute to our understanding of the differences among the three classes of slanderers? Explain your opinion.

2. Explain the Moderator's method, and tell why it is more insidious than that of the other two types.

3. Following Johnson's lead, divide one of these subjects into three classes, label them, and arrange them from least to worst type.

cheaters	bullies
liars	skeptics
ingrates	lechers

Advice, Warnings, Reminders

1. You must have an intelligent purpose for classifying and dividing a topic. For example, biologists classify humankind into races in order to study the sources of such genetic diseases as sickle-cell anemia and to study genetic changes and adaptations.

2. You can generate interest in a classification/division essay by selecting an unusual (but genuine) criterion. Consider, for instance, all of the bars you've been to. Although each was different, you could nevertheless discern three or four *types* of bars, and if you thought about them long enough you could come up with an interesting angle. Personally, I divide bars into two types: those that serve mayonnaise, and those that don't. I won't frequent a bar that serves the stuff.

3. Another way to generate interest is to give memorable labels to your classes. The labels you use are important because they reflect your attitude toward the topic and they are what readers will remember most prominently about your essay (such as Samurais and Wimps or Roarers, Whisperers, and Moderators). Be imaginative in your choice of headings, whether you are classifying librarians, underwear, or walking styles.

4. You have considerable opportunity for humor in this assignment, either by the labels you use, your attitude toward the material (as in the Lebowitz essay that follows), or by *intentional* overlapping (e.g., dividing college band members into music majors, nonmajors, and drummers, or dividing kinds of intelligence into animal, human, and military).

5. In our zeal for classifying ideas, objects, and persons, we must not ignore the uniqueness of the individual. We must be aware that although classes serve a purpose, they also disregard variations within the group and emphasize similarities. In other words, we should guard against stereotyping and pigeonholing.

6. One pitfall consists in dividing a subject into only two classes, so that an item must fit into one or the other, when in fact a third option exists. This is the fallacy of incomplete classification, sometimes called an "either/or" fallacy in argument. "You are either for us or against us" ignores the possibility of remaining neutral or indifferent. Consider these examples:

> Life is either a bed of roses or a path of thorns.
> Reading is either a means of escape or a means of arrival.
> Prisons are either for punishment or for rehabilitation.
> Men are either husbands or lovers.

What is wrong with those statements?
Some either/or statements, however, are real:

> A woman is either pregnant or not pregnant.
> Organizations are either profit or nonprofit.

Exercises

1. Divide these subjects and then subdivide your divisions:
   A. governments
   B. birds
   C. boats
   D. vacations

2. Place these individuals into classifications:
   A. Emily Dickinson, George Bernard Shaw, Rembrandt, Anna Pavlova, John Donne, Mozart, Twyla Tharp, Tennessee Williams, Vivaldi, William Faulkner, Picasso, Leonardo da Vinci, Mary Cassatt, Virginia Woolf, Baryshnikov, Renoir, Tolstoy, Isadora Duncan, Tchaikovsky, Nijinski, Shakespeare, Martha Graham, Whistler, Mark Twain, Jane Austen, Bach, Chaucer, Molière, Milton, Joan Didion, Lillian Hellman.

B. Skylark, Monte Carlo, Le Car, Vega, Rambler, Corolla, Hornet, Grand Prix, Malibu, Cutlass, Duster, Valiant, Civic, Maverick, Pinto, Stutz Bearcat, El Camino, Cordoba, Mustang, Nova, Dart, Edsel, Corvette, LTD, RX-7, TR3, LeMans, Cougar, Toronada, Camaro, Celica, Capri.

C. Southdown, Berkshire, razorback, basset, German shepherd, Angus, Persian, Doberman, Charolais, Siamese, English setter, duroc, guernsey, Appaloosa, leghorn, Clydesdale, Pekinese, Angora, Plymouth Rock, Morgan, Hampshire, holstein, Rhode Island Red, Tennessee walker, Santa Gertrudis, bantam, dorset

3. List the types of:
   A. politicians
   B. television comedies
   C. jeans
   D. wars

4. Make a diagram like the transportation diagram on page 228 on two of these topics, making at least four levels of the diagram. Bring your diagrams to class and compare them with others on the same topics. Formulate a thesis statement for one of your narrowed topics.
   A. sports
   B. music
   C. food
   D. communication
   E. fabrics
   F. healers

5. Types of people:
   A. Classify the people in your dormitory, neighborhood, or apartment building into several types.
   B. Classify current film actresses.

6. What, if anything, is wrong with each of the following classifications? In each instance, you must decide (1) what the criterion is, (2) whether the classes are complete, and (3) whether the classes are distinct and separate.

Subject	Classes
religions	Christianity, Buddhism, Judaism
musical instruments	winds, strings, horns, percussion
children	ill-behaved, worse-behaved
televisions	portable, black-and-white, color, 3D
working dogs	seeing-eye dogs, hunting dogs, watchdogs, herding dogs
daydreaming	productive, nonproductive

Subject	*Classes*
plants	algae, ferns, flowers, fungi, grains, grass, herbs, moss, shrub, trees, vines, weeds
deceptions	those intended to help the deceived party, those intended to harm others
freedom	internal, external
boots	Hessian boots, hip boots, ski boots, Wellington boots, half boots
sweaters	pullovers, turtlenecks, cardigans, V-necks
airplanes	gliders, biplanes, jets, hydroplanes
reds	crimson, scarlet, puce, claret
gems	precious, semiprecious
movies	horror, Western, foreign, romantic, comedy, musical
people	left-handed, right-handed

7. Write an outline for a classification/division essay on one of these topics:

jokes	teachers
eccentricities	sidekicks of Western stars
dates	thinking
escapes	boots

Suggested Writing Assignments

Write a classification and division essay either on the topic you outlined or on one of the following topics:

salespersons	marriages	discoveries
cowardice	disobedience	cunning
mental slowness	spectators	dullness
flattery	conformity	collectors
power	deviation	laughs
men who go to gyms	snobs	mothers
cabbies	rock music	fathers
women who go to gyms	male ballet stars	newscasters
Cary Grant movies	smiles	dentists
Western movies	test-takers	joggers
sports cars	retirees	vacations
female comedians	exaggeration	gifts
drivers	sci-fi movies	gum

Additional Readings

NICE GIRLS DON'T TWIRL BATONS

Laura King (first-year student)

I remember being six, driven off to ballet lessons on cold Thursday evenings after   1
school. The pink tights I can still feel as they scraped leg against leg; pink slippers
scuffed precisely over the dirty tile floor of the studio. And Madame Blake, the stern,
grey-sweatered instructor somehow melded in my mind with the arthritic feel of winter
blowing up under my coat as I ran from the car into the dance class. Stiffly, she
instructed us and disciplined racing minds and bodies fresh from free-form snow
angels.

Then there was Vicki Shubeck who learned to twirl a baton on bright Saturdays   2
at the high school. I would see her skipping down the sidewalk, her glittering baton
over her shoulder like a not-too-benevolent royal scepter. Sometimes stopping by the
marble-shooters' favorite sewer top, she flipped that stick in a whirl of color over her
head and caught it in one hand, shining. She marched in the Memorial Day Parade
wearing white boots, twirling her baton—a handful of fireworks.

"Baton is silly," my mother scoffed disdainfully. "Ballet lessons are for nice girls."   3

So Vicki and the rest of the sequined marchers in the parade became the local   4
sleazes by virtue of their Saturday baton lessons while we, the Thursday evening
ballerinas, occupied a station in life somewhere near princesses and eighth graders.

When I was in fourth grade, my mother presented me with a second-hand flute   5
and the proposition that I should learn music. Sitting on a wobbly, wooden chair
among the clutter of the stage in the All-Purpose Room, I took flute lessons. The
instructor was a weasel in glasses with a moustache who tapped my music stand
impatiently to let me know each time I had played the wrong note. His preoccupation
with the chastisement made me too nervous to express myself through beautiful
music. Moved to the periphery of the group, I became an avid music listener. But from
my observer's position in the class, I began to notice that the musically competent
students, the ones who licked their reeds so assuredly, were the ones who got picked
last for kickball, or were in the worst reading group, or didn't watch Batman. I decided,
at the age of nine, that this was just not the image I wanted to project. So I quit my flute
lessons and with two other girls took up Wendy Ward modeling classes.

As Wendy Ward girls we felt entitled to occupy our own private lunch table in   6
order to discuss upcoming fashion shows. Over peanut butter sandwiches and
Cheetos we made detailed plans to become movie stars and to drape ourselves

across the decks of yachts. The modeling classes themselves were boring. We sat in rows and listened to several Max-Factored women tell us that our beauty regimens were more important than our homework. Yawning through, we stayed simply for the prestige of having various boys inscribe our initials on the wall of the coatroom.

There were many lessons I saw only from the outside, like Cheryl Horner's   7 sewing classes that somehow conjured up images of her, aproned and motherly. Roller skating and ice skating were for the elite and very elite, respectively. Denise, who went to her ice skating class on Monday nights, practically glowed with celebrity. Tim Magruder took singing lessons and embarrassed everyone with his operatic rendition of the morning National Anthem while Larry Zachary threw spit balls at him, to everyone's satisfaction. A short stint with hula lessons brought Karen a passionate, if fleeting, popularity with the boys. I remember a particular group of her admirers who used to whisper feverishly about how hula dancers probably didn't wear anything under their grass skirts. Finding a picture drawn of herself on the blackboard, Karen abandoned her hula lessons in a rage of humiliation.

So we created images for ourselves, voluntarily or not, with our lessons. Lying   8 in bed at night, I was bouncing off to the car in my ice skating skirt or seen slipping into the basement where hula was taught. Just recently in a quiet moment of empty identity, I dug out my dust-creased ballet shoes from the bottom of a trunk. Small and pink, they took me right back to Madame Blake's classroom where the cocked blinds had staved off winter sunshine and I had strained to achieve a perfect point of the toes. But even stronger than that memory is the still rebellious desire to have been a sleazy baton twirler in the gaudy sunshine of the Memorial Day Parade. Here in my head like spilled glitter are the sparkling six-year-old Saturdays that will never fade.

1. Is the point of view that of Laura the child, Laura the college student, or a combination?

2. How would you describe her tone?

3. What structure does she use?

4. Is this essay basically one of classification or of division?

5. What role does light or absence of light play in the essay?

THE SOUND OF MUSIC: ENOUGH ALREADY

Fran Lebowitz

First off, I want to say that as far as I am concerned, in instances where I have not personally and deliberately sought it out, the only difference between music and Muzak is the spelling. Pablo Casals practicing across the hall with the door open— being trapped in an elevator, the ceiling of which is broadcasting "Parsley, Sage,

Rosemary, and Thyme"—it's all the same to me. Harsh words? Perhaps. But then again these are not gentle times we live in. And they are being made no more gentle by this incessant melody that was once real life.

There was a time when music knew its place. No longer. Possibly this is not music's fault. It may be that music fell in with a bad crowd and lost its sense of common decency. I am willing to consider this. I am willing even to try and help. I would like to do my bit to set music straight in order that it might shape up and leave the mainstream of society. The first thing that music must understand is that there are two kinds of music—good music and bad music. Good music is music that I want to hear. Bad music is music that I don't want to hear.

So that music might more clearly see the error of its ways I offer the following. If you are music and you recognize yourself on this list, you are bad music.

1. MUSIC IN OTHER PEOPLE'S CLOCK RADIOS

There are times when I find myself spending the night in the home of another. Frequently the other is in a more reasonable line of work than I and must arise at a specific hour. Ofttimes the other, unbeknownst to me, manipulates an appliance in such a way that I am awakened by Stevie Wonder. On such occasions I announce that if I wished to be awakened by Stevie Wonder I would sleep with Stevie Wonder. I do not, however, wish to be awakened by Stevie Wonder and that is why God invented alarm clocks. Sometimes the other realizes that I am right. Sometimes the other does not. And that is why God invented *many* others.

2. MUSIC RESIDING IN THE HOLD BUTTONS OF OTHER PEOPLE'S BUSINESS TELEPHONES

I do not under any circumstances enjoy hold buttons. But I am a woman of reason. I can accept reality. I can face the facts. What I cannot face is the music. Just as there are two kinds of music—good and bad—so there are two kinds of hold buttons—good and bad. Good hold buttons are hold buttons that hold one silently. Bad hold buttons are hold buttons that hold one musically. When I hold I want to hold silently. That is the way it was meant to be, for that is what God was talking about when he said, "Forever hold your peace." He would have added, "and quiet," but he thought you were smarter.

3. MUSIC IN THE STREETS

The past few years have seen a steady increase in the number of people playing music in the streets. The past few years have also seen a steady increase in the number of malignant diseases. Are these two facts related? One wonders. But even if they are not—and, as I have pointed out, one cannot be sure—music in the streets has definitely taken its toll. For it is at the very least disorienting. When one is walking down Fifth Avenue, one does not expect to hear a string quartet playing a Strauss waltz. What one expects to hear while walking down Fifth Avenue is traffic. When one does indeed hear a string quartet playing a Strauss waltz while one is walking down Fifth Avenue, one is apt to become confused and imagine that one is not walking down Fifth Avenue at all but rather that one has somehow wound up in Old Vienna. Should one imagine that one is in Old Vienna one is likely to become quite upset when one realizes that in Old Vienna there is no sale at Charles Jourdan. And that is why when I walk down Fifth Avenue I want to hear traffic.

4. MUSIC IN THE MOVIES

I'm not talking about musicals. Musicals are movies that warn you by saying, "Lots of music here. Take it or leave it." I'm talking about regular movies that extend no such courtesy but allow unsuspecting people to come to see them and then assault them with a barrage of unasked-for tunes. There are two major offenders in this category: black movies and movies set in the fifties. Both types of movies are afflicted with the same misconception. They don't know that movies are supposed to be movies. They think that movies are supposed to be records with pictures. They have failed to understand that if God had wanted records to have pictures, he would not have invented television.

5. MUSIC IN PUBLIC PLACES SUCH AS RESTAURANTS, SUPERMARKETS, HOTEL LOBBIES, AIRPORTS, ETC.

When I am in any of the above-mentioned places I am not there to hear music. I am there for whatever reason is appropriate to the respective place. I am no more interested in hearing "Mack the Knife" while waiting for the shuttle to Boston than someone sitting ringside at the Sands Hotel is interested in being forced to choose between sixteen varieties of cottage cheese. If God had meant for everything to happen at once, he would not have invented desk calendars.

EPILOGUE

Some people talk to themselves. Some people sing to themselves. Is one group better than the other? Did not God create all people equal? Yes, God created all people equal. Only to some he gave the ability to make up their own words.

—From *Metropolitan Life*

1. People react differently to Lebowitz's acid wit. Some find her irreverence funny, and others find it abrasive. What is your reaction? Explain why you react as you do (that is, why you find it funny or offensive).

2. Describe her tone, and use examples from the essay to illustrate your generalizations.

3. What criterion does Lebowitz apply to the classes of bad music?

4. Does the humor in each paragraph occur mainly at the beginning, the middle, or the end of the paragraph? Why?

5. Write a sixth example of bad music for Lebowitz's essay.

CHAPTER 8

Process Analysis

Process writing explains how something is done, such as baking a German chocolate cake or making a neutron bomb. It is utilitarian writing that tells readers either how to do something or how something complicated works; it gives either directions or explanations.

Without directions from someone with greater experience, we would have to undergo a trial-and-error method to learn procedures, gaining expertise the inefficient way, through experience. By providing directions to a novice, an experienced person passes along knowledge and thereby eliminates much unnecessary experimentation. The transference of practical knowledge from one generation to another keeps techniques alive and allows the next generation to build on that knowledge, instead of wasting energy by continually reinventing the wheel. Process writing is also a means of sharing: We lend our expertise in one area, and we draw from others' expertise in other areas.

Much of our education, informal as well as formal, involves imparting practical knowledge through directions. A grandparent shows how to build a birdhouse, a construction crew leader demonstrates how to build forms for a concrete foundation, and a professor explains how to locate oceanic oil, how to develop color film, how to write a research paper, or how to design a dam.

Audience

When writing directions of any sort, we must know our audience so that we can determine how much explanation and detail are needed. If we are writing a service manual for airplane mechanics, we may assume that they have a certain level of knowledge about the subject, tools, and general procedure; if we are providing directions for Harry Homeowner to install a microwave oven, we must assume another level of knowledge and competence. The best policy is to assume that lay readers have little technical understanding, and therefore we must make our directions absolutely clear.

From having read hundreds of directions, though, you have no doubt noticed that most of them are impossible to follow because they take too much for granted and are imprecise. When you take home from a department store a carton marked "Easy Assembly," you get the queasy feeling that piecing together the scattered parts will take three times as long as it should because of inane directions. For example, someone I know well, a reasonably intelligent fellow but slightly ignorant of mechanical contraptions, was snared one December 25th into putting together a glass-and-brass fireplace screen, a seemingly simple task. Although the "Easy-to-assemble directions" included diagrams and some details, this person could not properly erect the kit in the allotted 2 hours. The trouble was that there were 57 parts, including 32 screws. The directions said "Attach the pressure jaws with set screws." (What's a set screw?) "Fasten the slide frames with round screws." (What's the difference between a set screw, a sheet metal screw, a round head screw, and a pan head screw?) After a process of elimination, he successfully filled in all the holes with screws, but probably not the right ones. Then the final direction said "Secure the screen into the fireplace opening." (Secure how? With crazy glue? Bore a hole into the brick?) Whoever wrote the directions obviously aimed for an audience with a better knowledge of securing and screwing than my friend had, yet I daresay that, incompetent as he is in these areas, others had equal difficulty because the directions left out vital information.

Many men have the same trouble with cookbooks, which are usually written for persons who already know how to cook, or at least for persons with enough experience to understand basic terms and procedures. Many of us know little about preparing food, and therefore whenever we try to break away from our frozen-dinner routine, we encounter recipes that assume a level of competence far beyond our own. They direct us to "beat the egg whites till stiff but not dry," "fold them into the batter," and "pour into a flan ring"; the recipes contain such words as *coddle, sauté, dredge, score, steep, bruise, frizzle,* and *roux.* Defeated by the cookbook's jargon and our own ignorance, most of us wander back to the frozen-food aisle. A similar situation exists with women who have had little chance to acquire traditionally masculine skills. *The New York Times Guide to Home Repairs Without a Man,* obviously addressed to a female audience, assumes that its readers have limited experience with tools and materials, and therefore it is careful to define terms and explain general procedures that might be unnecessary for a male audience.

The following example explains to a lay audience a technically sophisticated procedure—landing astronauts on the moon. To an aeronautics engineer, the explanation would be an oversimplication because it omits details, substitutes common vocabulary for technical language, and streamlines the whole process. But the explanation is meant to be elementary: It is intended not for engineers but for persons like you and me, persons who are curious but unknowledgeable. Where in this explanation do the authors omit details in favor of generalization to keep from confusing readers with technical operations?

LANDING THE FIRST MEN ON THE MOON

Landing a space vehicle on a celestial body devoid of atmosphere, such as the moon, presents special technical problems of braking the vehicle's descent and accurately controlling the braking action. The conditions of entry are different from those presented by a major planet enveloped in a relatively dense atmosphere. For a moon landing the entire kinetic energy of the vehicle must be braked by a counteracting thrust developed by rockets.   1

On arrival in the vicinity of the moon, the spacecraft is first slowed down by firing its retro-rocket motors, so that it goes into a circular parking orbit round the moon. This applies more particularly to a manned spacecraft such as the Apollo which the Americans have used for landing men on the moon. In the case of the Apollo XI project the actual descent onto the moon's surface was made by two astronauts in a special mooncraft, the "lunar (excursion) module" (abbreviated as "LEM" or "LM"), which was detached from the orbiting spacecraft, in which one astronaut remained awaiting the return of the mooncraft.   2

The entire procedure of releasing the mooncraft, landing it at a predetermined site on the moon and then linking it once again to the spacecraft is one which requires precise control of the direction and velocity of both vehicles. When the spacecraft is accurately in orbit and in the correct position on its orbit to ensure a landing in the desired area, the mooncraft briefly fires its rocket motor so that it moves away from the spacecraft and goes into an elliptical orbit whose point nearest the moon is located some 10 to 20 miles before and six or seven miles above the planned landing area. The periodic time of the mooncraft in this elliptical orbit must be the same as that of the spacecraft in its circular parking orbit. This particular requirement is for the astronauts' safety: should the landing rockets fail to fire, the mooncraft will simply continue in orbit and automatically encounter the spacecraft: the latter can then be maneuvered into a docking position with the mooncraft, so that the two astronauts in it can return to the spacecraft that will take them back to earth.   3

When the mooncraft is in the correct position in its orbit, the actual landing maneuver can commence. The landing rocket motor of the mooncraft must be able to develop a thrust that can be suitably varied, because at the start of the landing operation the craft still carries its full load of rocket fuel, and its speed has to be slowed down from about 5000 mph to zero. In doing this, fuel corresponding to about two-thirds of the mooncraft's initial total weight (with full tanks) is consumed. The power and direction of the thrust developed by the motor are so controlled that the   4 craft lands at a predetermined point and at a predetermined speed. If the orbit in which the mooncraft is moving around the moon deviates a little from the specified orbit, corrections can be made by means of small steering rocket jets. In this way the horizontal and the vertical speed in relation to the landing area are reduced. When the horizontal speed has diminished to zero, the mooncraft will slowly sink towards the surface, the actual speed being kept under control by means of retroactive rocket motor thrust. By this time the astronauts have taken over manual control of the mooncraft. Scanning the lunar surface from an altitude of several hundred feet, they select a zone free from boulders, deep cracks or other hazards and then bring their craft gently down. The final operation calls for very accurate control of the thrust so that it almost exactly balances the mooncraft's weight. When the feet of the craft touch the surface, the motors are shut off.

On completion of their exploration of the lunar surface, the astronauts return to   5 their mooncraft. The lower half of the craft serves as a launching pad for the upper half, which is provided with a second, smaller rocket motor just under the crew cabin. This motor propels the ascent stage of the mooncraft back to the spacecraft, which will rendezvous and dock with it. The lunar astronauts then transfer to the spacecraft and jettison the mooncraft; the return flight to earth then begins.

—From *The Way Things Work*, Vol. II

From this five-paragraph explanation, we understand the basic steps involved in landing astronauts on the moon because the authors have clearly and succinctly outlined them. Fortunately for us, they realize that the kind and amount of detail permissible depend on their audience, and therefore they have dispensed with complex scientific theories and descriptions in favor of concentrating on the major steps.

Organizing a Process Essay

A common characteristic of process papers is that they involve a series of steps. In fact, the word *process* comes from the Latin prefix *pro*, meaning forward, and the noun *cessus*, meaning movement or steps. When describing a process, we move forward in time: first this step, then this, then another step, and so on until the process is complete. This arrangement, with material organized according to a time sequence, is chronological, which we have already encountered in narrative writing.

Look again at the lunar landing example and notice the chronological order. First the rocket is slowed down, next the lunar module is launched, then the landing rockets are fired, and so forth. Each step must occur in the correct order; otherwise, the whole mission fails, and the astronauts might be left orbiting the moon or drifting in space. Likewise, if we add melted chocolate to egg whites before beating the egg whites, we will end up with a concoction much different from chocolate mousse. Readers not only must be given the information in the correct order, but also must clearly understand one step before we present the next one because each step relies on the previous one; readers cannot comprehend step 4 if they do not understand step 3.

As an aid to arrangement on the writer's part, and as an aid to understanding on the reader's part, we should try to mark off our process into three or four stages, each consisting of several steps. For example, the lunar landing consists of perhaps eight steps, but the writers group them into phases: "releasing the mooncraft, landing it at a predetermined site on the moon and then linking it once again to the spacecraft." Dividing the process into stages avoids the monotonous "then, and then, and then" approach, and it gives emphasis to the major sections. Furthermore, readers come away with a sense of a pronounced structure instead of a series of unmemorable steps.

Another aid in process writing is outlining, which can help prevent us from omitting steps and help us to see major divisions in the process. Unlike with some writing in which we are trying to discover content as we compose, with process writing we must already know the process and the steps. If we cannot outline the paper before we start writing, we cannot write the paper.

In fact, because of their "recipe" nature, process papers sometimes take the form of an outline or a list. The serial actions of a process naturally fall into a numerical listing. A list has the advantages of visual emphasis and clarity, but it should not be used as a substitute for a comprehensive explanation. Often the skeletal steps are put into a list and then developed more fully in subsequent paragraphs, as in this example, which first outlines the basic steps of a study method and in subsequent pages (not reprinted here) develops them:

STEPS IN THE SURVEY Q3R METHOD

The title for this new higher-level study skill is abbreviated in the current fashion to make it easier to remember and to make reference to it more simple. The symbols Survey Q3R stand for the steps which the student follows in using the method: a description of each of these steps is given below:

SURVEY   1. Glance over the headings in the chapter to see the few big points which will be developed. Also read the final summary paragraph if the chapter has one. This survey should not take more than a minute and will show the three to six core ideas around which the discussion will cluster. This orientation will help you organize the ideas as you read them later.

QUESTION   2. Now begin to work. Turn the first heading into a question. This will arouse your curiosity and so increase comprehension. It will bring to mind information already known, thus helping you to understand that section more quickly. And the question will make important points stand out while explanatory detail is recognized as such. Turning a heading into a question can be done on the instant of reading the heading, but it demands a conscious effort on the part of the reader to make this a query for which he must read to find the answer.

READ   3. Read to answer that question, i.e., to the end of the first headed section. This is not a passive plodding along each line, but an active search for the answer.

RECITE   4. Having read the first section, look away from the book and try briefly to recite the answer to your question. Use your own words and name an example. If you can do this you know what is in the book; if you can't, glance over the section again. An excellent way to do this reciting from memory is to jot down cue phrases in outline form on a sheet of paper. Make these notes very brief!

   Now repeat steps 2, 3, and 4 on each succeeding headed section. That is, turn the next heading into a question, read to answer that question, and recite the answer by jotting down cue phrases in your outline. Read in this way until the entire lesson is completed.

REVIEW   5. When the lesson has thus been read through, look over your notes to get a bird's-eye view of the points and of their relationship and check your memory as to the content by reciting on the major subpoints under each heading. This checking of memory can be done by covering up the notes and trying to recall the main points. Then expose each major point and try to recall the subpoints listed under it.

These five steps of the Survey Q3R Method—Survey, Question, Read, Recite, and Review—when polished into a smooth and efficient method should result in the student reading faster, picking out the important points, and fixing them in memory. The student will find one other worth-while outcome: Quiz questions will seem happily familiar because the headings turned into questions are usually the points emphasized in quizzes. In predicting actual quiz questions and looking up the answers beforehand, the student feels that he is effectively studying what is considered important in a course.

—From Francis P. Robinson, *Effective Study*

Another feature found often in process papers but seldom in other essays is the use of visual aids: drawings, diagrams, and sketches. The adage that a picture is worth a thousand words is occasionally true; the visual materials, however, are intended to illustrate and support the prose, not to replace the prose explanation. The two explanations—one prose, one pictorial—complement one another, each performing an indispensable function. Usually the prose explanation refers to the drawings for clarification, and often just as the prose section is divided into steps, there is an accompanying drawing for each step or series of steps.

Types of Process Papers

There are two types of process papers, the difference between them being purpose. A descriptive process essay tells *how something is done;* a prescriptive process essay tells *how to do something.* The intention of a descriptive process paper is to help readers to understand, simply for the sake of knowledge, how a process works—for instance, how NASA landed astronauts on the moon. On the other hand, the intention of a prescriptive process paper is to show readers how to do the process themselves by following directions. The first resembles a narrative, the second, a recipe. The distinction between the two can be illustrated with these examples. A surgeon might explain to a heart patient how bypass surgery is done because the knowledge could ease the patient's anxiety. Obviously, the explanation would not be so detailed that a layman could go out and try it on a neighbor. But a physician might give the local boy scout troop a demonstration of how to set a broken bone so that, if a trooper hiking out in the mountains breaks his tibia, his fellow scouts can set it.

Prescriptive Essays

Instructional materials give us vital information: how to bring forth life (delivering a baby); how to save life (treating victims of choking or heart attack); even how to destroy life (loading and firing a pistol). Especially in the last few years we have become a "how-to" society, coupling a "can-do" spirit with a new interest in do-it-yourself projects. Books advising us how to do everything from saving our souls to making a million dollars proliferate today:

> *How to Build Special Furniture & Equipment for Handicapped Children*
> *How to Make an Electric Car Out of an Old Clunker*
> *How to Develop a Winning Personality*
> *How to Control Your Destiny*
> *How Not to Lose at Poker*

How to Adopt a Child
How to Raise a Puppy
How to Flatten Your Stomach
How to Cheat at Chess
How to Make Possum's Honey Bread
How to Read Tarot Cards

The following directions tell us how to replace a broken pane of glass, which is a repair that almost everyone has had occasion to do, yet few know how to do correctly.

REPLACING A BROKEN PANE OF GLASS

A broken pane of glass is not particularly difficult to replace yourself—in many cases doing the job yourself is easier than trying to find someone who will come promptly when you want them to. You can replace the glass without removing the sash, providing you can get at the window easily from the outside. If the window is on the second floor or where climbing to the outside might be difficult, your best bet is to remove the sash completely so you can work on it from inside. 1

The first thing you will have to do is remove all of the old, broken glass by pulling the pieces out gently. To avoid cutting your hands wear heavy work gloves or use several thick rags to grab hold of the glass slivers. In most cases the pieces will pull out easily but if you run across a stubborn section rock it back and forth gently to break the bond between the glass and the putty, then pull it straight out to remove it. 2

The next step is to remove all of the old, hardened putty by scraping it out with a small chisel or large screwdriver. If the putty is extra stubborn, you may have to tap the chisel with a hammer but work carefully to avoid gouging the molding in which the glass fits. Use a stiff brush or piece of steel wool to clean the wood thoroughly, then paint the rabbet (recess) with a coat of linseed oil or a light coat of thinned-down house paint. This coating is important to seal the wood so that when you apply fresh putty the pores will not draw all the oils out of the compound and thus leave it brittle. 3

Measure the opening in which the glass must fit, then have your hardware dealer cut you a new pane the right size. When measuring, remember that the piece of glass should be approximately ⅛ inch less in width and height than the actual opening in order to allow for a small amount of clearance on all sides. Before pressing the new piece of glass into place, apply a thin layer of glazing compound to the inside of the recess around all sides. . . . This "bed" of glazing material is necessary to ensure a water-tight seal after the glass is in place, as well as to cushion the glass and correct for irregularities in the frame. Although you can use either glazing compound or linseed oil putty, you'll find glazing compound a lot easier to work with—and it will not get as brittle as putty. 4

Press the glass firmly against the bed of glazing compound so it seats smoothly around all edges, then fasten it permanently in position by inserting glazier's points around the side. Glazier's points are small triangular shaped bits of metal which you 5 can buy where you get the glass, and small panes will usually require four to hold them properly—two on each vertical side. Larger pieces should have three or more equally spaced along each side, as well as at least one at the top and bottom (a rule of thumb is one glazier's point every 6 or 7 inches along each side).

Remember it is these glazier's points that are supposed to hold the glass in   6 place, not the glazing compound, so don't leave them out. They're not hard to install, you just push them in with the end of a putty knife or a screwdriver as shown in the drawing above. Some brands also have little flanges or bent-up edges which make it easier to push them into place without slipping.

With the glass secured, you're ready to finish off with glazing compound around   7 the outside. The easiest way is to first roll the material into strips a little thinner than a pencil, then lay these into the recess around the edge of the sash, pressing it in place with your fingers. Now use your putty knife to smooth it into a neat bevel that runs from the edge of the sash molding up onto the glass as shown. Properly done, this should form a triangular shaped bead that will be flush with the outer edge of the molding on the outside and will come high enough up on the glass to match the level of the wood molding on the inside. The main thing is to make certain that you pack the compound down firmly and leave no cracks or open seams into which water can seep.

—From Bernard Gladstone, *The New York Times Guide to Home Repairs Without a Man*

Consider the many qualities that contribute to the clarity of these directions, even without the original diagrams. First, the author addresses the reader directly: "You can replace the glass." Such directness creates an intimacy between reader and writer, who is cast in the role of instructor. Second, the steps are arranged in an unmistakable chronological order: "The first thing you will have to do is remove all the old, broken glass"; "the next step is to remove all of the old, hardened putty." To help readers get from one step to another, transitional markers indicating time are provided: *first, next, then, after, before, finally* (see the list in Chapter 3, on page 78). Third, the writer tells us not only *what* to do, but also *how* to do it, carefully explaining procedure, tools, and materials. Fourth, he tells us the *why* as well as the *what* and the *how;* that is, he explains the reasons behind the directions: The last sentence in paragraph 3, the penultimate sentence in 4, and the first sentence in 6 explain the functions of particular steps. A writer should explain reasons not only to be courteous, but also to ensure the success of directions, for readers will more likely follow directions if they understand their purpose. Fifth, the writer has anticipated difficulties that might arise: "if you run across a stubborn section" and "if the putty is extra stubborn." A good process paper warns readers where they are likely to encounter trouble, where they are likely to go amiss, and what to do in case they do. Sixth, he has given definitions where necessary *(rabbet, glazier's points)*. Seventh, he has given us expert tips, for example on measuring the pane opening. In short, the directions succeed because they are clear, precise, and comprehensive.

Although we are used to reading directions that give "just the facts, ma'am," process papers don't have to be dull and lifeless. Rather than being a bare listing of ingredients, tools, and steps, directions can be embellished with details and descriptions that make the essay more entertaining. Since each of us has our own way of doing things, we should let that individualism shine through. We shouldn't be afraid to insert our personal opinion, to state the directions in our own flavorful words, or to address readers as if they were sitting across a table from us.

In the following process essay, the writer adds charm and character to a potentially dull topic—how to make corn bread—by revealing her attitude and personality while explaining the recipe. What in the first paragraph informs readers that this isn't a typical, dull description of how to bake something? Most recipe writers don't reveal much about themselves, but Ronni Lundy does. What do we know about her from this article? Could a novice successfully follow this recipe, or are there terms and procedures that a novice might not know? (This essay was originally published in *Esquire*, whose main readers are male.)

CORN BREAD WITH CHARACTER

Ronni Lundy

There are those who will tell you that real corn bread has just a little sugar in it. They'll say it enhances the flavor or that it's an old tradition in the South. Do not listen to them. If God had meant for corn bread to have sugar in it, he'd have called it cake. 1

Real corn bread is not sweet. Real corn bread is not homogenized with the addition of flour or puffed up with excessive artificial rising agents. Real corn bread rises from its own strength of character, has substance, crust, and texture. Real corn bread doesn't depend on fancy cornmeal, buttermilk, or cracklings for its quality. Real corn bread is a forthright, honest food as good as the instincts of its cook and the pan it is baked in. 2

That pan had best be a cast-iron skillet, preferably one inherited from a forebear who knew how to wield it. My mother, who made real corn bread almost every day of my growing-up life, has a great pan, a square cast-iron skillet given by a great aunt. She also has an eight-slot corn stick pan I would be satisfied to find as my sole inheritance someday. In the meantime, I bake corn bread in a nine-inch round cast-iron skillet I grabbed up in a secondhand store because it already had a black, nasty crust on the outside and the proper sheen of seasoning within. 3

If you have to start with a pan fresh from the store, season it according to the instructions for cast iron, then fry bacon in it every morning for a month to add a little flavor. Pour the leftover bacon grease into an empty one-pound coffee can and refrigerate it. Wipe your pan clean with a paper towel and don't ever touch it with 4 anything as destructive as soap and water. When the inside starts to turn black and shiny, you're ready to start making corn bread.

It's not enough to have the right pan, however; you also need to know how to   5
heat it properly. Heating right is the most important facet of the art of making corn bread, because if you have your skillet and drippings just hot enough, you'll consistently turn out corn bread with a faultless brown and crispy crust.

"Just what are drippings?" you may ask here, thereby revealing that you have   6
never been closer than a pig's eye to a country kitchen.

In my family, drippings were the bacon grease my mother saved every morning   7
in coffee cans. If you've followed the directions for seasoning a new pan, you're in good shape here. But what if you've inherited a well-seasoned pan and want to start baking corn bread before your next breakfast? Or what if you've never eaten bacon in your life? Don't despair. You will learn, as I did during a brief flirtation with vegetarianism, that while bacon drippings impart a distinctive taste to corn bread cooked with them, they aren't essential to baking great corn bread. You can improvise a lot with grease.

If you feel extravagant, you can use half a stick of butter, but if you need to   8
conserve, you can use some not too flavorful oil with a teaspoon or two of butter for effect. If you like the taste, you can use peanut oil or the thick, golden corn oil sold in health food stores that tastes like Kansas in the heady throes of late August. But you can't use olive oil or sesame oil (too strong and foreign), and margarine won't heat right.

To heat the pan correctly, you must leave it in the oven until it and the drippings   9
are really hot but not smoking. Knowing just how long that takes is a trick you'll learn with time. A good rule of thumb: Leave the pan in the oven while you mix the other ingredients, but don't stir too slowly. A good precaution, in the early stages of making corn bread, is to check the pan frequently.

A final secret on the art of heating: It does not work to heat the corn bread skillet   10
on top of the stove. Doing so may save you from setting off the smoke alarm, but the burner will create circular hot spots in your skillet and when you flip it to get the corn bread out, the middle crust will stay behind, clinging to those spots.

You will need cornmeal, of course. You may want to invest in a sturdy little   11
grinder and pulverize the kernels yourself at home. Or you may want to cultivate a dark and narrow little store somewhere that sells only stone-ground cornmeal in expensively priced brown paper bags. Either method is fine. Both will bake up just as nicely as the commercially ground white cornmeal you can find in bags on any supermarket shelf. That's what my mother always used, and years of sampling gourmet grinds have given me no reason to scotch her preference.

In my mother's kitchen, where I learned to make corn bread, there were two   12
kinds of measurements: enough and not enough. If we owned anything as fancy as a measuring cup, I'm sure it was not taken down for an occurrence so everyday as the baking of dinner corn bread. I do know that we had a set of four measuring spoons in primary colors, because it made a dandy toy for visiting children, but I don't remember ever seeing it in my mother's hand as she sprinkled salt, baking powder, or soda into

the corn bread mixing bowl. In the interest of science, however, and for those unable to visit my mother's kitchen, her instinctive art is converted here to teaspoons, tablespoons, and cups. What follows is a recipe for real corn bread, enough to accompany dinner for six:

Turn on your oven to 450 degrees.   13

In a nine-inch round cast-iron skillet or a reasonable facsimile thereof, place   14
four tablespoons of the grease of your choice. Place the skillet in the oven and heat it until the grease pops and crackles when you wiggle the pan.

While the grease heats, mix together in a medium-sized bowl two cups of fairly   15
finely ground white cornmeal with one teaspoon of salt, one-half teaspoon of baking soda, and one-half teaspoon of baking powder. Use your fingers to blend them together well.

Crack one big egg or two little ones into the meal mixture.   16

Add one and a half cups of milk or buttermilk.   17

Stir until just blended.   18

Remove the skillet from the oven and swirl it carefully so the grease coats most   19
of the inside edges of the pan but not your hand. Pour the grease into the corn bread mixture, and if everything is going right it will crackle invitingly. Mix together well with a big wooden spoon, using about twenty-five strokes.

Pour the mixture back into the hot skillet and return it to the oven for twenty   20
minutes. Run the pan under the broiler for a few seconds to get a light-brown top crust, then remove it from the oven and turn it upside down onto a large plate. If your skillet is seasoned right, the bread will slide out in a hot brown slab. If not, then just serve it straight from the pan. It will taste every bit as good. (This recipe can also be baked in a corn stick pan, but the baking time is cut in half.)

Serve the bread with fresh sweet butter, or crumble it in a bowl and cover with   21
hot pinto beans, a green onion, and sweet pickle on the side. Now, that's real corn bread.

1. Why does the recipe begin with an assertion that corn bread doesn't have sugar in it, instead of with an explanation of what ingredients do go into corn bread?

2. About one third of the essay concerns the cooking pan. Does she explain why the pan is so important?

3. Every sentence in paragraph 2 starts with the same subject. Why does she do this, and what is the effect?

4. Where has Lundy taken into consideration exceptions or problems, and where has she discussed alternatives to the prescribed method?

5. Where has she provided the rationale for using a certain ingredient or doing something a certain way? Where, if at all, has she not provided a necessary rationale?

6. Paragraph 12 contributes nothing to the recipe itself. Why is it there?

Descriptive Essays

The purpose of a descriptive process paper is to help people understand how things work, especially things that affect their lives. Many people feel powerless and frustrated when they must deal with systems or mechanisms that are mysteries to them. They don't understand how the judicial system works, how engines run, how electricity works, how computers bill them, or how surgeons operate on them. Although we are certainly more technically knowledgeable than people were 100 years ago, we daily use mechanisms that are unintelligible to us, including microwave ovens, televisions, jet airplanes, and ball-point pens.

Descriptive process writing can cover a broad range of subjects. In addition to explaining the workings of a complex mechanism, such as a solar converter or a Trident missile, such writing might trace the steps of a social or political movement, such as the women's movement or the presidential campaign of George Bush. A descriptive process essay might also explain the development of a natural phenomenon—how the universe was formed or how volcanoes erupt. It might even explain how a professional performs a complicated task—for instance, laser surgery. Libraries are filled with books describing mechanical, scientific, social, and creative processes:

How a Market Economy Works
How Motion Pictures Are Made
How American Foreign Policy Is Made
How the Bible Came to Us
How the Brain Works
How the Greeks Built Cities
How Plants Are Pollinated
How Babies Are Made
How Heredity Works
How Insects Communicate
How the IRS Selects Individual Income Tax Returns to Audit

In the following example, S. I. Hayakawa explains the process of making a dictionary. How does this descriptive essay differ from the preceding prescriptive essays?

HOW DICTIONARIES ARE MADE

S. I. Hayakawa

States why the process needs to be explained: public misconception about dictionaries

It is an almost universal belief that every word has a "correct meaning," that we learn these meanings principally from teachers and grammarians (except that most of the time we don't bother to, so that we ordinarily speak "sloppy English"), and that dictionaries and grammars are the "supreme authority" in matters of meaning and usage. Few people ask by what authority the writers of dictionaries and grammars say what they say. The docility with which most people bow down to the dictionary is amazing, and the person who says, "Well, the dictionary is wrong!" is looked upon with smiles of pity and amusement which say plainly, "Poor fellow! He's really quite sane otherwise."

Let us see how dictionaries are made and how the editors arrive at definitions. What follows applies, incidentally, only to those dictionary offices where first-hand, original research goes on—not those in which editors simply copy existing dictionaries. The task of writing a dictionary begins with the reading of vast amounts of literature of the period or subject that it is intended to cover. As the editors read, they copy on cards every interesting or rare word, every unusual or peculiar occurrence of a common word, a large number of common words in their ordinary uses, and also the sentences in which each of these words appears, thus:

Margin note	
Clarifies what kind of dictionary he is discussing	
Phase I: collecting	
Step 1: reading	
Step 2: editors copy quotations	

---

pail

The dairy *pails* bring home increase of milk

Keats, *Endymion*

I, 44–45

Illustration for clarity

That is to say, the context of each word is collected, along with the word itself. For a really big job of dictionary writing, such as the *Oxford English Dictionary* (usually bound in about twenty-five volumes), millions of such cards are collected, and the task of editing occupies decades. As the cards are collected, they are alphabetized and sorted. When the sorting is completed, there will be for each word anywhere from two or three to several hundred illustrative quotations, each on its card.

Indicates magnitude of the job and amount of time it takes

Steps 3, 4, and 5: cards are collected, alphabetized, and sorted

To define a word, then, the dictionary editor places before him the stack of cards illustrating that word; each of the cards represents an actual use of the word by a writer of some literary or historical importance. He reads the cards carefully, discards some, re-reads the rest, and divides up the stack according to what he thinks are the several senses of the word. Finally, he writes his definitions, following the hard-and-fast rule that each definition must be based on what the quotations in front of him reveal about the meaning of the word. The editor cannot be influenced by what he thinks a given word ought to mean. He must work according to the cards, or not at all.

Phase II: defining

Step 6: editor reads cards

Step 7: selects cards

Step 8: categorizes meanings

Step 9: writes definitions

The writing of a dictionary, therefore, is not a task of setting up authoritative statements about the "true meanings" of words, but a task of recording, to the best of one's ability, what various words have meant to authors in the distant or immediate past. The writer of a dictionary is a historian, not a lawgiver. If, for example, we had been writing a dictionary in 1890, or even as late as 1919, we could have said that the word "broadcast" means "to scatter," seed and so on; but we could not have decreed that from 1921 on, the commonest meaning of the word should become "to disseminate audible messages, etc., by wireless telephony." To regard the dictionary as

Draws conclusion: dictionary writer is a recorder and historian, not a lawmaker

Example of word that changed meaning

Tells why the dictionary should not be regarded as an authority: it is a record of the past, and words change with time

an "authority," therefore, is to credit the dictionary writer with gifts of prophecy which neither he nor anyone else possesses. In choosing our words when we speak or write, we can be guided by the historical record afforded us by the dictionary, but we cannot be bound by it, because new situations, new experiences, new inventions, new feelings, are always compelling us to give new uses to old words. Looking under a "hood," we should ordinarily have found, five hundred years ago, a monk; today, we find a motorcar engine.

—From *Language in Thought and Action*

Just as in prescriptive essays, this descriptive essay follows a chronological order; proceeds in steps; uses transitional markers such as *when*, *as*, and *finally*; provides a diagram; and gives the "how" and "why" of the process. In a descriptive essay, however, the writer doesn't address readers directly (Hayakawa uses the third-person "he" instead of second-person "you") and the essay reads more like a story than an essay that give directions. Also, whereas prescriptive writing gives knowledge for an end, descriptive writing gives knowledge to satisfy intellectual curiosity.

In the next example, the process of how a star is formed and dies is explained. As you read this scientific explanation, consider the following questions:

1. Has the writer divided the explanation into stages? If so, what are the stages and where does each begin? If not, where would you make the divisions?

2. What kind of order does the writer use to organize the material?

3. What purpose do the first two sentences serve?

4. Give examples of the writer's simplifying an explanation or intentionally omitting the reasons that an event occurs. Why does he do this?

5. Point out any explanations that you do not totally understand. Is this lack of understanding due to terms not being defined or explanatory material being omitted?

6. To achieve transition between paragraphs, the writer uses two main techniques: references to time and repetition of terms (repeating a term from one paragraph at the beginning of the following paragraph). Point out two examples of each technique.

THE LIFE AND DEATH OF A STAR

Robert Jastrow

The stars seem immutable, but they are not. They are born, evolve and die like living 1 organisms. The life story of a star begins with the simplest and most abundant element in nature, which is hydrogen. The universe is filled with thin clouds of hydrogen, which surge and eddy in the space between the stars. In the swirling motions of these tenuous clouds, atoms sometimes come together to form small pockets of gas. These pockets are temporary condensations in an otherwise highly rarefied medium. Normally the atoms fly apart again in a short time as a consequence of their random motions, and the pocket of gas quickly disperses to space. However, each atom exerts a small gravitational attraction on its neighbor, which counters the tendency of the atoms to fly apart. If the number of atoms in the pocket of gas is large enough, the accumulation of all these separate forces will hold it together indefinitely. It is then an independent cloud of gas, preserved by the attraction of each atom in the cloud to its neighbor.

With the passage of time, the continuing influence of gravity, pulling all the 2 atoms closer together, causes the cloud to contract. The individual atoms "fall" toward the center of the cloud under the force of gravity; as they fall, they pick up speed and their energy increases. The increase in energy heats the gas and raises its temperature. The shrinking, continuously self-heating ball of gas is an embryonic star.

As the gas cloud contracts under the pressure of its own weight, the tempera- 3 ture at the center mounts steadily. When it reaches 100,000 degrees Fahrenheit, the hydrogen atoms in the gas collide with sufficient violence to dislodge all electrons from their orbits around the protons. The original gas of hydrogen atoms, each consisting of an electron circling around a proton, becomes a mixture of two gases, one composed of electrons and the other of protons.

At this stage the globe of gas has contracted from its original size, which was 10 4 trillion miles in diameter, to a diameter of 100 million miles. To understand the extent of the contraction, imagine the Hindenburg dirigible shrinking to the size of a grain of sand.

The huge ball of gas—now composed of separate protons and electrons— 5 continues to contract under the force of its own weight, and the temperature at the center rises further. After 10 million years the temperature has risen to the critical value of 20 million degrees Fahrenheit.* At this time, the diameter of the ball has shrunk to one million miles, which is the size of our sun and other typical stars.

Why is 20 million degrees a critical temperature? The explanation is connected 6 with the forces between the protons in the contracting cloud. When two protons are separated by large distances, they repel one another electrically because each proton

---

*Twenty million degrees is a very high temperature. For comparison, the temperature of the flame in the gas burner of the kitchen stove is 1,000 degrees, and the temperature of the hottest steel furnace is 10,000 degrees.

carries a positive electric charge. But if the protons approach within a very close distance of each other, the electrical repulsion gives way to the even stronger force of nuclear attraction. The protons must be closer together than one 10-trillionth of an inch for the nuclear force to be effective. Under ordinary circumstances, the electrical repulsion serves as a barrier to prevent as close an approach as this. In a collision of exceptional violence, however, the protons may pierce the electrical barrier which separates them, and come within the range of their nuclear attraction. Collisions of the required degree of violence first begin to occur when the temperature of the gas reaches 20 million degrees.

7   Once the barrier between two protons is pierced in a collision, they pick up speed as a result of their nuclear attraction and rush rapidly toward each other. In the final moment of the collision the force of nuclear attraction is so strong that it fuses the protons together into a single nucleus. At the same time the energy of their collision is released in the form of heat and light. This release of energy marks the birth of the star.

8   The energy passes to the surface and is radiated away in the form of light, by which we see the star in the sky. The energy release, which is one million times greater per pound than that produced in a TNT explosion, halts the further contraction of the star, which lives out the rest of its life in a balance between the outward pressures generated by the release of nuclear energy at its center and the inward pressures created by the force of gravity.

9   The fusion of two protons into a single nucleus is only the first step in a series of reactions by which nuclear energy is released during the life of the star. In subsequent collisions, two additional protons are joined to the first two to form a nucleus containing four particles. Two of the protons shed their positive charges to become neutrons in the course of the process. The result is a nucleus with two protons and two neutrons. This is the nucleus of the helium atom. Thus, the sequence of reactions transforms protons, or hydrogen nuclei, into helium.*

10   The fusion of hydrogen into helium is the first and longest stage in the history of a star, occupying about 90 percent of its lifetime. Throughout this long period of the star's life its appearance changes very little, but toward the end of the hydrogen-burning stage, when most of the hydrogen has been converted into helium, the star begins to show the first signs of age. The telltale symptoms are a swelling and reddening of the outer layers, commencing imperceptibly and progressing until the

---

*The transmutation of heavy hydrogen into helium and heavier elements has been duplicated on the earth for brief moments in the explosion of the hydrogen bomb. However, we have never succeeded in fusing hydrogen nuclei under controlled conditions in such a way that the energy released can be harnessed for constructive purposes. The United States, the Soviet Union and other countries have invested prodigious amounts of money and energy in the effort, for the stakes are high, but physics has not yet been equal to the task. The difficulty is that no furnace has yet been constructed on the earth whose walls can contain a fire at the temperature of the millions of degrees necessary to produce nuclear fusion. The only furnace that can do this is provided by nature in the heart of a star.

star has grown to a huge red ball 100 times larger than its original size. The sun will reach this stage in another 6 billion years, at which time it will have swollen into a vast sphere of gas engulfing the planets Mercury and Venus and reaching out nearly to the orbit of the earth. This red globe will cover most of the sky when viewed from our planet. Unfortunately we will not be able to linger and observe the magnificent sight, because the rays of the swollen sun will heat the surface of the earth to 4000 degrees Fahrenheit and eventually evaporate its substance. Perhaps one of the moons of the outer planets will be a suitable habitat for us by then. More likely, we will have fled to another part of the Galaxy.

Such distended, reddish stars are called *red giants* by astronomers. An example of a red giant is Betelgeuse, a fairly bright star in the constellation Orion, which appears distinctly red to the naked eye. 11

A star continues to live as a red giant until its reserves of hydrogen fuel are exhausted. With its fuel gone, the red giant can no longer generate the pressures needed to maintain itself against the crushing inward force of its own gravity, and the outer layers begin to fall in toward the center. The red giant collapses. 12

At the center of the collapsing star is a core of pure helium, produced by the fusion of hydrogen throughout the star's earlier existence. Helium does not fuse into heavier nuclei at the ordinary stellar temperature of 20 million degrees, because the helium nucleus, with *two* protons, carries a double charge of positive electricity, and, as a consequence, the electrical repulsion between two helium nuclei is stronger than the repulsion between two protons. A temperature of 200 million degrees is required to produce collisions sufficiently violent to pierce the electrical barrier between helium nuclei. 13

As the star collapses, however, heat is liberated and its temperature rises. Eventually the temperature at the center reaches the critical value of 200 million degrees. At that point helium nuclei commence to fuse in groups of three to form carbon nuclei, releasing nuclear energy in the process and rekindling the fire at the center of the star. The additional release of energy halts the gravitational collapse of the star. It has obtained a new lease on life by burning helium nuclei to produce carbon. 14

In stars the size of the sun, the helium-burning stage lasts for about one hundred million years. At the end of that time the reserves of fuel, composed now of helium rather than hydrogen, once again are exhausted, and the center of the star is filled with a residue of carbon nuclei. These nuclei, possessing *six* positive electrical charges, are separated by an even more formidable electrical barrier than helium nuclei, and collisions of even greater violence are required for its penetration. The 200-million-degree temperatures which fuse helium nuclei are not adequate for the fusion of carbon nuclei; no less than 600 million degrees are required. 15

Since the temperatures prevailing within the red giant fall short of 600 million degrees, the nuclear fires die down as the carbon accumulates, and the star, once again lacking the resources needed to sustain it against the weight of its outer layers, commences to collapse a second time under the force of gravity. 16

All stars lead similar lives up to this point, but their subsequent evolution and   17
manner of dying depend on their size and mass. The small stars shrivel up and fade
away, while the large ones disappear in a gigantic explosion. The sun lies well below
the dividing line; we are certain that it will fade away at the end of its life.

—From *Red Giants and White Dwarfs*

Incidental Process Writing

As in the case of other types of writing, such as definition and narration,
process writing can be used as substantiation to develop one point of a
larger structure. Instead of the entire essay being an explanation of how
something works, the process material may be only one or two paragraphs inserted in the essay to illustrate a secondary idea. For example, in
a discussion of Eskimo life, Annie Dillard explains briefly one of the
Eskimos' activities—capturing birds to make undershirts. Dillard's intent is not so much to describe the process as to illustrate the ingenuity of
the people and the cruelty of the process.

On St. Lawrence Island, women and children are in charge of netting little birds. They
have devised a cruel and ingenious method: after they net a few birds with great effort
and after much stalking, they thread them alive and squawking through their beaks'
nostrils, and fly them like living kites at the end of long lines. The birds fly frantically,
trying to escape, but they cannot, and their flapping efforts attract others of their kind,
curious—and the Eskimos easily net the others.
  They used to make a kind of undershirt out of bird skins, which they wore under
fur parkas in cold weather, and left on inside the igloos after they'd taken the parkas
off. It was an elaborate undertaking, this making of a bird-skin shirt, requiring
thousands of tiny stitches. For thread they had the stringy sinew found along a
caribou's backbone. The sinew had to be dried, frayed, and twisted into a clumsy
thread. Its only advantages were that it swelled in water, making seams more or less
waterproof, and it generally contained a minute smear of fat, so if they were starving
they could suck their sewing thread and add maybe five minutes to their lives. For
needles they had shards of bone, which got thinner and shorter every time they
pushed through tough skins, so that an old needle might be little more than a barely
enclosed slit.

—From *A Pilgrim at Tinker Creek*

Notice that Dillard doesn't tell how the Eskimos net the birds, how
they kill the birds, or how they tan the skins. This general level of
description is typical in essays where the process material is incidental to

the larger purpose. However, where the process is the main focus, we must describe each step in detail.

Advice, Warnings, Reminders

1. Select a topic that will have interest because it is useful or fascinatingly odd.

2. Estimate your readers' level of general knowledge in the subject area; if the process is a mechanical one, for instance, will they likely be acquainted with standard procedures, materials, and tools?

3. Define specialized terms.

4. Outline the steps, and group them into major classes.

5. Consider using diagrams and referring to them in the prose explanation.

6. If an explanation first depends on understanding a theory or principle, take the time to clarify the principle.

7. Warn readers of potential pitfalls in executing a process; you might offer advice as to what they can do in case they make a common mistake ("If *X* happens, try *Y*").

8. Explain the reason behind instructions. People will usually follow a direction if they know there is a logical reason for it; likewise, if they don't see the reason, they often won't bother to do it. For example, if you are explaining to your little brother how to change a tire, you might suggest that he place wedges in front of and in back of the tires on the ground. The reason: This will prevent the car from rolling when he jacks it up. Similarly, you should give an insider's tips and shortcuts.

9. If possible, avoid the "How to (verb) (noun)" title. Although it is revealing, it lacks originality.

10. For a humorous approach in a process essay, try writing a negative example: how to lose your shirt in the stock market, how to cultivate a heart attack before you reach 50, or, everybody's favorite book, *How To Choose the Wrong Marriage Partner and Live Unhappily Ever After.*

11. One pitfall in process essays is to present a highly complex process as if it is simple and easy. To suggest that persons can make a million dollars easily, change their personalities overnight, or achieve a perfect relationship in five *Reader's Digest* steps is to mislead by oversimplifying.

12. Accidentally leaving out a step would seem unlikely in writing a paper whose sole intent is to explain a chronological process. It does happen,

though. We sometimes know the process so well that we assume that what is obvious to us will be obvious to readers, and therefore we don't include it. Whereas with most types of writing we must be on guard against boring readers with the obvious, with process papers we must remember that obviousness is a relative concept; what is obvious to the writer may be news to readers. And omitting a step is like leaving the yeast out of bread dough—guaranteed failure.

Suggested Writing Assignments

Mechanical Processes

How drillers get oil out of the earth
How a cyclotron works
How helicopters fly
How a rotary engine works
How to make a telescope
How medieval cathedrals were constructed
How a Geiger counter works
How to make a sunscope
How record albums are made

Natural Processes

How coral is formed, or how atolls develop
How a volcano is formed
How continental drift occurs
How a tornado occurs
How black holes evolve
How photosynthesis or chemosynthesis works
How birds evolved
How the earth originated
How the hydrologic cycle works (global moisture cycle)
How the moon was formed

Sports

How to make duck decoys
How to teach a child to swim
How to make an Indian canoe
How to catch an alligator
How to set up a weight-lifting program

How to hang glide or wind surf
How to hunt squirrels
How to use the "veer T" offense in football

Politics

How laws are made in Congress
How India won its independence
How the Louisiana Purchase was negotiated
How the Soviet Union is governed
How political polls are conducted

Business

How to invest in bonds (silver, stocks)
How to set up a small business
How to conduct an interview
How to set up a roadside produce stand
How to buy a used car
How CBS decides which stories to air on the evening news
How to set up a family corporation for tax purposes

Arts and Crafts

How to make candles
How to restore antique furniture
How to make knives from old saw blades
How to construct a log cabin
How to quilt
How museums restore damaged paintings
How to plant an autumn garden
How to make a plant terrarium
How to construct a bluebird house
How to construct a greenhouse

Medical

How psychoanalysis is conducted
How hypnosis works
How to improve your memory
How to overcome stuttering
How the course of a disease, such as multiple sclerosis, proceeds

Miscellaneous

How to commit the perfect crime
How to train a dog
How to train a husband or wife
How to talk your way out of a traffic ticket

Negative Instructions

How to go bankrupt with your new business
How to flunk out of college in only two semesters
How to stay fat
How to get turned down when asking for a date
How to break your neck breaking in a horse
How to keep from being reinvited by your party host

Additional Readings

MUMMIFICATION

Herodotus (fifth century, B.C.)

When a family brings a body to the embalmers, they show the family wooden models of corpses that have been painted for likeness. First they show the most expensive manner of embalming; they then show the second, which is inferior and less expensive; and then the third, which is the cheapest. The family selects the way they wish the body to be prepared, agree on the price, and depart.

The most expensive manner of embalming is thus: First they draw out most of the brain through the nostrils with an iron hook and take out the remainder by infusing drugs. Then with a sharp Ethiopian stone, they make an incision in the side and take out the bowels; they then cleanse the abdomen and rise it with palm-wine, and sprinkle it with perfumes. Then the belly is filled with pure pounded myrrh, cassia, and other perfumes, frankincense excepted, and they sew it up. When they have done this, they immerse the body in natrum, leaving it in for seventy days, which is the maximum time allowed. At the end of the seventy days they wash the corpse and wrap it in bandages of flaxen cloth, smearing it with gum, which the Egyptians commonly use instead of glue. The family returns and takes the body, makes a wooden case in the shape of the human figure, and encloses the body in it; the body is fastened into the case and stored in a sepulchral chamber upright against the wall.

When the middle method is selected to avoid great expense, the embalmers use the following procedure. Rather than making an incision and removing the bowels, they inject oil made from cedar through syringes into the anus, preventing the injection from escaping. The body is immersed in natrum for the prescribed number of days, and on the last day they let out from the abdomen the oil of cedar. The oil is so powerful that it dissolves the intestines and vitals, which come out in liquid form; the natrum dissolves the flesh, and nothing of the body remains but the skin and the bones. When they have done this, they return the body without any further operation.

The third method of embalming is used only for the very poor. Having thoroughly rinsed the abdomen in syrmaea, they immerse it in natrum for the seventy days, and then deliver it to be carried away.

—Translated by Henry Cary, with alterations

1. Herodotus was a Greek writer who is considered the father of history. His histories are full of anecdotes and descriptions of foreign customs as well as records of battles and political strife. His purpose in this excerpt is to inform the Greeks about the Egyptians' embalming customs. Has he succeeded in describing the processes? Why, or why not?

2. He gives most attention to the first method, less to the second, and least to the third. Why?

3. How would you describe his tone: serious, charming, ghoulish, amused, shocked, or what?

The following process description takes readers into an operating room where Dr. James Brockman, chief of neurosurgery at a medical center, is performing brain surgery on a patient named Charlie White.

THE MUSIC LESSONS

Lawrence Shainberg

The first incision, a quick slice with a scalpel along the forward line of the flap, was made by Benny [Dr. Brockman's assistant] at eight forty, and the scalp was peeled away from the muscle beneath it about fifteen minutes later. Three layers of tissue— scalp, muscle, and the membrane called the galea—had to be severed before bone was reached and drilling begun to prepare the area that Brockman had called a trapdoor. Charlie's scalp was about a half inch and the bone about a quarter inch thick (it can be thicker or thinner at other points on the skull, and it also varies among individuals; two weeks earlier they had operated on a woman whose skull, according to Benny, was paper-thin). Altogether, it would take fifty-five minutes to complete the flap and expose the dura in preparation for Brockman's attack on the tumor.

Bleeding was heavy along the incision, and after the blood was suctioned and sponged, white plastic clips were installed to seal off the vessels. When the line of the flap had been incised, the tissue beneath it—called subaponeurotic—was sliced with a very sharp knife, then the flap was peeled back gently like the skin of an orange. There were many bleeding points on its underside, and as these were coagulated electrically, the now-familiar smell of burning skin filtered through the room.   2

The flap was wrapped like a package, first with a mesh-like material, then with gauze, then clamped to the drape on its bottom side, just above Charlie's ear. Since the skull bone was covered with the galea, it was not yet visible, but now the galea was cut with a Bovie loop and pushed back gently with an instrument called a periosteal elevator. At the bottom of the flap, there was muscle to be got through in addition to galea, and this was cut with a scalpel.   3

"Call the Boss," Benny said. "Tell him thirty minutes."   4

When the bone was exposed, six large holes, about the size of those in a bowling ball, were drilled along the line of the flap. The instrument in this case was a nitrogen-powered, stainless-steel cylinder called a craniotome that looked a lot like a space gun and whined like a baby pig when activated. It took a half-inch bit for drilling and a slicing tool which made horizontal cuts. In their arsenal now for the last ten years, the craniotome's great feature was that, being air-powered, it responded negatively to pressure. The harder the tissue it encountered, the more power it generated. Thus, the drill bit turned with maximum speed through the bone and stopped altogether when it met the soft tissue that lay beneath it.   5

Observing this procedure could increase one's respect for the human anatomy. The trait we call hardheadedness is not, it seems, entirely figurative. Benny had to get all his weight behind the craniotome to make it penetrate Charlie's skull. He leaned forward until his body was nearly thirty degrees off the vertical. The egglike shape of the skull is said to be inherently protective, distributing stress over the largest possible area, but the skullbone itself is tough as armor.   6

Shavings from the bone were kept in a paper cup on the instrument stand to plug the drill holes when the skull was reassembled. Each hole bled as drilled, and beeswax was applied as a sealer after it was suctioned and sponged. When Benny was done with the craniotome, he took up a hand drill that looked exactly like a carpenter's, enlarged each hole, then clipped at the jagged edges with an instrument called a rongeur. Finally, when the holes were smoothed and coagulated, he set about connecting them.   7

There were various tools used for this, and that morning, since Charlie's skull was especially hard, Benny required them all. Using the craniotome with its cutting bit, he sawed out the line between the holes, angling the blade so that later, when the flap was replaced, the beveled edge would help secure it. Once again he had to lean into the drill with all his weight. Against heavy resistance from the bone, the saw moved very slowly, sometimes imperceptibly, sending trails of smoke into the room and   8 generating so much heat that it required constant irrigation. Now, replacing the craniotome in its metal box, Benny threaded a flexible instrument called a dural protector between the holes and slid it back and forth several times to separate bone from the brain beneath it. He called for the rongeur again and clipped edges on the two holes closest to Charlie's ears, worked the space between them once again with the periosteal elevator, and finally, throwing the elevator onto the instrument stand, stood up—for the first time since his original incision—and surveyed his work.

"What's his pressure?" 9

"Ninety-five over seventy," Carla said. 10

"Can we take him down a point or two?" 11

"I'd rather not until we open the dura." 12

Benny shrugged his shoulders, rolled his head in a circle as if to stretch his neck, then looked up at Millie on the stand. "Chisels, please." 13

She handed him two stainless-steel instruments with blunt one-inch blades, slapping them between his thumb and forefinger. After working them first around the edges of the flap, Benny elevated it gently until he was certain it was coming off the dura, then grasped it with his fingers and lifted it clear. Now, for the first time, Charlie's brain was visible, framed by the flap and covered by the silky film of the dura like an embryo in its sack. Though the dura is protective and more opaque than transparent, one could discern quite clearly beneath it the interlacing of blood vessels on the surface of the brain and, just barely, the distinctive folds of the cortex. 14

The underside of the bone flap had grooves in it where the middle meningeal artery ran across the surface of the brain. This artery had been severed when Benny lifted the flap, and blood flowed heavily now until José suctioned it and Benny, using the cautery that passed current through the plate beneath Charlie's buttocks, sealed off the vessel. Now the flap was wrapped in moistened gauze, tied with rubber bands, and set up on the instrument stand, the dura irrigated, sponged, and dried, the drapes around the flap readjusted to prepare the neat, impersonal view which Brockman would require. 15

"What time is it?" Benny said. 16

"Nine twenty," Esther said. 17

"Anyone heard from the Boss?" 18

"He's on his way." 19

About the time that Benny was calling for the chisels, Brockman had arrived in the locker room. He had dressed quickly and headed down the hall to scrub. 20

As always Brockman took a scrub sponge into the O.R. and continued to wash, dripping suds on the floor, while he inspected the flap that Benny had turned. 21

"Looks good," he said. 22

He stood with his back to Millie while she dressed him, examined the angiograms while she pulled on his gloves, and finally stepped up between José and Benny and probed the dura with his finger. His face was eight to ten inches from Charlie's brain. 23

"What's his pressure?" 24

"Ninety-five over seventy," Carla said. 25

Stretching his hand toward Millie, Brockman requested Malis scissors and then   26
quickly opened the dura. Taut and resilient, it snapped out of the way, and the brain
pushed through the opening like a tiny fist. Fifteen years ago, this was a dangerous
moment in neurosurgery, because brains expanded drastically and often herniated
when the dura was opened, but nowadays, with steroids to control intracranial
pressure, the swelling was not problematic.

It was nine thirty-five. After making a small incision, the Boss inserted a strip of   27
Cottonoid between the dura and the brain and then continued cutting, using the
Cottonoid as a protective buffer, sliding it along as the incision progressed. In time he
cut out a piece of dura which more or less followed the flap, taking care not to use the
cautery too much, since it caused contraction in the dura that might make it too tight to
close. Finally, the dural flap was raised as the bone and muscle had been raised
before it, wrapped in moistened gauze, and clamped out of the way. In all its
convolution, oyster-gray and pink on its surface and almost black at the folds, the
cortex was visible at last. It was nine forty-five.

At the bottom of the exposure lay the tumor. Encapsulated like all meningiomas,   28
it was striated with blood vessels like the brain around it but still sharply distinct from it,
darker and smoother, clearly alien but inoffensive somehow, certainly anticlimactic.
Hard to believe that this walnut-sized collection of cells which the brain had produced
of its own accord had dropped Charlie to the floor more than four weeks ago when he
stood up from his desk.

One of the crucial variables with parasagittal meningiomas (since they originate   29
in the lining of the brain) is whether they've invaded the transparent membrane called
the arachnoid which lies beneath the dura. If so, a layer of brain must be removed
along with the tumor, and the chance of deficit in the aftermath of surgery is greatly
enhanced. Seeking this information, Brockman probed the arachnoid with a forceps,
then edged his retractor around the mass—bending it so that it followed the tumor's
contours—to determine as much as he could about its depth. When a good view had
been exposed, he called for the microscope and the videotape, and a moment later
Charlie's brain made its first appearance on television.

"Okay," said the Boss. "We're looking at this man's motor strip. That's leg and   30
that's arm. That's tongue. Since the tumor gave him a leg seizure, we know it's
growing to the falx. The arachnoid is involved, even some of the dura, I think, but
there's no reason from what I see that we shouldn't get it all."

It seemed to me that Charlie's chances had taken a sudden nose dive, but I was   31
wrong. As Benny explained later, the region in which the arachnoid and dura were
involved was not near enough to vital centers to endanger his motor function. Though
another surgeon might have been intimidated by a tumor so invasive, Brockman had
done so many over the years that he handled it with no timidity at all.

The first target with meningiomas is their blood supply. Since they're highly   32
vascular tumors, they can hemorrhage if entered directly, but once their principal
sources have been tied off, they can be manageable, even tame. In search of the
feeding vessels, Brockman worked his way around the tumor, using his retractor first

and then Cottonoid, coagulating with a hyphercator when vessels were small, a Bovie forceps when they were large. Once or twice, in what seemed to me an ingenious improvisation (I found out later it was common), he gripped his suction tube with his coagulating forceps so that he sent current down the barrel of the tube and coagulated as he drew off the loose tissue and blood that he'd produced.

With all that cutting they were using the suction tube a lot, and, as sometimes   33
happens, this led to misadventure. Suddenly a piece of normal brain got caught up and sucked—*whoosh!*—up the tube, gone forever into the central garbage receptacle that served the suction tubes in all operating rooms on the floor. With Brockman working in such proximity to Charlie's motor strip, I thought he'd sucked an arm or leg right up the tube. As it turned out, I was wrong again. The normal tissue came from the posterior side of the tumor, far from anything crucial, and the brain that disappeared would not be missed. To say the least, Brockman took its departure in stride.

"Shit," he said. "There go the music lessons."   34

Everyone in the room cracked up, Benny grunting behind his mask and Millie   35
convulsing on the stand, but the pleasure was short-lived because José got his suction tube entangled with the Boss's.

By ten o'clock Brockman had the tumor ligated and separated (with Cottonoid)   36
from the brain around it. To elevate or, as the surgeons say, mobilize the tumor, he sewed several sutures to it and then attached them to clamps, drawing them taut and lifting the tumor a bit from its cavity.

"Speech problem, you think?" José asked.   37

"I doubt it," Brockman replied. "Bayonet, please."   38

"Irrigation," Benny said.   39

"Oh, that's pretty, isn't it?" Brockman said. "Make a sharper bend in your   40
retractor, Benny. Yes, that's it. That's very nice. No, no. You take the retractor, José, and give me the sucker. When it's bleeding, I've got to control it myself."

When things were quiet like this, the sounds of the O.R. were musical and   41
hypnotic. The sizzle of the cautery, the flutelike beep of the oscilloscope, the sighs of the respirator, the conversation, the suction, the clink of instruments against each other like knives and forks at the dinner table—it was all repetitive, monotonous, constant in its rhythm as a fugue. If you listened with enough detachment, all of it merged in a sweet continuum that might have been made on a synthesizer.

Brockman came now upon the large draining vessel called the sagittal sinus,   42
which he'd mentioned to Charlie in their first interview. In certain cases parasagittal meningiomas invade crucial areas of this sinus, and if it is transected during surgery, the result can be coma or quadriplegia. (As Brockman had pointed out to Charlie, the danger was actually less if the tumor was blocking the sinus entirely.) In Charlie's case, as it turned out, the sinus vein was not invaded, but—equally dangerous—it blocked the only angle by which the tumor could be approached.

When the Boss had a good view of the sinus, he called for the videotape again   43
and pointed (with his forceps) to a vein which was actually connected to the sinus. "We must preserve this vein at any cost. It's draining the motor strip into the sinus."

Continuing the tape, since this was essential technique for students, he slipped   44
Cottonoid behind and in front of the vein, trying to isolate and secure it, but a moment
later it slipped forward anyway, and a bit of hysteria ensued.

"Move it! Move it! How many times I got to tell you, don't cross over me when   45
I've got cutting instruments in my hand."

As it turned out, the problem was a piece of dura which had been invaded by   46
tumor and was itself pulling on the vein. Once they amputated it and slipped more
Cottonoid between the vein and the adjoining tissue, everything was under control.

By ten fifteen they were extracting tumor.   47

Using a scalpel first and then a copper spoon, he broke through the tumor's   48
capsule and dug it out in small, bloody slivers, which he placed in the specimen glass
on the instrument stand. The inside of the tumor looked a lot like Cream of Wheat.
Once gutted, its walls collapsed, and the difficult points at which it was connected to
brain became accessible. By ten forty, half the tumor was in the specimen glass and
the rest had snaked away through the suction tube. The Boss was packing the empty
cavity with Gelfoam, a Styrofoam-like material that expands when it's wet and contracts as it dries, promoting coagulation in the areas beneath it. A few minutes later,
he said, "All right, let's get the hell out of there."

By the time he had showered and dressed and made his way to the ninth floor   49
where, to use his words for it, he played a bit of God for Mrs. White, Charlie was
almost reassembled.

Closing was tedious and time-consuming, more hazardous in certain ways than   50
opening. The danger of clots or postoperative bleeding was not a small one, and there
were no miraculous instruments to protect against it. No oscilloscope recorded a vein
left open, no lights blinked if a flap were improperly sealed. As usual, tension had
diminished with the Boss's departure, but, relaxed though the mood became, there
was no interruption of the burden or the concentration it required. ("The worst part of a
party," Benny said. "Cleaning up when it's over.") José and Benny had seen too many
mistakes to let that happen, too much postsurgical hemorrhage after perfectly successful operations, too many patients returning like unicorns, their bone flaps infected
and disfigured.

The Boss had closed the dura before he left and sewn a patch called Silastic   51
over the area he had amputated. Now Benny and José set about reconstructing the
rest of Charlie's skull, starting with the bone.

When the dura was cleaned and dried, a plastic tube, beginning at the highest   52
point on the skull, was laid across it to act as a siphon, a gravity-fed drain to draw off
excess fluid. Tiny, pinlike holes were drilled (with the craniotome) in the bone flap and
used to wire the flap to the skull, and stainless-steel sutures, threaded through these
holes, were twisted together and stuffed in nearby burr holes, there to remain—like
the Silastic patch—for the rest of Charlie's life. They were moving along, and Benny
was whistling behind his mask.

Burr holes were filled first with Gelfoam and then with the bone shavings that   53
had been collected during the original drilling. The bone was inspected carefully for

bleeding spots, and once it was attached, the inner surface of the muscle above it was heavily cauterized, then sutured to the muscle on the skull surrounding it. One small opening was left in the flap for the drain, which was pushed through a special hole (called a stab wound) made especially for it behind Charlie's ear. The drain would remain in place, attached to Charlie's bandage like a feather on a cap, for thirty-six hours, and then, if his intracranial pressure was satisfactory, they'd remove it and sew up the wound. The opening in the bone—actually one of the burr holes—was not considered problematic.

Esther was counting sponges aloud—"Ninety-one, ninety-two, ninety-three"— 54
tying them in packages of a hundred for disposal. During an operation like this they could go through, two, three, or even four such packages.

With the under layer of flap in place, they had continued to the muscle and 55
periosteum. Now they were restoring the scalp, and there was a lot of sewing to be done. Unlike their orthopedic colleagues, they couldn't use a staple gun, so each stitch was personal and meticulous handiwork, inserted by hand, knotted by hand, loose ends clipped by hand. Sutures were made of fine silk material (other specialties have opted for synthetics, but not the neurosurgeons) which had been threaded—in tiny U-shaped needles—by the manufacturer. Esther removed them one by one from their packages, installed them in a special instrument, and passed the instrument to Benny, who had pushed the needle through the edges he meant to knit, tied the knot, then passed it to José, who clipped the loose ends. The needle, like the sponges and syringes and Cottonoid, was thrown away. By the time they were done, they had taken more than one hundred and fifty stitches in Charlie's scalp.

They were standing in a pool of blood at least half an inch deep. . . . 56

—Abridged from *Brain Surgeon*

1. The essay combines narrative and process writing. What is the advantage of using narration to describe the surgery?

2. A brain operation is of course a complicated procedure, and explaining it requires technical language. How does the writer make these technical terms understandable to lay readers? Give examples.

3. In several places the narrator explains problems that might occur. Where and why does he do this?

4. Why does the writer periodically tell what the time is?

5. Are the last eight paragraphs anticlimatic? If so, why does the writer include them?

CHAPTER 9

Causal Analysis

In this chapter we will explore the journalistic question "why?" When we ask this question, we are seeking causes: Why does the Nile River run north? Why has there been an increase in the number of miscarriages among American women in the past decade? Why did the dinosaurs disappear? Why did the Space Shuttle *Challenger* explode?

When writing about events with causal relationships, we can focus on the cause, on the effect, or on both, depending on which one is uncertain and needs to be proved. When searching for causes, we start with the known effects and work backward in time to see why they happened; when searching for effects, we start with the known causes and go forward in time to determine consequences. In this chapter we will discuss causes, and in the following chapter we will discuss consequences.

Reasons for Studying Causation

In almost every course on campus, students are asked to write essays and exams on causes. In history, for example, you may be required to write on the causes of World War I, and you will have to distinguish among the main causes, the secondary causes, the immediate causes, and the remote causes. In psychology, you might study the causes of claustrophobia or schizophrenia. In political science, you might be asked to discuss why many Democrats voted for the Republican presidential candidate in the last few elections. In astronomy, you might have to explain why the universe is expanding, and in geology, why continental drift occurs. In sociology, the question of why the family unit is disintegrating might be explored, and in economics, why interest rates are going up or down.

Exploring cause-and-effect relationships is central to our comprehension of the world. Through observation and inference, we learn that events that lead regularly to other events have a special relationship, which we label *causation*. We assume that all things have a cause, and this assumption is called the principle of determinism. As we perceive it, the physical world operates according to mechanical causes, such as gravity; once discovered, these causes help us to understand our environment. Not only does everything have a cause, but series of causes and effects are intricately interlinked so that causation acts as "the cement of the universe."[1] We know about many physical causes today (for instance, the causes of lightning, sleeping sickness, lunar eclipses, and earthquakes), and although some causes remain hidden (such as the causes of aging, cancer, and the common cold), their numbers are decreasing. We also seek the causes of human behavior, but the social sciences are less exact than the physical sciences, and their findings are tentative. Still, the more we know about why people act as they do and why the world works as it does, the better we are able to understand and control our lives.

APPLICATION

1. Early human beings, not understanding the causes of such phenomena as solar eclipses, thunder, and diseases, felt compelled to explain the inexplicable by assigning them supernatural causes. Ancient tribes, for instance, attributed volcanic eruptions to displeased gods and, to appease them, sacrificed a virgin; the practice obviously had no effect on volcanic pressure. The ancient Chinese attributed solar eclipses to a dragon swallowing the sun, though we have since settled for the more likely explanation that the moon comes between the earth and the sun. The Norse attributed thunder to the god Thor throwing his hammer, not to gases expanding after an electrical discharge. In the Middle Ages the bubonic plague was thought to be caused by demonic possession, and therefore the cure was to lash oneself with whips to drive out the evil spirits; had someone only observed that the plague was transmitted by fleas on infected rats, 25 million people might have been saved from the Black Death.

   Find three other examples of prescientific explanations for diseases or occurrences of nature.

2. Although we are more sophisticated about causal matters than our ancestors, a few of us nonetheless have been known to attribute events to such irrelevancies as black cats and broken mirrors; and the entire nation watches every February 2 to discover whether the groundhog will see its shadow so we will know whether to expect a prolonged winter. Give three other examples of current superstitions.

[1]David Hume, eighteenth-century philosopher.

We study causation for purely intellectual reasons—to think more clearly, to understand more fully—and for practical reasons—to learn from the past and to solve problems. By studying causality, we encourage complex thinking: Causal analysis is an intellectual activity that forces us to expand our perception and to consider multiple factors and relationships. Studying causation also helps us to see the interconnectedness of our world and to see that disturbing one element often sets off a chain reaction. In addition, it teaches us to beware of short-sighted thinking that suggests easy, simplistic answers to challenging questions.

Our interest in causation is pragmatic as well as intellectual because causation helps us to interpret the past. If we are to learn from history, we must know what caused the failures in the past and what caused the successes. For example, analyzing the causes of the Great Depression prompted Congress to pass regulations stopping certain investment practices in order to ensure that such a catastrophic collapse would not happen again. Likewise, by discovering the causes of the Space Shuttle explosion, NASA has been able to correct the problems and to make future flights safer.

Causal investigation helps us to interpret facts and make inferences about the present as well as about the past. For instance, if you work in a hospital and notice that admissions for respiratory ailments such as asthma, emphysema, and bronchitis rise when a local sulphur plant is operating, what would you infer? If you notice that breast-fed infants in the hospital have a lower death rate from botulism than formula-fed infants, would you conclude that baby formulas cause botulism? (The explanation may be that breast feeding confers some protection against developing the disease; in that case, formulas would not be the cause.)

Causal analysis is the first step in problem-solving. Before we can suggest solutions to a problem, we must establish the causes of the problem. In this way, we use our knowledge of causal relationships either to produce or to prevent acts that are within our control. For example, medical researchers for decades sought a cure for migraine headaches. Recently, a group of Finnish scientists discovered that injecting doses of prostaglandins (unsaturated fatty acids) into subjects results in migraine attacks. The acids, they concluded, must cause migraines. They then worked under the principle of "remove the cause, and the effect will cease." Knowing that another acid—tolfenamic acid—can inhibit the production of prostaglandins in the body, they had the cure for migraines. In fact, they had had it all along, but they didn't know that it was the remedy because they didn't know the cause. This kind of problem-solving is used when an ill effect is known but its cause is not. We search for the cause, for within the cause lies the cure.

Principles of Causation

Causal relationships are, first of all, chronological: one event occurs after another one. Cause precedes effect in time.[2] The relationship is more than chronological, however, since the two events are linked to one another in a fixed pattern: Every time *A* occurs, *B* occurs. Scientists call this an invariant relationship because the relationship of *A* to *B* never changes. *A always* produces *B*.

Types of Conditions

When trying to determine causes, whether they are the causes of inflation, heart attacks, or meteor showers, we must distinguish among three types of conditions: necessary, sufficient, and contributory. A *necessary* condition is one that must exist for an event to happen, but it may not be strong enough to cause the event. For example, oxygen is a necessary condition for ignition, but oxygen alone does not cause a fire. A *sufficient* condition is one that is strong enough to produce the event, but it does not have to be present for the event to occur. For instance, a lighted match is sufficient to start a fire, but fires can occur without matches; fires can be caused by such sufficient conditions as lightning, flint sparks, magnified sunlight, friction, and so on. A *contributory* condition is one that helps to produce an effect but is neither necessary nor sufficient; gasoline, for example, contributes to making wood burn.

What do these principles have to do with writing? The answer is that, when generating a thesis and support for a causation essay, we must be careful not to confuse contributing conditions for sufficient conditions and not to forget that a sufficient condition is not automatically a necessary condition. Writers sometimes hit upon one sufficient condition and assume that it is *the* cause, when in fact there may be other sufficient conditions that also must be considered in order to determine which one or ones caused an event to occur. When we find what we think is the cause of an event, we should continue to explore the situation to see whether any other sufficient conditions were present. For example, in an attempt to explain the origin of life on earth, most biologists theorize that millions of years ago the planet was covered with a "primeval soup"—a sea of chemicals—and that under the sun's ultraviolet rays the organic substances combined into amino acids, and from those acids originated more complex nucleic acids, and so on until, after 100 million years of

---

[2]A rare example of simultaneous cause and effect was given by the German philosopher Immanuel Kant: When a lead ball is placed on a cushion, the cause (the ball descending) and the effect (the depression of the cushion) occur at the same time.

self-replication and evolution, higher life forms appeared. But the primeval soup was a sufficient condition, not a necessary one. An alternative evolutionary theory, more speculative and radical, is that molecular clouds floating through space distributed organic polymers that evolved into cells. The extraterrestrial dust clouds, like the primeval soup, may have been a sufficient condition but not a necessary one.

APPLICATION

Which of these are necessary conditions, which are sufficient conditions, and which are contributory conditions?

Condition	*Effect*
1. closing your eyes	sleeping
2. having low brake fluid in your car	hitting the car in front of you
3. raining lightly	hitting the car in front of you
4. studying hard	getting an A on an exam
5. having a cold	failing an exam
6. having a patient instructor	learning to drive
7. being sighted	learning to drive
8. eating candy every day	getting a cavity
9. being 20 pounds overweight	having a heart attack

Correlation, Coincidence, and Causation

The distinctions among correlation, coincidence, and causation are also important. *Correlation* means that two events are related but that neither causes the other. For example, there is a correlation between infectious hepatitis and liver cancer; where one is found, the other is often found. Rather than one causing the other, however, both may be caused by a similar virus. Similarly, a correlation exists between creases in ear lobes and heart attacks; a higher percentage of persons with creases in their ear lobes have heart attacks than those without. To suggest, however, that ear-lobe creases cause heart attacks is absurd; rather, the relationship between the two is probably that poor circulation, which is a symptom of heart trouble, causes skin to wrinkle in extremities. *Coincidence* is the accidental occurrence of two events. For example, during election years from 1952 to 1976, every time the American League pennant winner in baseball won the World Series, the Republican candidate won the presidential election; and every time the National League was victorious, so were the Democrats. Despite this 24-year streak of coincidence, no one suggested that the World Series decided the presidential election.

Errors in Causal Thinking

Writers of causal essays are frequently guilty of committing two types of errors, both of which result from pairing incomplete thinking with incomplete evidence. The first error falls under the generalized heading of oversimplification, and the second is referred to by the Latin phrase *post hoc.*

Oversimplification

Oversimplification means failing to consider *all* of the causes of an effect. "Why are there so many divorces in America today? More women are working." "What caused the Civil War? Slavery." "Why are so many farmers going bankrupt? They borrowed too heavily." Instead of perceiving that there are multiple causes, we present one cause as *the* cause; we see a part and call it the whole. Oversimplification is a tempting error because our minds would rather deal with one cause than with several; retaining several ideas simultaneously requires considerable mental effort. Oversimplification results from haste, laziness, and narrow vision; in an attempt to understand a situation immediately, we make it less complex than it actually is and fail to consider the whole picture. We seek an easy answer, and therefore we find an easy—and simplistic— answer. We fail to look at a problem from different angles and therefore overlook political, economic, or social causes. The effect of oversimplification is that instead of clarifying a situation for our readers, we unintentionally distort it.

Consider these examples of oversimplification:

> Theorists espouse single causes for all of humankind's motivation: for Marx, the cause of all behavior is economics; for Darwin, genetics; for Freud, sex; for Skinner, environment.

> The drop in SAT scores over the past two decades has been the result of more minority students taking the test. [A variety of factors contribute to the decline: public education in general, parental laxity, students' attitudes, and the influence of television.]

> A journalist asserts that grain sales to Russia caused beef prices in the United States to go up: "The higher prices of steak in American supermarkets in 1978 can be traced back to the sudden increase in the price of corn in 1973, and the costs this added to fattening the beef from which tender, marbled steaks are cut." [Although United States grain sales to Russia contributed to higher beef prices, the main reasons for higher prices were that the

United States beef cattle population dropped significantly in the early 1970s and that ranchers had higher operating costs because of inflation and higher-priced petroleum products, such as fertilizer and gasoline.]

Post Hoc

The phrase *post hoc, ergo propter hoc* translates as "after this, therefore because of this" and refers to the error of mistaking chronological coincidence for causation. The *post hoc* fallacy asserts that because *B* follows *A*, *A* must have caused *B:* Night follows day, and therefore day causes night. Whereas all causal relationships are chronological, not all chronological relationships are causal; and whereas all causes precede their effects, not all antecedents are causes. The *post hoc* fallacy, by confusing temporal sequence and causation, offers a causal explanation for what is simply a chronological relationship. For instance, if you walk under a ladder on Tuesday and break your leg on Wednesday, you might be tempted to attribute the accident to bad luck caused by walking under the ladder; after all, one event occurred, and then the other occurred. For another example, if every time you take two friends fishing with you, you catch no fish, you might call them a jinx and assume that they are the cause of your poor fishing.

Examples of *post hoc* fallacy are, unfortunately, easy to find:

A few years ago medical researchers announced that milk causes cancer, and they based their finding on the fact that people who drink lots of milk get cancer more than people who do not. As a result of the announcement, milk consumption decreased immediately. [As it turned out, however, people who drink large quantities of milk tend to live longer, and cancer disproportionately strikes old people. There was a correlation between drinking milk and getting cancer, but there is no direct causation.]

A religious leader on television repeatedly asserts that because prayers have been banned in public schools, crime has risen, assassinations have occurred, divorce has increased, and American morality has dropped.

A scholar claims that the Mary Tyler Moore Show caused "consciousness raising" among female television viewers: "During those first two seasons in which Mary Richards and Rhoda Morgenstern came to television, the level of public support among women for a female President increased more than among any other two-year—or ten-year—period since the 1930s." [Rather than causing women to think differently about a female president, the television show more likely merely reflected changing values among women.]

Major recessions are blamed on Republicans because every time a recession occurs, a Republican is in the White House. [Rather than Republicans causing recessions, it may be that the financial policies of the Democrats lead to recession, and when the economic situation worsens, people vote for the other party.]

APPLICATION

Evaluate the following assertions (or implications) to determine which constitute true causation and which do not. For those that are fallacious, explain what the error is.

1. A Smith-Corona typewriter advertisement states: "In an independent survey of high school and college instructors, fifty per cent agreed: STUDENTS WHO TYPE USUALLY RECEIVE BETTER GRADES." The implication is that typing creates better students and that buying one's children a typewriter will raise their grades.

2. World War I, World War II, the Korean War, and the Vietnam War all occurred during Democratic presidential administrations. I therefore conclude that the policies of the Democrats caused the wars.

3. The introduction of the birth control pill in the 1960s caused the increased promiscuity that began in the 1960s.

4. Lorne Greene promotes Alpo dog food by implying that his 14-year-old dog ("That's 98 dog years") owes her longevity to Alpo.

5. Newspaper headline:
"UNIVERSITY PRESIDENT RESIGNS AFTER STUDENT PROTEST"

6. Eisenhower won the 1952 presidential election because he was a father-figure to American women and they turned out in record numbers to vote for him.

7. Foreign imports are the cause of the decline in United States auto sales.

8. When I play tennis in my lucky T-shirt, I usually win.

9. Since I've been going to that new doctor, I haven't been sick as much.

10. "At My Lai, American GIs—young men who had grown up as members of the Television Generation—methodically shot and killed, or stood by and watched others shoot and kill, several hundred women." (From *Remote Control*)

11. People act more eccentric when there is a full moon. The moon therefore must cause insanity. After all, the word *lunacy* comes from *luna*, which means moon.

12. Until 1971, the Pittsburgh Steelers had never been in a play-off game; in 1971 they acquired Franco Harris, and they were in the play-offs for the next 9 consecutive years.

13. Last month my boss changed from a friendly and relaxed employer to a demanding and critical slave driver. Production dropped 2 percent. Serves him right.

14. "In the South, which is heavily armed, the burglary rate is lower than elsewhere." (William F. Buckley, "Gun Control: It Won't Work")

15. Mark Twain drank a Scotch every night to prevent toothaches, and it worked: He never had a toothache.

16. Last winter I had three colds. This winter I took vitamin C and didn't have a single cold.

17. In October 1965 in New York City there was an all-night electrical blackout. In June and July 1966 there was a substantial increase in births in New York City.

18. The infant mortality rate in the United States is thirteenth in the world. The reason the mortality rate is so high is that physicians tell women to keep their weight down during pregnancy, and American babies are underweight at birth.

19. Pregnant women living near airports have a higher abnormal birth rate than other women. Mrs. Andrews lived near La Guardia Airport when she was pregnant with Tommy, and that's why he is retarded.

20. As unemployment rises, so does the number of hospital admissions for mental illness. Recessions must cause mental illness.

21. People under stress have a statistical tendency to be ill. Stress causes illness.

22. People who drink coffee have a higher rate of cancer of the pancreas than people who don't drink coffee. Caffeine must cause pancreatic cancer.

23. My uncle drank and chased women until he was 68, at which age he got religion, gave up both, and within two months was dead. Virtuous living is fatal.

Invention: Systematic Investigation to Discover Causes

To guard against oversimplification and to ensure that we have explored all of the sufficient conditions, we should systematically investigate every possible field of influence:

political	scientific/technological
economic	religious
cultural	environmental/geographical
moral	social (family, community)
psychological/emotional	

Whether we are searching for the causes of the high dropout rate in urban high schools or the causes of the American Civil War, an examination of these fields of influence will prevent us from overlooking an important cause. Also, probing these areas serves as a mode of inquiry that will help us to generate ideas about our topic. Each area can be addressed in the form of a question: What were the economic causes of the Civil War? What were the technological causes of the war? What were the political causes? By probing each of the areas above, we will not only ensure a thorough investigation, but also generate new ideas. We wouldn't likely explore the technological advances that contributed to the Civil War unless we forced ourselves to consider that area.

The following is an example of how we might systematically explore the subject of "the causes of the Civil War."

1. *What were the economic causes of the Civil War?*

The North was industrialized and wanted protective tariffs for its emerging manufacturing; the South, which was primarily agricultural, wanted low tariffs because it feared that if the United States had high tariffs, other countries would retaliate with their own tariffs against American agricultural exports.

The North dominated national finance and controlled interest rates; the South resented the North's control of banking and therefore turned to England for credit; England bought the South's raw products, which English workers then used to manufacture products that competed with the North's products on the international market.

The economy of the South depended on cheap farm labor—slavery.

2. *What were the moral causes of the Civil War?*

Although the South saw slavery as an economic necessity, the North saw it as a moral issue. The South resented this stance of moral superiority by the North, which needed skilled workers for its factories, not the unskilled laborers the South needed.

The question of slavery is important as a cause mainly because it was a highly emotional issue and because it became a focal point of all other issues and contentions.

3. What were the psychological causes?

Southerners were afraid of slave uprisings, and John Brown's raid in 1859, which was an attempt to lead slaves in an uprising, intensified the South's fears of an insurrection of slaves, promoted by Northern "radicals."

4. What were the contributing geographical conditions?

In addition to the geographical differences between the North and South, there was the question of westward expansion, which was the stimulus that made slavery a heated issue. If it had not been for westward expansion, the North probably would not have forced the issue so strongly and the South would have gradually ended slavery because of economic and moral reasons. But each time a new Western territory was acquired, the nation had to decide whether the territory would be free or slave, and slavery became the test issue in an elaborate power struggle. For example, abolitionists wanted Kansas to be free as a sign that the whole West would be free; Southerners wanted it slave as a sign that they had sufficient political power. Bloody Kansas resulted, with each side sending in people and arms for the fight.

5. What were the contributing technological conditions?

Before the mid-nineteenth century, distance and poor transportation prevented real unity among the states and prevented centralized governing. Then the telegraph made communications easier, and the railroad collapsed distances. Increasingly, the federal government was becoming able to exercise strong authority over isolated states.

6. What cultural conditions contributed to war?

Much of the literature of the period bordered on propaganda; novels such as *Uncle Tom's Cabin* kindled antislavery sentiment. Also, penny newspapers fueled controversies and exaggerated events.

7. What were the political causes?

The major political parties became sectional parties, the Republican party being formed in 1854 on an antislavery platform.

Because the North had a larger population, it gained enough Congressional power to force the federal government to intervene in the South's affairs.

The South wanted power to remain at the state level; the North wanted power to be centralized. Lincoln's election in 1860 demonstrated that the North had the political power to dominate the republic. With a

Northern majority in Congress and a Northerner in the presidency, the South realized that the federal government had won the battle with states' rights.

Conclusion: Not wanting to adopt the North's values and morality, and bitterly resenting the Northern dominance, the South saw no reason to stay in a government that it thought was violating its rights.

Only through this kind of systematic exploration of all areas can we be assured of discovering all the sufficient and contributory conditions that caused an event to occur.

Our next step after generating all the possible causes is to analyze them to distinguish underlying causes from surface ones, and remote causes from immediate ones. For example, the underlying cause of the Civil War was the country's shift from a fragmented to a national society. Until the middle of the nineteenth century, individual states had little to do with each other and worked in relative independence. Then, however, the country's economy and population reached a size that made it necessary for the states to act as one. Differences in social, economic, and political structures, which had mattered little before this time, suddenly became apparent and important. As the country moved toward centralization and the federal government began to assume power, basic questions of economic, social, and political policy had to be faced.

Another example of an underlying cause being important concerns the economic success of Germany and Japan after World War II. Specific causes for their industrial successes include their technology, their emphasis on modern products such as electronics, and their modern factories. The *underlying* cause is that during World War II the Allies destroyed most of the old factories, so German and Japanese industry had to abandon antiquated processes and start over from scratch (with American aid). Often these underlying causes are difficult to discern because they are remote in time.

Remote causes (those separated in time from the effect) are often as important as *proximate* causes (those immediately preceding the effect). Because immediate causes are convenient and apparent, we tend to perceive those as the sole causes. Too often we latch on the causes nearest to the effect and fail to look further into the past for other, sometimes more significant, determinants. Occasionally an immediate cause is sufficient in itself, such as the Japanese attack on Pearl Harbor.

An interesting example of a recently discovered immediate cause has helped to explain a historical mystery: Why were only a few hundred Spanish soldiers able to conquer and enslave thousands of Aztecs and Incas? According to the historian who wrote the following excerpt, "The main destructive role was certainly played by epidemic disease."

The first encounter came in 1518 when smallpox reached Hispaniola and attacked the Indian population so virulently that Bartoleme de Las Casas believed only a thousand survived. From Hispaniola, smallpox traveled to Mexico, arriving with the relief expedition that joined Cortez in 1520. As a result, at the very crisis of the conquest, when Montezuma had been killed and the Aztecs were girding themselves for an attack on the Spaniards, smallpox raged in Tenochtitlán. The leader of the assault, along with innumerable followers, died within hours of compelling the Spaniards to retreat from their city. Instead of following up on the initial success and harrying the tiny band of Spaniards from the land, therefore, as might have been expected had the smallpox not paralyzed effective action, the Aztecs lapsed into a stunned inactivity. Cortez thus was able to rally his forces, gather allies from among the Aztecs' subject peoples, and return for the final siege and destruction of the capital.

Clearly, if smallpox had not come when it did, the Spanish victory could not have been achieved in Mexico. The same was true of Pizarro's filibuster into Peru. For the smallpox epidemic in Mexico did not confine its ravages to Aztec territory. Instead, it spread to Guatemala, where it appeared in 1520, and continued southward, penetrating the Inca domain in 1525 or 1526. Consequences there were just as drastic as among the Aztecs. The reigning Inca died of the disease while away from his capital on campaign in the North. His designated heir also died, leaving no legitimate successor. Civil war ensued, and it was amid this wreckage of the Inca political structure that Pizarro and his crew of roughnecks made their way to Cuzco and plundered its treasures. He met no serious military resistance at all.

—From William H. McNeill, *Plagues and Peoples*

Most events, however, are a long time in the making, developing slowly and ripening. To see these remote causes, we have to exercise extended vision and gaze back into time. Remote causes are difficult to discover not only because they are distant in time, but also because there are intermediary steps between them and the effect. Furthermore, remote causes are often of a general nature, and our tendency is to see the specific instead of the comprehensive. For example, saying that Hitler was the cause of World War II fails to consider the more general causes, such as the economic collapse of Europe and the imbalance of power:

Adolf Hitler was as evil a monster as the twentieth century has produced—which is saying a lot. But he was not the root cause of the second world war. The root cause of the second world war was an enormous upset in the balance of power. To be sure, the upset was *effected* by the aggressive German rearmament and the aggressive German policy of the '30s. But the upset was also flaccidly and needlessly *permitted* by the two responsible free nations of the period, Britain and France. By 1939, the upset in the balance of power had gone so far that Britain and France had only two choices: to accept a dependent relationship to Hitler's Germany, or to fight like cornered rats.

—From Joseph Alsop, "Losing the Balance of Power," *Newsweek*, Nov. 13, 1978

Whether to include remote causes in an essay or concentrate on immediate ones depends on the subject and on the significance of the remote causes. Conceivably, seeking remote causes can be an endless process because, all of history being an interrelated series of events, we could trace an event's originating cause back for generations, though that might not contribute substantially to the reader's understanding. On the other hand, in order to understand situations such as the Israeli-Arab or Irish-Anglo conflicts, readers must be given a long historical perspective because the roots of those conflicts go back hundreds of years, and today's tensions are as much the result of ancestral hatred as of current political and economic problems.

Causal Patterns

Causal relationships come in several different shapes (some are circular, some linear) and numbers (some are singular, some multiple). Identifying the various causal patterns will help us (1) to look for these patterns when exploring a subject and (2) to structure our materials once we begin writing.

One Cause, One Effect

The simplest form of causal relationship is one cause leading to one effect:

$$A \longrightarrow B$$

Because of the interconnectedness of twentieth-century life, this pattern is infrequent; usually there are multiple causes and multiple effects. Can you think of an example when a *single* cause produced a *single* effect?

One Cause, Several Effects

Another pattern is one cause leading to several effects:

This pattern we will reserve for the next chapter, which concerns consequences.

Circular Cause and Effect

A circular pattern is *A* causing *B*, but then *B* causing *A* to recur:

We have seen this pattern operate in the United States economy during times of high inflation. When inflation is high, many American companies do not earn sufficient profits to invest in research for future products; since they do not produce as many new technologies as do, for instance, Japan and West Germany, American companies lose out on the international market; when their international trade is low, their profits are also low, so they cannot afford to invest in research and development, which was the original cause. Furthermore, because the country imports more than it exports, the American dollar is worth less and inflation increases. The whole process is what we call a "vicious cycle."

Another example of this reciprocal causation concerns the effect that politics has on language and that, in turn, language has on politics. The opening of George Orwell's "Politics and the English Language" explains the pattern effectively:

Most people who bother with the matter at all would admit that the English language is in a bad way, but it is generally assumed that we cannot by conscious action do anything about it. Our civilization is decadent and our language—so the argument runs—must inevitably share in the general collapse. It follows that any struggle against the abuse of language is a sentimental archaism, like preferring candles to electric light or hansom cabs to aeroplanes. Underneath this lies the half-conscious belief that language is a natural growth and not an instrument which we shape for our own purposes.

Now, it is clear that the decline of a language must ultimately have political and economic causes: it is not due simply to the bad influence of this or that individual writer. But an effect can become a cause, reinforcing the original cause and producing the same effect in an intensified form, and so on indefinitely. A man may take to drink because he feels himself to be a failure, and then fail all the more completely because he drinks. It is rather the same thing that is happening to the English language. It becomes ugly and inaccurate because our thoughts are foolish, but the slovenliness of our language makes it easier for us to have foolish thoughts. The point is that the process is reversible. Modern English, especially written English, is full of bad habits which spread by imitation and which can be avoided if one is willing to take the necessary trouble. If one gets rid of these habits one can think more clearly, and to think clearly is a necessary first step toward political regeneration: so that the fight against bad English is not frivolous and is not the exclusive concern of professional writers.

—From *Shooting an Elephant and Other Essays*

Multiple Causes

When we trace an effect back to its origin, we are likely to discover several sufficient causes, for seldom does only one cause exist in a society as technologically complex and socially interrelated as ours. The pattern we most often find is:

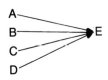

For example, to answer the question "What caused the sudden burst of daring exploration in the fifteenth century that led to Columbus' discovering America?" we must look not for one but for many causes. First, there was the navigation school set up by Prince Henry the Navigator in 1416. Second, because Italy controlled trade to the East, and because Spain, Portugal, and England wanted a part of that trade, their economic desire to find sea routes to Asia was strong. Third, shipbuilders were making faster, stronger, and larger ships that could withstand storms better and could carry the supplies necessary for long voyages. Fourth, sea captains had a better knowledge of astronomy, better instruments, and better maps. Finally, in 1453 the Turks closed the land trade routes to Asia, making it absolutely necessary to discover sea routes to the East.

In the following example, a historian explores why Europeans immigrated to America. He suggests that although there were multiple causes, the main ones were economic, social, and psychological—not, as previous history books have told us, religious and political.

The first paragraph is an overview of the various causes, which will be developed individually in the following paragraphs

The paragraph discusses not only why people migrated, but also who migrated

The discussion of immigrants is chronological: Spanish colonists settled first and therefore are discussed first; next come the English settlers; finally, other European immigrants

The impulse of migration may be described, negatively, as an impulse of escape. The American fled from a Europe where he could find no satisfying fulfillment of his energies and was confronted by conflicts and dilemmas that had no easy solution. The groups who came to all parts of the New World were, in general, those who were most acutely discontented with their status in European society and who had the least hope of being able to improve it. The Hispanic colonies were settled mainly by impoverished members of the lower nobility and by adventurers from the lower classes. Unable to achieve aristocratic status at home, they hoped to win riches, land, and glory for themselves in America. Most of the early immigrants to the United States

1

came from the petty bourgeoisie in the English cities or from the yeoman farmers; a few were motivated primarily by the desire to put into practice novel religious or political ideas, but the majority expected to improve their economic condition. The later migration from the other European countries into both North and South America was similar in character, including some religious and political refugees, but consisting mainly of ambitious younger sons of the bourgeoisie and of oppressed and land-hungry peasants from Ireland, Germany, Scandinavia, Italy, and the Austrian and Russian empires. All sought in the New World an environment where they could act more freely, without being restricted by traditional forms of authority and discipline or by a scarcity of land and natural resources.

Paragraph 2 discusses the most important cause, which has already been prepared for in paragraph 1

The writer explains the economic situation that made Europeans migrate: Demand exceeded supply

The chronology expressed in paragraph 1 is stated more explicitly here

Of the various factors that caused men to come to America, the economic was no doubt the most important. Throughout the period of the migrations, there was no free land in Europe; natural resources were limited; and the population was always in danger of increasing faster than the means of subsistence. Migration always occurred chiefly from areas of Europe where agriculture was still the chief occupation and where (owing to the growth of big estates or to genuine overcrowding) the demand for land was in excess of the supply. This was true of Spain in the sixteenth century, of England in the early seventeenth, and of Ireland, Germany, Scandinavia, Italy, and the Slavic countries of the east in the nineteenth.

Paragraph 3 discusses the next most important reason: the rigid social order

The writer relates this reason to the previous one: The class system caused the economic woes of peasants

The writer explains the history of the class system so readers will understand the background

An almost equally influential stimulus to migration was the European class system. This was, in fact, perhaps the chief cause of European economic privation, since the big estates of the aristocracy diminished the supply of land available for the peasants. Before the discovery of America, European society had been molded by feudalism into a tightly knit organic structure in which every individual, from the king at the top to the humblest peasant at the bottom, was expected to know his place and to perform the duties appropriate to it. These class differences had originated with the barbarian invasions during the fall of the Roman Empire, or even earlier, and for a thousand years they had been a deeply rooted part of the European consciousness. Ambitious and enterprising members of the middle and lower classes could sometimes improve their position, either individually or in groups, but the battle against aristocratic privilege was always difficult, and never reached a conclusion. For such persons the opening of the New World beyond the Atlantic promised an easier escape from frustration and the sense of inferiority.

The writer now qualifies his previous two reasons by stating that they do not usually determine human behavior

Privation and inequality weighed upon all underprivileged persons in Europe, but did not cause all of them to come to America. Human behavior is conditioned by economic and social factors in the sense that these establish the problems to be solved, but it is not determined by them: how particular individuals choose to act in a given situation depends upon deeper, more intangible, and more mysterious forces. Confronted by the same difficulties, some individuals preferred to submit to them or to continue struggling with them, while others, generally the more restless and adventurous, decided to come to the New World. Thus the settlement of America was a selective process that attracted those members of the European middle and lower classes who had the appropriate bent and disposition; it appealed not necessarily to the ablest or the strongest, but usually to the most enterprising. In a sense it may be said that America was from the beginning a state of mind and not merely a place.

The first two reasons had to be combined with psychological factors—a certain "disposition" and "state of mind"

—From Henry Bamford Parkes, *The American Experience*

As Parkes has done in this example, we should show the relationship among the causes if possible. Parkes, for instance, explains that the rigid social class actually was the cause of the economic deprivation, and he explains the relationship between individual disposition and social/economic reasons. When we encounter a situation in which there are several causes, we should also establish their relative importance—which is most important, which next, and so forth. In the immigration example, economic reasons were most important, social reasons were almost as important, and religious and political reasons were mentioned but were not important enough to discuss.

Instead of a hierarchy of causes, we may discover (as discussed earlier) many surface causes with one underlying cause. For example, after studying the causes of poverty, John Kenneth Galbraith finds that there may be numerous causes, but that one cause is pervasive:

There is no economic question so important as why so many people are so poor. There is none concerning the human condition to which so many different and conflicting answers are given with so much confidence and such nonchalance. The people are naturally lacking in energy and ambition. Their race or religion makes them so. The country is wanting in natural resources. The economic system—capitalism, socialism, Communism—is wrong. There is insufficient saving and investment. Property, profit or the rewards of toil are not secure. Education is inadequate. There is a shortage of technical, scientific or administrative talent. There is a legacy of colonial exploitation, racial discrimination, national humiliation. Every day in every part of the world every one of these explanations is offered. For mankind's most common affliction we have a multitude of diagnoses, each offered with the utmost casualness. Poverty is a painful thing. It would be well if we knew the cause.

There is no one answer—obviously. It is because so many explanations have a little truth that so many are offered. But one cause of poverty is pervasive. That is the relationship, past or present, between land and people. Understand that, and we understand the most general single cause of deprivation.

The reason is simple. Everything that allows of the first escape from privation— food, clothing, elementary shelter—comes from the land. If these cannot be provided, there is poverty. If they cannot be increased in relation to the numbers of the people, it endures.

—From *The Age of Uncertainty*

Causal Chain

Frequently what first appears to be several unrelated causes will upon further investigation turn out to be a causal chain. A *causal chain* is a series of events in which each intermediate effect becomes a cause itself; one cause produces an action that in turn produces another action, which itself produces a third action, and so forth until the reaction stops with a final cause.

A causes B; B, which is an effect, causes C; C, which also is an effect, causes D; and D causes E. It is a chain reaction, started by one action, resulting in many. Such chain reactions are common both in nature and in society, but to see them we must be looking for them.

For example, the burning of fossil fuels (coal, oil) sets off a causal chain that consists of many links, the last two of which are circular. Burning these carbons releases carbon dioxide into the atmosphere, raising the carbon dioxide content above what the oceans and vegetation can absorb. Increased carbon dioxide in the atmosphere lets less infrared radiation escape at night and therefore raises the earth's temperature slightly (this is called the "greenhouse effect"). The increased temperature causes greater evaporation of the ocean and raises the level of water vapor in the atmosphere. Water vapor, like carbon dioxide, has a greenhouse effect, and therefore the global temperature rises even higher, more water evaporates, and the cycle continues toward catastrophe unless something happens to break the chain.

Causal chains help to explain the political and social situation in many developing nations, such as those in Central and South America. Traditionally the countries in Central and South America were rural societies, growing and exporting bananas, coffee, cotton, and sugar. Industrialization and tourism, however, disrupted the agricultural society by encouraging workers to sell their small farms and to move to the cities, where wages were higher. Instead of finding new wealth in the cities, though, people found inflation, slums, unemployment, and hunger. The industrialists bought the vacated farmlands and therefore controlled all of the wealth, which they shared with the military class to protect against political coups. Although the gross national product of these countries increased, the common people's share actually decreased. The people became increasingly resentful as they perceived the injustice in the polarization of wealth and poverty, as they tired of poverty, and as they grew to hate their new lifestyles, which undermined traditional rural values. In reaction to the redistribution of wealth and the ensuing disadvantages, political leftists tried to reform the system but were frustrated by the power of the elite and the military. Frustration led to terrorism, guerrilla bands, and attempted revolution. One thing led to another—a causal chain.

To solve a problem that results from a causal chain, we must first determine and then prevent the first cause. Simply breaking one link—*C*, for instance—will not ultimately stop *E* from occurring because *A* will always cause *B*, and *B* will always cause *C*.

APPLICATION

1. Describe a circular causal relationship in nature.
2. Find an example of a causal chain in history or in business.
3. Give an example of a social, political, or economic situation in which there are many surface causes but only one underlying cause.
4. What were the multiple causes of some recent event in the news? Try to establish the relative importance of the causes.
5. Give an example of a situation in which remote causes are important.

Organizing a Causal Essay

Once we have determined which causal pattern is producing the effect, we can often translate that pattern into a corresponding structure. For example, if we discover a causal chain, our organization will be chronological. We would first discuss the original cause, then the effect (which itself becomes a cause), and then the second effect (which also becomes a cause), and so on until we reach the final effect. We use chronological order also to show immediate and then remote causes (or, remote and then immediate).

If, on the other hand, we discover that there are multiple causes contributing simultaneously to one major effect, we can group them according to common characteristics (as we did in Chapter 7, "Classification and Division") and then arrange the groups

> from most important to the least important,
> from the obvious causes to the lesser-known ones,
> from the simple causes to the complex ones,
> or from many surface causes to one underlying cause,
>   as in the Civil War example discussed on page 292.

Here is an outline that gives us a skeletal view of an essay on the causes of divorce:

  I. Sociological reasons: changing values
     A. In a mobile society, the extended family (parents, grandparents, aunts, uncles, etc.) exerts less influence, and couples don't feel bound by the morality and values of the family network.
     B. Divorce is acceptable these days in most groups; people feel less pressure from colleagues to stay married.
     C. The roles of men and women are changing.
        1. Women want equal status in marriage.
        2. Some men have difficulty accepting independent women; the men feel threatened.
     D. Working couples have greater demands on their time and energy.

 II. Economic reasons
     A. Wives are not as financially dependent on their husbands as they once were; a large percentage of wives are earning decent salaries.
     B. Men no longer have to pay alimony if they divorce.

III. Sexual reasons
     A. Extramarital affairs are on the increase.
     B. Being divorced doesn't necessarily mean being celibate, so the sexual consequences of being divorced don't seem drastic.

 IV. Legal reasons
     A. Divorce laws are lenient.
     B. Obtaining a divorce can be quick and inexpensive.

  V. Psychological reasons
     A. People enter marriage knowing there is an escape clause, and therefore their commitment through hard times may not be as strong.

  B. Young people sometimes enter marriage with unreasonably high expectations; they expect prolonged romantic love, a view that is reinforced by movies, television, and romance novels.

  C. Divorce may be a cyclical pattern: people raised in broken homes are more likely themselves to become divorced.

 VI. Underlying cause and thesis: The reasons cited above are all surface reasons. The underlying reason is that a lifelong emotional/social/spiritual/sexual/financial partnership is unnatural and unrealistic. People change as they go through their 20s, their 30s, their 40s, their 50s, their 60s, and their 70s and beyond; a man and woman cannot be expected to grow in the same direction for 40 or 50 years of marriage. We should not be alarmed at the divorce rate; rather, we should be amazed that it is as low as it is.

Why would a writer put the underlying cause at the end instead of the beginning in this essay?

APPLICATION

What organization is used in the following explanation of the causes of the tides?

TIDES

Rachel Carson

The tides are a response of the mobile waters of the ocean to the pull of the moon and the more distant sun. In theory, there is a gravitational attraction between every drop of sea water and even the outermost star of the universe. In practice, however, the pull of the remote stars is so slight as to be obliterated in the vaster movements by which the ocean yields to the moon and the sun. Anyone who has lived near tidewater knows that the moon, far more than the sun, controls the tides. He has noticed that, just as the moon rises later each day by fifty minutes, on the average, than the day before, so, in most places, the time of high tide is correspondingly later each day. And as the moon waxes and wanes in its monthly cycle, so the height of the tide varies. Twice each month, when the moon is a mere thread of silver in the sky, and again when it is full, we have the strongest tidal movements—the highest flood tides and the lowest ebb tides of the lunar month. These are called the spring tides. At these times sun, moon, and earth are directly in line and the pull of the two heavenly bodies is added together to bring the water high on the beaches, and send its surf leaping upward against the sea cliffs, and draw a brimming tide into the harbors so that the boats float high beside their wharfs. And twice each month, at the quarters of the moon, when sun, moon, and earth lie at the apexes of a triangle, and the pull of sun and moon are opposed, we have the moderate tidal movements called the neap tides. Then the difference between high and low water is less than at any other time during the month.

1

That the sun, with a mass 27 million times that of the moon, should have less   2
influence over the tides than a small satellite of the earth is at first surprising. But in
the mechanics of the universe, nearness counts for more than distant mass, and
when all the mathematical calculations have been made we find that the moon's
power over the tides is more than twice that of the sun.

The tides are enormously more complicated than all this would suggest. The   3
influence of sun and moon is constantly changing, varying with the phases of the
moon, with the distance of moon and sun from the earth, and with the position of each
to north or south of the equator. They are complicated further by the fact that every
body of water, whether natural or artificial, has its own period of oscillation. Disturb its
waters and they will move with a seesaw or rocking motion, with the most pronounced
movement at the ends of the container, the least motion at the center. Tidal scientists
now believe that the ocean contains a number of 'basins,' each with its own period of
oscillation determined by its length and depth. The disturbance that sets the water in
motion is the attracting force of the moon and sun. But the kind of motion, that is, the
period of the swing of the water, depends upon the physical dimensions of the basin.
What this means in terms of actual tides we shall presently see.

The tides present a striking paradox, and the essence of it is this: the force that   4
sets them in motion is cosmic, lying wholly outside the earth and presumably acting
impartially on all parts of the globe, but the nature of the tide at any particular place is
a local matter, with astonishing differences occurring within a very short geographic
distance. When we spend a long summer holiday at the seashore we may become
aware that the tide in our cove behaves very differently from that at a friend's place
twenty miles up the coast, and is strikingly different from what we may have known in
some other locality. If we are summering on Nantucket Island our boating and
swimming will be little disturbed by the tides, for the range between high water and
low is only about a foot or two. But if we choose to vacation near the upper part of the
Bay of Fundy, we must accommodate ourselves to a rise and fall of 40 to 50 feet,
although both places are included within the same body of water—the Gulf of Maine.
Or if we spend our holiday on Chesapeake Bay we may find that the time of high water
each day varies by as much as 12 hours in different places on the shores of the same
bay.

The truth of the matter is that local topography is all-important in determining   5
the features that to our minds make 'the tide.' The attractive force of the heavenly
bodies sets the water in motion, but how, and how far, and how strongly it will rise
depend on such things as the slope of the bottom, the depth of a channel, or the width
of a bay's entrance.

—From *The Sea Around Us*

Structure depends not only on the causes we find, but also on our
purpose for writing about those causes. Often our purpose is to correct a
common misperception about the causes of a situation. In that case, we
start by discussing the effect; then show that what most people consider

to be the cause is simply a surface cause; and finally present, as in the divorce example above, what we believe is the underlying cause or the real cause.

    I. Description of effect (and background provided if needed)
    II. Description of commonly held view of cause
    III. Explanation of why commonly held view is inadequate
    IV. Description of real causes
        A. Discussion of first real cause
        B. Discussion of second real cause
        C. Discussion of third real cause, etc.

Another purpose for writing about causes is to prepare for a solution to a problem. When trying to solve a problem, we first must establish the causes of that problem because the purpose of the solution usually is to prevent the causes. The structure of an essay that sets out to analyze a problem and offer a solution may proceed from problem to causes to solution:

    I. Statement of the problem, which is an effect
    II. Analysis of causes
    III. Explanation of solution

Causal essays are not mere lists of causes, of course. We must provide background, explain concepts, give examples, and, most important, demonstrate causal connections. We can't simply assert that *A* caused *B*—we must prove it did.

Interpretive Causes

We cannot always establish causes with absolute certainty because often we encounter variables that are so numerous and interlocking that disentangling them becomes a Herculean task. Is there a causal relationship, for example, between pornography and sexual crimes? Because pornography is only one of many variables to consider in sexual assault, sociologists are unable to verify that it is definitely a cause. Unlike a laboratory situation, where a researcher can isolate each variable to determine its effect, in life we must rely on our ability to see and weigh variables, and often we must settle for probable causes. In such fields as psychology, anthropology, political science, criminology, and economics, there is little certitude, and therefore the evidence is open to interpretation. Our task in these cases is to investigate the issue, pose an intelligent hypothesis, and convince readers that our thesis presents the most probable cause.

So many interdependent variables complicate national economics, for instance, that experts, even Nobel laureates, cannot agree on the causes of—and therefore on the cure for—inflation. One group says that inflation is caused by government deficit spending, which leads to government borrowing to finance the deficit, which in turn drives up interest rates. Another group maintains that inflation is caused by the wage-price spiral. Still another blames the Federal Reserve Board for increasing the quantity of money. The point here is that the elements—taxes, interest rates, business production, investments, unemployment, social services, wages, prices—are so interrelated that economists are unable to isolate individual factors to see which are necessary and sufficient conditions.

When we argue probable causes, we should be particularly careful to avoid dogmatism. Instead of taking an authoritarian stance, we should appear confidant but open-minded, assuming the role of the investigator rather than the dictator. Where an issue is open to interpretation, the side that seems both informed and broad-minded will likely be the one to win converts.

Occasionally we have to admit that, even after the evidence is examined, no hypothesis adequately accounts for cause, as in this investigation into the reasons for our primate ancestors' starting to walk upright. How would you describe the authors' tone, and how do they achieve it?

The most dramatic thing to have happened to *Ramapithecus* during that frustrating   1
fossil void is that it learned how to walk upright. We don't know how it got around the place before it adopted this highly unusual method of locomotion; maybe it moved smoothly on all fours, much as olive baboons do today. We don't know, and indeed, we shouldn't try to pin *Ramapithecus* down too precisely to what we can see in contemporary primates because, in all probability, the ancient hominid did its own thing. But by three million years ago our ancestors walked around the Pliocene landscape in much the same way as modern humans walk around modern cities.

By standing and walking upright, *Ramapithecus* would have freed its hand   2
wonderfully. It would have been able to carry things, to learn to throw accurately, to manipulate small objects with undreamed of precision, and perhaps even to invent a language of hand gestures. A whole new world is opened up when a primate learns to walk on two legs instead of four, and the evolutionary force propelling *Ramapithecus* into this unique position must have been pretty powerful because the new stance demands radical restructuring of the pelvis and leg anatomy. We are talking here of *habitual* upright walking, rather than *occasional* bipedalism, something that all apes are capable of, inelegant though it looks.

That it happened we know. That there are considerable advantages to be had   3
once one has stood up is incontrovertible. But *why* it should happen in the first place is a mystery because most of the advantages are apparent only when upright walking is very well advanced.

The arguments about bipedalism, as it is called, can be slotted into one of two   4
main categories: cultural and ecological, and so far neither is overwhelmingly convincing.

Tools are at the focus of one cultural argument. Some people suggest that the   5
need to fashion tools is sufficient to demand that ancient *Ramapithecus* should be
able to stand up. *Ramapithecus* stood up, that we know, but this particular line of
reasoning doesn't. First of all, the earliest stone tools don't appear in the archaeological
record until relatively late, around three million years, and these are extremely
crude, certainly not the work of hands tuned to fine precision. In any case, our
ancestors were fully accomplished bipedalists by this time and probably had been for
several million years. Unless one wishes to propose a culture centered on elaborately
carved sticks (which, of course, disappear without trace), then this particular culture-
based argument for bipedalism should probably be dropped.

What of ecology? One suggestion has been that as the forests shrank *Rama-*   6
pithecus set himself up as a hunter on the open savanna, and as he was such a
diminutive chap he got on much better by standing on his hind legs to peer over the
tall grass to spot the prey. This argument too is a nonstarter. First of all our ancestors
did not adopt an avaricious taste for meat at this time; indeed the teeth tell us quite the
opposite. Second, *Ramapithecus* developed his new way of walking while he was still
making a living in the forest fringes, or at least in woodland.

One attractive notion is that walking on two legs allows the animal to cover a   7
greater range more effectively. If *Ramapithecus* really did have to search high and
wide for its food and to have the wit to know what type of vegetation was ready to eat
where and when, then it probably would have to exploit an unusually large home
range. Walking on two legs would help, if it were cheaper than going around on four.
But it probably isn't. Bipedalism appears to consume more energy per mile than
quadrupedalism. Yet another simple theory is frustrated.

We have to admit to being baffled about the origins of upright walking. Probably   8
our thinking is being constrained by preconceived notions, by trying to make *Rama-*
pithecus fit into patterns we see around us today. The Miocene primates are not just
primitive versions of today's apes or of us. They had developed their own special
adaptation, and this is something we really must keep in mind when we're peering into
that fossil void trying to pick out some images of our ancestors' way of life.

—From Richard E. Leakey and Roger Lewin, *People of the Lake*

Advice, Warnings, Reminders

1. Once you have found a cause, don't stop the search: Always look for
   multiple causes.

2. Be aware of the possibility of causal chains.

3. Differentiate between immediate and remote causes, and between surface and underlying causes.

4. Be certain to demonstrate causality. The connection between cause and effect must be well substantiated.

5. To show a causal relationship in a sentence, use these connectives:

hence	as a result
consequently	because
so	thus
therefore	due to

6. Problems are effects. Before we can deal with such problems as alcoholism, drug addiction, and child abuse, we must know what causes them; otherwise, we end up treating symptoms instead of eliminating problems.

Exercises

1. As a class activity in assigning causes, speculate on the causes for these phenomena:
   A. Americans are saving less and less these days. Why?
   B. Most college freshmen gain weight, sometimes a great deal of weight. Why?
   C. Americans are living longer each decade. Why?
   D. There is a notable increase in bank robberies each year. Nationally, there are about 6,000 a year; in New York City alone there were 120 in 22 days in one year—10 in one day. Why are there so many?
   E. Why don't people read as much as they used to?
   F. What are the general causes of war?
   G. The 1980 census revealed an interesting demographic phenomenon: For the first time in the twentieth century, the United States population growth in rural areas is exceeding that in urban areas. What are the causes of this reversal?
   H. An increasing percentage of American women are choosing to remain childless (whereas in the past approximately 10 percent were childless, now about 30 percent are). Why is the proportion of childless women increasing?
   I. According to sociological surveys, people in the United States are less happy about themselves, their jobs, and their communities today than people surveyed in the 1950s. Why?
   J. What are the main causes of crime in America?
   K. Studies show that most working men who die suddenly die on Mondays. Why?

L. The suicide rate for urban dwellers is much higher than that for rural residents. What causes people in cities to commit suicide more?

2. Are the causal conclusions in the following passages valid or fallacious? If fallacious, explain why.

A. To most Americans, therefore, the upsurge in criminal violence that began around 1960 appeared to be an aberration from the norm rather than a return to it. The increase can be explained, in part, by a new and extraordinary demographic change that occurred between 1960 and 1975: the population aged fourteen to twenty-four grew 63 percent, more than six times the increase in all other age groups combined. In 1960, fourteen- to twenty-four-year-olds accounted for 69 percent of all arrests for serious crimes, although they comprised only 15.1 percent of the population. Without any change in young people's propensity for crime, the increase in their numbers alone would have brought about a 40 to 50 percent increase in criminal violence between 1960 and 1975. In fact, the number of serious crimes increased more than 200 percent. The change in the age distribution of the population thus accounts for only 25 percent of the increase; the rest is due to the greater frequency with which members of every age group, but particularly the young, commit serious crimes.

—From Charles E. Silberman, *Criminal Violence, Criminal Justice*

B. The truth as I see it is that contemporary marriage is a wretched institution. It spells the end of voluntary affection, of love freely given and joyously received. Beautiful romances are transmuted into dull marriages, and eventually the relationship becomes constricting, corrosive, grinding, and destructive. The beautiful love affair becomes a bitter contract.

The basic reason for this sad state of affairs is that marriage was not designed to bear the burdens now being asked of it by the urban American middle class. It is an institution that evolved over centuries to meet some very specific functional needs of a nonindustrial society. Romantic love was viewed as tragic, or merely irrelevant. Today it is the titillating prelude to domestic tragedy, or, perhaps more frequently, to domestic grotesqueries that are only pathetic.

Marriage was not designed as a mechanism for providing friendship, erotic experience, romantic love, personal fulfillment, continuous lay psychotherapy, or recreation. The Western European family was not designed to carry a lifelong load of highly emotional romantic freight. Given its present structure, it simply has to fail when asked to do so. The very idea of an irrevocable contract obligating the parties concerned to a lifetime of romantic effort is utterly absurd.

Other pressures of the present era have tended to overburden marriage with expectations it cannot fulfill. Industrialized, urbanized America is a society which has lost the sense of community. Our ties to our society, to the bustling multitudes that make up this dazzling kaleidoscope of contemporary America, are as formal and superficial as they are numerous. We all search for community, and yet we know that the search is futile. Cut off from the support and satisfactions that flow from community, the confused and searching young American can do little but place all of his bets on creating a community in microcosm, his own marriage.

—From Mervyn Cadwallader, "Marriage as a Wretched Institution,"
Atlantic Monthly, November 1966

C. By 1662, sugar consumption in England had zoomed from zero to some 16 million pounds a year, this in little over two centuries. Then, in 1665, London was swept by a plague. More than 30,000 people died that September. Since only one pest house, or hospital, existed for the entire city, sick people were locked up in their homes, under guard, behind doors painted with huge red crosses. Others fled the city; everything ground to a halt. While swarms of quacks sold worthless potions and pills, learned physicians used knives and burning caustic to lance the underarms and groin swellings. When their surgery did more harm than good, and the doctors themselves became infected, they stopped that treatment. In a year, the epidemic ran its course. The plague was named after its most obvious symptom, the swelling (or buboes), and became known as the bubonic plague. The swelling plague. The plague of boils.

People who lived in the country virtually without sugar seemed to escape the plague. Had anyone called it the city sugar plague, they might have been denounced as menaces to commerce and crown and strung to a gibbet.

—From William Dufty, *Sugar Blues*

D. A survey by the Law Enforcement Assistance Administration of ten thousand inmates of correctional facilities concluded that 13 percent of the inmates had used heroin at the time of their arrest. The same survey estimated between 13 and 60 percent of incarcerated criminals to have been heroin users. Although this kind of data suggests links between heroin use and crime, nothing was established in that survey to demonstrate that these individuals began to commit crimes because of their heroin use, nor does the study indicate whether the correctional population surveyed was typical of all those arrested, or of all committing crimes. It may indicate a tendency to jail heroin users in disproportionate numbers.

The studies which indicate that after the onset of opiate addiction individuals generally increase their criminal activity come closest to demonstrating a causal link between drug use and crime. These studies suggest that although an individual may have been a criminal before he used heroin, his heavy use led to an increase in criminal activity to meet the new income need. On its face, this implies a connection between heroin use and crime. However, there is an across-the-board increase in crime among men between ages eighteen and twenty-five, irrespective of drug use. Thus, any data suggesting increased crime because of heroin use would have to correct for the general increase in crime for this age bracket.

The evidence relating to a heroin-crime link could best be described as showing that regular, heavy opiate use in the United States probably means a higher rate of revenue-producing crime by the addict. Because of its broad political appeal, however, this connection has been repeatedly overstated and even misrepresented to support tough enforcement policies.

—From Drug Abuse Council, *The Facts about "Drug Abuse"* (this excerpt by John R. Pekkanen)

3. Find an example of each the following:
  A. A *post hoc* fallacy in a magazine article.
  B. An oversimplification in your campus newspaper.

Suggested Writing Assignments

1. Social:
  What are the causes of: alcoholism among teenagers?
  racial prejudice?
  the resurgence of fundamentalism in religion?

2. Historical:
  Why did feudalism arise as a social structure?
  What caused "McCarthyism" in the 1950s?
  What role did "yellow journalism" play in the United States declaring war against Spain in 1898?
  Why were dictators—Mussolini, Hitler, Franco, Stalin—able to seize power across Europe in the 1920s and 1930s?
  What caused Prohibition in America?
  What caused the Salem witch trials?

3. Medical/Psychological:
  What causes: hiccoughing
  seasickness
  stuttering
  kleptomania
  Trace the causes of some hang-up or mild phobia that you have.
  What are the psychological reasons for hunting animals?

4. Natural/Scientific:
  What causes the "northern lights" (aurora borealis)?
  What causes: earthquakes   magnetism
  deserts   comets
  Mars' redness   continental drift
  sunspots   supernovas
  tidal waves   tornadoes

5. Cultural:
   How do you account for the popularity of:
   Bogie or Monroe
   antiques
   professional football
   health foods

6. Choose a year that marked a sociological, cultural, political, or economic change and give the causes of the change. For example, in 1966 the Civil Rights Movement underwent a significant change. Why?

7. Why was there so much scientific discovery in the seventeenth century, especially in astronomy?

Additional Readings

WHO KILLED BENNY PARET?

Norman Cousins

Sometime about 1935 or 1936 I had an interview with Mike Jacobs, the prize-fight promoter. I was a fledgling newspaper reporter at that time; my beat was education, but during the vacation season I found myself on varied assignments, all the way from ship news to sports reporting. In this way I found myself sitting opposite the most powerful figure in the boxing world.   1

There was nothing spectacular in Mr. Jacobs's manner or appearance; but when he spoke about prize fights, he was no longer a bland little man but a colossus who sounded the way Napoleon must have sounded when he reviewed a battle. You knew you were listening to Number One. His saying something made it true.   2

We discussed what to him was the only important element in successful promoting—how to please the crowd. So far as he was concerned, there was no mystery to it. You put killers in the ring and the people filled your arena. You hire boxing artists—men who are adroit at feinting, parrying, weaving, jabbing, and dancing, but who don't pack dynamite in their fists—and you wind up counting your empty seats. So you searched for the killers and sluggers and maulers—fellows who could hit with the force of a baseball bat.   3

I asked Mr. Jacobs if he was speaking literally when he said people came out to   4
see the killer.

"They don't come out to see a tea party," he said evenly. "They come out to see   5
the knockout. They come out to see a man hurt. If they think anything else, they're
kidding themselves."

Recently a young man by the name of Benny Paret was killed in the ring. The   6
killing was seen by millions; it was on television. In the twelfth round he was hit hard in
the head several times, went down, was counted out, and never came out of the
coma.

The Paret fight produced a flurry of investigations. Governor Rockefeller was   7
shocked by what happened and appointed a committee to assess the responsibility.
The New York State Boxing Commission decided to find out what was wrong. The
District Attorney's office expressed its concern. One question that was solemnly
studied in all three probes concerned the action of the referee. Did he act in time to
stop the fight? Another question had to do with the role of the examining doctors who
certified the physical fitness of the fighters before the bout. Still another question
involved Mr. Paret's manager: did he rush his boy into the fight without adequate time
to recuperate from the previous one?

In short, the investigators looked into every possible cause except the real one.   8
Benny Paret was killed because the human fist delivers enough impact, when directed against the head, to produce a massive hemorrhage in the brain. The human
brain is the most delicate and complex mechanism in all creation. It has a lacework of
millions of highly fragile nerve connections. Nature attempts to protect this exquisitely
intricate machinery by encasing it in a hard shell. Fortunately, the shell is thick enough
to withstand a great deal of pounding. Nature, however, can protect man against
everything except man himself. Not every blow to the head will kill a man—but there is
always the risk of concussion and damage to the brain. A prize fighter may be able to
survive even repeated brain concussions and go on fighting, but the damage to his
brain may be permanent.

In any event, it is futile to investigate the referee's role and seek to determine   9
whether he should have intervened to stop the fight earlier. This is not where the
primary responsibility lies. The primary responsibility lies with the people who pay to
see a man hurt. The referee who stops a fight too soon from the crowd's viewpoint can
expect to be booed. The crowd wants the knockout: it wants to see a man stretched
out on the canvas. This is the supreme moment in boxing. It is nonsense to talk about
prize fighting as a test of boxing skills. No crowd was ever brought to its feet
screaming and cheering at the sight of two men beautifully dodging and weaving out
of each other's jabs. The time the crowd comes alive is when a man is hit hard over
the heart or the head, when his mouthpiece flies out, when blood squirts out of his
nose or eyes, when he wobbles under the attack and his pursuer continues to smash
at him with poleax impact.

Don't blame it on the referee. Don't even blame it on the fight managers. Put the   10
blame where it belongs—on the prevailing mores that regard prize fighting as a

perfectly proper enterprise and vehicle of entertainment. No one doubts that many people enjoy prize fighting and will miss it if it should be thrown out. And that is precisely the point.

—From *Saturday Review*, May, 6, 1962

1. We can look at a topic from many different angles. In earlier chapters, we created narratives about topics, defined topics, compared them to other subjects, and classified them. The death of Benny Paret was the subject of an earlier essay (page 67) by Norman Mailer. Both that piece and this one found the fight significant for one reason—a man was killed. Yet Mailer and Cousins approach that death in very different ways. Contrast these two fundamentally different approaches.

2. What is Cousins' thesis? Where does he state it explicitly?

3. What kind of evidence does he offer to substantiate his view?

4. Why does Cousins distinguish between cause and responsibility? Explain the difference.

5. What purpose does paragraph 7 serve?

6. Cousins categorizes fighters as either "killers" or "boxing artists." What is his purpose in limiting the classifications to these two? Is this an either/or fallacy? Substantiate your answer.

7. Why does Cousins spend the first two paragraphs describing the fight promoter?

8. Where does Cousins attempt to engage readers' emotions in the essay? What emotions is he trying to engage? Why? Is the appeal to emotions effective?

PASSIVE SMOKING

Ellen Goodman

I am, according to *The New England Journal of Medicine*, a passive smoker. I did not 1
mean to be one. My parents did not raise me to be one. But there you are. *The New England Journal of Medicine* says I am one, and it ought to know.

What I meant to be was a plain old nonsmoker. It fits my self-image better. It fits 2
my habits better.

I am, you see, one of the lucky people who choked on the first green-tipped, 3
personally labeled, sweet-sixteen cigarette that ever touched my lips in 1957. I count this as a piece of biological luck, not unlike my inability to get drunk.

Years ago, I discovered that I fell asleep before I ever found the right lamp   4
shade for my head. So, I end up dozing instead of drunk, the way I end up coughing
instead of cancerous.

It is not my virtue but my body chemistry which keeps me from falling down the   5
path of assorted evils. If my jaw would only lock at the sight of assorted chocolates, I
would be perfect.

But this morning I am in no position to gloat.   6

Two men from the University of California, San Diego, studied men and women   7
at work. Some of the 2,000 worked in smoky places and some in smoke-free places.
Now, the researchers have published the first study that proves what we knew all
along, deep down in our lungs: Nonsmokers are getting zonked by the smokers at
work.

Professor James White and Dr. Herman Froeb put it more carefully in their   8
paper. The way they figured it, nonsmokers have about the same amount of small
airways impairment as people who smoke up to about eleven cigarettes a day.
Sounding like the Surgeon General's warning, they wrote that "chronic exposure to
tobacco smoke in the work environment is deleterious to the nonsmoker."

Informally, Professor White said simply, "We know that if a person works   9
around another smoker for a period of time, he will experience lung damage. Now
whether it will impair him or cause emphysema, we don't know. But who wants it?"

Not I, said the little red hen. But, at this very moment, I am sitting here at my   10
desk passively smoking.

The man behind me, who is otherwise a charming neighbor, smokes cigars.   11
They are not really offensive, he has explained to me patiently and in some detail,
because they are *good* cigars. It's the cheap cigars that smell, he says, pointing one
stinking stogie at another. I fail to make this class distinction.

Three yards away, the environmental reporter sits attached to his pipe. The   12
smoke that surrounds it would make the EPA inspector condemn a plant. "It is," he
admits, puffing thoughtfully, "a contradiction."

All around me are cigarettes whose smoke is mysteriously attracted to my   13
magnetic personality. I am convinced that whenever I change desks in this city room,
the air currents in my office shift and I am once again drifting in the Smoke Stream.

My situation isn't the worst by far. I have a friend who goes home every night   14
and washes that Marlboro man right out of her hair. I have another who actually goes
into the garage for a breath of fresh air.

I sympathize with smokers, although I no longer buy them ashtrays. (I have a   15
friend who uses my daughter's dollhouse bathtub for his butts, but I promised not to
tell a soul.) I imagine that stopping smoking is like stopping eating.

So, I don't want to ban smoke just because I don't want to work with banned   16
smokers. But I don't want to inhale the stuff, either.

What I would like is to find the national scene more in line with the Minnesota   17
Clean Air Act. What I would like is to extend the airline policy to the ground, wherever
possible, and divide the work place into zones.

As *The New England Journal of Medicine* editorialized: ". . . the feelings and psychological reactions of smokers are as vehement as those of nonsmokers. But now, for the first time, we have a quantitative measurement of a physical change—a fact that may tip the scales in favor of nonsmokers." 18

Well, it's tipped my scale. This morning, at least, one more passive smoker is feeling aggressive. 19

—From *At Large*

1. What is the causal relationship that Goodman establishes in this essay?

2. Is there an implied argument that passive smoking causes cancer? Explain why you think there is or isn't an unstated argument at work in this essay.

3. What does Goodman do with her causal information? Is it an end in itself, or does she use it for a further end? What is her thesis, and why is it placed where it is instead of elsewhere?

4. In Chapter 1, we established that, to hold readers' attention, an essay must have a provocative subject, a challenging thesis, a lively style, dramatic facts, or some combination of these qualities. What holds readers' attention in this essay? Why?

5. What is the purpose of the first six paragraphs?

6. Point out instances of humor in the essay. Is the humor inappropriate? Why, or why not?

7. How would you describe Goodman's diction—as formal, colloquial, elegant, or informal? Contrast her diction to that of the *New England Journal of Medicine* article and editorial.

TRIGGERING THE GLACIERS

Isaac Asimov

The ice ages of the last million years have obviously not brought an end to life on the planet. They didn't even put an end to human life. *Homo sapiens* and its hominid ancestors lived all through the ice ages of the last million years without any noticeable interruption of rapid evolution and development. 1

Nevertheless, it is fair to wonder whether another period of glaciation is ahead of us or whether it is all part of the past. Even if an ice age does not mean an end to life or even to humanity, and is not catastrophic in that sense, the thought of almost all of Canada and of the northern quarter of the United States under a mile-deep glacier (to say nothing of portions of Europe and Asia similarly iced) might seem quite bad enough. 2

To decide whether the glaciers might return, it would help to learn first what   3
causes such periods of glaciation. And before trying to do that, we must understand
that it doesn't take much to start the glaciers moving; we don't have to postulate large
and impossible changes.

Right now, snow falls over much of northern North America and Eurasia every   4
winter and leaves all that region covered with frozen water almost as though the Ice
Age had returned. The snow cover, however, is only a few centimeters to a couple of
meters thick, and in the course of the summer it all melts. There is, in general, a
balance and on the average as much snow melts in the summer as falls in the winter.
There is no overall change.

But suppose that something happens which cools the summers just a bit,   5
perhaps only two or three degrees. There would continue to be warmer summers and
cooler summers in some random distribution, but the warmer summers would occur
less frequently and the cooler summers more frequently so that, on the average, the
snow that fell in the winter would not quite all melt in the summer. There would be a
net increase in snow cover from year to year. This would be a very slow increase and
it would be noticeable in the northern polar and subpolar regions and in the higher
mountainous regions. The accumulating snow would turn to ice and the glaciers that
exist in the polar regions and at higher elevations even in southerly latitudes would
extend farther in the winter and retreat less in the summer. They would grow from
year to year.

The change would feed on itself. Ice reflects light more efficiently than bare rock   6
or soil does. In fact, ice reflects some 90 percent of the light that falls on it, while bare
soil reflects less than 10 percent. This means that as the ice cover expands, more
sunlight is reflected and less is absorbed. The average temperature of the Earth
would drop a little farther, summers would grow a trifle cooler still, and the ice cover
would expand still more rapidly. As a result of a very small cooling trigger, then, the
glaciers would grow and turn into ice sheets that would slowly advance, year by year,
until finally they could cover vast stretches of ground.

Once an ice age had well established itself and the glaciers had reached far   7
southward, however, a reverse trigger, very small in itself, could initiate a general
retreat. If the average temperature of summer rose two or three degrees over an
extended period of time, more snow would melt in the summer than would fall in the
winter and the ice would recede somewhat from year to year. As it receded, the Earth
as a whole would reflect somewhat less sunlight and absorb somewhat more. This
would further warm the summers and the glacier retreat would be accelerated.

What we must do, then, is identify the trigger that sets off the glacial advance—   8
and retreat. This is not hard to do. The trouble is, in fact, that there are too many
possible triggers and the difficult task is to choose among them. For instance the
trigger may lie in the sun itself. Earlier, I mentioned that the Maunder minimum[1] came

---

[1]In an earlier chapter of Asimov's book, he has explained that *minima* are periods of solar
inactivity when few sunspots occur. In these periods, the sun may give off less heat. Maunder
minima are named after the astronomer E. W. Maunder.

at a time when Earth's weather was generally on the chilly side. The time is actually referred to, sometimes, as "the Little Ice Age."

If there is a causal connection, if Maunder minima cool the Earth, then perhaps 9 every hundred thousand years or so it may be that the sun goes through an extended Maunder minimum, one that doesn't last a few decades, but a few millennia. The Earth may then be chilly long enough to initiate and maintain an ice age. When the sun finally begins to spot again and experiences only short Maunder minima at most, the earth would warm up slightly and the glacial retreat begin.

There may be something to this, but we have no evidence. Perhaps further 10 studies of the solar neutrinos[2] and why they are so few in number may help us know enough of what is going on inside the sun to allow us to understand the intricacies of the sunspot cycle. We might then be able to match the sunspot variations with the periods of glaciation and be able to predict if and when another period will arrive.

Or, it might not be the sun itself, which might shine with beautiful steadiness. It 11 might, instead, be the nature of the space between the Earth and sun.

I explained earlier that there was only an incredibly small chance of a close 12 encounter with a star or any other small object from interstellar space, on the part of either the sun or the Earth. There are, however, occasional clouds of dust and gas between the stars here in the outskirts of our galaxy (and of other galaxies like it) and the sun in its orbit about the galactic center might easily pass through some of those clouds.

The clouds are not dense by ordinary standards. They would not poison our 13 atmosphere or us. They would not, in themselves, be particularly noticeable to the average observer, let alone catastrophic. Indeed, NASA scientist, Dixon M. Butler, suggested in 1978 that our solar system has passed through at least a dozen quite extensive clouds in the course of its lifetime and, if anything, this may be an underestimate.

Almost all the materials in such clouds are hydrogen and helium, which would 14 not affect us at all, one way or another. However, about 1 percent of the mass of such clouds consists of dust; grains of ice or rock. Each of these grains would reflect, or absorb and reradiate, sunlight, so that less sunlight than normal would make its way past the grains to fall on Earth's surface.

The grains might not blank out the light falling on Earth very much. The sun 15 would look as bright and perhaps even the stars would look no different. Nevertheless, a particularly dense cloud might blank out just enough light to cool the summers the proper amount to trigger an ice age. Moving out of the cloud might serve as the trigger for glacial retreat.

It may be that for the last million years the solar system has been passing 16 through a cloudy region of the Galaxy and that whenever we pass through a particularly dense cloud that will blank out just enough light, an ice age will start, and when

[2]Neutrinos (Italian for "little neutral one") are particles emitted when radioactive nuclei break down; although neutrinos are without electrical charge and probably without mass, they have energy.

we leave it behind us, the glaciers retreat. Prior to the last million-year period there was a 250-million-year period in which there were no ice ages, and perhaps during that time the solar system was passing through clear regions. Prior to that there was the Ice Age I mentioned as giving rise to the thought of Pangaea.[3]

It may be that every 200 to 250 million years there are a series of ice ages.   17
Since this is not very different from the period of revolution of the solar system about the galactic center, perhaps we are passing through the same cloudy region every revolution. If we have now passed through the region completely, then there may be no periods of glaciation for a quarter of a billion years. If not, another one—or a whole series of them—is due much sooner than that.

In 1978, for instance, a group of French astronomers presented evidence   18
leading to the possibility of another interstellar cloud just ahead. The solar system may be approaching it at a velocity of 20 kilometers (12.5 miles) per second, and at that rate, it may reach the edges of the cloud in about 50,000 years.

But it may not be either the sun directly or the dust clouds of interstellar space   19
that are the true trigger. It may be Earth itself, or rather its atmosphere, that offers the necessary mechanism. The sun's radiation has to pass through the atmosphere and that might affect it.

Consider that the sun's radiation reaching Earth does so chiefly in the form of   20
visible light. The peak of the sun's radiation *is* in the wavelengths of visible light and this passes through the atmosphere easily. Other forms of radiation, such as ultraviolet and x-rays, which the sun produces in lesser profusion are blocked by the atmosphere.

In the absence of the sun—as at night—the Earth's surface radiates heat away   21
into outer space. It does so chiefly in the form of long infrared waves. These pass through the atmosphere, too. Under ordinary conditions, these two effects balance and the Earth loses as much heat from its night-shrouded surface as it gains on its daylight-drenched surface, and its average surface temperature remains the same from year to year.

Nitrogen and oxygen, which make up virtually all the atmosphere, are easily   22
transparent to both visible light and to infrared radiation. Carbon dioxide and water vapor, however, while transparent to visible light are not transparent to infrared. This was first pointed out in 1861 by the Irish physicist John Tyndall (1820–93). Carbon dioxide makes up only 0.03 percent of the Earth's atmosphere and the water vapor content is variable but low. Therefore, they don't block the infrared radiation altogether.

Nevertheless, they do block the infrared radiation somewhat. If the Earth's   23
atmosphere lacked carbon dioxide and water vapor entirely, more infrared radiation would escape at night than does so now. The nights would be colder than they are

[3]Pangaea (Greek for "all Earth") is the name given to the land mass that existed on Earth millions of years ago when all the continents were joined into one huge continent; Pangaea broke up into smaller continents, which then drifted to their present positions.

now and the days, warming up from a colder start, would be cooler. The average temperature of the Earth would be distinctly less than it is now.

The carbon dioxide and water vapor in our atmosphere, even though present in small quantities, block enough of the infrared to act as appreciable conservers of heat. Their presence serves to produce a distinctly higher average temperature for the Earth than would otherwise be the case. This is called the "greenhouse effect," because the glass of a greenhouse works similarly, letting through the visible light of the sun and holding back the infrared reradiation from the interior. 24

Suppose, for some reason, the carbon dioxide content of the atmosphere goes up slightly. Let us suppose it doubles to 0.06 percent. This would not affect the breathability of the atmosphere and we would be unaware of the change in itself— only of its effects. An atmosphere with that slight increase in carbon dioxide would be still more opaque to infrared radiation. Since infrared radiation is held back, the temperature of the Earth would rise slightly. The slightly higher temperature would increase the evaporation of the oceans, raise the level of water vapor in the air, and that, too, would contribute to an increased greenhouse effect. 25

Suppose, on the other hand, the carbon dioxide content of the atmosphere goes down slightly, from 0.03 percent to 0.015 percent. Now the infrared radiation escapes more easily and the temperature of the Earth drops slightly. With lower temperatures, the water vapor content decreases, adding its bit to the reverse greenhouse effect. Such rises and falls in temperature could be enough to end or begin a period of glaciation. 26

But what could bring about such changes in carbon dioxide content of the atmosphere? Animal life produces carbon dioxide in great quantity, but plant life consumes it in equally great quantity, and the effect of life generally is to maintain the balance.* There are, however, natural processes on Earth that either produce or consume carbon dioxide independently of life and they may unbalance the equilibrium sufficiently to produce a trigger. 27

For instance, a great deal of atmospheric carbon dioxide can dissolve in the ocean, but carbon dioxide dissolved in the ocean can easily be given up to the atmosphere again. Carbon dioxide can also react with the oxides of the Earth's crust to form carbonates and there the carbon dioxide is more likely to stay put. 28

Of course, those portions of the Earth's crust that are exposed to air have already absorbed what carbon dioxide they can. During periods of mountain formation, however, new rock reaches the surface, new rock that has not been exposed to carbon dioxide, and this can act as a carbon dioxide-absorbing medium, reducing the percentage in the atmosphere. 29

On the other hand, volcanoes spew vast quantities of carbon dioxide into the atmosphere since the intense heat that melts rocks into lava breaks up the carbonates and liberates the carbon dioxide again. In periods of unusually high volcanic activity, the atmospheric content of carbon dioxide may go up. 30

Both volcanoes and mountain building are the result of the movements of the 31

*This is not entirely true of that portion of life that includes human activity.

tectonic plates, but there are times when the conditions for vulcanism are more common than for those of mountain formation and there are times when the reverse is true.

It may be that when mountain formation is more characteristic of a period in Earth's history, the carbon dioxide content goes down, the Earth's surface temperature drops, and the glaciers begin to advance. When it is vulcanism that predominates, the carbon dioxide content goes up, the Earth surface temperature rises, and the glaciers, if present, begin to retreat.   32

But just to show that things are not as simple as they might sound, if volcanic eruption tends to be *too* violent, large quantities of dust may be hurled into the stratosphere and this may produce so many "years without a summer" like 1816, that *this* may trigger an ice age.   33

From the volcanic ash in ocean sediments, it would seem that vulcanism in the last 2 million years has been some four times as intense as in the preceding 18 million years. Perhaps it is a dusty stratosphere, then, that is subjecting the Earth to its periodic ice ages now.   34

—From *A Choice of Catastrophes*

1. Does this essay have a thesis? If so, what is it? If not, what is the essay's purpose?

2. Does Asimov present his explanations as informed conjecture or as definite causal relationships? Explain your answer, drawing from his prose for substantiation.

3. Find an example of a circular pattern of causation and an example of a causal chain in Asimov's explanations.

4. Is there a reason for Asimov's presenting the possible causes in the order that he does? Explain.

5. Outline the essay to see its structure more clearly.

6. Why does Asimov tell who discovered the various ideas he cites?

CHAPTER 10

Consequential Analysis

This chapter on consequences must be considered as an extension of the previous chapter because cause and effect are cemented together in a fixed relationship. "Cause and effect, means and ends, seed and fruit, cannot be severed," Ralph Waldo Emerson contended, "for the effect already blooms in the cause, the end pre-exists in the means, the fruit in the seed."

Although separating cause and effect and drawing distinctions between them distort the unity of their relationship, there is something to be said for disentangling them for the purposes of analysis and writing. We almost always explore both when we analyze a subject, but our focus is usually more on one than the other. Whether we are searching for causes or for consequences depends on which of the two is unknown or uncertain.

Studying consequences is almost the same as studying causes, but our vision is reversed. Instead of starting with effects and tracing backward to causes, we start with causes and seek effects. In the same way that we assume that everything has a cause, we assume that every action has a consequence. Furthermore, the principles involved in establishing consequences are the same as those in establishing causes; therefore, studying effects requires an equally conscientious investigation of the facts and a vigilance against oversimplification.

Consequential Patterns

We encounter the same patterns here as in causal analysis, and having already discussed the first four patterns in the previous chapter, we will examine the last one in this chapter:

A ————————➤ B

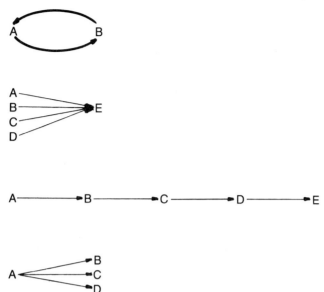

As noted earlier, effects are seldom singular; in a complex, in-terdependent society, an action usually has multiple effects. Think, for example, of some of the many domestic consequences resulting from one cause—OPEC's raising the price of crude oil in the 1970s:

Car sales dropped; Detroit concentrated on producing smaller autos.

Use of public transportation accelerated, as did the cost.

Research was intensified to discover alternative sources of energy.

Remote vacation spots (such as Florida, Colorado, and Las Vegas) were hard hit; fewer recreational vehicles, such as campers and power boats, were sold.

Farm costs and food costs rose with cost hikes in petroleum-based fertilizer and gas for tractors.

Heating and lighting bills increased; more insulation was installed; thermostats were lowered.

Air fares went up (Boeing 757 jets, which burn 30 percent less fuel than 727s, were in demand).

Truckers increased freight charges 5 percent for every 2-cent in-crease in gasoline.

Businesses of every kind passed along increased costs to consumers.

Inflation soared, and the dollar dropped on the international market (the causes of inflation and devaluation are multiple).

All of these consequences and many more were caused by the rise in oil prices. Some of these consequences in turn became intermediate causes themselves. For instance, because their costs increased, businesses raised prices, which in turn resulted in higher inflation. Likewise, the gas prices deterred consumers from buying large cars; without that intermediate consequent—sales being down—auto manufacturers would probably not have focused on producing smaller, more energy-efficient cars.

APPLICATION

In 1985 the price of crude oil dropped from $34 a barrel to $12 a barrel and has remained relatively low. What have been the major effects of the declining oil prices?

Invention: Systematic Investigation to Discover Effects

When we search for multiple consequences, we are asking the question "what?" We can apply this question to the major fields of influence that we used in the previous chapter:

political	social
economic	psychological/emotional
religious	scientific/technological
cultural	environmental/geographical
moral	

An equally productive question to ask is "Who?": Who is affected? We can combine the "what" and "who" to explore the consequences of almost any issue. For example, what have been the political effects of lower oil prices on such oil-producing countries as Saudi Arabia, Mexico, Libya, Kuwait, Iran, and Iraq? What have been the economic effects of lower oil prices on such oil-producing states as Texas, Oklahoma, and Louisiana? What have lower prices for Texas crude meant to the Texas educational system? Depending on our focus, we can explore any of the fields of influence and any population, whether it is international, national, state, city, community, group, family, or individual.

Immediate and Long-Range Effects

The interval between action and consequence may be quite long, and consequences that are slow to develop are referred to as *delayed effects*. For example, a boxer may take incredible beatings during his professional career, and the immediate results will be cuts over the eyes, a broken nose, a cauliflower ear, and so forth; but 20 years later, brain damage may result in the form of early senility and reduced memory.

When we trace consequences, we begin at the source and go forward, a seemingly easy task. Bloodhound-like, we go off sniffing and barking, following the scent from the cause in search of effects. But as with hounds, most of us find only the immediate prey. We're able to discover the effects that immediately follow an action, but often the long-range effects, which are as powerful and are longer lasting, elude us. What would be the effects, for instance, of an atomic war? The immediate effects are easy to envision—the mass confusion, destruction, radiation illness, lack of medical supplies, incinerated life—but the remote effects from the radiation fallout are just as disastrous—delayed environmental and biological effects, delayed casualties from leukemia, shortened life-spans, and genetic aberrations for generations. We must learn to look for such delayed consequences by consciously examining our subject at several chronological points to make certain that we have not, like a lazy hound, stopped at the first hare we've come to.

Myopic (shortsighted) thinking is dangerous, as Americans have discovered concerning our energy and environmental policies. Short-sighted policies from government and business and conspicuous consumption by all Americans have led to depletion of oil reserves, erosion of soil, loss of arable land, strip-mining, depletion of underground water level, streams polluted with chemicals, and air polluted with toxic fumes. If we don't consider long-range consequences as well as immediate needs, we eventually reap the ill effects of our actions. Today, for instance, we are experiencing the effects of a shortsighted transportation policy that Congress passed in the 1950s, when America was car-crazed. We allocated billions of dollars for an interstate highway system instead of realizing that America needed to invest in public transportation to conserve fuel and to prevent auto exhaust pollution. Perhaps today we are a little better at weighing present needs against future effects, since most Americans are conscious of environmental conservation, and conservation itself represents long-range thinking.

The problem, however, is that long-range effects are more difficult to fathom, even though they are often more significant than immediate effects. For example, to fatten poultry, pork, and beef, feed companies use wonder drugs, which have been proven to put weight on animals quickly; in fact, almost 40 percent of all antibiotics produced in the United States are used as fatteners. Although the immediate effects of these feed additives are positive—animals grow quickly—the long-range consequences are harmful. People who eat drug-fattened meat build up such high levels of antibiotics in their bodies that they develop an immunity to them; then when they contract a disease that should normally be cured by penicillin or tetracycline, they discover that the diseases have become resistant and the antibiotics are ineffectual.

Secondary and Unanticipated Consequences

Just as we can usually find the immediate effects, we have little trouble finding major and expected consequences. Often, however, minor consequences and unexpected consequences occur, and they are easy to overlook. An action will usually set off many reverberations, like a pebble tossed into a pond, the initial splash being the major effect and the series of waves being the secondary effects, some of which may be unanticipated. For example:

> The main effect of social security has been a guaranteed financial income for the elderly, but an unforeseen by-product of social security has been a decreased financial base for new business investment. Because people know that they will receive social security payments when they reach 65, they save less for their retirement years than they did in the past; savings in banks are the basis for businesses borrowing money for new development, so as that financial base dwindles, new development dwindles also, and the gross national product suffers.

> The main consequences of the oil shortage were higher gasoline prices and longer lines at the service stations, but one side effect was an increase in people being treated for gasoline poisoning—because more siphoning occurred.

> Although evidence about whether jogging promotes longevity is indecisive, researchers discovered that such strenuous exercise has the auxiliary benefit of slowing down the mental deterioration of aging because more oxygen is pumped to the brain.

> A quirky consequence of the many kidnappings in Italy by terrorists in the late 1970s was a sharp decline in Rolls Royce sales; once Rolls' largest European market, Italy imported 50 percent fewer of the cars in the 2-year period after kidnappings increased because

terrorists kidnap the wealthy, and rich Italians wanted to avoid ostentatious displays of wealth.

An unexpected consequence of Proposition 13 in California was an invasion of mosquitos: Lack of funds led to a cutback in personnel to catch African clawed frogs in Californian streams, so the frogs reproduced quickly and devoured their main prey, which is mosquito fish, whose main diet is mosquito eggs, the result being that more mosquitos hatched. The whole thing resembles a nursery tale: This is the referendum that reduced the personnel who caught the frogs that ate the fish that ate the eggs and caused a mosquito infestation.

The plague that ravaged in Europe in the fourteenth and fifteenth centuries, killing perhaps 25 million people, had a bizarre side effect—drunkenness. Desperate to find a preventative, people latched on to the idea that liquor helped ward off the plague. Most of Europe stayed in a state of intoxication as long as the plague continued, and although the liquor didn't prevent the disease, it no doubt eased people's worries to some degree.

As we can see, effects are not always predictable. Quite often consequences are unintended and unplanned for; in fact, sometimes programs result in consequences that are antithetical to those intended. In the 1930s, for instance, Roosevelt's Soil Conservation Program was intended to help the rural poor by allowing farmers to lease their land to the government, but the legislation hurt the poorest rural group, tenant farmers or sharecroppers, because when landowners put their acres into the Soil Conservation Program, tenant farmers had no place to work or even to live. Likewise, in the 1970s the program to cure heroin addicts by using methadone as a temporary substitute resulted in methadone addiction; by the second year of the program, more addicts died of methadone overdose than of heroin. Here is an illustration of a rodent control program that backfired:

An example of one poorly conceived biocontrol method was the introduction in the 1870s of the Indian mongoose into Jamaica, Puerto Rico, and other West Indian islands to combat rats on sugar cane plantations. Although the mongoose initially seemed highly effective, the rat population soon returned to pest levels. Farmers found mongooses were preying heavily on their chickens, and in the early 1940s the animals were incriminated as the vector of, and reservoir for, rabies. In addition to these new problems, the question remained as to why the mongoose, an animal that usually controlled rats, was suddenly ineffective.

At the time the mongoose was brought there, the rat population of the Caribbean Islands consisted of two species, the Norway, or brown, rat and its natural competitor, the tree, or black, rat. The Norway rat was then the dominant rat species because it generally drives out the tree rat and all rival rodents. Since the Norway rat nests in the ground, the introduced mongoose had ample opportunity to attack and control it on sugar plantations. Once the dominant species was controlled, tree rats easily became dominant since they no longer had a competitor. The mongoose, which cannot climb, could not reach the tree rat, and hence itself developed into a pest. On islands where the mongoose was not introduced, the Norway rat remains the dominant species.

Besides preying on chickens and carrying rabies, the mongoose destroyed ground-nesting birds and lizards. The reduction in lizard populations apparently resulted in an increase in populations of a sugar cane beetle. This example illustrates not only how far-reaching the effects of a biocontrol method can be, but also the importance of studying an entire established ecosystem before introducing any new species.

David and Marcia Pimentel, "The Risk of Pesticides," *Natural History*, March 1979

Usually effects are predictable, but there are so many variables in any given situation that consequences are sometimes totally surprising and disproportionate. Small actions can occasionally lead to great consequences. Who would have thought, for instance, that a bungled hotel break-in could have eventually led to the resignation of a United States president, or that using aerosol spray deodorant could erode the ozone layer and cause skin cancer?

We must learn to look not simply for the immediate, the expected, and the major consequences; we must also carefully study the possible long-range and secondary effects of an action. In short, we must be thorough hounds when we track consequences.

APPLICATION

1. What would be the effects of raising the minimum wage?

2. What were the effects of the discovery of the New World? (Divide the effects into immediate and long-range.)

3. What are the effects of extensive private car operation in the United States?

4. What are the effects of watching television? (Classify the effects under major headings—for instance, under groups of people affected or under such headings as *stereotyping, violence, race relations.*)

5. What are the effects of going to college?

6. What are the effects of drinking alcohol, short-term and long-range?

7. In 1970 the average life expectancy for females worldwide was 57 years and for men, 53; in 1980 the average had risen to 62.3 and 58.6 years, respectively. What are the consequences of the increasing life expectancy and of the longer lifespan for women over men? A similar statistic is that in 1900 only 4 percent of the United States population was 65 and older; in 1970, the figure was 10 percent.

8. By the year 2000, Hispanic Americans are expected to become the largest minority in the country. What effects will this growing population have on politics and society?

9. Defense attorneys are increasingly using social science techniques to manipulate the composition of juries. By determining what kind of person will be sympathetic to their client's case, they can effectively stack a jury. What effect do these techniques have on the jury system?

10. What effects would occur if _____? (Imagine some hypothetical situation, such as a prolonged severe drought along latitudes 40°–60°.)

   The following essay, by a first-year economics major named Harold, discusses the effects that illegal immigrants have on the United States. As you read the essay, consider these questions: Has Harold looked at the issue from all angles and discussed all of the major effects? Has he classified the effects, distinguished between primary and secondary effects, and put them into a logical order? Has he offered facts to support his generalizations and to prove his causal assertions?

EFFECTS OF ILLEGAL IMMIGRATION

Illegal aliens from Mexico and Central America are entering the United States in droves daily. Even though the border patrol captures many of them attempting to cross and rounds up others working at restaurants, construction sites, and sweatshops, only a small percentage gets caught and returned to their country, and then they come right back. The consequences of having an enormous population of illegal aliens are monumental and detrimental. These illegals cost U.S. citizens hundreds of millions of dollars each year.

   The worst consequence of having so many illegal aliens is that they take away jobs from U.S. workers, which is unfair to the Americans. Furthermore, illegal aliens usually take unskilled jobs, and therefore they take away jobs from Americans at the bottom of the work force, who can least afford to be unemployed. Even those unskilled American workers who are not displaced from the job market are hurt because the availability of cheap labor (illegal aliens are willing to work for lower than average wages) keeps wages low. Why should an employer pay a decent wage to an American worker when an illegal alien will do the job for less? For those Americans who lose their jobs to illegal aliens, or who cannot find a job because illegal aliens are hired instead, they must go on unemployment or welfare. Since unemployment and welfare are paid for with everyone's tax money, everyone ends up paying indirectly for the problems caused by the presence of illegal aliens.

Illegal aliens cost U.S. citizens in other ways. They use all kinds of social services, including, ironically, police protection. They also use public hospitals and their medical bills are paid for with taxpayer dollars. They seldom have car insurance, and when they are in an accident, the victim or the victim's insurance company must pay for damages; that drives up the price of auto insurance for everyone. Illegal aliens send their children to American schools, which are financed by local taxpayers. Since many of the children speak little or no English, public schools they attend must be bilingual, and bilingual education is expensive.

Another consequence of having a large illegal alien population is that they contribute heavily to crime. The crime rate in Miami, for instance, has increased dramatically in the last 10 years, and much of the increase has been due to the large number of Cuban immigrants; and Miami has become a shipping center for cocaine. The other city most affected is Los Angeles, which also has a high crime rate and a recognized drug problem. Besides making the streets less safe for Americans, this increased crime means that more police must be hired, and this means more taxpayer money. And when the aliens are caught perpetrating a crime, they go to trial, and you and I pay for the expense of that trial.

The consequences of not controlling our borders means that Americans end up losing jobs, paying for services for illegals, and living in a more dangerous world.

What can we point to in the essay that Harold has done well? For one thing, he logically has divided the body of the discussion into three paragraphs: Paragraph 2 deals with job displacement and resulting costs, paragraph 3 with other costs, and paragraph 4 with crime. For another thing, he considers not only direct and obvious costs, but also indirect costs, such as unemployment for displaced American workers and bilingual education. Paragraph 2 in particular demonstrates some solid thinking and analysis. Other commendable qualities are that Harold has provided topic sentences for his paragraphs, and his prose is clear and understandable.

The essay is far from perfect, however, and the problems stem from one source: Harold has not investigated the issue thoroughly. Because he has not looked at the issue from all sides, he has not given a balanced picture of the situation. I seriously doubt that he used the journalistic questions to explore this issue, or if he did, he asked only one kind of question: What are the disadvantages of illegal immigration?

Because of his bias, Harold sees only the negative effects that illegal immigrants have on our society. Asking a series of questions would have helped him to overcome that bias because they would have forced him to consider perspectives other than his own. For example, in addition to asking "What are the disadvantages?" Harold should have asked, "Are there any benefits from illegal immigration?" That question would have sparked other questions: Do illegal immigrants contribute to businesses and therefore help improve the economy? Do they pay taxes? Do they in fact pay more than they get back in services? Do they help create jobs as well as take them? He has examined the issue from the most obvious perspective only, and therefore he has not considered these less obvious questions.

Two other major problems are that Harold has offered us opinions instead of facts, and he has not established the connection between cause and effect, especially in the fourth paragraph. His assertion that Miami's crime has increased over the last 10 years is probably true, but has it increased more than the crime in other cities? How can we be certain that an increase in crime is due to illegal aliens? Are there statistics to substantiate this generalization? Are most of the Cuban immigrants even illegal? The essay is supposed to discuss the effects of *illegal* immigrants, not legal immigrants. The connection between illegal immigrants and drug-smuggling seems far-fetched, and the writer offers no evidence to prove a causal relationship.

In short, Harold needs to rethink the issue, use an inventional system to help him explore it better, and perhaps read some recent literature on the topic. Since he is an economics major and since his analysis of the economic consequences seems sound, he should probably limit the discussion to economic effects.

Analyze his revised essay. In what ways is this a more balanced and complete view of the topic? How does Harold demonstrate that he is knowledgeable about the subject? Why has his opinion changed from that in the first version? Does he have a thesis? If so, what is it and where it is stated? Explain whether the organization seems logical or not. How could Harold further improve his essay?

Illegal aliens from Latin America are crossing into the United States in bigger numbers each year. Although estimates of the number of illegal aliens are imprecise, one indication of their number is the number of them getting caught every year. In 1965, 110,000 illegals were captured and returned; in 1970, 320,000; now over 1,000,000 a year.[1] Estimates of the number of illegals currently living in the U.S. range from 2 million to 10 million.[2]

[1] James Fallows, "Immigration: How It's Affecting Us," *Atlantic Monthly* November 1983: 102.

[2] Tom Morgan, "Closing the Door?" *Newsweek* 25 June 1984: 19.

These illegal aliens affect all aspects of American life, but the most important consequences—and the ones that working Americans are most concerned about—are economic. Specifically, illegal aliens affect job availability, certain industries' stability, and local governments.

Although most Americans seem to view illegal aliens as a drain on the economy, that may not be the case. The evidence suggests that the benefits of having these cheap laborers may be substantial—and may even outweigh their liabilities. On the subject of jobs, for instance, most Americans feel that aliens take away jobs from U.S. workers, and that they particularly take away unskilled jobs from those Americans at the bottom of the work force who can least afford to be unemployed. Why should an employer pay a decent wage to an American worker when an illegal alien will do the job for less and for no fringe benefits? According to this view, American workers lose their jobs to illegals, or cannot find a job because aliens are hired instead, and therefore must go on unemployment or welfare. Since unemployment and welfare are paid for with everyone's tax money, everyone ends up paying indirectly for the presence of illegal aliens. Even though illegal immigration is primarily a regional (Southwest) concern, it indirectly affects workers in other states. If workers in Detroit or Seattle, for instance, are laid off, they might otherwise move to California or Texas to find jobs, but many industrial jobs in those states are being filled with aliens. Another indirect effect is that because of the availability of cheap labor in the Southwest, industries currently located in Pittsburgh or Kansas City might be attracted to Texas.

But this view overlooks certain facts. First, illegal aliens usually work in jobs that American workers do not want—sewing machine operators, maids, gardeners, crop pickers, and so forth. In these types of jobs, the illegals are not displacing U.S. workers; rather, they are filling unfilled jobs. It is true, however, that aliens are moving up in skill. Whereas they once worked primarily in agricultural jobs, they now are working in semi-skilled jobs, such as construction; former strawberry pickers may now be displacing U.S. carpenters. A 1979 study estimated that unemployed Americans could have filled 20% of the jobs held by aliens.[3] Even if they are displacing some U.S. workers, the displacement rate is not one to one because illegal aliens create jobs as well as take them. They create jobs because they are consumers—they buy food, rent housing, buy cars, use phones, pay for entertainment, buy clothes, and so on.

The issue of illegal aliens must also be looked at from the employers' viewpoints. M. S. Forbes, of *Forbes Magazine*, says that the economy of the Southwest is so dependent on the illegal alien labor market that it "would suffer a depression without them."[4] Farmers and owners of restaurants and hotels might not be able to fill menial jobs like fruit and vegetable pickers, maids, busboys and dishwashers if not for illegal aliens; or if they had to use U.S. workers, they would have to pay them much

[3]"Illegal Immigrants: The U.S. May Gain More Than It Loses," *Business Week* 14 May 1984: 126.

[4]M. S. Forbes, Jr., "Immigration," *Forbes Magazine* 17 June 1985: 31.

higher wages and pass along the costs to consumers. By helping to keep consumer prices down, cheap labor helps to keep inflation down. Some businesses, such as the garment industry, need cheap labor in order to compete on the international market with other nations, which use cheap labor. The garment industry in California, which grosses $3 billion annually, relies on aliens for two-thirds of its workers.[5] Such businesses would have to fold or relocate to foreign countries in order to compete. By having an illegal alien labor force, the U.S. is able to keep those industries here, where they contribute to the national economy.

Although illegal aliens may contribute to the overall economy, some people argue that they are a drain on public services such as hospitals, welfare, and education. This, too, is an oversimplification. On the one hand, illegal aliens do use county hospitals, local schools, and some social services. In 1984, illegal aliens left unpaid medical bills totaling an estimated $100 million in three Los Angeles public hospitals alone.[6] In Texas, the cost of providing education to children of illegal aliens was approximately $85 million in 1982, the year that the U.S. Supreme Court ruled that such children are entitled to free public education.[7]

On the other hand, illegal workers have income taxes deducted from their pay checks, but because of fear of detection, they seldom file income taxes even when they are due a refund. In other words, they pay state and federal income taxes just like everyone else, and perhaps even a higher percentage than they should. They are not, however, entitled to many federal benefits, including Medicaid, unemployment in- surance, food stamps, and Aid to Families with Dependent Children. In addition to paying income taxes, they have social security payments deducted from their paychecks, yet they cannot be issued a social security card and they will probably never receive social security payments. These aliens in fact are subsidizing our social security system by millions and millions of dollars each year.[8]

If there is an inequity between what aliens pay in taxes and what they receive in services, the inequity is due to where the tax money goes rather than to the amount the aliens pay. They pay the majority of their taxes to the federal government, but the state and local governments are the ones that foot the bill for most of the services. Although the federal government sets national policies about the rights of illegal aliens, state and local governments bear the burden of those policies. For example, the federal government decreed that the children of illegals must be provided not only with free education, but also bilingual education; the states and counties pay for these increased services.

The debate over the consequences of having a large illegal alien population is so complex that generalizations are difficult. The one certainty seems to be that the trend will continue. As long as population growth remains high and economic growth

[5]David Goody, "Illegal Immigrants: What They Cost, What They Contribute," *Scholastic Update* 6 Sept. 1985: 12.

[6]Goddy 13.

[7]Melinda Beck, "Costs and Benefits," *Newsweek* 25 June 1984: 23.

[8]Beck 23.

remains low, unemployment will remain high in Latin America. Mexico's population has tripled in the last 40 years to a labor force of 19 million people, and by the year 2000, its labor force will be 45 million; creating new jobs to keep pace with this population growth will be nearly impossible.[9] At present, almost 50% of the work force in Mexico is unemployed or working part-time, and the minimum wage is the equivalent of 55 cents an hour.[10] And as long as unemployment remains high, Latin Americans will travel north for jobs, higher pay, and a new life.

Thus far, the U.S. has been able to accommodate the influx of illegal workers, and perhaps they are even paying their way by paying taxes and contributing to the national economy. But at some point soon, our own country will become overcrowded, the unskilled job market will become filled, the increasingly skilled illegal workers will begin pushing U.S. workers out of more jobs, and the problems will be monumental.

[9]Richard D. Lamm, "Time to Change Course: The Urgent Need for Immigration Reform," *Vital Speeches*, 15 Oct. 1985: 5.

[10]George J. Church, " 'We Are Overwhelmed,' " *Time* 25 June 1984: 16.

Past Consequences

Consequences can be viewed in two ways: those that have already occurred, and those that are expected to occur at a future time. The distinction is important because writing about the former usually belongs to the realm of exposition, and about the latter, to argument.

When we discuss past effects, most often we are merely explaining what those effects were in order to make the past intelligible. Our purpose is less to argue a point of view than to inform others who haven't studied the subject as thoroughly as we and to share our knowledge and perceptions. We might, for example, study the sociological, political, and economic effects of the women's movement or, as in the following essay, the effects of World War II.

THE WAR EUROPE LOST

Ronald Steel

September 1939. For a few a searing memory. For most a dim recollection or a date in   1
a history book. The Luftwaffe spreading death and destruction from the air, Hitler's
Panzer divisions slicing through a hapless Poland. Britain and France, having refused
a year earlier to help a defensible country, Czechoslovakia, come to the aid of an
indefensible one. World War II is under way.

Forty years have passed, and yet the event has not been put into perspective.   2

We are still uncertain as to what it means. Young Germans, not even born when the war began, are only now learning the truths that their elders preferred not to think about, learning of the Holocaust from a commercial television program. The evil that was once unspeakable has now become historic and, judging from the current spate of books and films about Hitler, dramatically entertaining.

Unlike World War I, which was fought entirely in Europe and whose con- 3 sequences were largely confined there, the second war was truly a world war, one that undermined the authority of the vanquished European states and broke their imperial hold on the colonial world. In this sense the consequences of the war were at least as great, perhaps greater, outside Europe as within. A world centered on Europe and defined in terms of it—the "Near East," the "Far East," the "New World"—shifted in perspective as Europe's hold on its colonies and clients was broken.

The demise, or at least the precipitous decline, of Europe itself as a power 4 center and arbiter of the world's destiny was an event few could have predicted. Hitler's attempt to unify the continent in a Pax Germanica had cataclysmic consequences. It made Europe the instrument of the two victorious flanking powers, America and Russia, and destroyed the political and moral authority of the European state system. Europe, having been the predatory power, became the quarry, the object of others' diplomacy rather than the prime mover. One of the great unintended effects—and surely one of the most ironic—of World War II was to end the hegemony of Europe in the very act of trying to assert it.

Europe may rise again as a political power. But it will be in very different form. 5 And such revival can find its impetus only in an attempt to regain what has so incontestably been lost—lost not only to America and Russia, but, as hardly needs to be underlined, to colonial areas Europe once held in thrall. This condition has become so accepted that few anymore think it remarkable that the value of the pound sterling should be dependent on Arab deposits in British banks.

Although Europe indeed lost much as a result of World War II, it gained a great 6 deal—perhaps even more on balance. It gained liberation from its own colonies; liberation from the costly and often bloody pursuit of empire; liberation from the deadly rivalries of a state system perpetually out of balance because a unified Germany was simply too big and too powerful to contain. One of the few happy results of the war was the division of Germany, a division that solved the problem, temporarily at least, of how it would be possible to create a European balance Germany would neither dominate nor try to overturn. This development, most Germans would agree, has been as desirable for them as for their neighbors. It has provided an answer to the dilemma first posed a century ago when Bismarck created a Reich under Prussian dominance. What was achieved by the sword in 1870 was undone by the sword in 1945.

Thus it can be said that the result of World War II, unintended though it may 7 have been, was to save Europe from itself. Europe, as a political entity, lost the war it had brought on itself. America and Russia expanded to a global scale in quest of a balance that was no longer possible to maintain within Europe itself. The successor powers, America and Russia, not only gained control over Europe, but to protect their newfound role also developed a vested interest in the continued division of Europe. A divided Europe is of no harm to either superpower. A unified Europe, either allied to one of them or standing between them, represents an enormous and potentially threatening change in the world political balance.

Thus, looking back from the perspective of 40 years, we can see World War II   8 not only as a human tragedy, as all wars are, but as a political lesson. The war itself resulted from the attempt to resolve the German question. This problem had been left hanging ever since the Treaty of Versailles 20 years earlier, in 1919. World War I, for all its carnage, resolved nothing. It neither gave Germany the mastery of Europe, as the Kaiser and his generals hoped, nor removed Germany's power to seek that mastery once again. It could be argued that, if the United States had not entered the European war in 1917, the Allies would have been obliged to agree to a compromise peace giving Germany hegemony over Eastern Europe. Such a compromise in turn probably would have allowed Kerensky's parliamentary regime to have survived in Russia and avoided the conditions within Germany that allowed Hitler to come to power in 1933.

A concern with the European power balance is what brought the United States   9 into the Second World War, as into the first one. That concern was twofold, although we tend to forget the second part. It was, first, that Europe not fall under the control of an aggressive power hostile to the United States; and, second, that Europe not be dominated by *any* single power. The reason for the second concern is simply that a unified Europe with a single political will inevitably would have needs and ambitions different from, and even hostile to, those of the United States.

The sadistic brutality and maniacal racial practices of Nazi Germany gave a   10 moral patina, so far as Britain and America were concerned, to what was essentially a dynastic conflict. The United States, like Britain, was not drawn into World War II because it found Nazi evil insupportable. Had Hitler confined his genocide within the German frontiers fixed at Versailles, the democratic nations would have done no more to stop him than they did to stop his latter-day admirer, Idi Amin. Rather it was his attempt to overturn the European balance by force, to gain control of the continent, that brought Britain and France, and ultimately the United States and Russia, into belated alliance against him.

Thus it is worth remembering that the last European war, whose 40th an-   11 niversary we note this fall, was not about freedom versus slavery, but about more mundane considerations of the balance of power. The character of the Nazi regime, appalling and inhuman though it was, was not the question at issue. The question was whether that regime should be allowed to impose its authority by force of arms upon all of Europe. When that objective moved from the abstract to the verge of attainment, the United States set up the conditions by which it was drawn into the European war.

It is well to remember anniversaries like the current one, but there is danger in   12 overdrawing or misunderstanding their significance. World War II is not the cold war. Soviet Russia is not Nazi Germany. Angola is not republican Spain. History does not repeat itself. The person who overlearns its "lessons" is condemned to relive its chastisements. Conditions change, and so do alliances. If, as Palmerston said, nations have no allies, only interests, the definition of those interests changes with time and circumstance.

What happened on the plains of Poland 40 years ago represented the last   13 attempt to resolve the German problem within a strictly European context. It was a "world" war only as a result of its unintended consequences. That situation cannot recur because Europe has lost the mastery of its fate—precisely as a result of that war for the mastery of Europe. The slogans of World War II—"appeasement," "isolation," "neutrality"—are of no more value today than that war's antiquated tanks and Flying Fortresses.

—From *The New Republic*, Oct. 6, 1979

1. The *occasion* for this essay is the fortieth anniversary of the beginning of World War II. What is Steel's *purpose* in writing the essay?

2. Why does he discuss consequences and then causes, instead of causes first?

3. Is Steel concerned with immediate or remote effects? Major or secondary effects? Singular or multiple effects?

An essay on consequences need not have as its subject something as general or monumental as a war; its subject can be the effects of a personal experience, such as being the youngest in your family, growing up in the suburbs, or being raised in a certain religion. The value of analyzing the effects on us of a particular influence in our past is that we come to know ourselves a little better, and sharing that analysis with readers spurs them to think about similar influences on themselves.

Future Consequences

Investigating future consequences is inherently more speculative than explaining past consequences. Our goal in this kind of consequential analysis is to consider the *probable* effects of a project or policy that is currently in operation or that has been proposed. Your initial response may be that predicting future effects belongs in the realm of science fiction or fortune-telling, but in fact it is a pragmatic activity used by everyone in making decisions. You base many of the important decisions in your life on this type of consequential thinking: whether to major in the humanities or the sciences, whether to marry, whether to have children, and so on. The activity of projecting probable consequences is the basis of policymaking by business executives, who try to forecast long-range economic and marketing trends, and by legislators, who vote for or against a proposed bill, such as a treaty or an immigration policy, based on their informed predictions of whether the bill will be beneficial or detrimental. There is even a new field of study called *futurology* that uses computer simulation to forecast the social, political, economic, and ecological future of the nation and of the world.

We determine probable consequences by knowing (1) the history of the topic, (2) the current trend, and (3) the principles and agents that are at work. Just as a meteorologist predicts the weather by knowing meteorological principles, current conditions, and yesterday's weather, we gather information, make inferences based on the past and the principles involved, and predict consequences. Take, for example, the question of whether the United States should impose quotas on Japanese car imports in order to help domestic car sales and Detroit employment. To predict the consequences of an import quota, we must know the effects that former quotas have had, the current trade situation between the United States and Japan, some basic principles of economics, and Japanese attitudes toward quotas. Here is an excerpt from an editorial against imposing quotas:

> About all that could be expected from import quotas are that (1) foreign car prices would rise as demand for them exceeded supplies, (2) the buying public's freedom of choice would be arbitrarily curtailed and (3) the United States would quickly find itself in a protectionist battle with key foreign trading partners. The end results would be to eliminate jobs rather than to restore them, to add to rather than to lessen inflation, to force the consumption of more gasoline rather than to make it possible to use less.
>
> —From *The Los Angeles Times*, editorial, Apr. 29, 1980

Because we are dealing with probable effects, not certain ones, such speculation is seldom 100 percent accurate—"the best laid plans of mice and men . . ."—but it beats reading palms. By thoroughly analyzing a topic, we should be able to formulate an intelligent hypothesis on the plausible effects of a policy. Before deciding on a course of action— whether it is declaring war on Libya or buying stock in Xerox—we weigh the potential consequences and then, based on our evaluation, make a decision. On the basis of this educated, informed speculation, we argue for or against a policy; such an argument is called *conditional reasoning*. We state that if *A* (some decision) occurs, *B* (the probable consequences) will occur: If *A*, then *B*. For example, in an address to Congress, former President Carter predicted the following dire consequences if Congress did not approve a strategic arms limitation treaty (SALT):

The SALT II treaty must be judged on its own merits—and, on its own merits, is a substantial gain for national security and international stability. But it would be the height of irresponsibility to ignore the possible consequences of a failure to ratify the treaty.

These consequences would include: greatly increased spending for strategic arms; greater uncertainty about the strategic balance; vastly increased dangers of nuclear proliferation among other nations throughout the world; and increased political tensions between East and West, with a great likelihood that other inevitable problems could escalate into superpower confrontations.

Rejection would also be a damaging blow to the Western alliance. All of our European and other allies, including especially those most directly and courageously facing Soviet power, strongly support SALT II. If the Senate were to reject the treaty, America's leadership of the alliance would be compromised, and the alliance itself would be severely shaken.

In short, SALT II is not a favor we are doing for the Soviet Union. It is a deliberate, calculated move we are making as a matter of self-interest—a move that happens to serve the goals of both security and of survival, that strengthens both the military position of the United States and the cause of world peace.

—June 18, 1979

Obviously, no one has a monopoly on judging the probable effects of a decision. The opponents of SALT II outlined a very different scenario of what would happen if the treaty was approved: the United States would fall further behind in the arms race, the Soviet Union would become even more aggressive in the Middle East, Africa, and Southeast Asia, and the possibility of war would increase. The Reagan Administration, for example, opposed arms agreements with the Russians on the basis of past dealings with the Russians, the perceived imbalance between Russian and American power, and the principle that one should negotiate from a position of strength. Because there are two interpretations to every issue, writing about future consequences is considered to be argumentation.

The reading that follows is a statement on the predicted effects of nuclear war. It was drafted by eighteen scientists from eight nations, including the United States and Russia, on behalf of the Vatican.

1. Five United States scientists conceived the theory of the nuclear winter. Why did the Vatican enlist scientists from different nations instead of simply asking the five originators to draft the statement?
2. What is the tone of the piece? Is the tone appropriate? Why, or why not? What is the effect of this tone on readers?
3. Outline the causal chain that these scientists describe.

4. What is the purpose of paragraph 5?
5. What is the purpose of paragraph 6?
6. What is the purpose of paragraph 7?
7. Is the concluding paragraph effective? Would a more passionate appeal have been more effective? Why, or why not?

NUCLEAR WINTER: A WARNING

Nuclear war would include among its immediate consequences the death of a large   1
proportion of the populations in combatant nations. Such a war would represent a
catastrophe unprecedented in human history. Subsequent radioactive fallout,
weakening of the human immune system, disease, and the collapse of medical and
other civil services would threaten large numbers of survivors.

We must now issue an additional warning: newly-recognized effects of nuclear   2
war on the global climate indicate that longer-term consequences might be as dire as
the prompt effects, if not worse.

In a nuclear war, weapons exploded near the ground would inject large quanti-   3
ties of dust into the atmosphere, and those exploded over cities and forests would
suddenly generate enormous amounts of sooty smoke from the resulting fires. The
clouds of fine particles would soon spread throughout the Northern Hemisphere,
absorbing and scattering sunlight and thus darkening and cooling the earth's surface.
Continental temperatures could fall rapidly—well below freezing for months, even in
summertime—creating a "nuclear winter." This would happen even with wide variations in the nature and extent of nuclear war.

We have only recently become aware of how severe the cold and the dark   4
might be, especially as a consequence of intense and numerous fires ignited by
nuclear explosions, and from attendant changes in atmospheric circulation. This
would produce a profound additional assault upon surviving plants, animals and
humans. Agriculture, at least in the Northern Hemisphere, could be severely damaged for a year or more, causing widespread famine.

Calculations show that the dust and smoke may well spread to the tropics and   5
to much of the Southern Hemisphere. Thus non-combatant nations, including those
far from the conflict, could be severely afflicted. Such nations as India, Brazil, Nigeria,
and Indonesia could be struck by unparalleled disaster, without a single bomb
exploding on their territories.

Moreover, nuclear winter might be triggered by a relatively small nuclear war,   6
involving only a minor fraction of the present global strategic arsenals, provided that
cities are targeted and burned. Even if a "limited" nuclear war were initiated in a
manner intended to minimize such effects, it would likely escalate to the massive use
of nuclear weapons, as the Pontifical Academy of Sciences stressed in its earlier
"Declaration on Prevention of Nuclear War" (1982).

The general results seem to be valid over a wide range of plausible conditions,   7
and over wide variations in the character and extent of a nuclear war. However, there
are still uncertainties in the present evaluations, and there are effects which have not

yet been studied. Therefore, additional scientific work and continuing critical scrutiny of methods and data are clearly required. Unanticipated further dangers from nuclear war cannot be excluded.

Nuclear winter implies a vast increase in human suffering, including nations not directly involved in the war. A large proportion of humans who survive the immediate consequences of nuclear war would most likely die from freezing, starvation, disease, and, in addition, the effects of radiation. The extinction of many plant and animal species can be expected, and, in extreme cases, the extinction of most non-oceanic species might occur. Nuclear war could thus carry in its wake a destruction of life unparalleled at any time during the tenure of humans on Earth, and might therefore imperil the future of humanity.   8

Carlos Chagas, Brazil, *Chairman*
Vladimir Alexandrov, USSR
Edoardo Amaldi, Italy
Dan Beninson, Argentina
Paul J. Crutzen, FRG
Lars Ernster, Sweden
Giorgio Fiocco, Italy
Stephen J. Gould, USA
José Goldemberg, Brazil

S. N. Isaev, USSR
Raymond Latarjet, France
Louis Leprince-Ringuet, France
Carl Sagan, USA
Carlo Schaerf, Italy
Eugene M. Shoemaker, USA
Charles Townes, USA
Eugene P. Velikhov, USSR
Victor Weisskopf, USA

Organizing a Consequential Essay

The structure of a consequential essay will most often take this form:

I. Thesis statement
II. Explanation of issue or proposal
III. Effects—whether past, present, or future
   A. First effect
   B. Second effect
   C. Third effect

The order in which we arrange the effects—that is, which effect is the first effect?—will depend, of course, on the content and our purpose. The nuclear winter piece, for instance, was arranged chronologically, from immediate to long-term effects, and the long-term effects were in a causal chain:

I. Immediate effects
   A. Millions would die instantly.
   B. There would be short-term death due to fallout, lowered immune systems, and lack of medical attention.

II. Longer-term effects
   A. Dust and smoke would affect sunlight.
   B. Temperatures would decrease.
   C. Crops would fail.
   D. Mass hunger would result.
   E. Eventually the Southern Hemisphere would be affected.
   F. Some forms of plant and animal life might become extinct.
   G. Humankind's own existence might be imperiled.

Another structural pattern would be to divide consequences into favorable and unfavorable categories. This pattern is especially appropriate when we are arguing for or against a proposal, as we will see in Chapter 14. When urging readers to accept a proposal, we stress the benefits that will occur if it is approved and the harmful consequences that will occur if it is not approved; conversely, when opposing a proposal, we stress the harmful effects of its passage and the benefits of its rejection.

  I. Favorable effects
   A. First favorable effect
   B. Second favorable effect
   C. Third favorable effect
 II. Unfavorable effects
   A. First harmful effect
   B. Second harmful effect

Also, we can group the effects under major headings, such as political effects, economic effects, and so forth.

   I. Political effects
    A. On federal government
    B. On state governments
    C. On local governments
   II. Economic effects
    A. In the Northwest
    B. In the rest of the United States
  III. Social effects
    A. On the family
    B. On various ethnic groups
  IV. Cultural effects
    A. On literature
    B. On art
    C. On music

We can also switch the emphasis of the structure above and stress the effects on certain groups.

    I. Effects on the United States
      A. Political effects
      B. Economic effects
      C. Social effects
      D. Cultural effects
   II. Effects on Great Britain
      A. Political effects
      B. Economic effects
  III. Effects on Japan
  IV. Effects on Germany

Other organizational patterns would be to proceed:

> from most to least significant effects,
> from obvious to subtle effects,
> from those effects least likely to occur to those most likely to occur,
> or
> from effects that are important to others to those that have an
> impact on us.

Advice, Warnings, Reminders

1. To help generate ideas about a topic, return to the journalistic questions:

    > Who (was or will be affected?)
    > What (are the causes and the effects?)
    > When (did or will the effects occur?)
    > Where (are the effects felt or will be felt?)
    > Why (will the effects result from the situation?)
    > How (will the effects come about?)

2. Expectation often dominates perception; that is, we find what we expect to find. When we have a preconception of particular consequences, those are the effects we seek and therefore find. We should try to keep an open mind and avoid this kind of seeing-with-blinders-on because it limits our vision.

3. Before you begin writing, make two lists, one of negative consequences, the other of positive ones. These lists should force you to consider all possible effects and should keep you from oversimplifying the situation. Oversimplification is the major weakness in most consequential papers.

4. Explain connections between cause and effect thoroughly and substantiate them with details. Demonstrate, don't simply assert, the probability of the connection.

5. Although we have discussed the basic cause-effect patterns, our list has not been exhaustive. Some patterns are complex combinations of basic patterns. For example, we may encounter a situation in which multiple causes lead to multiple effects:

Another pattern might be one action resulting in clusters of effects and causal chains:

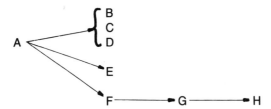

6. Predicting future consequences is a risky business. You must be especially careful to substantiate your claims by citing precedents, establishing current trends, and qualifying generalizations. Often you will have to allow for more than one possible option and make allowances for all the variables that can affect a situation. Although you cannot be absolutely certain that your predictions are accurate, your goal is to convince readers that there is a *high probability* of the consequences you discuss.

Suggested Writing Assignments

1. What are the effects or possible effects of:

   human cloning
   the 35-hour work week
   mandatory retirement at age 65
   raising the entrance standards at your college
   the increased divorce rate
   the election of a particular candidate for president
   the slowdown in school enrollment due to population decrease
   a recent Supreme Court decision
   euthanasia legislation

studying a foreign language
equal funding of women's sports

2. Find a real proposal that is currently being considered on any level—campus, community, state, or national—and argue for or against it based on its probable environmental, economic, social, or political effects. Write your argument as if it were going to be considered by the authorities empowered to accept or reject the proposal. Your paper, therefore, should address a definite audience.

3. Analyze the effect of some decision you have made, such as deciding to attend college.

4. Analyze the effect on your family of some government policy.

5. Discuss the consequences that a particular possession, such as your car, has had on you.

6. Analyze your worst fault and explain its effects on others and on yourself.

7. What are the physical and psychological effects of noise on human beings?

8. What are the consequences of the United States foreign policy toward Israel?

9. During the past 20 years the population in America has been gradually shifting from the Northeast and Midwest to the South and West; that is, the sunbelt is prospering, and the frostbelt is declining. What are the consequences of this shift in terms of economics, politics, and social trends?

Additional Readings

TOWARD LIVING IN CITIES AGAIN

Edmund N. Bacon

In the future we have to perceive ourselves as urban people. The mere acceptance of   1
the notion that we are an urban civilization will be an important revolution in thought,
because we still cling to the nostalgic idea that we are primarily rural.

We are assisted considerably in facing up to the problems of urban settlement   2
by the fact that the petroleum of the world is rapidly becoming exhausted. We are
going to have to move from a petroleum-base mobility to an electric-base mobility.
We've got to quit using petroleum for our basic way of getting around.

This has enormous consequences. The form of the cities will be different. The   3
future extensions of our cities, the future housing, will occur in relatively intense areas
clustered on electric-transportation lines. Since these lines will converge toward the
existing center of the city, it means that the center, which we think of at the moment as
decaying and being abandoned, will have a resurgence and will again become the
focal point of communication.

The great illusion of the suburban experience was that man can experience   4
nature by owning pieces of it. And that is fundamentally incorrect. Nature eludes
ownership.

Becoming more urban and less suburban will also reverse the rhythm of life, to   5
our great benefit. Right now a suburbanite goes daily in and out, leaving his nature in
the morning and coming home when the sun is setting and the children are going to
bed.

A genuinely urban civilization would have not a daily but a weekly rhythm. We   6
would spend the workweek, perhaps four days, in the highly social atmosphere of the
city, at the end of which we would move outward to the mountains and the sea and the
farm.

Low density of the suburbs is nothing but an insulation of human communica-   7
tion. Intensive development is necessary for the quality of the life of the children. They
should not have to depend upon their mothers being chauffeurs in order to make
contact with friends.

Let us visualize the re-utilized city. Blocks will be reorganized to represent   8
separate living communities. At the end of each block there will be electric buses and
electric taxicabs. The only reason for a vehicle will be to bring a baby home from the
hospital or to take a casket out. By this concept we lead people into a view of the
removal of petroleum as being not an obstacle, but a fine, creative thing.

There is more than plenty of space in our cities. In Philadelphia there are 28,000   9
abandoned houses and 12,000 vacant lots. It ends up that 40,000 units are abandoned in the middle of the city, with all the sewers and water and everything else
provided. Again there is a trend toward the concept of homesteading—not in the
praries, but in the wastelands of our inner cities.

We don't have to build new towns. The new technological town is a total dead   10
end. Besides, there is a whole series of middle-sized cities that have a new possibility
for creating new life-styles, including a more sympathetic approach to nature and less
consumptive ways of doing things. New perceptions of land are going to make for a
situation where private property versus control doesn't become the main conflict.

The American people are quite capable of being way ahead of the scientist,   11
technologists, and philosophers. Americans love their land, and they need to be
shown how better to cherish it.

—From *National Geographic*, July 1976

1. What will be the cause of our increasingly urbanized living, according to Bacon? Does that seem a sufficient cause to change our living patterns?

2. What kind of causal pattern does Bacon suggest will occur: A circular pattern? One cause, many effects? Many causes, many effects? A causal chain? Explain.

3. Does this futuristic urban living sound like "a fine, creative thing" to you? If not, what makes it seem less attractive, and what has Bacon done to make it seem less than desirable?

4. What is the purpose of paragraph 9?

5. What relationship between land and patterns of living does Bacon perceive? Has he made a good case for his argument that urbanization would result in better treatment of the land?

OLD AGE

Sharon Curtin

Like conspirators the old walk all bent over, as if hiding some precious secret, filled with self-protection. The body seems to gather itself around those vital parts, folding shoulders, arms, pelvis like a fading rose. Watch and you see how fragile old people come to think they are made. 1

Aging paints every action gray, lies heavy on every movement, imprisons every thought. It governs each decision with a ruthless and single-minded perversity. To age is to learn the feeling of no longer growing, of struggling to do old tasks, to remember familiar actions. The cells of the brain are destroyed with thousands of unfelt tiny strokes, little pockets of clotted blood wiping out memories and abilities without warning. The body seems to slowly give up, randomly stopping, starting again as if to torture and tease with the memory of lost strength. Hands become clumsy, frail transparencies, held together with knotted blue veins, fluttering in front of your eyes and reminding you of growing infirmity. 2

Sometimes it seems as if the distance between your feet and the floor is constantly changing, as if you walk on shifting and not quite solid ground. One foot down, slowly, carefully, force the other foot forward. Sometimes you are a shuffler, not daring to lift your feet from the uncertain earth but forced to slide hesitantly forward in little whispering movements. Sometimes you are able to really "step out" but this effort—in fact the pure exhilaration of easy movement—soon exhausts you. 3

The world becomes narrower as friends and family die or move away. To climb stairs, to ride in a car, to walk to the corner, to talk on the telephone; each action seems to take energy needed to stay alive. Everything is limited by the strength you hoard greedily. Your needs decrease, you require less food, less sleep, and finally less human contact; yet this little bit becomes more and more difficult. You fear that 4 one day you will be reduced to the simple acts of breathing and taking nourishment. This is the ultimate stage you dread, the period of helplessness and hopelessness, when any further independence will be over.

—From *Nobody Ever Died of Old Age*

1. Why does this piece carry such an emotional wallop?

STARVATION AS A WEAPON SHOULD BE OUTLAWED

Jean Mayer

There is no dearth of miseries inflicted on man by man. However, one practice that has disgraced mankind for centuries has been put aside for the moment: the attempt, by every possible means, to starve an opponent into surrender. For that very reason, this is a God-given time to strike a blow for human rights by putting a stop to it once and for all. 1

The use of starvation as a weapon is as old as the history of declared and undeclared warfare. Every student of Thucydides remembers the Athenian and Spartan expeditions across the Peloponnesus to ravage the enemy's crops. Many popular textbooks of medieval history tell of wasted citizens in besieged cities feasting on roasted rat. 2

Without the softening effect of time and story, the denial of food takes on a very different cast. It has been of interest to me as a nutritionist, but my misfortune as a man, to have been in a condition to witness (with only limited capacity to relieve) starvation on three continents. I can say flatly, from both historical studies and practical experience, that there has never been a famine or food shortage, whatever the cause, which has not first and foremost affected the small children. 3

Pictures of wide-eyed, living skeletons can sum up the horror, but they cannot describe its slow progression. The first and most obvious effect of starvation is the wasting of the body's fat deposits. The stomach and intestines, heart and lungs are affected next. The liver shrinks drastically. The lining of the intestines becomes thin and smooth, losing some of its capacity to absorb nutrients, and diarrhea results. 4

Starvation is a self-accelerating process, especially in children: Because of intestinal damage, the food that is available is poorly absorbed, and undernutrition increases correspondingly. The damaged stomach lining stops secreting hydrochloric acid, which is necessary for digestion. Blood pressure and pulse rate drop. 5

Early effects of starvation are cessation of menstruation in women and impotence and loss of libido in men. (In effect, the birth rate drops to zero). Hair grows dull and bristling, and in children abnormal hair grows on the forearms and back. The skin acquires the consistency of paper and shows the irreversible dusty brown splotches which will be the permanent marks of starvation—if the victim survives. In 6 extreme cases, particularly in children, cancrum oris devours tissues around the mouth, destroying the lips and part of the cheeks.

The diseases that accompany famine—typhoid, cholera, smallpox, tuberculo-   7
sis, malaria—are rampant. The weakened body is open to any infection. The psychologic state deteriorates rapidly; the individual becomes listless and apathetic, but self-centered and mentally restless—and obsessed with food. Murder is not uncommon. Even cannibalism may be seen.

As calorie requirements decline with the loss of weight, drop in blood pressure   8
and pulse rate and slowing of activity, a perilous physical equilibrium may be created that can endure for several weeks or even months. At the end, there is constant diarrhea. Death may come from cardiovascular collapse or from disease and infection.

The process is most rapid when the person is in a period of rapid growth or   9
weakened by age or disease, or has special nutritional needs. Death from starvation occurs first and overwhelmingly in small children, then in older children and the elderly (in a famine, anyone over 45 is "old.") Pregnant women not infrequently abort; lactating mothers always stop producing milk and the babies die. Adolescents are more likely to survive, although they are highly susceptible to tuberculosis. Adult men are least affected. Physiologically, young men are the most resistant to starvation, and armed men rarely starve—particularly since they can always justify requisitioning any remaining food by the nobility of their cause.

We have outlawed chemical and bacteriological methods of waging war, in part   10
because they are indiscriminate in their effects, jeopardizing civilian bystanders as much as armed enemies. Starvation preferentially attacks the most helpless and vulnerable bystanders.

But if we are going to continue to institutionalize war—and there is no sign that   11
we are not—the ethics of means will always pose difficult problems. Can the denial of food be defended as an effective military weapon, one that may prevent the greater suffering of a long-drawn-out conflict? Even a short examination of wars fought within the last hundred years argues that it cannot.

General Sherman's march through Georgia to the sea resulted in widespread   12
crop destruction and enmities that have endured to this day, but the Civil War was lost in the factories of the North and on the battlefield, at Gettysburg and Vicksburg.

For 129 days during the Franco-Prussian War, Paris was under siege by the   13
Germans. In the first week, 3,680 people died; in the third, 4,405. Epidemics, smallpox in particular, swept the city. Children died by the hundreds. But, according to contemporary records, the National Guard had enough to eat and more than enough to drink. The Paris garrison held, while the French lost the war at Sedan and Metz, in the Loire Valley and on the Swiss border.

At the beginning of World War I, the Allies blockaded the Central Powers in the   14
hope of bringing the war to a quick conclusion. The blockade had a devastating effect on the civilian population. In Vienna, the death rate from tuberculosis rose by 100 percent; excess civilian deaths during the war years over 1913 totaled almost

800,000. By 1918 famine edema (an increase in the water content of the body) was a common sight throughout Central Europe. But many of the men in the German army ate even better than they had as civilians. George A. Schreiner, an Associated Press correspondent who spent the first three years of the war in Germany, reported that "the army came first in all things." While thousands of the aged poor were going to a premature death, a decrease in the army's bread ration was made good by increasing their ration of meat and fat. But it is the great 1918 Allied offensive, bolstered by hundreds of thousands of fresh American troops, which broke the back of the Kaiser's armies.

During the three-year siege of Leningrad in World War II, almost a third of the   15 population was lost. Children died by the tens of thousands. The Red Army's rations were reduced, but the army was able to defend the city, and finally to break out to join the advancing relief force.

In the civil war in Nigeria, the Nigerians' final victory over the Biafrans was   16 clearly attributable to the military superiority, in arms and numbers, of the central government's army, not to the famine in Biafra, although in some areas every child under 7 had died. And in Vietnam, the efforts in crop destruction and interdiction had little effect on the Vietcong.

Denial of food in war constitutes a war measure directed almost exclusively at   17 children, the elderly, and pregnant and nursing women. Not only will innocent bystanders be hurt—they will be the *only* ones to be hurt. It is an ineffective weapon that is also a clear and particularly horrible violation of the rights of man.

Now, while no nation's survival may be supposed to depend on it, I propose that   18 we move for an international agreement, like that eliminating chemical and bacteriological warfare, against man-created starvation. Let us outlaw the use of starvation as a weapon of coercion or terror against large or small population groups, and supplement the agreement with one which will allow suitable organizations, such as UNICEF, to freely enter a famine area to feed and care for noncombatant victims of starvation.

—From *The Washington Post*, Nov. 15, 1978

1. What are Mayer's two basic arguments for outlawing starvation tactics?

2. What kinds of evidence does he offer to substantiate his arguments?

3. What type of organization does he use when describing the effects of starvation? Outline paragraphs 4–9.

4. In paragraphs 12–16, Mayer presents a long list of historical examples in which he asserts that starvation was ineffective. Do you accept his causal explanations? Why, or why not?

5. How does he make his argument pragmatic at the end, and why is this proposal an effective way of concluding the essay?

IV

ARGUMENT AND PERSUASION

We study argumentation for two reasons: to improve our ability to convince others of our beliefs, and to recognize and guard against false reasoning and propaganda. Argumentative skills are essential if we are to persuade others of the benefits of our ideas. If we believe, for example, that a certain chemical used in fattening chickens is harmful to the human beings who eat these chickens, we have an obligation to convince the public and the government of the truthfulness of our belief; and in order to do this we must know how to structure an argument, how to use evidence, how to appeal to readers, and how to project a good image of ourselves. The more we know about the subtleties of presenting and defending a proposition, the more extensive our influence will be in the free market of ideas.

Knowledge of argumentation offers a kind of self-protection as well as a kind of power because the more we know about the techniques used in propaganda, the less likely we are to be fooled by them. By developing a critical awareness, we fortify ourselves against persons who try to get us to act without thinking. Studying argumentation, then, strengthens our critical faculties and teaches us how to discern and advance truth.

Although we take for granted that the goal of argument is *to win*, there are degrees of winning. Granted, our ultimate aim may be to bring readers around to our way of thinking, but in reality we usually shoot for a much lower target. For example, instead of asking readers to discard their current opinion and adopt a whole new belief, we might try simply modifying that opinion. Even more modestly, our intention may be to narrow existing differences between views and to make our view more viable. The most noble goal of argument, which in the heat of controversy we often forget, is cooperation—not winning, but unifying the two sides by taking the best of both views and allowing each side to maintain its dignity. If arguments are conducted properly—that is, with a logical basis and a due respect for the other side—they can result in improved understanding and intelligent resolutions.

Differences Between Exposition and Argumentation

The traditional distinction between exposition and argument might be called a helpful distortion. Although there are real differences between the two, to suggest that they are totally separate is to oversimplify. Because each mode borrows from the other, essays tend to be combinations of exposition and argument. A particular piece of prose may be *mainly* expository or *mainly* argumentative, but we must realize that we are discussing gradations and that pure forms seldom exist. Even a paper whose purpose is to define a term has a slight argumentative edge to it because implicitly it argues for readers to accept the writer's way of understanding or seeing. Likewise, an argumentative paper contains a great amount of clarification and explanation in order to help readers understand the logic, to evaluate the evidence, and to reach the desired conclusion. For instance, if we propose to a lay audience that a nuclear power plant being built in their vicinity should be structured differently, we must explain about the structure in order to help the audience make an informed and intelligent judgment. The explanation is a necessary part of the argument, and the success of the argument depends to a considerable extent on the success of the explanation. An argument therefore may include various types of expository writing, such as definition, process analysis, and classification.

On the other hand, argument is very different from exposition in important ways. One important distinction is that argument implies an active controversy between conflicting opinions, while exposition does not. Also, their goals are different. Whereas exposition attempts only to clarify or inform, argument seeks to influence. Exposition informs readers about the nature of a subject; argument may inform readers about an issue, but only to persuade them to accept a certain view of the issue. Because their goals are different, the structures and styles may differ, also. The structure of an expository essay usually proceeds from general to specific; that is, the thesis is usually positioned in the beginning of the essay. Argument, by its inherent nature of disagreement, must be more strategic and therefore will often postpone the thesis until readers have accepted basic premises and evidence. Furthermore, argument must concern itself more with the psychology of the readers and with other viewpoints.

Differences Between Argumentation and Persuasion

Another distinction sometimes made is between argumentation and persuasion. *Argumentation* refers to discourse that uses reason to prove or disprove a proposition. Its appeal is exclusively to the intellect, and its goal is conviction. *Persuasion* appeals additionally to emotions, and its goal is usually behavioral. Argument uses *logic*, focuses on the *subject*, and seeks *truth*; persuasion uses *emotion* as well as logic, focuses more on the *audience*, and seeks *action*. In short, whereas argumentation appeals to the mind, persuasion appeals to the heart as well as the mind.

There are two types of persuasion: that which uses emotion in lieu of reason, and that which uses emotions to reinforce reason. The first type attempts to manipulate readers by bypassing their rational faculties and may resort to any means possible to motivate people. The second type of persuasion is usually more ethical because it is based on sound thinking and solid evidence. It attempts to vitalize and bolster reason with an emotional surge and to arouse readers in order to convert reasoned conviction into action. When I use the term *persuasion* in these chapters, I mean responsible persuasion that is founded in logic.

CHAPTER 11

Logical Strategies

It is a saying of the ancients, that "truth lies in a well"; and to carry on the metaphor, we may justly say, that logic supplies us with steps whereby we may go down to reach the water.

—Isaac Watts

The attitude that most students have toward logic is the attitude they usually reserve for opera and final exams. They think that logic is something invented by ancient philosophers in order to torture modern students with mumbo-jumbo like *syllogism, enthymeme,* and *argumentum ad hominem.* They think that in level of difficulty logic is akin to calculus; in usefulness, akin to Sanskrit. In brief, they consider it to be indecipherable and valueless, and they don't understand why they should have to study it at all, especially in a writing course.

Logic is nothing more than straight thinking; it is the study of the principles of reason. We study logic in a writing course because it helps us to reason more clearly, and the better we reason, the better we write. Although logic may seem theoretical, we study it for practical reasons: As an objective test of thinking, it provides us with a means of judging our own arguments and the arguments of others. We use logic (1) to test hypotheses and arrive at sound conclusions, (2) to help us structure our arguments so that readers can follow our thinking, (3) to anticipate and guard against attacks on our arguments, (4) to point out fallacies in our opponents' arguments, and (5) to protect us from being manipulated by sophistry (misleading arguments that appear plausible but are actually unsound).

This chapter is an elementary discussion of the principles of logic, the purpose being to offer an introduction to the basic concepts without going into the many subtleties. Although the study of logic entails much more than the rudimentary explanation offered here, the hope is that you gain a sufficient understanding to reason more clearly and to test arguments. In keeping with the elementary nature of this discussion, the use of technical terms has been kept to a minimum, though you will encounter a few.

The chapter is divided into the two major types of logic: deduction and induction. First we will discuss the principles of deduction, including the elements of a syllogism, the types of syllogisms, and the distinction between validity and truth; then we will analyze the limitations of deduction and the use of deductive reasoning in argumentative essays. Next we will examine the two types of induction, review different types of evidence in inductive arguments, and survey the types of fallacies to guard against, such as card-stacking and begging the question. Finally, we will explore how deduction and induction can work together in an argumentative essay, using the *Declaration of Independence* as an example.

Deduction

Deduction is a type of reasoning that presents two related statements and draws a conclusion from them. It applies (1) a generalization to (2) a particular case and draws (3) a conclusion about that case. The generalization is called the *major premise;* the second statement is the *minor premise;* and the third statement, the *conclusion.* Together, the three statements are called a syllogism.

There are several types of syllogisms, but for the sake of brevity we will consider only the two most common: categorical syllogisms and conditional syllogisms.

Categorical Syllogism

In a categorical syllogism, the major premise states that all members of a certain group have a certain characteristic; for example, "All men are mortal." The minor premise states that the individual case being considered is a member of that group: "Socrates is a man." And the conclusion drawn is that the individual case therefore shares the characteristic: "Socrates is mortal."

MAJOR PREMISE: All men are mortal.
MINOR PREMISE: Socrates is a man.
CONCLUSION: Therefore, Socrates is mortal.

To see the relationships more clearly, we can construct a diagram, using circles to show categories:

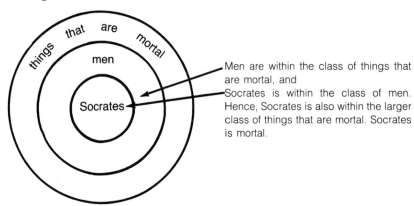

Men are within the class of things that are mortal, and Socrates is within the class of men. Hence, Socrates is also within the larger class of things that are mortal. Socrates is mortal.

This is an example of an affirmative categorical syllogism; it verifies that a member is included in a particular class. Socrates is in the class of men, and men are in the class of things that are mortal (a class that includes many other organisms, such as mosquitos, algae, and polar bears).

To understand how a syllogism works, we must know its parts.

MIDDLE TERM   MAJOR TERM
All cats   have   whiskers.

MINOR TERM   MIDDLE TERM
Sylvester   is a   cat.

MINOR TERM   MAJOR TERM
Sylvester   has   whiskers.

The middle term in an affirmative categorical syllogism is the one repeated in both the major premise and minor premise; the minor term is the subject of both the minor premise and the conclusion. The major term, appearing at the end of both the major premise and the conclusion, is the characteristic that all members of the class share. When diagrammed with circles, the minor term must always be within the circle of the middle term, which in turn must be encircled by the area of the major term.

Negative categorical syllogisms, on the other hand, verify that a member is *excluded* from the characteristics of a particular class. As the name suggests, these syllogisms are framed in negative statements.

                MAJOR TERM   MIDDLE TERM
major premise: No Angus cattle have horns.

                MINOR TERM   MIDDLE TERM
minor premise: This bull has horns.

                MINOR TERM   MAJOR TERM
conclusion: This bull is not an Angus.

Note the difference between a negative categorical syllogism and an affirmative one: In a negative categorical syllogism, the major premise begins with *No* rather than *All;* the middle term is at the end of the major premise; and the conclusion excludes the minor term from the class of the major term. Diagrammed, the syllogism consists of separate circles:

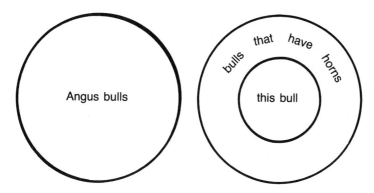

We can also have categorical syllogisms that mix an affirmative major premise and a negative minor premise.

> All Shetland ponies are under 42 inches at the shoulder.
> This pony is not under 42 inches at the shoulder.
> Therefore, this pony is not a Shetland.

Another kind of mixture uses *only:*

> Only those citizens registered can vote.
> D.J. is not registered.
> D.J. cannot vote.

Validity

A syllogism is valid if it is correct in form, and to be correct in form it must meet these rules:

1. There can be only three terms in a syllogism.

2. The middle term must be distributed at least once. (A term is *distributed* if it includes or excludes all of the members of a class. In the premise "All men are mortal," *men* is distributed because it includes every individual in the class of men. Likewise, in the premise "No Angus bulls have horns," the term *Angus bulls* is distributed because it excludes all Angus bulls from the characteristic of horns. If a term in the first half of a premise is preceded by *all, no, only, any,* or *every,* that term is distributed. Determining whether the predicate (the part of the premise following the verb) is distributed or undistributed is

more difficult. For now, we may simply accept two rules about predicates:

> The predicates of all affirmative statements are undistributed.
> The predicates of all negative statements are distributed.

3. If one premise is negative, the conclusion must be negative also.

4. For a term to be distributed in the conclusion, it must be distributed in one of the premises.

5. No conclusion can be drawn from two negative premises.

Now let's concentrate on the rule that the middle term must be distributed at least once. Analyze the following syllogism (the symbol ∴ means "therefore"):

> All gymnasts are muscular and agile.
> Kim is a gymnast.
> ∴ Kim is muscular and agile.

What is the middle term? Gymnasts. Is it distributed? Yes. Is the syllogism valid? Yes, because it follows the correct form. How about this one:

> All gymnasts are muscular and agile.
> Randy is muscular and agile.
> ∴ Randy is a gymnast.

What is the middle term? It is not *gymnasts* because *gymnasts* doesn't appear in the minor premise. The middle term is *muscular and agile.* Is the middle term distributed? No. Remember the rule: The predicates of affirmative premises are undistributed. Is the syllogism valid? No, it is not valid.

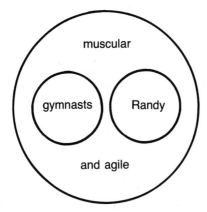

Within the large circle of people who are agile and muscular are many kinds of athletes, and Randy may be a swimmer or a dancer, not a gymnast.

Consider this syllogism:

No bats are birds.
This is a bird.
∴ This is no bat.

What is the middle term? "Birds." Is it distributed? Yes; the rule is that the predicate of a negative premise is distributed. The syllogism is valid.
How about this syllogism:

All racists oppose court-ordered busing to achieve desegregation.
Mr. Anderson opposes court-ordered busing to achieve desegregation.
∴ Mr. Anderson is a racist.

Forget your intuition and check the form. What is distributed? *Racists.* Is that the middle term? No; *oppose(s) court-ordered busing* is the middle term, and it is undistributed; therefore the syllogism is invalid. According to this syllogism, Mr. Anderson might be a racist, but he isn't necessarily one, and in a valid syllogism the conclusion must *necessarily* follow from the premises. The syllogism above would be valid only if its conclusion was that "Mr. Anderson *may be* a racist" or if its major premise was that *"Only* racists oppose busing."
Although such invalid thinking should convince no one, in fact it is used daily, and people accept it unthinkingly. We hear political candidates, for example, use it in this form:

All socialists support governmental subsidies to private industry.
My political opponent supports governmental subsidies to Amtrak and other companies.
Do you want a socialist to be your elected representative?

Many people, including the president and half the Senate, may favor certain forms of subsidy, but that doesn't mean they are socialists. Such syllogisms as the one above may *seem* logical to an uncritical mind, but they are as fallacious as the following one, which uses the identical form:

All elephants have large ears.
My Uncle Jake has large ears.
∴ My Uncle Jake is an elephant.

In both cases, the middle term is undistributed, and therefore the logic is not valid.

APPLICATION

Which of these syllogisms are valid and which invalid?

All state residents must pay a state income tax.

John and Mary are state residents.

∴ John and Mary must pay a state income tax.

No trains travel on water.

This vehicle travels on water.

∴ This vehicle is a boat.

All cowgirls get the blues.

Sue gets the blues.

∴ Sue is a cowgirl.

No hippopotamus can fly.

An eagle is not a hippopotamus.

∴ An eagle can fly.

Xemenia are lubgrify.

Codhyps are Xemenia.

∴ Codhyps are lubgrify.

Validity and Truth

In common usage, *valid* is often used as a synonym for *true*, and therefore we would think that an argument that is valid would also be truthful. But in the province of logic, validity and truth are two totally different qualities. Validity has to do with the *form* of a deductive argument; the content of the statements is irrelevant to validity. Truth, on the other hand, has to do with the individual statements within an argument: The premises may be true, or false, or probable.

This distinction between truth and validity confuses most students who are studying logic for the first time. To help clarify the distinction, let's examine some syllogisms that are valid but false and others that are invalid but true. Consider this one:

All men have three ears.

John is a man.

Therefore, John has three ears.

Is that a valid syllogism? Yes, because it adheres correctly to the form. Obviously, however, the major premise is not truthful, and therefore the conclusion is untruthful also. How about this syllogism:

All men have two ears.

John has two ears.

Therefore, John is a man.

Although all three statements are true, the form is incorrect because the middle term—*two ears*—is undistributed. An invalid argument that uses true premises, like this one, is the most deceptive argument because it appears to be reasonable. When both of the premises and even the conclusion are true, yet the form is invalid, the conclusion has been arrived at in a haphazard way. Consider the following syllogism:

> Greeks eat black olives.
> Zorba eats black olives.
> Therefore, Zorba is a Greek.

Here, the first two statements do not lead *necessarily* to the conclusion; it was arrived at accidentally, not logically. To demonstrate this fact, simply substitute "Hitler" for "Zorba."

> Greeks eat black olives.
> Hitler ate black olives.
> Therefore, Hitler was a Greek.

We can have true statements in an invalid argument and false statements in a valid argument. But a *good* argument must have both correct form and true premises; in such an argument, the conclusion is necessarily true.

APPLICATION

Which of these syllogisms are valid?

(All) fish walk on two legs.
Men are fish.
Therefore, men walk on two legs.

Fig trees grow in California.
Fruit trees grow in California.
Therefore, fig trees are fruit trees.

All cities in Illinois are smaller than Phoenix, Arizona.
Chicago is a city in Illinois.
Therefore, Chicago is smaller than Phoenix, Arizona.

Enthymemes

In daily conversation and reading, we seldom encounter full syllogisms such as those we have been analyzing. Instead, we usually encounter *enthymemes*, which are abbreviated arguments. An enthymeme omits one of the three statements because that statement is obvious and therefore unnecessary. For example, the statement "He's got to be dumb because he's a jock" is a condensed version of a syllogism:

> All jocks are dumb.
> He is a jock.
> Therefore, he is dumb.

The speaker realizes that listeners can mentally fill in the omitted statement—in fact, *enthymeme* comes from a Greek word meaning "to have in the mind."

An enthymeme can omit any one of the three statements of a syllogism. It can omit, for example, the major premise:

> State lotteries are an immoral way of raising public revenue because they encourage gambling by those people least able to afford to lose money.

What is the implied major premise in that argument? In the following enthymeme, the minor premise is omitted. What is that minor premise?

> Activities that encourage passivity in children are not allowed in my home. Therefore, my children aren't allowed to watch television.

Or an enthymeme can omit the conclusion:

> Boys should be encouraged to take classes in high school that traditionally have been only for girls. Sewing and cooking are examples of such courses.

The main point to remember when evaluating enthymemes is that we must carefully consider the implied statement in order to see whether, when expanded into a syllogism, the logic is valid.

Conditional Syllogism

Another kind of deduction besides categorical reasoning is conditional reasoning.[1] Conditional reasoning poses a possible situation and gives the result that will ensue if and when that situation occurs. The major premise always takes the form of an "if . . . then" statement, the "if" part

---

[1]Actually there is a third type of deductive thinking called *alternative syllogisms*, which arrive at conclusions from either/or statements.

> Either the President will cut the budget or he will raise taxes.
> He is not going to cut the budget.
> Therefore, he will raise taxes.

Or,

> Either the President will cut the budget or he will raise taxes.
> He will not raise taxes.
> Therefore, he will cut the budget.

The valid form is one of negating the minor premise:

A or *B*.	or	*A* or *B*.
Not *A*.		Not *B*.
Therefore, *B*.		Therefore, *A*.

being called the *antecedent,* the "then" part called the *consequent.* For example, here is a conditional major premise:

ANTECEDENT   CONSEQUENT
If Congress approves the current budget, taxes will have to rise.

The minor premise states that the antecedent is true:

Congress has approved the current budget.

And the conclusion is the consequent:

Therefore, taxes will have to be raised.

Conditional reasoning is valid only when the minor premise *affirms the antecedent* or *denies the consequent* of the major premise.

Affirming the antecedent:
If *X,* then *Y.*
X.
Therefore *Y.*

If it rains any more today, the creek will overflow.
It will rain some more today.
Therefore, the creek will flood (and we had better head for higher land).

Denying the consequent:
If *X,* then *Y.*
Not *Y.*
Therefore, not *X.*

If it rained last night, the creek would have overflowed.
The creek didn't overflow.
Therefore, it didn't rain last night.

But we cannot affirm the consequent and have a valid argument:

If you make a fortune, you will be happy.
Anne is happy.
Therefore, Anne has made a fortune.

This syllogism is not valid because although wealth may be a sufficient reason for happiness, it is not the only reason; Anne could be happy for any number of reasons. Nor can we deny the antecedent and have a valid argument:

If you make a fortune, you will be happy.
Anne did not make a fortune.
Therefore, Anne is not happy.

Again, the antecedent may be sufficient to cause the consequent, but it is not the only possible cause.

APPLICATION

According to the rules above, which of these arguments are valid?

If Congress approves the budget, income taxes will be raised.
Taxes have been raised.
Therefore, Congress has approved the current budget.

If the Son of God comes to Earth, he will be crucified.
Jesus was crucified.
Therefore, Jesus was the Son of God.
If Congress approves the current budget, income taxes will be raised.
Congress did not approve the budget.
Therefore, income taxes will not be raised.

If Puerto Rico becomes the 51st state, its economy will prosper.
Puerto Rico's economy has not prospered.
Therefore, Puerto Rico has not become the 51st state.

As in categorical arguments, validity and truth are not synonymous in conditional arguments; here again, validity concerns form. Therefore, we can have valid conditional arguments that contain false premises and false conclusions. Also as in categorical arguments, conditional reasoning may be stated as enthymemes.

APPLICATION

What part has been omitted in the following two enthymemes? Set up each argument as a syllogism.

If an occupation is dangerous, workers deserve high pay. That is why I support pay raises for coal miners.

If we want to lessen our dependence on foreign oil, we must drill for offshore oil.

Conditional reasoning has a multitude of uses. We have already encountered this kind of thinking in the chapter on consequences, and we will find it useful again in the chapter on proposals. Conditional reasoning is used not only in argument, but also in scientific investigations when scientists pose a hypothetical situation and then test the antecedent to see what happens. For example, when geologists were investigating the possibility of continental drift (the idea that the Earth's land masses move), they posed this hypothesis:

> If the fossils at the bottom of the Atlantic Ocean are not as old as those on the continents of Africa and South America, then those continents must have occupied at one time the area where the Atlantic Ocean is now.

Expeditions confirmed the antecedent:

> The fossils at the bottom of the Atlantic Ocean are not as old as those on the continents of Africa and South America.

So geologists accepted the conclusion:

> Africa and South America must have once been joined millions of years ago, and they occupied the area where the Atlantic Ocean now is.

APPLICATION

Here is an account of another scientific discovery that relied on posing and testing a hypothetical situation. Formulate a syllogism that reflects the thinking behind the discovery.

> Scientists believed that the length of the Earth's day has been increasing slightly over millions of years, and that the number of days in the year has subsequently decreased. To test this theory, a paleontologist named John Wells examined fossil corals that were over 400 million years old. (Because coral grows faster during the day than during the night and faster in the summer than in the winter, coral has shell markings, much as trees have annual rings, that indicate age.) Wells found that these fossil corals had almost 400 markings per year, indicating that 400 million years ago, the Earth's year was about 400 days long instead of the present 365, and consequently that the length of the day was approximately 22 hours, not 24. Hence, the length of the Earth's day has been increasing slightly.

Limitations of Deduction

Although deduction is an important tool for hypothesizing and for applying generalizations to individual cases, it has two limitations in writing arguments. One is the distinction between truth and validity. Even if our argument is valid (i.e., our form is correct), our conclusions are not necessarily true, and readers who disagree with one of our premises will disagree with a conclusion based on that premise. In such a case, regardless of the validity of the argument, we will not have convinced readers that our thesis is sound. For example, if representatives for the coal industry offer the following syllogism, we may reject their conclusion because we do not accept their major premise.

> If anything interferes with our lifestyle, we should eliminate that hindrance.
> Environmental regulations on strip mining interfere with our lifestyle.
> Therefore, we should eliminate environmental regulations.

Although the syllogism is valid, many readers will question the truthfulness of the major premise and therefore will reject the conclusion.

The other limitation of deduction is that although it is useful for establishing certainty, argumentative papers usually try to prove probability instead of certitude. If arguments dealt with certitude, they would not be arguments since argument implies that there are two viable sides to an issue. In an argument, each side tries to establish a high degree of probability that its thesis is right or its course of action is better. Because many arguments concern complex human affairs in which variables are numerous and certitude is impossible, deduction alone is sometimes an unsuitable vehicle for persuasion.

Using Deduction in Arguments

If deduction has such limitations, why bother to study it? To answer that question, we must look at our study of logic from the viewpoint of readers and then as writers. A knowledge of deduction helps us as *readers* to test the validity of others' syllogisms and enthymemes and to question the truthfulness of their premises. By reducing a long prose argument into syllogistic form, we can isolate the bare argument and analyze the reasoning to see whether it is sound. As *writers* we study deduction because it helps us (1) to establish common ground between our readers and us and (2) to structure our material.

To Establish Common Ground

Common ground is any belief or value that we share with our readers. Emphasizing this common ground is an effective way of aligning ourselves with readers and of gaining their trust, especially in the beginning of a persuasive essay. The connection between deduction and common ground is that our major premise can serve as a shared belief. If we are sufficiently inventive, we should be able to discover a principle that both we and our readers endorse and that, of course, is applicable to the minor premise.

To find a major premise that acts as common ground, we must first consider the nature of our thesis. Let's take the thesis that our college should include pluses and minuses on grade records. That thesis is not our major premise; it is the conclusion of our deductive syllogism. So far we have:

MAJOR PREMISE: ?
MINOR PREMISE: ?
CONCLUSION: The college should indicate pluses and minuses on official grade records.

Now we go in search of a major premise that readers will endorse because they believe that it is humane, fair, democratic, just, or some other admirable quality. We must locate the laudable traits that our thesis embodies—and surely it embodies some, or we wouldn't be supporting it—and formulate a major premise from those traits. Would adopting a plus/minus system be more humane, fair, democratic, or just? Yes; the reason to implement such a system would be to increase the accuracy and equity of recording grades. Most people would endorse a proposal that increases accuracy and equity, and therefore we base our argument on this major premise:

> Any grading system that is more accurate and equitable and is easily implemented should be adopted by the college.
> The plus/minus grading system is more accurate and equitable and is easily implemented.
> Therefore, the plus/minus grading system should be adopted by the college.

By opening with the basic principle of equity and accuracy, we base our argument on values that most readers will readily accept, and thereby we gain their initial consent. If they accept our major premise, they are forced to accept our conclusion, provided that we prove the minor premise—that in fact the plus/minus system *is* more accurate, more equitable, and easily implemented.

Before we can determine what major premise to use, we must of course know our audience because what one audience will accept as a truth, another will not. After we analyze the audience, the challenge is to find a principle contained in our thesis that readers will unhesitatingly accept. In this light, deduction can be considered an inventional device since it is a method of generating strategies for reaching readers.

To Structure an Argument

Deduction can also be considered a form of structure because an argumentative essay can be set up as a fleshed-out syllogism. The major premise becomes the introduction of the essay, the minor premise and its proof constitute the body, and the thesis is the conclusion. A syllogism, therefore, is the basis not only for the reasoning in an essay, but also for the organization. We can map out our logic in syllogistic form and then insert our evidence within that framework. A bare syllogism, such as the plus/minus syllogism above, no doubt seems simplistic and therefore unrelated to the complex argumentative papers we write. Inside many extended arguments, however, is a deductive skeleton holding the argument together, although the buried syllogism may not be readily apparent because the premises are separated by evidence and supporting enthymemes.

Here is how we might expand the plus/minus syllogism into an outline for an essay:

I. Introduction: The college should be open to new administrative ideas and to systems that improve equity and accuracy on campus.

II. Plus/minus grading is such a system.
   A. The current grading system is inaccurate.
      1. Professors award pluses and minuses for greater accuracy.
      2. The registrar's office, which uses only letter grades, loses that accuracy.
   B. There is as much as a nine-point difference between a B+ and a B–, and it is unfair to give two students a simple B when one student had an 89 average and the other an 80.
   C. In four years, the difference in overall grade point average affects a student's chances for professional school.

III. Implementation would be easy and inexpensive.
   A. The campus computer director confirmed that she can program a system that will accept and average pluses and minuses.
   B. The initial cost for writing a program and the cost for extra running time would be minimal.

IV. Therefore, the college should adopt the plus/minus system.

Exercises

1. Expand the following enthymemes into full syllogisms, and decide whether they are valid:
   A. David can't attend the university because his grades are low.
   B. He should have a complete physical examination each year because both of his parents have angina.
   C. The current mortgage rates are preventing Americans from buying homes.
   D. Democrats who refuse to support the party platform shouldn't be allowed to vote at caucuses; Henry shouldn't be allowed to vote at this caucus.
   E. Unless we want convicted criminals back on the streets, we should support the bill to finance new state prisons. So support the bill.
   F. My Uncle Thom is a real sleaze. He hangs around pool halls all of the time.
   G. Ed retired early; he must not have liked his job.
   H. Gifted children should be grouped in separate classrooms; when they are placed in heterogeneous classes, they get bored.
   I. "Please do not shoot the pianist. He is doing his best." (Oscar Wilde)

J. How can you say that I cheat at cards if I never win?

K. "I think we ought to have a draft. . . . It's very clear that the all-volunteer military has failed to attract and retain a sufficient number of quality people." (Congressman Paul Trimble, Virginia)

2. Which of the following arguments are valid, and which are not valid? To determine validity, you will have to set up each argument as a syllogism. If you do not agree with an argument (i.e., you don't think it is true), which premise do you think is false?

A. Capital punishment is injurious by the example of barbarity it presents. If human passions, or the necessities of war, have taught men to shed one another's blood, the laws, which are intended to moderate human conduct, ought not to extend the savage example, which in the case of a legal execution is all the more baneful in that it is carried out with studied formalities. To me it seems an absurdity that laws, which are the expression of the public will, which abhor and which punish homicide, should themselves commit one; and that, to deter citizens from private assassination, they should themselves order public manslaughter.

—From the Marquis of Beccaria, Cesare Bonesana, *Against Capital Punishment*

B. Perhaps the best cure for the fear of death is to reflect that life has a beginning as well as an end. There was a time when we were not: this gives us no concern—why, then, should it trouble us that a time will come when we shall cease to be?

—From William Hazlitt, "On the Fear of Death"

C. It has been thought a considerable advance towards establishing the principles of freedom to say, that government is a compact between those who govern and those who are governed; but this can not be true, because it is putting the effect before the cause; for as man must have existed before governments existed, there necessarily was a time when governments did not exist, and consequently there could originally exist no governors to form such a compact with.

The fact therefore must be that the individuals themselves, each in his own personal and sovereign right, entered into a compact with each other to produce a government: and this is the only mode in which governments have a right to arise, and the only principle on which they have a right to exist.

—From Thomas Paine, *Common Sense*

D. Conservatives often complain that the law provides insufficient deterrents to violent behavior, but few of them support the one legal deterrent likely to be the most effective: handgun control. There now are 100 million guns in the hands of the civilian population. In 1978, over 63 percent of reported murders involved firearms, but less than one-quarter of all reported aggravated assaults involved firearms. The rest involved knives, blunt instruments, hands, fists, feet, and other less efficient weapons. The more frequent use of firearms is the main difference—apart from the result—

between murder and aggravated assault. There is little reason to believe that as a rule, some attackers carefully set out to kill and others merely to injure. They just attack, using whatever force is convenient. Therefore, even if handgun control cannot be expected to reduce the frequency of violent attacks, it could lead to the use of less efficient weapons. We could expect fewer murders and more aggravated assaults, which certainly would be an improvement. One study has estimated that, if knives rather than firearms were used in attacks, there might be 80 percent fewer fatalities. Less speculatively, a 1975 Massachusetts law that mandates a one-year minimum prison term for carrying a gun without a license has resulted in substantial decreases in gun-related murders, assaults, and robberies—and increases in non-gun assaults and robberies.

—From Lynn A. Curtis, "What's New in Murder," *New Republic,* Jan. 26, 1980

E. The world of religion and philosophy was shocked recently when Henry P. Van Dusen and his wife ended their lives by their own hands. Dr. Van Dusen had been president of Union Theological Seminary; for more than a quarter-century he had been one of the luminous names in Protestant theology. He enjoyed world status as a spiritual leader. News of the self-inflicted death of the Van Dusens, therefore, was profoundly disturbing to all those who attach a moral stigma to suicide and regard it as a violation of God's laws.

Dr. Van Dusen had anticipated this reaction. He and his wife left behind a letter that may have historic significance. It was very brief, but the essential point it made is now being widely discussed by theologians and could represent the beginning of a reconsideration of traditional religious attitudes toward self-inflicted death. The letter raised a moral issue: does an individual have the obligation to go on living even when the beauty and meaning and power of life are gone?

Henry and Elizabeth Van Dusen had lived full lives. In recent years, they had become increasingly ill, requiring almost continual medical care. Their infirmities were worsening, and they realized they would soon become completely dependent for even the most elementary needs and functions. Under these circumstances, little dignity would have been left in life. They didn't like the idea of taking up space in a world with too many mouths and too little food. They believed it was a misuse of medical science to keep them technically alive.

They therefore believed they had the right to decide when to die. In making that decision, they weren't turning against life as the highest value; what they were turning against was the notion that there were no circumstances under which life should be discontinued.

—From Norman Cousins, "The Right to Die," *Saturday Review,* June 14, 1975

F. It now remains to see what should be the methods and conduct of a prince in dealing with his subjects and his friends. And because I know that many have written on this topic, I fear that when I too write I shall be thought presumptuous, because, in discussing it, I break away completely from the principles laid down by my predecessors. But since it is my purpose to write something useful to an attentive reader, I think it more effective to go back to the practical truth of the subject than to depend on my fancies about it. And many have imagined republics and principalities that never have been seen or known to exist in reality. For there is such a difference between the way men live and the way they ought to live, that anybody who abandons what is for what ought to be will learn something that will ruin rather than preserve him, because anyone who determines to act in all circumstances the part of a good man must come to ruin among so many who are not good. Hence, if a prince wishes to maintain himself, he must learn how to be not good, and to use that ability or not as is required.

—From Machiavelli, *The Prince* (translated by Allan H. Gilbert)

Induction

Induction is the method by which we reach generalizations. It is the type of reasoning that begins by examining individual instances and empirical data and ends by making a generalization about those items. It is through induction that we have learned most of what we know, whether from first-hand experience or from scientific research. Through the scientific method, which is nothing more than systematized induction, scientists form universal principles; by examining repeated occurrences, they have discovered causes, effects, and generalizations, including such useful knowledge as the cure for smallpox, ways of preserving food, ways of predicting the weather, and the effects of smoking.

On a more mundane level, here is an example of how we use induction. During her life, Natalie has eaten shrimp, trout, crab, bass, sole, haddock, clams, salmon, and lobster. Somewhere along the way she formed the generalization that she likes seafood. She has moved from specific instances to a general statement concerning all seafood, including those she has not yet tried. Conceivably, however, there is some seafood she hasn't yet tried that she won't like—octopus, for example, or eel. Her inductive generalization, which is based on a reasonable sampling of seafood, is not 100 percent certain; it is, instead, highly probable.

The limitation of induction is that there is almost never certainty—only degrees of probability. Inductive conclusions approach certainty without reaching it. We move from a sampling of *some* instances to a generalization about *all* instances. Because we examine only a portion of the evidence, the generalization exceeds the evidence.

Because we usually must draw a conclusion based on partial evidence, induction involves a certain intellectual danger. We cannot be absolutely certain that the unobserved instances will not contradict our generalization. To reach certainty, we would have to examine each instance, but a comprehensive examination is usually unnecessary and often impossible. We need not eat *every* species of fish to decide that we like seafood. Gallup pollsters cannot interview every American for an opinion, so they interview a representative sample. To reach the conclusion that all fingerprints are unique, researchers didn't examine the fingerprints of every person in the world; they examined a sample, and from that evidence formed a general principle.

The rational jump from a few instances to a general statement about all instances is called an *inductive leap*. For example, if we eat a grapefruit and find that it is extremely tart, and eat another grapefruit and find it tart, and then another and another, eventually we will leap from the individual instances to the conclusion that all grapefruits are extremely tart. After we find the same characteristic repeatedly, we conclude that this characteristic will appear in the whole class; we assume that what is true of observed instances will hold true for all instances. At some point we must stop looking at individual instances and draw a conclusion, even though there will be a gap between our evidence and our conclusion. If we are careful, we can leap over that gap successfully, but we must have a firm springboard of facts in order to make the inductive leap to generalization.

Sometimes inductive leaps turn out to be wrong. For example, after examining all available birds, early Europeans may have concluded that all birds can fly. Later exploration, however, revealed that the ostrich in Africa, the rhea in South America, and the dodo in Mauritius are birds that cannot fly. If we examined scores of mammals—dogs, rats, tigers, antelope, moles, sheep, beavers, pandas, chimpanzees, buffalo, cows, chipmunks, human beings, donkeys, hippos, moose, kangaroos, rabbits, cats—we might conclude that all mammals have two knees. But we would have leaped to a premature conclusion because whales have no knees and elephants have four. When we use induction, we have no assurance that our conclusion is true.

Although making an inductive leap is dangerous, we must take the risk at some point. Without the generalization, the data do not make sense and the facts are useless. The whole purpose of examining facts is to reach a conclusion from which we can make predictions to apply to new instances. Without induction we wouldn't be able to learn from our experiences because each instance would seemingly have no bearing on similar instances, and each instance we encounter would be totally new. For instance, when we were children, if we burned our fingers on a candle, then burned them with a match, and later burned them on a gas stove, before long we made the leap and concluded that fire burns. That is the manner in which we reached most of our beliefs—for instance, that studying hard increases the chances for high grades; that the Salk vaccine prevents polio; that the sun will rise in the east tomorrow; that crime doesn't pay; that a little humor helps a speech immensely; that physical exercise promotes good health; that alcohol in the bloodstream decreases one's reaction time. We hold such beliefs because we observed the individual instances time and time again until we reached a generalization concerning them.

Categorical Induction

The type of induction that we have been examining thus far might be called *class induction* or *categorical induction* because it concerns items within one class. We examine one grapefruit, another grapefruit, another, and so on—all items belonging to the same class—and then we make a generalization about that class. For a class inductive conclusion to be sound, the evidence must meet certain requirements:

1. The evidence must be known and available.
2. There must be a sufficient number of instances in the sample.
3. The instances used must be typical.
4. Exceptions must be shown to be atypical.

Evidence Must Be Known

Where the evidence is unknown or unavailable, there can be no inductive generalization. Thus, arguments that there is intelligent life elsewhere in the universe, that Big Foot exists, or that the John F. Kennedy assassination was a conspiracy cannot be proved because there is no evidence to support the propositions.

APPLICATION

Can you think of two other examples of arguments for which the evidence is unknown?

Sample Must Be Sufficient

Before we can safely make the inductive leap to a generalization, we must examine a sufficient number of examples. The question is, how many is "sufficient"? How large must our sample be for the generalization to be reliable? At what point can we leap from specific instances to a general statement? The number will vary, depending on (1) the attitude of our readers (skeptical readers will insist on a large sample) and (2) the size of the population—that is, the total number of instances in a class. If we are investigating a small population, such as United States senators, we might examine each instance since in this case there are only 100. With a large population, however, polling every example is impossible, so we must settle for a sample, provided that the sample is large. If the population is 10,000 we might canvass 500, or 15 percent; if the population is only 1,000 we might poll 250, or 25 percent. Naturally, if we poll 500, our sample will be more representative than if we poll only 100.

The fallacy that we must guard against in this regard is *hasty generalization*, which is jumping to a conclusion on the basis of insufficient evidence. For example, if we are trying to determine whether couples who live together for more than a year before marrying have a lower divorce rate than couples who marry before living together, we cannot reach a reliable conclusion if we limit the examination to five couples we know. Rather, we would have to conduct a rather extensive poll, examining a large sample. Conclusions based on only a few instances are always suspect and often incorrect.

Sample Must Be Typical

Besides being sufficient in number, the instances in the sample must be typical of the whole population that we are investigating. If the instances that we examine are not typical, our conclusion will be a *faulty generalization*. For example, if we are testing our hypothesis that premarital cohabitation decreases the likelihood of divorce, and we poll 100 married couples on campus who first lived together, will our ensuing conclusion be reliable? It will not be reliable for the entire American population because college students are not representative of the American public: They are more highly educated, younger, and less affluent than the "average" American. In addition, the college is located in a particular area, and that area may not be representative of the rest of the country. Hence, the generalization will be reliable only for married couples at colleges in that region.

An example of a generalization that has been criticized because of its unrepresentative sample is the famous Kinsey report, which described the sexual behavior of American women in the 1950s. Although the sample was sufficient (5,940 cases), the women interviewed did not represent a cross section of American women because they were predominantly well educated, Protestant, and middle class. Also, all of them were willing to discuss their sex lives with strangers, and that prerequisite itself makes for an atypical sample because it eliminates those women who were too shy to talk, and those women might have been more conservative than the sample. The result was a faulty generalization that shocked many people because it portrayed American women as being more sexually liberated than they probably were.

Another kind of unrepresentative sample is an isolated population. For example, if a statistic indicates that 80 percent of teenagers from broken homes admit to having smoked marijuana, drunk hard liquor, and had premarital sex, can we draw any conclusion from that statistic? Does it prove that broken homes cause adjustment problems in teenagers? Maybe not. The statistic lacks significance because it isn't a representative sample; for it to be meaningful, we would have to know that 80 percent is higher than the proportion for the general teenage population. If 80 percent of all teenagers—those with married parents as well as those with divorced parents—smoked marijuana, drank alcohol, and had sex, then the statistic is meaningless.

The key to representative sampling is random selection. The Gallup and Harris polls work by canvassing fewer than 2,000 Americans, but because everyone in America has an equal chance of being selected, the samples are fair and representative. These polls can predict within 3 or 4 percent what the entire American population, 240 million strong, thinks on an issue; in presidential elections, for instance, these polls are usually within 2 percent of predicting the final outcome.

Exceptions Must Be Accounted For

If there are exceptions to our generalization, we must either prove that they are unrepresentative of the population or modify our generalization. For example, if our generalization is that all crows are black, and someone points out that there is a white crow on display in the zoo, we must account for that white crow: It is an albino and therefore is not typical. If our generalization is a statistical one—288 out of 310—we must qualify the generalization or give the precise percentage: *almost all* professors have at least a Master's degree, or 87 percent of the United States Congress are lawyers.

We should not exclude or suppress evidence that doesn't support our conclusion. Negative instances cannot be ignored. If we try to ignore them, the opposition will most certainly bring them up, and therefore it is in our best interest to mention them ourselves and to show that they are atypical, insignificant, and infrequent. For example:

Mortimer: PBS doesn't interfere with programming by inserting annoying interruptions and commercials. That's why I watch it.

Henrietta: That's not true. I tuned in last night and they interrupted repeatedly with a fund drive.

Mortimer: But they have those fund drives only two weeks a year.

A negative instance doesn't mean that we must abandon our generalization; it means, however, that we must modify it: "Except for the fund drive twice a year, PBS does not. . . ."

Exercises

1. Which of the following generalizations would you accept? Which ones would you not accept, and why not—no evidence? inadequate sample? atypical sample? needs qualifying? To which generalizations can you add further evidence in support?

   A. Jack Ruby, who knew he was dying of cancer, was recruited by the FBI to assassinate Lee Harvey Oswald in order to keep Oswald from exposing a conspiracy. The fact that Ruby died of cancer shortly after the assassination proves this.

   B. The business school on this campus is terribly inferior. I had three different professors and they all were drones.

   C. Mortimer decides to shop at a new grocery store. He buys the same brands that he buys at the store where he usually shops. He discovers that the jelly costs 8¢ less at the new store, the milk 11¢ less per half gallon, the sugar 20¢ less, the sirloin 28¢ less per pound, and the apples 10¢ less per pound. Mortimer tells Henrietta that from now on they will shop at the new store because it is less expensive.

   D. Because 20 percent of the basketball team is on scholastic probation, I conclude that basketball interferes with scholastic achievement and should be banned.

   E. Houston cops are notoriously brutal. There was an article in the paper just yesterday about a young Chicano who died as a result of internal bleeding from a cop—wearing cowboy boots—having kicked him in the stomach repeatedly.

   F. The Bermuda Triangle is a magnetic field where UFOs operate.

   G. Most scholarly research is a waste of tax money. Some governmental agency awarded a $90,000 grant to study the mating habits of the South American tree frog.

   H. The United States dropped the atomic bomb on Hiroshima not to make the Japanese surrender—surrender was inevitable and imminent—but to show the Russians that we would not hesitate to use nuclear weapons. It was intended as a warning and was nothing more than a power play in the mounting confrontation with the communists.

   I. *Mortimer, Jr.*: "I don't know why I should finish high school. Lots of successful people never finished even grade school."
      Mortimer, Sr.: "Oh, yeah? Like who?"
      Mortimer, Jr.: "Mark Twain, Stanley (who found Dr. Livingston), Sean

O'Casey, Andrew Carnegie, Buffalo Bill, Charlie Chaplin, Charles Dickens, Thomas Edison, and John Philip Sousa."

J. The students on this campus are more interested in partying than in learning. On weekends there is a party in every house on fraternity row, one in the student union, and hundreds of students down on the main strip drinking and dancing at the local bars.

K. To find out students' attitudes about the mandatory health fee, Henrietta asked every tenth student going through registration if he or she objected to the fee. Seventy-eight percent said that they objected to the fee.

L. The oil companies have discovered how to make cheap synthetic fuels, but they are keeping the formula a secret because it would ruin the oil market.

M. American law enforcement agencies are incompetent. There are areas in New York City where drug dealers openly sell marijuana, cocaine, and heroin on street corners and in public parks.

2. What is wrong with the following conclusions?
   A. In the Napoleonic Wars, only 35,000 soldiers were killed by the enemy, but 270,000 died of epidemic diseases. In the Crimean War, 35,000 died of battle wounds, and 190,000 died of typhoid, smallpox, and other diseases. In the American Civil War, three times as many died from diseases as from enemy action. The same is true of the Crusades, the Wars of the Roses, the Punic Wars, the Greco-Persian Wars, and other wars. It is safe to say, therefore, that epidemic disease is a more dangerous enemy in war than are the opposing troops.
   B. Case histories of 7,000 people dying of stomach cancer in 1983 reveal that 57 percent of them had regularly consumed cola during the 5 years years prior to their deaths. Clearly, cola causes stomach cancer.
   C. In 1936 the *Literary Digest* conducted a poll to predict the outcome of the upcoming presidential race between the Republican candidate Landon and the Democratic candidate Roosevelt. The sample was large—over 2 million responses. The pollsters randomly chose names from phone directories across the country, and the result of their poll indicated that Landon would win by a considerable margin. Of course, Roosevelt won. What went wrong? (*Hint:* Remember where the pollsters got their sample. Who was likely to be listed there in the Depression years? Who traditionally votes Republican?)
   D. Of the 400 people with whom I graduated from high school, 200 attended a recent reunion. Seventy percent of those attending were in professional jobs—doctors, lawyers, professors, business executives, and so forth. I therefore conclude that the majority of the people with whom I graduated from high school have successful careers. (*Hint:*

Besides the difficulty of defining *successful*, there is difficulty about the numbers. Who is more likely to attend a class reunion—those who have become successful, or those who have failed?)

E. Clinical studies show that the odds of quitting smoking and staying off tobacco are quite small. After studying the results of dozens of programs designed to help smokers break their addiction, researchers report that only 60 percent of the smokers kicked the habit, and that of those who managed to quit, 75 percent start smoking again within two years. If you try to quit smoking, you will likely fail. (*Hint:* Does the sample include *all* smokers?)

Interpretive Induction

There is another type of nondeductive logic that we might call *interpretive induction* because it *evaluates* evidence to reach a conclusion. Instead of examining items within a class, this inductive process accumulates and examines related facts and draws a conclusion from them, much as a detective examines the facts of a crime and tries to discover the identity of the criminal. We gather all types of evidence— statistics, testimony, examples, parallel cases—and then see what they add up to. For example, based on available evidence, an archaeologist concludes that human beings are descended from killer apes; an economist forecasts that the recession will end within the next 14 months; a history professor reasons that the behavior of those thought to be under the spell of witches in Salem in 1692 was caused by poisonous fungus. These conclusions weren't pulled out of a magician's hat; they are the result of examining evidence and making a judgment based on facts.

What would you conclude from these sets of facts:

A. The bank is missing $275,000.

The bank president during the past year bought a new boat and a new car and vacationed in Europe for a month.

He is known to be keeping a mistress who likes expensive things.

He and his mistress have flown to Argentina without notice.

B. Military satellites show Nicaraguan troop movement along the Honduras border.

Cuban and Russian military advisors have been training Nicaraguan troops.

The President of Honduras flew to Washington, D.C. for an emergency meeting with the President of the United States.

The United States has granted additional military aid to Honduras.

Are conclusions other than the obvious one possible? If so, what?

Exploring Alternative Explanations

A different interpretation of the same evidence can often yield a different conclusion; therefore, before we leap to a conclusion and proclaim that it is the only one, we should explore the possibility of alternative conclusions. For example, with reference to the earlier conclusions about killer apes, witch spells, and the economy, we can reach alternative, competing conclusions based on the same facts. Another archaeologist has concluded that human beings are descended from basically peaceful hunters and gatherers and are not innately aggressive; another historian has concluded that the aberrant behavior attributed to witchcraft was caused not by poisoned fungus but by religious hysteria; and a different economist may conclude that the recession will continue for 2 more years. We must consider all options and then decide which one seems most plausible.

Because interpretive conclusions are based on judgment and often involve complex situations, we must qualify them according to the degree of certainty. Absolute statements *(all, never, always)* can be dangerous; we don't want to abuse the evidence by trying to pour a 10-gallon conclusion into a 5-gallon data bucket. We want to make the strongest claim we can for our evidence, of course, but we must proceed with caution. Moving from evidence to conclusion requires prudence and qualifying remarks *(seemingly, usually, probably, most likely, many, often, apparently,* and so forth).

Accumulating Sufficient Evidence

The amount of evidence needed to convince readers depends on the degree of our readers' skepticism and on the forcefulness of our evidence. Some types of evidence are more convincing than others, and occasionally one very strong proof is sufficient. Usually, however, we need an entire arsenal of facts. Since readers proportion their belief to the evidence we present, we want the sheer number of proofs to overcome any skepticism they harbor.

Arguments convince because of the force, the amount, and the order of their evidence. If the proofs are arranged in a progression—each proof a little more forceful than the previous one—there is a sense of momentum in an argument, and readers are swept along toward conviction. We progressively build up their trust, turning their skepticism to openness and then to acceptance.

The importance of having an abundance of facts in our arguments cannot be overemphasized. Before readers will accept our proposition, they want to see our facts, and therefore we must back up with facts any assertion we make. In short, evidence establishes the truth of our proposition, and facts are the bricks that conviction is built on. Producing a fact is like laying down a brick of conviction: After enough bricks are laid, we have a solid argument.

Writers who have facts to substantiate assertions can make a good case for their thesis even when readers are initially skeptical of that thesis. For example, in an article opposing gun control, Don B. Kates asserts that where handgun training programs exist, crime is lower, and therefore what is needed is not gun restriction but gun training. He substantiates his opinion with hard facts:

In the year after Orlando, Florida, had a highly publicized training program in which 6,000 civilian women mastered handgun combat skill, rape dropped 90 percent there—though it rose precipitously across the country. Aggravated assault and burglary also declined by 25 percent each, making Orlando the only city in the country of over 100,000 population to enjoy a decline in major crime in 1968. Similar programs have had the same result elsewhere. Thus in Highland Park, Michigan, armed robberies dropped from a total of eighty in a four-month period to zero in the succeeding four months, after police there instituted a highly publicized firearms training program for retail merchants. In Detroit such a program was carried on by a grocers' association over the opposition of the police chief. The program received extensive publicity, first through the chief's denunciations of it, and subsequently when seven robbers were shot by grocers. Grocery robberies in Detroit dropped 90 percent. In 1971, publicity for a firearms training program for New Orleans pharmacists was credited by police and federal narcotics agents with causing pharmacy robberies to drop from three per week to three in six months there.

—From "Gun Control: The Real Facts," *Field and Stream*, July 1979

Do the writer's facts convince you that his proposition is true and that he knows what he is writing about?

Facts contribute to our argument in two ways: by serving as proof, and by establishing our credibility. The first function is obvious—we need facts to substantiate our assertions. But the second function is almost as important. By presenting relevant facts about our subject, we convince readers that we know what we are writing about, and when they are assured that we are knowledgeable and reliable, they more readily accept our proposition. (There will be more about this function in the next chapter under "Ethos.")

Arguments that fail to convince readers usually fail because they lack facts. Instead of offering hard evidence to prove a proposition, many student writers offer a series of assertions that are substantiated only by other assertions. They think they are offering facts when in reality they are merely offering opinions.

Distinguishing Between Fact and Opinion

Opinions trying to masquerade as facts are a major weakness in many arguments. Part of the problem is that some writers don't understand the precise distinction between opinions and facts. The distinction is simple: Facts can be *objectively verified*, and opinions are *judgments*. Facts stand up under scrutiny and cannot be successfully challenged. We can test and empirically verify them. For example:

> Possums are marsupials.
>
> More women in the United States die of breast cancer than of any other form of cancer.
>
> The Neptunian moon Triton revolves retrograde to the planet's rotation.
>
> A Hoosier is a person from Indiana.
>
> Tennessee Williams won the drama Pulitzer Prize in 1948 for *A Streetcar Named Desire* and in 1955 for *Cat on a Hot Tin Roof.*
>
> William McKinley, the 25th president of the United States, was a mess sergeant in the Civil War, but he was given a commission for preparing hot food to troops in action.
>
> Although the Sears Tower in Chicago and the World Trade Center in New York are both 110 stories high, the Sears Tower is 104 feet taller.

Opinions, on the other hand, are subjective judgments and are open to debate. For example:

> Men are equal to women.
>
> Space exploration is a waste of money.
>
> Clark Gable was handsome.

Although we may hold these opinions with confidence and maintain that they are true, they are nonetheless evaluative, and different persons can hold opposing opinions. Some opinions are based on arbitrary impressions and on emotions, but many are based on evidence. Even informed opinions, though, are interpretations of evidence that can be viewed several ways. For example, here is one opinion on economics:

> The way to stimulate the national economy is to reduce individual income tax rates by 10 percent so that consumers will spend more money, which in turn will increase business sales, which in turn will create more productivity and more jobs.

Here is the opposing opinion:

> Rather than stimulating the economy, income tax reductions cause greater inflation, and the increased inflation eats away the 10 percent decrease in taxes so that consumers do not actually get to

spend it; hence, there is no increase in buying, productivity, or jobs.

The reason that persons—even experts—can hold different opinions on the same issue is that the evidence may be ambiguous. Sometimes there are so many factors involved that experts have difficulty evaluating the evidence, and sometimes precise measurements are difficult, as in the realm of human behavior.

Another reason for differing opinions is that persons use subjective criteria.

Life is better in the Sun Belt than on the East Coast.

What criteria do we use to make such a determination? Someone else may use other criteria.

Clark Gable was handsome.

What one person finds handsome another may not. Usually an opinion contains an evaluative word (an adjective such as *handsome, bad, unethical*) indicating that the statement is a subjective judgment. For example, which words are evaluative here?

Baseball players make excessive salaries.
The major issue in the 1984 presidential election was the budget deficit.
Television has become more sophisticated over the years.
The mayor is an effective politician.

When evidence is vague, determining whether a statement is a fact or an opinion may be difficult. For instance, we have accepted as fact that the Wright brothers were the first men to fly an airplane, but now other contenders for that honor are being proposed, such as Albert Santos-Dumont, Clément Ader, and Samuel Pierpont Langley. Should we accept the Wright brothers' being first as a fact or as an opinion?

APPLICATION

Which of the following are facts, and which are opinions?

1. Rocky Marciano was the greatest heavyweight boxer of all times because he was the only heavyweight champion who never lost a fight; he won all 49 of his bouts, including 6 title defenses, and 43 of the 49 were by knockout.
2. The Taft-Hartley Act restricted the actions of unions by prohibiting "closed shops," outlawing federal employee strikes, restricting political contributions of unions, and allowing for temporary court injunctions against strikes.
3. The Irish Republican Army (IRA) is an Irish national and terrorist organization.

4. Sea horses are rare among animals in that the male carries the eggs until they hatch.
5. Pornography contributes to sexual assaults.
6. Although Christmas carols are religious in origin, they have become culturally significant and therefore do not violate the separation of church and state; hence, they can be sung in public schools.
7. Chiang Kai-shek, who succeeded Sun Yat-sen as leader of the Chinese Nationals, defeated the Chinese warlords who had controlled China for generations, but in turn Chiang lost his country to Mao Tse-tung's communist forces.
8. The Beatles influenced popular music.
9. The Moral Majority was a reaction against the social liberalism of the 1960s and early 1970s.
10. The most popular television show in 1953 was "I Love Lucy."
11. The Olympics foster international goodwill.
12. Marilyn Monroe committed suicide.
13. Import quotas are counterproductive: They keep prices high by prohibiting competition from inexpensive foreign products and they cause other countries to set import quotas against our country.
14. Buster Keaton's famous 1926 film *The General* was panned by the critics when it first was issued.
15. Chimpanzees are sexually promiscuous.
16. Because there have been several false alarms triggered by malfunctions in the United States Air Force's computer defense system, the Air Force should have a dual system.
17. The Matterhorn, the 14,690 foot peak in the Pennine Alps, is more difficult to climb than Mt. McKinley in Alaska, which is 20,320 feet high.
18. Strict gun control laws would cut the homicide rate.
19. By the year 2000 there will be a surplus of doctors in the United States.
20. Prostitution is a sin.

Moving from Evidence to Inference

Facts are meaningless by themselves. They acquire significance only when we use them to support a generalization or when we draw inferences from them.

To understand the process of inference—that is, of examining a fact and drawing a conclusion from it—we might defer to that genius of inference, Sherlock Holmes. The following passage from "The Adventure of the Blue Carbuncle" illustrates the detective's masterful powers of reasoning. Holmes gives Dr. Watson an old hat and bids him to look upon it "as an intellectual problem" to solve. The facts are that on Christmas morning a presumably intoxicated man was mugged, leaving at the scene his hat and a roasting goose with a card tied to its leg: "For Mrs. Henry

Baker." Because there are hundreds of Henry Bakers in London, Holmes needs to discover the correct Henry Baker in order to return the hat and goose. Holmes hands Watson the hat:

"Here is my lens. You know my methods. What can you gather yourself as to the individuality of the man who has worn this article?"

I took the tattered object in my hands, and turned it over rather ruefully. It was a very ordinary black hat of the usual round shape, hard, and much the worse for wear. The lining had been of red silk, but was a good deal discoloured. There was no maker's name; but, as Holmes had remarked, the initials "H. B." were scrawled upon one side. It was pierced in the brim for a hat-securer, but the elastic was missing. For the rest, it was cracked, exceedingly dusty, and spotted in several places, although there seemed to have been some attempt to hide the discoloured patches by smearing them with ink.

"I can see nothing," said I, handing it back to my friend.

"On the contrary, Watson, you can see everything. You fail, however, to reason from what you see. You are too timid in drawing your inferences."

"Then, pray tell me what it is that you can infer from this hat?"

He picked it up, and gazed at it in the peculiar introspective fashion which was characteristic of him. "It is perhaps less suggestive than it might have been," he remarked, "and yet there are a few inferences which are very distinct, and a few others which represent at least a strong balance of probability. That the man was highly intellectual is of course obvious upon the face of it, and also that he was fairly well-to-do within the last three years, although he has now fallen upon evil days. He had foresight, but has less now than formerly, pointing to a moral retrogression, which, when taken with the decline of his fortunes, seems to indicate some evil influences, probably drink, at work upon him. This may account also for the obvious fact that his wife has ceased to love him."

"My dear Holmes!"

"He has, however, retained some degree of self-respect," he continued, disregarding my remonstrance. "He is a man who leads a sedentary life, goes out little, is out of training entirely, is middle-aged, has grizzled hair which he has had cut within the last few days, and which he anoints with lime-cream. These are the more patent facts which are to be deduced from his hat. Also, by the way, that it is extremely improbable that he has gas laid on in his house."

"You are certainly joking, Holmes."

"Not in the least. Is it possible that even now when I give you these results you are unable to see how they are attained?"

"I have no doubt that I am very stupid; but I must confess that I am unable to follow you. For example, how did you deduce that this man was intellectual?"

For answer Holmes clapped the hat upon his head. It came right over the forehead and settled upon the bridge of his nose. "It is a question of cubic capacity," said he; "a man with so large a brain must have something in it."

"The decline of his fortunes, then?"

"This hat is three years old. These flat brims curled at the edge came in then. It is a hat of the very best quality. Look at the band of ribbed silk, and the excellent lining. If this man could afford to buy so expensive a hat three years ago, and has had no hat since, then he has assuredly gone down in the world."

"Well, that is clear enough, certainly. But how about the foresight, and the moral retrogression?"

Sherlock Holmes laughed. "Here is the foresight," said he, putting his finger upon the little disc and loop of the hat-securer. "They are never sold upon hats. If this man ordered one, it is a sign of a certain amount of foresight, since he went out of his way to take this precaution against the wind. But since we see that he has broken the elastic, and has not troubled to replace it, it is obvious that he has less foresight now than formerly, which is a distinct proof of a weakening nature. On the other hand, he has endeavoured to conceal some of these stains upon the felt by daubing them with ink, which is a sign that he has not entirely lost his self-respect."

"Your reasoning is certainly plausible."

"The further points, that he is middle-aged, that his hair is grizzled, that it has been recently cut, and that he uses lime-cream, are all to be gathered from a close examination of the lower part of the lining. The lens discloses a large number of hair ends, clean cut by the scissors of the barber. They all appear to be adhesive, and there is a distinct odour of lime-cream. This dust, you will observe, is not the gritty, grey dust of the street, but the fluffy brown dust of the house, showing that it has been hung up indoors most of the time; while the marks of moisture upon the inside are proof positive that the wearer perspired very freely, and could, therefore, hardly be in the best of training."

"But his wife—you said that she had ceased to love him."

"This hat has not been brushed for weeks. When I see you, my dear Watson, with a week's accumulation of dust upon your hat, and when your wife allows you to go out in such a state, I shall fear that you also have been unfortunate enough to lose your wife's affection."

"But he might be a bachelor."

"Nay, he was bringing home the goose as a peace-offering to his wife. Remember the card upon the bird's leg."

"You have an answer to everything. But how on earth do you deduce that the gas is not laid on in his house?"

"One tallow stain, or even two, might come by chance; but, when I see no less than five, I think that there can be little doubt that the individual must be brought into frequent contact with burning tallow—walks upstairs at night probably with his hat in one hand and a guttering candle in the other. Anyhow, he never got tallow stains from a gas jet. Are you satisfied?"

—From Sir Arthur Conan Doyle, *The Adventures of Sherlock Holmes*

Do you accept Holmes' inferences about head size, perspiration, sedentariness, and wifely affection? Has the clever detective failed to consider alternative inferences from the evidence? For instance, what alternative explanations might be given for a man wearing a fine-quality hat that is now 3 years old and in poor condition?

Although we might take issue with the certainty of Holmes' conclusions, his inspection of the hat demonstrates the process of moving from evidence to inference. Like Watson, we too often see everything but fail to reason from what we see. We must be alert to the significance of our evidence, and we must have some expertise in the subject to understand the evidence.

Consider this example: A farmer in East Africa uncovers a fossilized primate skull. To the laborer, the skull means nothing, but to archaeologists it becomes evidence from which numerous inferences can be made. First, the experts are able to date the skull as being between 3 million and 4 million years old. Second, by examining the teeth, they can infer the creature's diet: The large, flat teeth indicate that it ate mainly vegetables, probably fiberous vegetables that required considerable grinding—roots, stalks, and seeds—instead of fruits and leaves. Hence, this being was not likely a tree dweller; it may have even left the forests for the woodlands and plains. The teeth also tell whether the creature had a prolonged childhood: The first molar shows more wear than the second molar, the third even less. This evidence suggests that the being's molars developed one at a time over several childhood years. Third, a lump in the skull over the front left portion of the brain—the region called Broca's area—suggests that this prehistoric ancestor was developing language because Broca's area is where the neural center for language is housed. From physical facts, observant and informed persons can make intelligent, reasonably certain inferences.

Many scientific discoveries were nothing more than drawing plausible inferences from available facts. For example, even when the Earth was considered to be flat, people could see the Earth's round shadow on the moon during a lunar eclipse, and some had the intelligence to make the logical inference. Likewise, William Harvey, the seventeenth-century physician credited with conceiving the theory of pulmonary circulation, merely applied sound thinking to facts already known—that the arteries carry blood, that blood passes through the lungs, and that valves exist within the heart. From those facts, Harvey inferred the cause and purpose of circulation. The facts had been known for centuries, but the significance of the facts was not known until Harvey reasoned them through.

APPLICATION

What inferences would you draw from these facts:

A man who has blood type AB notices on his daughter's birth certificate that she has type O blood. The man knows that an offspring of an AB male can be only A, B, or AB.

A Norse penny, dating around the eleventh century, was found near an ancient Indian village near Blue Hill, Maine, several years ago. Can you think of three possible inferences?

People tend to remember their dreams more during periods of stress. Can you think of two explanations?

The suicide rate in the 15 to 24-year-old age group for Americans has increased sharply over the past few decades. Suicide ranks third as a cause of death among young people (next to accidents and homicides). Each year, about 6,000 youths aged 15 to 24 commit suicide, according to a surgeon general's report. What can you infer from this statistic?

Keep in mind that evidence is open to interpretation, and that the inferences drawn from evidence can be widely different.

Translating Facts to Fit Audience

A fact is meaningless until we demonstrate its relevance to our readers. Before a fact acquires significance for them, they must know how it can affect them or of what value it is to them. Our task, therefore, is to show why a fact is important to them, and to accomplish this task, we must know not only the evidence but also the audience.

The best way to reach readers is to find facts that apply specifically to them. For example, if we are trying to convince a black urban civic group that they should support gun control, we should match our evidence and our audience. Instead of giving general population statistics, we should give the statistics specifically for the black population:

Murder is the number-one cause of death of black men between the ages of 25 and 35. From 1960 to 1970, the average life expectancy of black males aged 20 or younger declined by one year, mainly as a result of the increase in the murder rate in inner cities. More blacks were killed by other blacks in 1977 (5734) than died in nine years in Vietnam (5711).

—From Lynn A. Curits, "What's New in Murder," *New Republic*, Jan. 26, 1980

From the mass of evidence available when we research a subject, we must select those proofs that relate to our specific audience. We must find the right evidence for the right audience.

Another way to reach readers is to translate facts into terms that will be intelligible to them. Because a statistic means nothing to readers who don't know if the number is relatively large or small, we have to translate it into some other measurement in order to make it comprehensible. For example, if we say that Japan exports over $100 billion in goods each year, readers don't know whether that amount is large or small in relation to other countries' economies: $100 billion is a meaningless sum. If, on the other hand, we say that Japan's $100 billion in exports exceeds the combined gross national products of Puerto Rico, Venezuela, and Denmark, readers begin to get an idea of the magnitude of Japan's exports.

In addition to translating a statistic by comparing it with other figures, we can dramatize it by enlarging it—that is, we can show what its enlarged effects would be over long periods. For example, during a drought, a city government might try to impress upon citizens the necessity of repairing leaky faucets in order to save water. It can dramatize the fact by saying: "A faucet that drips once every second wastes 7,000 gallons of water a year." That statistic makes a seemingly insignificant drip suddenly sound like an incredible waste, and it may motivate citizens to put new washers in their faucets.

APPLICATION

1. Consider these strategies of translating or molding evidence to convince an audience. Explain the technique used and the effect of each.

   When the President severely cut the budget for the National Endowment for the Arts, arts administrators appealed to Congress to restore the funds by pointing out that the whole NEA budget was only one-seventh the cost of a single jet fighter. They also pointed out that their budget was less than what the President had allocated for military bands.

   "Every day 12 square miles of America's farmlands vanish forever. Where crops, barns, and silos once stood, roads, subdivisions, and shopping centers have sprouted. In the past decade we have lost farmlands equivalent to the combined areas of Vermont, New Hampshire, Massachusetts, Rhode Island, Connecticut, New Jersey, and Delaware. Today we still have 24 million acres in reserve—currently unfarmed land that could be brought under cultivation within a short time. If the present rate of loss continues, however, that reserve will evaporate by 1990." (Peter J. Ognibene, "Vanishing Farmlands: Selling Out the Soil," *Saturday Review*, May 1980)

   When Ronald Reagan first ran for the presidency, critics said that he was politically inexperienced because he had never held a national office. Reagan tried to maximize his experience by responding that he had been a two-term governor of California, and that California is equivalent in population to many nations, such as Czechoslovakia, Australia, Holland, Saudi Arabia, Peru, Canada, and Algeria.

To encourage Americans to support a nuclear arms limitation agreement with the Soviet Union, Jimmy Carter told them that a nuclear holocaust would be the equivalent to all the bombs of World War II exploding at the same time—every second that a nuclear war lasted. More people would die, he said, than in all the previous wars throughout history.

The disease that John Merrick, the Elephant Man, had (neurofibromatosis) is still prevalent today. "An estimated 100,000 Americans suffer from NF— more than the combined number of patients with cystic fibrosis, Tay-Sachs disease, sickle-cell anemia and Huntington's chorea." (*Newsweek*, March 24, 1980)

2. How would you translate these facts to make them impressive to readers: Preschool children watch an average of 3.8 hours of television a day.

In a typical summer, forest fires in the United States destroy over 3 million acres.

In 1986, Americans purchased an estimated $45 billion of marijuana and cocaine.

Commuters on congested expressways in Los Angeles, Houston, and Washington, D.C. spend an average of 8 minutes for every mile they commute.

Each year, over 20,000 Americans are killed with handguns.

The average American adult is 7 pounds overweight.

Every year over 50,000 Americans die in traffic accidents.

Using Different Types of Evidence

There are numerous types of evidence—including examples, reasons, parallel cases, precedents, testimony, narratives, humor, and statistics— and in an argument we usually use several types because each has a slightly different effect. For instance, statistics sound absolute and incontrovertible, narratives often appeal to readers' emotions, and precedents tend to dispel any refutation by the opposition. What follows is a discussion of the various types of evidence, with examples of each type.

Examples. Citing examples is probably the most common form of proof for substantiating a generalization. If we say, for instance, that many of the best mystery writers have been women, we must be prepared to back up that generalization with examples: Agatha Christie, Dorothy Sayers, P. D. James, Josephine Tey, Ngaio Marsh, Margery Allingham, Ruth Rendell, and Amanda Cross.

In the following paragraph, a writer uses examples to substantiate his claim that using interpreters can lead to misunderstandings among nations (and hence diplomats should learn several languages):

Everyone remembers when the Soviet leader Nikita Khrushchev told us, "We will bury you." Everyone remembers wrong. The correct translation is, "We will survive you." Although neither statement is pleasant to hear, the one we thought we heard is substantially more ominous sounding than what was actually said. Such nuances make a substantial difference in anger and misunderstandings. When President Jimmy Carter visited Poland, the world guffawed at the translation errors. President Carter's wish to "learn your opinions and understand your desires for the future" came out "I desire the Poles carnally." It caused embarrassment to the President and to our country. Wrong translations between potential enemies, however, can lead to difficulties much more serious than minor embarrassments.

—From Paul Simon, *The Tongue-Tied American: Confronting the Foreign Language Crisis*

APPLICATION

1. Provide examples for these generalizations:
   A. Numerous actors are trying their hand at film directing these days.
   B. Western television series today tend more toward humor than those of the 1960s.
   C. Rulers over the age of 60 make good leaders.
   D. Prominent political figures are often targets for assassination.
   E. Sequels to movies are seldom as good as the originals.

2. Examples can also be effective for refuting the opposition's evidence. When the opposition gives examples to support its case, we should try to counter with examples that disprove its case. For instance, to the generalization that "sequels to movies are seldom as good as the originals," we could offer counterexamples: *Return of the Thin Man, Godfather II, Destry Rides Again, The Bride of Frankenstein, Star Trek II,* and *Rocky III*. Can you provide counterexamples for statements B and C above?

Reasons.   Enumerating reasons for or against a case is another frequently used technique, but usually the reasons are conclusions themselves. For instance, if we are endorsing a political candidate, we might list as reasons that he or she:

1. has solid legislative experience
2. has supported education enthusiastically
3. has a commendable record on cutting taxes
4. is endorsed by respected leaders in the community.

Each of these reasons in turn requires further evidence because readers expect us to prove that the person has supported funding for education or has cut taxes.

If we find ourselves citing reasons, we should decide whether the reasons themselves need to be substantiated or whether readers will accept them as being apparent and commonsensical.

APPLICATION

1. Provide reasons for these assertions:
   A. The insanity plea should be reconsidered.
   B. The United States needs (or does not need) the equal rights amendment.
   C. The United States should (or should not) develop satellites that can launch nuclear warheads from space.
   D. The government should (or should not) subsidize Olympic athletes.

2. Which reasons that you list need substantiation?

Parallel Case. Arguing by parallel situation is different from and more acceptable than arguing by analogy. An analogy is a figurative correspondence between unlike things—for example, comparing a nation to a human body. The comparison points out isolated similarities between essentially unrelated things, and inferences drawn from analogies are frequently fallacious. (See pages 202–207 for a discussion of analogy.) By contrast, to argue from parallel cases is to draw comparisons between situations whose natures are fundamentally similar. For example, some medical personnel argue that we should use medical support teams composed of doctors' aides and paraprofessionals for perfunctory problems and preventive care. They argue that paraprofessionals have been successful in other health-care areas: Dental hygenists act as substitutes for dentists in certain activities, optometrists examine patients and make prescriptions but refer difficult cases to ophthalmologists, and paramedics are used in the armed forces and on ambulance calls. The situations are fundamentally comparable, and therefore the argument has merit. Of course, no two situations are identical, and therein lies the potential weakness of arguing by parallel case.

APPLICATION

Which of these arguments are acceptable, and which are vulnerable to refutation? (Remember that for a parallel argument to hold, there must be a close similarity between the two situations, both in general and in details.)

1. The reporter-informant relationship is similar to the lawyer-client, the physician-patient, and the priest-parishioner relationships, all of which are protected by law. Therefore, reporters shouldn't be required by law to reveal their confidential sources.

2. The United States should not intervene in Central America because the political and military situation is similar to that in Vietnam, and intervention would lead to the same kind of futile war.

3. If we found a person lying in the street unconscious, would we call an ambulance or a hearse? Certainly, we would give the person the benefit of the doubt and at least check to see if he or she is alive. Then why do we assume the opposite about fetuses? Legalized abortions assume that fetuses are not alive, when in fact there is reasonable doubt.

4. "In June, 1934, President Franklin D. Roosevelt signed the National Firearms Act, which outlawed civilian ownership of machineguns. Perhaps this is the law that best illustrates the way in which legislation can effectively restrain the availability of firearms. Since enactment of that measure over 40 years ago, machineguns have been virtually eliminated in the United States. Obviously, a machinegun has no legitimately useful place in a civilized society. Easily concealed pistols and revolvers are also out of place in today's highly urbanized and complex society." (Edward M. Kennedy, *Current History*, July/August 1976)

5. "When I was seventeen, a rabbi tried to convince me that there was some sort of afterlife. Try to explain to a fetus, he said, what it's going to be like to live in the world, what the next stage of its life is going to be. The fetus just won't understand. When you die, he said, you are like the fetus, entering into a new realm that you couldn't possibly have anticipated." (Robert Epstein, *Harvard Magazine*, July/August 1981)

Precedents.   Precedents are similar to parallel cases, and in fact example 4 above could be considered a precedent. A *precedent* is an instance in the past that is nearly identical to an incident currently being considered, so that the event in the past becomes an example by which to judge the present case. In argument, as in law, we can use a historical event to determine what course to take in subsequent similar events. For example, sending American troops into Korea without declaring war on that country became a precedent that later presidents used to justify sending troops into other countries; President Kennedy used the Korean precedent as part of his argument for sending troops into Vietnam. Similarly, when Detroit was hard hit by recession a few years ago, it considered applying for a federal loan to help out the municipal government. Officials argued that since the federal government had extended a loan to New York City, it should give other ailing cities loans. The New York City loan became a precedent. Precedents are especially useful in proposals, when we are offering a plan of action. (See Chapter 14, "Proposals," for a further discussion of precedents.)

APPLICATION

Cite a precedent for each of these cases:

1. altering the Constitution of the United States
2. severing diplomatic ties with a country
3. granting statehood to Puerto Rico

Testimony. The informed, expert testimony of an authority on a subject can be potent evidence. The authority doesn't necessarily have to be a person; it can be a book, such as the *Encyclopeadia Britannica,* or even an institution, such as the Brookings Institute. For example, if we are arguing against a proposal by our local utility company to use coal instead of oil to generate electricity, we might quote a respected authority to support our view that coal is an environmental and health hazard:

> The National Academy of Sciences has in fact stated that "Coal is by far the most destructive fuel in ecological and public health terms, and the likelihood of large increases in its use presents some unpleasant prospects."

In effect, we are saying "If you don't believe me, believe this expert." Most readers will accept the opinion of a reliable expert, and therefore testimony usually functions as convincingly as hard evidence, such as statistics.

In addition to serving as evidence, testimony enhances our ethos (image) because it shows that we are well informed and that we have read the right sources. Furthermore, quoting a respected authority shows readers that we think along the same lines as this authority, and by association our general credibility increases.

For testimony to be acceptable and convincing, the sources must meet certain requirements:

1. They should be bona fide experts. Their credentials must be impeccable and their professional standing solid.

2. The sources must be giving testimony in their own field.

3. Readers must recognize the authority's name and respect it. Hence we must choose our experts with our readers in mind since one authority may have a different influence on different audiences. For example, quoting George Wallace in a letter to the Selma, Alabama, Lion's Club may carry a great deal of weight, but quoting him to the Boston Lion's Club may have a negative effect. Likewise, quoting Northrup Frye at a literary convention may carry weight, but at a business luncheon the reference would have little impact because most executives probably would not have heard of the distinguished scholar. Executives would more likely recognize a famous economist or entrepreneur—Keynes or Morgan, for example. The point is, we should

select respected authorities from the audience's circle. The more prestige they have, the better.

4. Sources must be impartial. If they are being paid for their endorsement or if they have something to gain, their testimony will be questioned. If readers suspect that an expert's motivation is self-interest, they will consider it biased and therefore will not accept it. We should use unbiased sources not only because they are usually more accurate, but also because readers will more likely accept them. For example, if the president of American Airlines goes on television and announces that American is the best commercial airline to fly, we might be a little skeptical. But if the Federal Aviation Administration says that according to their records American has fewer accidents, cheaper rates, and timelier service than its competitors, we would believe that American is the best airline to fly.

5. The expert's testimony must not be taken out of context and distorted. The testimony must be representative of the authority's true opinion.

6. The testimony must be current or still valid.

APPLICATION

Which of the following are good authorities for the stated audiences or subjects?

1. Ralph Nader on consumer fraud.
2. An ad blurb on a book jacket stating that this book is one of the best romantic novels of the decade.
3. Robert Redford endorsing a political candidate.
4. Jane Fonda on physical exercise.
5. A group of distinguished older Americans—artists, entrepreneurs, actors, adventurers, military men, diplomats, sociologists—testifying against forced retirement before a hearing of the House Committee on Aging.
6. Quoting Darwin at a fundamentalist religious meeting.
7. Quoting J. Edgar Hoover at a meeting of the American Civil Liberties Union.
8. Quoting Vince Lombardi at a sports dinner.
9. Quoting Harry Truman at the Republican national convention.
10. Quoting Abe Lincoln at the Republican national convention.

We should keep in mind that even experts within a field disagree and that their testimony is often opinion—informed opinion, but nevertheless opinion. Supreme Court justices, for instance, disagree on the constitutionality of laws, medical researchers on the effects of saccharine, economists on the causes of inflation, and scientists on the origin of life. Furthermore, experts endorse different schools of thought: In psychology, there are Freudians, Jungians, and behaviorists; in politics, Republicans and Democrats; in economics, Marxists, capitalists, and so forth.

Narrative.   We sometimes overlook ourselves as authorities. In formal argument, we tend to neglect our own experience as a source of evidence and assume that only such evidence as statistics and examples is appropriate. The knowledge we have obtained through experience and direct observation is not only legitimate, but also convincing because it has the truth of "I was there" behind it. For example, if you could say, in an argument concerning offshore drilling, that you had had a summer job as an oil hand, your views on the subject would take on greater authority because yours would be an informed opinion. If you served in the Peace Corps or lived in another country, your first-hand knowledge of that society and its politics would be convincing. Of course, you have to guard against the potential danger of drawing a hasty generalization from limited experience, but if the experience is substantial, don't hesitate to offer your first-hand knowledge as evidence. (Review the section on "Narrative for Expository and Argumentative Purposes" on page 91.)

Humor.   Humor can be a devastating weapon in argument, but it is more useful as a means of attacking opposing ideas than of promoting our own ideas. The tone of an argument can be humorous throughout, in which case the argument usually becomes a satire or a parody, or the humor can be isolated in the form of a joke, anecdote, or barb. The effect in any case is to diminish the opposition and to make their ideas seem silly and inconsequential. Laughter is often a form of criticism, and when we get readers to chuckle at our adversary's ideas, we decrease their respect and approval of those ideas. The potential danger of attempting humor is that if our attempt fails we seem adolescent, or if our remarks are too caustic we appear petty and mean. Ridicule is a fine-honed edge that can slice an opponent to pieces, but we can inadvertently cut our own throats with it if we aren't careful.

In the following passage, Mark Twain effectively pokes fun at James Fenimore Cooper, the author of *The Pathfinder* and *The Deerslayer:*

Another stage-property that he pulled out of his box pretty frequently was his broken twig. He prized his broken twig above all the rest of his effects, and worked it the hardest. It is a restful chapter in any book of his when somebody doesn't step on a dry twig and alarm all the reds and whites for two hundred yards around. Every time a Cooper person is in peril, and absolute silence is worth four dollars a minute, he is sure to step on a dry twig. There may be a hundred handier things to step on, but that wouldn't satisfy Cooper. Cooper requires him to turn out and find a dry twig; and if he can't do it, go and borrow one. In fact, the Leather Stocking Series ought to have been called the Broken Twig Series.

—From "Fenimore Cooper's Literary Offences," *In Defense of Harriet Shelley and Other Essays*

Statistics. Numerical data impress readers because statistics seem to reflect and record an objective reality. In the age of computers, quotas, and polls, we put a special value on numerical measurements because we have been trained to respect the accuracy of statistics. Numbers sound absolute, real, and incontrovertible, so only when items are quantifiable do we have faith in their importance.

Because they are believable, statistics are highly effective evidence when we are trying to substantiate a proposition and to convince readers of our command of a subject. For instance, the assertion that television has become an integral part of American life becomes almost an understatement when writers give the figures to support the assertion:

Statistics begin to give us an idea of what has happened. Ninety-seven per cent of all American households have at least one television set, more than are equipped with refrigerators or indoor toilets. Forty-one per cent of the households have two or more television sets. Nearly 100 million Americans are regular television viewers, and the average set is on for about six hours and fifteen minutes each day. A study subsidized by the National Institute of Mental Health estimates that "about one-third of all American adults watch an average of four or more hours of television per day."

—From Frank Mankiewicz and Joel Swerdlow, *Remote Control:*
Television and the Manipulation of American Life

Where does a writer find such statistics? They are available in various specialized books and reference works (see pages 563–569); here are several handy sources:

Facts on File
Statesman's Year-Book
Vital Statistics of the United States
The New York Times Encyclopedic Almanac
Statistical Abstract of the United States
The World Almanac and Book of Facts
Information Please Almanac, Atlas, and Yearbook

If we can produce relevant statistics in an argument, we sound immensely knowledgeable about the subject. For instance, to assert that the 55-mile-per-hour speed limit should not be repealed because it saves gas and lives is not especially convincing because it is too general. But to say that, according to the Department of Transportation, the 55-m.p.h. speed limit has saved 9,000,000 gallons of gas a day since it was enacted and has been the biggest factor in reducing highway fatalities by 7,000 a year is to convince readers that the assertion is true.

For a statistic to be useful and to have significance, it must be explained and must be related to a generalization. Consider this statistic: In 1981, the United States imported approximately 5.3 million barrels of oil per day. "So what?" you say. The figure is meaningless until we combine it with other statistics and relate them to a generalization:

> The United States is becoming less dependent on foreign oil because of conservation and domestic production. In 1978, the United States imported approximately 8.8 million barrels a day; 8.4 in 1980; 5.3 in 1981. The United States cut its oil consumption by 8 percent from 1979 to 1980, and cut its oil importation by 19 percent.

Isolated statistics, when combined into a pattern and used to support a generalization, suddenly become important because they have the power to convince readers.

We think of statistics as being almost unbelievably boring, but statistics are versatile things that can be used inventively and provocatively. For example, in the following defense of the rising cost of health care, a physician compares health costs to selected other costs:

Despite what you have been led to believe, physicians' fees have not kept pace with inflation. During the past ten years, while the price of postage increased 150 per cent and of hamburger 148%, the increase in physicians' office fees was 116 per cent.

—From Dr. Joel Posner, "What Price Health?" *Newsweek*, Dec. 10, 1979

Here is another example of using numbers in a convincing way:

Consider the numbers. Our galaxy is only one of billions; yet in our galaxy alone, several hundred billion stars are shining. To suppose the sun is the only star accompanied by planets, and that our planet is the only one on which life emerged, smacks a bit of the medieval church, which put men to death for daring to suggest that the earth was not the center of the universe. It has only been in the lifetime of men still living and working that we have figured out where we stand in the galaxy, and where the galaxy stands in this part of the universe.

The numbers argument was put in cogent form by Harlow Shapely, one of the first to accurately measure the galaxy. He calculated that if only one star in a thousand had any planets at all, and if only one in a thousand of these had planets at a suitable distance, and if an atmosphere developed on only one in a thousand of these, and if the right chemicals were present in the oceans and atmosphere of only one in a thousand of these, we would still be left with a hundred million planets suitable for life. And that's just in our galaxy.

—From John P. Wiley, Jr., "Intelligent Life in the Universe," *Natural History*, February 1972

Because such statistics are surprising and dramatic, they jolt readers and leave a lasting impression. We want to find statistics that contradict common belief or that dramatize an issue. For example, most people are shocked when pro-choice advocates in the abortion issue point out that abortions are safer than live births—there are 3.2 deaths per 10,000 abortions, but 12.8 per 10,000 births. Another dramatic statistic is that in the last 20 years more Americans have been killed by handguns (over half a million) than were killed in World War II.

However, statistics must be carefully analyzed to determine whether they are being used correctly. In the following passage, for instance, an author refutes the contention that the justice system is ineffective by showing that the statistics have been misinterpreted:

At first glance, the [statistics seem] to confirm the thesis that the courts permit the overwhelming majority of criminals to escape scot-free: some 2,780,000 Index crimes reported to the police in 1965 resulted in 63,000 offenders going to prison, a punishment rate of only 2.3 percent. If one begins with the number of arrests, rather than of reported crimes—a more appropriate starting point if we are to assess the role of the courts, rather than of the police—punishment still seems to be a rare event. (The courts cannot be blamed for the fact that the police cleared only 26 percent of reported Index crimes through arrest.) Although 727,000 arrests were made for an Index crime, only 177,000 people were formally charged with a felony; the statistics imply that only one felon in four was prosecuted, and one in twelve actually punished.

The statistics are grossly misleading. The fact that only one arrested suspect in four was prosecuted for a felony does not mean that the other three were turned loose. Some 260,000 arrestees were transferred to juvenile court—a mandatory procedure when the police arrest someone below the age at which the criminal courts have jurisdiction. Of the 467,000 adults who were arrested for an Index crime—the proper base from which to analyze the performance of the adult courts—charges were dropped against 128,000, or 27 percent.

That left 339,000 people—73 percent of the total—who were prosecuted for a crime. Charges were reduced to a misdemeanor in 162,000 cases, in exchange for a guilty plea; of the 177,000 who were charged with a felony, 130,000 pleaded guilty and another 30,000 were convicted after a bench or jury trial. All told, therefore, 322,000 defendants were convicted on either a felony or misdemeanor charge—69 percent of all those who were arrested, and 95 percent of those who were prosecuted.

—From Charles E. Silberman, *Criminal Violence, Criminal Justice*

Although they are the most convincing evidence, statistics are also the most easily manipulated evidence. "There are three kinds of lies," Benjamin Disraeli said: "lies, damned lies, and statistics." When someone uses statistics in an argument, we as readers should carefully analyze how the numbers are being used. Often what statistics say is not as important as what they don't say.

If statistics are simply numbers, how can they distort? Numbers can be made to appear large or small depending on how we use them because they can be expressed in various ways. Statistics can be expressed as percentages, averages, absolute numbers, and so on. Consider this statistic: In a one-year period, national unemployment among white teenagers rose 25 percent but rose only 6 percent among nonwhite teenagers. From these percentages, we would assume that nonwhite teenagers were better off than white teenagers. Not so. The 25 percent increase for white teenagers was from an unemployment rate of 15.4 percent to 19.3 percent, but the 6 percent increase among nonwhite teens was from 37.5 percent to 39.6 percent. The 25 percent and 6 percent figures don't tell the whole story because they represent rate of increase, not the actual rate of unemployment. Similarly, the increase in unemployment from one year to the next for adult white males was 29 percent, and for nonwhites, 30 percent. That sounds like equality—until we examine not the percentage of increase but the actual percentages: 7.1 percent unemployment for white men and 15.1 percent for nonwhite men—over twice the white unemployment rate.

We must also be careful of the terms *mean, mode,* and *median. Mean* is arithmetic average, *mode* is the number occurring most frequently in a series, and *median* is the number in the middle of a series. Say, for example, we interview thirteen married physicians, aged 40 to 45, and thirteen married attorneys, aged 50 to 55. We ask them individually and confidentially how many extramarital affairs they have had, and they report as follows:

physicians: 0, 0, 1, 2, 2, 3, 3, 4, 5, 5, 9, 9, 9
attorneys: 0, 1, 2, 3, 3, 4, 5, 6, 7, 8, 11, 13, 15

What statements could we make about the data? The mean for doctors is 4, for lawyers, 6; the mode for doctors is 9, for lawyers, 3; and the median for doctors is 3, for lawyers, 5. By using different terms, we come up with widely divergent figures. Also, if we concluded from these figures that the average lawyer is more adulterous than the average physician, our conclusion would be unreliable because (1) the age groups are different and (2) the sample is limited to only thirteen in each profession.

Even when we're dealing with averages we must be cautious. For instance, the average annual income in a small town could be $52,500 per family, but that average could represent 100 families at $100,000 each, and 100 other families at $5,000 each. The average suggests a wealthy little town where everyone shares in the affluence, but in reality it is a town of extreme wealth and extreme poverty. Averages can be misleading. A person can drown crossing a river that has an average depth of 2 feet.

A final warning about statistics is that quality can seldom be translated accurately into quantity, and we should realize that most attempts to do so fall short. Although we live in an era when numbers and quantities are the valued measures, there are few measurements for quality. Individuals, groups, and even institutions are too complex to be captured precisely in numbers, and statistics based on human observation often fail to capture truth because human observation is subject to error and bias.

Logical Fallacies

> The most perfidious manner of injuring a cause is to vindicate it intentionally with fallacious arguments.
>
> —Friedrich Nietzsche

We study *valid* arguments to learn how to argue correctly, but we should also study *fallacious* reasoning—not only to avoid it in our own writing, but also to avoid being manipulated by other writers and to be able to refute their specious arguments. Although fallacious reasoning should convince no one to accept a proposition, it can appear plausible and therefore can be unreasonably persuasive. Sometimes the illogic is unconscious and unintentional, but just as often it is a deliberate attempt to deceive. Because advertisers, politicians, and editorialists are not too scrupulous to resort to illogical appeals to advance their cause, we must learn to recognize fallacious arguments that are masquerading as sound arguments and to counter them; such recognition can make the difference between being thoughtful and being manipulated.

There are two kinds of fallacies in logic: formal fallacies, which concern improper syllogistic form, such as undistributed middle term or affirmed consequent; and informal fallacies, which concern content instead of form. Having discussed formal fallacies in the section on deduction, we will now name and discuss informal ones. Knowing the name of a fallacy helps us to remember the fallacy, to recognize it when we encounter it, and to strip it of its persuasive force.

Erroneous Appeal to Authority

Although testimony from qualified authorities in a field is legitimate and effective evidence, testimony from experts outside their field is useless.

For example, when Nobel laureates in economics testify about the dangers of nuclear energy, or when famous novelists endorse a political candidate, they are trying to transfer their prestige from one field to another field, where they have no expertise.

When the person is a celebrity, the attempt is to transfer the person's ethos to the thing being endorsed. Advertising has long recognized the importance of ethos in selling products by getting an audience to associate the qualities of the celebrity—honesty, beauty, elegance—with the product. Joe Namath testifies to a cologne's sexiness; Robert Young ("Father Knows Best" and "Dr. Welby") says that Sanka is tasty and relaxing; and Joe DiMaggio, the former baseball great who beams of all-American honesty, uses his own image of goodness to sell numerous products.

To be accepted as authorities in an argument, people must establish their credentials and be experts in the direct area of discussion.

Attacking the Person

Attacking the person, or *argumentum ad hominem*, is a diversionary tactic whereby a writer attacks the opponent instead of the opponent's ideas. The attempt is not only to divert attention from the issue, but also to discredit the opponent by using negative remarks regarding his or her character. Discrediting an opponent is a legitimate tactic, but a writer should discredit the person's expertise, facts, or reasoning, not the person.

This fallacy can take several forms, all of which are designed to circumvent both the issue and the reasoning process:

Name-Calling.   One particularly odious tactic is to call the opponent a derogatory name. The writer first finds out the audience's biases and then labels the opponent accordingly. Each political group, for instance, has names for its opponents: right-wingers call liberals "subversives" or "Communist sympathizers"; liberals call conservatives "reactionaries," "fascists," or "rednecks." The writer tries to get readers to react emotionally to a prejudice instead of thinking rationally about the issue. Labeling as a means of discrediting an opponent doesn't have to be as obvious as referring to the person as an imbecile, traitor, coward, or criminal. In fact, obvious name-calling can backfire on a writer because readers recognize it as a smear tactic. Subtle name-calling, however, can be insidiously effective—for example, calling someone an interloper, elitist, militarist, die-hard, regionalist, isolationist, stickler, pawn, crony, and so forth.

Personal Attack.   There are various ways writers may try to discredit an opponent by offering as evidence personal traits that have nothing to do with the issue. Mentioning irrelevant facts about a person's private life in order to cast doubt on his or her character tends to discredit the opponent as a reliable source, even though personal life may have little bearing on expertise.

> How can we accept Francis Bacon's ideas on education and philosophy as being trustworthy when everyone knows he was removed from the chancellorship because of bribery?

Another tactic for discrediting an opponent is to suggest that the person's motives are selfish or ignoble. For example, in a discussion of Norman Mailer as a writer, George F. Will resorts to personal attack by mentioning that Mailer has been divorced several times and by suggesting that he writes in order to pay off alimony debts:

Alimony laws make the costs of serial monogamy steep, so Mailer wrote "Marilyn" with an eye cocked on his former wives' lawyers.

—*The Pursuit of Happiness and Other Sobering Thoughts*

A third tactic is "guilt by association." A writer mentions an opponent in the same sentence with a notorious group, hoping that readers will believe that the opponent is either a member of that group or has the same unsavory characteristics of that group.

> When my political opponent was lieutenant governor, he was repeatedly seen in the company of underworld figures.
>
> The attorney general's policies—wiretapping phones of federal employees, issuing blanket warrants, and using the FBI to investigate political dissenters—are reminiscent of Gestapo tactics.

Without thinking, readers are supposed to transfer their negative feelings about the group to the person being attacked; they are to assume that the person is guilty simply by having his or her name associated with a disreputable group. Such tactics, which work mainly through innuendo, can unfortunately persuade readers.

Shifting the Issue

An evasive tactic similar to *argumentum ad hominem* is to try to change the subject from the central issue to an irrelevant issue. The writer attempts to gloss over weak points in the argument by flattering the audience, by pointing an accusatory finger at someone else, or by referring to traditional values. Here is a good example of evasive tactics from NBC News' "Meet the Press" (January 18, 1976), in which the moderator is interviewing presidential candidates:

Mr. Monroe: Senator Bentsen, some Democrats are concerned that a Democrat coming out of Texas might be a little hawk-like in his approach to military matters, for example.

I know this is going back a long way, but is it correct that in 1950 as a Congressman you urged President Truman to threaten North Korea with an atomic bomb unless the North Koreans got out of South Korea within one week?

Senator Bentsen: You are looking at a much wiser and more mature man today and a very different change of circumstances, and obviously that sort of thing can't be done with both sides having the enormous power that you see today.

But let me touch just for a minute on this other question of growth in this country, which I think is a very material one. My grandfather came to this country and homesteaded because he was seeking opportunity. Homesteaded in South Dakota—first home built out of sod walls. We have got to keep alive that hope in this country of ours. I think we can, and the realists in our country have been optimists. We can continue to improve the standard of living in our country and we can make technological advances where we can get more out of less and we can make the cars that will give us better gasoline mileage and we can learn how to conserve energy in our homes, and at the same time we do this we will reject the extremes of both sides in favor of those things that work.

You know, I can recall a panel of so-called experts that wrote long ago that it wouldn't be many years before one out of every two women were going to have to be telephone operators in this country because of the increased usage, but they didn't prophesy the invention of the dial telephone.

We can have economic policies that will let this country grow and clean its water and clean its air and give people opportunity. That is what you have to keep alive in our country.

Mr. Monroe: Senator, to get back to this matter of to what extent you are a hawk, . . .

As with many politicians when asked a direct question that they feel will expose an unpopular opinion or an error in judgment, Bentsen resorts here to flag-waving and shifting the subject.

Irrelevant Emotional Appeal

Appeals to emotions such as pity or fear may be appropriate in some instances, but appealing to emotions can also be just a diversionary tactic. When writers have little evidence to support their thesis, they sometimes try to bypass the rational faculties and engage the readers' feelings, hoping to win emotional support where they cannot muster intellectual support. (Emotional appeals are discussed more fully in Chapter 12.)

Hasty Generalization

Hasty generalization is formulating a general rule on the basis of isolated examples. Because the sampling is unrepresentative or insufficient, the resulting broad assertion is invalid.

> Redheads really do have fiery tempers. I know. My Aunt Lucy has red hair, and jeepers does she ever have a temper!

> All politicians are crooks. Within the last few years Watergate, Koreagate, Abscam, and other scandals have proved that politicians are corrupt. Representatives Ozzie Myers, Charles Diggs, and Wayne Hays, and Senators Herman Talmadge, Edward Brooke, Daniel Brewster, and Adam Clayton Powell have all faced charges of corruption.

Card-Stacking

The philosopher John Locke said that "Hunting after arguments to make good one side of a question, and wholly to neglect those which favour the other, is wilfully to misguide the understanding; and is so far from giving truth its due value, that it wholly debases it." He was discussing what we call *card-stacking*, which is giving a one-sided argument. By suppressing material damaging to one's thesis and by misrepresenting the opponent's thesis, the writer is guilty of distortion that approaches falsehood.

> We should legalize gambling in Arizona because it would be a source of revenue, encourage tourism, and cost the citizens nothing. The only opponents of legalized gambling are a loud-mouthed minority of Baptists who want to stop progress within the state.

Bandwagon

To urge readers to accept a proposition because many other people believe in it is to commit the fallacy known as *bandwagon*. Even in a democratic society, what the majority believes or does is not necessarily what is good and just. This fallacy intends readers to assume that common consent means wisdom and for them to feel pressure to join the crowd and hop on the bandwagon of popular opinion. Appealing to the herd instinct occurs in advertising when companies boast that their product outsells all other brands two to one, in publishing when a book jacket reports that a bestseller has sold 2 million copies, and in politics when candidates announce that the latest Gallup poll shows that 58 percent of the voters favor them over their opponents. No doubt we used the technique ourselves in earlier years: "Aw, c'mon, Dad, all the other kids my age get to drive and to stay out past midnight." To illustrate the fallacy of equating general acceptance and wisdom, we need only consider that 73 percent of all Americans believe that UFOs are spaceships. Does that make it true?

Begging the Question

This is the fallacy of arguing in a circle: Gentlemen prefer blondes because they are attracted to women with fair hair. The premise and the conclusion say the same idea in different terms; the premise itself assumes the conclusion. Whereas logic uses one statement to prove another statement, begging the question uses a statement in support of itself and therefore proves nothing. In essence, begging the question says that A is true because A is true, but usually the argument is more subtle and complex: A is true because B is true, B is true because C is true, and C is true because A is true. When stated at length, this kind of circular thinking can be difficult to detect, especially when the writer inserts numerous intermediate steps and the conclusion is couched in different terminology.

> Cooperation is advantageous for society because when people work together society flourishes.

> "The will to live is not irrational. It is also natural. Attachment to life is not a delusion. It is very real. Above all, life has a purpose. To seek to defeat that purpose is a sin. Therefore suicide is very rightly held to be a sin." (Mahatma Gandhi)

Fallacy of the General Rule

There are exceptions to almost all generalizations, and to disregard those exceptions is to commit the fallacy of the general rule. What is true under normal circumstances is not always true under special circumstances.

> Jogging is good for people; therefore, Mr. Jones should jog, even though he has a heart condition, and so should Mrs. Burke, despite her bursitis.

Complex Question

The question "Do you still snort coke?" is framed in such a way that it presumes that a controversial issue has already been decided—that you once used cocaine. It is a loaded question because it involves two questions but demands a single reply.

When will you stop cheating on exams?

Why did you hire someone to throw a pie in the dean's face?

False Either/Or Situation

(See page 244 for previous discussion.) Although there are legitimate either/or situations, some either/or dilemmas are false because they suggest that only two options exist when in fact others also exist. Usually the false either/or dilemma works this way: The writer tells readers that they must choose between two options, one being the writer's scheme, the other being an undesirable alternative. This is a fallacy if it ignores other alternatives, as the adage "sink or swim" ignores the possibility of floating.

"America: Love It or Leave It" (a bumper sticker that ignores the possibility of criticizing the government in order to improve it)

You're either for me or against me.

If you support capital punishment, you are either unthinking or uncivilized.

False Cause

(See the sections on oversimplification and *post hoc* in Chapter 9, pages 288–290.)

False Analogy

As discussed in Chapter 6, analogies that are clever and striking can enliven an essay, but they seldom serve as proof in an argument because important differences exist between even very similar situations. A false analogy asserts that because two things are similar in one respect, they are similar in another respect, disregarding fundamental differences while emphasizing superficial similarities. A false analogy presses the comparison between two situations beyond the legitimate limits and insists that the analogical resemblances constitute proof. In argument, the fallacy usually occurs when writers compare their idea to something favorable, or their opponent's idea to something absurd or unfavorable.

According to Darwin's principle of natural selection, the survival of the fittest is the way that species evolve and prosper. War is the means of evolution among nations. The strongest nations survive, and the weakest perish. This is as it should be for civilization to evolve.

Exercises

Decide whether the following statements are fallacies, and if they are, name the fallacy and explain exactly why they are fallacies.

1. "A biological axiom explains that progress is made only through differences. The breeders of race horses succeed only because some animals are born different from the ordinary. The same is true of roses or potatoes or grapefruit—or thinkers! If we all tend to think, or appear to think, the same way, under compulsion or from any other motive, the laws determining intellectual evolution cease to operate." (Claude M. Fuess, "The Perils of Conformity," *Saturday Review*, Jan. 12, 1952)

2. Of course advocates of evolution want to discredit the biblical version of creation; they are atheists.

3. The West wasn't won with a registered gun.

4. Register Communists, not Guns!

5. There are only two courses open to us. We may accept the leadership of our great President and enact unamended this legislation which he has laid before us, or we may turn our backs on progress, reject the bill outright, and assume the responsibility for the disasters that would surely follow.

6. There's no sense coddling children. The neighbors on each side of me are opposed to spanking, and their kids are terrible.

7. You favor resumption of the draft only because you're too old to serve.

8. The beauty and order that we see on Earth are proof that God exists, for only a divine being could have created the millions of forms of life and perfected the ecological balance that exist on our planet.

9. The District Attorney is not interested in my client's innocence. He is enthusiastically prosecuting the case because he knows that if he wins, he will get publicity, gain political prominence, and be able to run for state attorney general.

10. Do you want to be a good boy or do you want to go to bed?

11. Why do you read pornography?

12. Freedom of the press is one of our most cherished rights, and therefore censors should not be allowed to prohibit obscene books from elementary school libraries.

13. Democracy is the best form of government for advanced societies because, on the whole, where citizens have reached a high level of scientific, tech-

nological, and cultural consciousness, a representative political system is appropriate as well as desirable.

14. Does Alan Brady wear his toupee at home?

15. Senator Jones has not condemned the Ku Klux Klan and did not endorse the Equal Rights Amendment. Doesn't that suggest that he is a racist and a sexist?

16. Nuclear power plants are unsafe; look what happened at Three Mile Island and at Chernobyl.

17. Which are you: a boob or a jerk?

18. Pakistani women think they are something special. There are two of them on our campus and they walk around with their noses in the air and consider themselves too good to date American men.

19. It should be against the law to fire a woman because she gets pregnant. They don't fire a man for fathering a child.

20. People who refuse to accept the theory of evolution are like those ignorant people in the sixteenth century who refused to accept that the Earth is round.

21. "Organizations such as the *Fund For Animals* and *Friends of Animals* frantically recruit for funds and members, as do the *Defenders of Wildlife* and others. Close examination of their yearly expenditures shows that an alarming amount of money goes into salaries, advertising, office expenses, mailings, fund raising, and such vague categories as 'humane education,' but very little ever seems to be done for the animals these groups claim to be worried about." (Jack Samson, editorial in *Field and Stream*, April 1979)

22. *Literary Critic:* Your novel fails to develop a believable hero and the structure is anticlimatic.
    Author: I guess you could write a better one?

23. The environment is like an airplane. Losing one plant or animal species may not be disastrous, just as removing one rivet from an airplane may do little harm. But if we remove another rivet, and another, and another, eventually the plane will crash.

24. Biblical creationists who say that evolution is a myth because you cannot see evolution occurring are ridiculous. You cannot see a tree growing, but it does.

25. "To be sure, some drugs are more dangerous than others. It is easier to kill oneself with heroin than with aspirin. But it is also easier to kill oneself by jumping off a high building than a low one. In the case of drugs, we regard their potentiality for self-injury as justification for their prohibition; in the case of buildings, we do not." (Thomas S. Szasz, M.D., "The Ethics of Addiction," *Harper's*, April 1972)

26. Human beings were created for cooperation. The feet acting together allow us to walk; the eyelids close together; the hands work together; the upper and lower teeth fit together. Therefore cooperation, not war, is human beings' nature.

Relationship of Induction and Deduction

Thus far we have considered induction and deduction as modes of logic that work independently of each other, but in practice they usually work together. Instead of using either deduction *or* induction exclusively, we usually use both in an argument. Induction is the logic by which we discover generalizations; deduction is the logic by which we use those generalizations. Through induction we reach conclusions that in turn can act as premises in a syllogism. For example:

> INDUCTION: My fern needs water to live.
> My ivy needs water to live.
> My begonia needs water to live.
> My hibiscus needs water to live.
> My cactus needs water to live.
> I conclude that all plants need water to live.

Now I take that generalization and apply it to a specific case.

> DEDUCTION: All plants need water to live.
> My azalea is a plant.
> Therefore, my azalea needs water to live.

Deduction applies generalizations to specific instances; induction is the means of reaching those generalizations in the first place.

Individually, induction and deduction are of limited use. The limitation of induction is that once we reach a generalization, it is of little benefit unless we can then apply it to specific cases; the limitation of deduction is that readers may not accept one of our premises and therefore will not accept our conclusion. The solution is to combine the two modes: Set up an argument deductively, but prove the premises inductively. The majority of arguments are deductive, with a syllogism forming their skeleton, but the major *portion* of an argumentative essay is spent proving one of the premises, and that proof is inductive. Hence, although the basic form of most arguments is deductive, the greater part of the argument is the evidence that establishes the truth of the premise.

In deduction, we must either use premises that our readers will accept as true or prove premises that they are skeptical of. Since argument implies controversy, we may assume that our conclusion is disputable, and because the conclusion is based on premises, at least one of the premises is at issue. If both premises were already acceptable to readers, the conclusion would be self-evident and there would be no need to write an argument; we would simply present the syllogism. What is debatable in an argument is the truth of a premise. Consider the following syllogism:

> If the proposed submarine missile system will increase national security, Congress should approve it.
> The proposed submarine missile system will increase national security.
> Therefore, Congress should approve it.

This is a valid syllogism, but validity and truth, we have discovered, are not synonymous. Readers may not accept the conclusion because they may question the truthfulness of one or both of the premises. Some readers may feel that the major premise is unwise or uninformed; they may maintain that national security is satisfactory at present and that we spend too much on defense and too little on social problems. Other readers may disbelieve our minor premise; they may assert that the proposed submarine system will not increase national security because the system can be easily disabled by enemy weapons, or they may say that it will not increase national security because the communists have a similar system that they will implement if we approve this one, and in effect adopting the plan will encourage the arms race and decrease everyone's chances of survival. Suffice it to say that readers are skeptical folks who seldom let a premise go unchallenged. Instead of taking our word that our premises are true, they want proof. That is where induction comes in: We prove any questionable premise with induction.

Proving the Premise with Induction

Which premise or premises we must inductively prove depends on our audience. We must know our audience's attitude on the subject in order to know what they are likely to accept and what they are likely to question. For example, for the syllogism above we have to know the audience's attitude toward defense spending. The same syllogism may meet with agreement from one set of readers and opposition from another because their basic assumptions are different. Here is a valid syllogism that many people would accept as truthful:

> If life begins at conception, abortion is murder.
> Life begins at conception.
> Therefore, abortion is murder.

Other people would disagree with the minor premise and therefore with the conclusion, and no amount of arguing will convert them to another view. We must know which basic principles readers endorse before we broach a subject.

Would you accept the following premises and conclusion?

All harmful drugs should be illegal.
Heroin is a harmful drug.
Heroin should be illegal.

How about this syllogism?

All harmful drugs should be illegal.
Alcohol is a harmful drug.
Alcohol should be illegal.

If possible, we want one of our premises to be indisputable because having to prove both premises can be strenuous and lengthy. Usually it is preferable to have the major premise the acceptable premise because it occurs first and we can establish common ground with it and then ease into the proof of the minor premise. The major premise should be an acknowledged truth for that particular audience.

APPLICATION

Here are several major premises on current issues. Which ones would you accept, and which ones would you expect the writer to substantiate?

If a country is our ally, we should support it regardless of its form of government.

The United States should take whatever action is necessary to prevent Central America from turning communist.

Any community that allows pornography stores in its midst can expect an increase in rape.

An unjust law lessens citizens' respect for laws in general.

If a company sponsors a television show that is immoral, the public should boycott that company's products.

An example of a convincing argument that uses both deduction and induction is the *Declaration of Independence*, which, in addition to being an affirmation of the natural rights of humankind, is a valid logical argument. What are the major premise, the minor premise, and the conclusion? Which premise is assumed to be indisputable, and which premise needs to be proved? How does the induction complement the deduction? How objective are the facts that Jefferson offers? Are there any logical fallacies in the Declaration?

When, in the Course of human events, it becomes necessary for one people to 1
dissolve the political bands which have connected them with another, and to assume, among the Powers of the earth, the separate and equal station to which the Laws of

Nature and of Nature's God entitle them, a decent respect to the opinions of mankind requires that they should declare the causes which impel them to the separation.

   We hold these truths to be self-evident, that all men are created equal, that they   2
are endowed by their Creator with certain unalienable Rights, that among these, are Life, Liberty, and the pursuit of Happiness. That, to secure these rights, Governments are instituted among Men, deriving their just Powers from the consent of the governed. That, whenever any form of Government becomes destructive of these ends, it is the Right of the People to alter or to abolish it, and to institute new Government, laying its foundation on such Principles, and organizing its Powers in such form, as to them shall seem most likely to effect their Safety and Happiness. Prudence, indeed, will dictate that Governments long established should not be changed for light and transient causes; and, accordingly, all experience hath shewn, that mankind are more disposed to suffer, while evils are sufferable, than to right themselves by abolishing the forms to which they are accustomed. But, when a long train of abuses and usurpations, pursuing invariably the same Object, evinces a design to reduce them under absolute Despotism, it is their right, it is their duty, to throw off such Government, and to provide new Guards for their future Security. Such has been the patient sufferance of these Colonies; and such is now the necessity which constrains them to alter their former Systems of Government. The history of the present King of Great Britain is a history of repeated injuries and usurpations, all having in direct object the establishment of an absolute Tyranny over these States. To prove this, let Facts be submitted to a candid world.

   He has refused his Assent to Laws the most wholesome and necessary for the   3
public good.

   He has forbidden his Governors to pass Laws of immediate and pressing   4
importance, unless suspended in their operation till his Assent should be obtained; and when so suspended, he has utterly neglected to attend to them.

   He has refused to pass other Laws for the accommodation of large districts of   5
people, unless those people would relinquish the right of Representation in the Legislature, a right inestimable to them and formidable to tyrants only.

   He has called together legislative bodies at places unusual, uncomfortable, and   6
distant from the depository of their public Records, for the sole purpose of fatiguing them into compliance with his measures.

   He has dissolved Representative Houses repeatedly, for opposing with manly   7
firmness his invasions on the rights of the people.

   He has refused for a long time, after such dissolutions, to cause others to be   8
elected; whereby the Legislative powers, incapable of Annihilation, have returned to the People at large for their exercise; the State remaining in the mean time exposed to all the dangers of invasion from without, and convulsions within.

   He has endeavoured to prevent the population of these States; for that purpose   9
obstructing the Laws for Naturalization of Foreigners; refusing to pass others to encourage their migrations hither, and raising the conditions of new Appropriations of Lands.

He has obstructed the Administration of Justice, by refusing his Assent to Laws   10
for establishing Judiciary powers.

He has made Judges dependent on his Will alone, for the tenure of their offices,   11
and the amount and payment of their salaries.

He has erected a multitude of New Offices, and sent hither swarms of Officers   12
to harass our people, and eat out their substance.

He has kept among us, in times of peace, Standing Armies without the Consent   13
of our legislatures.

He has affected to render the Military independent of and superior to the Civil   14
power.

He has combined with others to subject us to a jurisdiction foreign to our   15
constitution, and unacknowledged by our laws; giving his Assent to their Acts of
pretended Legislation:

For Quartering large bodies of armed troops among us: 16

For protecting them, by a mock Trial, from punishment for any Murders which   17
they should commit on the Inhabitants of these States:

For cutting off our Trade with all parts of the world: 18

For imposing Taxes on us without our Consent: 19

For depriving us in many cases, of the benefits of Trial by Jury: 20

For transporting us beyond Seas to be tried for pretended offenses: 21

For abolishing the free System of English Laws in a neighbouring province,   22
establishing therein an Arbitrary government, and enlarging its Boundaries, so as to
render it at once an example and fit instrument for introducing the same absolute rule
into these Colonies:

For taking away our Charters, abolishing our most valuable Laws, and altering   23
fundamentally the Forms of our Governments:

For suspending our own Legislatures, and declaring themselves invested with   24
Power to legislate for us in all cases whatsoever.

He has abdicated Government here, by declaring us out of his protection, and   25
waging War against us.

He has plundered our seas, ravaged our Coasts, burnt our towns, and de-   26
stroyed the Lives of our People.

He is at this time transporting large Armies of foreign Mercenaries to compleat   27
the works of death, desolation and tyranny, already begun with circumstances of
Cruelty and perfidy scarcely paralleled in the most barbarous ages, and totally
unworthy the Head of a civilized nation.

He has constrained our fellow Citizens, taken Captive on the high Seas, to bear   28
Arms against their Country, to become the executioners of their friends and Brethren,
or to fall themselves by their Hands.

He has excited domestic insurrections amongst us, and has endeavoured to   29
bring on the inhabitants of our frontiers, the merciless Indian Savages, whose known
rule of warfare, is an undistinguished destruction of all ages, sexes and conditions.

In every stage of these Oppressions, We have Petitioned for Redress, in the   30 most humble terms: Our repeated Petitions, have been answered only by repeated injury. A Prince, whose character is thus marked by every act which may define a Tyrant, is unfit to be the ruler of a free People.

Nor have We been wanting in attentions to our British brethren. We have   31
warned them from time to time of attempts by their legislature to extend an unwarrant-able jurisdiction over us. We have reminded them of the circumstances of our emigration and settlement here. We have appealed to their native justice and magnanimity, and we have conjured them by the ties of our common kindred, to disavow these usurpations, which, would inevitably interrupt our connexions and correspondence. They too have been deaf to the voice of justice and consanguinity. We must, therefore, acquiesce in the necessity, which denounces our Separation, and hold them, as we hold the rest of mankind, Enemies in war, in Peace Friends.

WE, THEREFORE, the Representatives of the UNITED STATES OF AMERICA, in   32
GENERAL CONGRESS assembled, appealing to the Supreme Judge of the World for the rectitude of our intentions, DO, in the Name, and by Authority of the good People of these Colonies, solemnly PUBLISH and DECLARE, That these United Colonies are, and of Right, ought to be FREE AND INDEPENDENT STATES; that they are Absolved from all Allegiance to the British Crown, and that all political connexion between them and the State of Great Britain, is and ought to be totally dissolved; and that, as FREE and INDEPENDENT STATES, they have full Power to levy War, conclude Peace, contract Alliances, establish Commerce, and to do all other Acts and Things which INDEPENDENT STATES may of right do. AND for the support of this Declaration, with a firm reliance on the protection of divine Providence, we mutually pledge to each other our Lives, our Fortunes, and our sacred Honour.

The basic form of the Declaration is deduction, and Jefferson launches into his syllogism immediately. After advancing the supremacy of unalienable rights, he explicitly states the major premise, based on the idea of government as a social contract: "That, whenever any form of Government becomes destructive of these ends, it is the Right of the People to alter or to abolish it, and to institute new Government." The deductive argument takes the form of a conditional syllogism, and the minor premise is that the King has taken away the people's rights and established "an absolute Tyranny." The conclusion necessarily follows therefore that "it is their right, it is their duty, to throw off such Government."

MAJOR PREMISE: If a government destroys the rights of the people, then the people have the right to revolt.

MINOR PREMISE: King George has destroyed the rights of the colonists.

CONCLUSION: Therefore, the colonists have the right to revolt.

As stated previously, in order to gain acceptance of any conclusion, we must either use premises that everyone recognizes as true or prove the premises ourselves. In the Declaration, Jefferson assumes that his major premise will be uncontested, though to ensure its acceptance he moves from "self-evident" truths to the idea of government as social contract and then to the major premise. The minor premise, however, he must prove, and he sets out to prove it inductively by enumerating facts. The lengthy middle section of the document (27 of its 32 paragraphs) catalogs the King's malevolent deeds and overwhelms readers into accepting the conclusion that he is a tyrant. That inductive conclusion—that the King has destroyed the colonists' rights—Jefferson then inserts as the minor premise of the deduction.

Although the Declaration is a valid argument, it isn't necessarily a truthful one because the opposition might question the colonists' interpretations of the King's actions and therefore question the factuality of the articles of indictment. What Jefferson offers as facts, the British may interpret as opinions.

Jefferson is consciously guilty of using one main logical fallacy: card-stacking. He distorts the argument by presenting only the convincing evidence in favor of the colonists and by suppressing any of their actions that may have provoked the British government. Likewise, he fails to mention any of Parliament's conciliatory gestures, and he simplifies some issues and evades others in order to emphasize the moral distinctness of the questions at hand. In short, he deliberately presents a clear-cut case of good and evil to force readers to side with the oppressed colonists against a tyrant.

Suggested Writing Assignments

1. Using the Declaration as a logical and strategical model, draft an argument proposing the independence of a particular group—women, salespersons, blacks, secretaries, gays, taxi drivers, children, men—by beginning with an accepted truth (a common ground of belief that will serve as a major premise), and then gradually easing into the minor premise, which you will prove with a list of forceful facts. The conclusion of your essay might be an impassioned plea for equality and a call for reformative action.

2. Write an editorial for your campus newspaper, modeled on the Declaration, calling for either a student boycott of some business or product, or a student protest because of administrators' disregard of student grievances.

3. Put yourself in Thomas Jefferson's position. Your group, a well-organized but minority faction on campus, has selected you to draft a political manifesto.

Your purpose is to convince the majority of students through this document to back your proposal for funds from the student government association. Following the form of the Declaration, you first need to establish a philosophical bond with the rest of the students, then list the reasons they should support your project, and conclude with an appeal for action or a call for a referendum.

Additional Readings

BRING BACK FREEWHEELING

Jack Avins

We could reduce our gasoline consumption by as much as 15 per cent if we were to provide incentives for the auto industry to revive freewheeling, which was widely used in the early 1930s. The savings could approach 1 million barrels of oil daily and an annual reduction in our oil bill of some $10 billion.   1

Freewheeling eliminates the waste of energy that occurs when engine drag in a conventional car prevents it from coasting freely and thereby using the energy stored in the momentum of the vehicle. When properly implemented, freewheeling does not compromise safety: the driver retains complete power to brake or accelerate the car.   2

In bicycles, freewheeling makes it unnecessary to keep pumping the pedals when there is enough momentum to carry the rider at the speed he wishes to travel. Freewheeling is thus familiar to anyone who has ever ridden a bike, whether of the single-speed or the ten-speed variety.   3

For the past 45 years, the auto industry has designed its cars so that, unless gas is continually fed to the engine, the engine will slow down the car under conditions where it would otherwise continue to coast freely. This engine drag is greatest in cars with manual transmissions and least at cruising speeds in cars having automatic transmissions. A freewheeling device eliminates this drag without adding significantly to the cost of the vehicle.   4

The story of why we have continued to build cars without freewheeling provides a fascinating chapter in automotive history.   5

In 1932 virtually every auto manufacturer used freewheeling, including Chevrolet, Oldsmobile, Lincoln and Chrysler, as well as less-familiar names since vanished   6 from the scene: Auburn, Dusenberg, Franklin, Hupmobile, Marmon, Pierce Arrow, Studebaker and Willys-Knight. The foremost exponent and pioneer in freewheeling was a distinguished engineer, D. G. Roos, a president of the Society of Automotive Engineers and the chief engineer of the Studebaker Corp.

The primary reason for freewheeling was the desire to save fuel. The industry's   7
experience during this period established beyond any doubt that freewheeling reduced fuel consumption by more than 15 per cent.

The safety issue was addressed head-on from the start. In the Journal of the   8
Society of Automotive Engineers for January 1931, Roos reported that, before production began, "cars equipped with freewheel transmissions were submitted to many state motor-vehicle officials for trial and comment. Without exception the approval was unanimous and enthusiastic."

Although freewheeling was demonstrably as safe as conventional transmis-   9
sions because of the ease of engaging engine braking in a lower gear, the safety issue continued to be a negative psychological factor in the eyes of the public. In addition, gasoline was then cheap (about 20 cents a gallon) and environmental pollution was not a problem. For these reasons, together with the fact that the auto industry concluded it could save money by dropping freewheeling, by 1935 freewheeling had virtually disappeared.

A number of recent developments suggest that the revival of freewheeling   10
would be in the public interest:

● The reduction in fuel consumption made possible by freewheeling and related   11
improvements is now critical to our national defense and our economic stability. Because we have to import so much of the oil that we consume, we are highly vulnerable to any stoppage of the flow of oil from the Middle East. And even if there should be no such interruption, we clearly cannot continue to pay the cartel-imposed price without adding substantially to inflation.

● Freewheeling opens the door to further reductions in fuel consumption. In combina-   12
tion with an electronically controlled gas pedal that automatically closes the throttle when engine torque is not required, without the driver having to remove his foot from the accelerator pedal, freewheeling accomplishes even greater fuel savings. Additional savings are possible by designing the vehicle so that the engine can be safely turned off under certain conditions and by providing for automatic restarting when the accelerator pedal is depressed.

● Improved techniques are available for making freewheeling autos as safe as the   13
cars we now drive. In particular, the normal reflex of stepping on the brake pedal can be made to automatically provide full engine braking. Freewheeling is restored when the accelerator pedal is depressed.

To determine whether freewheeling is in the public interest, an industry-   14
government committee should be set up. If the decision is in the affirmative—and the evidence points overwhelmingly in this direction—new EPA mileage-rating schedules should be designed to evaluate and give credit for the fuel savings realized under actual driving conditions. (Ultimately, these are the ratings that appear on the windows of new cars.) Without usurping any of the prerogatives of the auto industry or

adding to government regulations, this would provide the needed incentive for manufacturers to adopt freewheeling and related improvements. The need is urgent and
the program should be implemented without delay.

—From *Newsweek*, March 23, 1981

1. Is the logic of "Bring Back Freewheeling" inductive, deductive, or both? If it is
   deductive, write out the syllogism. Is it a valid syllogism? Is it a syllogism or
   an enthymeme? If the logic is inductive, does the evidence warrant the conclusion? If it is both, which premise does the induction seek to prove?

2. What kinds of evidence does the writer use: testimony, narration, reasons,
   statistics, parallel case, examples, precedents, humor? Does he use facts that
   grab the readers' attention?

3. Is the author guilty of card-stacking? If freewheeling is safe and economical,
   why isn't it currently being used?

4. Does the argument convince you? Why, or why not?

THE MAGNIFICENT POSSIBILITY

Gina Cerminara

Ptolemy said—and the Church accepted and taught his pronouncement—that the sun   1
revolved around the earth; yet the instruments which Copernicus invented and used
showed it was the earth, instead, that revolved around the sun. Aristotle—whose
psychology and science the Church fully embraced—wrote that if two objects of
differing weights were dropped, the heavier of the two would reach the ground first,
yet by a simple experiment from the top of the Tower of Pisa, Galileo demonstrated
that two objects of similar volume but of differing weights, when dropped, reach the
ground at the same time. Numerous phrases in the Bible—together with the most
obvious of common-sense observations—indicated that the earth was flat; yet Columbus and Magellan and other explorers of the fifteenth century quietly overthrew this
conviction by the unanswerable accomplishment of sailing West and arriving East.

By these and a hundred other demonstrations, men came gradually to see that   2
the ancient authorities could be wrong. Thus was the attitude of science born, and
thus came about the skepticism of the modern mind. Discovery after discovery
disarranged the neat world-picture in which man had believed. Spirit? Nobody has
ever seen a spirit. Soul? No one has been able to detect a soul, either lurking in
protoplasm or sitting on the pineal gland, where Descartes had said it ought to be.
Immortality? Who has ever come back to tell us about it? Heaven? Our telescopes
show no evidence thereof. God? A colossal assumption; a projection of a mind that
needed a father-substitute. The universe is a great machine. Man is a little machine,
made possible by an accidental arrangement of atoms and a naturalistic evolutionary

process. Suffering is man's inescapable lot in his struggle for survival. It has no "meaning" other than that; no purpose. Death is a dissolution of chemical elements; nothing else remains.

For the authority of the Great Man, then, or the Great Book, or the Great Teacher, the authority of our own five senses has been substituted. Science has enlarged the range of our senses, to be sure, with microscopes and telescopes and X-rays and radar; and science has systematized our five-sense observations with reasoning, mathematics, and repeatable techniques of experiment. But basically the testimony of science and of reason is the testimony of our five senses. The edifice on which science is built rests on the eye, the ear, the nose, the tongue, and the touch of man. 3

In the past few decades, however, we have grown still more sophisticated and still more skeptical of what we know or what we think we know. The instruments which we have created with our brave, proud senses have ironically turned and showed us that this sense equipment itself is imperfect and inadequate to acquaint us with the world as it really is. Radio waves, radio-activity, and atomic energy, to name but a few phenomena of our times, demonstrate beyond the shadow of doubt that we are surrounded by invisible waves and pulsations of energy, and that the minutest particles of matter contain forces of a magnitude so great that our imagination cannot embrace them. 4

Somewhat humbled, we know now that we are looking out at the world through our eyes and ears as through tiny peepholes in the narrow cell of our body. Our vibratory sensitivity to light enables us to receive only a small fraction of the total number of light vibrations that exist. Our vibratory sensitivity to sound brings us only a narrow octave, so to speak, of the whole keyboard of sound in the universe. A dog whistle, bought at the store for fifty cents, will summon our dog, yet it will be inaudible to us because its vibratory frequency is above our uppermost limit of sensitivity. There are many other animals, and many birds and insects, whose range of hearing or seeing or smelling is different from our own; consequently their universe contains much that we do not and cannot perceive. 5

A thinking man begins to wonder at this curious spectacle of proud man— exceeded by animals and insects and birds and his own ingenious inventions in the perception of reality; and he begins to speculate on the possibility of seeing for himself some of these great invisibilities. . . . Suppose, for example, that we could somehow train or improve our sensory equipment in such a way that our vibratory sensitivity to light and to sound were only slightly enlarged: Would we not then become aware of many objects that were previously unavailable to us? Or suppose that a few persons among us were born with a slightly enlarged sensitivity range: Would it not be natural for them to see and hear things which the rest of us do not see or hear? Might they not hear at a distance, as if with an interior radio receiving set, or see at a distance, as if with an interior television screen? 6

The vast, incredible, invisible world of object and energy which our twentieth-century instruments have uncovered compels us to think about such possibilities, and—casting back into the long, strange history of man—we find that there are many 7 cases in recorded history where such an enlarged perception seems actually to have existed. We learn that Swedenborg, the great eighteenth-century mathematician and scientist, is said by his biographers to have developed in later years a supernormal perceptive gift. One instance of his television-like perceptive power is particularly well known, since it is attested to by many distinguished persons, including the philosopher Immanuel Kant.

At six o'clock one evening Swedenborg, while dining with friends in the town of Gothenburg, suddenly became excited and declared that a dangerous fire had broken out in his native city of Stockholm, some three hundred miles away. He asserted a little later that the fire had already burned the home of one of his neighbors and was threatening to consume his own. At eight o'clock of that same evening, he exclaimed with some relief that the fire had been checked three doors from his home. Two days later, Swedenborg's every statement was confirmed by actual reports of the fire, which had begun to blaze at the precise hour that he first received the impression.   8

Swedenborg's case is only one among hundreds of similar instances recorded in history and biography of the great, the near-great, and the obscure. At some time in their lives Mark Twain, Abraham Lincoln, Saint-Saëns, to name but a few, had, according to their biographers and in some cases their own accounts, strange sudden visions of events taking place at a distance, or events that took place, down to the last minute detail, months or years later in their own lives. In the case of Swedenborg the ability to see at a distance developed later into a powerful and sustained faculty; in most other cases, the heightened perceptivity seemed to arise only in a moment of crisis.   9

We in the Western world have tended to look askance and with some slight suspicion upon such occurrences. However well substantiated they are, however well attested to by honorable and intelligent persons, however frequently they occur, we have tended to dismiss them with a raised eyebrow, a shrug, the word "coincidence," or the adjective "interesting"—and let it go at that.   10

The time has come, however, when we can no longer so lightly dismiss them. To a mind alert to the possibilities of high discovery within an unexplained event, to a mind aware of the great scientific currents and necessities of our times, the whole subject of the strange potential faculties of man is of tremendous import and interest.   11

Among the far-seeing scientists who have considered extra-sensory phenomena worthy of systematic laboratory investigation, and who have actually undertaken such investigation, is Dr. J. B. Rhine of Duke University. Since 1930 Dr. Rhine, with his associates, has been making extensive studies of the telepathic and clairvoyant faculties of man. Using closely controlled, repeatable experiments and adhering rigidly to scientific method, Rhine has discovered that many individuals can demonstrate extrasensory powers of perception under laboratory conditions. Careful statistical techniques have been used to evaluate Dr. Rhine's experiments, and, mathematically speaking, it has been found that the results obtained could not possibly be attributed to chance. (For details of Dr. Rhine's methods and results, see his book, *The Reach of the Mind,* published in 1947.) Other scientific investigators, such as Warcollier in France, Kotik in Russia, and Tichner in Germany, also using   12 laboratory methods, have come independently to the same conclusions as Rhine, and the growing body of scientific evidence is slowly undermining the prevailing doubts in the Western world that there exist in man's mental makeup powers of a telepathic and clairvoyant nature.

From three points of view, then, there would seem to be reason to believe that   13
the narrow slits of man's sense perceptions can be enlarged. Inferentially, it is reasonable to believe such an enlargement possible; historically, a great accumulation of authentic anecdote demonstrates that in many instances it has occurred; scientifically, there is a growing body of laboratory data that testifies, by repeatable experiments, that man can experience awareness beyond the normal range of the senses.

—From *Many Mansions*

1. What is the writer trying to prove? Does she use induction, deduction, or both? Explain the logic.

2. In paragraph 1, what is the purpose of listing the errors and discoveries? In what way is paragraph 4 parallel to paragraph 1?

3. Is her argument for the existence of extrasensory perception convincing?

The editorial printed below is included not only because it offers a multitude of syllogisms and fallacies, but also because it was written years ago; examining a current political endorsement would result in bogged-down debates about the issues and the candidate instead of about the form, logic, and techniques. To avoid focusing on content, we will examine a 1964 editorial on the Johnson-Goldwater presidential race.

WHY LYNDON JOHNSON MUST BE ELECTED

A healthy, vigorous two-party system is absolutely indispensable to the survival of   1
American democracy. Its proper functioning requires each of the major parties to put forth a man who is unmistakably and unquestionably qualified to be trusted with the incalculably grave and terrible powers of the Presidency.

In the presidential election of 1964, the two-party system has been seriously   2
endangered. One of the great parties, the Democratic, has fulfilled its duty by putting forth a man, Lyndon B. Johnson, who has many flaws and leaves much to be desired, but who is unquestionably as well qualified to be President as any tried and tested leader the Democratic Party now affords.

The other great party, the Republican, has shirked and betrayed its duty by   3
putting forth a man, Barry Goldwater, who is manifestly unqualified to be President and whose unsuitability for this awesome responsibility becomes clearer with every passing day and with every feckless word he utters.

The two-party system has thus been endangered because this misfeasance on   4
the part of the Republican Party has left the enlightened, the rational, the prudent, the responsible American voter no acceptable other choice in this election. He is not even given the option of an echo. He is given only the option of a question mark, of a man who is seemingly congenitally unable to say what he means or even know what he says, to say anything clearly or to hold the same conviction two days in a row. Barry Goldwater's tongue is like quicksilver; his mind is like quicksand.

The Post therefore urges the election of Lyndon B. Johnson as President.   5

It urges, even more strongly, the defeat of Barry Goldwater.   6

We are confident that Johnson will make a good President because he already   7
is a good President. In the 10 brief months he has held the highest office, he has shown an ability unmatched in this century to bring all the diverse and warring factions of Congress behind the enactment of positive, progressive and needful legislative programs. In his greatest test as Commander-in-Chief—the attack on our Navy in the Gulf of Tonkin—he has acted with both the forcefulness and restraint which is required in the man who alone controls the ultimate weapon and bears all the fearful responsibility which that entails.

We are equally confident that Goldwater would not make a good President. He   8
has not even made a good Senator. He has been in the Senate 11 years and not one piece of memorable legislation attaches to his name. He has been in its councils through the most momentous and revolutionary decade in the history of this Republic as we have strained every seam and fabric of our traditional habits and thinking to keep abreast of an age when all the supposed boundaries of man's environment are being broken, gravity defied, space penetrated, the moon reached, the riddle of the human cell being unraveled. Merely to understand, much less to master, this surge and change, heavy with unguessed new treasures of technology to increase man's wealth, has required and will require government entry into areas never before imagined. But Barry Goldwater has managed to live through this whole tremendous epoch with his back turned squarely to the past, his eyes closed, and his mind preoccupied with one—and only one—idea: somehow to shrink the Government back into the familiar and comfortably small proportions of his Arizona youth. Barry Goldwater has left no mark in the Senate because, as he has truthfully declared, he sought to erase marks rather than to make them: "I have little interest in streamlining government or in making it more efficient, for I mean to reduce its size. I do not undertake to promote welfare, for I propose to extend freedom. My aim is not to pass laws, but to repeal them. It is not to inaugurate new programs, but to cancel old ones. . . ." He is like the Cincinnati kettlemaker who, when first hearing of Kentucky ironmaker William Kelly's use of air to make steel, exclaimed, "I want my iron made in the old way or not at all." His mind is surely not in phase with today's world.

Goldwater changes his "convictions" almost as often as his shirt. One day he is   9
for abolishing Social Security, the next day for strengthening it, one day for giving field commanders control over nuclear weapons, the next day for restricting control to the NATO supreme commander. Many of statements are inherently contradictory non-

sense—e.g., to cut all government expenditures, while expanding defense (which already takes more than half of every tax dollar spent)—like advertising a car that is bigger on the inside but smaller on the outside. Some of his statements, if they have any meaning at all, are rather frightening in the subconscious thought which seems to lie behind them, particularly those concerning his strange love affair with German prowess: *"With all due respect to American military leaders, Germany would have won both world wars if she had not been badly led." "I think it was the Germans who originated the modern concept of peace through strength."* This last remark prompted Hamilton Fish Armstrong, editor of *Foreign Affairs,* to ask *The New York Times* to clarify whether it was Hitler's or the Kaiser's "peace through strength" that Goldwater had in mind. However, it is always possible that he really had *nothing* in mind, as when he told reporters who briefly boarded his cruising *Sundance,* "I've thought for some time that talks with the Red Chinese might be profitable." He later radioed ashore that what he really meant was that the U.S. should be ready to threaten the Chinese, telling them that "if they didn't stop, then you would blow up a bridge or show some other sort of force." He finally cleared everything up by adding, "I'm not really recommending this, but it might not be an impossible idea."

Goldwater is a grotesque burlesque of the conservative he pretends to be. He is   10
a wild man, a stray, an unprincipled and ruthless political jujitsu artist like Joe McCarthy, whose last-ditch defender he remained even when three fourths of the Senate had voted to condemn their Red-hunting colleague. He still defends McCarthy, well knowing that he imputed treason to General Marshall and to President Eisenhower. He will not condemn the John Birch Society, though knowing that its leader, Robert Welch, has called Eisenhower a Communist agent. Yet, in order to get Eisenhower's vacuous blessing, Goldwater was capable of a tongue-in-cheek erasure of his infamous "extremism" slogan, a statement that was not written in haste but with extreme care, and gone over time and again by Goldwater before he uttered it. These words can, and should, forever symbolize the total fraudulence of his claim to be a true conservative: "Extremism in the defense of liberty is no vice, and . . . moderation in the pursuit of justice is no virtue." That statement deserves to be the "Rum, Romanism and Rebellion" of this election, and Barry Goldwater deserves to be defeated for it alone, no matter how much he tries to clown it away. He knew what he meant by it, and so does every John Birch fanatic and Ku Klux vigilante.

For the good of the Republican Party, which his candidacy disgraces, we hope   11
that Goldwater is crushingly defeated. It was clear, from poll after poll, that the rank and file of Republican voters overwhelmingly preferred other leaders to Goldwater. It was equally clear that the fanatical Goldwater bias of a majority of convention delegates revealed the capture of the Republican Party by a new breed of so-called "leaders" whose selection had been steam-rollered by extremist, well-heeled types. The men who have most deserved to lead the Republican Party, by virtue of their long, distinguished and responsible service in it, and to the country, have been made to feel unwelcome, hissed and hated in it, as they were repudiated by it. A crushing defeat for Goldwater will drive the fanatic saboteurs of the Republican Party back into

the woodwork whence they came. It will provide the opportunity for the party's true leaders to build anew from the wreckage that these heedless, reckless, ill-mannered and arrogant men are sure to leave. Then the two-party system can be restored, and the voter will again have a choice, not a calamity.

—From *The Saturday Evening Post,* Sept. 19, 1964

1. The strategy of the editorial is a lesser-of-two-evils endorsement. Why would the editors use that approach? Which sentence is the thesis statement?

2. Why does the syllogism concern the two-party system? What are the purpose and strategy behind using the two-party system in this editorial? Which voters is *The Saturday Evening Post* hoping to sway (examine the final paragraph)?

3. Paragraph 7 opens with an enthymeme. Which part of the syllogism has been omitted? Write out the full syllogism. Which premise do the editors try to prove? Do they offer facts or opinions as proof?

4. Paragraph 8 opens with a similar enthymeme. Expand it into a syllogism. How do paragraphs 9, 10, and 11 relate to paragraph 8 in terms of logic?

5. The editors attempt to use fear as a means of motivating voters against Goldwater. Point out statements intended to evoke fear.

6. Explain the logic of the last paragraph.

7. Point out the various fallacies in the editorial.

8. How would you refute this editorial, based solely on the logic? Is the logic valid? Is it truthful (that is, are the premises truthful and substantiated)? Is the proof reliable and factual?

CHAPTER 12

Psychological Strategies

This chapter analyzes the psychological side of persuading readers. We will investigate two psychological persuaders: ethos (the image of the writer) and pathos (emotional appeals and adaptation). Certainly an argument needs an intelligent thesis, hard facts, and valid reasoning above all else, but we must also acknowledge the enormous contribution of psychological strategies: presenting a good image of ourselves to readers, using emotions when appropriate, and adapting the presentation to fit the audience.

Modifying belief, which is the intent of argument, is a difficult business. First, just getting people to read our argument is a challenge because most people will not read arguments that run contrary to their beliefs. In general, people are not open to opposing ideas, regardless of how logical our argument is or how many convincing facts we muster in support of our proposition. Obviously, if people do not read our argument, we cannot succeed in persuading them.

Second, even if we succeed in getting them to read our argument, people are hesitant to change their beliefs—and for good reason. They base their beliefs on their values, and they define themselves by their values; therefore, when we argue that they should change their beliefs, they see our argument as an attack on their value system and on their identity. Attacking their beliefs is perceived as attacking *them*, and naturally no one appreciates being assaulted. Although readers' defensiveness is frustrating because it interferes with communication, it is not entirely an inappropriate response. After all, we are asking them not only to invest some time in our paper, but also to be willing to leave the safety of their current beliefs and to make themselves somewhat vulnerable. We shouldn't be surprised if they hold onto their beliefs with a passion and are more intent on mounting counterarguments than on listening to our facts and logic.

Furthermore, people generally think that changing their beliefs represents a kind of defeat. No one wants to admit to being wrong, which is implicit in giving in to another's opinion. *We* don't want to accept *their* beliefs; they are likewise unwilling to give up their views for ours. Think of the last argument you had with someone. Did either of you accept the other's view? Why didn't you accept the other person's view? Probably because you thought it was wrong. Why didn't your opponent accept your view? Probably for the same reason. Did the two of you reach a compromise? Did either of you even consider altering your thinking?

All of this does not mean that we cannot influence people through argument. It does mean that we cannot move them in any direction we like as if they were chess pieces on a board. Every reader—regardless of how skeptical at the outset—is a potential convert to our point of view, but we must find a way to reach readers and develop that potential for change. Of course, we need facts and logic to modify beliefs, but cold logic alone is not always successful in overcoming defensiveness and hostility.

Writers must be psychologists as well as logicians. We must learn how to put readers at ease, how to make it easy for them to alter their beliefs, and how to touch them and motivate them. To overcome the readers' skepticism and defensiveness, we must somehow alleviate their apprehension and assure them that we are their allies, not their enemies. We must create a climate conducive to change—a climate that is nonthreatening, friendly, accommodating, and sincere.

Persuasion is a little like seduction, and since wooing readers is not unlike wooing lovers, the process is no doubt familiar to you. In order to gain the readers' acceptance of our proposition, we must actively court them. We must coax them along, convince them of our sincerity and integrity, and make our ideas alluring. We must convince them that there is no risk involved in accepting our proposition. We accomplish this by showing that our ideas are very similar to theirs, that no shifts in values are necessary, and that they have something to gain from our proposition. In essence, we make them want to change by showing that change is in their best interest.

Ethos

Definition

Whether we intend to or not, we reveal a great deal about ourselves when we write. We reveal our values, our personal philosophy, our character, and our blemishes. Through what we say and how we say it, we project an image of ourselves in an essay, and this image is called our *ethos*. Ethos is the implied character of the writer; it is the readers' perception of the author behind the words. Readers unconsciously draw inferences and form judgments about our integrity and intelligence based on our language and ideas. For example, from having read parts of this book, you have reached certain generalizations about my character—whether I am rational, cranky, informed, stodgy, flexible, ironic, and so forth.

Ethos is important in any kind of discourse because it helps to establish our credibility. Readers accept our ideas based on their perception of our character almost as much as on our ideas. From the voice we project in our prose, they infer what we are like and decide whether we are reliable sources. They trust writers who seem to have good character, good will, and good sense, and because of this trust, readers more readily accept the propositions of such writers. If our ethos is good—that is, if readers perceive us as honest and reliable sources—they will be more inclined to accept our reasoning and conclusions. Likewise, if our ethos is poor—if they perceive us as biased, closed-minded, or uninformed—they will be hesitant to accept our conclusions. Our goal, therefore, is to assure them that we are neither radicals who want to turn their world upside down nor simpletons who don't understand the issues and consequences. We want them to perceive that we are intelligent, moral, and open-minded.

In essence, writers themselves become a type of proof or evidence, which we call ethical proof, and it is one of the most persuasive yet least discussed proofs. Arguments are effective largely because writers demonstrate, often in subtle ways, that they are ethical, trustworthy persons. By offering ethical proof, writers win an audience's trust and that in turn helps to ensure acceptance of factual and logical proofs. Why is it, for instance, that of two writers who use the same thesis, evidence, and structure, one convinces us and the other does not? Why is it that we sometimes accept one speaker's proposition even though its substantiation may be sparse, but we withhold acceptance from another speaker who has ample evidence? For the most part, the answer in each case is credibility, which is established through an effective ethos.

What kind of ethos does the author of the following passage convey? What can we infer about his character? Does he sound intelligent? Informed? Reasonable? Benevolent? How do we determine these opinions?

An elm in our backyard caught the blight this summer and dropped stone dead, leafless, almost overnight. One weekend it was a normal-looking elm, maybe a little bare in spots but nothing alarming, and the next weekend it was gone, passed over, departed, taken. Taken is right, for the tree surgeon came by yesterday with his crew of young helpers and their cherry picker, and took it down branch by branch and carted it off in the back of a red truck, everyone singing.   1

The dying of a field mouse, at the jaws of an amiable household cat, is a spectacle I have beheld many times. It used to make me wince. Early in life I gave up   2 throwing sticks at the cat to make him drop the mouse, because the dropped mouse regularly went ahead and died anyway, but I always shouted unaffections at the cat to let him know the sort of animal he had become. Nature, I thought, was an abomination.

Recently I've done some thinking about that mouse, and I wonder if his dying is necessarily all that different from the passing of our elm. The main difference, if there is one, would be in the matter of pain. I do not believe that an elm tree has pain receptors, and even so, the blight seems to me a relatively painless way to go even if there were nerve endings in a tree, which there are not. But the mouse dangling tail-down from the teeth of a gray cat is something else again, with pain beyond bearing, you'd think, all over his small body.   3

There are now some plausible reasons for thinking it is not like that at all, and you can make up an entirely different story about the mouse and his dying if you like. At the instant of being trapped and penetrated by teeth, peptide hormones are released by cells in the hypothalamus and the pituitary gland; instantly these substances, called endorphins, are attached to the surfaces of other cells responsible for pain perception; the hormones have the pharmacologic properties of opium; there is no pain. Thus it is that the mouse seems always to dangle so languidly from the jaws, lies there so quietly when dropped, dies of his injuries without a struggle. If a mouse could shrug, he'd shrug.   4

I do not know if this is true or not, nor do I know how to prove it if it is true. Maybe if you could get in there quickly enough and administer naloxone, a specific morphine antagonist, you could turn off the endorphins and observe the restoration of pain, but this is not something I would care to do or see. I think I will leave it there, as a good guess about the dying of a cat-chewed mouse, perhaps about dying in general.   5

—From Lewis Thomas, "On Natural Death," *The Medusa and the Snail*

The writer's ethos develops gradually over the five paragraphs. We can't tell much about his values or knowledge based solely on the first paragraph, which is an objective narrative about an elm dying of the blight, but from the simplicity and clarity of the language (there are no words over three syllables) we can infer that Thomas is an unpretentious person and that he is not trying to impress us; his intention seems to be clear communication. So far, though, that's about the only opinion we can venture.

What does paragraph 2 add to our knowledge about the author? For one thing, his reaction to the field mouse's death—"It used to make me wince"—suggests that he is humane and sympathetic. He threw sticks at the cat not to injure it but to save the mouse, and after he discovered that the mouse always died anyway, he simply threw "unaffections at the cat." Also, by juxtaposing his attitudes "early in life" with his current attitudes, the author gives the impression that we are listening to a more tolerant, more knowing, and more philosophical person than he once was; we sense a maturity that comes with experience and thoughtfulness.

What strikes us about paragraph 3, which thematically ties together the two preceding paragraphs, is the modest and relaxed manner in which he puts forth his reflections and speculations. He does not insist that his words are gospel, he does not force his ideas on us, and he is not dogmatic. Rather, he offers an idea for our consideration: "I wonder if . . ." he muses. The ethos conveyed is that of broad-mindedness and tolerance, the author inviting us to follow his speculations on a subject he has contemplated.

The fourth paragraph continues in a tolerant vain. He suggests that there are "plausible reasons" for believing one interpretation "if you like," and he invites us to consider this interpretation. Because he offers it to us in such a conditional, soft-sell manner, we are more likely to listen to this interpretation. Thus far his ethos is one of benevolence and tolerance, but the second sentence of paragraph 4 introduces a new element that further increases the writer's credibility: his expertise. His technical description of the chemical processes indicates that he has special knowledge, and because his explanation sounds sensible, we begin to trust him not only as a thoughtful and humane person, but also as an informed person.

In the final paragraph, Thomas further wins our trust by honestly admitting his uncertainty, and he again proves his humane affections by preferring not to cause pain as part of an experiment. "I think I will leave it there," he concludes, again demonstrating his flexibility with such expressions as "a good guess" and "perhaps."

In short, the writer has conveyed an effective ethos: benevolent, informed, and credible. He has successfully encouraged us to enter his world for a moment, to accept his values, and to share the way he sees this subject.

We, too, must invite readers to enter our world when we write. That world holds a truth—our thesis—but if readers don't enter our world, they will not become acquainted with our truth. Inhabiting the same world requires that readers accept our values and premises, and they will do that only if they trust us. To gain their trust, we must present a good ethos.

How Ethos Works in Argument

Ethos is important in any kind of writing, but it is especially important in argument, where readers are often skeptical. In an argument, we must immediately establish a good ethos so that we can overcome their initial skepticism. If we can get readers to see that we are well intentioned and intelligent, we have a chance of ushering them into our world and of showing them the validity of our thesis.

For an example of an effective ethos, we can turn again to the *Declaration of Independence*. Jefferson had a difficult task in attempting to establish a sympathetic ethos because he had to justify rebellion against a monarch (which was a radical idea in the eighteenth century) and yet not offend other monarchies in Europe. The Founding Fathers wanted to use the Declaration not only as a statement of political philosophy, but also as a persuasive document (1) to present to the world their case for revolution; (2) to gain the sympathies of European nations whose recognition, commerce, and aid they would need for survival; and (3) to unify the thirteen colonies, on whom ratification of the Declaration depended.

Jefferson's strategy for achieving these goals is to portray the colonists not as traitors but as oppressed patriots, and to portray the Founding Fathers not as radicals but as men of principle and sound judgment. Knowing that they could not afford to be viewed as impulsive rebels or as political extremists, he is careful to present an image of them as respectable citizens, motivated by a sense of idealism and moral courage. To this end, his language is dignified, his assertions are substantiated, and his logic is clear and convincing. Also, he makes a special effort to show that they realize the seriousness of their action: "Government long established should not be changed for light and transient causes."

His main strategy, however, is to take the offensive: The Declaration is as much an attack on the King of England as it is a vindication of the colonists' severing ties with England; the ethos in the document depends almost as heavily on portraying the King as a tyrant as it does on presenting the colonists as people of rationality and principle. Jefferson states that they have long endured "abuses and usurpations" with "patient sufferance" rather than abolish the present system of government: "In every stage of these Oppressions We have Petitioned for Redress in the most humble terms: Our repeated petitions have been answered only by repeated injury." In other words, here is a people who wants to remain loyal, who has tried to remain loyal, but who has been forced to "throw off such government," absolve allegiance to this despot, and form a more humane government. Jefferson portrays them not as rebels, but as defenders of the rights of people all over the world by asserting that they are free human beings living under self-evident and universal laws; he constantly stresses the human element over the political. By setting up criteria by which to judge governments and then by giving evidence to substantiate that the King has not met those standards, Jefferson makes the King appear the illegal one. By contrast, he implies that the colonists have lived up to their contract as citizens, and therefore they are the righteous ones who are on the side of authority. To pen an argument that first declares revolution against the mother country and then emerges on the side of authority is no small task, but Jefferson accomplishes it by demonstrating high morals, sound judgment, and clear thinking.

The Qualities of a Good Ethos

The four qualities that make for an effective ethos are good sense, high morals, good will, and human warmth. Together, these qualities create an image that assures readers of our worth and reliability. Readers judge us based on our intelligence and knowledge, our integrity, our intentions, and our amicability.

1. Good Sense. Because readers must believe that we are qualified to write on a subject before they will accept our ideas, we must establish that we are intelligent and knowledgeable. We do this by offering provocative ideas, by demonstrating valid reasoning, and by presenting conclusive evidence. Once we establish our competence through our command of the subject, and once readers see that we are informed and perceptive, they more readily accept our ideas. Demonstrating good sense is absolutely essential for establishing a convincing ethos.

2. High Morals. We must convey to readers that we are virtuous as well as knowledgeable. Before they will accept our proposition, readers must perceive us as being principled and honest, and we communicate those qualities by endorsing conventional values, by basing our major premise on proven principles, and by stating the truth.

Truthfulness is a powerful virtue, particularly when the truth is difficult to admit. For example, in 1975 when Gerald Ford gave his first State of the Union message, the United States had gone through a tumultuous period—the Vietnam war, dissension, high inflation and unemployment, political scandals, the Vice President's resignation, Watergate, and finally the President's resignation. Americans obviously realized that the state of the nation was not good, but they expected to hear the traditional bombast, flag-waving, and exaggerated appraisal of the country's power and virtue from the new president. Instead, this is what they heard:

> Twenty-six years ago, a freshman Congressman, a young fellow, with lots of idealism who was out to change the world, stood before Speaker Sam Rayburn in the well of this House and solemnly swore to the same oath you took yesterday. That is an unforgettable experience, and I congratulate you all.

Two days later, that same freshman sat in the back row as President Truman, all charged up by his singlehanded election victory, reported as the Constitution requires on the State of the Union.

When the bipartisan applause stopped, President Truman said:

"I am happy to report to this Eighty-first Congress that the State of the Union is good. Our Nation is better able than ever before to meet the needs of the American people and to give them their fair chance in the pursuit of happiness. It is foremost among the nations of the world in search for peace."

Today, that freshman Member from Michigan stands where Mr. Truman stood and I must say to you that the State of the Union is not good.

Millions of Americans are out of work. Recession and inflation are eroding the money of millions more. Prices are too high and sales are too low.

Such a candid and realistic evaluation of the state of the nation struck most Americans as being refreshingly honest, and it gave them hope that Ford's administration would be characterized by this kind of candor.

3. Good Will. We must communicate to readers that our intentions are not to manipulate them or to promote our own interests but to help readers or society in general. If our motivation appears to be selfish or malicious, readers will surely reject our ideas. We need to assure them that we are motivated by public spirit, patriotism, or a sense of justice, not by self-interest.

Not only must our intentions be honorable, but also our tone must be humane and compassionate. If we sound cruel, vindicative, or simply uncaring, readers will question our character and consequently be hesitant to accept our proposition. Consider this example from Mary Shelley's *Frankenstein*, in which the monster pleads with his creator for a mate, although the monster has already proved himself to be a killer.

"I do refuse it," I replied; "and no torture shall ever extort a consent from me. You may render me the most miserable of men, but you shall never make me base in my own eyes. Shall I create another like yourself, whose joint wickedness might desolate the world. Begone! I have answered you; you may torture me, but I will never consent."

"You are in the wrong," replied the fiend; "and instead of threatening, I am content to reason with you. I am malicious because I am miserable. Am I not shunned and hated by all mankind? You, my creator, would tear me to pieces and triumph; remember that, and tell me why I should pity man more than he pities me? You would not call it murder if you could precipitate me into one of those ice-rifts and destroy my frame, the work of your own hands. Shall I respect man when he condemns me? Let him live with me in the interchange of kindness, and instead of injury I would bestow every benefit upon him with tears of gratitude at his acceptance. But that cannot be; the human senses are insurmountable barriers to our union. Yet mine shall not be the submission of abject slavery. I will revenge my injuries; if I cannot inspire love, I will cause fear, and chiefly towards you my arch-enemy, because my creator, do I swear inextinguishable hatred. Have a care; I will work at your destruction, nor finish until I desolate your heart, so that you shall curse the hour of your birth."

A fiendish rage animated him as he said this; his face was wrinkled into contortions too horrible for human eyes to behold; but presently he calmed himself and proceeded, "I intended to reason. This passion is detrimental to me, for you do not reflect that *you* are the cause of its excess. If any being felt emotions of benevolence towards me, I should return them a hundred and a hundredfold; for that one creature's sake I would make peace with the whole kind! But I now indulge in dreams of bliss that cannot be realized. What I ask of you is reasonable and moderate; I demand a creature of another sex, but as hideous as myself; the gratification is small, but it is all that I can receive, and it shall content me. It is true, we shall be monsters, cut off from all the world; but on that account we shall be more attached to one another. Our lives will not be happy, but they will be harmless and free from the misery I now feel. Oh! My creator, make me happy; let me feel gratitude towards you for one benefit! Let me see that I excite the sympathy of some existing thing; do not deny me my request!"

I was moved. I shuddered when I thought of the possible consequences of my consent, but I felt that there was some justice in his argument.

Notice the monster's awareness of ethos. His basic argument is that he has murdered in the past because humankind hates him, and that if he had a mate he would no longer be lonely and vengeful. He wants to project an ethos of rationality and benevolence, but his rage bursts out at the end of paragraph 2, and he realizes that he is showing himself to be malicious: " 'I intended to reason. This passion is detrimental to me.' " Even a monster knows that an audience is not persuaded by anger and accusations. It is worth noting that Frankenstein consents to the monster's request.

4. Human Warmth. As in other social activities, we should be friendly and entertaining in our writing, and readers should enjoy getting to know us as well as our ideas. What holds readers' attention is a human being emerging through the language, and that personality should help to make an essay interesting—whether the personality is warm and tolerant or feisty and witty. Getting to know the complex and ingenious being who created the world that readers step into is partly what keeps them reading, and therefore they should find something in our personality that attracts them.

What qualities make the following excerpt hold your interest? How would you describe the author, Judith Wax?

My queenly bridal gown has been preserved in pink tissue for twenty-seven years now. The satin shoes that match it are nearly virginal, and so was I the day I teetered down the aisle in them. Last New Year's Eve I broke the old shoes out; they'd come back in style and looked quite contemporary (everyone said so). But the fragile wedding gown will never march again. Though my daughter is nearly old enough to wear it, if Claudia ever chooses to marry, it's not likely that she'll do so wearing my bridal finery. Just as well. The sweeping train and those layers of lace might look strange with her leg warmers and combat boots.

I took the old gown out and stared at it a few days before our latest anniversary. It unnerved the silver-haired groom, who thought I might be plotting one of those renew-the-vows ceremonies you read about . . . where midlife couples get into their ancient wedding attire and summon friends, relatives, and progeny to witness romantic history reenacted. He needn't have feared. I had disinterred my gown because I was thinking about old marriages, wondering what keeps them going, why some stay happy, what my own was *really* like. It was thorny stuff, and I suppose that staring at the gown was my idea of scholarly investigation. (Besides, I'd finished my research into whether, if you listen closely, you can hear your own arteries hardening, and you can't.)

The trouble is, my investigative credentials are tainted by a traitorous streak of romanticism. Not that my heart leaps up for Marabel Morgan, though if such fluffy philosophies keep other people happy and juicy, it's okay with me. But if *I* were dressed in nothing but a garter belt when Shel, my husband, limped home from the office, he'd be right in assuming that once again I'd forgotten to do the laundry. Now that I work full time, he's surprised enough to find dinner ready; a preheated wife would be excessive.

—From "Old Valentines, Old Marriages," *Starting in the Middle*

Is this an effective ethos? How does the humor help to create the ethos? What is it that makes us trust a person who sees herself as part of the human comedy?

Of course, this kind of ethos is not appropriate for all forms of discourse. Reports, for instance, allow for little display of wit or warmth; the ethos that a report strives for is usually objectivity, authority, and accuracy. Almost any essay or argument, however, invites a touch of humanness and individuality, regardless of the topic.

APPLICATION

Here is a scientific explanation of one step in evolution, told in a manner that reflects an individual imagination. How does the author keep from sounding like a characterless, cold scientist? What kind of ethos does the writer have? Describe it and substantiate your description with references to the passage.

It began as such things always begin—in the ooze of unnoticed swamps, in the darkness of eclipsed moons. It began with a strangled gasping for air.   1

The pond was a place of reek and corruption, of fetid smells and of oxygen-starved fish breathing through laboring gills. At times the slowly contracting circle of the water left little windrows of minnows who skittered desperately to escape the sun, but who died, nevertheless, in the fat, warm mud. It was a place of low life. In it the human brain began.   2

There were strange snouts in those waters, strange barbels nuzzling the bottom ooze, and there was time—three hundred million years of it—but mostly, I think, it was the ooze. By day the temperature in the world outside the pond rose to a frightful intensity; at night the sun went down in smoking red. Dust storms marched in incessant progression across a wilderness whose plants were the plants of long ago. Leafless and weird and stiff they lingered by the water, while over vast areas of grassless uplands the winds blew until red stones took on the polish of reflecting mirrors. There was nothing to hold the land in place. Winds howled, dust clouds rolled, and brief erratic torrents choked with silt ran down to the sea. It was a time of dizzying contrasts, a time of change.   3

On the oily surface of the pond, from time to time a snout thrust upward, took in air with a queer grunting inspiration, and swirled back to the bottom. The pond was doomed, the water was foul, and the oxygen almost gone, but the creature would not die. It could breathe air direct through a little accessory lung, and it could walk. In all that weird and lifeless landscape, it was the only thing that could. It walked rarely and under protest, but that was not surprising. The creature was a fish.   4

In the passage of days the pond became a puddle, but the Snout survived.   5
There was dew one dark night and a coolness in the empty stream bed. When the sun rose next morning the pond was an empty place of cracked mud, but the Snout did not lie there. He had gone. Down stream there were other ponds. He breathed air for a few hours and hobbled slowly along on the stumps of heavy fins.

It was an uncanny business if there had been anyone there to see. It was a   6
journey best not observed in daylight; it was something that needed swamps and shadows and the touch of the night dew. It was a monstrous penetration of a forbidden element, and the Snout kept his face from the light. It was just as well, though the face should not be mocked. In three hundred million years it would be our own.

—From Loren Eiseley, "The Snout," *The Immense Journey*

How to Establish Ethos

Sometimes the writer's ethos is already established. For example, if you had known that Eiseley had won the Pulitzer Prize or that he is known as an historian of science, you would already believe that he is knowledgeable and would tend to be open to his ideas. In another instance, an ethos already is established when a writer is personally known to the audience, whether the relationship is student to instructor, executive to client, or child to parent. When an ethos is already established, our task is not so difficult as when the audience doesn't know us at all, but we need to reinforce our ethos. Although they already know whether we are ethical and trustworthy, we can always put our best foot forward, improve our ethos, and impress upon them that we are more informed on an issue than they had realized.

Usually, however, we must establish our ethos from point zero, and establishing that we are rational and benevolent in a discourse addressed to readers who don't know us is considerably more challenging. Since they don't know that we are a reliable source, they cannot be expected to accept our ideas immediately; our first task, therefore, is to prove that we are a reliable source. The question is, how do we communicate our good sense, good will, high morals, and humanity in order to win readers' approval?

Because our ethos emerges through our style, logic, substantiation, and all other aspects of writing, our ethos will be good if we do a good job with everything else. In fact, the relationship is circular: Effective writing creates a good ethos, and a good ethos in turn makes readers view our proposition more favorably.

Ethos is partly a product of logical and imaginative thinking. If our thesis is provocative and if our arguments are inventive, readers assume that we are original thinkers. If our inferences and conclusions are sound, and if our organization is clear and logical, readers assume that these reflect a logical mind. We gain readers' respect by carefully thinking out our ideas, being aware of their consequences, and seeing their relationships. The harder we work on invention, logic, and structure, the more readers will respect us and accept us as reasonable persons, and the easier it is to persuade them.

Another way in which we establish our ethos is by providing authoritative evidence. Our main purpose for providing evidence, of course, is to substantiate generalizations, but a by-product of good evidence is good ethos. Presenting convincing facts, introducing the latest finding in the field, citing respected authorities, providing statistics—all of these not only prove our assertion, but also convey to readers that we have a command of the subject. Knowing the vital information demonstrates that we know the field and establishes our expertise.

Ethos is also closely related to tone. By striking a conciliatory tone and using modest language, we convey an ethos of tolerance and reasonableness, and we communicate our respect for readers. If we treat readers with respect, they will reciprocate; if we treat them with anger and arrogance, they will respond with anger and will quit reading. The Golden Rule applies to writing as well as to other forms of social behavior. If we start with the notion that readers are as intelligent as we are, we will have a better chance of making friends out of strangers.

Present Credentials

In addition to ensuring that tone, invention, logic, and evidence are appropriate, we can employ several techniques to help achieve an effective ethos. One obvious way to establish our ethos is to present our credentials early in the discourse, since the early part of an essay introduces readers not only to the subject, but also to us. In order to inform readers that we are qualified to write on a particular topic, we can discreetly allude to special experience or training that we have in that area. The situation is analogous to court witnesses giving expert testimony at a trial; such professionals as psychologists and chemists establish their credibility by presenting their credentials so the jury will accept them as experts. To convince readers that we are reliable and informed, we too can mention any relevant experience or education, since readers are in effect our jury—they are the ones who will decide our case.

When trying to establish ourselves as competent sources, we must be careful not to sound boastful because that will undermine our ethos instead of increasing our credibility. The best way to handle remarks about ourselves is to insert them in subordinate clauses or in phrases:

> Having grown up in a ghetto, I know what a Boy's Club means to urban youths. It means . . .
>
> As chairman of the student court, I have seen . . .
>
> Having participated in Junior Olympics, . . .
>
> During the 5 years that I played in a band, . . .
>
> "Having served first on one of the Congressional Committees that oversee our intelligence apparatus, and later as Secretary of Defense, I am familiar with some of the accomplishments of our intelligence services." (Melvin Laird, "Let's Stop Undermining the CIA")

These tactfully inserted self-introductions help to convince readers that we know what we are writing about.

Communicate Perspective

A second technique specifically calculated to establish a favorable ethos is to give an overview of the problem being discussed and of the tentative solutions. The purpose here is to communicate a sense of perspective on the issue. Outlining the problem, the causes, and the suggested solutions demonstrates our knowledge of the subject and also educates readers about the issue. We want to assure readers that we have a comprehensive understanding of the issue, that we are mindful of the complexity of the subject, and that we have formed an opinion only after carefully considering alternative opinions. If readers perceive that we have an encompassing view of the issue, they will more readily accept us as an informed source.

Consider this passage from the *Final Report of the National Commission on the Causes and Prevention of Violence,* which analyzes, among other things, the effects of television on violence in America. The Commission is careful to qualify its statements, to note that there are multiple causes of violence, and to list the problems inherent in measuring the impact of television. Which statements can you point to that demonstrate the Commission's sense of perspective?

We approach this question with great care. In our concern about violence and its causes, it is easy to make television a scapegoat. But we reemphasize what we said in our Progress Report last January: there is no simple answer to the problem of violence—no single explanation of its causes, and no single prescription for its control. We urge that those who read this chapter do so carefully, without exaggeration of its findings, remembering that America also experienced high levels of crime and violence in periods before the advent of television.

The problems of balance, taste, and artistic merit in entertainment programs on television are complex. We cannot countenance government censorship of television. Nor would we seek to impose arbitrary limitations on programming which might jeopardize television's ability to deal in dramatic presentations with controversial social issues. Nonetheless, we are deeply troubled by the television's constant portrayal of violence, not in any genuine attempt to focus artistic expression on the human condition, but rather in pandering to a public preoccupation with violence that television itself has helped to generate.

Experience with pervasive mass communications—and particularly television—is so recent that at present there is much that is not fully understood and little that is proven beyond a reasonable doubt about the full social impact of the mass media. It is difficult to design studies linking human behavior or personality formation to media content, in view of the vast array of other variables in the social environment that converge to shape a person's conduct and values. Television is but one powerful element in a complex nexus of social forces impinging on people's lives. Consequently, we have seen our principal task as being one of clarifying the issues surrounding the problem of television violence and its effects, weighing the evidence in light of the risks of continuing the recent volume and style of violence portrayed on television, and framing recommendations appropriate to a problem that is as yet imperfectly understood.

We do not and cannot answer all of the questions raised by television programs that contain violence. But we do believe that our findings are adequate to support the recommendations which we offer to the broadcasting industry, to the government, and to the public. Questions of social policy can rarely be resolved beyond a reasonable doubt—but when we know enough to act, there is no excuse for inaction.

Find Common Ground

A final technique designed to create a favorable ethos is to form an initial bond with the audience by pointing out the common ground that exists between them and us. As discussed in the previous chapter, common ground means any values, principles, emotions, or experiences that we and our readers share. The purpose of establishing common ground is (1) to cultivate a sense of similarity and kinship and (2) to start the discourse on a note of agreement.

Readers tend to trust writers whom they perceive as being similar to themselves; in fact, similarity is the basis of most alliances. Since readers are quick to determine whether we are friend or foe in an argument, our emphasizing the common ground between them and us—a shared concern, a shared attitude, a shared goal—encourages them to perceive us as allies. When they recognize our values as being their values, they identify with us and extend their trust. Assuring readers that we are similar to them, therefore, enhances our credibility.

In order to find common ground, we must search the audience's general characteristics. With audiences whom we don't know personally, this task entails analyzing such characteristics as religion, political affiliation, social class, education, and so forth. Once we discover which convictions we share with them, we base our argument on premises that we know they will endorse. We can also explicitly point out experiences or attitudes that we share with the audience. For example, citing our military experience in an argument addressed to members of the Veterans of Foreign Wars establishes an immediate bond between that audience and us.

Starting an argument on any common ground has the additional advantage of encouraging even those readers who are against our thesis to consider it. People ordinarily will not read arguments that advocate an opinion opposite to their own because they are too threatened by opposing ideas to listen to them. By starting arguments with a point of agreement, however, we sometimes can get opponents to listen because common ground helps overcome readers' initial skepticism and defensiveness. Once we have formed a bond between our readers and ourselves and have laid a foundation of trust, we can ease into areas of disagreement without losing readers. In this way, ethos can be extremely strategic.

APPLICATION

1. What common ground can you generate on the subject of federal funding of training programs for low-income youths if your audience is (1) blue collar workers, (2) business executives, or (3) elderly retirees?
2. In the following introduction to a nine-page argument in favor of nuclear energy, the author assumes that many of his readers are against nuclear energy, and he knows that he must overcome their initial attitude. What is his strategy? What emotional common ground does he hope to establish with his readers? Why does he begin by admitting that he is frightened by "all massive concentrations of energy?" What is the purpose of the anecdote about the gas tanks near his boyhood home?

I write of nuclear power as a self-confessed coward in the face of all massive concentrations of energy. Lightning frightens me. A surge in the wind's strength makes me uneasy in an airplane. And I cannot stand at the base of a 200-foot dam without thinking of the force of gravity stored up behind it, waiting to sweep everything before it.

When I was 10 years old, I was leery of the two large tanks in which cooking gas was stored not far from my home in uptown Manhattan. I had been instructed that playing with matches was bad, particularly near stoves; lighting the oven was a hazardous chore reserved for adults. If an oven could go off with a bang, I thought, what would exploding gas tanks do?

Yet it was clear that my mother, timorous in the face of other perils—deadly poisoning by a lunch eaten elsewhere than Schrafft's, for example—did not fear those gas tanks. And I, too, might have made my peace with them if I had known what she knew, that they were an essential part of the basically beneficent petroleum-energy system that produced hot cocoa on cold afternoons. Now, sensing the approaching demise of that system, I am steeling myself for its successor. Without broadened use of nuclear power, I see little long-range hope for the achievement of decent living standards everywhere.

—From Roger Starr, "The Case for Nuclear Energy," *New York Times Magazine*, Nov. 8, 1981

If we search, we can always find some pertinent belief that we share with readers, and this common ground can become highly persuasive material. However, we should not *pretend* to share attitudes with readers because feigning beliefs in order to manipulate readers is hypocritical. We should not misrepresent our values, falsify our experience, or camouflage our attitudes in order to gain their support.

Ethicality of Using Ethos

A good ethos, we decided earlier, is one that reveals that we are intelligent, benevolent, and virtuous, but in fact none of us is always knowledgeable, kind, and moral. When we emphasize our virtues and charm, and hide our selfishness and irascibility, aren't we distorting our true character and intentionally projecting a false image? The answer is—yes, and no.

When we write to persuade, we inevitably improve on our character a little. When we are aware of the effects of every statement we write, we are consciously projecting a desirable image, and to the extent that that image is conscious and calculated, it is inauthentic. The dilemma that good argumentative writers face is that the anticipated reader reaction influences everything from structure to diction and requires that writers adapt accordingly; simply being aware of readers affects our ethos and makes total authenticity impossible. To reach readers, we must present our best side, and since that side presents only a partial view of our character, we are not expressing our real, full character.

On the other hand, we are not misrepresenting our character and not presenting a false image. As in any social situation, in writing we want to be on our best behavior, and therefore we cultivate the best parts of our character. Naturally, whenever we want to make a good impression and win someone's approval, we put our best foot forward; it's not false or inauthentic because it's still our foot. If readers perceive us as being altruistic, informed, and principled, they are more likely to accept our truths than if they perceive us as being selfish, narrow-minded, and unscrupulous. Thus, it is a matter of practicality for us to present our best side.

To some degree, then, we reach a compromise between wooing readers with a desirable image and presenting our full character. As much as possible we should be ourselves, freckles and all, though prudence suggests that we show our best profile to readers.

Ineffective Ethos

There are at least three ethos stances that automatically alienate readers: the angry ethos, the superior ethos, and the official ethos.

The angry ethos results when we believe so intensely in our cause that we allow our temper to overrule us and our tone to become belligerent. Although we want to communicate the depth of our conviction on an issue, we have to be careful not to let the tone get out of hand and not to shake our fists in readers' faces. Instead of persuading readers, such tactics usually have the opposite result. Writers who figuratively stick out their tongues at those readers who hold differing views only antagonize those readers and further widen the ideological split. Instead of convincing readers of the justness of our cause, we make them hostile to it. Consider the ethos conveyed in this letter to a college dean from an involved student:

> Dear Dean Boone:
>
> Your refusal to allow the marching band to travel to Florida for the Gator Bowl game is just another example of your ridiculous and dictatorial policies.
>
> We band members practiced long hours all season, played well at the games, and should be rewarded by getting to perform at halftime on national TV.
>
> But no. You want to destroy our school spirit and to send the football team all the way to Florida alone. Such idiotic decision-making is typical of the administration at this college.
>
> I'm so disgusted with it all that I don't care whether the team wins or loses.
>
> > Bill M. Polight
> > Bassoonist

Mr. B. M. Polight no doubt has a legitimate complaint, but his strategy is ineffective, the consequences being that instead of helping his cause, he is hurting it. How would you describe his ethos? What will be the dean's probable response to this letter? Clearly, shouting and sticking one's tongue out at the person one intends to persuade is no way to win friends and influence deans.

APPLICATION

Rewrite the letter to Dean Boone so that you create a favorable ethos and make a more persuasive appeal.

An equally offensive stance is the superior ethos, whereby our tone is condescending and abusive. If our readers hold an opposing view, and if we treat their ideas disdainfully or attack them as being ridiculous, what will their reaction most likely be? The writer who in effect says "I'm right and you're not only wrong but stupid" has a great deal to learn about (1) good manners and (2) persuasion. If our goal is to achieve cooperation and to win converts to our view, we cannot afford to be disrespectful of others' ideas. Readers are more likely to listen to, and eventually give in to, a reasonable and compassionate opponent who does not humiliate them and who treats them as intelligent persons of judgment. No one wants to be ravished, but most of us don't mind gentle seduction.

The third ineffective stance, the official ethos, is a calculated attempt to impress readers by sounding grandly intellectual. In a desire to appear knowledgeable and important, we may fall into the trap of thinking that big words are the sign of a grand intelligence, and we hide behind verbose prose and double-talk. The tone is unnecessarily formal, the diction is inflated, and the meaning is obscure. The official ethos unfortunately seems to be on the increase these days, and it is practiced by educators, lawyers, bureaucrats, and social scientists. Usually an official ethos backfires because instead of sounding intellectual and authoritative, the writer sounds pompous and phony.

APPLICATION

Here is an example of a writer who uses an official ethos in an attempt to sound important. What is the effect of the language and tone? How would you describe the writer as he presents himself in this letter? If you can, translate the writer's message in plain English.

Dear Mayor Stone:

Confronted with the prodigious and, one disquietedly observes, incremental indebtment of the municipal government, one is hesitant to acquiesce to the commission of a sculptural verisimilitude of the intrepid peripatetic who founded our metropolis.

The solicitation of such a disbursement during a protracted interval of fiscal delinquency seems irrefutably unconscionable. Any contractual ratification requires the approbation of the municipal executive council, and such ratification heretofore has not been bestowed.

The abandonment of the enterprise's development would seem of the utmost sagacity, in consideration of the solitariness of your unpropitious sentiment and the imminence of the mayoral election.

                                        Your friend,
                                        Councilman Alfred Dolt

Instead of capturing the voice of one human being talking to another, the letter sounds as if it were written by some bloodless thing with a dictionary where its soul should be.

The best advice about ethos is to be yourself. Communicate your unique personality, letting readers see that you have a sense of ethics and of irony, that you have moments of perception, that you are practical and judicious, and that you have an inquisitive mind and a conviction about your ideas. Talk to them in a friendly and unaffected manner. They are much more likely to accept your information as truthful and to accept your expertise on a subject if they are convinced that you are an authentic, breathing human being than if they perceive you as being a frigid, pretentious, and faceless entity.

Advice, Warnings, Reminders

1. Ethical proof is obviously only one of several considerations in persuasion. Regardless of how winning our ethos is, readers must see that the issue is significant to them and that they have something at stake in the issue.
2. One of the chief obstacles to communication is that readers are too threatened by opposing ideas to listen to them. A good ethos helps to overcome those feelings, to gain trust, and to gain readers.
3. Introductions of arguments must gain not only readers' attention, but also their consent.
4. We don't establish our ethos once and for all in an essay; it emerges and develops throughout the discourse, and any slips into intolerance, illogic, or malice can destroy our ethos.
5. Although we need not be experts in a field to discuss the subject intelligently, we must have special knowledge of some sort and be more informed than the audience. We shouldn't overlook the value of firsthand knowledge; remember Orwell's personal narrative "A Hanging," which is a persuasive argument. Usually, though, we must study a subject and research it some before writing; then we demonstrate our knowledge by citing statistics, examples, and authorities.
6. Don't be afraid to admit that you have shortcomings or that you don't know something. Concessions sometimes help our ethos.
7. Don't insult your readers or imply that they are stupid because they believe something different.
8. Factual errors, misspellings, contradictions, and muddled prose destroy our ethos.
9. Modesty is a winning virtue, but false modesty, which is easily detected, alienates readers.

10. Readers judge us based on:
    whether we appear to see the world as they do,
    whether we seem informed,
    whether we seem fair and open-minded,
    whether we seem moral and altruistic,
    whether we are logical, and
    whether we treat them with respect.

Exercises

1. Analyze the ethos projected in an essay presented earlier in the text—for example, by one of these writers: Tom Wolfe, Fran Lebowitz, Norman Cousins, Phyllis Theroux, Sharon Curtin, or John Bunzel.

2. In order to see how ethos works, try to imitate the ethos of an easily recognizable person. Assume that you are writing a speech to a graduating college class on the subject of success and that you are one of these persons:
   A. Muhammad Ali
   B. Howard Cosell
   C. Suzanne Somers
   D. Ronald Reagan
   E. Richard Pryor
   F. Barbara Walters
   G. Phyllis Theroux
   H. Harry Crews
   I. Fran Lebowitz
   J. Isaac Asimov

3. Exchange papers anonymously in class and criticize someone else's ethos.

4. Bring to class one essay or editorial that you consider to have an effective ethos and another that you consider to have an ineffective ethos.

5. Find an example of an advertisement that relies on a celibrity's ethos to sell a product.

6. Companies, organizations, and products as well as writers have an ethos. Describe the ethos of the following:
   A. Pepsi Cola
   B. National Rifle Association
   C. Ivory soap
   D. NAACP
   E. Calvin Klein jeans
   F. Marlboro cigarettes
   G. Rolls Royce

7. Describe the ethos of some national speaker: Jack Kemp, Jesse Jackson, Geraldine Ferraro, George Bush, or someone similar.

8. Can you think of an occasion when an angry ethos or a formal ethos might be appropriate?

9. The following three passages are excerpts from autobiographies. The first is by Billy Martin, the former Yankee baseball player and manager; the second

is by Roger Wilkins, a civil rights advocate, columnist, and former Assistant Attorney General; and the last is by John Kenneth Galbraith, an economist and former ambassador. Based solely on these passages, what kind of ethos does each man project?

A. During my entire playing career as a Yankee I never once felt secure because the whole time I knew that Yankee general manager George Weiss hated my guts. It didn't matter how well I played, or how many pennants we won, I always knew that as soon as Weiss could find a way to get rid of me, he would.

  I came up to the Yankees in 1950, and though I felt I should have been the starting second baseman, I was on the bench and Jerry Coleman was playing. I'd play every once in a while, and when I got in, I'd drive in a couple runs or make a good play in the field, and so in late April when our manager, Casey Stengel, told me the Yankees were sending me down to Kansas City, I was a little upset.

  —From Billy Martin and Peter Golenbock, *Number 1*

B. In a sense, I have been an explorer and I sailed as far out into the white world as a black man of my generation could sail. A New York law firm, State, Commerce, Justice, Ford, *The Washington Post, The New York Times,* the Hamptons, Johannesburg and Paris were some of my ports of call along with a number of beds, some warm, some luxurious, some both. I could not stand white people shutting doors in my face, so I pushed through plenty of them. My life wasn't always neat and tidy, and I didn't always do the right thing, but because the fish were guiding me, even when I didn't know it or want it, there were some good things.

  After I left and they put some more blacks, some women and some young people on the board of the Ford Foundation, Mac Bundy told Kenneth Clark, "I didn't know one man could change an institution as much as Roger did, but he did it." Warren Christopher, when he was Deputy Attorney General, once told my staff that I was the conscience of the Department of Justice. I liked that, and I like the fact that Ben Bradlee gives me credit for helping him learn better the need for more racial openness at the *Post.* Once, at the *Times,* I was told that a column of mine had convinced President Carter to add $667 million to his budget request for education aid to disadvantaged children.

  —From Roger Wilkins, *A Man's Life: An Autobiography*

C. My academic success somewhat lessened my need to be in Washington. But now in Cambridge I did need to make everyone aware of my eminence. The FBI files to which I earlier adverted cover numerous investigations of my character, credit standing, sobriety, marital fidelity, friends and associates. All reports were uniformly favorable. But nearly all of my colleagues and professional acquaintances, after conceding my affirmative qualifications, said that I had an unduly well-developed view of my own intellectual excellence. Many years later, in 1961, when I was about to go to India, the

New York Times ran a profile of the new ambassador. At breakfast that day President Kennedy asked me how I liked it.

I said it was fine, but I didn't see why they had to call me arrogant.

"I don't see why not," said the President, "everybody else does."

—From John Kenneth Galbraith, *A Life in Our Times*

10. The following are the openings of two argumentative essays. Explain how each writer attempts to present an ethos of impartiality and fairness.

A. Miss Horsefield introduced me to the metric system in her third-grade class at DuBois School in Springfield, Ill., 25 years ago. I didn't find it awesome or difficult to understand then, and I don't now. The interrelationship of distance, volume and weight is impressive. What a pity the United States didn't adopt it 100 years ago when we joined in the signing of the International Metric Convention.

Now, however, I wonder with growing horror what lunacy propels us to go metric at this late date.

—From Lisa Shillinger, "Kill the Metric!" *Newsweek,* Nov. 8, 1976

B. Freud's ambivalence toward female sexuality has often (too often) been cited simplistically as evidence of male chauvinism. This conclusion is not only unfair to the powerful and analytic mind of Freud but, more important, it short-circuits our understanding of his work and deters us from mining it for perceptions that can be very useful in any examination of the position of women today. In my discussion of his 1931 paper, *Female Sexuality,* I shall call attention to some ambiguities and, indeed, some outright inaccuracies of speech; but it is for a positive purpose. I believe that these faults can reveal, as geological "faults" do for the earth, positions of strain in Freud's structure of concepts which tell us a great deal about the society in which he lived and to which we are the heirs, as we are the heirs to his thought. In raising questions of motivation and of emotive personal relationships I am not seeking to discredit Freud's enormous achievements but rather to put these in perspective, so that we can more readily call on their dynamic energy.

—From Elizabeth Janeway, "Freud's View of Female Sexuality," *Women and Analysis*

11. Describe the qualities that make these writers likable and charming. What about them captures our affection and entices us to continue reading? Be specific and point out words and phrases that effect this response from us.

A. It is one of the great surprises of my adult life that I am not particularly good at doing the Double-Crostic. When I was growing up, I thought that being able to do the Double-Crostic was an adult attribute, not unlike buying hard-cover books, and that eventually I would grow into it. My mother, who was indirectly responsible for this misapprehension, was a whiz at Double-Crostics and taught me how to do them. In those days, the Double-Crostic was available through three sources: every week in the *Saturday Review,* every other week in the *New York Times Magazine* and twice a year in a Simon and Schuster anthology containing fifty or so new puzzles. The first two puzzles in each anthology were geared to beginners—to idiots, to be more precise—and I could usually solve one of them in about a month, using an atlas, a dictionary, a thesaurus, a Bartlett's and an occasional tip from my mother, who would never have been caught dead using any source material at all. There are many things I will never forgive my mother for, but heading the list is the fact that she did the Double-Crostic in ink.

—From Nora Ephron, "Double-Crostics," *Scribble, Scribble*

B. I have just come in from planting chrysanthemums, fourteen full-blooming plants of them. The edges of my porches are covered with their colors, my mood is still full of the tart, sweet odor of chrysanthemums, and there is still a smudge of dirt on my fingers, but let no man mistake me for an honest gardener, for I raise nothing from seed. These are the days of instant flowering. I bought my plants grown and blossomed from a mild-eyed and loam-knuckled man who lives near us and who spends his serene retirement in raising for his neighbors what they are too lazy to raise for themselves. These days my kind of gardening comes to little more than just-add-tap-water-and-set. It is to the flowering world what instant powder is to coffee, with the minor difference that the flower water should not be boiling, and with the major difference that the flowering result is as authentic as if the process were real.

Perhaps we no longer have time for the full process of a green reality. Yet there was a time when I knew my garden up from seed. My mother and aunt used to set out a huge kitchen garden when I was growing up and I was automatically its chore boy, even to the point of suffering the ridicule of my fellow hoodlums when we managed to corner a load of manure. At such times, I was appointed as the local substitute for the McCormick spreader while the boys stood by the fence and let me know how suitably I was occupied.

—From John Ciardi, "Chrysanthemums," *Manner of Speaking*

12. How does the following writer communicate his tolerance and humanness?

The burning question around here now is what I am going to do about my deer. They always speak of it as "my" deer, and it has come to seem just that. I often think of this not impossible animal, walking statelily through the forest paths and wearing a studded collar with "E. B. White, phone Waterlot 40 Ring 3," engraved on it.

"You goin' to get your deer?" I am asked by every man I meet—and they all wait for an answer. My deer-slaying program is a matter of considerable local import, much to my surprise. It is plain that I now reside in a friendly community of killers, and that until I open fire myself they cannot call me brother.

The truth is I have never given serious thought to the question of gunning. My exploits have been few. Once I shot a woodchuck that my dog had already begun to take apart; and once, in the interests of science, I erased a domestic turkey—crouching silently on a log six feet from the bird's head, as cool as though I were aiming at my own cousin. But by and large my hunting has been with a .22 rifle and a mechanical duck, with dusk falling in gold and purple splendor in the penny arcades along Sixth Avenue. I imagine I would feel mighty awkward discharging a gun that wasn't fastened to a counter by a small chain.

This business of going after some deer meat is a solemn matter hereabouts. My noncommittal attitude has marked me as a person of doubtful character, who will bear watching. There seems to be some question of masculinity involved: until I slay my dragon I am still in short pants, as far as my fellow-countrymen are concerned. As for my own feelings in the matter, it's not that I fear buck fever, it's more that I can't seem to work up a decent feeling of enmity toward a deer. Toward *my* deer, I mean. I think I'd rather catch it alive and break it to harness.

—From E. B. White, "Clear Days," *One Man's Meat*

Emotional Appeal

Argument, which appeals to the intellect, sometimes fails to motivate readers because sound logic and evidence, while convincing, may be lifeless and unmoving. Therefore writers often appeal to emotions as well as to reason. Logic and emotion together, Richard Whately suggests, form a sword in which the logical argument is the sturdiness of the metal and the emotion is the sharpness of the cutting edge. A stout sword that is dull will not pierce the flesh; a sharp rapier of inferior metal will break.

Because emotional appeals bypass the reasoning processes, some individuals object to their use. They believe that arguments should be based exclusively on logic, and since emotions are nonrational they find them unacceptable. However, the case *for* emotions being admissible in many persuasive essays is strong.

Rationale for Using Emotional Appeals

If human beings were totally rational creatures who reached beliefs through logical processes alone, appealing to reason alone would be sufficient. But human beings are dualities: half intellect, half emotions. And therefore reason does not conquer all. For writers to ignore half of human nature is not only naive, but also impractical; to disregard the emotional side of an issue and the emotional nature of our readers is a disservice to our thesis because we fail to employ all legitimate means of advancing that thesis. Not using emotional appeals amounts to surrendering a forceful weapon.

This is not to say that we should appeal to emotions *instead of* reason; we should appeal to emotions *in addition to* reason if we wish to reach the total person. We must appeal to both sides of human nature since both faculties play a part in forming opinions. Emotional appeals are to the heart what logical proofs are to the understanding. The relationship is complementary. Through emotion we touch readers and cause them to understand the human side of an issue. Logic convinces the mind; emotions move readers to act. Logic promotes certainty; emotions promote forcefulness. Whereas logic is reflective, emotions are impulsive; the one causes readers to ponder and contemplate, while the other arouses readers immediately. A dual appeal—rational and emotional—will be more effective than an appeal to only one faculty.

Emotional appeals serve several purposes. They motivate readers to act on our thesis, they help to counter the opposition's emotional appeals, and they promote a mental state conducive to change.

If readers already hold an opinion, and if they reached that opinion emotionally, we will have little success in dissuading them from that opinion by appealing solely to their rational faculties. "It is useless," Jonathan Swift observed, "to attempt to reason a man out of an opinion that he was never reasoned into." Not being founded in reason, emotionally held views are seldom destroyed by reason alone. We will have more success countering emotions with other emotions.

Techniques for Arousing Emotions

Because enlisting readers' emotions generates strong and immediate support for our thesis, we must learn how to kindle our readers' affections. Most of us are old hands at emotional appeals; we have manipulated our parents' emotions, played on the emotions of teachers and employers, and responded to the emotions of friends. From experience and observation you already know the basics of emotional appeals, though you may not have practiced them much in writing.

Emotions must be aroused indirectly. Straightforwardly telling readers that they should feel anger, pity, or anxiety concerning an issue doesn't work because feelings cannot be dictated. Furthermore, ordering readers to feel an emotion sounds as if we are preaching to them or admonishing them, and they are likely to resent that. Such orders carry with them an implied moral superiority that makes us appear contemptuous and arrogant, and that is not the image we wish to project.

We must make readers *experience* the intended sentiment. One way to achieve this is to use highly connotative language—words that are so heavily laden with associations that readers respond to them automatically. Such words as *liberty, honor, tyrant, fascist,* and *communist* have acquired emotional overtones so that whenever we use those words, we are assured of eliciting particular sentiments. Even an unimpassioned, logical document such as *The Declaration of Independence* uses highly emotive language to reinforce its reasoning. When referring to the colonists, for example, Thomas Jefferson uses such terms as "patient sufferance," "manly firmness," "free people," and "good People of these colonies"; but when referring to the King of England, he uses negative terms: "absolute Despotism," "abuses and usurpations," "arbitrary government," "injuries and usurpations," "absoute Tyranny," and "barbarous." Jefferson's intent is to present the conflict as being not between a king and his subjects, but between a tyrant and abused citizens. To gain readers' sympathy for the colonists and to elicit anger at the King, Jefferson presents images of violence and injustice practiced by the British and suffered by the Americans: "He has plundered ours seas, ravaged our Coasts, burnt our towns, and destroyed the lives of our people"; "he is at this time transporting large Armies of foreign Mercenaries to compleat the works of death, desolation, and tyranny"; "[he] has endeavoured to bring on the inhabitants of our frontiers, the merciless Indian Savages, whose known rule of warfare, is an undistinguished destruction of all ages, sexes and conditions." Such words as "plundered," "ravaged," and "tyranny" arouse readers' anger; and images of savages indiscriminantly murdering women and children arouse readers' sympathy. Jefferson is cautious, however, not to use excessive or exaggerated language because ranting calls attention to itself and destroys the emotional impact.

Even more effective than using highly connotative language is describing an emotional scene and allowing readers voluntarily to respond to it. For example, if we are urging city council members to fund a community day center where the elderly can gather for lunch, games, and afternoon television, our best strategy is to describe a few isolated, lonely old people in order to break through the council's financial concerns to their humanity. We could give an example of an old man on our block, living alone, existing day by day in seclusion, not knowing people his own age, feeling friendless and deserted, and so forth. We dramatize the scene and give vivid details to stir the readers' imaginations and sentiments. A descriptive illustration translates the issue into human terms and reaches through the official city council masks to the human beings behind them. Simply telling council members that they should have pity on the 213 elderly persons within the community who are solitary and unvisited does not have the impact of a concrete description of forsakenness. The former they accept as faceless statistics; the latter they react to as human circumstances.

If we describe a situation of injustice, readers will feel anger; if we describe a scene of suffering, they feel pity. We must use images and details that make readers vicariously experience the situation and that draw out the intended sentiment.

Detailed descriptions or narratives are effective persuaders. Remember, for instance, how Orwell uses narration in "A Hanging" (page 95) to persuade readers of the inhumanity of capital punishment. Here is an excerpt from Martin Luther King, Jr.'s "Letter from Birmingham Jail" in which he uses description to arouse readers' compassion. King is responding to praise that Birmingham police received from King's fellow ministers for preserving order and preventing violence during a freedom march.

> I doubt that you would have so warmly commended the police force if you had seen its dogs sinking their teeth into unarmed, nonviolent Negroes. I doubt that you would so quickly commend the policemen if you were to observe their ugly and inhumane treatment of Negroes here in the city jail; if you were to watch them push and curse old Negro women and young Negro girls; if you were to see them slap and kick old Negro men and young boys; if you were to observe them, as they did on two occasions, refuse to give us food because we wanted to sing our grace together.

Why does King describe maltreatment of the elderly and the young? Why does he include the image of "dogs sinking their teeth into unarmed, nonviolent Negroes"?

Here is an anecdote from Mark Twain's *Autobiography* that immediately sparks feelings of pity for a child slave:

In my school-boy days I had no aversion to slavery. I was not aware that there was anything wrong about it. No one arraigned it in my hearing; the local papers said nothing against it; the local pulpit taught us that God approved it, that it was a holy thing, and that the doubter need only look in the Bible if he wished to settle his mind—and then the texts were read aloud to us to make the matter sure; if the slaves themselves had an aversion to slavery, they were wise and said nothing. In Hannibal we seldom saw a slave misused; on the farm, never.

There was, however, one small incident of my boyhood days which touched this matter and it must have meant a good deal to me or it would not have stayed in my memory, clear and sharp, vivid and shadowless, all these slow-drifting years. We had a little slave boy whom we had hired from some one, there in Hannibal. He was from the Eastern Shore of Maryland and had been brought away from his family and his friends, halfway across the American continent, and sold. He was a cheery spirit, innocent and gentle, and the noisiest creature that ever was perhaps. All day long he was singing, whistling, yelling, whooping, laughing—it was maddening, devastating, unendurable. At last, one day, I lost all my temper and went raging to my mother and said Sandy had been singing for an hour without a single break, and I couldn't stand it, and *wouldn't* she please shut him up. The tears came into her eyes and her lip trembled, and she said something like this:

"Poor thing, when he sings it shows that he is not remembering, and that comforts me; but when he is still I am afraid he is thinking and I cannot bear it. He will never see his mother again; if he can sing, I must not hinder it but be thankful for it. If you were older, you would understand me; then that friendless child's noise would make you glad."

It was a simple speech and made up of small words but it went home, and Sandy's noise was not a trouble to me any more.

We respond emotionally to several different things in this simple tale: to the child himself, to the mother's tears and trembling lip, to her simple wisdom, and to Twain's recognition and compassion.

Emotional appeals in arguments are placed most often either at the beginning or at the end of the essay. If readers are unlikely to listen to reason, we might open with an emotional scene to engage their concern. If they are already engaged, however, we might lay a foundation of solid reasoning and save the emotional pitch for the conclusion. An impassioned appeal that evokes the emotions warranted by an issue provides a fitting climax and motivates the audience to action.

APPLICATION

1. How could you evoke these emotions in readers:
   patriotism
   pity
   anger

2. How could you appeal to readers' emotions on each of these issues, and what emotion would be best?
   A. executing criminals with a lethal injection
   B. stronger penalties for drunk drivers
   C. amnesty for illegal aliens who have been here more than 5 years
   D. financial aid for Haiti
   E. increasing social security benefits
   F. mandatory prison terms for persons who dump toxic wastes

3. Find an editorial in a magazine or newspaper that uses emotional appeal and bring the editorial to class. Analyze the appeal: Where is the emotional appeal positioned in the editorial? Why is it positioned where it is? What proportion of the editorial is devoted to logic and what to emotion?

Ignoble Emotional Appeals

We can appeal to any number of noble affections: compassion, sense of justice, gratitude, altruism, honor, public good, and so on. But we can also appeal to less noble affections: revenge, prejudice, self-love, greed, jealously, vanity, and snobbery. The question is, should writers appeal only to virtues, or should we also appeal to readers' baser tendencies? Being a moral consideration, the issue is a matter of individual ethical standards, and therefore I cannot presume to dictate an answer. But I can outline the issue for you.

On the one hand, some writers believe that using any means available is fair, including appeals to readers' pettiness, selfishness, and unscrupulousness. Endorsing the adage that "the end justifies the means," these writers adopt a code of ethics akin to that of advertising. Another class of writers believes that such emotions as revenge and envy are improper, but they nonetheless believe that if the opponent uses them, so should they. They contend that one should fight fire with fire.

On the other hand, many writers consider such emotions improper and unethical in any situation, and they feel that taking advantage of readers' frailties is at best unseemly and at worst dishonest. They suggest that by appealing to negative emotions in response to an adversary's negative appeal, we lower ourselves to our opponent's level, thereby injuring our image by showing that we are as unscrupulous as our adversary. For example, when a political candidate attacks an opponent with mud-slinging tactics, the public usually loses respect for the candidate. If the opponent turns around and uses the same tactics, the public loses respect for both of them. We implicitly endorse our opponents' code when we use their tactics.

Irrelevant Emotional Appeals

Emotional appeals are either legitimate or fallacious depending on their intent and on the issue being discussed. A legitimate appeal reinforces the logical appeal by pointing out the emotional side of an issue. A fallacious appeal tries to divert readers' attention away from the issue.

Emotional appeals in an argument that contains an emotional issue are legitimate and sometimes unavoidable. In fact, *not* touching readers' emotions is often impossible because emotions naturally attend some issues, and when we address those issues, we necessarily address the accompanying sentiments. For example, fear is a natural and involuntary response to an essay exposing fire hazards in nursing homes, and pity is a relevant emotion when discussing aid to homeless children. There is nothing unscrupulous about pointing out the human side of an issue and kindling readers' pity at suffering, indignation at injustice, and anger at inequity—so long as the issue warrants those emotions.

However, emotions can be used as a tactic for dodging an issue instead of as a means of addressing it. When emotions are intended as a smokescreen to obscure a weak case, they are fallacious. For instance, lawyers frequently use emotional appeals to shift a jury's focus from the issue (the defendant's guilt or innocence of a crime) to an irrelevant object (the man's wife and children, who will go hungry if he is convicted). Politicians also have been known to resort to irrelevant emotional appeals in order to manipulate audiences, as in Richard Nixon's infamous "Checkers Speech." Accused of accepting $18,000 in illegal contributions when he was a vice-presidential candidate in 1952, Nixon responded by giving a televised speech denying any misconduct. As a diversionary tactic to win public sympathy, he appealed at one point to the audience's affection for dogs and little girls:

> One other thing I probably should tell you, because if I don't they'll probably be saying that about me too, we did get something—a gift—after the election. A man down in Texas heard Pat on the radio mention the fact that our two youngsters would like to have a dog. And, believe it or not, the day before we left on this campaign trip we got a message from Union Station in Baltimore saying they had a package for us. We went down to get it. You know what it was? It was a little cocker spaniel dog in a crate that he sent all the way from Texas. Black and white spotted. And our little girl—Trisha, the six-year-old—named it Checkers. And you know the kids love the dog and I just want to say this right now, that regardless of what they say about it, we're gonna keep it.

What bearing does a black-and-white cocker spaniel have on the issue of a vice-presidential candidate's integrity?

Writers resort to irrelevant emotional appeals because they lack sufficient evidence to support their proposition and feel that the only way to gain support is to use emotions. Such attempted manipulation is ultimately ineffective because readers detect the empty intensity and reject it.

Just because emotions can be misused, however, is no reason to reject their use altogether. As the eighteenth-century rhetorician George Campbell pointed out: "Our eyes and hands and feet will give us the same assistance in doing mischiefs as in doing good; but it would not therefore be better for the world, that all mankind were blind and lame."

Exercises

1. To what emotions do these advertisements appeal?

   A. Virginia Slims cigarettes usually show an attractive, fashionably dressed, young professional woman holding a cigarette. The slogan says: "You've come a long way, baby."

   B. Karl Malden appears in ads for American Express traveler's checks. The scene typically shows a pickpocket stealing a tourist's wallet, a vacation cabin burning with a couple outside in bathrobes huddled in the cold night air, a man accidentally dropping his billfold into the ocean on a cruise, or a similar catastrophe.

   C. An ad publicizing the need to help poor children in Third World countries shows individual photographs of small children, and under each photo is the child's name and a description of his or her difficulties: "Ani lives in a ghetto in Brazil; his father has been unemployed 3 years, and Ani must beg for food."

   D. To sell paper cups, a company presents a scene with a mother and 3-year-old barefoot child in the bathroom. The mother reaches for a glass to get the child a drink and the glass falls to the floor and shatters all over the floor.

   E. A bank that sells individual retirement accounts (IRAs) shows an elderly person looking destitute in a dingy room. The ad suggests that social security isn't enough to live on and that people in their thirties and forties should start an IRA immediately.

   F. A tire company shows a woman and child driving in a rainstorm late at night. The ad, however, is targeted at a male audience since it asks "Aren't they worth the best protection available?" The ad recommends that the husband buy a certain radial tire.

2. Find two ads that appeal to emotion and bring them to class. Analyze their appeal and their effectiveness.

3. Analyze the emotional appeal in each of the following passages. Which emotion is being appealed to? How effective is the appeal?

   A. The Greek philosopher Socrates was tried in 399 B.C. for religious heresy and for corrupting youth with his ideas; he was convicted, was sentenced to death, and drank poison. At his trial, which is recorded by his pupil Plato, Socrates made the following clever appeal:

Well, Athenians, this and the like of this is nearly all the defence which I have to offer. Yet a word more. Perhaps there may be someone who is offended at me, when he calls to mind how he himself, on a similar or even a less serious occasion, had recourse to prayers and supplications with many tears, and how he produced his children in court, which was a moving spectacle, together with a posse of his relations and friends; whereas I, who am probably in danger of my life, will do none of these things. Perhaps this may come into his mind, and he may be set against me, and vote in anger because he is displeased at this. Now if there be such a person among you, which I am far from affirming, I may fairly reply to him: My friend, I am a man, and like other men, a creature of flesh and blood, and not of wood or stone, as Homer says; and I have a family, yes, and sons, O Athenians, three in number, one of whom is growing up, and the two others are still young; and yet I will not bring any of them hither in order to petition you for an acquittal. And why not? Not from any self-will or disregard of you. Whether I am or am not afraid of death is another question, of which I will not now speak. But my reason simply is that I feel such conduct to be discreditable to myself, and you, and the whole State. One who has reached my years, and who has a name for wisdom, whether deserved or not, ought not to debase himself. At any rate, the world has decided that Socrates is in some way superior to other men. And if those among you who are said to be superior in wisdom and courage, and any other virtue, demean themselves in this way, how shameful is their conduct! I have seen men of reputation, when they have been condemned, behaving in the strangest manner: they seemed to fancy that they were going to suffer something dreadful if they died, and that they could be immortal if you only allowed them to live; and I think that they were a dishonor to the State, and that any stranger coming in would say of them that the most eminent men of Athens, to whom the Athenians themselves give honor and command, are no better than women. And I say that these things ought not to be done by those of us who are of reputation; and if they are done, you ought not to permit them; you ought rather to show that you are more inclined to condemn, not the man who is quiet, but the man who gets up a doleful scene, and makes the city ridiculous.

But, setting aside the question of dishonor, there seems to be something wrong in petitioning a judge, and thus procuring an acquittal instead of informing and convincing him. For his duty is, not to make a present of justice, but to give judgment; and he has sworn that he will judge according to the laws, and not according to his own good pleasure; and neither he nor we should get into the habit of perjuring ourselves—there can be no piety in that. Do not then require me to do what I consider dishonorable and impious and wrong.

—From Plato's *Apology,* translated by Benjamin Jowett

B. In this argument from "Opinion on the Draft" (1863), Abraham Lincoln endorses a draft law because the Union needs soldiers to fight in the Civil War.

The principle of the draft, which simply is involuntarily, or enforced service, is not new. It has been practiced in all ages of the world. It was well known to the framers of our constitution as one of the modes of raising armies, at the time they placed in that instrument the provision that "the congress shall have power to raise and support armies." It has been used, just before, in establishing our independence; and it was also used under the constitution in 1812. Wherein is the peculiar hardship now? Shall we shrink from the necessary means to maintain our free government, which our grand-fathers employed to establish it, and our own fathers have already employed once to maintain it? Are we degenerate? Has the manhood of our race run out?

> C. The following example is from a speech by David Lloyd George, who later became Prime Minister of Britain during World War I, in which he urges England to go to Belgium's defense in 1914 after Germany invaded that country.

Belgium has been treated brutally. How brutally we shall not yet know. We already know too much. What had she done? Had she sent an ultimatum to Germany? Had she challenged Germany? Was she preparing to make war on Germany? Had she inflicted any wrong upon Germany which the Kaiser was bound to redress? She was one of the most unoffending little countries in Europe. There she was—peaceable, industrious, thrifty, hard-working, giving offense to no one. And her cornfields have been trampled, her villages have been burnt, her art treasures have been destroyed, her men have been slaughtered—yea, and her women and children too. Hundreds and thousands of her people, their neat comfortable little homes burnt to the dust, are wandering homeless in their own land. What was their crime? Their crime was that they trusted to the word of a Prussian King.

> D. Clarence Darrow, the famous trial lawyer, pleas for the court to sentence his clients, Loeb and Leopold, to life in prison rather than to death. His 1924 appeal was successful.

Here is Leopold's father—and this boy was the pride of his life. He watched him, he cared for him, he worked for him; the boy was brilliant and accomplished, he educated him, and he thought that fame and position awaited him, as it should have awaited. It is a hard thing for a father to see his life's hopes crumble into dust.

Should he be considered? Should his brothers be considered? Will it do society any good or make your life safer, or any human being's life safer, if it should be handed down from generation to generation, that this boy, their kin, died upon the scaffold?

And Loeb's, the same. Here are the faithful uncle and brother, who have watched here day by day, while Dickie's father and his mother are too ill to stand this terrific strain, and shall be waiting for a message which means more to them than it can mean to you or me. Shall these be taken into account in this general bereavement?

E. After World War II, the French philosopher Jean-Paul Sartre argued that the French people should set up a republic and should preserve the fierce love of freedom that they had demonstrated when the Nazis occupied France. He recalls the valor, principles, and suffering of those in the Resistance who fought for France's freedom.

In all circumstances they were alone. They were hunted down in solitude, arrested in solitude. It was completely forlorn and unbefriended that they held out against torture, alone and naked in the presence of torturers, clean-shaven, well-fed, and well-clothed, who laughed at their cringing flesh, and to whom an untroubled conscience and a boundless sense of social strength gave every appearance of being in the right. Alone. Without a friendly hand or a word of encouragement. Yet, in the depth of their solitude, it was the others that they were protecting, all the others, all their comrades in the Resistance. Total responsibility in total solitude—is this not the definition of our liberty?

F. Ellen Goodman argues for increasing control over the power that parents have to put their children into mental institutions. She begins the essay this way:

First, consider the stories.

An eleven-year-old retarded boy was brought to a mental hospital with a teddy bear under his arm. His parents were, they said, going on a two-week vacation. They never came back.

A twelve-year-old "tomboy" and truant was committed to a mental hospital by her mother after school authorities threatened the woman with prosecution.

A seven-year-old boy's mother died one year, and he was committed the next year by his father—two days before the man's remarriage. The diagnosis: a reaction of childhood.

Consider, too, the story of one child committed because he had "school phobia," another because she was "promiscuous," a third and fourth because they were "difficult" or even "incorrigible."

—From "Checks on Parental Power," *At Large*

Audience and Adaptation

Audience Analysis

Here is one of the few commandments in argumentative writing: Know thy audience. In order to know which emotional appeals will work, what common ground to establish, and what barriers we must overcome, we first have to identify our readers and their opinions, values, and characteristics. Selecting and analyzing our audience should be one of the first steps in persuasive writing, and determining whether readers are for or against our proposition is our first priority.

Readers' Attitude toward Thesis

Whoever our readers are, they probably already have some opinion on the issue we plan to discuss. Failure to realize this fact is one of the biggest mistakes that beginning writers make in argumentation. To assume that readers are empty vessels, sitting around with indifferent thoughts waiting for us to fill them with new opinions, is to ignore reality. Readers usually have information about the issue and an alignment before we begin writing. Even when they have little opinion about the issue we have chosen to discuss, though, they will have an opinion about the premises on which we base our thesis. For example, they may have never heard of the MX missile system, but they probably have a ready-formed opinion about defense spending and about national security; or readers may have no knowledge about a particular magazine that the courts are censoring, but they have a definite opinion about freedom of the press, pornography, and censorship. The larger opinion encompasses and influences readers' acceptance of our thesis.

People have what we might call fundamental premises upon which opinions are built. These beliefs are an interrelated combination of moral, religious, political, social, and economic beliefs, and these basic beliefs are at the bottom of readers' opinion toward our thesis. As writers, we must realize that we are dealing not with one issue but with underlying principles as well, and we must analyze those fundamental premises. Knowing these premises is important because readers are disinclined to accept a thesis that runs counter to a basic belief and, conversely, they are likely to accept a thesis that appears to be based on one of their fundamental premises. Readers accept an idea because it fits in with their other ideas.

Because of fundamental premises and of opinions derived from them, our thesis is seldom given impartial consideration. Even if readers don't have a preconception about the subject itself, they will have one about our premise. Whether they favor our proposition or not depends on whether their fundamental premises are compatible with ours.

Favorable Readers.   Usually we write arguments to change opinions from other viewpoints to ours, but occasionally we might wish to reinforce a viewpoint or to rally our readers to action. For example, most student editorials against the college administration are not written to convince students that the administration is uncaring and incompetent—students already believe that—but to solidify that belief, to cement and strengthen the bonds of harmony, and to motivate students to protest against a particular policy. Most arguments addressed to fellow believers resemble cheerleading: They are rallying cries to unify forces and to increase fervor. In addition, they serve to negate any attempts from the opposition to win converts, and they provide fellow believers with material to oppose nonbelievers.

Writing to readers who share our opinion presents few difficulties because there are no obstacles to overcome and no elaborate strategies to invent. Usually we can announce the thesis straightforwardly, outline the evidence, and conclude with considerable emotion.

Neutral Readers.   If readers are neutral—that is, they neither support nor oppose our thesis—we should first find out *why* they are neutral. The reason for their neutrality will determine what we must do to change them from a neutral to a favorable stance. Neutrality may be the result of ignorance, uncommitment, or apathy.

Sometimes readers have no opinion on an issue because they have no knowledge about it. They may have heard of psychokinetic research, for instance, but they are unaware of any controversy surrounding it and hence haven't formed an opinion about it. They are neutral because they are uninformed. These readers are easy converts to our side because our task is simply to inform them and simultaneously convince them of the soundness and justness of our cause.

Uncommitted readers are those who know something about both sides of the issue but are undecided as to which side they should support. When the merits of each side are nearly equal, as in an election with evenly matched candidates, there will be many uncommitted readers. Polls indicate that in the final week of most elections, nearly 40 percent of the voters are still undecided; whichever side wins the undecided vote usually wins the election—it's that significant. It is these voters whom editorialists go after because these readers are more open-minded than readers who have chosen a side. In fact, undecided readers often want to be convinced that one side is better, and they therefore invite evidence that will help them to make up their minds. This does not mean that undecided readers aren't skeptical, but because they are searching for an allegiance, they are more receptive than decided readers. It is easier to win an undecided vote than it is to change a vote from one side to the other. Undecided readers are interested in discovering truth; decided readers are usually more interested in defending their position.

A third type of neutrality results from apathy, which is very difficult to overcome. Readers are apathetic about three kinds of subjects: those subjects they think do not concern them personally, those that they realize affect them but that they believe they cannot in turn affect, and those that have received so much publicity that readers are numbed by the exposure. In the first instance, our task is to demonstrate that the issue—for example, tariffs—does affect our readers; we show how tariffs affect wages, taxes, and job security. We create interest by presenting effects. In the second case, our task is to show that our readers' involvement does count and that they have the power to effect change but that they are not using their power. For example, many people do not vote in political elections because they feel that their one vote will not matter. Consequently, in order to motivate citizens to vote, Democrats point out that a single vote can be of great importance: If one more person in each precinct across the nation had voted for Hubert Humphrey in 1968, Richard Nixon would not have become president. That statement causes people to reconsider their options of voting or not voting because it proves that each vote has power.

In the final case, when readers have grown indifferent through overexposure to an issue, our task is to stimulate unresponsive readers with a new approach to the issue. Sometimes the most challenging argument is the one that everyone has heard and ignored, so the wrong still exists. How does a writer enliven an old grievance? Take the issue of women's rights as an example. Many Americans, especially males, turn a deaf ear to what they consider to be a worn issue. "Oh, *another* essay on women's rights," they groan. The writer's task therefore is to put the issue into a fresh light, translate the facts into more meaningful terms, and make the inequality real. Here is a refreshing and effective letter from the National Women's Political Caucus that does just that:

Dear Friend:

If we elected the President, the Senate and the House of Representatives only from the eastern half of the country, nobody would consider it fair.

If the President, in appointing federal judges and other officials, considered only people from the western half of the country, there would be loud cries of discrimination.

But for all practical purposes, we <u>do</u> choose our government from only one half of the country.

The male half.

The offices of President, Vice-President and Supreme Court Justice are exclusively male. The Senate and the federal judiciary have only token female representation. The Cabinet right now has its largest number of women in our history—two. The U.S. House of Representatives has only 16 women out of 435 members. In our state governments we have only two women governors and six women lieutenant governors; only 10% of the state legislative seats are held by women.

That's not only unfair. It is a waste of half the talent in America. Today, we can't afford to waste talent that might be helping to guide and administer our country's affairs.

I want to ask you to join the National Women's Political Caucus. We're working to put that wasted talent into our government, where we need it.

This letter dramatizes the inequality and appeals to readers' democratic sense of fairness and justice. By opening this way, the letter gains a sympathetic reading and makes readers more likely to consider the request for membership and dues, which is the purpose of the letter.

Unfavorable Readers.   Readers who oppose our thesis and who believe in a contrary view are the most difficult readers to sway because we have two interrelated tasks: to overcome a current opinion and to replace it with our own opinion. In addition, readers tend not to read opposing arguments in the first place, and if they do, they tend to reject opposing evidence without due consideration. Consequently, unfavorable readers require a special effort on our part in presenting an argument. Although substituting one opinion for another can be accomplished, the chances of succeeding are not as high as they are with neutral audiences. Realistically, we can hope only to chip away at the other side's credibility, plant a seed of doubt in readers' minds, make our thesis more viable, and cause readers to reconsider the issue and give our thesis a less biased examination.

Some unfavorable audiences are more vulnerable to change than others. The least susceptible to change are those readers who are well informed about the issue and who have reached their opposing opinion only after careful analysis and weighing of both sides. These thoughtful readers tend to be unpliable, and we should not have high expectations about dislodging their beliefs. An easier opponent to persuade is the one who has not been exposed to our side's arguments but has reached a conclusion based on partial, one-sided evidence. This fact was proved during the Korean War when American prisoners of war were subjected to brainwashing techniques by the North Koreans and Chinese. Those POWs who saw both sides of the political issue—that is, who already realized that there are weaknesses in the American democratic and capitalistic system and that there are advantages to a socialistic system—were less susceptible to alteration of political beliefs; they knew both sides and concluded that the American system, although imperfect, is better. However, those POWs who had unquestioningly accepted that capitalism is good and socialism is evil turned out to be highly impressionable. Because they had not critically examined both systems, because they saw political ideologies in black and white terms, and because they had accepted on faith the superiority of the American way, some of them actually changed their convictions under intensive propaganda and coersive indoctrination. I'm not recommending that we resort to brainwashing, of course, but we can learn something about persuasion from this example: If readers have not properly considered both sides, we might be able to cause them to reconsider their position by giving them the full picture.

Reader Profile

In addition to knowing whether readers are for or against our thesis, we need to know their basic characteristics. One audience may differ widely from another intellectually, morally, and emotionally. Different upbrings, educations, values, religions, and occupations give people different perspectives and incline them to think differently.

Depending on our subject, we may have to know and take into account any number of factors about our readers: level of education, social class, income, religion, political ideology, occupation, ethnic background, age, and region. You might ask why knowing their religion is essential, or their occupation. Perhaps it isn't, but if our subject is abortion, knowing whether the audience is predominantly traditional Catholic will matter significantly. On the subject of tariffs, farmers will have different views from industrialists. Basic assumptions differ not only with each audience, but also with each issue. On the subject of welfare, for instance, a conservative Republican banker, an unemployed auto worker, and an aeronautics engineer might have widely divergent views, while on the subject of defense spending they might wholeheartedly agree.

Of course, there are differences within an audience because no audience is composed of identical readers. Nevertheless, the individual readers within almost any audience have some characteristics in common. Seldom do we address a universal audience; more likely, readers share a common interest, live in the same community, belong to a specific group, and so on.

Even when we address readers so diverse that their only similarity is that they are Americans, we can rely on traditional American values. In general, Americans:

1. take pride in their country (American way of life, American know-how, American prestige and power)
2. believe in representative democracy—the two-party system, constitutional government, elected officials, trial by jury
3. revere the Ten Commandments
4. espouse justice, fair dealings, honesty, straightforwardness
5. glorify the traditional family
6. treasure individual rights
7. regard hard work as the key to personal success
8. believe in education for everyone as the door to opportunity
9. emphasize money and material things (house, cars, clothes)
10. admire efficiency
11. respect common sense and pragmatism
12. believe that competition is good, especially in business and sports.

But rather than addressing all Americans, we usually address a limited and specific audience, most often a group whose members have common characteristics. Recognizing group allegiance and identity is important in writing. If we can determine which groups the readers belong to, we can get a better idea of their probable beliefs.

Let's say that you decide to enter a student essay contest offered by the *Wall Street Journal*, the winning essay of which will be printed on the editorial page of the *Journal*. Who is your audience? First, you start narrowing down your readers from the other 5 billion people on this globe. For one thing, 99 percent of the *Journal's* readers are Americans, and as diverse as Americans are, we have certain values and experiences in common. Next, you can specify who among the 240 million Americans reads the *Wall Street Journal:* mainly urban professional people, predominantly business persons, and for the most part managers and executives. Therefore, the editorialists for the *Journal*, despite their large readership, write for a fairly select audience whose concerns and interests are reasonably distinct.

Consider another example: If we write an argument against sex education being taught to sixth graders in the local elementary school, and if we address our argument to parents whose children attend the school, what assumptions can we make about this audience? First, most parents of elementary school children fall into a certain age range, say between 25 and 40. Second, because elementary schools are in local neighborhoods, the families are usually in similar economic and social classes. Third, being parents, they have a vested interest in the issue, and they are concerned about their children's moral welfare as well as education.

APPLICATION

What traits would you expect these audiences to have, and what interests would they have?

1. your college's faculty senate
2. Junior Chamber of Commerce (JCs)
3. members of the local National Rifle Association
4. senior citizens' association

Our reasons for analyzing an audience are twofold: to understand and to motivate. By understanding readers' feelings, needs, and concerns, we are better able to identify with them and to empathize with them. Once we understand why readers hold a certain view, we can put ourselves in their position and see the issue more comprehensively and with less bias. Empathy also gives us a new respect for readers, and when that respect is communicated by our tone, readers reciprocate by treating our argument with greater respect. Empathy helps us to see their side of the issue, and a more comprehensive vision of the issue promotes better understanding.

The other reason for analyzing an audience is to discover how susceptible they are to change and how we can motivate them to change. This is what ad agencies and political pollsters do; they investigate consumers' or voters' opinions and needs, and then capitalize on those opinions and needs. In our case, learning readers' main concerns and needs tells us how to reach those readers because such knowledge helps us to generate a strategy. We learn (1) what ideas we share with the readers so we can begin on common ground, (2) what emotions to appeal to, (3) what barriers there are to overcome, (4) what subjects to avoid, and (5) where to draw examples from. Knowing the pyschological terrain, then, is absolutely essential.

Incentives That Motivate Readers

What motivates readers? Are there standard goals that everyone seeks? Although exceptions exist, most people are motivated by these objectives:

money	social status	self-image, self-esteem
sex	power	family welfare
success	emotional security	national welfare

If we can relate our thesis to one of these incentives and show that our proposition will gratify one of these needs, we have a good chance of gaining readers' endorsement. With almost any topic, readers consider how it affects them and what they have to gain or lose.

Self-interest, then, is the greatest psychological motivator. This view may seem cynical, but it is realistic, and as writers we may as well recognize it and act on it. But we should also realize that self-interest is not necessarily a negative trait; *self-interest* and *selfishness* are not synonymous. The whole American system of capitalism is based on self-interest, and through self-interest the human race has not only survived but excelled. To act in our own best interest does not mean that we do not also act in the best interest of others. For example, because it is in our self-interest to breath clean air, we might write an editorial encouraging readers to write to their congressional representative in support of an antipollution bill. We act from self-interest and we appeal to their self-interest. It is when we appeal to interests that are against society or are at the expense of others that we move into morally ambiguous persuasion, and self-interest becomes selfishness.

To appeal to readers' self-interest, our proposition must carry an implicit promise either to gratify a need or to avoid displeasure. Readers must believe that by endorsing our thesis they will fulfill a desire or avoid pain. The psychology is no more complex than motivating a burro: We offer a carrot or a whip. We must demonstrate to readers (1) that if they support our proposition, good will result, or (2) that if they do not support our proposition, bad will result. Knowing what they consider to be good and bad is where audience analysis comes in. For example, if we support a city revenue bill for public transportation, we might urge commuters in the city to support it because a monorail system would be cheaper, faster, and more relaxing than driving a car. We might urge retired persons to support the same bill by using another approach—if they don't approve it, car pollution will continue to rise, affecting elderly people who have pulmonary and respiratory ailments. Sometimes we promise reward; sometimes we threaten.

Which is more effective—promise of reward or threat of penalty? They seem to be equally effective, and most arguments both promise that readers will receive pleasure if they act on the proposition *and* threaten that they will encounter displeasure if they do not.

Implicit warnings work on a fear principle. We point out that something that readers dread will occur as a result of their not accepting our proposition. What, then, do people fear? Most of us fear harm to family, loss of or failure to find love, loss of political freedom, war (especially nuclear war), professional failure, loss of job and money, illness, death, divine retribution (punishment by God), loss of social status, and personal inadequacy.

Adaptation

Thus far we have discussed readers' attitude toward our thesis, readers' traits, standard incentives, and the role of self-interest in argument.

Unless we make use of the knowledge we gain from these preparatory investigations, though, we have been wasting our time. Gradually we have been leading up to the purpose for all these preliminary considerations: adapting our argument to a particular audience. Of the many lines of argument we could use, of the storehouse of evidence we could use, and of the various structures we could use, we must select those that will work on the specific audience we are to address. We must strategically invent ways of reaching that special audience.

Writers are like strategists in any other field—sports, diplomacy, war, or courtship. For example, a baseball pitcher doesn't throw identical pitches to every batter; he learns to throw breaking curves to one batter and low fast balls to another, and by knowing his batters he improves his strike-out record. Muhammed Ali adapted his boxing style to his opponent's strengths and weaknesses. With Joe Frazier, for instance, he floated and jabbed, danced and circled; with George Foreman, he leaned against the ropes, covered up, and let Foreman pound away until exhausted. American diplomats conduct negotiations with China one way, with Uganda another way, and with France still a third way. Even an animal has enough savvy to use different strategies in different situations: Sometimes a 'possum runs for its life, and sometimes it rolls over and plays dead. The point is obvious—by knowing our audience, we learn which evidence to include, which rewards or penalties to put forward, which emotions to appeal to, and how to structure it all. We devise a strategy based on our knowledge of human nature in general and of the audience being addressed in particular.

Persuasion is a little like war, and the most persuasive writers are like military strategists, though writers battle over ideas instead of territories. The greatest military leaders have been those who carefully devised battle strategies based on a knowledge of their own strengths and weaknesses, the terrain, and the enemy's strengths, weaknesses, and traits. Each battle requires an individual plan of attack. Alexander the Great, for example, defeated the seemingly invulnerable city of Tyre, situated a quarter mile out to sea, by having his engineers build a stone pier—which is still in existence today—to reach the island fortress. Hannibal won repeated battles against the Romans because, realizing that his cavalry was superior, he elected to fight in the plains regions, where cavalry tactics were favorable. Robert E. Lee, battling against superior numbers, won an audacious victory at Chancellorsville by splitting his army and encircling the Union troops. Sam Houston, after losing half his army at the Alamo and having to retreat from Santa Anna's superior numbers, easily beat the Mexican army by attacking at the right time— during siesta. Finally, Patton, totally disregarding classic military rules, knifed his Third Army through German defenses to attack at the heart of the enemy. Good generals adapt their tactics to the situation and to the enemy.

In rhetorical battles, the writer must develop a plan of attack and defense based on the particular situation, just as a general does. We must know, for instance, which premises the readers will accept and which ones we will need to prove; on what points we must defend ourselves against the opponent's claims, and when to counterattack; which appeals will be effective; where to draw examples from; and what structure will be most effective.

In the following chapter, we will examine how to adapt structure for different audiences—where to place the thesis statement, where to place our strongest evidence, when and where to refute the opposition's arguments, and when and where to concede points to the opposition.

Exercises

1. Explain the strategy at work in these examples.

   A. In the period 1920–1936, 80 percent of the cigar manufacturers in the United States went out of business because cigar-smoking had a bad image from the movies, which invariably portrayed villains smoking stogies. The Cigar Manufacturers Association launched a major campaign to reverse the image. First, they discreetly offered monthly cash prizes to photo journalists for the best photos in newspapers of men puffing on cigars, preferably such famous men as Churchill, Babe Ruth, and movie stars. Second, the cigar industry offered the movie industry free advertising of new movies that portrayed villains without and heroes with cigars. Suddenly, Gary Cooper, Tyrone Power, and Clark Gable were seen in the cinema with a gun in one hand and a cigar in the other.

   B. In the 1970s, when gas supplies became short and gas lines became long, auto manufacturers started advertising for the first time "miles per tankful."

   C. A computer school advertises on television that over 50 percent of their applicants fail the school's entrance exam.

   D. Life insurance companies appeal to men to take care of their health. The approach is to tell men: "If you won't do it for yourself, do it for your wife and children."

   E. A French brandy distiller advertised in Hong Kong that brandy increases men's virility and that whiskey causes impotence.

   F. After World War I, to encourage men to attend Sunday School, some ministers held Sunday School in the local armory.

2. What strategy can you devise to convince the specified audiences to endorse the following thesis statements? How can you show these audiences that their self-interest is at stake?

    A. Audience: the college administration
         Thesis: A college newspaper should be able to print anything that it wishes without the approval of the faculty advisors or the administration.

    B. Audience: local Little League managers' association
         Thesis: Each team in the local Little League should be required to have at least two girls on the roster, and the girls should be guaranteed to play three innings each game.

    C. Audience: taxpayers
         Thesis: Instead of being sent to prison, nonviolent criminals should be sentenced to a lengthy period of public service, according to their skills. For example, convicted persons would serve as aides in nursing homes, as mechanics for state-owned cars, as garbage collectors, and so forth.

    D. Audience: your dean
         Thesis: College students should be given representation on committees that hire such nonacademic employees as counselors, coaches, student center directors, directors of security, directors of housing, and even dean of students.

    E. Audience: your local VFW (Veterans of Foreign Wars)
         Thesis: Both the United States and the USSR should neutralize—or hand over to a neutral nation, such as Switzerland—all of their nuclear weapons.

    F. Audience: a local judge
         Thesis: Unwed fathers who have maintained emotional and economic ties to their child should have legal rights regarding the raising of that child.

    G. Audience: senior citizen group
         Thesis: If a terminally ill patient asks to be given a lethal injection by his or her physician, the physician should be legally allowed to give the injection.

    H. Audience: your congressperson
         Thesis: During wartime, women should be allowed, on a volunteer basis, to serve in combat roles such as flying helicopters and operating tanks.

I. Audience: city council
   Thesis: The city should contribute 50 percent of the funds to help
             set up a battered-women's center that provides temporary
             shelter and professional counseling.

J. Audience: fellow students
   Thesis: The college should add to its curriculum a research and
             writing course that students would be required to take in
             their junior year; the course would be taught by professors
             in the students' major department.

Additional Reading

Reprinted below is the text of a speech that President Reagan delivered on national television, March 16, 1986. The purpose of the address was to gain support for a $100 million aid proposal for the rebels (the contras) fighting the Nicaraguan Sandinista government. Analyze the psychological strategies used in this argument.

1. How does the President try to show that giving aid to the contras is in the best interest of Americans?

2. What traditional American values does he appeal to? Give specific examples.

3. Find an example of an appeal to pity.

4. How does Reagan use fear as a means of urging support for the bill?

5. Where does he appeal to individual groups of Americans?

6. Give examples of highly connotative language that is intended to evoke emotional responses.

7. What does the President suggest will be the consequences of Congress disapproving the funds?

8. Why does he refer to John F. Kennedy?

9. Why does he quote Qaddafi and Gromyko?

10. How does Reagan use comparisons in the argument? Give examples.

AID TO THE CONTRAS

Ronald Reagan

My fellow Americans, I must speak to you tonight about a mounting danger in Central America that threatens the security of the United States. This danger will not go away; it will grow worse, much worse, if we fail to take action now.   1

I am speaking of Nicaragua, a Soviet ally on the American mainland only two hours' flying time from our own borders. With over a billion dollars in Soviet-bloc aid, the Communist Government of Nicaragua has launched a campaign to subvert and topple its democratic neighbors.   2

Using Nicaragua as a base, the Soviets and Cubans can become the dominant power in the crucial corridor between North and South America. Established there, they will be in a position to threaten the Panama Canal, interdict our vital Caribbean sea lanes and, ultimately, move against Mexico. Should that happen, desperate Latin peoples by the millions would begin fleeing north into the cities of the southern United States, or to wherever some hope of freedom remained.   3

The United States Congress has before it a proposal to help stop this threat. The legislation is an aid package of $100 million for the more than 20,000 freedom fighters struggling to bring democracy to their country and eliminate this Communist menace at its source. But this $100 million is not an additional $100 million. We are not asking for a single dime in new money. We are asking only to be permitted to switch a small part of our present defense budget—to the defense of our own southern frontier.   4

Gathered in Nicaragua already are thousands of Cuban military advisers, contingents of Soviet and East Germans and all the elements of international terror—from the P.L.O. to Italy's Red Brigades. Why are they there? Because, as Colonel Qaddafi has publicly exalted: "Nicaragua means a great thing, it means fighting America near its borders. Fighting America at its doorstep."   5

For our own security the United States must deny the Soviet Union a beachhead in North America. But let me make one thing plain, I am not talking about American troops. They are not needed; they have not been requested. The democratic resistance fighting in Nicaragua is only asking America for the supplies and support to save their own country from Communism.   6

The question the Congress of the United States will now answer is a simple one: Will we give the Nicaraguans' democratic resistance the means to recapture their betrayed revolution, or will we turn our backs and ignore the malignancy in Managua until it spreads and becomes a mortal threat to the entire New World?   7

Will we permit the Soviet Union to put a second Cuba, a second Libya, right on the doorsteps of the United States?   8

How can such a small country pose such a great threat? It is not Nicaragua alone that threatens us, but those using Nicaragua as a privileged sanctuary for their struggle against the United States.   9

Their first target is Nicaragua's neighbors. With an army and militia of 120,000 men, backed by more than 3,000 Cuban military advisers, Nicaragua's armed forces   10 are the largest Central America has ever seen. The Nicaraguan military machine is more powerful than all its neighbors combined.

Now let me show you the countries in Central America where weapons supplied   11 by Nicaraguan Communists have been found: Honduras, Costa Rica, El Salvador, Guatemala. Radicals from Panama—to the south—have been trained in Nicaragua. But the Sandinista revolutionary reach extends well beyond their immediate neighbors; in South America and the Caribbean, the Nicaraguan Communists have provided support in the form of military training, safe haven, communications, false documents, safe transit and sometimes weapons to radicals from the following countries: Colombia, Ecuador, Brazil, Chile, Argentina, Uruguay and the Dominican Republic. Even that is not all, for there was an old Communist slogan that the Sandinistas have made clear they honor: the road to victory goes through Mexico.

If maps, statistics and facts aren't persuasive enough, we have the words of the   12 Sandinistas and Soviets themselves. One of the highest-level Sandinista leaders was asked by an American magazine whether their Communist revolution will—and I quote—"be exported to El Salvador, then Guatemala, then Honduras, then Mexico?" He responded, "That is one historical prophecy of Ronald Reagan's that is absolutely true."

The Soviets have been no less candid. A few years ago, then Soviet Foreign   13 Minister Gromyko noted that Central America was "boiling like a cauldron" and ripe for revolution. In a Moscow meeting in 1983, Soviet Chief of Staff, Marshal Ogarkov, declared: "Over two decades ago there was only Cuba in Latin America. Today there are Nicaragua, Grenada and a serious battle is going on in El Salvador."

But we don't need their quotes; the American forces who liberated Grenada   14 captured thousands of documents that demonstrated Soviet intent to bring Communist revolution home to the Western Hemisphere.

So, we are clear on the intentions of the Sandinistas and those who back them.   15 Let us be equally clear about the nature of their regime. To begin with, the Sandinistas have revoked the civil liberties of the Nicaraguan people, depriving them of any legal right to speak, to publish, to assemble or to worship freely. Independent newspapers have been shut down. There is no longer any independent labor movement in Nicaragua nor any right to strike. As A.F.L.-C.I.O. leader Lane Kirkland has said, "Nicaragua's headlong rush into the totalitarian camp cannot be denied by any who has eyes to see."

Like Communist governments everywhere, the Sandinistas have launched   16 assaults against ethnic and religious groups. The capital's only synagogue was desecrated and firebombed—the entire Jewish community forced to flee Nicaragua. Protestant Bible meetings have been broken up by raids, by mob violence, by machine guns. The Catholic Church has been singled out—priests have been expelled from the country, Catholics beaten in the streets after attending mass. The Catholic Primate of Nicaragua, Cardinal Obando y Bravo, has put the matter forthrightly: "We want to state clearly that this Government is totalitarian. We are dealing with an enemy of the church."

Evangelical pastor Prudencio Baltodano found out he was on the Sandinista hit   17
list when an army patrol asked his name: "You don't know what we do to the
evangelical pastors. We don't believe in God," they told him. Pastor Baltodano was
tied to a tree, struck in the forehead with a rifle butt, stabbed in the neck with a
bayonet—finally his ears were cut off, and he was left for dead. "See if your God will
save you," they mocked. Well, God did have other plans for Pastor Baltodano. He
lived to tell the world his story—to tell it, among other places, right here in the White
House.

I could go on about this nightmare—the blacklist, the secret prisons, the   18
Sandinista-directed mob violence. But, as if all this brutality at home were not enough,
the Sandinistas are transforming their nation into a safe house, a command post for
the international terror.

The Sandinistas not only sponsor terror in El Salvador, Costa Rica, Guatemala   19
and Honduras—terror that led last summer to the murder of four U.S. marines in a
cafe in Salvador—they provide a sanctuary for terror. Italy has charged Nicaragua
with harboring their worst terrorists, the Red Brigades.

The Sandinistas have been involved themselves in the international drug trade.   20
I know every American parent concerned about the drug problem will be outraged to
learn that top Nicaraguan Government officials are deeply involved in drug trafficking.
This picture, secretly taken at a military airfield outside Managua, shows Federico
Vaughn, a top aide to one of the nine commandantes who rule Nicaragua, loading an
aircraft with illegal narcotics, bound for the United States.

No, there seems to be no crime to which the Sandinistas will not stoop—this is   21
an outlaw regime.

If we return for a moment to our map, it becomes clear why having this regime in   22
Central America imperils our vital security interests.

Through this crucial part of the Western Hemisphere passes almost half our   23
foreign trade, more than half our imports of crude oil and a significant portion of the
military supplies we would have to send to the NATO alliance in the event of a crisis.
These are the choke points where the sea lanes could be closed.

Central America is strategic to our Western alliance, a fact always understood   24
by foreign enemies. In World War II, only a few German U-boats, operating from
bases 4,000 miles away in Germany and occupied Europe, inflicted crippling losses
on U.S. shipping right off our southern coast.

Today, Warsaw Pact engineers are building a deep-water port on Nicaragua's   25
Caribbean coast, similar to the naval base in Cuba for Soviet-built submarines. They
are also constructing, outside Managua, the largest military airfield in Central America—similar to those in Cuba, from which Russian Bear bombers patrol the U.S. East
Coast from Maine to Florida.

How did this menace to the peace and security of our Latin neighbors—and   26
ultimately ourselves—suddenly emerge? Let me give you a brief history.

In 1979, the people of Nicaragua rose up and overthrew a corrupt dictatorship.   27
At first the revolutionary leaders promised free elections and respect for human rights.

But among them was an organization called the Sandinistas. Theirs was a Communist organization, and their support of the revolutionary goals was sheer deceit. Quickly and ruthlessly, they took complete control.

Two months after the revolution, the Sandinista leadership met in secret, and in what came to be known as the "72-hour document," described themselves as the "vanguard" of a revolution that would sweep Central America, Latin America and finally the world. Their true enemy, they declared: the United States. 28

Rather than make this document public, they followed the advice of Fidel Castro, who told them to put on a façade of democracy. While Castro viewed the democratic elements in Nicaragua with contempt, he urged his Nicaraguan friends to keep some of them in their coalition—in minor posts—as window dressing to deceive the West. That way, Castro said, you can have your revolution, and the Americans will pay for it. 29

And we did pay for it. More aid flowed to Nicaragua from the United States in the first 18 months under the Sandinistas than from any other country. Only when the mask fell, and the face of the totalitarianism became visible to the world, did the aid stop. 30

Confronted with this emerging threat, early in our Administration I went to Congress and, with bipartisan support, managed to get help for the nations surrounding Nicaragua. Some of you may remember the inspiring scene when the people of El Salvador braved the threats and gunfire of Communist guerrillas—guerrillas directed and supplied from Nicaragua—and went to the polls to vote decisively for democracy. For the Communists in El Salvador it was a humiliating defeat. 31

But there was another factor the Communists never counted on, a factor that now promises to give freedom a second chance—the freedom fighters of Nicaragua. 32

You see, when the Sandinistas betrayed the revolution, many who had fought the old Somoza dictatorship literally took to the hills, and like the French Resistance that fought the Nazis, began fighting the Soviet bloc Communists and the Nicaraguan collaborators. These few have now been joined by thousands. 33

With their blood and courage, the freedom fighters of Nicaragua have pinned down the Sandinista Army and bought the people of Central America precious time. We Americans owe them a debt of gratitude. In helping to thwart the Sandinistas and their Soviet mentors, the resistance has contributed directly to the security of the United States. 34

Since its inception in 1982, the democratic resistance has grown dramatically in strength. Today it numbers more than 20,000 volunteers and more come every day. But now the freedom fighters' supplies are running short, and they are virtually defenseless against the helicopter gunships Moscow has sent to Managua. 35

Now comes the crucial test for the Congress of the United States. Will they provide the assistance the freedom fighters need to deal with Russian tanks and gunships—or will they abandon the democratic resistance to its Communist enemy? 36

In answering this question, I hope Congress will reflect deeply upon what it is the resistance is fighting against in Nicaragua: 37

Ask yourselves, what in the world are Soviets, East Germans, Bulgarians, North 38

Koreans, Cubans and terrorists from the P.L.O. and the Red Brigades doing in our hemisphere, camped on our own doorstep? Is that for peace?

Why have the Soviets invested $600 million to build Nicaragua into an armed   39
force almost the size of Mexico's, a country 15 times as large, and 25 times as populous? Is that for peace?

Why did Nicaragua's dictator, Daniel Ortega, go the Communist Party Con-   40
gress in Havana and endorse Castro's cause for the worldwide triumph of Commun-ism? Was that for peace?

Some members of Congress asked me, Why not negotiate? Good question—   41
let me answer it directly. We have sought—and still seek—a negotiated peace and a democratic future in a free Nicaragua. Ten times we have met and tried to reason with the Sandinistas. Ten times we were rebuffed. Last year, we endorsed church-mediated negotiations between the regime and the resistance. The Soviets and the Sandinistas responded with a rapid arms buildup of mortars, tanks, artillery and helicopter gunships.

Clearly, the Soviet Union and the Warsaw Pact have grasped the great stakes   42
involved, the strategic importance of Nicaragua. The Soviets have made their de-cision—to support the Communists. Fidel Castro has made his decision—to support the Communists. Arafat, Qaddafi, and the Ayatollah have made their decision—to support the Communists. Now, we must make our decision. With Congress' help, we can prevent an outcome deeply injurious to the national security of the United States.

If we fail, there will be no evading responsibility; history will hold us accountable.   43

This is not some narrow partisan issue; it is a national security issue, an issue   44
on which we must act not as Republicans, not as Democrats, but as Americans.

Forty years ago, Republicans and Democrats joined together behind the Tru-   45
man Doctrine. It must be our policy, Harry Truman declared, to support peoples struggling to preserve their freedom. Under that doctrine, Congress sent aid to Greece just in time to save that country from the closing grip of a Communist tyranny. We saved freedom in Greece then—and with that same bipartisan spirit we can save freedom in Nicaragua today.

Over the coming days, I will continue the dialogue with members of Congress,   46
talking to them, listening to them, hearing out their concerns. Senator Scoop Jackson, who led the fight on Capitol Hill for an awareness of danger in Central America, said it best: On matters of national security, the best politics is no politics.

You know, recently one of our most distinguished Americans, Clare Booth   47
Luce, had this to say about the coming vote.

"In considering this crisis," Mrs. Luce said, "my mind goes back to a similar   48
moment in our history—back to the first years after Cuba had fallen to Fidel. One day during those years, I had lunch at the White House with a man I had known since he was a boy—John F. Kennedy. 'Mr. President,' I said, 'no matter how exalted or great a man may be, history will have time to give him no more than one sentence. George Washington—he founded our country. Abraham Lincoln—he freed the slaves and preserved the union. Winston Churchill—he saved Europe.'

" 'And what, Clare,' John Kennedy said, 'do you believe my sentence will be?'   49

"Mr. President," she answered, "your sentence will be that you stopped the   50
Communists—or that you did not.' "

Tragically, John Kennedy never had the chance to decide which that would be.   51
Now, leaders of our own time must do so. My fellow Americans, you know where I
stand. The Soviets and the Sandinistas must not be permitted to crush freedom in
Central America and threaten our own security on our own doorstep.

Now the Congress must decide where it stands. Mrs. Luce ended by saying: 52
"Only this is certain. Through all time to come, this, the 99th Congress of the United
States, will be remembered as that body of men and women that either stopped the
Communists before it was too late—or did not."

So tonight I ask you to do what you have done so often in the past. Get in touch   53
with your representatives and senators and urge them to vote yes; tell them to help
the freedom fighters—help us prevent a Communist takeover of Central America.

I have only three years left to serve my country, three years to carry out the   54
responsibilities you have entrusted to me, three years to work for peace. Could there
be any greater tragedy than for us to sit back and permit this cancer to spread, leaving
my successor to face far more agonizing decisions in the years ahead? The freedom
fighters seek a political solution. They are willing to lay down their arms and negotiate
to restore the original goals of the revolution. A democracy in which the people of
Nicaragua choose their own government, that is our goal also, but it can only come if
the democratic resistance is able to bring pressure to bear on those who have seized
power.

We still have time to do what must be done so history will say of us, We had the   55
vision, the courage and good sense to come together and act—Republicans and
Democrats—when the price was not high and the risks were not great. We left
America safe, we left America secure, we left America free, still a beacon of hope to
mankind, still a light onto the nations.

Thank you and God bless you.   56

CHAPTER 13

Structural Strategies

When writing an argument, we must make important decisions about where to position its various parts. Should the strongest evidence come first or last? Why do some arguments open with the proposition and others postpone it until later? Should the refutation invariably follow the confirmation? As always, subject, purpose, and audience will determine which arrangement we should use since no single structure works in all situations. Structure is a matter of strategically positioning the parts in an argument, like troops in a battle, where they will have the greatest impact.

Classical Structure

The classical structure of argument, so called because it was practiced by the ancient Greeks and Romans, is still a frequently used form and can be effective with certain audiences. We study it because it offers an easy-to-follow, prefabricated form that has proved to be an excellent way of arranging argumentative material. We study it also as an inventional device. If we consider the individual parts of this comprehensive structure, we will have covered all the elements of argument and will likely generate approaches for presenting our ideas and evidence. The classical structure consists of the following parts:

> Introduction
> Background
> Confirmation
> Concession
> Refutation
> Conclusion

We should remember, however, that this is not a soufflé recipe; we do not have to use all of the ingredients or to place them in the order of the classical structure. If, for example, the audience is familiar with the background, we can omit that section. Sometimes we can even make the body of the essay all refutation. We have numerous possibilities available and should not become locked into one rigid structure.

Introduction

An introduction to an argument should accomplish several goals. As discussed later (see pages 724–732 for types of introductions), an introduction to any essay should gain readers' attention, announce the subject, establish the significance of the issue, and set the tone. The introduction to an *argument* must also make readers receptive to a point of view that they may consider controversial or even contrary to their own opinion. It is essential that we quickly gain their trust and make them open to what they are about to read. In order to create a favorable disposition toward us and our proposition, we must impress upon the readers our good will and our selfless interest in truth. In addition to creating a favorable ethos at the outset, we should appeal to readers' interests in order to establish a bond between them and ourselves so that they will accept us, our judgment, and ultimately our proposition.

A major consideration in an argumentative introduction is how much to announce about the proposition. Should we state our thesis outright, or should we announce only the subject to be discussed and reserve our thesis till later? In the classical structure, an essay opens with the proposition; there are situations, however, when delaying the proposition is more prudent and effective (see page 502–505).

The placement of the proposition depends on the *readers'* attitude toward that proposition. If the readers are *uncommitted* to a view, and if they are *unprejudiced* toward our proposition, we should consider opening with a direct statement of the proposition. Examine, for instance, the advantages of beginning a newspaper editorial with this direct assertion:

> The Supreme Court of the United States, at the seeming peak of its powers, badly needs reform.
>
> —From Arthur S. Miller, *The Washington Post*, Jan. 11, 1976

Advantage 1: This opening highlights the proposition. There is no chance of the main point becoming lost amid proofs and premises. The editorialist's opinion here is inescapably clear, and he has firmly implanted it in the readers' minds. Furthermore, the tone from the very beginning of the argument is one of confidence; the strong opening statement carries with it a sense of conviction and assures readers of the depth of the writer's belief.

Advantage 2: Unlike the openings of essays that delay the proposition, this opening immediately orients readers so that they know what to expect in the editorial. Especially if the subject is complex and will be difficult to follow, the proposition-first approach helps readers to keep clearly in their minds how our individual proofs and minor propositions relate to the whole argument. The writer shows them an overview before giving the evidence; that way, when readers encounter a piece of evidence, they relate it to the main proposition and see how it fits into the whole argument. They are better able to evaluate the proofs when they know what the proofs are supporting.

In a delayed-proposition structure, on the other hand, readers do not know the main point of the argument until late in the argument. This means they must mentally store evidence piece by piece until the end. For some readers, such retention is a struggle and a hardship. The other problem with the delayed proposition is that readers may not understand the proofs because they do not yet understand the purpose of those proofs.

Therefore, to ensure clarity and to help readers, the classical structure opens with the proposition. The writer poses the proposition as a hypothesis at the beginning, proves that hypothesis in the body of the argument, and restates it as a conclusion:

Hypothesis
Proof
Conclusion

This general-to-specific structure is perhaps the most common method of presenting an argument, but *it is most effective with neutral or favorable audiences.*

Placing the proposition up front is especially useful when we wish to advocate a new approach to a problem. Our strategy is to cite the inadequacies of previous views and then to offer a fresh solution. By citing previous failures, we dismiss those analyses and provide a context for our own thesis, which comes at the end of the first paragraph or the beginning of the second.

How should one go about assessing the degree of sophistication of a given society— the Greek, say, or nineteenth-century Europe, or the present-day world community? A purely economic assessment is one way, in terms of gross product and so on. This method is useful in comparing slightly different conditions of society, this year with last year. But it tends to fail badly if we use it to compare widely different conditions. It failed to assess the true strength of Russia in the period between the two world wars. It failed to assess the recuperative power of Germany after the Second World War.

A quite simple method, one that contains no very great measure of sophistication it is true, but one that never seems to go far wrong, is given by the rate of energy consumption. Energy consumption has increased more or less exponentially over the last few centuries. There is a good one-to-one correspondence between energy consumption and technology.

—From Fred Hoyle, *The New Face of Science*

A similar writing situation arises when we wish to demonstrate that our case has been misstated by the opposition or misunderstood by the public. This might be effective even with an antagonistic audience because what we are saying to them is that their opinion of us is based on incorrect information and distortion. Here, for example, is how a senator might try to correct a mistaken view of his or her policy:

Although the liberals have implied that I advocate a substantial cut in next year's budget for social programs, they have misunderstood, or even intentionally distorted and misrepresented, my budgetary recommendations. Actually, I have recommended a 6 percent increase in educational, medical, and welfare programs. The liberals are angry that I have proposed a larger increase in the defense budget in order to keep up with the increased military spending of the Soviets. Because we have fallen behind in the arms race, we must allocate more funds for defense over the next several years, or we must resign ourselves to continued communist intervention in Asia, Africa, and the vital Mideast.

This clarification allows the writer to restate his or her view and perhaps also to cast doubt on the opposition's credibility.

Another time to open with the thesis is when that thesis is novel or perhaps shocking, as in this editorial suggesting that the United States should reserve its food for its own citizens:

The United States should remain an island of plenty in a sea of hunger. The future of mankind is at stake. We are not responsible for all humanity. We owe more to the hundreds of billions of *Homo futurans* than we do to the hungry millions—soon to be billions—of our own generation.

—From Johnson C. Montgomery, "The Island of Plenty," *Newsweek*, Dec. 23, 1974

Such a thesis challenges the reader to question a traditional belief. Our strategy in this case is to astonish readers and to lure them by our boldness. It whets their curiosity because they want to know why we make such a statement and how we can back it up.

Background

The background material, which comes after the introduction, provides readers with the facts necessary to understand the argument. Just as a district attorney's first duty is to inform a jury of the relevant circumstances in a case, so too must we give readers information that will enable them to understand the issue.

The amount and kind of background that we provide depends on the extent of the readers' sophistication and their current knowledge of our subject. Sometimes we can omit this stage of an argument because the readers are familiar with the issue. If they are not familiar with it, though, the background is an essential step because it enables them to understand and evaluate our proofs. Even an audience familiar with the facts may appreciate a brief summary.

Nobel economist Milton Friedman, arguing that the government should not use concealed taxes to compensate for reductions in visible taxes, puts his topic into perspective by summarizing American requests for government to cut taxes:

The widespread tax revolt has already led seven states to adopt constitutional amendments limiting taxes or spending by state and local governments. Similar provisions are pending in most of the other states. It has led some 30 states to request Congress to convene a constitutional convention to propose an amendment requiring a balanced budget. It has led the National Tax Limitation Committee (NTLC) to draft an amendment to the U.S. Constitution to limit spending. The amendment has been introduced in Congress by bipartisan sponsors and has been endorsed by more than 1.2 million citizens who have signed petitions being circulated by the NTLC.

—From "Our New Hidden Taxes," *Newsweek*, April 14, 1980

The kind of background material needed will vary from case to case. Usually we outline the issues and explain the circumstances; sometimes we must also explain the principles involved in the issue. We might define crucial terms ("How many a dispute could have been deflated into a single paragraph," Aristotle said, "if the disputants had dared to define their terms"). The background conceivably could describe a procedure, such as how acid rain affects lakes, or it could explain an administrative structure, telling who is responsible for what. Often background is a history of a movement or a narration of events leading up to the current situation, as in this example concerning a Supreme Court ruling that amplified an earlier decision:

That earlier ruling held that a public figure claiming to have been libeled by published or broadcast material must show the material was prepared with malice, in the sense of "reckless disregard for truth." It is not sufficient to show that errors were published or broadcast.

This week's ruling authorizes public figures who seek to prove the existence of malice to call journalists to testify under oath concerning their personal state of mind while preparing an allegedly libelous news article or broadcast.

—From *The Ann Arbor News*, April 20, 1979

Brevity, clarity, objectivity: these are the virtues of background material. We want to keep it as succinct as possible because we do not want readers' attention to flag early in the argument; hence, we eliminate all but the most relevant facts. Because understanding the rest of the argument depends first on understanding the issue, the background must be presented in a clear style, and relationships and concepts must be explicit. Also, we must present the facts as objectively as possible in order to convince readers of our fairness. We don't want to color the facts or attempt to interpret them at this point.

The background, in short, prepares readers for our evidence by giving them a context, orienting them to the subject, setting forth pertinent facts, and bringing them up to date on the situation. Our goal is to inform uninformed readers or to remind informed readers by giving an overview of the facts. Our purpose at this stage is to instruct, not to persuade.

Confirmation: Proving the Argument

Whereas in the background stage we report facts, in the confirmation stage we evaluate facts. The confirmation is the body of the argument, where we prove our proposition. We lay out our logic and present the various sorts of evidence—testimony, analogy, statistics, and so forth—as discussed in Chapter 11.

We convince in three ways: through the arguments themselves (how ingenious we are at discovering them), through our style, and through the arrangement of the arguments. It is the last of these—the internal arrangement of the arguments—that we will now consider.

The most common structure for presenting our evidence is a hierarchy. Such an arrangement gradually builds from the least to the most important, the effect being that the argument gains strength as it progresses so that at the end we have reached the strongest argument. Each argument must be slightly stronger than the preceding one to keep readers' interest mounting and gradually to overwhelm readers with evidence. An argument should build up momentum and should intensify in strength and pace.

An inherent drawback, however, in starting with the weakest argument and growing progressively stronger is that the beginning of the confirmation stage is low in interest. Because it comes immediately after the background stage, which also tends to be a little flat and lifeless, there is a possibility of losing momentum and, with it, our readers. To prevent reader apathy, we might start with our *second* strongest argument, then pick up the *least* strong and advance progressively toward the *strongest:*

> Introduction
> Background
> Confirmation
>   second strongest argument
>   least strong
>   fourth strongest
>   third strongest
>   strongest

In other words, instead of presenting the order 5, 4, 3, 2, 1 (1 being the strongest), try 2, 5, 4, 3, 1. This solves the decline in interest yet retains the sense of mounting to a climax. It also places the lesser arguments in the middle, where they are less conspicuous; they contribute to the proposition by their number, not their placement.

In the confirmation, it is important that we show readers the stages of thinking that lead to the conclusion. They must understand how each argument relates to the main proposition. Also, they must perceive each argument as being separate and distinct instead of as a disorganized clump; if they can see the arguments as distinct, they will retain a sense of the variety of our arguments and be able to mark off the stages of thought. No single argument should be extended so much that it interferes with the momentum or the progression of ideas. Furthermore, if several minor arguments individually do not carry enough weight to be worthy of development, we can put them together in one paragraph and use them as one collectively forceful step in the argument.

The confirmation stage is mainly an appeal to reason. Although one step of this section may be an emotion-packed example, in general the confirmation should be directed to the intellect. Our goal is to convince readers of the inherent justice and the inescapably sound reasoning of our proposition.

Concession

To *concede* means to acknowledge the opposition's strong points. The question is, should we concede those points or should we conceal them? Many students feel that acknowledging the adversary's strengths introduces the opposition unnecessarily and also undermines the writer's own argument. They ask, and rightly so, "Why should a writer bring up the other side's strengths?"

A case can be made for including a concession. In fact, instead of being detrimental to our argument, concession can be rhetorically effective, and evading evidence that is damaging to our side can be detrimental. If readers are familiar with the opposition's argument, and if we fail to acknowledge the strengths in that argument, readers will probably assume that either (1) we hold our view because we fail to see the advantages of the other side or (2) we are trying to deceive them by suppressing the truth. By conceding certain inescapable points, we let readers know that we see both sides but that the opposing side's few advantages do not outweigh its many disadvantages or our side's many advantages. Readers have a new respect for us because of our honesty and our knowledge of the issue—our ethos gets a boost. They realize that we are aware of the complexities of the discussion we have initiated. Furthermore, if readers later encounter the other side's strong points, they are less likely to shift their loyalty from us to the other side.

The dilemma with concession is how to acknowledge the truth of the opposition's valid points without giving them undue emphasis and without weakening our own argument. The solution is (1) to concede only one or two points, (2) to subordinate those points within our own discussion, and (3) to come back always with a series of our own strong points. A concession should be followed by a "But . . ." that lists either the opposition's weaknesses or our strengths. We deemphasize the concession by placing it between two proofs of our own argument. That way, we can give the devil his due without hurting our case.

The following concessive paragraph comes from a book that successfully exposes and attacks the multinational grain companies' monopoly of the world grain market. After admitting in the first paragraph that the trade companies have helped some countries, the author goes on in the second paragraph to show how they have also created hunger and economic dependence. He allocates one paragraph to concession and the rest of the chapter to attack:

It would be wrong to suggest that the unprecedented growth of the America-centered postwar grain trade is without its benefits. It often has helped hungry people avoid starvation, and it has helped economies to modernize and progress during times of international change, development, and recovery from war. American food has been a source drawn upon by almost every country in the world. The world would be quite unrecognizable today without American grain surpluses—and quite likely a less happy and hospitable place than it now is.

But fundamental questions have not been resolved in the global food economy. Foremost among those are the questions of how to reform the system to make it more responsive to the needs of the poor, the malnourished, and the vast majority of underprivileged peasants.

—From Dan Morgan, *Merchants of Grain*

Another approach is to concede not the opposition's strong points but our weak points. We should use this strategy, however, only if we can show that the apparent weakness is actually not a weakness at all. For example, in an essay on rising medical costs, a physician concedes in one paragraph that health costs have increased more than other costs, "But," he adds in the next paragraph, there is a good reason:

Medical care has gone up also. The cost of medical care for each American has increased to 244 per cent of 1967 levels, whereas the cost of all consumer goods and services has gone up somewhat less to 223 per cent of 1967 levels.

But this comparison, which suggests that the cost of medical care has risen faster than other costs, is misleading. It ignores a vital and often overlooked distinction: whereas the cost increase of most goods and services since 1967 has been for products that were available but cheaper then, today's medical care is very different from that fifteen years ago.

—From Joel Posner, "What Price Health?" *Newsweek*, Dec. 10, 1979

Dr. Posner goes on to point out that while food, clothing, cars, and houses are not much better today than they were in 1967, today's medical care is far superior to that of 1967. People are paying for improved service, and that is a good reason to pay higher prices.

When we bring up a concession, we should remind the reader of two things. First, our side has more advantages; second, that one objection to our proposition does not invalidate our proposition, which is still by far the better solution.

Refutation

To *refute* means to prove something incorrect. In the refutation section of an argument, we (1) defend our proposition against the other side's charges and (2) point out the weaknesses in their proposition.

All of us are familiar with the idea of refutation because we use it in daily discussions. For example, imagine that a person innocently asks a friend what his weekend plans are, and the friend replies that he is going deer hunting. Because the first person opposes hunting, a friendly argument gradually arises about the issue, with each person defending his viewpoint and attacking the other's viewpoint. We eavesdrop on the conversation:

Hunter: I like hunting because I enjoy being outdoors, tromping through the morning woods, feeling at one with nature.

Nonhunter: How can you feel at one with nature if you're out there killing nature's creatures? A person doesn't have to kill animals to enjoy the outdoors. I'm an outdoor person as much as you, but I don't hunt.

Hunter: Yeah, but there's something thrilling about hunting. Last weekend, for instance, I bagged a beautiful 8-point buck.

Nonhunter: That's barbaric. And you're going back to kill another defenseless deer this weekend? Hunting is such a wasteful sport. Senseless slaughter has almost eliminated the buffalo; has made endangered species of the grizzly bear, whooping crane, and mountain lion; and has made extinct the Eastern elk and the passenger pigeon.

Hunter: I agree that the excessive hunting in the nineteenth century was senseless. But since the creation of modern wildlife programs—many founded by hunting organizations—not one species has been threatened with extinction. In fact, the return of the buffalo and the transplanting of elk, antelope, and bighorn sheep are in large part due to enlightened hunting organizations.

Nonhunter: These "protective measures," as hunters call them, are doubly cruel: You merely transplant herds to kill them.

Hunter: Is it more cruel to kill a deer than to kill a cow so long as one eats the meat? Society lives on beef that is raised solely for consumption. Just because you entrust the killing to the butcher doesn't change the fact that you're responsible for the killing.

Nonhunter: But cows aren't wounded and don't suffer lingering deaths the way crippled deer do and the way ducks die of lead poisoning from buckshot.

Hunter: If hunters didn't harvest the excess animals, the whole herd would suffer, and animals would starve during the winter. Hunting is essential for balanced populations. You speak of a lingering death—starvation is the cruelest death I know of. By maintaining a stable animal population, hunters are simply continuing man's natural role over the millenia as predators.

Nonhunter: If hunters wouldn't kill natural predators like the mountain lion and grizzly bear, there would be a natural balance in the animal world. Furthermore, natural death takes the weakest animals, leaving the healthiest to live and breed. Hunters, however, kill the healthy animals, the "trophies," like your 8-point buck.

Hunter: You simply don't understand the spiritual nature of hunting, the sense of totem, the primitive ritual being acted out in
confronting an animal in its own habitat, of participating in an
age-old tradition and recapturing the spirit of the frontier life of
America.

Nonhunter: You're absolutely right, I don't understand why any
civilized, mature adult would take joy in invading an animal's
habitat with a high caliber rifle and bushwacking defenseless
animals. It is a sport to convince insecure men that they are
macho.

Both the hunter and the nonhunter offer evidence to support their views
(confirm), they answer the other's charges (defend), and they point out
weaknesses in the other's thinking (attack). While a written argument is
not a direct debate because the opponent is absent, the opponent is
nonetheless real; if there were no opponent, there would be no argument
since argument is based on a difference of opinion.

Defending Against Opponent's Attacks

If the opposition has attacked parts of our argument, and if readers are
familiar with those attacks, we must counter them in order to dispose of
readers' doubts about the soundness of our proposition. Ignoring those
charges is like admitting that they are true. For example, in his bid for the
presidency, Ronald Reagan realized that his age had become an issue.
Noting that at 69 he would be the oldest inaugurated president, critics
questioned his mental and physical endurance. Reagan knew that ignoring their persistent verbal assaults would be damaging to his campaign,
and therefore his aides came up with an ingenious refutation: Because life
expectancy has increased by 20 years in the last 150 years, Reagan at age
69 was physically and mentally younger than such former presidents as
John Adams (61), Jackson (61), Taylor (64), Buchanan (65), and Harrison
(68).

Occasionally it is possible to turn an attack around and to reverse
the accusation. The best defense, the adage goes, is a strong offense. For
example, if the opposition contends that our proposition will result in
financial hardship for the public, we turn the accusation around and point
out that in actuality the opposition's proposition will cause a financial
hardship because it does not alleviate a long-term problem. Another
effective reversal is to show that what the opposition has labelled a
disadvantage within our argument is really an advantage. For instance,
when the Federal Aviation Administration proposed deregulating the
airline industry, critics argued that airlines would discontinue service to
cities that had few air passengers. The FAA responded that it was true

that airlines might drop such unprofitable routes or decrease the number of flights; in fact, the FAA said, that was one of the intentions of deregulation. By dropping unprofitable flights, the airlines would be able to lower prices on other flights. A similar example arose during the civil rights movement when whites labelled Martin Luther King, Jr. an extremist. King decided that the best way to deal with the label was not to deny it but to make it an attribute. He pointed out that Jesus Christ, Saint Paul, Martin Luther, John Bunyan, Thomas Jefferson, and Abraham Lincoln were extremists, also. "So the question is not whether we will be extremists, but what kind of extremists we will be," King stated. "Will we be extremists for hate or for love? Will we be extremists for the preservation of injustice or for the extension of justice?"

We refute some charges with logic and evidence, we dismiss some with irony, and we let others pass without refutation. We must use our judgment in each case.

Attacking Opponent's Proposition

Student writers often question whether they should try to refute the opposition's main points or simply ignore them. Studies suggest that it is better to confront and dispose of the opposition, regardless of whether readers know the opposing view. If readers are well informed on the issue and are familiar with the competing view, we must show them the deficiencies of that view before they will finally accept our view. Exposing the fallacious reasoning of the opposition enhances our case in comparison. We prove our case, then disprove the other case.

Even when readers are unaware of the opposing view, however, we should introduce and confute it in order to make readers more resistant to later persuasion from the opposition; this is what psychologists call *attitude immunization.* For example, if you had not heard the common argument for capital punishment that capital punishment is justified on the basis of tradition, you might consider that to be a good justification if you read it in an argument advocating the death penalty. If, however, you had encountered that line of reasoning in an argument *against* capital punishment, in which the writer had refuted that reasoning, you would not likely accept it when you later read it in the argument advocating capital punishment. You would have been exposed to it and immunized. Here is a refutation by former Supreme Court justice Abe Fortas from an argument against capital punishment.

It is also argued that capital punishment is an ancient sanction that has been adopted by most of our legislatures after prolonged consideration and reconsideration, and that we should not override this history.

But the argument is not persuasive. If we were to restrict the implementation of our Bill of Rights, by either constitutional decisions or legislative judgments, to those practices that its provisions contemplated in 1791, we would indeed be a retarded society. In 1816, Thomas Jefferson wrote a letter in which he spoke of the need for constitutions as well as other laws and institutions to move forward "hand in hand with the progress of the human mind." He said, "We might as well require a man to wear still the coat which fitted him when a boy, as civilized society to remain ever under the regimen of their barbarous ancestors."

—From "The Case Against Capital Punishment," *The New York Times*, Jan. 23, 1977

One way of attacking the opposition is to point out the logical fallacies that they use, such as false analogy, flag-waving, and a false either/or situation. By citing a case of false causation, the author of the following piece effectively undermines one proposition of his opponent's argument:

A 1971 study at England's Cambridge University confounds one of the most widely believed non sequiturs: "Banning handguns must work, because England does and look at its crime rate!" (It is difficult to see how those who believe this can resist the equally simple-minded pro-gun argument that gun possession deters crime: "Everybody ought to have a machine gun in his house because the Swiss and the Israelis do, and look how low their crime rates are!")

The Cambridge report concludes that social and cultural factors (not gun control) account for Britain's low violence rates. It points out that "the use of firearms in crime was very much less" before 1920 when Britain had "no controls of any sort." Corroborating this is the comment of a former head of Scotland Yard that in the mid-1950s there were enough illegal handguns to supply any British criminal who wanted one. But, he continued, the social milieu was such that if a criminal killed anyone, particularly a policeman, his own confederates would turn him in. When this violence-dampening social milieu began to dissipate between 1960 and 1975, the British homicide rate doubled (as did the American rate), while British robbery rates accelerated even faster than those in America. As the report notes, the vaunted handgun ban proved completely ineffective against rising violence in Britain, although the government frantically intensified enforcement and extended controls to long guns as well. Thus, the Cambridge study—the only in-depth study ever done of English gun laws—recommends "abolishing or substantially reducing controls" because their administration involves an immense, unproductive expense and diverts police resources from programs that might reduce violent crime.

—From Don B. Kates, Jr., "Against Civil Disarmament," *Harper's*, Sept. 1978

In addition to undermining one individual point, an effective refutation undermines the opponent's credibility on all other points. Readers will begin to question the opposition's command of the facts: If they were wrong on one proof, they could be wrong on others. This, in fact, is one of the goals of refutation—to discredit the opposition without resorting to personal attack.

In the refutation section of an argument, we try to discredit the opposition by disproving their argument. Rather than attacking each proposition and piece of evidence, we usually select those individual errors and inconsistencies in their argument that will demonstrate to readers that our opponents are unreliable sources. For instance, in an editorial refuting former Congresswoman Bella Abzug's accusation that the federal government is ignoring an urban crisis in America, columnist George F. Will casts doubt on her information and credibility:

It is frequently said by Ms. Abzug and others that "70 percent of Americans live in cities." True, any place with 2,500 people is officially classified as an "urban place." More pertinent facts are: The percentage of Americans living in cities of 250,000 or more is about what it was in 1920. Population density in urban areas has declined from 5,408 per square mile in 1950 to 3,376 in 1970. Thirty percent of Americans live in central cities, down from 35 percent twenty-five years ago. Most parts of most central cities are not in what can properly be called a "crisis."

—From "The Dispersal of Cities," *The Pursuit of Happiness, and Other Sobering Thoughts*

Knowing *which* arguments to refute depends on the importance of each argument and the nature of our audience. Refuting every argument is unnecessary; in fact some arguments cannot be refuted, as in the earlier debate over hunting, in which each side decided not to refute one of the other's arguments. We usually choose one or two that are particularly important to our intended audience and concentrate on disproving them.

Knowing *how* to refute particular arguments will be determined by the arguments themselves and our own ingenuity. Although there is no formula for attack, it helps to focus on one or more of these areas: our opponents' methods of reaching the goal; the goal itself; their evidence; and their logic. We want to demonstrate the following points about our opponents:

Their methods are expensive or unjust.
Their goal is selfish, unjust, short-sighted, or dangerous to the readers or their institutions.
Their statements are uninformed, untrue, or contradictory.
Their logic is unsound (either one of the premises is false or the conclusion does not follow from the premises).

Examine these examples of how to attack an idea:

> Critics of the federal government claim the bureaucracy has become so large that its goals have become contradictory. They point out that at the same time that the Department of Health and Human Services is carrying on a strong antismoking campaign, the Department of Agriculture is subsidizing tobacco farming.

> Advocates of active euthanasia say that an inconsistency exists in society's laws about euthanasia. To allow passive euthanasia and to reject active euthanasia is inconsistent because both are in effect decisions to end a painful and hopeless life. What is the moral difference, they ask, between withholding treatment or taking away a life-support system on the one hand and injecting a fatal drug on the other?

> Skeptics of women's ability to serve in combat-related roles are referred to precedents: American women fought bravely against Indians in the 1800s, Israeli women are used in the military and perform heroically, and American female pilots flew bombers from the United States to European bases in World War II.

APPLICATION

How would you refute the following arguments?

1. Women should not be paid the same salary as men because men, being heads of households, need to make more money to support their families. (Refute this idea in several ways.)
2. At the Constitutional Convention in 1787, Benjamin Franklin argued against paying the president and other federal officials because high salaries would attract persons of questionable motives. Franklin believed that the honor of serving one's country and the respect conferred by the office should be sufficient reward, and he noted that George Washington had served 8 years as General of the Army without pay, as did the High Sheriff in England and the Counsellor in France. If you had been present at the Convention, how would you have refuted his proposed amendment to the Constitution?
3. Convicted murderers should be executed. It is more humane to end their misery than to cage them for life. Besides, it's expensive—$25,000 a year—to keep a prisoner, and the prisons are already severely overcrowded.
4. Guns are more dangerous to others than are barbiturates, but anyone can buy a gun, and barbiturates are given out only with a medical prescription.

Conclusion

The conclusion of a persuasive essay differs from the conclusion of other essays in that it often uses emotion and seeks to motivate.

At the end of an argument, after we have laid down our reasoning and proofs, we frequently can reinforce that reasoning by adding emotion to it. Emotional appeals at the end of an argument elevate the readers' belief. The *reasoning* should convince readers of the justice and worth of our proposition, but the *emotion* stimulates them and drives home the point. The proper emotion depends on the situation; sometimes pity is effective, sometimes fear, and sometimes, as in the conclusion of Winston Churchill's Dunkirk address, patriotism:

I have, myself, full confidence that if all do their duty, if nothing is neglected, and if the best arrangements are made, as they are being made, we shall prove ourselves once again able to defend our Island home, to ride out the storm of war, and to outlive the menace of tyranny, if necessary for years, if necessary alone. At any rate, that is what we are going to try to do. That is the resolve of His Majesty's Government—every man of them. That is the will of Parliament and the nation. The British Empire and the French Republic, linked together in their cause and in their need, will defend to the death their native soil, aiding each other like good comrades to the utmost of their strength. Even though large tracts of Europe and many old and famous States have fallen or may fall into the grip of the Gestapo and all the odious apparatus of Nazi rule, we shall not flag or fail. We shall go on to the end, we shall fight in France, we shall fight on the seas and oceans, we shall fight with growing confidence and growing strength in the air, we shall defend our Island, whatever the cost may be, we shall fight on the beaches, we shall fight on the landing grounds, we shall fight in the fields and in the streets, we shall fight in the hills; we shall never surrender, and even if, which I do not for a moment believe, this Island or a large part of it were subjugated and starving, then our Empire beyond the seas, armed and guarded by the British Fleet, would carry on the struggle, until, in God's good time, the New World, with all its power and might, steps forth to the rescue and the liberation of the old.

—From *Blood, Sweat and Tears*

Usually it is preferable to balance emotion and logic. Although we want to stimulate readers, we mainly want them to remember our sound reasoning when they later think about the issue in an analytic, dispassionate mood.

Several options are available for closing an argument (in addition to those enumerated on pages 736–740):

1. Restatement and reinforcement of the proposition and main proofs. By encapsulating in general terms the points we have made throughout the argument, we reemphasize those ideas that we want readers to remember. For example, in an editorial that asks "Are Lab Courses a Waste of Time?" the author summarizes his beliefs in the concluding paragraph:

By offering a genuine, unvarnished scientific experience, a lab course can make a student into a better observer, a more careful and precise thinker, and a more deliberate problem solver. And that is what a college education is all about.

—From Miles Pickering, *Chronicle of Higher Education*, February 19, 1980

2. A call for action or for a new attitude.   In these conclusions, we encourage readers to view an issue in a new light and to adopt a new policy toward the subject. Usually these conclusions are recommendations; they call for and offer a correction to the current way of doing business. For example, in an essay entitled "Opportunity in Adversity," the writer calls on national leaders to adopt a new psychology, to be less pessimistic, and to have greater faith in Americans' ability to adjust to hardships:

I believe it is essential that economists, politicians and journalists learn to understand just how capable most people are of responding in positive ways to change. "Future Shock" notwithstanding, people not only survive, they adapt. They make the best of things. When the President mandates lower building temperatures, sweaters become not merely a necessity but the hottest thing in fashion. We have this immeasurable capacity to make an opportunity of adversity, and it is incumbent upon our leadership to capitalize on that and not to sabotage it.

—From Arnold Brown, *Newsweek*, April 7, 1980

3. Warnings.   Occasionally we might wish to end an argument by pointing out the negative consequences that will ensue if our proposition is not acted on. This is basically an appeal to fear, for we hope to motivate readers by showing the harmful effects of neglecting the issue. Here is the conclusion to an argument urging military action against terrorist groups:

> If we do not strike out against terrorist organizations in their training camps, they will strike out at us. The U.S. has been fortunate that terrorist acts have not occurred here, but it is just a matter of time. Acts of sabotage, assassination, and general bloodshed will happen in our country if we don't take stronger action against these fanatics now.

4. Inference drawn.   In an argument that reserves the thesis until the end, the conclusion states explicitly what the evidence in the body of the argument has been leading to. For example, in an argument against United States intervention into foreign affairs, Pulitzer Prize editorialist Robert Lasch ends the essay by drawing the conclusion he has been building up to throughout the essay:

Between the two world wars, our country retreated into isolationism, which failed. After the second war we swung to the other extreme, becoming an international busybody bent on directing the course of social and economic development everywhere in the world. This policy, too, has failed.

It is long past time that we began walking the middle road, which means accepting our full responsibilities as a decent (and wealthy) world citizen, while leaving it to the people of every country to pursue their own destiny, socialist or otherwise.

—From "Lessons of Korea and Vietnam," *Newsweek*, Feb. 18, 1980

Alternative Structures

Although the classical structure offers a convenient mold for arguing, we should recognize that it is not always the most appropriate structure. To assume that all arguments should follow this design is to assume that all audiences, issues, and situations are alike. Just as an architect would not build one kind of house and force homeowners and their family, furniture, and dog into it, architects of persuasion should not unthinkingly use a prefabricated form that is effective only in certain cases.

The classical structure is particularly effective with audiences who have little knowledge of or opinion on an issue, but it isn't as effective with audiences who are already informed to some extent. It became the standard structure in antiquity because of the nature of classical speeches: The speaker, a learned person, was addressing the populace, who were uneducated and needed a comprehensive explanation and analysis. Today in America, because of mass education and mass media, citizens are better informed. Arguments, therefore, must take into account readers' current knowledge and opinion.

Of the two basic ways of conducting and arranging an argument—the direct approach and the indirect approach—the classical structure is a direct approach. It opens with the proposition, outlines it, and then proves it: one, two, three—as straightforward as a sermon. The indirect method, however, delays the major proposition until we gain the readers' confidence and until they have accepted assumptions that will lead to the proposition.

Although the placement of the proposition—at the beginning or at the end of the argument—might seem to be an inconsequential and arbitrary decision, it is actually the structural key to our whole argumentative strategy for reaching a particular audience. Placing the proposition at the head of the argument works well for neutral readers; but for readers whose opinions differ from ours, the proposition-first approach can cost us the argument before they finish the first paragraph. The reason is this: People seldom read arguments against their own viewpoints. Therefore, if we open our argument with a blunt declaration of the proposition, hostile readers will immediately know that we are advocating what they think is the wrong view, and they will read no further.

Delayed Proposition

In cases when we ascertain that our proposition is contrary to the readers' current opinion, we should postpone stating the proposition. We may announce the *issue*, but we should not yet reveal our viewpoint on that issue until we have gained their confidence. Before readers will listen to us, they must feel that we are nonthreatening. We want them to recognize us as an ally, and to that end we assist them to see an alignment between their views and ours. Once they accept us as an ally, they will be more relaxed, less skeptical, and more receptive to our ideas. If we can get readers who are predisposed against our thesis to listen to us for a while—to open their minds, if only a centimeter—we have a chance of convincing them. And the best way to gain a hearing is to proceed gradually to the proposition. Instead of appearing to argue, we appear to analyze objectively and disinterestedly the issue at hand. Our stance should be that of an investigator, not that of a debater.

In the process of investigating the issue, our strategy is to analyze the issue point by point and to make minor conclusions as we proceed. We lead readers through the steps of our reasoning and through the facts, from one truth to another, in a chain that leads inevitably and naturally to the conclusion. The readers draw the conclusion at the same time that we appear to, and they accept it because they have discovered it with us. The investigation has been a kind of joint adventure in evaluation. In fact, a major reason for choosing the delayed proposition approach is to allow readers to undergo the process of discovery that we originally underwent.

An indirect argumentative approach can take one of several forms: options, installments, principles, or concessions. All four share the advantages of opening with a point of agreement with the readers and of postponing our proposition until we have gained the readers' favor and trust. Also, each progresses gradually from analysis into pure argument.

Options

The strategy here is to list the various ways of viewing a situation, explain them individually, and weigh their advantages and disadvantages. This strategy is particularly effective when there are several competing solutions to one problem. We present all options as if our purpose is not to advance a predisposed opinion but to discover which option is the best. We assume the character of an investigator who is exploring and evaluating the solutions, though in fact we have of course discovered in advance which is the best solution. Nevertheless, this approach has the psychological advantage of inviting readers to share in our analysis and evaluation and to deliberate with us the possible plans.

For example, in an address to the nation concerning which energy source the United States should invest in for the future, a president might explain the pros and cons of each source: oil (problems: limited supply, cost, OPEC); coal (problems: air pollution and health hazard, strip mining); nuclear (problems: nuclear waste disposal and nuclear accidents); and synthetic fuels (problems: cost, still in research stages). After extensively discussing these possible alternatives and pointing out their weaknesses, he or she would turn to his or her preference—solar energy—and list its advantages: unlimited and accessible, clean, safe, and inexpensive once the initial cost is defrayed.

The structure of this argument-by-options approach is called *elimination of alternatives.* We evaluate and reject in turn all of the plans competing with our solution. Although we present advantages as well as disadvantages with each option, we emphasize the weaknesses of the alternatives and show that our plan has more advantages and fewer disadvantages than the others. The elimination of alternatives takes this form:

A. Enumeration and brief explanation of options
B. Option 1 and its weaknesses
C. Option 2 and its weaknesses
D. Option 3 and its weaknesses
E. Our solution and its strengths

A similar structure when there are only two plans, ours and an alternative, is:

A. Explanation of both sides
B. The alternative and its weaknesses
C. Our plan and its strengths

(This is a whole-to-whole comparison/contrast structure, which we discussed in Chapter 6.)

Installments

In this approach, instead of each segment of the argument being another option, each segment is one part of the proposition to be proved. As the eighteenth-century rhetorician Richard Whately suggested, "it will often be advisable to advance very gradually to the full statement of the Proposition required, and to prove it, if one may so speak, by instalments; establishing separately, and in order, each part of the truth in question." The argument is a chain of reasoning that we advance in stages, each step often building on the previous ones and leading to the major proposition. As with the options approach, we do not commit ourselves by stating the proposition until we have laid down the proof. Although this tactic will not guarantee acceptance of the thesis, it at least prevents immediate rejection.

This is an inductive structure: It explains the issue, presents the proofs, and then draws the conclusion, which is the main proposition.

A. Explanation of issue
B. Proof 1
C. Proof 2
D. Proof 3
E. Conclusion (which follows from the evidence presented)

Principle-first, or Deduction

In this approach, we begin with a broad principle that we believe the readers will endorse, then apply that principle to the issue under discussion, and at the end of the argument draw the conclusion, which is our thesis. By opening with a basic principle that readers agree with, we secure a reading of our argument; most people will read an argument that they think will lead them to a conclusion to which they are predisposed. Once readers have accepted the opening premise, they place themselves into the position of accepting all propositions based on that principle. There is a subtle psychological pressure exerted here because if the readers accept the principle but not the application of it, they must admit to being either illogical or hypocritical, neither of which makes for a comfortable self-image.

This is the strategy that civil rights leaders used in the 1960s when they appealed to whites based on the moral principle that all persons are created equal and on the religious principle that we are all God's children. The strategy was intended to place segregationists in a moral dilemma: They had to deny the principles or grant blacks their equal rights. A similar approach was used in *The Declaration of Independence.* The first few paragraphs of the Declaration lay down the principles upon which the argument will proceed: Everyone has certain inalienable rights; governments are formed to protect those rights; when a government destroys those rights, the people may form a new government. The structure of this approach is that of a deductive syllogism:

A. Major premise (an accepted principle)
B. Minor premise (an assertion that must be proved)
C. Conclusion (the thesis)

Concession-first

Sometimes, to gain hostile readers' confidence, it is politic to open with an affirmation of the opposition's valid points. Although hostile readers will not likely listen to a direct statement of our thesis, they will listen to an argument that coincides with their own views; therefore, it is essential that these readers perceive us initially as being *on their side*. Once they are assured that we are rational (because we think as they do), we say: "But wait a minute; the other viewpoint has some interesting evidence and deserves consideration." We thereby gain access to their minds and then gradually move from the opposition's strengths to its weaknesses, and finally to our own proposition, whose merits become obvious as we enumerate the proofs. With this structure, the proposition occurs not at the end but near the middle:

A. Concession
B. Refutation
C. Proposition
D. Proofs

APPLICATION

Examine the following newspaper editorials to discover which delayed-proposition structure they use.

1. This first editorial discusses the 55-mile-per-hour speed limit. With which side of the issue do most Nevadans agree? Where is the proposition, and why is it placed there instead of elsewhere? Of the four approaches—options, installments, principles, and concessions—which one or ones does the writer employ?

Once again, the 55-mile-per-hour speed limit is under attack in the West, where the miles stretch out forever—and so does the time for drivers pushing their way across endless and desolate stretches of landscape.

The issue conjures up states' rights, wasted hours, wasted lives, and wasted gasoline. Like Billy Martin in the televised beer commercial, it is easy to feel strongly both ways.

A number of western states feel strongly one way: they claim the law makes no sense in their wide-open regions. They also feel very strongly that the federal government has no business dictating speed limits to them.

This feeling is especially strong among Nevadans, who never had a state speed limit to contend with before the 1973 oil crisis and the federal law that grew out of it. Nevadans were accustomed to flooring the pedal when they hit the road and getting their long drives over with as quickly as possible. There's no doubt that the law—if obeyed—makes long-distance travel more tedious.

It is also true that federal interference is an especial irritant to Nevadans, who dislike federal ownership of large blocks of land and IRS attempts to collect income tax on tips, to name just two areas of contention.

So many Nevadans will be pleased to see that bills have been introduced in both the Assembly and the Senate to get rid of the 55-mile-per-hour speed limit in this state. AB 252, introduced by Michael Fitzpatrick of Las Vegas, would eliminate all reference to the 55-mile speed limit, and would in effect leave Nevada with no limits at all. SB 176, introduced by Keith Ashworth of Las Vegas, would raise Nevada's state speed to 65 miles per hour.

But despite the joy these proposals will create, there is much to be said for opposition to them.

For one thing, there is no doubt that lower speed limits have increased traffic safety. This is not just an idle statistic, with little relevance to our everyday lives. It relates directly to every person who gets behind the wheel of a car. It means that when you're out on the road, you're a little safer from yourself and a little safer from the other guy. Time is important, but not as important, perhaps, as lives and whole bodies.

Of course, not everyone is driving 55 and under. But even those who exceed the speed limit generally drive slower than they did when there was no limit. If the speed limit is raised, the speeders can be expected to drive even faster; and if there is no limit, there will be a mass return to high and dangerous speeds.

And the accident rate will climb.

Then there's the energy problem. Gasoline remains a once-only commodity. Nobody knows how much fuel is out there under the ground, but it will run out someday. The more we save now, the longer we will have it around. And, as we all know, there is no truly effective alternative power source on the horizon for automobiles.

Also, the deteriorating political situation in the Mideast could lead to another gasoline shortage at any time. This nation could see gas rationing or long lines at service stations, and not enough fuel to go around. Yet Nevadans, like other Americans, have not yet taken to heart the need to conserve.

Any number of national leaders have stressed the need for some sacrifices in the energy area, not only to conserve but to help this nation reduce its burdensome trade deficit and help bolster the dollar internationally. Yet Nevadans, like other Americans, have not yet taken to heart the need to conserve. It is time they did, and one way to do so is to drive more slowly.

So at this point in time, the needs of safety and conservation seem to outweigh states' rights and convenience. The wiser course would be to retain the 55-mile speed limit, at least for the time being.

—From *Reno Evening Gazette,* Feb. 4, 1979

2. This next editorial concerns Congress' allocating several million dollars of the defense budget for development of chemical weapons. Analyze the structure and the writer's reasons for using this particular structure.

Both the Senate and the House have voted overwhelmingly in favor of a $3 million fund to build a new plant capable of producing weapons for chemical warfare.

Both houses must take further action on the proposal because it surfaced in two separate bills. Before final action can be taken, however, the continued debate is certain to split the nation into two mutually antagonistic camps, divided along emotional if not strategic lines.

Proponents, as well as critics, will acknowledge that chemical warfare, particularly the use of nerve gas, is most horrible to contemplate. At that point agreement ends, and persuasion moves in opposite directions.

The measures contemplate the construction of a plant at Pine Bluff, Ark., which would be capable of producing binary nerve gas. . . . The binary process provides for the production of two components which, of themselves, are harmless but which, when mixed together, become toxic. The mixing would take place only after the firing of the artillery shell containing the components in separate chambers. This process renders the storage, transportation, handling and ultimate detoxification of the chemical weapon relatively safe.

Proponents of renewed production of U.S. chemical weapons insist the measure is necessary to counter the Soviet Union's chemical weapon superiority. U.S. intelligence has promulgated redundant evidence that Soviet forces have used nerve gas and, probably, other chemical weapons in the course of their military action in Afghanistan.

Furthermore, four years of negotiations has failed to generate a word of agreement between the United States and the U.S.S.R. in their quest for a treaty limiting or prohibiting the use of chemical weaponry.

It is difficult to refute the argument of Sen. Gary Hart, D-Colo., that the United States should give first priority to defensive measures to protect its own troops, not to mention friendly civilian populations, from chemical warfare. Proponents argued, of course, that in the absence of a viable defense, the capability of the United States to retaliate in kind would be the strongest deterrent to the use of chemical weaponry by a potential enemy.

We find greater merit in the arguments of Rep. Jack Edwards, R-Ala., and Sen. Henry M. Jackson, D-Wash.

Said Edwards: "It is a terrible weapon, but this is a terrible bill. I wish we did not have to discuss nuclear destruction and these other (chemical) programs. But we have to live in a real world."

Sen. Jackson insisted that seed money for the proposed Pine Bluff plant is not a commitment to produce nerve gas but, instead, a four-year moratorium offering both opportunity and incentive for progress toward a chemical arms treaty. Then he added: "This debate is not of bricks and stones. It's of how you negotiate with the Soviet Union, and you don't deal with them from a position of inferiority."

—From *Albuquerque Journal*, Sept. 20, 1980

The Ethics of Indirection

Is concealing or camouflaging our proposition dishonest? Although it lacks the straightforwardness that we associate with truthfulness, and although it is based on cunning rather than on openness, it is neither distortion nor falsification. We can perhaps rationalize the practice by saying that beginning any discourse with a point of agreement rather than disagreement is a matter of diplomacy and good manners. Even more to the point, though, is the justification that, by delaying our opinion until we have laid a foundation favorable to communication, we help readers to overcome their own prejudice. Our motivation is not only to advance our cause, but also to enrich the readers and to show them a truth that they will not even read unless they are coaxed into it.

Extensive Refutation

In addition to the delayed-proposition approaches, two other alternatives to the classical structure are sometimes effective. Like the classical structure, these are direct, proposition-first structures, but instead of following the classical pattern exactly, they emphasize the refutation stage.

The first of these is an alternating confirmation/refutation structure, which, instead of reserving all the refutations till the end of the argument, interweaves the refutations with the proofs. The time to use this structure is when we feel that the readers know the opposing arguments so well that, instead of paying attention to the forcefulness of our arguments, they will be preoccupied considering objections to our side. If they are already distracted by the arguments of the other side, we should make use of their preoccupation and turn it to our advantage. As we present a minor proposition, we should also anticipate and rebut the objections to it and attack the deficiencies of the other side on this point. The strategy is defense and attack, defense and attack, defense and attack. This approach forces readers to confront the strengths of our side and the weaknesses of the other side on every issue. The readers accept our proofs more readily once we dispose of a contending view that they have in mind. With this point-by-point confirmation/refutation, we build up our own case by demolishing the opposing case. As with every other structure, this one puts the evidence where it counts for a particular type of audience.

A. Introduction
B. Background
C. Proposition 1 and refutation
D. Proposition 2 and refutation
E. Proposition 3 and refutation
F. Conclusion

Usually refutation is one stage of a multidimensional argument, or, as in the structure above, a supporting element, but it can be the basis for a whole argument. This approach is especially effective when the opposition has attacked and distorted our view; in response, our best strategy is to meet each accusation with a counterstatement. Our goal is to correct fallacious statements and to present a side that the opposition omitted or distorted. After correcting and dismissing the distortions, we go on to present our full argument:

A. Introduction
B. Refutation of distortion 1
C. Refutation of distortion 2
D. Refutation of distortion 3
E. Confirmation
F. Conclusion

The procedure is to open with the objections to our point of view and then to counter each objection. This has the advantage of capturing the attention of the undecided and the hostile readers, both of whom are interested in seeing how we can refute the opposition.

Here are two arguments that employ a refutative strategy. After stating his thesis, each writer lists the objections to that thesis.

The four main arguments advanced against the death penalty are: 1. punishment for crime is a primitive idea rooted in revenge; 2. capital punishment does not deter; 3. risk; 4. a civilized state, to deserve its name, must uphold, not violate, the sanctity of human life.

I entirely agree with the first pair of propositions. . . . The uncontrollable brute whom I want to put out of the way is not to be punished for his misdeeds, nor used as an example or a warning; he is to be killed for the protection of others.

—From Jacques Barzun, "In Favor of Capital Punishment," *American Scholar*, Spring 1962

A writer must decide which arguments to refute among the ones the opposition offers. Barzun, for example, chooses to attack only the second two; his attempt in the essay is to demonstrate that those who oppose capital punishment are illogical, naive, and inconsistent in their views.

A similar strategy is taken in an essay by Senator Edward Kennedy; the entire essay is in the form of a refutation. This is the opening of the essay, in which he outlines the objections against his proposition:

The arguments used to oppose gun controls are old and hackneyed. The same lament has been used in one of the following forms time and time again:

First. Gun controls cannot limit the supply of guns enough to reduce violence.

Second. The Constitution protects the citizen's right to bear arms.

Third. There is no need to ban guns because guns are not killers; people do the killing.

Fourth. Criminals will always find a way to obtain guns. Thus, controls will only disarm those who obey the law.

Fifth. Registration and licensing procedures are so cumbersome and inconvenient that they would create unfair burdens for legitimate gun owners.

Opponents of effective gun controls believe that these objections are valid. But a thorough examination of each of these claims reveals that not one of them is well founded.

—From "The Need for Gun Control Legislation," *Current History*, July/Aug. 1976

Kennedy then tackles each objection and offers evidence against it.

Exercises

Below are eight questions concerning controversial issues. Select one issue about which you have a strong opinion, and use the journalistic questions to generate facts and reasons to substantiate your view. Then write two outlines for your argument: one for a hostile or skeptical audience, the other for a more sympathetic audience. Briefly discuss which type of structure you use for each audience, and give your rationale for choosing each structure.

1. Should students be given representation on faculty committees that decide tenure and promotions for professors?

   possible audiences: the college board of directors
                        the faculty senate
                        the college student government

2. Should your state impose mandatory life sentences in prison for habitual criminals? (The term *habitual criminal* would require definition, such as a person convicted of five felonies or four violent crimes.)

    possible audiences: a liberal state legislator
    the local police association
    your English class

3. To encourage voter turnout, should national elections be switched from Tuesday to Sunday, when most people do not work?

    possible audiences: your parents
    the League of Women Voters
    a minister

4. Should parents be allowed veto power over teachers' textbook selection in public schools?

    possible audiences: the school board
    a concerned parent group
    average newspaper readers

5. Should a spouse who has stayed home, raised the children, cooked for the family, and kept the house be entitled to a portion of his or her working spouse's pension if the couple divorces?

    possible audiences: your mother
    your father
    a local labor union

6. Should the federal government (specifically, the Federal Communications Commission) have the power to regulate television programming to the extent of requiring the major networks to offer a minimum number of hours of educational programming for children?

    possible audiences: parents of young children
    viewers in general

7. Should the President prohibit Americans from visiting a foreign country that is hostile to the United States, such as Libya or Iran?

    possible audiences: students on your campus
    a local travel club
    your senator

8. Should the federal government give tax breaks to parents who send their children to private schools?

possible audiences: the local parent-teacher association
                      parents with children in private schools

CHAPTER 14

Proposals

Proposals usually take one of two forms: (1) requests, such as a request for an exemption or for funds, or (2) solutions to problems. Anyone with an idea worthy of financial backing or with a solution to a vexing problem needs proposal-writing skills. An executive may recommend to the president of the company a way of increasing productivity or sales; a scientist may request research money from a corporation or endowment; citizens may put forward an idea on which they wish their city council to act. Presenting our ideas in a convincing, thorough, and clear manner is mandatory if our proposal is to be put into action.

The goal of other types of argument may simply be to change readers' attitudes, but the purpose of a proposal is to get readers to act. "The finest eloquence is that which gets things done," the British statesman David Lloyd George said. In that case, proposal writing is the most eloquent form of argument; a proposal is a bid for change and a blueprint for implementation.

A proposal can be one section of an argument, or it can stand alone. As part of a longer argument, it comes as the final step: The first section is an evaluation of the current situation and problem, the next step is an argument in favor of a particular view of the problem, and the last phase is a proposal that outlines changes. When there is agreement that a problem exists and that a particular goal is desired, we can dispense with steps 1 and 2 and present only the proposal.

Invention

Usually we don't have to search for a proposal topic—it finds us. Proposals spring from needs: Either we need something (money for a project, approval from an official) or we see a correctable flaw in a system. Since all of us have many needs and live in an imperfect world full of imperfect systems, finding a need to fulfill shouldn't be too much of a problem. For example, one afternoon while standing in line at the college administration building, waiting to straighten out a computer foul-up or a billing problem, you become fed up with the run-around you're getting and say to yourself: "What the college *should* do is appoint one person in each administrative section as an ombudsman (mediator) to take care of students' complaints and problems." There is your proposal. Write it up and send it to the appropriate official.

All the gaps between the way things *now* work and the way things *ought* to work are subjects for proposals. We have to reflect on all the gaps between what is and what should be in our daily encounters with the college, public transportation, the local police, the facilities for the elderly in our community, and so on. Our own experiences and frustrations are our best source for finding holes that need to be filled with intelligent solutions.

Using the journalistic questions should help us to think of the defects in systems that we have encountered in our community. The two main questions are "What needs to be changed in _____ ?" and "What is a better way?" Other questions are "Who is empowered to make change?" "What kinds of appeals can I make to this person?" and "What objections to my proposal will he or she have?"

Appeals to Use

Because readers judge proposals mainly on their expediency (is the proposal easy to implement?) and utility (is it useful?), those are the qualities a proposal writer should stress. The proposal that benefits the greatest number of people in the fastest and most economical way will win approval. Since utility is a priority, we should emphasize practical benefits rather than stressing the moral superiority or the purely intellectual benefits of our proposal. For example, if we were to propose an extensive lunar exploration program, we should base our argument not on the broadening of theoretical knowledge but on the practical benefits that could result: beaming down to earth large quantities of solar energy in the form of microwaves, controlling air traffic, surveying crop production and weather and military installations, using a lunar base for mining asteroids, and colonizing.

Emotional appeals are effective but should be subordinated to practical benefits. The writer can appeal to reader emotion in personal requests—for example, by stressing a personal situation such as finance or health. In problem-solving proposals, appeals to public virtues—patriotism, altruism—can be effective.

Anticipating and Countering Readers' Objections

More than with any other kind of argument, readers of a proposal look for drawbacks to our plan. At every conceivable point they will look for obstacles that can thwart our plan, and if they find any, they will conclude that the plan will not work. Sometimes even a minor objection can change readers' minds or can give skeptical readers an excuse to dismiss our proposal. We must therefore anticipate and refute those snags so that readers will not have the opportunity to say no. We must make them an offer they can't refuse.

The way to invalidate objections is to give a blueprint of our idea that is so detailed that it considers all possible challenges to implementing the idea. The plan must explicitly state what steps are to be taken, what the reasoning is for each step, how a particular action will be done, and who will do what. For example, if you are proposing a new course in your department, go to various professors and ask them whether they have the expertise and the desire to teach such a course; if they respond positively, put their responses in the proposal. This takes away the chairperson's objection: "Oh, it sounds like a good idea, but we don't have anyone qualified to teach or interested in teaching it." Besides taking away the readers' chance to veto our idea, we are informing them and, by doing all the investigating, performing a service for them.

Arguing by Precedent

The most effective evidence that a writer can muster in a proposal is to cite a precedent because that eliminates the opposition's rebuttal: "It can't be done." The precedent proves beyond a doubt that it can be done because it has been done. The readers' only reply to citing a precedent is to claim that the situations are not comparable; therefore, we have to demonstrate the similarity of situation for the precedent to be effective.

Once the precedent is established, it can even serve as a model. For instance, if you are planning on holding a fund-raising event to convert an old building into a teen canteen, you can cite what a neighboring community did and follow their success. Judge for yourself how precedents work in real life examples:

> In a proposal that the phone company include in its public directories of all major cities an emergency medical guide explaining what to do in case of heart attack, electrical shock, choking, burns, or poisoning, the writer points out that this is being practiced currently by Pacific Telephone and Telegraph.

A group of concerned citizens goes before the local judge, who is known to be a staunch conservative in juvenile sentencing, with a proposal to find alternatives to juvenile sentencing. He listens as they unfold a plan whereby misdemeanor offenders are referred to a court diversion program. To his skeptical "I doubt if such a plan will have much community backing or if it will work," the group produces a petition signed by 2,000 residents and endorsed by businesses, fraternal organizations, local attorneys, and churches. Then they cite precedents: the East Palo Alto Community Youth Responsibility Program in California; the Family Reception Center in Brooklyn; the La Playa Center for Orientation and Services in Puerto Rico. Because the group has done a thorough job researching and has come loaded with ammunition, the judge can hardly deny their request. He agrees to a pilot program, loosely using those programs as models.

A group of engineering and business majors presents a plan to the college administration: As a special project, they propose to study the college's structure, operations, equipment, and expenditures in order to find ways of improving services and reducing costs. In addition to helping the college, the students would gain practical experience. If a college is truly a learning institution, they argue, it should let students try their skills. The college should utilize its own resources (i.e., students) and make use of the expertise and intelligence at its disposal. Then they cite precedents: (1) Daytona Beach Community College allowed students in its technical school to work on the campus' air conditioning and heating equipment to give them practical experience; the result was also better service and lower heating and cooling bills, a savings of $37,000 in one year; (2) SUNY—Albany invited its graduate students in business administration to analyze the campus administration and, as a result, saved an estimated $43,000 as well as improving organization and efficiency.

Types of Proposals

Request proposals and solution proposals share basic characteristics, but they differ enough in their intent to warrant separate consideration. In fact, even the two types of request proposals—personal requests and grant requests—will be discussed separately because they differ in audience and content.

Request Proposals

Whether we are writing a personal request or a grant proposal, the elements we should stress are our intentions, our reasons for wanting to do whatever it is we are proposing, and the benefits to be derived from the proposal. Also, the evidence we use in both types of requests is usually information we gather through interviews with people instead of through library research.

Personal Requests

On the most personal level, a proposal can be a private request. These are usually characterized by a one-to-one appeal, often in the form of a letter, and can be anything from a petition that the dean exempt you from a course to a plea that your dad quickly send you $100. Because of the personal nature of these requests, they use emotional appeals more frequently than other types of proposals, though they should be based firmly on sound reasoning and convincing evidence.

The best way to demonstrate the "how-to" of proposal writing is to walk through the process on several examples to see the decisions that occur at each stage and the ways of gaining approval. For the first instance, imagine that you are a biology major who has applied for work at and been accepted by a medical research center near the college. You would like to get academic credit for the work, but the center is not an educational institution. Your first step is to find out whether the possibility exists of treating the work as an internship. After contacting the appropriate persons on campus and at the medical research center to obtain relevant information, you write your proposal to the chairperson of your department.

Dear Professor Howard:

I have an opportunity to work with a biological research institute in the vicinity, the Reedick Center, under the renowned Dr. J. R. Bancroft. I am a senior in Biological Sciences with a grade point average of 3.67.

Because such practical experience will broaden my understanding of my discipline, I am requesting your approval for the University to award academic credits for the work. In order to accommodate experiences like this, the University provides two mechanisms, and I seek your advice as to which would be more appropriate. According to the

[margin notes:]
Introduction of topic and self
Mention of famous researcher
GPA included to establish credentials

Thesis: the plea

Deference: "seek your advice"

Experiential Learning Center, credits could be awarded through their program under ELC 486 and 487. Or, within the Biological Sciences department, I could arrange an independent studies project (BIO 499) sponsored by a professor, for example, Dr. Daniel Watkins. Because the actual work pertains to the major, I prefer the second option, but I leave the decision to you. Precedents certainly exist in either case: Last year the department accepted field experience for five different projects, and other science departments on campus have a standardized mechanism, administered by the chief academic advisor, to allow for these types of experience.

Options outlined—a service to readers; options make it easier for them to say "yes" simply by choosing one

Preference inserted

Precedents showing that this is standard operating procedure

I feel that the department has prepared me to meet such an opportunity. As you can see from the attached transcript, I have taken most of the required courses to complete my major and several additional advanced laboratory courses. I plan to complete the final courses next year: Biochemistry and Lab III and Pathogenic Microbiology in the fall, Biochemistry and Lab IV and Virology in the spring. However, I would like to substitute my experience at the institute for Lab IV because that experience will duplicate the lab course curriculum. Lab IV, according to the course description, investigates "the chemistry and metabolism of nucleic acids, carbohydrates, proteins, and lipids." These are the kinds of experiments that I will be performing at the Center.

Emphasizes department's role

Attach relevant documents

Details of the request and rationale for substitution

Quotation from official document

In addition to providing appropriate study and experience in microbiology, Reedick would introduce me to the newest equipment and most current research and would allow me to work with another set of great minds. Their research in bacterial genetics and microbial fermentations is widely known. This type of research is particularly applicable to my education because I plan to focus on immunology in graduate school.

Convincing reasons enumerated

Application to specific goal

This prestigious institute takes two interns each year, out of over 100 applicants. (Attached is a copy of the Center's acceptance.) The interns' duties will be to prepare and classify slides, to assist in experiments, and to write up results, and they will work directly under Dr. Wayne Federick Scott, who has supervised the internship program for eight years in association with colleges throughout the nation. (I have the honor of being the first student from our college accepted into the internship program.) He will provide monthly evaluations to my academic advisor and submit a final evaluation at the end of the term. In addition to being supervised and evaluated, I would write a ten-page paper each term outlining my experience and would submit my lab experiments.

Indicates the distinction of the award

Description of duties

Length of program, implying its validity

Means of evaluation provided

Realizing that experiences at nonacademic institutions present some technical problems, I offer some tentative solutions for your consideration. The number of academic credits awarded for such work logically should depend upon the actual number of hours at the Center and upon comparable credits for college course work. The internship stipulates a minimum of 12 hours per week for 36 weeks. Usually academic labs award 1 credit for 3 hours of lab; 4 credits per term would therefore seem appropriate, 2 to substitute for Lab IV, 2 for electives or special topic courses. The grade would be awarded by a faculty sponsor based on the evaluation and the paper. Because the evaluation will be by a nonfaculty member, perhaps a precise letter grade would be difficult to determine; therefore, I would accept a pass/fail grading option if you think that is more appropriate.

Admission of potential difficulties, with solutions suggested

Rationale for number of credits

The logic and math of the suggestion

Willingness to compromise

I have discussed this opportunity with my faculty advisor, Dr. Watkins, and it was he who encouraged me to petition you because he said that it would be great preparation for graduate school and for work in biochemical research. The combination of classroom and work experience will give me an ideal education, the kind that the University itself no doubt would like to provide if it had the money and facilities. Professor Watkins views the experience as analogous to a doctor's internship or an engineer's apprenticeship: It is the practical experience that comes from on-the-job training in a stimulating environment. It is the kind of experience, too, that Dean Kolmerten referred to recently as "balancing the theoretical and the pragmatic, joining the University and the professional fields."

Faculty member's endorsement makes rejection more professionally and politically difficult

Analogy

Testimony by higher ranking official

The question is not whether I should accept the internship, but whether I can afford to accept it. If I do not receive academic credit for the experience, I may not be able to accept. I must take 14 credits each semester because I am on a Senatorial scholarship, but I do not believe that I can take a full credit load on campus and work at Reedick and perform both at a level of excellence. In addition, because the scholarship is for only 8 semesters, I cannot postpone my graduation one semester since my family is unable to finance my education.

Personal appeal: reasons explaining that if plea is rejected, student cannot accept opportunity (puts burden on chairperson)

Considering the advantages of such an educational opportunity and also considering my personal dilemma, I urge you to accept my work at the Reedick Center for academic credits.

Respectfully,

Richard Miller

Enclosures

If you were the department chairperson, would you accept this student's request? Can you think of any objections to it that the writer has not countered?

Grant Requests

Grant proposals are a means of securing financial backing for a person or group to research or implement an idea. Quite simply, we have the idea but not the money. The federal government, corporations such as Mobil Oil, Ford, and Xerox, and various nonprofit foundations support research and creativity by funding projects that they deem worthwhile to society. These are sources that creative thinkers should be aware of so we can put into motion our plans to improve the world an iota. Competition for funds is intense, however. What distinguishes one grant proposal from another is not only the originality and usefulness of the idea, but also the presentation of that idea. No doubt many worthwhile ideas have died because the originators' written proposals weren't sufficiently persuasive to gain the necessary financial support.

After we have our idea, we need to pinpoint a funding agent. Consulting several reference works will help to identify an appropriate sponsor:

Directory of Research Grants lists foundations, by field of interest, that award money for research projects to either individuals or organizations.

Catalog of Federal Domestic Assistance gives information concerning, among other things, grants offered by the federal government.

Annual Register of Grant Support is a thorough catalog of grant programs sponsored by government and private endowments, by fields of interest.

Foundation Grants to Individuals lists over 1,000 foundations that contribute to persons seeking financial promotion for research.

Once we locate several possible grantors, we should write to them requesting specific information about their grants: purpose, necessary qualifications, application form if needed, scope of grant, types of grants (some are highly specialized, some broad), and duration of grant. If possible, we should obtain a sample written proposal that was funded by that agency in the past. After receiving the agency's response, we can follow its directions and a few basic principles about grant writing. We should:

Try to tailor the written proposal to the agency's specifications, showing how our proposal fits into its stated objective. We must stress the connection between our idea and the agency's purpose.

Emphasize the benefits to be derived.

Specify our means of assessing the success of our project as well as specifying our objectives.

Provide a detailed budget of everything from personal stipend to travel expenses and photocopying.

Give a descriptive but brief title.

Present the logic of why the agency should fund us. Much of our proposal might be a justification of our request for funds: originality of idea, probable results, the need for such work.

Set a feasible timetable.

Outline our idea in a step-by-step form.

Let's say that you are a fine arts major—music, dance, art, or drama—and you want to form a performance group—a classical quartet, a small modern dance company, a mobile gallery, or a small acting company. You have the talent, but you need funds, audience, performance space, and official backing. Let's say, specifically, that it is a seven-member dance company. Here are the preliminary steps you might go through before setting pen to paper. First, approach a faculty member who likely will act as a sponsor or artistic director; if he or she agrees that the idea has merit, you and the sponsor go to the dean, who perhaps will be willing to allocate some money from the college budget for a pilot program. The main financing, you realize, must come from other sources. After days of thinking about funding, you hit on the idea of a college-affiliated company to serve the entire state educational system. Because it would be statewide, you can solicit funds from the State Board of Education; because it is an arts program, you can also solicit funds from the State Council for the Arts, whose responsibility is to promote the arts in your state. After calling the respective offices to request information about available funds and application procedures, you sit down to write a proposal to the State Council for the Arts. These are the considerations: what the agency's needs are, whether there is a modern dance company already in the region, how much money you would need, how the money would be spent, whether company members would be paid, how your project would promote dance in the state, how often and where you would perform, and who would be members. After working out the particulars in your own mind, you write several drafts until you come up with the following proposal.

Dear Council Members:

I am requesting guidance and funds from the State Council for the Arts to form a modern dance company to serve the people of our state. Because dance is one of the fine arts that your agency

Thesis ("guidance" included to gain favor of Council)

promotes, and because currently there are only ballet companies within the state, I believe that this proposal is worth consideration.

I propose to establish a semiprofessional, seven-member modern dance company that will tour within the state, performing at intermediate schools, high schools, colleges, and community playhouses. The best way to promote the arts, it seems to me, is to cultivate an appreciation for them within young people. An exposure to the arts at an early age improves the likelihood of people enjoying them throughout their lives. Youngsters have interest and curiosity when they attend a concert, unlike adults who, unless they have been educated to the art form, are often closed-minded. The period at which to cultivate their aesthetic sensibility, and in this case an appreciation of movement and form, is at the stage when they are still forming their tastes.

Education about dance is what our group will provide. At various schools throughout the state we will give lecture/demonstrations that define modern dance and explain its vocabulary, both in words and in movement. After such a demonstration, we will answer questions from students and perform two short pieces from our repertoire.

The company will be providing an educational experience not only to young people within the state, but also to the company members. Performance experience for the members, who are college juniors and seniors, will provide them an opportunity to continue their professional growth. This, too, falls under the aegis of the Arts Council: "The Council has responsibility for developing artistic talent within the State by awarding grants, arranging for apprenticeships, and organizing community artistic programs" (from the Council charter). As the members graduate from college and advance from semiprofessional to professional status, the company membership will change, allowing new members to gain experience. We might make a provision, however, to retain one graduating senior each year to perform half-time with the company and to teach half-time at the college. This person, who will act as dance captain, will be paid, but the other members will simply receive academic credit for their time. Developing teachers is yet another way of promoting the discipline.

Precedents for such college-associated modern dance groups are UCLA and the University of Maryland. Faculty members within my own college have volunteered to work in various capacities, including Chairwoman Dorine Sprague as artistic director and Ms. Florence Miller as rehearsal mistress. The college has officially endorsed the

---

Marginal annotations:

Establishes the uniqueness of this company within the state

Proposal encapsulated

Rationale presented: education through early exposure

Typical school performance outlined

Additional educational benefits

Quote from official document applies Council's own policy to this situation

Minor but relevant details explained, suggestions offered

How members will be rewarded

Again aligning proposal to Council's purpose

Precedents

Listing faculty volunteers implies that the department endorses the project

project and has even contributed a small amount ($500) to help launch the company. However, because we will serve the entire state and not just the students of this college, Dean Covalt feels that principal financing should come from a state agency. Because of the company's dual role—performing and teaching—we are requesting equal funds from the Arts Council and the State Department of Education. Dr. Sharon Edwards, Commissioner of Education, has given initial approval, but we need funds from both agencies in order to operate.

Official backing lends credibility and respect
Rationale for state funding
Noting that one agency has approved it increases likelihood of approval here

Although our annual budget will be $20,000, we are requesting only $7,500 from the Council. With an equal sum from Education, we will still lack $5,000, which we plan to raise from business and personal contributions, the college, and admission to our public concerts— several community playhouses have already voiced an interest in our performing. We arrive at the total amount by computing our anticipated expenses:

Presenting larger figure first makes $7,500 seem small
Accounts for additional funds

transportation (use once weekly of a minibus; gasoline for approximately 6,000 miles a year)	$1,600
costume material and maintenance (we will design and make costumes)	800
fee to choreographers (we will choreograph most of the dances, but would like to buy perhaps two dances per year from professional companies)	2,000
part-time stage manager	4,500
part-time lighting director	4,500
half-time teacher/dance captain	5,000
miscellaneous (insurance, scenery, guest dancers)	1,600
	$20,000

Itemized costs, all possible expenditures included
Communicates to Council that proposer has carefully thought out the idea and has a good head for business

We think that, considering the performance schedule and the extensive work, this is a modest budget. We realize that because of state tax reforms the Council's budget has been limited and that competition for funds is intense, but how many projects guarantee an annual audience of over 75,000?

Recognition of funding shortage, but appeal by numbers

Modern dance is almost nonexistent in the state, and therefore many people have little idea of what it is. Of the major arts, modern dance is the least represented. Yet people are interested in it. For example, last year the Paul Taylor Company and this year the Nikolais Dance Theater performed to full houses in the capitol.

Need and interest illustrated

Examples cited

The good that can come out of such a program is inestimatable. We believe that our project is practical and our scheme is logical. We welcome, of course, any suggestions that Council members can give us from your years of dealing with arts programs.

Continued ethos
of rationality and
pragmatism

Respectfully,

Gisela D'Anunzio

Problem-Solving Proposals

There are three steps in developing a problem-solving proposal: analysis of the problem, discovery of the solution, and presentation of the solution.

Analysis and discovery are interrelated because the solution is buried in the problem, and therefore before we can hope to unearth a solution we must know the problem inside and outside. Problem solving requires intensive, in-depth analysis, but people usually settle for a superficial investigation and end up seeing only one side of a problem, or seeing the surface but not the underlying problem. The result of seeing partial problems is offering partial solutions. A different sort of analytical shortcoming is to assume that all problems have easy solutions. Failing to understand the complexities of a situation, people seek immediate and simple solutions to problems that will take years to conquer. Easy answers are seldom lasting answers. Sometimes problems have not one but multiple solutions that require a series of actions, and in such cases, we contribute a part to a larger scheme. For example, responses to dwindling oil supplies require creative thinking on many different fronts: The auto industry uses lighter metals (aluminum, magnesium) and manufactures smaller cars; such cities as Washington, D.C., build new transit systems; petroleum engineers perfect new drilling techniques to liquefy lignite, to recover oil from the ocean, and to reach greater depths; and scientists seek alternative energy sources from the wind, the sun, the tides, even from plants.

In addition to inadequately analyzing the problem, people have difficulty seeing solutions because they think in the patterns established by others. As discussed in Chapter 2, thinking in conventional ways can be limiting, but there are ways of encouraging and nurturing creative thinking. In problem solving, the tendency is to think in accordance with current solutions and to follow the general path of predecessors. It is astounding how similar the offered solutions to a problem usually are because people fall into a set mold and think in the same way. If the tentative solutions all seem to be inadequate and to have the same weaknesses, we must break the mold and think in unorthodox ways in order to escape from the pattern and be independent. Although unconventionality is not always the answer, it may lead us to see the problem differently and may take us in new directions. For example, unorthodox thinking about energy conservation led engineers at Texas A&M University to discover a way of capturing wintry weather and preserving it until summer. During the winter, they spray water into the freezing air to chill it, then pump it into huge storage tanks 60 feet deep until summer, when it is used in cooling systems. By breaking the conventional pattern, they arrived at a useful and economical solution.

Once we have hit on a solution, we must carefully work out the details, paying particular attention to practical objections readers may find to our solution. The most likely objections encountered are "It can't be done," "It's too expensive," and "I know a better plan." We take care of the first objection by giving a detailed plan that shows, step by step, how the solution *can* be implemented. Here is how to counter the other two objections.

Paying for the Solution

Cost is the saboteur of many proposals. Writers like to ignore the cost of projects, but cost is a major consideration in solving problems since society weighs benefits against costs. We put a price tag on everything, even on the poor, the elderly, and the environment. Anyone can propose an ideal way to clean up America's air, but the cost prevents the solution from being adopted. For example, the Environmental Protection Agency sets emission control standards for automobiles, but the auto manufacturers maintain that the cost of achieving those high standards would prohibitively increase car prices. We have to consider the cost of implementing and maintaining the project and the subsequent indirect costs, if any, to the consumer and to business. For instance, if a project is to be funded through taxes, we must determine how much taxes will increase and what kind of taxes to target—income, sales, or property taxes. We must cite figures because they convince people and increase our credibility. If our proposal is to be privately funded, we must state whether we already have the backing lined up, or whether approval is pending. We have to demonstrate that a proposal is worth the dollars it will cost. In fact, we must show that it is a bargain by proving that in the long run, *not* implementing it will cost more than implementing it.

Refuting Alternatives

When we argue that our proposal is the best one available, we are implicitly arguing *against* other plans as much as we are arguing *for* our own. Because we must demonstrate, not simply assert, the superiority of our plan, we must point out somewhere in our proposal the weaknesses of competing solutions. There are several ways to do this, depending on the number and strength of the alternatives. If there is already a currently favored solution, our strategy might be to attack and then defend: to argue against that plan and then to argue for a new plan. Also, we might use a point-by-point comparison of the plans, showing the superiority of our plan over the alternative. (Chapter 6 suggests structures for comparing.) If there are several strong contending designs, we can consider one at a time, showing the weaknesses of each, and then present our suggestion; this approach is called eliminating alternatives. (Chapter 13 discusses this approach and methods of refuting.) The most common technique for refuting other options is to group them into one paragraph and rapidly list their deficiencies, the attempt being to dismiss them from the readers' consideration.

Sample Problem-Solving Proposal

The following proposal, which is intended to be read at a town meeting to decide what to do with the community funds, presents and argues for a particular community project.

Fellow Townspeople:

I suggest that our project for this year be the renovation of this town hall that we are in tonight. Look around you at the state of disrepair we have let this old building fall into: The floor is worn and uneven, the wooden steps leading into the building are dangerously rotten, the roof leaks and is damaging the interior, the exterior walls need painting, and the benches that you are sitting on, wobbly with age, are the ones originally built nearly a century ago.

Thesis presented immediately and straightforwardly

The problem is self-evident; deficiencies enumerated

Since this town hall was built in 1898, all that has been done to improve it has been to put in electricity in 1933, install butane heating in 1939, and paint it every 4 years. We should take more pride in this old structure that our great-grandfathers built and then built their town around. It has been the center of the political and social life of this town. Standing in the physical center of town, it is today

History of repairs to show that little has been done

Appeal to civic pride

an eyesore instead of a symbol of pride in our community. If for
nothing but historical significance, we should renovate it.

But there are more pragmatic reasons for renovating it. If we don't
do some work on it soon, the old place is simply going to be unsafe,
destroyed from neglect. We depend upon it too much to let it decay.
We have our town meetings here, weddings, bazaars, annual play,
concerts, ice-cream suppers, chess and other game tournaments,
Thursday bingo, poetry readings, campaign debates, and club meetings like the Rotary and Lions. Where will we hold these activities?
Not at any of the local churches because some of the activities are
inappropriate for religious settings; not at the school auditorium because it is available only at limited times. We need this building. And
we cannot afford to replace it if it falls into ruin. Replacing it would
cost approximately $48,000 according to estimates furnished by Mr.
Pyncheon at Seven Gables Construction, and that includes only materials, no labor. We have in our coffers right now $8,654. Can we
realistically expect to raise another $40,000 when this building is no
longer fit for use? I think not.

Restoring the town hall, however, would cost substantially less. We
can make all of the necessary repairs for about $6,000, one-eighth
the replacement cost. Commissioner Autry says there is even a
possibility of getting county funds to help finance a restoration project. Most of the materials can be purchased at wholesale prices,
which is a policy that local businesses have for nonprofit organizations. The $6,000 estimate covers only materials; the labor would
have to be volunteer, but members of the community with whom I
have talked are willing to donate time on weekends to fix up the
building.

The $6,000 estimate includes $800 for a new roof; instead of replacing the old roof, we can simply place shingles over it. Similarly, we
can lay vinyl tiles on the present wooden floor; 900 square feet of
this material will run about $1,600. Ready-made cement steps at both
entrances will cost $240, and a cement sidewalk in front (about 4
yards of concrete) will cost another $200; this amount, however, will
not have to come from our treasury because Jim Hayes has already
offered to pay for these projects. Another donation comes from
Kennon Vaughan, who has offered to pay for and install fiberglass
insulation in the attic. As for replacing the old benches, we can buy
some excellent and sturdy benches, pews, chairs, and four tables from
a furniture outlet in Columbus for about $2,000.

That leaves only the outside walls. Instead of painting the exterior, which is weathering badly, I suggest that we put vinyl siding on it. The siding is guaranteed for 20 years and will pay for itself by our not having to pay $500 every 4 years to have the building painted. The siding costs $1,600, and a group of citizens has already volunteered to put it on. The siding is durable and attractive, it matches the present wood design, and it cleans off with a water spray. In addition, it will act as a good insulator, will protect the original wood walls, and will not burn.

Explains that paying now is cheaper than paying later

Enumerates advantages of siding

I realize that there are other worthwhile projects under consideration, like entering a float in the Rose Bowl Parade and starting a scholarship fund for three outstanding local students each year, and I assure you that I will endorse these proposals next year. But these other projects can be postponed one year without detrimental consequences. Time is running out for us to save this landmark, this symbol of our civic involvement. We have put it off and put it off until it is almost too late. For a fraction of its material worth, to say nothing of its sentimental worth, we can at once beautify, preserve, and make safe for us and our children this historic building that has seen four generations of families meet and socialize and enjoy. Will we be the generation that lets it fall into ruin? Will we be the last generation to enjoy this old structure? Let's not procrastinate any longer. Thank you.

Reasonable stance toward alternative plans

Stresses greater need

Heightened emotional appeal: symbol, children, historic, generations, etc.

Ethos

In addition to projecting an image of honesty, sincerity, intelligence, and expertise, in a proposal we want to stress that we are (1) practical and (2) concerned about the welfare of others. We must communicate that we have perceptively analyzed the situation, fairly evaluated the evidence, examined current solutions, and reached a solution that, in view of our thorough study, is the best plan of action. Our rhetorical stance is one of serving: We present our solution because we want to serve the community or humanity. One of the differences between a request proposal and a solution proposal is the stance: In a solution proposal we are giving, not requesting something—serving, not seeking.

Organizing a Proposal Essay

As with other forms of writing, proposals may be organized in any number of ways, depending on the audience, purpose, and subject, but typically they follow variations of these structures:

1. Classical Arrangement (This is the structure used in the town hall proposal.)

   Clear statement of the proposition

   Presentation of idea (step-by-step blueprint showing how it is to be implemented and why it will be successful)

   Meeting objections and disposing of alternatives

   Confirmation

   Summation

2. Elimination of Alternatives (Discussed in Chapter 13)

   Brief statement of the problem

   Solution 1 and its weaknesses

   Solution 2 and its weaknesses

   Solution 3 and its weaknesses

   Our solution and its advantages

   Possible brief concession

   Conclusion

3. Point-by-Point Comparison (Discussed in Chapter 6)

   Introduction to problem and to competing solutions, encapsulated

      Criterion 1 (e.g., cost)

       Alternative plan

       Our plan and advantages

      Criterion 2 (e.g., side effects)

       Alternative plan

       Our plan and advantages

      Criterion 3, etc.

Introductions in proposals are usually brief, being little more than a statement of the thesis. However, if readers are not familiar with the problem, the first part of the paper must be an explanation of the problem and of the desired goal. The reader movement should be from awareness of the problem to knowledge about it, and then to conviction and action.

Exercises

Discuss as a group one of these topics, suggesting the kind of evidence, appeals, structure, and rhetorical stance that would be most effective. Then come up with a detailed outline of the proposal.

1. Suggest a ban on the sale of war toys by United States manufacturers. The underlying assumption would be that children who play with toy guns learn that war is an accepted practice; it conditions them by making them think

that violence is a routine way to solve problems. You will also have to refute the opposition's contention that military toys give children a way of venting their aggression in harmless play instead of sublimating it. For a precedent, examine Sweden's 1979 ban of all war toys modeled after twentieth-century weapons.

2. Draft a proposal to your employer suggesting that the company implement flextime or the 10-hour, 4-day work week.

3. Because the House and Senate Ethics Committees seemingly refuse to regulate their colleagues adequately—and you should give several examples—propose the formation of a citizens' committee to set standards, regulate abuse, and prosecute violations.

4. Take a solution to one problem and apply it to another problem. For example, apply the concept of foster homes to the elderly. We have foster homes instead of orphanages so that parentless children will have a home and a family; in return, the family receives financial aid for the child's upbringing. The same solution might be tried with the elderly. Instead of placing the elderly in taxpayer-supported nursing homes, we could place them in foster homes, which are not as impersonal, regimented, or crowded as nursing homes. Room and board in an adult foster home would be about 75 percent less than in a nursing home. Find a problem that is similar to another problem and see if a parallel solution will work.

5. A major problem confronting most large cities these days is getting qualified candidates for their police forces. Propose to your mayor that your city (or a large city near you) offer scholarships to qualified students who in return would serve 3 or 4 years on the police force after graduation. Also, the students would attend summer training at the police academy, for which they would receive an hourly wage. When they graduate, they would receive a rookie cop's pay but would not receive other benefits. Flesh out the details, including finances, qualifications, and so forth, and then draft the proposal. You might model the program after the ROTC concept that the military services use.

Suggested Writing Assignments

1. To provide a better sense of a college community, to make learning fun, and to create an environment of intellectual stimulation, propose scholastic contests between faculty and students. A new group would battle each week; professors would not be allowed to answer questions in their own discipline. Think of other ways to stimulate student-faculty involvement and interaction.

2. Set up a shuttle bus system around your campus and the nearby neighborhoods. Solicit funds from your student government association and find precedents at other colleges.

3. Suggest a change in a campus policy, such as the athletic fee, parking, pass/fail grading option, or recording grades with a plus or minus.

4. Come up with a way to raise donations for your college. For example, Unity College in Maine sold 25¢ chances to throw a pie in a professor's or administrator's face (with his or her permission). When 100 chances were sold, they drew to see who got to heave the pie.

5. Suggest that professors at your college volunteer one day a year to give a talk to elementary students to introduce pupils to a particular discipline, arouse their curiosity, and start them thinking positively about college. Precedent: "Meet the Professor" series at East Tennessee State University.

6. Petition your dean or department chairperson to accept for academic credit your volunteer experience with some professional group: as an apprentice with the city ballet company, as an intern with a law firm, as a volunteer on the local newspaper. The emphasis of your proposal will be on the rationale for accepting this nonacademic work for academic credit.

7. To keep theater tickets from going unused, and to provide free tickets to students, suggest that the entertainment committee on campus announce on local radio stations that if theater patrons find (at the last minute) that they cannot make it to a concert or play, they can call a number on campus and someone will get to use their tickets. The committee can announce availability to the dorms. Work out the details such as who would answer the phone, who would get the tickets, and how they would receive the tickets.

8. Propose a freshman essay contest with the bookstore offering gift certificates as prizes.

9. Write to your state legislator advocating that textbooks be exempted from state sales tax. Determine how much the average college student spends each year on texts, how much book prices are increasing annually, how much education costs the individual student per year, and how much of a savings per student the exemption would result in. You will have to offer a definition of *textbook*.

10. Now that you're in a college writing course, write a letter to the head of your high school English program suggesting ways of better preparing students for this course.

11. Propose to college administrators that entering students be allowed to pay tuition for all four years, like paying for hospital fees before the baby arrives. Explain the advantages to both sides and refute potential objections.

12. Petition your dean to change a certain requirement in your degree program. For example, if you are a special education major, and the degree requirements specify that all education students must take music theory and art practice, you might recommend substitutions geared to children with learning disabilities. You must present your rationale: Special-ed children have short attention spans and become frustrated with complex projects, such as mac-

rame and origami; some of the materials in the art class are dangerous (razor blades, rubber cement); music theory is too technical to be applicable to these children. Alternatively, suggest that a course be added to the current degree program, such as a course for drama majors in stage sound technique.

13. Propose to your community that you collectively form a co-op of some sort.

14. Write to your phone company suggesting that it give free dual spouse listing in its directory, for example "Doe, John/Mary." The current practice is chauvinistic and surrenders the wife's identity, though she is equally responsible for the bill. Cite precedents and test cases in court.

15. Recommend to the Olympic Committee that skateboarding become an Olympic sport. You will have to familiarize yourself with the requirements for admitting a new sport and know which countries would likely support such a bid. Or, suggest that, instead of moving the Olympics from country to country, they be held in Athens permanently. Discuss the financial, security, and political advantages; refute anticipated objections.

16. Many mayors invite citizens to give their views on the city's problems at a monthly luncheon. If your mayor invited you to the forum, what would you advocate?

17. Think of a way to use certain government workers in a new way. For example, West Germany uses mail carriers as parasocial reporters, keeping an eye on the elderly and the ill along their routes and conveying complaints to the proper authorities.

18. Request funds from the city council to set up one of these programs: a battered-wife center for counseling and temporary refuge; a day center for the elderly where they can meet, exercise, eat a hot lunch, play checkers, and watch television; a children's hotline phone service, which would be a kind of informational clearing house to answer emotional, educational, and sexual inquiries.

Sample Proposals

A NATIONAL INHERITANCE PLAN

David Hackett Fischer

Instead of supporting elderly people by grants of income at the end of life, it would be   1
cheaper, easier, and less disagreeable in many ways to give each American a grant

of capital at the beginning of life instead. Small capital payments would be more effective than large payments in the form of income.

Some American banks offer seven-year savings certificates which pay interest 2 at a nominal rate of 9 per cent a year. Real interest rates are lower (by 3%) because of inflation. But both are abnormal by the measure of experience over the past 300 years.[1] Let us assume that on long term investments, interest of 6 per cent will be generally available. Suppose that every American received at birth a sort of "national inheritance"—a gift of capital in the amount of $4400. The gift would be surrounded with many restrictions. It could never be spent, loaned, borrowed, alienated, expended, or employed as collateral in any way. This capital sum would be invested— perhaps in a savings account, or in government securities. The money would not be taxable. It would be left to earn compound interest until the infant who originally received it reached the age of sixty-five. At 6 per cent, over sixty-five years, the original $4400 would grow to $225,000![2]

At the age of sixty-five, the income from the $200,000 would provide an old age 3 pension. At 6 per cent the pension would be more than $12,000 for each American— far more than Social Security provides today. A husband and wife together would have a non-taxable household income of more than $25,000 a year. Upon their death, the money would return to the Treasury.

Yet the cost to the public would consist only of the initial payment of the original 4 capital sum to each American child. In 1975, approximately three million children were born in the United States. If each child had received a "national inheritance" of $4400, the total annual expense of the plan would have been $13.2 billion—a small fraction of present expenditure for social insurance. In 1974 alone the American government

[1]Everything depends on real, rather than nominal interest rates. Today, real interest is 2–3% because of inflation. But over the past three centuries, it has averaged about 6%. See Homer, *History of Interest Rates* (New Brunswick, N.J., 1977).
[2]For a fixed return of $200,000 at age 65, the size of the initial capital grant would be determined by the real interest rate. Even if real interest falls as low as 3%, the plan would be cheaper than our present arrangements.

Real rate of interest	Initial grant	Annual cost
3.0%	$28,600	85.6 billion
4.0	$15,200	45.6 billion
5.0	$ 8,000	24.0 billion
6.0	$ 4,400	13.2 billion
7.0	$ 2,400	7.2 billion
8.0	$ 1,300	3.9 billion

At the present rate of increase, by 1984 the cost of old age security will rise to $400 billion.

spent roughly $100 billion for that purpose—nearly $60 billion for Social Security alone—and costs were rising at a rate of more than 16 per cent a year. At such a speed social insurance expenditures will double in less than five years!

The administrative cost of a "national inheritance" system would also be cheaper than present arrangements. The huge Social Security Administration could be dismantled. No new bureaucracy would be required; the Treasury Department would simply deposit a check for $1400 in a long-term savings account at a federally insured bank, or issue government securities in a suitable form. No supervision would be necessary beyond the existing machinery for bank inspection. The banks themselves could be required to meet the minimal administrative requirements of the system—which would be no greater than that for any other savings account. The returns to the banks could be very great. Certainly, the old age of bankers would be most plentifully provided for. But rates and payments could be fixed at levels sufficient to guard against excess profits—enough to allow banks a fair return for their services, but nothing more.

The effect of this new plan upon the entire society would be as salutary as its effect upon the individual. The capital stock of the nation would be enormously invigorated—and a growing economic problem resolved. The national economy faces the prospect of a serious shortage of capital—a "capital gap," which is not entirely a fiction invented by the banking industry. A capital gap would make it difficult for new factories, houses, schools, and hospitals to be constructed. Many major reforms, such as urban renewal and environmental improvement, require heavy capital investment. But in America today capital is becoming scarce. The national inheritance plan would provide a powerful remedy.

Inflation, of course, could destroy the plan. But if it were set up properly, the plan could destroy inflation. The "national inheritance" system would itself serve as a more powerful weapon against inflation than any economic instrument we presently command. Inflation today has many causes—increased demand, administered prices, the growth of oligopoly. But probably most powerful are the repeated deficits which American government has run in the past forty years, and the debt it has accumulated. In the single month of October 1975 alone, the Treasury Department reported an operating deficit of $13 billion.

The national inheritance plan would create something new in public finance—a major program which was funded *before* the money is spent! The effect on prices would be the opposite of deficit spending. The accumulation of a surplus in the form of a national inheritance, rather than a deficit in the form of a national debt, would tend to reduce inflation—possibly even to reverse it.

Moreover, each person's capital would return to the Treasury, where it could be used to reduce the national debt, which is now rising out of control. The national inheritance plan could thus become an enormous sinking fund, such as Alexander Hamilton proposed in 1790, to restore the public credit of the Republic.

There will be many major difficulties in the enactment of the plan. The first and greatest—so great that many practical social planners will regard it as laughable—is the fact that the plan would not take effect for sixty-five years after its first enactment.

We would have to maintain our present system, or something like it, for a very long time. That will be extremely expensive for us to do—not so much because of added cost of the national inheritance plan, which is a very modest addition to existing expenditures, but rather because of the weaknesses inherent in our present system of social insurance. But this is not an argument against the plan; rather, it is still another indictment of the present system. We must hope to purchase time (at ruinous expense) by piecemeal reform, at the same time that we design a more fundamental and lasting solution.

A very long period—nearly a lifetime—would separate the enactment of the   11
national inheritance plan from its first operation as a system of old age insurance. This presents a problem of politics. If the plan would not produce results for sixty-five years, virtually everyone in the electorate would be dead before it begins to work. Its passage would therefore be an altruistic act, of a sort which the history of American politics has taught us not to expect.

The plan will succeed only if the electorate is given a stake in the outcome. That   12
could be done by enlarging it to include other measures—themselves equally important to our society. There is, among many other things, a growing economic problem in the American system of higher education. The demand for college education is increasing at a rapid rate, but the costs are already near or at a level which most American families cannot afford to pay.

The educational problem could be eased by an extension of the national   13
inheritance plan. In addition to the $1400 granted for old age support, another sum of $1400 could be granted under similar restrictions to every newborn child. In twenty years, it would grow to $6900, which might be used to pay part of the cost of college education. That would require another investment of $4 billion a year—a very large sum, but less than the cost of most other proposals for aid to higher education and a small fraction (about 4 per cent) of present educational expenditures in America.

This addition (and others like it) will give at least part of the present generation a   14
motive for supporting the plan, from which otherwise they would have nothing to gain. It would bind their interest to the future of the Republic. But even so, the enactment of the plan would require Americans to tax themselves for the sake of their posterity. Most people who voted on the question would gain from it less than they would be asked to give. If American politics is merely a calculus of private interests, then the plan has small chance of success. To that difficulty is added another—the tendency on the part of many Americans to live entirely in the present, without thought for either the past or the future. The spirit of pragmatism in American thought is, among other things, a way of separating today from yesterday and tomorrow. Americans can no longer allow themselves to remain secure in the comfortable illusion that the future will take care of itself. We must plan for it, work for it, study it as part of the long continuum of events in which we live.

The enactment of the national inheritance plan is highly problematical. Many   15
people will actively oppose it. Doctrinaire capitalists will resist another federal "give-away," even though it could help to sustain capitalism for many generations. Socialist intellectuals will condemn a form of welfare which is associated with private capital,

though it could create an instrument of social welfare more powerful than any collectivist alternative. Labor leaders will see in it a threat to their own pension plans. Social scientists will discover a dozen technical ways of proving that it could not possibly work. Practical politicians will waffle and delay until the existing welfare system collapses upon their heads, and if the plan is enacted they will undertake to destroy its fiscal integrity in every election year.

Those difficulties are compounded by the fact that the plan must be enacted in the form of a Constitutional Amendment—to protect it from future changes which could easily destroy it. In any election year some political leaders will be tempted to remove restrictions on the use of the capital, and thus ruin the integrity of the plan. Obviously, therefore, the plan presents many practical difficulties—but fewer than any other arrangement. The American government is presently committed to an expensive program of social welfare, but it cannot pay the bills. If it continues to operate with heavy deficits, sooner or later the Treasury will be unable to find purchasers for its notes. When that happens, the American government—not New York City or New York State, but the United States of America—will fall into bankruptcy. Many nation-states have done so in the past. Our own government actually came close to bankruptcy in the Revolutionary era, and again in 1860. The government of England approached insolvency in 1639; the government of France was virtually bankrupt in 1787; the government of Russia was nearly so in 1916, as was the government of China in the 1940's. We might profit by their example. Deficit spending was not invented in the twentieth century. It was often tried in the past, and when the experiment was prolonged, the results were always and inevitably the same. We *must* find an alternative to our present system of social welfare. Though the national inheritance plan is difficult, our present arrangements are impossible. Those who scoff at the practicability of the national inheritance plan may be invited to think of a better way.

16

—From *Growing Old in America*

1. Do you find the writer's solution to the problem innovative, or is his thinking in the same mode as other proposed solutions?

2. What kind of structure does the writer use to present his ideas? What are the major sections of the proposal, and what paragraphs does each section include?

3. How is Fischer able to counter the "first and greatest" difficulty in paragraph 10?

4. Why does he devote almost a third of the argument to the objections to his plan? Doesn't that undermine his proposal? Why, or why not? Does he try to counter each objection as he presents it? If so, give examples. If not, why not?

5. What incentives does Fischer build into his plan to encourage the current generation to accept it? Is this an effective strategy?

6. What emotion is he indirectly appealing to in the last paragraph when he discusses governments going bankrupt? Is the appeal effective? Explain.

The following essay, "A Modest Proposal" (1729) by Jonathan Swift, is a masterfully crafted piece that gives a detailed scheme, counters objections, cites financial and social benefits, appeals to emotions, and develops a credible ethos. But it is an ironic proposal; that is, it isn't proposing what it seems to be proposing. Instead of being a modest proposal, it is a savage and outrageous proposal intended to expose the brutality of the English treatment of the Irish people.

A MODEST PROPOSAL

For Preventing the Children of Poor People in Ireland from Being a Burden to Their Parents or Country, and for Making Them Beneficial to the Public

Jonathan Swift

1   It is a melancholy object to those who walk through this great town or travel in the country, when they see the streets, the roads, and cabin doors, crowded with beggars of the female-sex, followed by three, four, or six children, all in rags and importuning every passenger for an alms. These mothers, instead of being able to work for their honest livelihood, are forced to employ all their time in strolling to beg sustenance for their helpless infants, who, as they grow up, either turn thieves for want of work, or leave their dear native country to fight for the Pretender in Spain, or sell themselves to the Barbadoes.

2   I think it is agreed by all parties that this prodigious number of children in the arms, or on the backs, or at the heels of their mothers, and frequently of their fathers, is in the present deplorable state of the kingdom a very great additional grievance; and therefore whoever could find out a fair, cheap, and easy method of making these children sound, useful members of the commonwealth would deserve so well of the public as to have his statue set up for a preserver of the nation.

3   But my intention is very far from being confined to provide only for the children of professed beggars; it is of a much greater extent, and shall take in the whole number of infants at a certain age who are born of parents in effect as little able to support them as those who demand our charity in the streets.

4   As to my own part, having turned my thoughts for many years upon this important subject, and maturely weighed the several schemes of other projectors, I have always found them grossly mistaken in their computation. It is true, a child just dropped from its dam may be supported by her milk for a solar year, with little other nourishment; at most not above the value of two shillings, which the mother may certainly get, or the value in scraps, by her lawful occupation of begging; and it is exactly at one year old that I propose to provide for them in such a manner as instead of being a charge upon their parents or the parish, or wanting food and raiment for the rest of their lives, they shall on the contrary contribute to the feeding, and partly to the clothing, of many thousands.

There is likewise another great advantage in my scheme, that it will prevent   5
those voluntary abortions, and that horrid practice of women murdering their bastard
children, alas, too frequent among us, sacrificing the poor innocent babes, I doubt,
more to avoid the expense than the shame, which would move tears and pity in the
most savage and inhuman breast.

The number of souls in this kingdom being usually reckoned one million and a   6
half, of these I calculate there may be about two hundred thousand couple whose
wives are breeders; from which number I subtract thirty thousand couples who are
able to maintain their own children, although I apprehend there cannot be so many
under the present distresses of the kingdom; but this being granted, there will remain
an hundred and seventy thousand breeders. I again subtract fifty thousand for those
women who miscarry, or whose children die by accident or disease within the year.
There only remain an hundred and twenty thousand children of poor parents annually
born. The question therefore is, how this number shall be reared and provided for,
which, as I have already said, under the present situation of affairs, is utterly impossible by all the methods hitherto proposed. For we can neither employ them in
handicraft or agriculture; we neither build houses (I mean in the country) nor cultivate
land. They can very seldom pick up a livelihood by stealing till they arrive at six years
old, except where they are of towardly parts; although I confess they learn the
rudiments much earlier, during which time they can however be looked upon only as
probationers, as I have been informed by a principal gentleman in the county of
Cavan, who protested to me that he never knew above one or two instances under the
age of six, even in a part of the kingdom so renowned for the quickest proficiency in
that art.

I am assured by our merchants that a boy or a girl before twelve years old is no   7
salable commodity; and even when they come to this age they will not yield above
three pounds, or three pounds and half a crown at most on the Exchange; which
cannot turn to account either to the parents or the kingdom, the charge of nutriment
and rags having been at least four times that value.

I shall now therefore humbly propose my own thoughts, which I hope will not be   8
liable to the least objection.

I have been assured by a very knowing American of my acquaintance in   9
London, that a young healthy child well nursed is at a year old a most delicious,
nourishing and wholesome food, whether stewed, roasted, baked, or boiled, and I
make no doubt that it will equally serve in a fricassee, or a ragout.

I do therefore humbly offer it to public consideration, that of the hundred and   10
twenty thousand children already computed, twenty thousand may be reserved for
breed, whereof only one fourth part to be males, which is more than we allow to
sheep, black-cattle, or swine, and my reason is that these children are seldom the
fruits of marriage, a circumstance not much regarded by our savages, therefore one
male will be sufficient to serve four females. That the remaining hundred thousand
may at a year old be offered in sale to the persons of quality, and fortune, through the
kingdom, always advising the mother to let them suck plentifully in the last month, so
to render them plump, and fat for a good table. A child will make two dishes at an

entertainment for friends, and when the family dines alone, the fore or hind quarter will make a reasonable dish, and seasoned with a little pepper or salt will be very good boiled on the fourth day, especially in winter.

I have reckoned upon a medium, that a child just born will weigh twelve pounds, and in a solar year if tolerably nursed increaseth to twenty-eight pounds. 11

I grant this food will be somewhat dear, and therefore very proper for landlords, who, as they have already devoured most of the parents, seem to have the best title to the children. 12

Infant's flesh will be in season throughout the year, but more plentiful in March, and a little before and after, for we are told by a grave author, an eminent French physician, that fish being a prolific diet, there are more children born in Roman Catholic countries about nine months after Lent than at any other season; therefore reckoning a year after Lent, the markets will be more glutted than usual, because the number of Popish infants is at least three to one in this kingdom, and therefore it will have one other collateral advantage by lessening the number of Papists among us. 13

I have already computed the charge of nursing a beggar's child (in which list I reckon all cottagers, laborers, and four-fifths of the farmers) to be about two shillings *per annum,* rags included, and I believe no gentleman would repine to give ten shillings for the carcass of a good fat child, which, as I have said, will make four dishes of excellent nutritive meat, when he hath only some particular friend or his own family to dine with him. Thus the Squire will learn to be a good landlord and grow popular among his tenants, the mother will have eight shilling net profit, and be fit for work until she produces another child. 14

Those who are more thrifty (as I must confess the times require) may flay the carcass; the skin of which artificially dressed will make admirable gloves for ladies, and summer boots for fine gentlemen. 15

As to our city of Dublin, shambles may be appointed for this purpose in the most convenient parts of it, and butchers we may be assured will not be wanting; although I rather recommend buying the children alive, and dressing them hot from the knife as we do roasting pigs. 16

A very worthy person, a true lover of his country, and whose virtues I highly esteem, was lately pleased in discoursing on this matter to offer a refinement upon my scheme. He said that many gentlemen of this kingdom, having of late destroyed their deer, he conceived that the want of venison might be well supplied by the bodies of young lads and maidens, not exceeding fourteen years of age nor under twelve, so great a number of both sexes in every county being now ready to starve for want of work and service; and these to be disposed of by their parents, if alive, or otherwise by their nearest relations. But with due deference to so excellent a friend and so deserving a patriot, I cannot be altogether in his sentiments; for as to the males, my American acquaintance assured me from frequent experience that their flesh was generally tough and lean, like that of our schoolboys, by continual exercise, and their taste disagreeable; and to fatten them would not answer the charge. Then as to the females, it would, I think with humble submission, be a loss to the public, because they soon would become breeders themselves: and besides, it is not improbable that 17 some scrupulous people might be apt to censure such a practice (although indeed very unjustly) as a little bordering upon cruelty; which, I confess, hath always been with me the strongest objection against any project, how well soever intended.

But in order to justify my friend, he confessed that this expedient was put into 18
his head by the famous Psalmanazar, a native of the island Formosa, who came from thence to London above twenty years ago, and in conversation told my friend that in his country when any young person happened to be put to death, the executioner sold the carcass to persons of quality as a prime dainty; and that in his time the body of a plump girl of fifteen, who was crucified for an attempt to poison the emperor, was sold to his Imperial Majesty's prime minister of state, and other great mandarins of the court, in joints from the gibbet, at four hundred crowns. Neither indeed can I deny that if the same use were made of several plump young girls in this town, who without one single groat to their fortunes cannot stir abroad without a chair, and appear at the playhouse and assemblies in foreign fineries which they never will pay for, the kingdom would not be the worse.

Some persons of a desponding spirit are in great concern about that vast 19
number of poor people, who are aged, diseased, or maimed, and I have been desired to employ my thoughts what course may be taken to ease the nation of so grievous an encumbrance. But I am not in the least pain upon that matter, because it is very well known that they are every day dying and rotting by cold and famine, and filth and vermin, as fast as can be reasonably expected. And as to the young laborers, they are now in as hopeful a condition: they cannot get work, and consequently pine away for want of nourishment, to a degree that if at any time they are accidentally hired to common labor, they have not strength to perform it; and thus the country and themselves are happily delivered from the evils to come.

I have too long digressed, and therefore shall return to my subject. I think the 20
advantages by the proposal which I have made are obvious and many, as well as of the highest importance.

For first, as I have already observed, it would greatly lessen the number of 21
papists, with whom we are yearly overrun, being the principal breeders of the nation as well as our most dangerous enemies; and who stay at home on purpose to deliver the kingdom to the Pretender, hoping to take their advantage by the absence of so many good Protestants, who have chosen rather to leave their country than stay at home and pay tithes against their conscience to an Episcopal curate.

Secondly, The poor tenants will have something valuable of their own, which by 22
law may be made liable to distress and help to pay their landlord's rent, their corn and cattle being already seized, and money a thing unknown.

Thirdly, Whereas the maintenance of 100,000 children from two years old and 23
upward, cannot be computed at less than *10s.* a-piece per annum, the nation's stock will be thereby increased £50,000 per annum, beside the profit of a new dish introduced to the tables of all gentlemen of fortune in the kingdom who have any refinement in taste. And the money will circulate among ourselves, the goods being entirely of our own growth and manufacture.

Fourthly, The constant breeders, beside the gain of *8s.* sterling per annum 24 by the sale of their children, will be rid of the charge of maintaining them after the first year.

Fifthly, This food would likewise bring great custom to taverns, where the vintners will certainly be so prudent as to procure the best receipts for dressing it to perfection, and consequently have their houses frequented by all the fine gentlemen, who justly value themselves upon their knowledge in good eating; and a skilful cook, who understands how to oblige his guests, will contrive to make it as expensive as they please.   25

Sixthly, This would be a great inducement to marriage, which all wise nations have either encouraged by rewards or enforced by laws and penalties. It would increase the care and tenderness of mothers toward their children, when they were sure of a settlement for life to the poor babes, provided in some sort by the public, to their annual profit instead of expense. We should see an honest emulation among the married women, which of them would bring the fattest child to the market. Men would become as fond of their wives during the time of their pregnancy as they are now of their mares in foal, their cows in calf, their sows when they are ready to farrow; nor offer to beat or kick them (as is too frequent a practice) for fear of a miscarriage.   26

Many other advantages might be enumerated. For instance, the addition of some thousand carcasses in our exportation of barrelled beef; the propagation of swine's flesh, and improvement in the art of making good bacon, so much wanted among us by the great destruction of pigs, too frequent at our tables, are no way comparable in taste or magnificence to a well-grown, fat yearling child, which roasted whole will make a considerable figure at a Lord Mayor's feast, or any other public entertainment. But this and many others I omit, being studious of brevity.   27

Supposing that one thousand families in this city would be constant customers for infants flesh, besides others who might have it at merry meetings, particularly weddings and christenings; I compute that Dublin would take off annually about twenty thousand carcasses, and the rest of the kingdom (where probably they will be sold somewhat cheaper) the remaining eighty thousand.   28

I can think of no one objection that will possibly be raised against this proposal unless it should be urged that the number of people will be thereby much lessened in the kingdom. This I freely own, and it was indeed one principal design in offering it to the world. I desire the reader will observe, that I calculate for my remedy *for this one individual Kingdom of* Ireland, *and for no other that ever was, is, or, I think, ever can be upon earth.* Therefore let no man talk to me of other expedients: *Of taxing our absentees at five shillings a pound: Of using neither clothes, nor household furniture, except what is of our own growth and manufacture: Of utterly rejecting the materials and instruments that promote foreign luxury: Of curing the expensiveness of pride, vanity, idleness, and gaming in our women: Of introducing a vein of parsimony, prudence, and temperance: Of learning to love our country, wherein we differ even from* Laplanders, *and the inhabitants of* Topinamboo: *Of quitting our animosities and factions, nor act any longer like the* Jews, *who were murdering one another at the very moment their city was taken: Of being a little cautious not to sell our country and consciences for nothing: Of teaching landlords to have at least one degree of mercy*   29 *towards their tenants.* Lastly, *of putting a spirit of honesty, industry, and skill into our shopkeepers, who, if a resolution could now be taken to buy only our native goods, would immediately unite to cheat and exact upon us in the price, the measure and the goodness, nor could ever yet be brought to make one fair proposal of just dealing, though often and earnestly invited to it.*

Therefore I repeat, let no man talk to me of these and the like expedients, till he   30
hath at least a glimpse of hope that there will ever be some hearty and sincere attempt to put them in practice.

But as to myself, having been wearied out for many years with offering vain,   31
idle, visionary thoughts, and at length utterly despairing of success, I fortunately fell upon this proposal, which as it is wholly new, so it hath something solid and real, of no expense and little trouble, full in our own power, and whereby we can incur no danger in disobliging England. For this kind of commodity will not bear exportation, the flesh being of too tender a consistence to admit a long continuance in salt, *although perhaps I could name a country which would be glad to eat up our whole nation without it.*

After all I am not so violently bent upon my own opinion as to reject any offer,   32
proposed by wise men, which shall be found equally innocent, cheap, easy and effectual. But before some thing of that kind shall be advanced in contradiction to my scheme, and offering a better, I desire the author, or authors, will be pleased maturely to consider two points. First, as things now stand, how they will be able to find food and raiment for a hundred thousand useless mouths and backs? And secondly, there being a round million of creatures in human figure, throughout this kingdom, whose whole subsistence put into a common stock would leave them in debt two millions of pounds sterling; adding those who are beggars by profession, to the bulk of farmers, cottagers, and labourers with their wives and children, who are beggars in effect; I desire those politicians who dislike my overture, and may perhaps be so bold to attempt an answer, that they will first ask the parents of these mortals whether they would not at this day think it a great happiness to have been sold for food at a year old, in the manner I prescribe, and thereby have avoided such a perpetual scene of misfortunes as they have since gone through, by the oppression of landlords, the impossibility of paying rent without money or trade, the want of common sustenance, with neither house nor clothes to cover them from the inclemencies of weather, and the most inevitable prospect of entailing the like, or greater miseries upon their breed for ever.

I profess in the sincerity of my heart that I have not the least personal interest in   33
endeavouring to promote this necessary work, having no other motive than the *public good of my country, by advancing our trade, providing for infants, relieving the poor, and giving some pleasure to the rich.* I have no children by which I can propose to get a single penny; the youngest being nine years old, and my wife past child-bearing.

1. Of course, this an ironic argument, but how do you know that it is ironic? When does the first ironic statement occur?

2. Why does Swift advance his proposal by degrees instead of straightforwardly stating his proposition in the opening? What does he accomplish in the introduction (the first seven paragraphs)?

3. What is Swift's purpose in referring to people as "dams," "breeders" and "yearling child"?

4. Is the narrator Swift or is it a mask that Swift has created? Do the narrator's views coincide with Swift's at any points?

5. Describe the narrator's ethos. What are his primary traits and values? Is he rational? Emotional? How does his preoccupation with the economics of the problem affect his ethos? The narrator's ethos changes after paragraph 6; describe the ethos in paragraphs 1 through 6.

6. Give examples of the narrator's attempts to demonstrate that he is open-minded.

7. How do the calculations throughout the argument contribute to the satire?

8. Part of the horror about this argument is the shocking contrast between the tone and the proposal, which advocates cannibalism. How would you describe the tone?

9. Swift follows a classical structure. Outline the argument, showing which paragraphs belong to each section of the classical structure.

10. Has the narrator anticipated objections to his scheme and offered refutations? Give examples.

11. Explain the speaker's logic. Is it valid?

12. What purpose does the last paragraph serve?

Additional Argumentative Essays

STICKING UP FOR MARSUPIALS

Stephen Jay Gould

I am annoyed that the rapacious ways of my own species have irrevocably prevented   1
me from seeing the dodo in action, for a pigeon as large as a turkey must have been
something else, and stuffed, moldy specimens just don't carry conviction. We who

revel in nature's diversity and feel instructed by every animal tend to brand *Homo sapiens* as the greatest catastrophe since the Cretaceous extinction. Yet I would argue that the rise of the Isthmus of Panama a mere two to three million years ago must rank as the most devastating biological tragedy of recent times.

South America had been an island continent throughout the Tertiary period (for 2 seventy million years before the onset of continental glaciation). Like Australia, it housed a unique suite of mammals. But Australia was a backwater compared with the range and variety of South American forms. Many survived the onslaught of North American species after the isthmus rose. Some spread and prospered: the opossum moved as far as Canada; the armadillo is still making its way north.

Despite the success of a few, extirpation of the most dramatically different 3 South American forms must be ranked as the dominant effect of contact between mammals of the two continents. Two entire orders perished (we group all modern mammals into about twenty-five orders). Think how our zoos would have been enriched with a liberal sprinkling of notoungulates, a large and diverse group of plant-eating mammals, ranging from rhino-sized *Toxodon,* first exhumed by Charles Darwin on shore leave from the *Beagle,* to rabbit and rodent analogues among the typotheres and hegetotheres. Consider the litopterns with their two subgroups—the large, long-necked camel-like macrauchenids and the most remarkable group of all, the horse-like proterotheres. (Proterotheres even repeated some of the evolutionary trends followed by true horses: three-toed *Diadiaphorus* preceded *Thoatherium,* a single-toed species that outdid Man 'O War by reducing its vestigial side toes to a degree never matched by modern horses.) They are all gone forever, victims in large part of faunal disruptions set in motion by the rising isthmus. (Several notoungulates and litopterns survived well into the glacial epoch. They may even have received their *coup de grâce* from early human hunters. Still, I do not doubt that many would still be with us if South America had remained an island.)

The native predators of these South American herbivores also disappeared 4 completely. The modern carnivores of South America, the jaguars and their allies, are all North American interlopers. The indigenous carnivores, believe it or not, were all marsupials (although some flesh-eating niches were occupied by the phororhacids, a remarkable group of giant birds, now also extinct). The marsupial carnivores, although not as diverse as placental carnivores in northern continents, formed an impressive array, from fairly small animals to bear-sized species. One lineage evolved in uncanny parallel with the saber-toothed cats of North America. The marsupial *Thylacosmilus* developed long, stabbing upper canines and a protecting flange of bone on the lower jaw—just like *Smilodon* of the La Brea tar pits.

Although it is not commonly bruited about, marsupials are not doing badly in 5 South America today. North America may only boast the so-called Virginia opossum (actually a South American migrant), but opossums in South America are a rich and varied group of some sixty-five species. In addition, the caenolestids, pouchless "opossum rats," form a separate group with no close affinity to true opossums. But the third great group of South American marsupials, the carnivorous borhyaenids, were completely wiped out and replaced by northern cats.

The traditional view—though I dedicate this essay to opposing it—attributes the 6 extirpation of carnivorous marsupials to the general inferiority of pouched versus placental mammals. (All living mammals except marsupials and the egg-laying platypus and echidna are placentals.) The argument seems hard to beat. Marsupials flourished only on the isolated island continents of Australia and South America where large placental carnivores never gained a foothold. The early Tertiary marsupials of North America soon disappeared as placentals diversified; South American marsupials took a beating when the Central American corridor opened for placental immigration.

These arguments of biogeography and geological history gain apparent support   7 from the conventional idea that marsupials are anatomically and physiologically inferior to placentals. The very terms of our taxonomy reinforce this prejudice. All mammals are divided into three parts: the egg-laying monotremes are called Prototheria, or premammals; placentals win the prize as Eutheria, or true mammals; the poor marsupials lie in limbo as Metatheria, or middle mammals—not all quite there.

The argument for structural inferiority rests largely upon differing modes of   8 reproduction in marsupials versus placentals, bolstered by the usual smug assumption that different from us is worse. Placentals, as we know and experience, develop as embryos in intimate connection with a mother's body and blood supply. With some exceptions, they are born as reasonably complete and capable creatures. Marsupial fetuses never developed the essential trick that permits extensive development within a mother's body. Our bodies have an uncanny ability to recognize and reject foreign tissues, an essential protection against disease, but a currently intractable barrier to medical procedures ranging from skin grafts to heart transplants. Despite all the homilies about mother love, and the presence of 50 percent maternal genes in offspring, an embryo is still foreign tissue. The maternal immune system must be masked to prevent rejection. Placental fetuses have "learned" to do this; marsupials have not.

Marsupial gestation is very short—twelve to thirteen days in the common   9 opossum, followed by sixty to seventy days of further development in the external pouch. Moreover, internal development does not proceed in intimate connection with the mother, but shielded from her. Two-thirds of gestation occurs within the "shell membrane," a maternal organ that prevents the incursion of lymphocytes, the "soldiers" of the immune system. A few days of placental contact follow, usually via the yolk sac. During this time, the mother mobilizes her immune system, and the embryo is born (or, more accurately, expelled) soon after.

The marsupial neonate is a tiny creature, equivalent in development to a rather   10 early placental embryo. Its head and forelimbs are precociously developed, but the hind limbs are often little more than undifferentiated buds. It must then undertake a hazardous journey, slowly pulling itself along through the relatively great distance to mother's nipples and pouch (we can now understand the necessity of well-developed forelimbs). Our embryonic life within a placental womb sounds altogether easier and unconditionally better.

What challenge can then be offered to these biogeographical and structural   11 accounts of marsupial inferiority? My colleague John A. W. Kirsch has recently marshaled the arguments. Citing work of P. Parker, Kirsch contends that marsupial reproduction follows a different adaptive mode, not an inferior path. True, marsupials never evolved a mechanism to turn off the maternal immune system and permit a completed development within the womb. But early birth may be an equally adaptive strategy. Maternal rejection need not represent a failure of design or lost evolutionary opportunity; it may reflect an ancient and perfectly adequate approach to the rigors of survival. Parker's argument goes right back to Darwin's central contention that individuals struggle to maximize their own reproductive success, that is, to increase the representation of their own genes in future generations. Several highly divergent, but equally successful, strategies can be followed in (unconscious) pursuit of this goal. Placentals invest a great deal of time and energy in offspring before their birth. This commitment does increase the chance of an offspring's success, but the placental mother also takes a risk: if she should lose her litter, she has irrevocably expended a large portion of her life's reproductive effort for no evolutionary gain. The marsupial mother pays a much higher toll in neonatal death, but her reproductive cost is small. Gestation has been very short and she may breed again in the same season. Moreover, the tiny neonate has not placed a great drain upon her energetic resources, and has subjected her to little danger in a quick and easy birth.

Turning to biogeography, Kirsch challenges the usual assumption that Australia and South America were refugia for inferior beasts that couldn't hang on in the placental world of the Northern Hemisphere. He views their southern diversity as a reflection of success in their ancestral homeland, not as a feeble effort in peripheral territory. His argument relies upon M. A. Archer's claim for close genealogical relationship between borhyaenids (South American marsupial carnivores) and thylacines (marsupial carnivores of the Australian region). Taxonomists have previously regarded these two groups as an example of evolutionary convergence—separate development of similar adaptations (as in the marsupial and placental saber-tooths, mentioned previously). In fact, taxonomists have viewed the Australian and South American radiation of marsupials as completely independent events, following the separate invasion of both continents by primitive marsupials pushed out from northern lands. But if borhyaenids and thylacines are closely related, then the southern continents must have exchanged some of their products, probably via Antarctica. (In our new geology of drifting continents, southern hemisphere lands were much closer together when mammals rose to prominence, following the dinosaurs' demise.) A more parsimonious view imagines an Australian center of origin for marsupials and a dispersal to South America following the evolution of thylacinids, rather than two separate marsupial invasions of South America—borhyaenid ancestors from Australia, and all the others from North America. Although the simplest explanations are not always true in our wondrously complex world, Kirsch's arguments do cast considerable doubt on the usual assumption that marsupial homelands are refugia, not centers of origin.

Yet I must confess that this structural and biogeographical defense of marsupials falters badly before one cardinal fact, prominently featured above: the Isthmus of Panama rose, placental carnivores invaded, marsupial carnivores quickly perished,

12

13

and the placentals took over. Does this not speak for clear competitive superiority of North American placental carnivores? I could sneak around this unpleasant fact by ingenious conjecture, but I prefer to admit it. How then can I continue to defend marsupial equality?

Although the borhyaenids lost big, I find no scrap of evidence to attribute defeat   14
to their status as marsupials. I prefer an ecological argument predicting hard times for any indigenous group of South American carnivores, marsupial or placental. The real victims happened to be marsupials, but this taxonomic fact may be incidental to a fate sealed for other reasons.

R. Bakker has been studying the history of mammalian carnivores throughout   15
the Tertiary. Integrating some new ideas with conventional wisdom, he finds that the northern placental carnivores experienced two kinds of evolutionary "tests." Twice, they suffered short periods of mass extinction, and new groups, perhaps with greater adaptive flexibility, took over. During times of continuity, high diversity of both predators and prey engendered intense competition and strong evolutionary trends for improvement in feeding (quick ingestion and efficient slicing) and locomotion (high acceleration in ambush predators, endurance in long-distance hunters). South American and Australian carnivores were tested in neither way. They suffered no mass extinctions, and the original incumbents persisted. Diversity never approached northern levels, and competition remained less intense. Bakker reports that their levels of morphological specialization for running and feeding lie far below those of northern carnivores living at the same time.

H. J. Jerison's studies of brain size provide an impressive confirmation. On   16
northern continents, placental predators and prey evolved successively larger brains throughout the Tertiary. In South America, both marsupial carnivores and their placental prey quickly plateaued at about 50 percent of brain weight for average modern mammals of the same body sizes. Anatomical status as marsupials or placental seems to make no difference; a relative history of evolutionary challenge may be crucial. If, by happenstance, northern carnivores had been marsupials and southern carnivores placentals, I suspect that the outcome of isthmian exchange would still have been a rout for South America. North American faunas were continually tested in the fiery furnaces of mass destruction and intense competition. The South American carnivores were never strongly challenged. When the Isthmus of Panama rose, they were weighed in the evolutionary balance for the first time. Like Daniel's king, they were found wanting.

—From *The Panda's Thumb*

1. What kind of structure does Gould use, and why? Where does he first state his thesis? Why is less than half of the essay a direct defense of his thesis?

2. Why does he present the traditional view before presenting his thesis? When presenting that conventional view, how does he inform us, indirectly as well as directly, that he considers this view to be incorrect?

3. Paragraph 13 opens with an apparent concession. Why does Gould introduce this apparent concession?

4. Is the logic inductive, deductive, or a combination? Explain the logic.

5. Does he offer sufficient evidence to prove his thesis? What types of evidence does he use?

6. Describe Gould's ethos. Substantiate your description with references to the essay.

7. Gould doesn't define certain terms such as neonate, carnivorous, extirpation, taxonomy, morphological or even (until paragraph 8) marsupial and placental. But he does define terms such as borhyaenids, notoungulates, and evolutionary convergence. What kind of audience do you think he is writing to? (This essay originally appeared in *Natural History*.)

8. Do you find the argument interesting and ingenious? Why, or why not?

DEEPER INTO ABORTION

Bernard N. Nathanson, M.D.

In early 1969 I and a group of equally concerned and indignant citizens who had been 1
outspoken on the subject of legalized abortion, organized a political action unit known
as NARAL—then standing for National Association for Repeal of Abortion Laws, now
known as the National Abortion Rights Action League. We were outspokenly militant
on this matter and enlisted the women's movement and the Protestant clergy into our
ranks. We used every device available to political-action groups such as
pamphleteering, public demonstrations, exploitation of the media and lobbying in the
appropriate legislative chambers. In late 1969 we mounted a demonstration outside
one of the major university hospitals in New York City that had refused to perform
even therapeutic abortions. My wife was on that picket line, and my three-year-old son
proudly carried a placard urging legalized abortion for all. Largely as a result of the
efforts of this and a few similar groups, the monumental New York State Abortion
Statue of 1970 was passed and signed into law by Governor Nelson Rockefeller. Our
next goal was to assure ourselves that low cost, safe and humane abortions were
available to all, and to that end we established the Center for Reproductive and
Sexual Health, which was the first—and largest—abortion clinic in the Western world.
Its record was detailed in these pages in February, 1972.

Some time ago—after a tenure of a year and a half—I resigned as director of 2
the Center for Reproductive and Sexual Health. The Center had performed 60,000
abortions with no maternal deaths—an outstanding record of which we are proud.
However, I am deeply troubled by my own increasing certainty that I had in fact
presided over 60,000 deaths.

There is no longer serious doubt in my mind that human life exists within   3
the womb from the very onset of pregnancy, despite the fact that the nature of
the intrauterine life has been the subject of considerable dispute in the past.
Electrocardiographic evidence of heart function has been established in embryos
as early as six weeks. Electroencephalographic recordings of human brain activity has been noted in embryos at eight weeks. Our capacity to measure signs of
life is daily becoming more sophisticated, and as time goes by, we will doubt-
less be able to isolate life signs at earlier and earlier stages in fetal development.

The Harvard Criteria for the pronouncement of death assert that if the subject is   4
unresponsive to external stimuli (e.g., pain), if the deep reflexes are absent, if there
are no spontaneous movements or respiratory efforts, if the electroencephalogram
reveals no activity of the brain, one may conclude that the patient is dead. If any or all
of these criteria are absent—and the fetus does respond to pain, makes respiratory
efforts, moves spontaneously, and has electroencephalographic activity—life must be
present.

To those who cry that nothing can be human life that cannot exist in-   5
dependently, I ask if the patient totally dependent for his life on treatments by the
artificial kidney twice weekly is alive? Is the person with chronic cardiac disease,
solely dependent for his life on the tiny batteries on his pacemaker, alive? Would my
life be safe in this city without my eyeglasses?

Life is an interdependent phenomenon for us all. It is a continuous spectrum   6
that begins in utero and ends at death—the bands of the spectrum are designated by
words such as fetus, infant, child, adolescent, and adult.

We must courageously face the fact—finally—that human life of a special order   7
is being taken. And since the vast majority of pregnancies are carried successfully to
term, abortion must be seen as the interruption of a process that would otherwise
have produced a citizen of the world. Denial of this reality is the crassest kind of moral
evasiveness.

The fierce militants of the Woman's Liberation evade this issue and assert that   8
the woman's right to bear or not to bear children is her absolute right. On the other
hand the ferocious Right-to-Life legions proclaim no rights for the woman and absolute rights for the fetus.

But these "rights" that are held to be so obvious and so undeniable are highly   9
suspect. None of us have "rights" that go beyond the inter-related life that is our
common heritage on this planet. Our "rights" exist only because others around us care
enough about us to see to it that we have them. They have no other source. They
result from no other cause.

Somewhere in the vast philosophic plateau between the two implacably op-   10
posed camps—past the slogans, past the pamphlets, past even the demonstrations
and the legislative threats—lies the infinitely agonizing truth. We are taking life, and
the deliberate taking of life, even of a special order and under special circumstances,
is an inexpressibly serious matter.

Somehow, we must not deny the pervasive sense of loss that should accom-   11 pany abortion and its most unfortunate interruption of life. We must not coarsen our sensitivities through common practice and brute denial.

I offer no panacea. Certainly, the medical profession itself cannot shoulder the burden of this matter. The phrase "between a woman and her physician" is an empty one since the physician is only the instrument of her decision, and has no special knowledge of the moral dilemma or the ethical agony involved in the decision. Furthermore, there are seldom any purely medical indications for abortion. The decision is the most serious responsibility a woman can experience in her lifetime, and at present it is hers alone.

Can there be no help for the pregnant woman bearing the incalculable weight of this moral tension? Perhaps we could make available to her—though it should by no means be mandatory—a consultative body of unique design, much like Saint-Simon's Council of Newton. To meet the new moral challenges of the abortion decision, we may very well need specialists, some of new kinds, to serve on such a body—a psychohistorian, a human ecologist, a medical philosopher, an urbanologist-clergyman. The counseling that such a body could offer a pregnant woman would be designed to bring the whole sweep of human experience to bear on the decision—not just the narrow partisanship of committed young women who have had abortions and who typically staff the counselor ranks of hospitals and clinics now.

My concern is increased by the fact that the sloganeers, with their righteous pontifications and their undisguised desires to assert power over others, have polarized American reactions into dimly understood but tenaciously held positions. The din that has arisen in our land has already created an atmosphere in which it is difficult, if not impossible, for the individual to see the issues clearly and to reach an understanding free from the taint of the last shibboleth that was screamed in her ear.

Our sense of values has always placed the greatest importance upon the value of life itself. With a completely permissive legal climate for abortion (and I believe that we must have such a climate—that abortion must be unregulated by law) there is a danger that society will lose a certain moral tension that has been a vital part of its fabric. In pursuing a course of unlimited and uncontrolled abortion over future years, we must not permit ourselves to sink to a debased level of utilitarian semiconsciousness.

I plead for an honest, clear-eyed consideration of the abortion dilemma—an end to blind polarity. We have had enough screaming placards and mindless marches. The issue is human life, and it deserves the reverent stillness and ineffably grave thought appropriate to it.

We must work together to create a moral climate rich enough to provide for abortion, but sensitive enough to life to accommodate a profound sense of loss.

—From *The New England Journal of Medicine*, Nov. 28, 1974

1. What is the purpose of the lengthy first paragraph? What is the effect of the last sentence of the second paragraph?

2. Is the comparison in paragraph 4 sound? Are the comparisons in paragraph 5 sound? Disregarding their correctness, are the comparisons in those two paragraphs persuasive?

3. Describe the argument that is built in stages from paragraph 3 through paragraph 7.

4. Describe Nathanson's ethos. Is he informed? Tolerant? Open-minded? Angry? Concerned? Benevolent? Point to specific statements to support your description.

5. How does he establish himself as a moderate on this issue?

6. What is Nathanson arguing for?

7. Is there any emotional appeal in the article? Is the appeal or lack of appeal related to the fact that his audience is other physicians? Why would that matter?

8. Is his proposal clear? Is it practical? Does he provide sufficient details about it for readers to be convinced?

9. Does his argument seem contradictory in that he admits that abortion is "the deliberate taking of life," yet he endorses a "permissive legal climate for abortion"?

10. What kind of structure does he use?

NOTES FROM A FREE-SPEECH JUNKIE

Susan Jacoby

It is no news that many women are defecting from the ranks of civil libertarians on the issue of obscenity. The conviction of Larry Flynt, publisher of *Hustler* magazine—before his metamorphosis into a born-again Christian—was greeted with unabashed feminist approval. Harry Reems, the unknown actor who was convicted by a Memphis jury for conspiring to distribute the movie *Deep Throat*, has carried on his legal battles with almost no help from women who ordinarily regard themselves as supporters of the First Amendment. Feminist writers and scholars have even discussed the possibility of making common cause against pornography with adversaries of the women's movement—including opponents of the Equal Rights Amendment and "right to life" forces.

All of this is deeply disturbing to a woman who believes, as I always have and still do, in an absolute interpretation of the First Amendment. Nothing in Larry Flynt's garbage convinces me that the late Justice Hugo L. Black was wrong in his opinion that "the Federal government is without any power whatsoever under the Constitution to put any type of burden on free speech and expression of ideas of any kind (as distinguished from conduct)." Many women I like and respect tell me I am wrong; I cannot remember having become involved in so many heated discussions of a public issue since the end of the Vietnam war. A feminist writer described my views as those of a "First Amendment junkie."

Many feminist arguments for controls on pornography carry the implicit convic-   3
tion that porn books, magazines, and movies pose a greater threat to women than similarly repulsive exercises of free speech pose to other offended groups. This conviction has, of course, been shared by everyone—regardless of race, creed, or sex—who has ever argued in favor of abridging the First Amendment. It is the argument used by some Jews who have withdrawn their support from the American Civil Liberties Union because it has defended the right of American Nazis to march through a community inhabited by survivors of Hitler's concentration camps.

If feminists want to argue that the protection of the Constitution should not be   4
extended to *any* particularly odious or threatening form of speech, they have a reasonable argument (although I don't agree with it). But it is ridiculous to suggest that the porn shops in Times Square are more disgusting to women than a march of neo-Nazis is to survivors of the extermination camps.

The arguments over pornography also blur the vital distinction between expres-   5
sion of ideas and conduct. When I say I believe unreservedly in the First Amendment, someone always comes back at me with the issue of "kiddie porn." But kiddie porn is not a First Amendment issue. It is an issue of the abuse of power—the power adults have over children—and not of obscenity. Parents and promoters have no more right to use their children to make porn movies than they do to send them to work in coal mines. The responsible adults should be prosecuted, just as adults who use children for backbreaking farm labor should be prosecuted.

Susan Brownmiller, in *Against Our Will: Men, Women and Rape,* has described   6
pornography as "the undiluted essence of anti-female propaganda." I think this is a fair description of some types of pornography, especially of the brutish subspecies that equates sex with death and portrays women primarily as objects of violence.

The equation of sex and violence, personified by some glossy rock record   7
album covers as well as by *Hustler,* has fed the illusion that censorship of pornography can be conducted on a more rational basis than other types of censorship. Are all pictures of naked women obscene? Clearly not, says a friend. A Renoir nude is art, she says, and *Hustler* is trash. "Any reasonable person" knows that.

But what about something between art and trash—something, say, along the   8
lines of *Playboy* or *Penthouse* magazines? I asked five women for their reactions to one picture in *Penthouse* and got responses that ranged from "lovely" and "sensuous" to "revolting" and "demeaning." Feminists, like everyone else, seldom have rational reasons for their preferences in erotica. Like members of juries, they tend to disagree when confronted with something that falls short of 100 per cent vulgarity.

In any case, feminists will not be the arbiters of good taste if it becomes easier   9
to harass, prosecute, and convict people on obscenity charges. Most of the people who want to censor girlie magazines are equally opposed to open discussion of

issues that are of vital concern to women: rape, abortion, menstruation, contraception, lesbianism—in fact, the entire range of sexual experience from a woman's viewpoint.

Feminist writers and editors and filmmakers have limited financial resources: 10
Confronted by a determined prosecutor, Hugh Hefner will fare better than Susan Brownmiller. Would the Memphis jurors who convicted Harry Reems for his role in *Deep Throat* be inclined to take a more positive view of paintings of the female genitalia done by sensitive feminist artists? *Ms.* magazine has printed color reproductions of some of those art works; *Ms.* is already banned from a number of high school libraries because someone considers it threatening and/or obscene.

Feminists who want to censor what they regard as harmful pornography have   11
essentially the same motivation as other would-be censors: They want to use the power of the state to accomplish what they have been unable to achieve in the marketplace of ideas and images. The impulse to censor places no faith in the possibilities of democratic persuasion.

It isn't easy to persuade certain men that they have better uses for $1.95 each   12
month than to spend it on a copy of *Hustler?* Well, then, give the men no choice in the matter.

I believe there is also a connection between the impulse toward censorship on   13
the part of people who used to consider themselves civil libertarians and a more general desire to shift responsibility from individuals to institutions. When I saw the movie *Looking for Mr. Goodbar,* I was stunned by its series of visual images equating sex and violence, coupled with what seems to me the mindless message (a distortion of the fine Judith Rossner novel) that casual sex equals death. When I came out of the movie, I was even more shocked to see parents standing in line with children between the ages of ten and fourteen.

I simply don't know why a parent would take a child to see such a movie, any   14
more than I understand why people feel they can't turn off a television set their child is watching. Whenever I say that, my friends tell me I don't know how it is because I don't have children. True, but I do have parents. When I was a child, they did turn off the TV. They didn't expect the Federal Communications Commission to do their job for them.

I am a First Amendment junkie. You can't OD on the First Amendment, because   15
free speech is its own best antidote.

—From *The Possible She*

1. Who would you say is the intended audience? Does Jacoby attempt to woo the audience, or does she launch immediately into her logic?

2. Jacoby's argument is based mainly on a contradiction in her opponents' argument. What is that contradiction?

3. Is she attacking her opponents' major premise, minor premise, or conclusion? What is her point in paragraph 4?

4. How would you describe Jacoby's ethos—knowledgeable? Emotional? Intolerant? Logical? Support your description with statements from the argument.

5. Does her argument depend mainly on emotion, ethos, or logic?

6. What kind of evidence does she predominantly use—testimony, statistics, examples, narrative, parallel case, precedent, or reasons? Explain your answer.

7. Does Jacoby appeal to feminists' self-interest as a way of gaining their support? Explain.

8. What is her point in paragraphs 13 and 14? Are those paragraphs directly relevant to her main argument, or are they tangential? Do those paragraphs make a good conclusion?

V

RESEARCH SKILLS

CHAPTER 15

The Investigative Paper

The research paper—"Oh no, the dreaded research paper!" Now wait a second there. What we need is a little attitude adjustment about the much-maligned research project. Try to view it as an opportunity to explore in depth a subject about which you have a natural curiosity. Investigation should be part of the educational process, and this is your chance to become an aggressive learner. Academic education is too often a passive activity: sitting in classrooms, listening to lectures, following whatever intellectual path the instructors take. By contrast, investigative projects are active learning experiences in which students who are interested in a specialized subject go out on their own and discover knowledge that is new to them.

The obvious reasons for doing library research are to enhance your understanding of a subject, to draw conclusions from information you find, and to muster evidence to bolster a thesis. Investigative projects usually begin with (1) a question, for which you seek an answer; (2) a problem, for which you seek a solution; or (3) a thesis, for which you seek substantiation. As well as a gathering process, though, research can be a type of inventional device. In the process of accumulating facts, we encounter provocative ideas that in turn spark us to think of new ideas. As is so often the case, reading stimulates our minds, and we react to others' ideas by generating our own. A final benefit of an investigative project is that it allows you independence since it is *your* project: You choose the subject, you limit the scope, you set the pace, you control the direction, and you decide on the message. This type of independent study can be the most rewarding kind of education because when you discover something for yourself, as opposed to being told it, that knowledge is more memorable and lasting.

To become an aggressive learner, you must know how to retrieve knowledge from a library, and that is why in this chapter you will study investigative skills. The knowledge of the world has expanded to such a degree that no one can possibly keep abreast of everything; we can't carry around in our heads all the information known to humankind. Almost everything that is known, however, is accessible to us in a good library,

560

and college-educated persons should know how to locate any information they need. A library is simply a storehouse of data—ideas, events, and facts—there for the taking. Because you have to be something of a detective to find specific answers you need from this vast storehouse, this chapter is intended to help you build on the investigative skills you've acquired thus far in your schooling.

Investigative writing creates special problems and therefore places special demands on writers. In addition to the ordinary challenges of generating a thesis, organizing ideas, wrestling with paragraphs, and composing emphatic sentences, you have to research your subject thoroughly, integrate ideas from many sources, and document those ideas in a paper that is somewhat longer than your usual essay. Since most students find the investigative paper to be the most demanding, it is reserved until the end of the course so that you will have progressed in dealing with structure and substantiation before tackling this project.

The investigative paper often seems alien to students because many of the ideas in it are external, the composing process is fragmentary, and the format of the paper is somewhat mechanical. Previously, you have written primarily from your own knowledge and experience; that is, most of your writing up to this point has been self-generated. By contrast, this paper relies heavily on external knowledge, gathered from a variety of reference works. Hence, you may find that you will be dealing with a body of information that is more complex and comprehensive than what you are used to; and because this body of information is new to you, you will have to digest it and master it—within a short time frame—before you start composing. Even the composing process in investigative writing is different from your usual practice. Instead of the organic, associative process of writing as ideas occur to you, now you will be using a step-by-step methodology and drafting from note cards. Not only is it difficult to juggle the cards and draft simultaneously, but also the material on those cards often is disparate or downright contradictory. Finally, the investigative paper requires that you learn to document ideas that you borrow. You must learn both what to document and how to document it.

Formulate a Hypothesis and Test It

Before you have begun investigating an issue, you often have formed a hypothesis, or a tentative conclusion, based on your partial knowledge of the issue. The hypothesis is your initial belief that the evidence will yield a certain generalization. Having a hypothesis is useful because it helps to set the scope of the investigation, and it serves as a guide early in the investigation so that you have a general idea of what evidence is relevant and what is not. By giving an initial focus and helping you to evaluate information early in the investigation, a hypothesis prevents you from going off on tangents and rambling unnecessarily. Without a hypothesis, investigation would be exceedingly disorderly at the outset.

However, a hypothesis can be a potential problem if, instead of treating it as a trial thesis, you form a loyalty to it and dedicate yourself to proving it, even in the face of contrary evidence. Sometimes, rather than setting out to test a hypothesis, writers set out determinedly in search of evidence to substantiate that hypothesis. At that point, the hypothesis has become a hardened opinion, and the writers have become opinionated and biased. No longer seeking truth, they are simply trying to justify their version of reality. When writers seek evidence only to bolster a bias, they tend (1) to ignore evidence that doesn't support their views and (2) to try to mold the evidence to fit their hypothesis, instead of molding the hypothesis to fit the evidence.

You must follow the evidence, not the hypothesis, because the goal of investigation is to discover truth. Following the evidence requires that you remain objective, open-minded, and flexible enough to alter the hypothesis when the facts do not support it. Facts don't cease to exist just because you ignore them. "Facts are stubborn things," John Adams wrote, "and whatever may be our wishes, our inclinations, or the dictates of our passions, they cannot alter the state of facts or evidence." Instead of adhering to a hypothesis at all costs, learn to accept facts and to tolerate evidence that conflicts with your hypothesis. Hence, if you discover, after you begin examining evidence, that you need to modify your hypothesis, obviously you should modify it. The more contrary evidence you find, the more you have to modify the hypothesis; at some point you may even have to abandon it in favor of another hypothesis, one that the evidence suggests.

You should end the investigative stage with a complex understanding of the issue and with a conclusion that has been reached through objective evaluation of the evidence.

Reference Works

After narrowing the topic and formulating a hypothesis, you go to the library to research the topic. Before you start taking notes, however, I suggest that you read any background or general material that you can find, such as encyclopedias, yearbooks, and biographical dictionaries, to become acquainted with the topic and to acquire a basic understanding. Only after having done this background reading will you have an overview of the topic, understand its context, and know what to look for as you later browse through books and periodicals, read their information, digest it, take notes, and test your hypothesis.

The two library sources that most students consult when they launch into their research project are the card catalog and the *Readers' Guide to Periodical Literature.* In doing so, they seldom find the most useful books and articles on their topic, and they usually waste considerable time in their search. If you look up your topic in the card catalog, you may find fifty or more books listed. How do you know which ones will be relevant to your specific thesis? Do you try to guess from the titles? Probably you will select a few from the fifty and then go rummaging through the stacks, flipping through the books to see what is in them. This random skimming is a hit-and-miss process that seldom produces much except acute frustration and eye strain. Consulting the *Readers' Guide* for articles is also of limited value because it does not index scholarly and specialized journals. It indexes some fine periodicals, such as *Atlantic Monthly, Harper's, Scientific American, Newsweek,* and *Saturday Review,* but most of its entries are popular magazines, such as *Vogue, Seventeen, Field and Stream, Glamour, Better Homes and Gardens, Reader's Digest,* and *Creative Crafts.* To find listings of more specialized publications, you have to consult a subject index. For example, the *Humanities Index* lists many periodicals not found in the *Readers' Guide,* including *American Historical Review, American Literature, Civil War History, Film Quarterly, Journal of Negro History,* and many others. Each field, such as art, education, political science, chemistry, and psychology, has its own index, and you will save yourself time and energy if you go straight to that index or to a reference bibliography.

Reference Bibliographies

A reference bibliography is a list of books and articles on a particular subject, usually compiled by experts in the field. Not only have these bibliographers already searched journals and books for all the relevant materials, but also they have often annotated the entries; that is, they tell what the book covers and they evaluate its usefulness. You should probably begin your search by consulting the following works.

GENERAL BIBLIOGRAPHIES

Bibliographic Index, published annually
Guide to Reference Books (9th ed.), Eugene P. Sheehy
How and Where to Look It Up: A Guide to Standard Sources of Information, Robert W. Murphy

Reference Books: How to Select and Use Them, Paul Galin and
  Peter Spielberg
A World Bibliography of Bibliographies (5 vols.), Theodore
  Besterman

YEARBOOKS, ALMANACS, CURRENT EVENTS

The Americana Annual: An Encyclopedia of Current Events
  (1923 to present)
The Britannica Book of the Year (1938 to present)
*The Statesman's Year-Book: Statistical and Historical Annual
  of the States of the World* (1864 to present)
Yearbook of the United Nations (1947 to present)

Information Please Almanac (1947 to present)
World Almanac and Book of Facts (1868 to present)

Editorials on File (published weekly)
Facts on File: A Weekly Synopsis of World Events (1940 to present)
New York Times Index (1913 to present)

BIOGRAPHY

*Biography Index: A Quarterly Index to Biographical Material in
  Books and Magazines* (1946 to present)
*Biography News: A Compilation of News Stories and Feature
  Articles from American News Media Covering Personalities
  of National Interest in All Fields* (1974 to present)
Current Biography (1940 to present)
Dictionary of American Biography (20 vols.)
Dictionary of National Biography (British; 63 vols.)
*Index to Women of the World from Ancient to Modern Times:
  Biographies and Portraits*
International Who's Who (1935 to present)
Who's Who (British; 1849 to present)
Who's Who in America (1899 to present)

ART

American Art Directory (1952 to present)
Art and Architecture: Including Archaeology
Art Books: A Basic Bibliography on the Fine Arts
Art Index (1929 to present)
Dictionary of Art (5 vols.)
Encyclopedia of World Art (15 vols.)

Oxford Companion to Art
Who's Who in American Art
Who's Who in Art (British)

BIOLOGICAL SCIENCES

Biological Abstracts (1926 to present)
Biological and Agricultural Index (1964 to present)
Biological Sciences
Botanical Bibliographies
Encyclopedia of the Biological Sciences
Guide to the Literature of the Zoological Sciences
Science Reference Sources

BUSINESS AND ECONOMICS

American Business Dictionary
Business Periodicals Index (1958 to present)
A Classification of Business Literature
Economic Almanac (1949 to present)
Encyclopedia of Management
International Bibliography of Economics (1955 to present)
Literature of Executive Management: Selected Books and Reference
    Sources for the International Businessman
Sources of Business Information

DANCE

Dance Encyclopedia
Dictionary of Modern Ballet
Guide to Dance Periodicals
Research in Dance

EDUCATION

Current Index to Journals in Education (1969 to present)
Dictionary of Education
Digest of Educational Statistics (1962 to present)
Education Abstracts (1936 to present)
Education Index (1929 to present)
Encyclopedia of Education
International Yearbook of Education (1948 to present)
The Literature of Education: A Critical Bibliography, 1945–1970
Research in Education (1967 to present)

Who's Who in American Education (1928 to present)
World Year Book of Education (1932 to present)

HISTORY

*Bibliographies in American History: Guide to Materials for
    Research*
Bibliography of Modern History (13 vols.)
Cambridge Ancient History (12 vols.)
Cambridge Medieval History (8 vols.)
Cambridge Modern History (13 vols.)
Guide to Historical Literature
*Harper Encyclopedia of the Modern World: A Concise Reference
    History from 1760 to the Present*

LITERATURE—GENERAL

Humanities Index
Handbook to Literature
*MLA International Bibliography of Books and Articles on the
    Modern Languages and Literature* (1921 to present)
A Reference Guide to English Studies
*Selective Bibliography for the Study of English and American
    Literature*

AMERICAN LITERATURE

Articles on American Literature, 1900–1950
Articles on American Literature, 1950–1967
Literary History of the United States (3 vols.)
Oxford Companion to American Literature

BLACK LITERATURE

*Black American Literature: A Critical History of the Major Periods,
    Movements, Themes, Works, and Authors*
No Crystal Stair: A Bibliography of Black Literature

BRITISH

Cambridge Bibliography of English Literature (5 vols.)
Cambridge History of English Literature (15 vols.)
A History of the English Novel (11 vols.)
A Literary History of England

Oxford Companion to English Literature
Oxford History of English Literature
Year's Work in English Studies

MUSIC

American Music: An Information Guide
Dictionary of Music and Musicians
Encyclopedia of Country and Western Music
Encyclopedia of Rock
Harvard Dictionary of Music
International Cyclopedia of Music and Musicians
Music Article Guide (1966 to present)
Music Index (1949 to present)
Oxford History of Music (8 vols.)
Popular Music: An Annotated Index of American Popular Songs

PHILOSOPHY

Bibliography of Philosophy
Dictionary of Philosophy
Encyclopedia of Philosophy
Guide to Philosophical Bibliography and Research
A History of Philosophy (8 vols.)

PHYSICAL SCIENCES—GENERAL

Applied Science and Technology Index (1958 to present)
McGraw Hill Encyclopedia of Science and Technology
McGraw Hill Yearbook of Science and Technology
Reference Sources in Science and Technology
Scientific and Technical Books in Print
Technology (2 vols.)

PHYSICAL SCIENCES—SPECIFIC

Chemical Abstracts
A Dictionary of Geology
Dictionary of Mathematics
Encyclopaedic Dictionary of Physics (9 vols.)
Encyclopedia of Chemistry
Encyclopedia of Physics (54 vols.)
Engineering Encyclopedia
Engineering Index Annual

Geologic Reference Sources
Handbook of Chemistry and Physics
An International Bibliography on Atomic Energy
International Computer Bibliography

POLITICAL SCIENCE

A Guide to Library Sources in Political Science
Information Sources of Political Science
The Literature of Political Science: A Guide for Students,
    Librarians, and Teachers
Political Science: A Bibliographical Guide to the Literature
Political Science Bibliographies
Stateman's Yearbook
United Nations Yearbook
Yearbook of World Affairs

PSYCHOLOGY

Annual Review of Psychology (1950 to present)
Dictionary of Psychology and Related Fields
Encyclopedia of Psychology
Guide to Library Research in Psychology
Harvard List of Books in Psychology
Psychological Abstracts
Psychology Almanac: A Handbook for Students

RELIGION

A Bibliography of Bibliographies in Religion
Cambridge History of the Bible
The Catholic Encyclopedia (18 vols.)
Dictionary of the Bible
A Dictionary of Non-Christian Religions
An Encyclopedia of Religion
Index to Religious Periodical Literature
Universal Jewish Encyclopedia and Reader's Guide (11 vols.)

SOCIOLOGY

Current Sociological Research
Dictionary of Sociology and Related Sciences
Encyclopedia of Social Work
International Bibliography of Sociology

Social Science Index
Sociological Abstracts

WOMEN'S STUDIES

Bibliography on Women: With Special Emphasis on Their Roles in Science and Society
Who's Who of American Women (1965 to present)
Women: A Bibliography
Women's Right Movement in the U.S., 1948–1970
Women's Studies Abstracts
The World's Who's Who of Women

Bibliography Cards

When you find a source that sounds promising in a reference work, write down the essential information about that book or article on a 3-by-5 inch index card (one book or article per card). For a book, for instance, the bibliography card will contain such information as author's name, title of book (underlined), place of publication, publisher, and date published.

```
                                          353.03
                                            C



          Califano, Joseph A. Jr.
          A Presidential Nation
          New York: Norton, 1975.
```

After you have made a bibliography card for each book that seems relevant to your subject, you can look up the books in your library's card catalog and write down the call number in the upper right corner of the card, as shown above.

Likewise, for each journal article that you find in an index or bibliography and wish to read, you should make a bibliography card that contains the following information: author, title of article (in quotation marks), name of journal (underlined), date, and the inclusive pages of the article.

```
Morris, Edward A.
"The One-Term Presidency."
Center Magazine
May/June 1981: 45–55.
```

For the form of other types of books and periodicals and for the form governing encyclopedias, newspapers, and book reviews, consult the examples on pages 578–580.

Consider bibliography cards your working bibliography or preliminary bibliography, which you will then explore to see which items are useful and which are not. Very likely this working bibliography will expand because the more you read, the more sources you will encounter. One source will often refer you to another; when it does, make a new bibliography card.

The reasons for using bibliography cards are, I think, persuasive. First, being systematic is convenient in the long run because you avoid the confusion that can result from dealing with many different books and articles. By keeping the cards in alphabetical order according to author's last name, you can quickly locate any one of them. Second, this system allows you to keep track of which books and articles you have consulted; as soon as you examine a source and decide whether it is valuable to you or not, put a check mark above the call number to remind yourself that you have looked at it. Third, these bibliography cards correspond to note cards that you will make later, and since you have already recorded the full information on the bibliography card, you won't have to repeat all that information on each note card. Fourth, when you begin documenting your paper much later, the bibliography card will supply necessary information. Fifth and finally, when at the end of your paper you compile a list of sources you cited in the paper, all you will have to do is to copy the information from those bibliography cards.

Note-Taking

Once you have completed the first stage—making a list of possible sources—the next stage is to find those sources, determine whether the information in them is relevant to your topic, and, if it is, record the information. Since the success of your paper ultimately depends on the quality of the sources you use and on the accuracy of your notes, this stage is especially important. If I could give you only two pieces of advice about this process, they would be:

1. Read widely and intensely before you take a single note.
2. Have a system for recording the information after you assess it.

Although note-taking is important, don't forget that extensive reading is equally important.

The tendency will be to begin taking notes immediately. Restrain yourself. Don't take notes prematurely because you simply will not know which information is relevant until you have read broadly about the topic. Once you have an overview from reading background material, you can move on to specialized sources and be better able to assess their appropriateness for your project.

Even when you are examining such specialized sources as articles and books, learn to scan before taking notes. With a book, for example, read the table of contents to see what the chapters are about; if a chapter sounds promising, read the opening and concluding paragraphs, and if they seem relevant, scan the whole chapter by reading the first and last sentences of each paragraph. This will give you an overview of the chapter and will help you to locate the most pertinent information. Also look at the index in the back of the book to find out on which pages major topics are discussed. Then carefully read the material you have located and digest it: You must understand the information and evaluate it before you can take intelligent notes. Only now are you ready to take notes.

Here is where the trouble begins for most students. Although they have listened to their instructor imploring them to use note cards and to adhere to a logical system that will keep the subtopics separated from each other, they ignore these sage warnings and launch into note-taking haphazardly. They open their spiral notebooks and start writing, not believing that they are using a method of note-taking that is so inefficient that they will have to buy several bottles of aspirin when the time comes to draft the paper. The problem with the spiral-notebook approach is that the students must record the information in the order that the author presents it instead of the order that they need it. Also, this approach means putting on the same page information that doesn't belong together, and later they have difficulty locating a particular piece of information because it is buried in a mass of other notes.

Don't be one of those students.

Note Cards

The most efficient, flexible, and convenient system is to use index cards (either the 4-by-6 or 5-by-8 inch size). You can place separate information on separate cards, you can label the information in order to find it quickly and in order to place related cards together, and you can shuffle the cards in order to consider different arrangements of information when you start to outline your paper. Here is a typical set of note cards:

---

budget constraints—Califano, 1 of 2

Under the current system, a new president has to wait 21 months from the time he enters office to have his own budget. The budget during his first 9 months in office will be his pre-decessor's, which Congress has already approved. Even the budget for the following fiscal year will have been developed by his predecessor and already sent to Congress. The new president

Califano, Presidential Nation

---

budget constraints—Califano, 2

starts operating under his own budget about halfway through his 4-year term. pp. 297–98.

"The president who desires significantly to reorder national priorities by shifting the expenditure of federal resources faces an almost insurmountable time problem in the confines of a four-year term." p. 299

Califano, Presidential Nation

---

reelection

Califano suggests allowing the president to run for reelection after serving 6 years, but only for one other term. The second term doesn't have to be 6 years; it could be 4 years. p. 296

Making the president ineligible for a second term would make him less responsive and less accountable. p. 302

[Did the constitution of the Confederate States of America, which called for a 6-year presidency, allow reelection—if so, for how many years?]

Califano, <u>Presidential Nation</u>

Notice several important facts about these cards:

(1) Each card contains information about only one topic. Even though the information is all from the same source, Joseph Califano's *A Presidential Nation*, each idea should get a separate card.

(2) Each card should be labeled with a key word or phrase designating its contents, such as *budget constraints* or *reelection*. These headings not only inform you at a glance what is on each card, but also allow you to file the cards by subject, grouping together all the cards on "budget," even though they may be from different sources. In addition, by grouping together cards on common topics, you can quickly see on which topics you have sufficient information, and on which topics you need additional research.

The headings should be as specific as possible because general headings don't distinguish sufficiently between subtopics. At first, when gathering information on the proposal for a one-term 6-year presidency, for instance, you might sort all the note cards into either "pro" or "con" categories, depending on whether the author supports or opposes the proposal. But such broad labels don't allow you to differentiate among the many arguments that might be mustered either in favor of or against the proposal. "Con" arguments might be subdivided into "perpetual lame duck," "too long," "lack of accountability," "president would be unresponsive," and "ineligibility for reelection."

Putting your notes into specific categories is a kind of preliminary classifying process that will help you later when you start to organize the paper. What you are doing when you separate notes into headings is dividing a mass of information into manageable pieces, and eventually these headings will become sections in an outline from which you will draft the paper. How you classify notes, therefore, affects how you organize your final product. This early classifying of information helps you to forecast how you will use the notes and allows you gradually to see an initial shape to your paper.

(3) Always, always include the page number where you found the material. Why? Because later when you have to document the source in your paper, you will know what page number to put in the note. If you forget to record the page number on your note card, you'll have to make an additional trip to the library, look up the book (if it's not checked out or misplaced), and flip through it searching for the material again. Research is difficult enough without having to do it twice. Save yourself the double effort and put the page number on the card.

(4) Cards may contain both paraphrased material and direct quotes. Be certain to distinguish between the two, and double check to make sure that the quoted material is quoted exactly. In general, paraphrase and summarize where possible, and quote only material that is cleverly or eloquently stated. If quoted material runs from one page to another in your source, mark where the break occurs.

(5) Sometimes you will want to react to the notes you have recorded and insert your own ideas on the card. That's acceptable, of course, but place your own thoughts in brackets to distinguish them from the author's ideas.

(6) Don't use both sides of a card because it's too easy to overlook the back later when you're composing from the note cards. If you have more information than will fit onto one card, use another card and indicate on both cards that they belong together.

(7) At the bottom of each note card should appear the author's last name and the title of the source so that you will know where the information came from. Because you already should have a full entry among your bibliography cards, repeating all of the source information on each note card is unnecessary.

(8) Be certain that you have a bibliography card to match a note card. When you have examined a source from your working bibliography, regardless of whether it turns out to be useful, remember to put a check mark on the bibliography card to remind yourself that you have looked at that source.

Documentation

Why Document?

You should document materials for two reasons: to give credit to the person whose ideas or words you are borrowing, and to tell readers precisely where to find the passage so that they can read further if they wish. Without acknowledging that the material comes from another source, you are guilty of plagiarism because you present the ideas as if you had thought of them yourself. Also, unless you give readers the source and page number, they cannot inspect the material themselves and read the surrounding pages.

What to Document

Several different types of material require documenting: direct quotes, paraphrases, data accumulated by someone else, apt phrases, and even another person's line of reasoning. In fact, you must document everything except common knowledge and your own ideas. You have to use quotation marks not only for entire sentences that you borrow directly, but also for parts of sentences where you quote over four consecutive words. Distinctive phrases coined by an author must be credited to that person even if the phrase is only two words. Such important phrases as "dialectical materialism," "shame culture, guilt culture," "affective memory," "objective correlative," "collective unconscious," "cognitive dissonance," and "hot medium, cold medium" must be identified as belonging to their respective originators: Friedrich Engels, Ruth Benedict, Konstantin Stanislavski, T. S. Eliot, Carl Jung, Leon Festinger, and Marshall McLuhan. When you borrow ideas from authors, give them credit. Ideas and phraseology can belong to individuals just as cars and stereos do, and borrowing those ideas and words without documenting them is against the law.

Although students realize that they must document sentences that they quote verbatim, they sometimes aren't aware that they must give credit when they borrow other material as well. Failure to footnote borrowed material or to put quotation marks around verbatim borrowings is plagiarism, even when the plagiarism is unintentional. Plagiarism is a serious infraction, and in the professional world it results in severe legal penalties; in your world, it can result in failure in a course and even academic dismissal.

How to Paraphrase and Avoid Plagiarism

Plagiarism can occur in two ways: when you take material from an author but fail to document the source, or when you document the source but fail to indicate that the phraseology is not your own. The first is not only the more blatant but also the more reprehensible offense because it is premeditated theft and misrepresentation, but the second is also a type of piracy and therefore a violation of law. The second type occurs when the writer has documented a source but either (1) has stolen whole passages verbatim without putting them in quotation marks or (2) has failed to paraphrase properly. Students seem surprised to learn that they can be guilty of plagiarism even when they document material, especially when in case 2 the offense was unintentional and they had tried in fact to avoid plagiarism by rearranging the author's phrases.

This type of plagiarism occurs because students do not fully understand what paraphrasing means or how to do it. To *paraphrase* is to restate another person's ideas in your own words. To paraphrase effectively, you must read the author's material carefully, digest its essence, and then transform those thoughts into your own style so that the material blends into the rest of your paper. Most students believe that paraphrasing means simply shifting around a few words, using synonyms here and there, and switching the order of a couple of phrases, but these minor alterations don't constitute paraphrasing because much of the author's original diction and structure remain. The problem arises because students try to paraphrase while looking at the original passage; instead, you should close the book or periodical and put the ideas down in a totally new way—your way. If you truly comprehend what the author is saying, you should have no problem restating it.

Below, for example, is an excerpt from an article by Arthur M. Schlesinger, Jr., that might be paraphrased:

Even if a single term could elevate a President above politics, is this what we want in a democracy? The argument for insulating the presidency is profoundly anti-democratic in its implication. It assumes that the President alone knows what is best for the country and that the voters are so wrong-headed and ignorant that a President should be enabled to disregard them. It assumes that the democratic process is the obstacle to wise decision.

—From "Reforming the American Presidency," *The Wall Street Journal*, 7 April 1981: 34

Here is an attempted paraphrase that is so close to the original that it constitutes plagiarism:

Even if having a President serve one term would place him above politics, it may not be what we want in a democracy because the President would be insulated. The argument for putting the President above politics is profoundly anti-democratic because it assumes that he alone understands what is good for the nation and that he should be able to disregard voters, who may be wrong-headed and uninformed. The assumption is that the democratic process interferes with wise decision-making.

Notice how closely parallel the second version is to the first. Although some of the diction has been altered, the structure has been essentially copied and there are significant portions that are reproduced verbatim from the original. This degree of similarity in structure and phraseology amounts to appropriating the author's own words and is little more than thinly disguised literary piracy.

Here is an example of a more effective paraphrase of the same passage:

> Schlesinger argues that the proposal for a one-term 6-year presidency goes against basic democratic principle because the President could rule—and, this proposal suggests, should rule—without considering the views of the public that elected him. The proposal implies that the opinions of the public are not worth regarding, that national sentiment should not influence the President's decisions on important issues, and that only his opinions matter.

Because plagiarism is a serious offense, you will want to be uncommonly careful when paraphrasing and documenting. Plagiarism is usually detected because professors can tell when students use someone else's words, and the risk is not worth the penalty. I was in charge of student academic affairs at a university for several years, and my most unpleasant duty was to conduct hearings against students accused of plagiarism by their professor. They had borrowed someone else's ideas, wording, or data and presented it as their own, and therefore they found themselves before a panel charged with academic dishonesty. The penalties ranged from an "F" on the plagiarized paper to an "F" in the course, to suspension from college. In all cases, the offenses were noted in the students' permanent academic files and kept some of them from gaining admission into law school or medical school. Remember, you are responsible for your words.

Bibliography

The easiest and least disruptive way to document material is to give a brief reference within the text that corresponds to a full reference in the list of works cited (the bibliography) at the end of the paper. In the following example, the writer inserts a parenthetical note after using borrowed material; the note, which consists of the author's last name and the page the material comes from, relates to the book, periodical, or other source in the bibliography that is listed under that last name.

> World War II introduced the concept of total war, which disregarded moral principles altogether (Lown 985).

Readers at once know who the author is, and if they want to know the full name, the title, and the date, they can flip to the bibliography, where they will find:

> Lown, Bernard. "Nobel Peace Prize Lecture: A Prescription for Hope." *New England Journal of Medicine* 314 (1986): 985–987.

Because the complete source is found only in the bibliography, it is extremely important to record the bibliographic entries precisely. The forms for various types of reference works are illustrated below.

BOOKS:

One author:
> Johnson, Lyndon B. *Vantage Point.* New York: Holt, 1971.

Two or three authors:
> Corwin, Edward, and Louis W. Koenig. *The Presidency Today.* New York: New York UP, 1956.

> Minow, Newton N., John Martin, and Lee Mitchell. *Presidential Television.* New York: Basic, 1973.

More than three authors:
> Campbell, Angus, et al. *The American Voter.* New York: Wiley, 1960.

Two or more books by the same author:
> Reedy, George E. *The Presidency in Flux.* New York: Columbia UP, 1973.

> ———. *The Twilight of the Presidency.* New York: World, 1970.

Corporate author:
> American Political Science Association Committee on Political Parties. *Toward a More Responsible Two-Party System, A Report.* New York: Rinehart, 1950.

Other than first edition:
> Cronin, Thomas E. *The State of the Presidency.* 2nd ed. Boston: Little, Brown, 1980.

Republication:
> Ford, Henry Jones. *The Rise and Growth of American Politics: A Sketch of Constitutional Developments.* 1898. New York: Da Capo, 1967.

Anthology:
> Moynihan, Daniel P. "The President and the Press." *Commentary* 51 (1971): 41–52. Rpt. in *The Presidency Reappraised.* Ed. Rexford G. Tugwell and Thomas E. Cronin. New York: Praeger, 1974. 148–167.

Multivolume work:
> Richardson, James D., ed. *Messages and Papers of Presidents, 1798–1897.* 20 vols. New York: Bureau of National Literature, 1896–1911.

Translation:
> Machiavelli, Nicolò. *The Prince and Other Works.* Trans. Allan H. Gilbert. New York: Hendricks, 1964.

Article in a reference work:
> "The Constitution of the United States." *Compton's Encyclopedia.* 1983 ed.

> Frey, Frederick Ward. "Political Power." *Encyclopaedia Britannica: Macropaedia.* 1984 ed.

PERIODICALS:

Journal with continuous pagination:
> Palmer, Norman D. "The United States and the Western Pacific." *Current History* 85 (1986): 145–148.

Journal that paginates each issue separately (issue number follows volume—38.6):
> Udall, Morris K. "A Six-Year Presidency?" *Progressive* 38.6 (1974): 19–20.

Monthly or bimonthly periodical:
> Edward A. Morris. "The One-Term Presidency." *Center Magazine* May/June 1981: 45–47.

Weekly or biweekly periodical:
> "A Change in Presidential Terms Favored." *Newsweek* 4 Feb. 1974: 11.

> Valenti, Jack. "A Six-Year Presidency." *Newsweek* 4 Feb. 1974: 11.

Daily newspaper:
> Schlesinger, Arthur M., Jr. "Reforming the American Presidency." *The Wall Street Journal* 7 April 1981: 34.

Review:
>   Commager, Henry Steele. "The Presidency After Watergate." Rev. of *The Living Presidency*, by Emmett John Hughes. *New York Review of Books* 18 Oct. 1973: 49–53.

To compose the bibliography, you can simply arrange your 3-by-5 bibliography cards in alphabetical order and then record them. All of the sources are arranged in alphabetical order according to the author's last name or, for unsigned works, according to the first word in the title (disregarding *A, An,* and *The*). As in these examples, the first line of each bibliographic item should be flush with the left margin, and if more than one line is needed, the subsequent lines are indented five spaces. Single-space within each entry, but double-space between entries, and don't number the entries.

The following sample bibliography will give you an idea of how a finished bibliography should look.

BIBLIOGRAPHY

American Political Science Association Committee on Political Parties. *Toward a More Responsible Two-Party System, A Report.* New York: Rinehart, 1950.

"A Change in Presidential Terms Favored." *Newsweek* 4 Feb. 1974: 11.

Commager, Henry Steele. "The Presidency After Watergate." Rev. of *The Living Presidency*, by Emmett John Hughes. *New York Review of Books* 18 Oct. 1973: 49–53.

"The Constitution of the United States." *Compton's Encyclopedia.* 1983 ed.

Corwin, Edward, and Louis W. Koenig. *The Presidency Today.* New York: New York UP, 1956.

Cronin, Thomas E. *The State of the Presidency.* 2nd ed. Boston: Little, Brown, 1980.

Ford, Henry Jones. *The Rise and Growth of American Politics: A Sketch of Constitutional Developments.* 1898. New York: Da Capo, 1967.

Frey, Frederick Ward. "Political Power." *Encyclopaedia Britannica: Macropaedia.* 1984 ed.

Johnson, Lyndon B. *Vantage Point.* New York: Holt, 1971.

Machiavelli, Nicolò. *The Prince and Other Works.* Trans. Allan H. Gilbert. New York: Hendricks, 1964.

Minow, Newton N., John Martin, and Lee Mitchell. *Presidential Television.* New York: Basic, 1973.

Richardson, James D., ed. *Messages and Papers of Presidents, 1798–1897.* 20 vols. New York: Bureau of National Literature, 1896–1911.

Schlesinger, Arthur M., Jr. "Reforming the American Presidency." *The Wall Street Journal* 7 April 1981: 34.

Udall, Morris K. "A Six-Year Presidency?" *Progressive* 38.6 (1974): 19–20.

Valenti, Jack. "A Six-Year Presidency." *Newsweek* 4 Feb. 1974: 11.

Parenthetical Notes

To avoid the complicated procedure of footnoting, you may simply note within the text the essential information that will allow readers to match the parenthetical note with the bibliographic entry. Usually all that is needed in a parenthetical note is the author's last name and the page number:

(Johnson 103)

If there is no author, an abbreviated title should be used:

("Change" 11)

If there are two or more works in the bibliography by the same author, include a brief title as well as the author's last name:

(Reedy, *Twilight,* 213–215)

If there are two authors with the same last name, include an initial to distinguish them:

(T. Cronin 53)

If the material cited is part of a multivolume work, include the volume as well as the page:

(Richardson 4: 79–80)

Simply use common sense when deciding what to include in a parenthetical note. Unless there is a reason to include additional information, insert only the author's last name and the page number. If there is a chance that readers will become confused for any reason, clarify the note with additional information.

Footnotes

You or your instructor may prefer to use footnotes instead of parenthetical notes; footnote forms are illustrated below.

First Reference

BOOKS

One author:
    [1]Lyndon B. Johnson, *Vantage Point* (New York: Holt, 1971) 344.

Two or three authors:
    [2]Edward Corwin and Louis W. Koenig, *The Presidency Today* (New York: New York UP, 1956) 113.

    [3]Newton N. Minow, John Martin, and Lee Mitchell, *Presidential Television* (New York: Basic, 1973) 94.

More than three authors:
    [4]Angus Campbell et al., *The American Voter* (New York: Wiley, 1960) 33.

Other than first edition:
    [5]Thomas E. Cronin, *The State of the Presidency*, 2nd ed. (Boston: Little, Brown, 1980) 353.

Reprint:
    [6]Henry Jones Ford, *The Rise and Growth of American Politics: A Sketch of Constitutional Developments* (1898; New York: Da Capo, 1967) 84–86.

Anthology:
    [7]Norman C. Thomas, "Reforming the Presidency: Problems and Prospects," *The Presidency Reappraised*, ed. Thomas E. Cronin and Rexford G. Tugwell, 2nd ed. (New York: Praeger, 1977) 334.

Edited work of more than one volume:
    [8]James D. Richardson, ed., *Messages and Papers of the Presidents, 1798–1897*, 20 vols. (New York: Bureau of National Literature, 1897) 7: 49.

Translation:
    [9]Nicolò Machiavelli, *The Prince and Other Works*, trans. Allan H. Gilbert (New York: Hendricks, 1964) 49.

Encyclopedia:
    [10]F[rederick] W[ard] F[rey], "Political Power," *Encyclopaedia Britannica: Macropaedia*, 1984 ed.

Association as author:
    [11]American Political Science Association Committee on Political Parties, *Toward a More Responsible Two-Party System, A Report* (New York: Rinehart, 1950) 51.

PERIODICALS

Journal with continuous pagination:
    [12]Norman D. Palmer, "The United States and the Western Pacific," *Current History* 85 (1986): 146.

Journal that paginates each issue separately (issue number follows volume—38.6):
    [13]Morris K. Udall, "A Six-Year Presidency?" *Progressive*, 38.6 (1974): 19.

Monthly or bimonthly periodical:
    [14]Edward A. Morris, "The One-Term Presidency," *Center Magazine* May/June 1981: 46.

Weekly magazine:
    [15]Jack Valenti, "A Six-Year Presidency," *Newsweek* 4 Feb. 1974: 11.

Unsigned article:
    [16]"A Change in Presidential Terms Favored," *Nation's Business* April 1977: 16.

Newspaper:
    [17]Arthur M. Schlesinger, Jr., "Reforming the American Presidency," *The Wall Street Journal*, 7 Apr. 1981: 34.

BOOK REVIEW:

    [18]Henry Steele Commager, "The Presidency After Watergate," rev. of *The Living Presidency*, by Emmett John Hughes, *New York Review of Books*, 18 Oct. 1973: 49.

Subsequent References

Once you have cited a source and given readers the full information about the source, there is no need to repeat all of the information in subsequent footnotes. An abbreviated form is sufficient, so long as there is no confusion. You may simply use the author's last name followed by the page number, whether the source is a book, a periodical, a newspaper, or an encyclopedia. For example:

    [19]Johnson 211.

If there is any confusion, follow the same logic as for parenthetical notes and include additional information as needed.

Drafting the Investigative Paper

Because of their concern with such nonwriting tasks as library research and documentation, students often forget that the investigative paper is more than a mechanical process. The investigation itself is an essential preliminary activity, but it is a means to an end, not an end in itself. Although documentation is important, it is purely a matter of form, which any intelligent person can follow. These mechanical activities, however, can at times monopolize your attention and consume all of your energy; you may find that you become so preoccupied with documenting who said what that you will slight the drafting stage and neglect rhetorical concerns.

The drafting stage of the investigative paper is typically a cut-and-paste stage for most students. Instead of assuming the role of writer and creating a unified, coherent paper, they become tailors who sew together odd remnants of prose into a quilt that belongs to other authors. There is a difference between splicing and drafting. When you draft, you develop a logical argument, emphasize primary ideas and subordinate secondary ones, integrate material that is drawn from diverse sources, create a uniform tone and style, and connect the parts so that the paper reads smoothly. Although the ideas may come from many sources, the investigative paper is the product of one mind—yours—and should bear the individual stamp and style of that mind.

As with any other paper, this one has to be focused, organized, unified, coherent, and, if possible, even graceful. To achieve these qualities, keep in mind the principles that you have learned from earlier writing assignments:

> You must have a strong thesis—good writing starts with having
>   something worthwhile to say. Most research papers suffer from

lack of a central proposition or point of view, and therefore they offer dozens of facts, but not in support of a focused thesis.

Topic sentences are especially important in paragraphs in the investigative paper because support sentences may each be from a different source and therefore may seem unrelated. By opening a paragraph with a strong topic sentence and controlling idea, you point out for readers the common thread between the sentences and forge them into a unified paragraph.

Repetition of key terms is a fundamental way of achieving coherence. In paragraphs composed of paraphrased sentences that come from several authors, coherence is particularly difficult to achieve because the authors often will have used slightly different key terms in their sentences. If that is the case, you must paraphrase their ideas using the same key terms in each sentence, thereby forming a bridge between the sentences.

When drafting your paper, you might also ask yourself the following questions about structure, logic, evidence, and audience, and if necessary refer to other chapters to refresh your understanding of these concepts:

Who is my audience? (Perhaps you will want to define explicitly an intended audience.) How much knowledge about my subject do they have? Is the audience likely to be hostile, sympathetic, or indifferent to my thesis? What obstacles in their belief system must I overcome, and which beliefs can I appeal to? (Chapter 12)

Should I open with my thesis, or build up to it inductively and present it in the conclusion? (Chapter 13)

What tone should I adopt? Should it be strictly formal, or will a less formal tone be more effective? (Chapter 16)

What kind of ethos am I projecting in this paper? Do I sound stuffy and pedantic, or do I come across as an inquisitive, honest human being? (Chapter 12)

Have I focused on the main issues? (Chapters 1 and 11)

Have I given my readers assertions alone, or have I substantiated assertions with sufficient evidence? (Chapter 11)

What types of evidence will be most convincing—statistics, testimony, personal experience, comparisons? How can I translate facts into meaningful terms for my readers? (Chapters 1 and 11)

Am I biased in my interpretation of the evidence? Am I guilty of presenting only the benefits of one side and only the disadvantages of the other? (Chapter 11)

Have I committed any logical fallacies—post hoc, oversimplification, or hasty generalization? Have I relied on emotionally connotative language to sway readers? (Chapter 11)

Are emotional appeals appropriate in this paper, or would they be irrelevant and manipulative? (Chapter 12)

Have I sufficiently established the link between cause and effect? Have I discovered the underlying causes or just surface causes? Have I identified long-term consequences as well as immediate consequences? (Chapter 9)

Have I provided enough background information for my readers to follow my discussion? (Chapters 1 and 13)

What terms need to be defined? Are my technical descriptions clear? Have I included all the steps in any processes that I explain? (Chapters 5 and 8)

If my paper examines a problem, have I offered a viable solution or outlined the pros and cons of the available solutions? (Chapter 14)

Is my language concrete and precise? Have I avoided clichés? (Chapter 16)

Are my sentences emphatic, concise, and clear? (Chapter 17)

Exercises

1. Find the answers to the following questions, and tell where you found them:

    A. What was the gross national product last year for the United States?
    B. What was the date of birth of Louise Brown, the first test-tube baby?
    C. Who was the physicist who created the neutron bomb?
    D. Who choreographed the antiwar dance "Green Table" (1932)?
    E. What happened of historical significance October 22–28, 1962?
    F. Who was the spokesperson for the free silver movement in the United States presidential elections of 1896 and 1900?
    G. How many troops constitute the United States Rapid Deployment Joint Task Force?
    H. What are the titles of three nineteenth-century Gothic romances?
    I. Who painted the work *Guernica*?
    J. In what publication were Bret Harte's short stories and poems first published?

K. Who was the British physician who first explained the blood circulation system in 1628?

L. Who killed Wild Bill Hickok?

M. Who won the Academy Award for Best Actress in 1961, and what is her real name?

N. In what year was the Environmental Protection Agency established?

O. What was the last year that Japan paid reparations to the United States for damages during World War II?

P. Under which American presidents was the office of the vice president vacant for more than one year?

Q. What was the main cause of the Barons' War in England?

R. Which is the larger airplane, the Boeing 737 or the McDonnell Douglas DC8?

S. What country has the highest suicide rate in the world, and what is that rate?

T. Who was the first black senator in the United States?

U. Who was the first woman Cabinet member?

V. Who first danced the lead role in Diaghilev's "Afternoon of a Faun" in 1912?

W. In 1808, the first duel between two representatives in Congress was fought. Who were the duelists, what was the outcome, and why did they duel?

X. Next to the United States, which country exports the most military armaments—France, the United Kingdom, or West Germany? How many millions of dollars in arms did that nation export last year?

Y. What was the first motion picture to gross $50 million?

Z. In what gallery does the Dutch painter Aelbert Cuyp's *Piper with Cows* hang?

2. Put the following information in correct bibliographic form, and arrange the entries in the proper order:

A. November 17, 1980 a one-page article (p. 32) entitled "Is the One-Term Presidency a Trend?" appeared in *Newsweek*. No author.

B. Library of Congress Catalog Number: 60-14230. Printed in the United States in 1960. *The Presidency*. Subtitle: *Crisis and Regeneration*. Herman Finer. Published by University of Chicago Press.

C. In a book entitled *Congress Against the President* edited by Harvey C. Mansfield, Sr. is an essay by Max M. Kampelman, "Congress, the Media, and the President," pp. 85–97. Mansfield's book was published by Praeger Publishers in New York in 1975. The material used was on page 88.

D. *The President of the United States*. First edition published in 1963. This second edition published in 1972 by McGraw-Hill in New York.

Author is Rowland Egger, who is Professor of Politics and Public Affairs at Princeton University.

E. On November 17, 1980, appeared an article on p. 64 of *U.S. News & World Report* by D. C. Bacon entitled "One More Disposable President." The article concerns the defeat of Jimmy Carter.

3. Paraphrase the following excerpts on note cards:

A. Many have sought to reform the primary by changing the President's term of office. Closely linked to that is the proposal to change the terms of congressmen and, in some versions, senators as well. Limiting the President to a single six-year term was discussed at the Constitutional Convention and proposed to Congress as a constitutional amendment as early as 1826. It has been reintroduced into Congress more than a hundred times since then, most recently in 1971, when both the Senate majority leader, Mike Mansfield (Democrat of Montana), and the venerable Senator George Aiken (Republican of Vermont) sponsored it jointly. As recently as February 1979 the then attorney general of the United States, Griffin Bell of Georgia, and a prominent Republican candidate for the presidency, John Connally of Texas, both came out for the six-year term, which was favored by former President Lyndon Johnson and by no fewer than nine other Presidents.

The case for a single six-year term is in part humanitarian: the burdens of the office are so heavy, it is argued, that no man should be asked to carry them for more than six years. A more convincing case for six years rests on the belief that too much of a President's time in the White House is taken up with working [p. 250/p. 251] for his reelection. The President and his men are preoccupied with reelection, the argument goes, to the detriment of the national interest; reduce the proportion of the first term that is under the shadow of the coming election, and to that extent you free the President to concentrate on what ought to be his proper concerns. The White House is too preoccupied with reelection. But merely by removing the pressures of reelection, you do not necessarily remove the need or the temptation to be "political." If the image developed in these pages is accepted—that of a President reduced to trading for his political requirements because his ability to get them any other way is so restricted—then the six-year single term would not remove all the temptations to excessively "political" behavior. Indeed, another school of thought attacks the six-year proposal on the grounds that there is nothing wrong with the White House being political. George Reedy, for example, who also worked for Lyndon Johnson, dismisses this and indeed most other reform suggestions altogether, on the grounds that they are naive and fail to take account of existing "power relationships in society." The art of politics, says Reedy, is to reconcile these relationships with social needs. Any other approach must fail. Many other critics share his view. Only the constant need to take every political pressure into account, this counterargument goes, can ensure that the presidency will remain democratically responsive to what the people want. "Political," for many of this opinion, has become almost a synonym for "democratic."

—From Godfrey Hodgson,
All Things to All Men: The False Promise of the Modern American Presidency

B.   The Founding Fathers' anxiety about the President's term of office was reflected in their adoption at successive junctures of a term first of seven, then of six, and finally of four years. If Congress chose the President, as many favored, a long term without eligibility for re-election seemed best, because a President otherwise might become a Congressional yes-man in courting re-election. But once the electoral college system had been adopted, a shorter term with unlimited eligibility was agreed upon.

The Founding Fathers expected that George Washington would become the first President and would willingly serve the rest of his days. Their acceptance of the principle of indefinite eligibility ran counter to another American political principle deeply ingrained since Revolutionary [p. 63/p. 64] times, when George III was regarded as the symbol of monarchical tyranny: that rotation in executive office is essential to liberty.

The principle of unlimited eligibility for reelection was innocently but irreparably undermined in practice by the man in whose behalf it had been established, George Washington himself. Washington announced upon completing his second Presidential term that it was his personal wish not to serve another. Thomas Jefferson brought the weakened principle crashing to the ground when, after admiring state legislatures earnestly asked him to continue for a third term, he declared he would not. If there were no limitation on office, understood if not required, he said, the office would be held "for life" and would degenerate "into an inheritance." "Truth also requires me to add," Jefferson continued, "that I am sensible of that decline which advancing years bring on, and feeling their physical I ought not to doubt their mental effect." By the Civil War, Presidential observance had established the two-term principle in the core of American political doctrine.

The two-term practice has occasionally been under siege, however. One assault is the proposal that a President be limited to a single term. Such a doctrine was preached, for example—though certainly not practiced—by Andrew Jackson. And as late as 1912 the Democratic platform endorsed a single Presidential term, a pledge that its nominee, Woodrow Wilson, quickly repudiated. This was by no means the last to be heard of the subject. Dwight D. Eisenhower, both before and after assuming office, found the notion intriguing. Convinced that he could establish in a span of four years his cherished concepts of moderate government, a free economy, and a balanced budget and mindful of his own advanced years, he proposed to hand over the reins after a single term to a younger man. Eisenhower came within an eyelash of incorporating this proposal into his first inaugural address. At the last minute he was talked out of it, but as his term wore on he often reverted to it in private conversation.

—From Louis W. Koenig, *The Chief Executive*

Appendix I

STYLE

In this unit, we will explore the elements of style and the various ways of improving our style. First, however, we need to nail down the definition of style. Style can be defined either broadly to include such elements as reasoning, evidence, word choice, organization, paragraph construction, and sentence structure, or narrowly to include only word choice and sentence structure. For our purposes, we will use the more narrow definition, and in the next chapters we will see how words and sentences determine style and how style affects meaning.

That differences in diction and sentence structure result in different prose styles can be seen in the following short passages, all by well-known writers. How would you characterize each style, and what (besides content) creates the obvious differences among these passages?

On Saturday nights we all go to the picture show, even my mother; Westerns are her favorite kind of movie. Back home, "on the ranch," we pretend we are Tom Mix, Hopalong Cassidy, Lash LaRue (we've even named one of our dogs Lash LaRue); we chase each other for hours rustling cattle, being outlaws, delivering damsels from distress. Then my parents decide to buy my brothers guns. These are not "real" guns. They shoot "BBs," copper pellets my brothers say will kill birds. Because I am a girl, I do not get a gun. Instantly I am relegated to the position of Indian. Now there appears a great distance between us. They shoot and shoot at everything with their new guns. I try to keep up with my bow and arrows.

One day while I am standing on top of our makeshift "garage"—pieces of tin nailed across some poles—holding my bow and arrow and looking out toward the fields, I feel an incredible blow in my right eye. I look down just in time to see my brother lower his gun.

—From Alice Walker, "Beauty: When the Other Dancer Is the Self,"
In Search of Our Mothers' Gardens

A mood of constructive criticism being upon me, I propose forthwith that the method of choosing legislators now prevailing in the United States be abandoned and that the method used in choosing juries be substituted. That is to say, I propose that the men who make our laws be chosen by chance and against their will, instead of by fraud and against the will of all the rest of us, as now. But isn't the jury system itself imperfect? Isn't it occasionally disgraced by gross abuse and scandal? . . . It has its failures and its absurdities, its abuses and its corruptions, but taking one day with another it manifestly works. It is not the fault of juries that so many murderers go unwhipped of justice, and it is not the fault of juries that so many honest men are harassed by preposterous laws. The juries find the gunmen guilty: it is functionaries higher up, all politicians, who deliver them from the noose, and turn them out to resume their butcheries.

—From H. L. Mencken, "A Purge for Legislatures," *Prejudices: Sixth Series*

Great pals we've always been. In fact, there was a time when I had an idea I was in love with Cynthia. However, it blew over. A dashed pretty and lively and attractive girl, mind you, but full of ideals and all that. I may be wronging her, but I have an idea that she's the sort of girl who would want a fellow to carve out a career and what not. I know I've heard her speak favourably of Napoleon. So what with one thing and another the jolly old frenzy sort of petered out, and now we're just pals. I think she's a topper, and she thinks me next door to a looney, so everything's nice and matey.

—From P. G. Wodehouse, *The Inimitable Jeeves*

. . . when John Wayne rode through my childhood, and perhaps through yours, he determined forever the shape of certain of our dreams. It did not seem possible that such a man could fall ill, could carry within him that most inexplicable and ungovernable of diseases. When John Wayne spoke, there was no mistaking his intentions; he had a sexual authority so strong that even a child could perceive it. And in a world we understood early to be characterized by venality and doubt and paralyzing ambiguities, he suggested another world, one which may or may not have existed ever but in any case existed no more: a place where a man could move free, could make his own code and live by it; a world in which, if a man did what he had to do, he could one day take the girl and go riding through the draw and find himself home free, not in a hospital with something going wrong inside, not in a high bed with the flowers and the drugs and the forced smiles, but there at the bend in the bright river, the cottonwoods shimmering in the early morning sun.

—From Joan Didion, "John Wayne: A Love Song," *Slouching Towards Bethlehem*

Good writers are those who have intelligent ideas, know their intended audience, and make informed decisions about which words to choose and how to arrange those words. Put simply, style is a matter of choices. We become good writers by seeing the stylistic options that are available in a given situation, judging the implications of each option, and then selecting the best option based on our purpose, audience, and content. In the next chapters, we will explore some of those stylistic options and their implications.

A

Diction

Mortimer strolled into the room and closed the door. Henrietta glanced up from her novel and then returned to her reading. Mortimer poured himself a healthy Scotch and water, tossed the cat on the floor, and sat down in the rocker with a sigh. "How was your day?" she asked. "Don't ask," he grimaced; "I'm trying to forget." He picked up the newspaper, and she returned to her novel. It would be another evening of tranquility at home.

Notice how a few minor changes in diction alter the whole meaning of this brief narrative. By changing six words, we achieve a different tone and communicate a different message.

Mortimer *stomped* into the room and *slammed* the door. Henrietta *glared* up from her novel and then returned to her reading. Mortimer poured himself a healthy Scotch and water, *threw* the cat on the floor, and sat down in the rocker with a sigh. "How was your day?" she asked. "Don't ask," he grimaced; "I'm trying to forget." He *snapped* up the newspaper and she returned to her novel. It would be another evening of *indifference* at home.

As we can see from these two passages, diction is important because differences in diction amount to differences in meaning, and different words have different effects on our readers. The effect of *stomped* instead of *strolled, slammed* instead of *shut, threw* instead of *tossed,* and so on is to change readers' perception of a situation. The shades of meaning between closely related words such as these are what precise communication is all about. As Mark Twain once said, "The difference between the right word and the almost right word is the difference between lightning and the lightning bug." We have many words, for example, to convey the act of walking in addition to *stroll* and *stomp*—*amble, strut, toddle, clump, shuffle* and so forth—and each conveys something slightly different.

Our language offers several words to refer to almost any idea or object. Certainly we can find examples of one word for one idea—no word other than *guillotine* refers to an instrument for beheading criminals—but for most ideas, we have multiple words. For instance, a place where one drinks beer can be called a *pub*, a *bar*, a *beer joint*, a *honky-tonk*, a *tavern*, a *saloon*, a *cocktail lounge*, or a *rathskeller*. The meaning of each word differs slightly because we associate each with a slightly different setting and patron.

APPLICATION

1. Find five words that, like *guillotine*, refer so exclusively to an idea or object that they have no synonyms.
2. For each of the following words, list two other words that have similar meanings; that is, two synonyms:

eliminate   information
rowdy   saber
horse   usual

Although this diversity in our language makes choosing the right word all the more difficult, it also makes communication more precise. By having several words that refer to the same idea, we can choose the one that conveys our tone and meaning exactly. For example, *imply* and *insinuate* both refer to imparting thoughts indirectly. *Imply* means to convey an unstated idea by stating explicitly another idea that allows the audience to deduce the implied part. *Insinuate*, however, suggests expressing veiled malice through slyness. Although the two verbs are closely related in meaning, the difference is important in terms of both precision and tone. Consider the differences among these statements:

The Senator implied that the CIA was involved.
The Senator insinuated that the CIA was involved.
The Senator hinted that the CIA was involved.
The Senator suggested that the CIA was involved.
The Senator intimated that the CIA was involved.

The shades of meaning among the five statements are subtle but significant since readers are atuned to these fine distinctions and nuances. Naturally, we too must be aware of these nuances in order for our words to express our intended meaning.

Here are four words that refer to someone who avidly supports a cause: *enthusiast, zealot, extremist, fanatic.* Each word has definite boundaries, and each varies in degree of passion and degree of social acceptance. *Enthusiasts* are those who wholeheartedly give themselves to whatever engages their attention, and usually the word applies to small matters, such as sports. *Zealots* are those whose commitment is stronger, and usually the commitment is to an ideological cause. *Zealot* is much stronger than *enthusiast*, and the feeling that accompanies it is less positive. To call someone an *enthusiast* is a compliment; to call someone a *zealot* communicates that the person becomes excessively passionate about a cause and pursues it a little too ardently. To understand fully the term *zealot*, we have to trace its etymology back to biblical times: A zealot was a member of a militant Jewish sect that opposed the Romans in Palestine. Hence, *zealot* has militant overtones. *Extremist* and *fanatic* come close to being true synonyms: Both refer to those who lack restraint and who exceed the norm by going beyond an acceptable limit in belief and behavior. *Extremists* are radicals—people who advocate unreasonably severe measures. *Fanatics* likewise are people who have an intense, uncritical devotion to an idea. The subtle difference between the two is that *extremist* implies that even though a person's beliefs and actions are excessive and perhaps drastic, the person is nevertheless rational and in control. *Fanatic*, however, implies that the person has lost rationality and control. We think of fanatics as people who are wild-eyed and anarchistic. Their outlook is immoderate to the point of monomania, and their behavior is characterized by unpredictability and randomness.

APPLICATION

In the same manner that I have distinguished among *enthusiast, zealot, extremist*, and *fanatic*, try to articulate differences among these sets of synonyms:

clever	foolish
shrewd	ignorant
cunning	gullible
ingenious	asinine

Connotation and Denotation

Words have two types of meaning. The first, called denotation, is the dictionary definition. For example, the dictionary may define cocker spaniel as a long-haired, medium-sized dog with drooping ears, originally bred in England for bird hunting. But when we think of the words *cocker spaniel*, we have definite associations—cockers are affectionate, cuddly, devoted dogs—and those associations are the connotative meaning. We respond to words not only intellectually, but also associatively. Denotatively, a mother is a female parent, but the word has connotations of security, warmth, affection, home, family, and so forth.

Some words elicit favorable responses, some words are neutral, and others are derogatory. *Slender* is positive; *skinny* is negative. *Embellish* is positive; *exaggerate*, negative. *Bloody* is negative; *ensanguined* is neutral. *Imperfect* is slightly negative, but *defective* is more so. *Discontinued* is neutral, but *abandoned* is negative. Being called a *violinist* is nicer than being called a *fiddler*. To *plan* is good; to *plot* isn't. To be *uncompromising* is not necessarily negative, but to be *inflexible* usually is. To be *indirect* is not so bad as to be *deceitful*, and *wagering* is not as bad a vice as *gambling*. Most words, like those below, evoke some degree of associative response. Define these terms denotatively, and then give their associations.

American flag	income tax
parrot	diplomat
lily	rose
oak	rat

Even words whose denotative meanings are similar can have different connotations, such as *pretend* and *feign*, *strength* and *potency*, and *agriculturist* and *farmer*. Articulate the connotative difference between the following pairs of words:

pro-abortion/pro-choice	burp/belch
enemy/adversary	confess/acknowledge
food/cuisine	peek/peer
creek/brook	snapshot/photograph

Even people's names carry connotations. Consider the differences among these names:

John, Jack, Johnny, John-Boy, Jonathan, Jacky
Elizabeth, Betsy, Bess, Lizzie, Beth, Liz
Margaret, Maggie, Meg, Marge, Margie, Peggy
Father, Dad, Daddy, Pop, Pappy, Daddums, Pappa

The following words have favorable connotations. Find a similar word for each that means the same denotatively but has an unfavorable connotation. For example: lawyer—shyster; youthful—immature; candid—blunt.

suave	fame	philanthropist
the public	humble	fastidious
daring	laugh	delicate
ingenuous	patriotic	svelte
self-controlled	traditional	natural

All of these exercises are simply to show that judgments are inherent in words. Words not only give information, they also express an attitude. For example, when we refer to television as the *boob tube,* we are expressing an opinion. We communicate as much by associative meaning as by surface, denotative meaning.

We choose words to influence our readers' attitudes as well as to reflect our own attitude. One way to persuade readers to accept our perceptions and beliefs is to couch them in favorable language—that is, in words that have positive connotations. For example, the World Health Organization has officially substituted the term *drug dependence* for *drug addiction* because *drug addiction* elicits a more negative response from the public. For another example, the United States Congress decided to change the name of its legislative breaks from *recesses,* which has the connotation of playtime, to *district work periods.* In addition to using favorable language to promote our beliefs, we can couch opposing views in unfavorable language. Political conservatives, for instance, say that they want to bring the costs of social programs "under control" to achieve "prudent fiscal management"; liberals contend that the conservatives want to "slash funds for the needy" in order to "inflate the defense budget." The highly connotative language is intended to influence voters so they will endorse one ideology over another. Language conveys the writer's opinion; it also influences readers' perceptions.

To illustrate that changes in diction can alter perceptions, Bertrand Russell wrote the following propositions: "I am firm; you are stubborn; he is pig-headed." The three adjectives mean essentially the same thing, but the attitude reflected by each statement is increasingly uncomplimentary. Here are a few additional examples:

I am concerned.
You are worried.
She is fearful.

I am weighing alternatives.
You are being indecisive.
He is confused.

I am tolerant.
You are lenient.
He is indulgent.

I am open-minded.
You are impressionable.
They are gullible.

I am sensitive.
You are petulant.
She is cantankerous.

APPLICATION

Try your hand at composing sets of propositions that reflect different levels of acceptance:

I am conciliatory.	I am demonstrative.	I am an epicurean.
You are _____	You are _____	You are _____
She is _____	He is _____	They are _____
I am _____	I am _____	I am _____
You are a politician.	You are defensive.	You are hard to please.
He is _____	She is _____	They are _____
I am _____	I am _____	I am _____
You are _____	You are _____	You are _____
She is sly.	He is cheap.	They are arrogant.

We must be aware of the associations that different words convey and must use the word that expresses our attitude, on the one hand, and elicits the exact response we wish on the other hand.

Levels of Diction

Bertie Wooster: "You agree with me that the situation is a lulu?"
Jeeves: "Certainly a somewhat sharp crisis in your affairs would appear to have been precipitated, sir."

—From P. G. Wodehouse, *Code of the Woosters*

Besides having different meanings and associations, words can differ in their degree of formality. *Intoxicated,* for example, is more formal than its synonym *drunk.* We can classify words according to their relative formality on a continuum ranging from slang at one extreme to elevated diction at the other:

slang—colloquial—mainstream—formal—elevated

For instance, *friend* is a mainstream word; i.e., it is neither formal nor informal, but middlebrow. As we move toward informality, we encounter the colloquial *buddy;* further down the line we find the slang term *sidekick.* Going the opposite direction, we encounter the more formal term *comrade;* and the most elevated term of all is *consociate.* Each term not only has a different connotation, but also is of a different social class. However, just because a word is slang doesn't mean that it has a negative connotation. A negative slang word for *friend* is *crony;* a positive slang word for *friend* is *chum.* We can classify other words in the same way—for example, *man:*

> dude—fellow—man—male—gentleman

Which level of diction we use in an essay depends on the occasion and the audience. Certain occasions, such as funerals and inaugural ceremonies, are necessarily formal and require formal diction. Likewise, certain audiences are more formal than others, and we must choose the diction level to suit the audience. We would not use the same language in a letter to a grandmother that we would to a sister, even if we reported on the same events. In the granny letter, we would probably use mainstream diction; in the other letter, we would more likely use colloquial and sometimes slang diction, full of ungrammatical constructions and stuff like, you know, that old gram wouldn't pick up on. (More on this under "Tone," on page 622.)

Maintaining a consistent level of diction in an essay is important in order to achieve a unified style. If we use different levels of diction in the same essay or letter, we unintentionally startle and confuse readers, as here:

> Mr. Holbron has been an exceptional employee during his 12 years with our firm. He not only has sedulously striven to achieve excellence, but has also contributed imaginatively to our product design. The boss has never had to chew him out for screwing off.

The shift from formal language to slang in the final sentence jolts readers, who were expecting to read something more along these lines:

> Management has never had to reprimand Mr. Holbron for laxity.

The two guidelines governing level of diction are: (1) use the level appropriate to the occasion and audience, and (2) be consistent in using that level.

APPLICATION

1. In the following pairs of synonyms, which is the more formal?

endeavor—try	sleep—slumber
rain—precipitation	ameliorate—improve
itinerary—route	fireworks—pyrotechnics
liar—prevaricator	sagacious—wise
thesbian—actor	atmosphere—ambience

2. At what level of diction are these terms?

danger	sawbones	okay
satisfactory	loophole	premeditated
sucker	movie	gabby
mentor	edify	tease
malarkey	clairvoyant	adage
accessible	refute	ransack
cognition	puke	equestrian

3. Arrange the following sets of words according to formality, from least to most formal.

cop	difficult	substitute
law enforcement agent	problematic	stand-in
police officer	tough	surrogate
flatfoot	hard	pinch hitter
fuzz	arduous	proxy

insane	neophyte	haughty
disturbed	greenhorn	arrogant
crazy	rookie	supercilious
luny	novice	snobbish
psychotic	beginner	snooty

4. Here are several mainstream words; supply synonyms for the other levels.

Slang	*Colloquial*	*Mainstream*	*Formal*	*Elevated*
		vicinity		
		food		
		gift		
		prison		
		salesperson		

5.   My immediate reaction when a head studded with aluminum rheostats confronted me over the garden gate last Tuesday morning was one of perplexity. That it belonged to a courier from outer space was, I felt, improbable, for nobody of such transcendent importance would have chosen a weedy Pennsylvania freehold to land on. Its features, moreover, were much too traditional for an interplanetary nuncio; instead of the elephant ears and needle-sharp proboscis that science fiction had prepared me for, the apparition exhibited a freckled Slavic nose and wattles ripened by frequent irrigations of malt. In the same instant, as I straightened up, giddy with the effort of extricating a mullein from the cucumbers, I realized that the spiny coiffure was in actuality a home permanent and the bulging expanse of gingham below it the rest of Mrs. Kozlich, our current cleaning woman.

—From S. J. Perelman, "Monomania, You and Me Is Quits," *The Rising Gorge*

A. Is Perelman's diction contrived, formal, colloquial, scientific, mainstream, slang, or what?

B. Why do you suppose he chose to use such words as *rheostats, nuncio, proboscis, mullein,* and so forth? (Look up any words that you don't know.) What is the effect of using this diction?

C. Does the fact that this is the introductory paragraph of an essay published in *The New Yorker* matter? How would you characterize the readers of that magazine?

D. Is his sentence structure as uncommon as his vocabulary, or is it typical of most prose in magazines? Substantiate your answer.

Contrived Diction

A lamentable trend in language over the past few decades has been the use of inflated and contrived diction to impress readers instead of to communicate with them. In lieu of a simple word that will precisely convey an idea, technocrats prefer to use two or more elevated words that sound important but that actually obscure meaning, as illustrated by the following phrases, which are substantial in sound but simple in meaning:

Contrived	*Plain English*
air vehicles with lower noise emission characteristics	quieter airplanes
unlawful or arbitrary deprivation of life	murder
second-party credibility	hearsay
effectuate enhancements to socioeconomically disadvantaged individuals inhabiting distressed urban areas	help the poor who live in slums

The more words of this type that writers use, the less meaning they convey.

Writers use this contrived diction because they are trying either to sound authoritative or to camouflage the truth. In the first instance, their technique is usually overstatement; in the second, understatement.

Overstatement

Some writers use overstated, inflated diction in a desperate attempt to convince readers that they know what they are writing about. Usually this type of writing occurs when writers aren't confident of their ideas. Because their ideas aren't original enough or perceptive enough to impress readers, these bluffers resort to pompous language to try to instill importance into their drab thoughts on a drab subject. By using big, grandiose terms and involved sentence constructions, they hope to elevate their subject, their ideas, and themselves. Through a surplus of words, they seek to bolster their image, convince readers of their great knowledge on a topic, and, in short, bamboozle the world.

Examples of inflated diction come from bureaucrats, educators, sociologists, politicians, lawyers, psychologists, and business persons:

Inflated Diction	*Plain English*
traffic expediter	cop
statutory aftercare of released individuals	parole
directive actions for the improvement of child behavior	discipline
nonpersistent chemical irritant	tear gas
voluntary interruption of pregnancy	abortion
children in need of supervision	juvenile delinquents
written vehicles of postal communication	letters
temporary cessation of gainful employment	job layoff

Educational journals contain such language as "the time-critical motivational aspects of underachievers on the self-realization continuum." In business reports we can read about "suboptimization agreements on the impact of downscaling the systems analysis division of the primary infrastructures." Bureaucrats "conduct feasibility studies on the cost-effectiveness of facilitating the prioritization of procedural safeguards." From the United States Congress we get the tortured prose of the Energy Policy and Conservation Act, which is supposed to give the President "a substantial measure of administrative flexibility to craft the price regulatory mechanism in a manner designed to optimize [oil] production from domestic properties subject to a statutory parameter requiring the regulatory pattern to prevent prices from exceeding a maximum weighted average."

What does it all mean? It is "full of sound and fury, signifying nothing." It represents the feeble attempts of feeble minds to bolster feeble thoughts.

This language is formed in several ways. The simplest is to take a noun, change it into an adjective, and connect it to a deadwood noun:

politics—political arena
motivation—motivational aspects
overcrowding—overcrowding scenario
implementation—implementation phase

A similar trick is to change a verb into a noun and substitute a weaker noun:

motivate—effect motivation
assess—make an assessment of
deter—is a deterrence to
implement—is in implementation

Notice that the converted noun usually ends in *-ation, -ment,* or *-ence* and is further encumbered by a preposition. Another way that technocrats botch up language is to use highly formal diction, for example substituting "educational facility" for "school," "pictorial erotic stimuli" for "pornography," or "protective coating laboratory" for "paint shop." A final method for lending importance to the mundane is to borrow words from science, so that a parachute becomes an "aerodynamic personnel decelerator," and brushing teeth regularly becomes, thanks to the American Dental Association, "a conscientiously applied program of oral hygiene."

The problem with stuffy prose is that it is always wordy, usually vague, sometimes unintelligible, and ultimately ineffective. Readers are put off by the pomposity because it simply confuses them. The attempt to bolster ordinary ideas by couching them in pompous language results in obscuring the message rather than clarifying it, and that is the main problem with using inflated language. Readers are also put off because they view the writer as a pretentious know-it-all. When writers don the mask of a self-important authority, they cover up their own personalities, and that is a mistake because we communicate most effectively when readers perceive a real person behind the pen instead of an anonymous phrasemonger.

We are most effective when we use concise, accurate, honest language.

APPLICATION

1. For what simple words are these contrived phrases substitutions?
   polygraph interview
   inventory leakage
   domestic engineer
   unauthorized use of a motor vehicle
   municipal relief station
   individuals preferring same-sex affection
   high tolerance for deviation in child rearing

2. Translate the following sentences into plain English.
   A. The dissociation of myself from my previous professional position was attributable to my temporarily expropriating certain assets.

B. I have no certain recollection of a private conversation offering inducement in the form of currency to any legislative or executive branch official to maximize the fiduciary opportunities of my corporate group.

C. An inmate of the county retraining center made an unauthorized departure from the correctional institution by exhibiting a tallow-sculpted facsimile of a manual high-velocity weapon.

D. "A dishonored check will cause assessment of a substantial penalty." (California Department of Motor Vehicles)

E. Regardless of the vapidity and fuliginousness of the edifice, no other tenantable structure is commensurate in affective quality with one's own inimitable abode.

3. Try your hand at translating these plain English statements into gobbledygook.

A. "Broadly speaking, the short words are best, and the old words best of all." (Winston Churchill)

B. A stitch in time saves nine.

C. Opposites attract.

D. "Take the course opposite to custom and you will do well." (Jean Jacques Rosseau)

E. "Let both sides [East and West] seek to invoke the wonders of science instead of its terrors. Together let us explore the stars, conquer the deserts, eradicate disease, tap the ocean depths and encourage the arts and commerce." (John F. Kennedy)

F. "When in doubt, tell the truth." (Mark Twain)

G. "An army marches on its stomach." (Napoleon)

H. Times change, and we change with them.

I. Supply determines demand.

J. He that fights and runs away may live to fight another day.

Understatement

Whereas the motivation for using overstated pretentious language is to impress readers, the motivation for using understated pretentious language is to conceal truth from readers; and whereas the former is used primarily by bureaucrats to pump up mundane ideas, the latter is used primarily by politicians and militarists to downplay bad situations. The one tries to make what is routine sound significant; the other tries to make what is horrendous sound routine.

This understated language, which is used by such institutions as the Pentagon and the CIA, is designed to be intentionally confusing and incomprehensible so that the public doesn't understand what the government is doing. For instance:

Contrived Diction	*Plain English*
enhanced radiation hardware for maximum termination capability	bigger bombs to kill more people
clandestine operations by electronic surveillance and surreptitious entry	spying, wiretapping, and burglary
civilian irregular defense soldiers on per diem contracts	mercenaries

The linguistic game of hiding truth with double-talk is morally akin to lying.

This type of linguistic deception is especially used to try to gloss over embarrassing situations. For example, when a government agency issues a report containing false assertions that are later uncovered, it doesn't say, "We made a mistake"; it says instead, "The certainty of our conclusions may not have been warranted by the specificity of our data." The meaning of the sentence is purposely lost in gobbledygook because the agency doesn't want anyone to understand that it blundered. Another example is that a hospital, not wanting to state that "a patient died," might couch the fact this way: "We experienced a case of negative patient outcome." Again, the statement is intentionally indecipherable. When the CIA is caught telling a whopper, it says "that was a case of terminological inexactitude" or "that information is no longer operative"— instead of admitting that "we lied." In wartime, the Defense Department (once called the War Department) uses such gibberish as "accidental delivery of friendly ordnance" to keep from saying "we mistakenly bombed our own troops." "Accidental delivery of friendly ordnance" sounds as if a supply sergeant sent an order of bedpans to the wrong battalion; it totally hides the fact that people were maimed and killed.

Wars seem to spawn nonsense coinages, and the less popular the war, the more double-talk is needed to mollify citizens. Although World War II, which most Americans supported, coined few weasel words, the Korean War, which was less popular, introduced several understated terms. The most memorable linguistic invention was the phrase *police action* for war; whereas *war* has negative connotations, *police* suggests protection and *action* is purposely neutral. Another substitution for *war* that emerged was *conflict*, which suggests disagreement instead of killing, though 33,629 American soldiers were killed in the Korean "conflict."

The most cunning weasel words were needed to sell the Vietnam War to the public because many Americans questioned our involvement there. To gloss over the violence and brutality of the war, and to make the war seen routine, the Pentagon used inoffensive and vague language to describe the war. An American invasion into Cambodia, for example, was called an *incursion* because the connotation was less negative than *invasion*; when American pilots bombed Laos, the air raid was called *area denial* or *limited air interdiction*; if American troops retreated at any time, it was called *retrograde maneuvers*; and when Vietnamese villages were burned, the official version read that they were *neutralized.*

What these terms have in common is that (1) they are polysyllabic substitutions for common, explicit, concise words such as *invade, bomb, retreat,* and *destroy*; (2) they are so vague that unless we already know their intended meaning, we wouldn't guess it; (3) they are so abstract that none of them conjures up mental images that might cause readers to react emotionally; and (4) they all avoid negative connotation as much as possible. In short, these elaborate phrases are smokescreens designed to interfere with communication and to dilute readers' emotional responses.

We must learn to be skeptical, we must refuse to accept sounds without meaning, we must learn to recognize smokescreens, and we must try to see what is *not* being said. Ask, "Why the smoke?" Where's there's smoke, there's fire, and our job is to look for the fiery truth.

APPLICATION

1. What would you guess these military and CIA phrases mean?
   air-to-ground encounters
   terminated with extreme prejudice
   favorable redefinition of frontiers
   antipersonnel device
   protective reaction aerial run
   compulsory transfer of native population to resettlement centers
   maximum bipolar superpower strategic exchange
   military research occupational illness
   destabilization of a politically nonfriendly government through
      disinformation and clandestine operations
   pacification of an environment

2. Translate this imaginary explanation of how the CIA protects the President from involvement in "destabilizations."

To limit the President's level of accountability and to maximize procedural safeguards, the U.S. intelligence community issues the chief executive a sanitized document when it undertakes to destabilize an uncordial foreign government and liberate their populace. They also provide the Administration with a plausible denial to counterfoil political accusations in the event that the operation has a negative conclusion.

How to Improve Diction

There is no single way of achieving a clear, emphatic writing style. Lively writing isn't so much a matter of rules as it is of energetic thinking, of refusing to be satisfied with dullness and stodginess, and of strenuous revising. I know of no shortcuts. We can, however, strive to meet certain standards, and we can avoid a few common weaknesses. Used together, the following suggestions will pep up a style considerably:

> use strong verbs
> avoid clichés
> try figurative language occasionally.

Use Strong Verbs

Dynamic verbs can invigorate prose by quickening the pace and animating ideas. In the following excerpt, for example, pay particular attention to the brisk verbs the author selects.

Even as adults, wolves play tag with each other or romp with the pups, running about a clearing or on a snowbank with a rocking-horse gait. They scare each other by pouncing on sleeping wolves and by jumping in front of one another from hiding places. They bring things to each other, especially bits of food. They prance and parade about with sticks or bones in their mouths. I recall how one Alaska evening, the sun still bright at 11:30 P.M., we watched three wolves slip over the flanks of a hill in the Brooks Range like rafts dipping over riffles on a river. Sunlight shattered on a melt pond ahead of them. Spotting some pintail ducks there, the wolves quickly flattened out in the blueberries and heather. They squirmed slowly toward the water. At a distance of fifty feet they popped in the air like corks and charged the ducks. The pintails exploded skyward in a brilliant confusion of pounding wings, bounding wolves, and sheets of sunburst water. Breast feathers from their chests hung almost motionless in midair. They got away. The wolves cavorted in the pond, lapped some water, and were gone. It was all a game.

—From Barry Holstun Lopez, *Of Wolves and Men*

Because it expresses the action, the verb is the most important word in a sentence. Too often, though, we insert a feeble verb and thereby weaken the whole sentence. Instead of a verb that acts, we favor ones that merely indicate a state of being. For some reason we shy away from strong, active verbs such as *collide, destroy,* and *gyrate;* we prefer *have a collision, is destructive,* and *make a gyrating motion.* We overuse motionless verbs such as *occur, have, consider, remain, determine, tend,* and so on.

Some linguists contend that verbs reflect our philosophy of life and that a style dominated by passive and weak verbs suggests that we see ourselves as lacking vivacity and dynamism. Regardless of the validity of this view, we must admit that weak verbs create a sinewless and flaccid prose style. Whereas strong verbs enliven prose, weak verbs deaden it.

Avoid Linking Verbs

Linking verbs are verbs that simply connect the subject to other parts of the sentence; examples are forms of the verbs *to be, to seem,* and *to become.* Instead of expressing an action, they merely act as a link to tie together groups of words. Whenever we use verbs such as *am, is, are, be, being, been, was, were, appears, seems,* or *becomes* in a sentence, we should look again to see whether another verb might strengthen the sentence and more forcefully communicate our idea. This is not to say that linking verbs don't have a useful purpose; it simply means that we use them too quickly and freely. A discourse filled with linking verbs lacks punch: Instead of an essay that scuttles along, we end up with one that is static and sluggish.

Compare the following versions of the same story and notice the number of linking verbs in the first version.

> The hostility in the office *is* pervasive. The female workers claim that they *are* discriminated against by their male supervisor. The male supervisor *is* an insecure person who *is* threatened by any subordinates who *are* industrious. In addition, the night crew *feels* that the day shift *is* lazy and doesn't do as much work as the night crew, so there *is* friction between them. And two of the secretaries *are* constantly at each other's throats over salaries, duties, and lunch hours. If something *is* not done soon, there will *be* war on the seventh floor.

To transform this paragraph into a more energetic and direct story, we merely locate the real action in each sentence and emphasize it by changing the verb:

> Hostility *pervades* the office. The female workers claim that their insecure male supervisor *discriminates* against them and that any initiative by subordinates *threatens* him. In addition, the night crew *accuses* the day shift of loafing and of not accomplishing as much work as the night crew;

hence, friction results. And two of the secretaries constantly *bicker* over salaries, duties, and lunch hours. If management *fails* to correct the situation, the seventh floor will *erupt* into open warfare.

With a little effort, we can almost always substitute action verbs for linking ones. The effect in any one sentence will not be monumental, but the cumulative effect will be substantial: Our prose will have spryness and snap.

Avoid Hidden Verbs

In the following example, the real action of the sentence is hidden in the form of a noun:

> ORIGINAL: The guards conduct hourly inspections of the cell blocks because such inspections can act as a deterrent to escape attempts.

> REVISION: The guards hourly inspect the cell blocks because inspections deter escape attempts.

Besides being more direct and emphatic, the revision contains 40 percent fewer words. In the original, the verbs *inspect* and *deter* have been changed into *conduct inspections of* and *act as a deterrent to*. This process of changing verbs into nouns, called nominalizing, sabotages the action of a sentence and results in limp, inactive, and wordy prose. We take perfectly good verbs, change them into nouns (usually ending in *-ation*, *-ment*, or *-ence*), and substitute weaker verbs: *change,* for instance, becomes *experience a change; prepare* becomes *make preparations for;* and *negotiate* becomes *carry on negotiations.*

To reverse nominalization, we must consciously seek out the imprisoned verb within the phrase and liberate it.

APPLICATION

Locate the hidden verbs in these phrases:

make a suggestion	commit robbery
hand in one's resignation	make a recommendation
achieve mechanization	make an adjustment
is an illustration of	cause a reduction
bring about a result	make a withdrawal of funds
act as a moderator	give a response

In the following paragraph, the nouns not only blur the action, but also require a number of prepositional phrases and extra words.

To *make the assumption* that Congress *gives unfair treatment to* farmers is to *make an unjust accusation*. We Congressional members *take legislative action on* agricultural programs each year: we *facilitate the development of* rural hydroelectric plants; we *establish communications* with potential importers of American farm goods; we *make available* the latest research by *issuing publications*; we *commit funds for* long-term weather forecasting; and we even *make purchases of* excess agricultural products like wheat and milk and *give subsidies to* tobacco farmers. We *are hopeful* that we can *lend assistance in* all areas of American farming, and in turn we *are hopeful* that American farmers will *give their approval to* our policies in other areas.

In every clause of this paragraph, the real verb has been transformed into a noun, and a deadwood verb, such as *make* or *are*, has been substituted. By rescuing the imprisoned verbs in the paragraph, we restore life to the sentences and effect a more straightforward and concise paragraph.

APPLICATION

Revise the following passage by finding and reinstating the hidden verbs. How many words does your revision eliminate from the original?

The method of awarding student loans is currently dependent on the parents' income. The new method, which could cause an increase in the number of eligible applicants, contains the stipulation that the financial aid officer make a decision as to what percentage of the students' incomes is derived from the parents. Students who make application for a loan must give a description of their finances and needs and then give their consent to an audit of their banking and income tax records. If students are in possession of other funds, such as an endowment, the financial aid officer can make the assumption that the students are not in need of a loan. An attorney may act as representative for a student if the student and the financial aid officer do not reach an agreement.

Avoid Clichés

Clichés are stock phrases that have lost their impact through overuse. They are expressions that are as old as the hills, and at every opportunity they rear their ugly heads; we use them left and right and make Shakespeare turn over in his grave. Here are a few words to the wise: Steer clear of clichés. You're free to pick and choose among words, so stand on your own two feet, take the bull by the horns, and turn over a new leaf. Put your best foot forward. Left to your own devices, you too can write without clichés, and it stands to reason that you will give your prose a shot in the arm.

We revert to clichés (like the ones in the preceding paragraph) because they are ready-made and easy to use—so easy, in fact, that we don't have to think about them. That is the main problem with clichés: They deactivate the mind and encourage trite thinking. By relying on mechanical expressions, we invite mechanical thinking, and we fail to give readers fresh ideas in fresh language. Our duty is to interest readers, but we sometimes give them hackneyed language that bores them. We use clichés because they are handy and we are lazy. When our imagination is asleep, or when we don't have the energy to search for a new way of expressing an idea, we adopt a commonplace phrase that already exists instead of communicating the individuality of our thoughts; then our perception seems trite because our expression of that perception is trite. When we have fresh ideas, we should express them in fresh language. We should refuse to write ready-made combinations of words that quickly come to mind.

Here is one way to recognize clichéd phrases: If we were to leave out a key word and anyone could supply it, the phrase is probably overused. Here are a few examples; you supply the missing words:

straight from the horse's _____
hit the nail on the _____
beyond a shadow of a _____
the land of milk and _____
last but not _____
put all my eggs in one _____
cast pearls before _____
jump from the frying pan _____ _____ _____
keep a stiff upper _____
can't see the forest for the _____
kill two birds with one _____
on the tip of one's _____
bit off more than one could _____
killed the goose that laid _____ _____ _____
don't count your chickens before _____ _____ _____
give him an inch and he'll _____ _____ _____

When clichés were first used, they were catchy and many of them conveyed a striking image. After years of using them, however, we no longer associate the expression with the original image, and therefore the phrase loses its reason for being used. For example, the verb phrase *drummed out,* meaning to be expelled, originally referred to dishonorable dismissal from military service to the beat of a drum; the phrase carried the flavor of the whole procedure of drums rolling, uniform being stripped of ensignia, and the person being publicly shamed. Today, however, we have dissociated such expressions from their original action, and their impact is diminished. Repetition and familiarity have killed their significance and their effectiveness.

The only way to make a cliché fresh again is to change it slightly or make a pun out of it. Transforming a cliché and turning it around has the effect of grabbing the readers' attention. For example:

People should have the courage of their confusions.
He has a heart of mold.
She has mace up her sleeve.
The partners stayed together through thin and thin.
Absence makes the heart go wander.

Show a little imagination by turning a cliché around or by avoiding clichés altogether; communicate your fresh experience with fresh expression.

APPLICATION

1. Explain the original meaning of these phrases (consult the *Oxford English Dictionary* if necessary):

feather in one's cap
to badger
Achilles' heel

when one's ship comes in
red-letter day
lock, stock, and barrel

2. Can you think of two clichés that once conveyed a visual image but that have since lost their impact?
3. Try to transform one of these clichés into a pun or a fresh image:

Truth is stranger than fiction.
Keep a civil tongue in your head.
A little learning is a dangerous thing.
To err is human; to forgive, divine.
Fools rush in where angels fear to tread.

4. Point out the clichés in this narrative:

The McCormicks and the McLeans have fought tooth and nail for over 40 years. The sheriff, who is caught between a rock and a hard spot, has tried to persuade them to bury the hatchet, but they turn a deaf ear to his appeals. No one even remembers the original bone of contention, and as a matter of fact at this point in time it doesn't matter who cast the first stone.

The feud between old Jack McCormick and Ben McLean, who are like two peas in the same pod, flared up again last month. Jack, Jr., who is a chip off the old block, nearly sealed his doom when he went to town on a Saturday night, dressed to the nines, to meet the youngest McLean daughter, Nancy Jane, who is the apple of her father's eye. Young Jack is a real ladies' man who burns the candle at both ends. His father had put his foot down and told him to stay away from the girl, but the advice had gone in one ear and out the other. He had fallen head over heels in love with Nancy Jane, and wild horses couldn't have dragged him away from her. They were to meet in a little soda shop off the beaten path, and Jack, Jr. knew he was playing with fire by meeting her. He should have smelled a rat when he walked into the soda shop and Nancy Jane wasn't there and the place got so quiet that you could have heard a pin drop. Her brothers were lying in wait for him, and to make a long story short, they beat him to a pulp, and he escaped by the skin of his teeth.

At this point the plot thickens. The McCormicks decided to strike while the iron was hot and to give the McLeans a dose of their own medicine. As luck would have it, the next day, when it was raining cats and dogs, three McCormick boys saw Tommy McLean hoofing it down the road and they gave chase. Although Tommy was born and bred in those hills and knew where everyone lived, neighbors are few and far between, and before he made it to help, they caught him and beat him black and blue.

Things have gone from bad to worse. Far be it from me to criticize, but one and all around here agree that the sheriff has to take the bull by the horns and jail the whole kit and caboodle of them before more blood is spilled.

Use Figurative Language

Words can be used in a literal or a figurative sense. The literal sense is the ordinary, actual meaning of a term or expression; the figurative sense is an imaginative use of an expression. For example, in *Othello* when Othello is about to kill his wife Desdemona, he says he will "Put out the light, and then put out the light." The first use of the word *light* is literal; Othello is going to snuff out the candle. The second *light*, though, is figurative—that is, rather than referring to an actual light, such as a candle or torch, Othello refers to Desdemona's life, which he is also going to snuff out. If we were to rewrite the line to be strictly literal, it would read: Put out the light, and then kill Desdemona. But Shakespeare's play on words—life as a kind of illumination—is infinitely more satisfying.

The two main figures of speech are metaphor and simile. Both are comparisons, but a simile is a overt comparison and a metaphor is an implied one. Also, a simile uses *like* or *as* to introduce the comparison, and the metaphor does not. For example:

> METAPHOR: "Man is only a reed, the weakest thing in nature; but he is a thinking reed." Pascal

> SIMILE: "My saliva became like hot bitter glue." Ralph Ellison, *The Invisible Man*

A metaphor takes the name of one thing, such as *reed*, and gives it to another thing, in this case *man*, thereby transferring a characteristic from the one to the other. The one thing lends its associations to the other for a moment and reveals their shared quality.

APPLICATION

In each of the following metaphors, what term that usually signifies one concept is being used to designate another concept? What characteristic is being transferred in each example?

"A hospital bed is a parked taxi with the meter running." (Groucho Marx)

"War is the faro table of governments, and nations the dupes of the games." (Thomas Paine)

"Satire is a sort of glass [mirror], wherein beholders do generally discover everybody's face but their own." (Jonathan Swift)

"The moon was a ghostly galleon [ship] tossed upon cloudy seas. . . ." (Alfred Noyes)

Whereas a metaphor identifies one thing with another, a simile directly compares the two things. It reveals a resemblance by stating that *A* is like (or as) *B* in one respect; or, said another way, something in *A* is like something in *B*. By connecting the two items, we draw out a similarity and, as with metaphor, transfer a quality from one thing to another. For instance:

"It [a shot of whiskey] gave me a good shiver, then settled broadly in my middle and began to spread through my body like a fire creeping in short grass." (Walter Van Tilburg Clark, *The Ox-Bow Incident*)

"He shook hands as though it were a karate maneuver." (Richard Condon, *Winter Kills*)

". . . when she walks, she holds her body erect and along a straight line, as though her soul were liquid and could spill with ease." (Larry Woiwode, *Beyond the Bedroom Wall*)

"The miner sat very still in his chair, his face going hard and remote. He was evidently thinking over something that was stuck like a barb in his consciousness, something he was trying to harden over, as the skin sometimes hardens over a steel splinter in the flesh." (D. H. Lawrence, "Jimmy and the Desperate Woman")

We use figurative language constantly, describing hair "as white as snow," feet "as cold as ice," an intellect "as sharp as a tack," a new father "as proud as a peacock," and so forth. The problem is that most of our figurative expressions are ones that we've picked up from other people, and therefore they are not fresh. To be effective, figurative language must be original and striking, and that means we must strain our imaginations a little. We should always be thinking in terms of comparisons and asking ourselves, "What is this like?" when we are writing.

APPLICATION

Try your hand at completing these similes:

Television is like _____.
The nuclear arms race is like _____.
College is like _____.
Going on a blind date is like _____.

Perhaps the best advice about figurative language is that you should jot down the first comparisons that pop into your mind—and then throw them into the trash. First thoughts tend to be obvious thoughts, and easy thinking produces clichés. Hard thinking produces fresh figurative language.

Although resemblance is at the heart of metaphorical language, the things being compared (*A* and *B*, we will call them) are usually basically dissimilar. In fact, the most striking similes are those in which *A* and *B* are not simply dissimilar, but radically dissimilar. The further apart the two elements, the greater the impact on readers because the comparison is unexpected. "A simile may be compared to lines converging at a point," Samuel Johnson said, "and is more excellent as the lines approach from a greater distance." In other words, a previously unseen connection between separate elements is all the more novel when *A* and *B* seem to have no common characteristic. For example, we wouldn't think that earrings and two people making love would have anything in common, yet John Updike deftly joins the two in this simile:

> "They were in this garage renovated to bachelor's quarters, my organist and my curate, one of each sex, like inter-locked earrings in a box too large for such storage." (*A Month of Sundays*)

Such similes are linguistic collisions whereby two radically different concepts cross paths and merge just long enough for the associations and implications of one concept to be transferred to the other. From the abrupt interaction between *A* and *B* springs a new perception, and readers are granted a striking way of comprehending or, as this example, of visualizing:

"Jones was perched on a wooden stool, his legs bent under him like ice tongs ready to pick up the stool and boldly carry it away before Mr. Watson's old eyes." (John Kennedy Toole, *A Confederacy of Dunces*)

Good similes and metaphors are difficult to create because, on the one hand, the more dissimilar the two elements, the more striking and novel is the effect, but on the other hand, to be appropriate the comparison should be drawn from the physical or psychological environment of the subject. Freshness is one criterion by which to judge similes, but we shouldn't strive only for novelty because the resulting comparison may be strained and inappropriate. For example:

The child was clinging to its mother like a sweaty shirt to a laborer's back.

Although the two things have clinging in common, this comparison doesn't work because "sweaty shirt" violates the image that we have of children nestling into their mothers' bosom. When we compose similes, B should somehow be harmonious with the connotations of A. In the following description, for instance, the writer is describing a scene on a Texas ranch:

"When I woke up Dad was standing by the bed shaking my foot. I opened my eyes, but he never stopped shaking it. He shook it like it was a fence post and he was testing it to see if it was in the ground solid enough." (Larry McMurtry, *Leaving Cheyenne*)

Besides giving us an image of how the man is shaking his son's foot—briskly, matter-of-factly—the writer reinforces the idea that the setting is the American West: The fence post reminds us of ranch life, and the father's manner reveals his rough, outdoor nature. Rather than simply being ornamental, the simile adds texture to the scene. Think what a different effect—and what an inappropriate one—this sentence would have: "He shook it like a Grand Prix driver shifting gears." Appropriateness, then, is the governing principle for metaphors and similes; B should relate to the social manner, the physical environment, the surrounding action, or the emotional context of A.

APPLICATION

Here are several examples of fresh and appropriate similes. From the brief introduction to each, determine why each is appropriate.

A child describing survivors of a concentration death camp after the Nazi downfall: "I clutched Yury's hand and looked into the gray faces of these people, with their feverishly burning eyes shining like pieces of broken glass in the ashes of a dying fire." (Jerzy Kosinski, *The Painted Bird*)

A description of tranquillized asylum inmates who usually follow orders mechanically but who suddenly are confronted with a dilemma: "I could see them twitch with confusion, like machines throttled full ahead and with the brake on." (Ken Kesey, *One Flew Over the Cuckoo's Nest*)

A fallen minister, whose obsession with women has caused him to be sent to a desert retreat, looks down the blouse of an attractive nurse: "The glimpse burned in me like a drop of brandy in the belly of an ostensibly reformed alcoholic." (John Updike, *A Month of Sundays*)

In each of these examples, the comparison not only reinforces the meaning and the context, but also maintains a logical and imaginative consistency.

Writers use figurative language because (1) it assists comprehension, (2) it conveys an image, (3) it is concise, and (4) it is enjoyable. First, figurative language is a means of extending description and explanation because capturing certain sensations is difficult except by comparison. How do you directly describe, for instance, the taste of kiwi fruit, the pain of breaking up a relationship, the excitement of parachuting, or the wail of a blue-tick hound on the trail of a raccoon? When there is no literal form to convey a precise meaning, we often try to explain what a thing is by saying that it resembles something else:

"Hear Old Jim? Hear that high keen, like a Comanche squaw at a burial? He's leading the pack now, over across the next ridge." (Douglas C. Jones, *Elkhorn Tavern*)

By using a simile, the writer has made the sound real to us.

The second reason for using figurative language is that it is visual and therefore improves readers' chances of seeing what we are describing. By conveying an image, a simile helps readers to picture an object with a clarity and vividness that might otherwise be impossible. For example, in this description of a man being repeatedly shot by policemen, the writer effectively uses a simile to convey the convulsive movements of his body as it continues to be riddled with bullets:

"The body jerked about the street in a sequence of attitudes as if it were trying to mop up its own blood." (E. L. Doctorow, *Ragtime*)

The action is immediately and strikingly vivid—we *see* the frenzied body fiercely twitch and writhe and tumble in its own red ooze.

Third, because metaphorical language is imagistic, it is also concise and economical. If a picture is worth a thousand words, then so is a simile because it conveys a picture.

> "Poppa laid his hand in the middle of Mr. Allnut's back and sort of guided him across to the door as if he was showing a little boy the way to the bathroom." (J. R. Salamanca, *Embarkation*)

The simile transfers the quality of lost-little-boyness to a grown man and thereby characterizes not only Mr. Allnut, but also the relationship between the two men. The image quickly and concisely conveys a characterization that might otherwise have taken a full paragraph of literal description to capture.

Consider the following description of a man trying to break into a conversation about marriage:

> "He was gathering toward speech, like a man about to rumba, waiting to feel the beat." (Leonard Michaels, *The Men's Club*)

To describe the hesitancy, the approach to social contact, and the facial expression of a man about to broach a very personal topic would have taken considerable space, but Michaels achieves this with a single simile.

Fourth, ingenious metaphors and similes are a source of enjoyment for readers, who approach essays with an appetite not only for new ideas and insights, but also for inventive and clever phrasing. Good prose, like superior chocolate, satisfies the person who devours it. Since imaginative comparisons are downright scrumptious, it can't hurt to sprinkle a few metaphors and similes over an essay to add a gratifying richness for readers to savor.

Although simile and metaphor are considered literary devices, their use certainly is not limited to fiction and poetry. We find figurative language in the writings of scientists, politicians, anthropologists, and historians. The following example is by a political analyst who is describing the Louisiana politician Huey "Kingfish" Long:

> "He broke the state to his saddle, yanked the cinch tight, slammed his spurs into its flanks, and set about the business of government, as he understood it: helping friends and hurting enemies." (George F. Will)

Notice how the strong verbs in Will's description—*broke, yanked, slammed*—communicate the implied comparison that Huey Long was a political bronc buster.

APPLICATION

1. Try your hand at creating similes by filling in the comparison:
   - **A.** harmless as _____   easy as _____
     awkward as _____   lucky as _____
     lonely as _____   gloomy as _____
   - **B.** bright green, like _____   brownish pink, like _____
     burnt orange, like _____   dull silver, like _____

2. Fill in the blanks to fit the situations:
   - **A.** Eating by candlelight is _____.
   - **B.** Reading a book of quotations is like _____.
   - **C.** Her hangover was _____.
   - **D.** After making a touchdown, the fullback performed an end-zone movement that was _____.
   - **E.** Running into a former lover at a party is like _____.
   - **F.** Wearing contact lenses is like _____.
   - **G.** Canned dog food smells like _____.
   - **H.** Like _____, the bus driver ordered the crotchety old man off his conveyance.
   - **I.** The stream meanders through the glen like _____.
   - **J.** He looked at me skeptically, as if _____.
   - **K.** After the little boy spilt hot chocolate on the nun's lap, she patted the little ruffian's head as if _____.
   - **L.** A morning without coffee is like _____.
   - **M.** Speaking a foreign language is like _____.
   - **N.** She puckered up for her first kiss like _____.
   - **O.** Swinging the ax like _____, Darlene chopped off the chicken's head.
   - **P.** Her nose, crinkled up like _____, led me to believe that she didn't care for my cooking.

3. Evaluate the freshness of these similes:
   - **A.** "They stood in a little desert of asphalt, where some kids were running about making a noise like a battle in a railway tunnel." (Joyce Cary, *The Horse's Mouth*)
   - **B.** "He sat hunched, bitterly smiling, as always, his muscles taut as old nautical ropes in a hurricane." (John Gardner, *Grendel*)
   - **C.** [A butler fetching for his employer a pair of purple socks, which the butler disapproves of] "He lugged them out of the drawers as if he were a vegetarian fishing a caterpillar out of the salad." (P. G. Wodehouse, *The Inimitable Jeeves*)
   - **D.** "I couldn't seem to get my thoughts straight; they kept jumping around like musical notes on a white page." (Louise Shivers, *Here To Get My Baby Out of Jail*)

E. "What a series of discarded selves each of us is, or selves we think we have discarded but which lurk, one beneath the other, like successive paintings on a single canvas." (Peter DeVries, *Sauce for the Goose*)

F. "Her mother's pride in the girl's appearance led her to step back, like a painter from his easel, and survey her work as a whole." (Thomas Hardy, *Tess of the D'Urbervilles*)

G. "Fame is like a shaved pig with a greased tail, and it is only after it has slipped through the hands of some thousands, that some fellow, by mere chance, holds on to it!" (Davy Crockett, *Autobiography*)

Tone

Like tone of voice for speakers, tone in prose reflects a writer's attitude toward a subject and toward an audience, and there are as many tones as there are attitudes. Our tone can be angry, conciliatory, casual, impersonal, dignified, ironic, erudite, amused, contemptuous, somber, complacent, festive, and so forth.

The tone of any discourse usually is easily identifiable. That is, we normally have no difficulty telling whether a writer is being whimsical or indignant, compassionate or ironic. For example, the tone of the following passage is clearly whimsical; the author is treating her subject with good-natured humor:

My friend Merithew, who was raised in California, where only cars are truly happy, is herself truly happy only in cars. She describes them as if they were jewelry or ex-lovers, gives them pet names, and has been known to flirt shamelessly with elderly convertibles old enough to be her trade-in. Last Christmas I gave Merithew a whole fleet of shiny foreign limousines (chocolate, wrapped in colored foil). An hour later, she was hungry for a Mustang.

—From Lois Gould, "Queasy Rider," *Not Responsible for Personal Articles*

APPLICATION

How would you characterize the tone of each of these passages?

1. A choreographer's comments on dance critics:

Critics usually write about their feelings and ignore the intent of the choreographer, and are generally incapable of dealing with choreographic structure. I have taught and watched thousands of improvisation classes and thousands of composition classes over the years, and I cringe at the arrogance and inadequacy of the dance press regarding choreography. The press today has had a considerable hand in aborting the developments in the field. Critics hover over the creative pasture waiting like the early bird, anxious for the head of any little creative worm to break the ground. Then down they swoop and tug and tug until they succeed in pulling their victim out of his germinal bed and out of all proportion.

—From Murray Louis, "On Critics," *Inside Dance*

2. On the technological subordination of women:

Data from the first national study of technological change generally support hypotheses that link sex stratification to occupational and technological stratification. Contrary to popular belief, relatively more women than men operate machines that perform repetitive tasks and restrict their physical mobility. Relatively more men operate machines that require skill and permit work autonomy. These differences in worker-machine relations parallel differences in work control patterns. Women's work is more impersonally controlled by their equipment, the assembly line, and workflow devices, while more of men's work is under the control of the operator or work group. These findings hold for both blue- and white-collar work.

—From William Form, *Divided We Stand: Working-Class Stratification in America*

3. From a feminist's book on rape:

Pornography has been so thickly glossed over with the patina of chic these days in the name of verbal freedom and sophistication that important distinctions between freedom of political expression (a democratic necessity), honest sex education for children (a societal good) and ugly smut (the deliberate devaluation of the role of women through obscene, distorted depictions) have been hopelessly confused. Part of the problem is that those who traditionally have been the most vigorous opponents of porn are often those same people who shudder at the explicit mention of any sexual subject. Under their watchful, vigilante eyes, frank and free dissemination of educational materials relating to abortion, contraception, the act of birth, and female biology in general is also dangerous, subversive and dirty. (I am not unmindful that a frank and free discussion of rape, "the unspeakable crime," might well give these righteous vigilantes further cause to shudder.) Because the battle lines were falsely drawn a long time ago, before there was a vocal women's movement, the anti-pornography forces appear to be, for the most part, religious, Southern, conservative and right-wing, while the pro-porn forces are identified as Eastern, atheistic and liberal.

—From Susan Brownmiller, *Against Our Will*

4. From a review of the movie *The Empire Strikes Back:*

There is a romantic subplot in which Han and Leia play the love-hate game of 1930s screwball comedies, where, at least, the hero and heroine ended up in a conjugal bed. Here a chaste kiss or two is the ultimate consummation, as tepid and infantile as the repartee that preceded it. *Infantile* is the operative word, for nothing in *Empire* must interfere with the blessed infantilism of children and the blissful regression of adults. Nevertheless, at film's end, when Han Solo is carbon-frozen into an oversized paperweight and carried off by a bounty hunter for undisclosed purposes, Leia seems to veer back to Luke, and simple-minded triangularity is restored.

This witless banality is made even less bearable by the nonacting of the principals. Harrison Ford (Han) offers loutishness for charm and becomes the epitome of the interstellar drugstore cowboy. Mark Hamill (Luke) is still the talentless Tom Sawyer of outer space—wide-eyed, narrow-minded, strait-laced. Worst of all is Carrie Fisher, whose Leia is a cosmic Shirley Temple but without the slightest acting ability or vestige of prettiness. Though still very young, she looks, without recourse to special effects, at least fifty—the film's only true, albeit depressing, miracle. It turns out, as part of the movie's barbershop Freudianizing, that Darth Vader is really Luke's father; by the time we get to the next episode, Leia may easily be his mother.

—From John Simon, "Mythopoeic Madness," *Reverse Angle*

Although recognizing the tone of a written piece is fairly easy, deciding what tone we should adopt with a particular topic and audience is not.

Tone Depends on Subject, Attitude, and Audience

The usual advice about tone is that serious subjects should be treated seriously, and light subjects, lightly. So far as it goes, it's not bad advice. Certainly subjects that everyone agrees are serious—cancer research, child abuse, poverty, the holocaust, racial discrimination, and toxic wastes—allow little room for humor. But are subjects such as marriage, the Olympics, opera, and gun control always serious? The controversy over gun control, for example, would seemingly demand serious discussion, but as Art Buchwald demonstrates, such is not necessarily the case:

The Handgun Control lobbyists maintain that guns kill people. The Right to Bear Arms crowd says that guns don't kill people—people kill people. Both groups are wrong. According to Arnold Crocus, a lethal weapons expert, bullets kill people.

To back up his theory, Arnold invited me to his laboratory, where he had an array of guns on the wall. He took one off the rack and told me to point it at a target and pull the trigger.

I did, and the gun went "click."

"Nothing happened," Crocus said, "therefore we know that guns don't kill people. Now pretend the target is someone you really hate."

I thought of someone, and stared at the target with all the anger I could muster. Once again nothing happened.

"This proves," said Arnold, "that people, at this distance, cannot kill people. Now I am going to place a round of ammunition in your gun, and I want you to pull the trigger."

I did as I was told. There was a loud explosion and the bullet went right through the target's heart.

"Well," said Arnold, "what do you conclude?"

"The only conclusion I can come to is that the bullet was the deadly weapon."

"Right. Now it's true that the bullet would not be able to penetrate the target unless it was fired through the barrel of the gun. And it is also true that the gun could not have been fired unless someone pulled the trigger. But without the bullet, the target would not have suffered any injury."

"That means," I said, "that the real problem America faces is not the plethora of handguns in this country, nor the people who use them, but the ammunition that is available to anyone who wants it."

"You got it. What this tells us is that it may be possible to satisfy both the Right to Bear Arms crowd and the Handgun Control people at the same time. By permitting the sale of guns, but prohibiting the manufacture or sale of ammunition, you make both sides happy."

"But the gun lovers will say that there is no sense owning a firearm if you can't fire anything out of it."

"Let them say it. They don't have a legal leg to stand on. There is nothing in the Constitution that says Americans have a right to bear bullets."

—From "Ban the Bullet," *Laid Back in Washington*

How would you describe Buchwald's tone? How do you know that he is not serious in his proposal? Why does he adopt such a tone—that is, what is his intention?

Few subjects absolutely dictate the manner in which they should be treated, and many subjects allow writers several options in tone. Hence, the subject itself is usually not such an influence over tone as is (1) our attitude toward the subject and (2) our readers' attitude toward the subject. To decide what tone to adopt, we first have to discover what our attitude is, and that means discovering not only whether we are for or against (or indifferent to) a topic, but also how the topic affects us emotionally. In other words, what do we *think* about the issue, and how do we *feel* about it?

Tone has a great deal to do with the individual personality, philosophy, and perspective of the writer. Some writers see humor in almost everything, some in almost nothing; some of us are by nature cynical, others optimistic. Our basic natures strongly affect our attitude on a particular topic, and that attitude translates into our tone in writing. Although we achieve tone through word choice, we must first decide what that tone should be, and once we have determined that, we select words to convey that tone. The nineteenth-century essayist Alexander Smith said that an essay "is moulded by some central mood—whimsical, serious, or satirical. Give the mood, and the essay, from the first sentence to the last, grows around it as the cocoon grows around the silkworm."

Knowing what tone to adopt also depends on knowing our audience's beliefs. Different audiences may view the same subject differently, and these different views require different tones on our part. For example, people who strongly endorse health foods, professional football, or the Miss America Pageant regard those subjects earnestly, but other people may see elements of humor in those topics and therefore may treat them facetiously. Not only should we be aware of our specific audience's attitude toward the subject that we will discuss, but we should also respect that attitude. Since writing is a social activity, we must be considerate of our audience's feelings and intellect, and since the goal of writing is agreement, we want to use a tone that will encourage readers to view our ideas favorably. In short, we must sometimes modify our tone to reach an audience. Although we want our tone to reflect our attitude, we also usually want the audience to approve of our tone and to accept our thesis. Our initial emotions on a topic, therefore, are not always the most effective for persuading. If our emotion is harsh and purely negative, as with anger or contempt, it is wise to temper the raw emotion—unless our intent is to shock or shame instead of to seduce.

Tone in argumentative writing requires even more attention to audience than tone in expository writing because often in argument we and the readers start from points of disagreement, and we want our tone to help overcome their defensiveness and hostility. The kind of tone we choose, therefore, depends greatly on our audience's stance. If our audience is antagonistic, our tone should be respectful and conciliatory, not angry or sarcastic. This doesn't mean that we must change our views on a topic; it means that of the tones available, we choose the one that will best advance our view. If, for example, we oppose federal mortgage assistance to home-buyers, we can voice our opposition by using one of several tones: We can be ironic, indignant, or pensive. If we are writing to a neutral or friendly audience, our choices of tone broaden because we concern ourselves less with offending our readers, although we still want our tone to be effective in winning readers' approval.

Tone can be a persuasive means by which to secure endorsement of our proposals. For example, put yourself for a moment in the position of an elementary school teacher who has a failing student in class. The teacher wants to write to the child's parents stating the problems (low grades due to apathy and lack of discipline) and suggesting solutions (a conference, tutoring, encouragement). If the teacher wrote a note reflecting his or her direct attitude, it might take this tone:

Johnny is a failure as a pupil. He is lazy, his behavior in class is disruptive, and you are not giving him support or encouragement at home. I don't understand why you are not concerned with your child's low achievement. I suggest that you report to my office for a conference as soon as possible.

Now put yourself in the position of the parents. What kind of response would this summons elicit? Would the tone help resolve the problems and help the child? Not likely. Although the tone here may represent the teacher's attitude, it is not very effective in achieving a working relationship between teacher and parents. The goal of communication is cooperation, but a note of this sort will result in increased tension and conflict because the tone is negative and accusatory.

If the teacher truly wishes to help the child, he or she will communicate not anger but concern:

I am concerned that Johnny is failing in several of his subjects at school. He has the potential to do satisfactory work, but he is unmotivated and his behavior in class is disruptive. Because these are problems that require efforts both in class and at home, I hope that you and I can meet soon to discuss ways of improving his study habits and attitude.

As in the first note, this one communicates the problem and outlines a course of action, but the effect is totally different. Whereas the earlier one alienates the parents and worsens the problem, the second note lays a foundation for trust and cooperation. Modifying the tone can do wonders for interpersonal relations.

Tone Affects Meaning

Tone not only helps our message win approval, it is also *part of* our message. Because tone reflects attitude, our tone communicates our feelings about the topic being discussed. The tone that is built up gradually in a discourse makes a statement in itself.

The tone tells readers how to interpret statements and contributes to the meaning. We can make the same statement in two different tones and mean totally opposite things. For instance, if you're at a baseball game and the umpire calls a player safe at second base, and you agree with the call, you might say "Good call, ump." If you disagreed with the call and thought that the player was undoubtedly out, you might sarcastically say "Good call, ump," and your tone of voice would communicate that you actually think the ump needs glasses. Tone in writing is equally important. If readers misunderstand the tone of an essay, they misinterpret the message of the essay.

The following essay is a good example of how tone affects meaning. What is the tone of this piece, and what is the message?

PURER THAN PURE

Carl Bode

I expect you've noticed how glossy my hair has been getting. And that I've grown heftier around the shoulders and leaner around the middle, and that I seem to be flexing my muscles all the time. And that my stride lengthens with a new purpose. And that my smile is more brilliant than ever.

Let me make the reason for all this perfectly clear. It's that I've finally started to eat organic foods. Organic foods, as even the check-out clerks now know, are grown without chemical fertilizers and processed without chemical additives. One of my daughters has long been an Organic Food Freak. With the tireless zest of a Muslim missionary she's been laboring to gather me into the fold. For quite a while she's been dropping newspaper articles on my desk about the dire effect of hexo-something or other. Whenever I've savored Maryland seafood she's talked to me about what mercury does to the human gizzard. While I've been peeling Florida oranges she's been pointing out the disconcerting fact that the orange coloring comes off on my hands. While I've been salting my steak she's been reading the label of the saltbox to me in tones of doom.

I'm just about convinced. So, I recognize, are many thousands of others. More organic food stores open in my neighborhood all the time; the local health-food emporium which was teetering on the brink of bankruptcy is now abustle. Even the rather scruffy supermarket in the next block has seen the light. Why not? The organic items seem to cost twice as much as the chemically assisted ones.

So I suffer, as do all of us poor, when I pay at the check-out counter. Yet the pain is eased by the thought of all the glossiness and vigor I'm gaining. Besides, I get a pastoral pleasure from reading the labels on the organic foods. "I, Otto Ogontz," a label on a lettuce box tells me, "to the best of my knowledge have raised this lettuce without an iota of chemical fertilizer." Otto, I believe you and munch your Emerald Iceberg with a hearty appetite.

No sex-starved hens have laid the organic eggs I addle. The cardboard carton standing on my sink says, "One Dozen Fertile Eggs from Free Running Hens Fed Natural Feed." These eggs hail from the henhouses of W. I. Wifmacher, of Mennonite Country. I can visualize Farmer Wifmacher clearly, a stout man who watches his hens with a patriarchal smile while they run freely, with one of the roosters in hot pursuit. The eggs I buy now are laid by fulfilled hens, not nattering neurasthenics. The roosters, now likewise fed on organic feed, show a fresh gloss in their plumage; they haste to the henhouse with the highest purpose; and they impress everyone for miles with the brassy brilliance of their crowing.

Their strength is as the strength of ten because their feed is pure.

—From *Highly Irregular*

Does Bode unconditionally believe in the power of organic foods, or does he think that organic foods are an expensive hoax, or does he consider them to be generally healthful but consider their proponents to be a little too avid? To understand the author's message, we must first decide what his tone is since the tone determines the meaning. Is he absolutely serious? Is he totally ironic? Is he slightly serious and slightly ironic?

I suggest that Bode is a slightly skeptical convert who accepts the superiority of organic foods over chemically processed foods but considers their powers somewhat exaggerated. From that half serious, half ironic position, he is good-naturedly poking fun at the mania surrounding organic foods and the exaggerated claims of their effects. He even includes himself in the comedy by implicitly comparing his new gleam and strength to that of the roosters—both he and they are virile and glossy due to organic food, and like them, he is crowing about it.

Unless we recognize that the tone is slightly ironic, we miss the message. The tone, by telling us how to interpret the author's statements, becomes part of the message itself. In essence, we interpret the message using the tone as a decoding device. In this instance, it takes a fairly sophisticated reader to understand the tone.

Exercises

1. Write three one-paragraph essays on the following topic. You may either endorse or oppose the idea, but the tone of each miniature essay must be different: One must be angry, one must be serious and rational, and one must be ironic.

   Topic: Human organ brokers. (Organ brokers are companies that sell human organs for transplants. They act as paid intermediaries that find organ donors for people who need a transplant operation. Healthy donors, recruited from poor countries overseas or from the poorer classes in America, can have an organ removed and sell it through a brokerage company to someone needing a transplant to survive.)

2. Sometimes treating traditionally serious subjects in a light manner can be rhetorically effective. Give an example of a topic that might be treated irreverently, and suggest how you might write such an essay.

3. Describe the tone of each of the following examples, analyze how each writer achieves the tone, and evaluate the effectiveness of the tone.

   A. Prehistoric man, without tools or fire to be thinking about, must have been the most anxious of us all. Fumbling about in dimly lit caves, trying to figure out what he ought really to be doing, sensing the awesome responsibilities for toolmaking just ahead, he must have spent a lot of time contemplating his thumbs and fretting about them. I can imagine him staring at his hands, apposing thumbtips to each fingertip in amazement, thinking, By God, that's something to set us apart from the animals—and then the grinding thought, What on earth are they for? There must have been many long, sleepless nights, his mind all thumbs.

It would not surprise me to learn that there were ancient prefire committees, convened to argue that thumbs might be taking us too far, that we'd have been better off with simply another finger of the usual sort.

—From Lewis Thomas, "On Transcendental Metaworry," *The Medusa and the Snail*

B. American social scientists are also involved in nationalism. We have no party of the left in this republic and no left-wing economists or sociologists to speak of. The economic expert sent abroad is expected to expound free enterprise and to make democracy work in undeveloped countries. As new nations arise, we think of them as enlisting on our side only as they develop representative governments resembling our own or that of the British, even though the representation be formal only. Our economic missions tacitly assume that the backwardness of a foreign people has some mysterious connection with its lack of industrialization—one speculates about what we would have recommended to the Athens of Pericles—and that mind would be, indeed, daring which ventured to inquire into the philosophic difference between the propaganda of the Americans and the propaganda of the Communist countries as theorists of happiness.

—From Howard Mumford Jones, "Goal for Americans," *Saturday Evening Post,* July 1, 1961

C. Apparently this man had treacherously killed the son of an influential farmer and the father had decided to punish the murderer in the old-fashioned manner. Together with his two cousins the man brought the culprit to the forest. There they prepared a twelve-foot stake, sharpened at one end to a fine point like a gigantic pencil. They laid it on the ground, wedging the blunt end against a tree trunk. Then a strong horse was hitched to each of the victim's feet, while his crotch was leveled with the waiting point. The horses, gently nudged, pulled the man against the spiked beam, which gradually sank into the tensed flesh. When the point was deep into the entrails of the victim, the men lifted the stake, together with the impaled man upon it and planted it in a previously dug hole. They left him there to die slowly.

—From Jerzy Kosinski, *The Painted Bird*

D. Pocket Calculators: It Took Me Three Years to Learn How to Do Long Division and So Should They

1. The rigors of learning how to do long division have been a traditional part of childhood, just like learning to smoke. In fact, as far as I am concerned, the two go hand in hand. Any child who cannot do long division by himself does not deserve to smoke. I am really quite a nice girl and very fond of children but I do have my standards. I have never taught a child to smoke before he has first taken a piece of paper and a pencil and demonstrated to my satisfaction that he can correctly divide 163 by 12.

2. Pocket calculators are not inexpensive and, generally speaking, parents would be better off spending the money on themselves. If they *must* throw it away on their offspring they would do well to keep in mind that a pack of cigarettes rarely costs more than seventy-five cents.

3. It is unnatural for *anyone,* let alone a *child,* to be able under any circumstances whatsoever to divide 17.3 by 945.8.

4. Pocket calculators encourage children to think that they have all the answers. If this belief were actually to take hold they might well seize power, which would undoubtedly result in all of the furniture being much too small.

—From Fran Lebowitz, "Digital Clocks and Pocket Calculators:
Spoilers of Youth," *Metropolitan Life*

E.   The Korean War engaged 5.7 million servicemen (twice as many as in World War I), of whom more than 54,000 died—and what did it accomplish? We have been burdened with a military occupation of our client state ever since. It can hardly be contended that our security, or that of what we laughingly call the free world, has been enhanced in any basic way. Cheap shirts, maybe, but not security.

—From Robert Lasch, "Lessons of Korea and Vietnam," *Newsweek,* Feb. 18, 1980

F.   Most people coming out of a war feel lost and resentful. What has been a minute-to-minute confrontation with yourself, your struggle with what courage you have against discomfort, at the least, and death at the other end, ties you to the people you have known in the war and makes, for a time, all others seem alien and frivolous. Friends are glad to see you again, but you know immediately that most of them have put you to one side, and while it is easy enough to say that you should have known that before, most of us don't, and it is painful. You are face to face with what will happen to you after death.

—From Lillian Hellman, *An Unfinished Woman*

G.   TO THE RIGHT HONOURABLE THE EARL
OF CHESTERFIELD

February 7, 1755.

My Lord

I have been lately informed, by the proprietor of *The World,* that two papers, in which my Dictionary is recommended to the publick, were written by your Lordship. To be so distinguished, is an honour, which, being very little accustomed to favours from the great, I know not well how to receive, or in what terms to acknowledge.

When, upon some slight encouragement, I first visited your Lordship, I was overpowered, like the rest of mankind, by the enchantment of your address; and could not forbear to wish that I might boast myself *Le vainqueur du vainqueur de la terre;*—that I might obtain that regard for which I saw the world contending, but I found my attendance so little encouraged, that neither pride nor modesty would suffer me to continue it. When I had once addressed your Lordship in publick, I had exhausted all the art of pleasing which a retired and uncourtly scholar can possess. I had done all that I could; and no man is well pleased to have his all neglected, be it ever so little.

Seven years, my Lord, have now past, since I waited in your outward rooms, or was repulsed from your door; during which time I have been pushing on my work through difficulties, of which it is useless to complain, and have brought it, at last, to the verge of publication, without one act of assistance, one word of encouragement, or one smile of favour. Such treatment I did not expect, for I never had a Patron before.

The shepherd in Virgil grew at last acquainted with Love, and found him a native of the rocks.

Is not a Patron, my Lord, one who looks with unconcern on a man struggling for life in the water, and, when he has reached ground, encumbers him with help? The notice which you have been pleased to take of my labours, had it been early, had been kind; but it has been delayed till I am indifferent, and cannot enjoy it; till I am solitary, and cannot impart it; till I am known, and do not want it. I hope it is no very cynical asperity not to confess obligations where no benefit has been received, or to be unwilling that the Publick should consider me as owing that to a Patron, which Providence has enabled me to do for myself.

Having carried on my work thus far with so little obligation to any favourer of learning, I shall not be disappointed though I should conclude it, if less be possible, with less; for I have been long wakened from that dream of hope, in which I once boasted myself with so much exultation, my Lord,

> your Lordship's most humble,
> most obedient servant,

SAM: JOHNSON

H.   I hope you will be very happy as members of the educated class in America. I myself have been rejected again and again.

As I said on Earth Day in New York City not long ago: It isn't often that a total pessimist is invited to speak in the springtime. I predicted that everything would become worse, and everything has become worse.

One trouble, it seems to me, is that the majority of the people who rule us, who have our money and power, are lawyers or military men. The lawyers want to talk our problems out of existence. The military men want us to find the bad guys and put bullets through their brains. These are not always the best solutions—particularly in the fields of sewage disposal and birth control.

I demand that the administration of Bennington College establish an R.O.T.C. unit here. It is imperative that we learn more about military men, since they have so much of our money and power now. It is a great mistake to drive military men from college campuses and into ghettos like Fort Benning and Fort Bragg. Make them do what they do so proudly in the midst of men and women who are educated.

When I was at Cornell University, the experiences that most stimulated my thinking were in R.O.T.C.—the manual of arms and close-order drill, and the way the officers spoke to me. Because of the military training I received at Cornell, I became a corporal at the end of World War Two. After the war, as you know, I made a fortune as a pacifist.

You should not only have military men here, but their weapons, too—especially crowd-control weapons such as machine guns and tanks. There is a tendency among young people these days to form crowds. Young people owe it to themselves to understand how easily machine guns and tanks can control crowds.

There is a basic rule about tanks, and you should know it: The only man who ever beat a tank was John Wayne. And he was in another tank.

Now then—about machine guns: They work sort of like a garden hose, except they spray death. They should be approached with caution.

There is a lesson for all of us in machine guns and tanks: Work within the system.

How pessimistic am I, really? I was a teacher at the University of Iowa three years ago. I had hundreds of students. As nearly as I am able to determine, not one of my ex-students has seen fit to reproduce. The only other demonstration of such a widespread disinclination to reproduce took place in Tasmania in about 1800. Native Tasmanians gave up on babies and the love thing and all that when white colonists, who were criminals from England, hunted them for sport.

I used to be an optimist. This was during my boyhood in Indianapolis. Those of you who have seen Indianapolis will understand that it was no easy thing to be an optimist there. It was the 500-mile Speedway Race, and then 364 days of miniature golf, and then the 500-mile Speedway Race again.

My brother Bernard, who was nine years older, was on his way to becoming an important scientist. He would later discover that silver iodide particles could precipitate certain kinds of clouds as snow or rain. He made me very enthusiastic about science for a while. I thought scientists were going to find out exactly how everything worked, and then make it work better. I fully expected that by the time I was twenty-one, some scientist, maybe my brother, would have taken a color photograph of God Almighty—and sold it to *Popular Mechanics* magazine.

Scientific truth was going to make us *so* happy and comfortable.

What actually happened when I was twenty-one was that we dropped scientific truth on Hiroshima. We killed everybody there.

—From Kurt Vonnegut, Jr., "Address to Graduating Class at Bennington College, 1970,"
Wampeters, Foma, & Granfalloons

1. Why does Vonnegut couch a very serious message in a slightly flippant style? What is the effect? Is the style appropriate to the audience?

2. How do the directness and simplicity of his diction contribute to his message?

I. There was a snake at the quarry with me tonight. It lay shaded by cliffs on a flat sandstone ledge above the quarry's dark waters. I was thirty feet away, sitting on the forest path overlook, when my eye caught the dark scrawl on the rocks, the lazy sinuosity that can only mean snake. I approached for a better look, edging my way down the steep rock cutting, and saw that the snake was only twelve or thirteen inches long. Its body was thick for its length. I came closer still, and saw the unmistakable undulating bands of brown, the hourglasses: copperhead.

The young copperhead was motionless on its rock. Although it lay in a loose sprawl, all I saw at first was a camouflage pattern of particolored splotches confused by the rushing speckles of light in the weeds between us, and by the deep twilight dark of the quarry pond beyond the rock. Then suddenly the form of its head emerged from the confusion: burnished brown, triangular, blunt as a stone ax. Its head and the first four inches of its body rested on airy nothing an inch above the rock. I admired the snake. Its scales shone with newness, bright and buffed. Its body was perfect, whole and unblemished. I found it hard to believe it had not just been created on the spot, or hatched fresh from its mother, so unscathed and clean was its body, so unmarked by any passage.

Did it see me? I was only four feet away, seated on the weedy cliff behind the sandstone ledge; the snake was between me and the quarry pond. I waved an arm in its direction: nothing moved. Its low-forehead glare and lipless reptile smirk revealed nothing. How could I tell where it was looking, what it was seeing? I squinted at its head, staring at those eyes like the glass eyes of a stuffed warbler, at those scales like shields canted and lapped just so, to frame an improbable, unfathomable face.

—From Annie Dillard, *A Pilgrim at Tinker Creek*

1. Point out specific words or phrases that capture the essence of a snake. What makes this description so vivid and realistic?

2. Are there any metaphors or similes in this excerpt?

3. How would you describe the tone? Give specific examples to substantiate your description.

4. Articulate the differences in meaning among the following words:

   A. abolish
      repeal
      nullify
      rescind

   B. partner
      colleague
      accomplice
      ally

   C. stout
      sturdy
      strong
      robust

   D. predicament
      plight
      dilemma
      quandary

   E. humble
      modest
      submissive
      unassuming

   F. effeminate
      feminine
      feminist
      womanly

5. For each of these words that has a positive connotation, find a counterpart that means the same but has a negative connotation. For example, *petite* is positive, but *shrimp* and *small-fry* are negative.

self-confident	humanitarian
free spirit	hard worker
Italian	smile
energetic	pooch
resolute	impassioned

6. Explain the differences between these sentences:
   A. Hotdogs are not good for you.
      Hotdogs are bad for you.

   B. My philosophy is to enjoy life.
      My philosophy is to have fun in life.

   C. Two children, one cleaner than the other, stood on the street corner.
      Two children, one dirtier than the other, stood on the street corner.

   D. You didn't mention her contribution.
      You omitted her contribution.

7. In each sentence, at least one word isn't quite right connotatively. After you have located the inappropriate word(s), see if you can find a substitute whose connotation better suits the sentence.
   A. I suppose I'm a little oafish because I believe whatever anyone tells me.
   B. A good administrator learns to regulate his or her employees by complimenting their efforts, rewarding productivity, and encouraging them to participate in decision-making.
   C. In order to compensate for inferior troop numbers, Robert E. Lee frequently segregated his troops into three groups when he encountered Union forces.
   D. The concept of equal pay between men and women in identical jobs has been stretched to include jobs that are of comparable worth but are not identical.
   E. Good literature makes demands on readers by requiring that we fancifully participate in the literary experience.
   F. Donald shops at the army surplus store because he says that the prices are frugal and that fatigues are fashionable.
   G. The reason that most men aren't cat lovers is that cats, unlike dogs, are free animals, and men prefer to have their love-objects dependent on them.
   H. Elizabeth has been climbing telephone poles for almost a year, but the veterans on the repair crew still consider her to be a starter.

I. As a child I frequently brooded about becoming an astronaut, and it never occurred to me that being claustrophobic would invalidate me.

J. Horror films must increasingly rely on gory immoderation in order to attract moviegoers.

8. Identify the clichés in this passage. What is the problem with using clichés?

No one said that marriage was going to be a bed of roses, but Mortimer gets up on the wrong side of the bed every morning, and Henrietta would try the patience of Job with her whining, so they are splitting the blanket. Today Henrietta and Mortimer aren't on speaking terms; they never see eye to eye on any issue, and they fight like cats and dogs. Mortimer thought that separation would give him a new lease on life and that he would sow some wild oats, but he is a shell of his former self because, let's face it, without her he can hardly keep body and soul together. All things considered, Henrietta is doing as well as can be expected, but she's bored to tears because she hasn't met any men (she's no spring chicken, you know), and she's having trouble making ends meet.

Absence makes the heart grow fonder. Neither of them, however, will make the first move and break the ice because they feel as though they've burned their bridges behind them. Finally, though, Mortimer calls and offers to mend his ways; Henrietta says that she too has had a change of heart. They vow to turn over a new leaf.

Their first week back together he complains that the house is a long ways from being spic and span, and she says that she's tired of waiting on him hand and foot. Rather than nipping the argument in the bud, they make a mountain out of a molehill. I have a sneaking suspicion that this is the shape of things to come: There will be more trials and tribulations, and they will continue to hang their dirty linen in public. Que sera.

B

Sentence Structure

Idea, word choice, and word order: those are the ingredients of a sentence. First we must have something intelligent to say, then we must select the words to communicate that thought, and finally we must arrange those words in an order that emphasizes the most important words in the sentence. The order in which we put the words—that is, the sentence structure—contributes to the meaning of the sentence; far from being simple decoration, the form is a vital part of the message.

The reason we have difficulty deciding how to structure our sentences is that there are many ways to state an idea, and each way is slightly different in emphasis and therefore in effect. The sentence is a malleable structure, and we can mold it almost any way we wish as we develop, expand, and qualify the central thought. Since there is no preset blueprint for building sentences, we develop the structure as we go, all the while trying to fit the form to the idea. Writing is a challenge not because there is one way to express a thought, but because there are so many options that settling on one that suits our needs is no easy matter.

Consider the following sentences that use almost identical words to communicate the same ideas but that lay the stress in different places, thereby changing the relative importance among the parts:

A. I haven't balanced my checkbook in 4 months. I managed okay until my calculator broke. I also shirk other responsibilities. These include washing the clothes, dishes, and kids.

B. There are two things hated by me: (1) washing the clothes, dishes, and kids, and (2) balancing my checkbook, which I haven't done in over 4 months because my calculator broke.

C. Of the many duties I shirk, including washing the clothes, dishes, and kids, the one duty I postpone the longest is balancing my checkbook, which I haven't done in 4 months because my calculator broke.

D. I was managing okay until my calculator broke, which was a good reason not to balance the checkbook that hasn't been balanced in over 4 months; washing the clothes, dishes, and kids is another duty that I shirk.

E. Having a broken calculator and staying busy shirking duties such as washing the clothes, dishes, and kids are my main excuses for not having balanced my checkbook in over 4 months.

F. I always procrastinate balancing my checkbook, though another reason for not having balanced it in 4 months is that my calculator broke, but I also shirk other duties, including washing the clothes, dishes, and kids.

By emphasizing different main topics, each of these options communicates a slightly different message, and each option differs in ease of reading, in clarity, and in logic. These differences are due to which idea we place first, what we select as the main clause, whether we subordinate certain ideas to others, how many sentences we break the information into, where we put the main clause, and which items we make parallel. These concerns comprise the focus of this chapter.

Version A, for example, allocates a complete sentence to each thought, and therefore each idea receives equal emphasis. This version is appropriate if we want to give all the ideas the same emphasis, but usually some ideas are more important than others. Version A is also slightly choppy, and it doesn't specify the relationship between sentences 1 and 2. Version B breaks up the sentence with a colon, but the main clause is unemphatic because it starts with deadwood ("There are") and uses passive voice. Version C balances the subordinate material on each side of the main clause, which is "one duty I postpone the longest is balancing my checkbook." Version D has two main clauses: "I was managing okay," which gets the primary emphasis because it opens the sentence, and "washing . . . is another duty." Every other idea in the sentence is subordinated in one way or another.

APPLICATION

Analyze versions E and F to determine where their emphases lie, how they subordinate ideas, how they structure the material, and how clear they are.

This chapter stresses that you have a variety of structures from which to choose, helps you to recognize a wide variety of options, suggests different ways of putting ideas together, and helps you to use those structures. The focus of this chapter, therefore, is on revising and improving sentences rather than on grammar or the elementary rules of composing sentences. I assume that by this stage in your education you know how to write complete sentences and that, although you may not remember the terminology, you understand the basic grammar of the sentence. If you are a native speaker, you already have an intuitive grasp of many of the intricacies of the English language, and I want to draw upon that knowledge, make you conscious of your expertise, and build on it.

The purpose of this chapter, therefore, is to bring to the forefront your current knowledge of sentence structure, to enhance your versatility in composing sentences, and to make your sentences more effective through informed revision. We will examine different types of sentences, the effects that those different types have, ways of achieving emphasis in sentences, ways to vary sentences, weaknesses to avoid when composing sentences, and suggestions for revising sentences.

Sentence Types

As you no doubt already know, sentences can be classified according to the number and types of clauses they contain. A sentence with only one clause, for instance, is called a simple sentence:

> Henrietta despises her existence.

A simple sentence doesn't have to be as bare as the one above; we can expand it by elaborating on the subject, on the verb, or on the direct object:

> Finding herself rapidly approaching mid-life and having no outside interests besides a minimal relationship with her husband, Henrietta despises her increasingly drab existence, with its predictable routines and unexciting interruptions, despite her comfortable split-level home in the comfortable, secure suburbs, a good salary as a bookkeeper for an interior decorating firm, and charge accounts at every department store from Sears to Saks.

Although the sentence above is complicated and long, it has only one clause and therefore is a simple sentence. *Simple* in this sense doesn't have to mean "ordinary" or "uncomplicated" because we can create very complicated simple sentences by elaborating on any part of the sentence and then modifying the elaborations. We can even have dual subjects and dual verbs:

> Mortimer and Henrietta quarrel and make up.

The fact remains, however, that the simple sentence communicates only one main idea.

We can also take two simple sentences—two main clauses—and combine them into what is called a compound sentence. To connect the two clauses, we use *and, but, or, nor,* or *yet* (coordinating conjunctions).

Henrietta despises her existence,
and Mortimer is going through his second childhood.

Whereas a simple sentence has one idea, a compound sentence has two or more.

    simple sentence: Idea A
    compound sentence: Idea A + Idea B

Compound sentences can also be formed with a semicolon followed by a conjunctive adverb, such as *however, therefore, furthermore, besides, moreover, also, consequently, hence,* and *nevertheless:*

    Mortimer wanted to enjoy the weekend;
    therefore, he went to Atlantic City, alone.

Another way to compose compound sentences is to use a semicolon without a conjunction:

    Henrietta stayed at home;
    she wanted to practice her pouting.

Finally, we can connect main clauses by using paired words, such as *either . . . or, neither . . . nor,* and *not only . . . but also* (correlative conjunctions):

    Either Mortimer will play blackjack for 15 hours a day,
    or some leggy blonde will entice him to spend his money
       in other ways.

Complex sentences, a third type of sentence structure, combine a main clause and a subordinate clause (a clause that cannot stand by itself and that is introduced by a word such as *although, that, who, which, because, while, since,* or *when*).

    Idea A (subordinate) + Idea B (main)
    While Henrietta pouts, Mortimer plays.

The fourth type of sentence is the compound-complex, which connects one or more subordinate clauses to two or more main clauses.

    Idea A (subordinate) + Idea B (main) + Idea C (main)

    Although Mortimer and Henrietta have decided to take a joint
      vacation this year, she wants to fly to Greece and cruise through
      the Aegean Sea, *but* he prefers to go rafting down the Green River
      in Utah.

APPLICATION

What type of sentence is each of the following? Identify main clauses and any subordinate clauses.

1. "He had graduated from Yale, but when Melee once asked him if he liked Thackeray he said sincerely and politely that he had never tasted any." (John Cheever)

2. "The business man who assumes that this life is everything, and the mystic who asserts that it is nothing, fail, on this side and on that, to hit the truth." (E. M. Forster)

3. "A young man may well find quite as many enchantments in a first intrigue as in a first true love." (Honoré de Balzac)

4. "He was a child, dark-eyed and grave, birthmarked upon his neck—a berry of warm brown—and with a gentle face, too quiet and too listening for his years." (Thomas Wolfe)

5. "He was tall and heavily muscled in the shoulders, narrow in the waist and flanks, and he was infinitely buttoned, strapped, harnessed into a uniform as tough and unyielding in cut as a straitjacket, though the cloth was fine and supple." (Katherine Anne Porter)

6. "The lights grow brighter as the earth lurches away from the sun, and now the orchestra is playing yellow cocktail music, and the opera of voices pitches a key higher." (F. Scott Fitzgerald)

7. "She never thought about God, herself, but she had a sleeping regard for Him, as a Being who thought very much as she herself did, though more potently." (Robertson Davies)

8. "Mysteriously and rather giddily splendid, hidden in a grove of sycamores just above the Pacific Coast Highway in Malibu, a commemoration of high culture so immediately productive of crowds and jammed traffic that it can now be approached by appointment only, the seventeen-million-dollar villa built by the late J. Paul Getty to house his antiquities and paintings and furniture manages to strike a peculiar nerve in almost everyone who sees it." (Joan Didion)

9. "I was roosting at the bar over a beer, dressed in a tan corduroy jacket and a life-affirming tie, eye-sparring with a girl in a raspberry-colored coat seated in a nearby booth." (Peter DeVries)

10. "He was, as are most sportsmen, obsessively neat with instruments, and obsessively messy with rooms." (Lillian Hellman)

Loose and Periodic Sentences

Another way to examine sentence structure is by the location of the main idea in the sentence. In the loose sentence, which is the prevalent pattern, the main subject and verb appear near the opening of the sentence, and the details (subordinate clauses, modifying phrases) follow the subject and verb. By placing the main subject and verb up front, we quickly communicate our primary thought and then explain and qualify it:

"She stood there, hands deep in the pockets of her tweed coat, looking down at me broodingly, her eyes narrow, the line of her mouth equally hard and straight." (Iris Murdoch)

The subject and verb are the first two words of the sentence, but the descriptive phrases pile up one after another to develop the way she stood.

A periodic sentence, on the other hand, uses the opposite structure: It delays the main subject and verb until just before the sentence closes. By presenting qualifications first and postponing the main statement until the end, the periodic sentence develops a certain amount of suspense, and the main thought serves as the awaited climax of the sentence:

"In about the time a person unaccustomed to bodily labour would have decided upon which side to lie, Farmer Oak was asleep." (Thomas Hardy)

The ultimate difference between loose and periodic sentences is emphasis—the loose sentence is a more natural order that flows evenly, but the periodic sentence is more emphatic and is slightly more calculated and self-conscious. The loose sentence, which is the usual pattern of conversational sentences, seems more familiar and natural to readers' ears, and it is also less formal. In general, loose sentences serve our purposes well since we usually want to plant our main idea like a solid tree at the beginning of the sentence so that we can then hang details, qualifiers, and subordinate material from it without interfering with the focus on the main idea.

Because the structure of the loose sentence seems natural, many writers tend to use it exclusively and never consider reversing the pattern with an occasional periodic sentence. The problem with using all loose sentences is that the repetition of subject-verb-modification over a span of ten or fifteen sentences can lull readers into the early stages of sleep. Lack of variety causes monotony in prose as well as in food, work, and music. Like a change of chord in a song, a periodic sentence once in a while changes the pace, and the readers' attention perks up. Therefore, when we have an idea that invites a climactic ending or demands special emphasis, we shouldn't hesitate to cast that idea in a periodic structure so that the details build toward the main subject-verb.

APPLICATION

1. Classify the following sentences as loose or periodic, and analyze the effect of the structure.

A. "I feel exquisite pleasure in dwelling on the reflections of childhood, before misfortune had tainted my mind and changed its bright visions of extensive usefulness into gloomy and narrow reflections upon self." (Mary Shelley)

B. "Gold could remember whole mornings and afternoons idled away on the bathroom-tiled floor, with his sister Joannie just outside the plateglass window in a baby carriage for as long as the sunlight fell there, his mother whizzing away at the Singer sewing machine or stitching by hand with a thimbled finger, while his father hummed or sang bouncy dance tunes as he darted about in disorder or shouted horrible imprecations at the presser." (Joseph Heller)

C. "Made properly, with the right tequila, the right liqueur, fresh Mexican limes (above all), the drink shaken with ice cubes in a cocktail shaker and strained (lest the ice cubes make it too watery) into a chilled stemmed (lest the heat from your hand warm the drink) glass (not a wine glass with its inward curving rim), the rim rubbed with a cut lime and pressed just the right way into a plate of salt so that it is coated (not caked), no drink dissolves tribulations and sets you up better." (William Brinkley)

D. "Fighting with the squalling gale, stumbling over stones, falling into trenches and waterlogged pits, I reached the forest." (Jerzy Kosinski)

E. "That was the Thirties when nobody was young any longer and next to nobody was rich and a great many people had nothing at all to do and almost as many had less than they should have had to eat and there was room to spare in the subways and scarcely a seat in the parks and the heart smoldered with indignation like a peat fire under-ground in the wet moss and the dead leaves but smoldered too with a kind of fiery hope so that men and women walked the streets together or sat around tables together and talked of a new world, a new and better beginning, and tried to make it happen in a theater somewhere, or in a fresco on a post-office wall, or a government plan to refinance farmers or to get the textile industry off its back." (Archibald MacLeish)

F. "His statement, however, that as he sprinted across the first field he distinctly saw a rabbit shoot an envious glance at him as he passed and shrug its shoulders hopelessly, I am inclined to discount." (P. G. Wodehouse)

G. "Mrs. O walked the quarter-mile down the road to their house and arrived slightly breathless, her bosom lifting and falling beneath her faded cotton dress, pale and innocent in pattern, like a dress she had worn as a child and that had enlarged and aged with her." (John Updike)

H. "Jenny had come upon Freytag standing alone, leaning slightly at the waist, one hand in pocket, watching the dancers, or pretending to, his features set in the strange frowning blind stare, the whites of his eyes sometimes showing all round the iris, that look Jenny had seen often by now, at first with perfect belief and indignant sympathy, and of late, always of two minds about it—first that his suffering was real, and second, that he was perhaps being a touch theatrical about it." (Katherine Anne Porter)

I. "During that period I spent happy evening hours cultivating the friendship of a middle-aged lawyer of aristocratic attitudes, huge and cosmopolitan erudition, and gentle manner, a bachelor crippled in his kindergarten days by polio who managed nevertheless to drive a specially built car and to fly an Ercoupe, which required no pedal motion, the ailerons having been synchronized with the wheel." (William F. Buckley, Jr.)

2. Change these periodic sentences into loose sentences. What is the effect of the change?

Example:

ORIGINAL (periodic): Because her bills were high, because her retirement check from her old job was small, and because her social security barely paid the rent, which had increased 20 percent in the last two years, the old lady took in typing from students.

REVISION (loose): The old lady took in typing from students because her bills were high, because her retirement check from her old job was small, and because her social security barely paid the rent, which had increased 20 percent in the last two years.

EFFECT: Since the main clause ("the old lady took in typing") isn't dramatic, there is no need to postpone it until the end. The revision is easier to read because the multiple subordinate clauses don't muddle the beginning of the sentence.

A. When my cat Elizabeth was 14 years old and had begun to lose her hair and teeth and mind, I had her put to sleep.

B. Flying low to the landscape, headed to a foreign country, full of power and stealth, the new missiles are almost unstoppable.

C. With the sun bobbing like an orange ball on the New Jersey horizon and with the tops of clouds still golden as the darkness begins to fill the woods, lovers wisely leave Central Park.

3. Change these loose sentences into periodic ones and describe the difference in emphasis.

Example:

ORIGINAL (loose): Mortimer bought a new turquoise car after scraping the old paint off the garage, putting on a primer coat, and then applying two coats of turquoise finish.

REVISION (periodic): After scraping the old paint off the garage, putting on a primer coat, and then applying two coats of turquoise finish, Mortimer bought a new turquoise car.

EFFECT: By postponing the main idea until the end, we have emphasized the cause-and-effect relationship of the actions and thereby added more humor to the sentence.

A. The rodeo rider stayed on the bull although it twisted and whirled its powerful 2000-pound frame and although the rider tore a ligament in his shoulder.

B. Rio is a city of sharp contradictions, with its luscious beaches and adjacent repelling slums, its gaiety and high unemployment and crime, its many consumer goods but few consumers, its intense natural beauty crowded with 8 million residents, and its decaying old buildings juxtaposed to modern skyscrapers.

C. I almost never read as a child because I was always too busy playing baseball or horseback riding on my favorite pony, a buckskin mare named Gypsy, or swimming in the river, even as late as October, or perhaps building a go-cart or a tree house.

Subordination and Coordination

Subordination and coordination are ways of combining clauses into one sentence to avoid a series of short clauses and to show the relationship between the clauses. Consider, for instance, the two clauses below:

> Wyatt Earp lived a violent life.
> He died of natural causes at the age of 80.

If we wish to show that the two clauses are of equal importance, we can do that structurally by making them into a compound sentence:

> Wyatt Earp lived a violent life, but he died of natural causes at the age of 80.

By placing the clauses in equal grammatical constructions—each is a main clause—we stress that they are coordinate: equal in significance.

If we wish to show that one clause is more important than the other, we can also do that structurally by making them into a complex sentence. One clause is subordinated to the other:

Although Wyatt Earp lived a violent life, he died of natural causes at the age of 80.

The first clause is subordinate because it is introduced by the subordinate conjunction *although* and therefore cannot stand by itself. The stress falls on the second clause because it is the main clause.

To demonstrate the versatility offered by subordination and coordination, we can take the following three short clauses and combine them in various ways.

A. George Washington Carver was born a slave.
B. He contributed significantly to agriculture and to the position of blacks.
C. Americans recognize him as a great man.

We can combine them in at least 7 different ways and a total of 42 configurations.

We can make all three of them main clauses in a compound sentence to show that they are of equal importance:

1. A, B, and C

"George Washington Carver was born a slave, he contributed significantly to agriculture and to the position of blacks, and Americans recognize him as a great man."

Alternative configurations:

B, A, and C
C, B, and A
C, A, and B
B, C, and A
A, C, and B

We can make one subordinate to the other two, for example:

"Although George Washington Carver was born a slave, he contributed significantly to agriculture and to the position of blacks, and Americans recognize him as a great man."

2. A (sub), B and C
3. A (sub), C and B
4. B (sub), C and A

We can change the configuration by placing the subordinate clause either between or after as well as before the other two.

We can also subordinate two and emphasize the third clause, for example:

"Although George Washington Carver was born a slave, Americans recognize him as a great man because he contributed significantly to agriculture and to the position of blacks."

5. A (sub), C, B (sub)
6. C (sub), B, A (sub)
7. B (sub), A, C (sub)

The main clause can be not only between, but also before or after the subordinate clauses.

APPLICATION

Combine these three clauses in as many as possible of the configurations demonstrated above:

A gas leak caused an explosion.
Six persons were seriously injured.
One man was killed.

The decision of whether to emphasize one idea over another, however, should be neither mechanical nor arbitrary because it is a matter of logic and value. We assign emphasis based on whether we want readers to perceive equality or inequality between ideas. To show inequality, of course, we use subordination, and there are several features about subordination that we should consider.

1. Subordination is, to some extent, a reflection of values because when we subordinate an idea we implicitly state that this idea is less important than another idea: *subordinate* after all means secondary in importance. Through subordination, we structurally de-emphasize material that we see as being less important by putting it in secondary positions. To demonstrate how subordination reflects values, consider these two clauses:

The firefighters battled the blaze all night.
They were unable to save seven children.

Which of these two clauses is the more important? Most of us would agree that the lives of seven children are more important than the firefighters having worked long hours. To express the relative value of the two ideas, we can subordinate one clause to the other:

> Although the firefighters battled the blaze all night, they were unable to save seven children.

Reversing the subordination would reflect a different value system, one that would seem inappropriate to most people:

> The firefighters worked all night although they were unable to save seven children.

What we implicitly communicate with this second construction is that we consider human life to be subordinate to firefighters' time. Using subordination, therefore, is not merely a technique for joining clauses into one sentence, but a way of achieving proper emphasis among our ideas. When we place main ideas in subordinate positions, or secondary ideas in main clauses, we emphasize or de-emphasize the wrong ideas, and the result is a disharmony between structure and content. Instead, our sentence structure should reinforce our content.

2. Which clause we subordinate may depend on the context of the paragraph in which the sentence appears as well as on our values. The controlling idea of a paragraph dictates the focus of the individual sentences in that paragraph, and therefore what would seem to be appropriate subordination in the context of one paragraph might be inappropriate subordination in another paragraph. For example, let's fuse these two clauses into a complex sentence:

> I was shot in the shoulder in 1974.
> I was simply driving down Concord Avenue in the South Bronx.

The clause to subordinate would logically seem to be the second one, since getting shot is infinitely more significant than a drive through the South Bronx. The resulting complex sentence would probably read:

> I was shot in the shoulder while I was driving down Concord Avenue in the South Bronx in 1974.

There could also, conceivably, be a situation in which the subordination would be reversed. For example, if a cop were writing about his or her experiences with the New York Police Department and opened a paragraph with the topic sentence "In my 15 years on the force, I have been shot five times while on duty—once in 1974, twice in 1979, once in 1981 and again in 1985," one of the support sentences might read "When I was shot in 1974, I was simply driving down Concord Avenue in the South Bronx." The logic of an individual sentence cannot be fully understood out of the context of the paragraph since each sentence is part of that larger unit. The paragraph certainly influences the structure, tone, and emphasis of its individual parts.

APPLICATION

Consider the subordination in the following paragraph. First, point out the subordinate clauses and the main clauses, and then decide whether each sentence carries forth the emphasis laid out in the topic sentence. Which sentences employ appropriate subordination? Which sentences, if any, are incorrectly subordinated? Can you recast those sentences to reflect the proper emphasis?

Paris is an enjoyable place to visit. Although the food is incomparable, many Parisian restaurants are so expensive that they are beyond most tourists' budgets. Because the museums house some of the most exquisite art in the world, the lines are always long, and the museums are always crowded. The Eiffel Tower has been called one of the world's ugliest edifices, though the view from the top gives one a sight of the entire city. Although taxis are sometimes scarce, the subway system, which operates between 5:30 A.M. and 12:30 A.M., is clean, dependable, and cheap. Nightclubs in Paris are different from those in the United States, for Parisian clubs have become expensive tourist traps, especially the Moulin Rouge, the Crazy Horse, the Lido, and the Follies Bergere, but one can still find great jazz clubs on the Left Bank.

3. Besides deciding which clause to subordinate, we must decide which conjunction to use to introduce the subordinate clause. The subordinating conjunction is extremely important because it establishes the relationship between the clauses. Consider the radical difference in meaning between these sentences:

> *Although* his mother helped him bake it, the cake was an absolute disaster.
> *Because* his mother helped him bake it, the cake was an absolute disaster.

In the first sentence, the cake fails despite the mother's help; in the second, the mother is the cause of the failure. By changing one word—the subordinating conjunction—we can totally change the meaning of a sentence. Subordinating conjunctions can show different types of relationships between the clauses, including relationships of time, contrast, condition, causation, or place, and we can draw from a pool of words to show any one of these relationships:

> *Causation:* as, because
> *Contrast:* although, though, even though
> *Condition:* if, unless, whether, provided that, assuming that
> *Place:* where, wherever
> *Time:* before, after, until, till, while, when, once, since, as soon as, as long as

Which subordinating conjunction we use to connect the clauses depends, of course, on what our message is and on what relationship we want to show between the clauses.

APPLICATION

For each sentence below, select an appropriate subordinating conjunction to show the relationship indicated. Then articulate the differences in meaning between the pairs of sentences.

  1. [*Causation*] the Academy Awards have become something other than a self-congratulatory ceremony, I will watch them.
  [*Time*] the Academy Awards have become something other than a self-congratulatory ceremony, I will watch them.

  2. [*Condition*] I like people, I will go to great lengths not to loan them money.
  [*Contrast*] I like people, I will go to great lengths not to loan them money.

  3. I usually bathe on Saturdays [*condition*] I need it.
  I usually bathe on Saturdays [*place*] I need it.

  4. [*Contrast*] he was a meek little man, his signature was bold and exaggerated.
  [*Causation*] he was a meek little man, his signature was bold and exaggerated.

   4. The final point about subordination is that the subordinate clause can be placed almost anywhere in the sentence: beginning, middle, or end.

>   *Beginning:* Because humankind's current evolution is cultural and informational more than genetic, our evolution could be reversed within one generation.
>   *Middle:* Humankind's current evolution, so long as it remains cultural and informational more than genetic, could be reversed within one generation.
>   *End:* Humankind's current evolution could be reversed within one generation because it is more cultural and informational than genetic.

The placement of subordinate clauses is one of the factors that determines whether sentences are loose or periodic: In a loose sentence the subordination and modification follow the main clause, but in a periodic sentence they precede the main clause.

   A subordinate clause at the opening of a sentence is especially useful to achieve transition from a preceding sentence. Another reason to put a subordinate clause at the beginning of a sentence is to keep a loose sentence from becoming a long train of strung-together clauses and phrases, as in this example:

Gold-hungry Americans inundated the Yukon Territory at the end of the nineteenth century to pan nugget-filled creeks, mine surrounding mountains, and encounter winters so severe that many died after gold was discovered in 1896 in the Klondike region, where over the next decade thousands of miners took out an average of $10 million a year in gold.

Placing all of the subordination after the main clause makes the sentence not only lopsided but also illogical because the time sequence is backwards. To ease the overcrowding at the end of the sentence and to clarify the chronology, we can position one of the subordinate clauses at the beginning and change the final subordinate clause into a main clause:

After gold was discovered in the Klondike in 1896, thousands of gold-hungry Americans inundated the Yukon to pan nugget-filled creeks, mine surrounding mountains, and encounter winters so severe that many died, but those who survived took out $10 million in gold over the next decade.

The main use of subordination and coordination is to combine short clauses so that our prose doesn't become choppy and disjointed. The following clauses, for instance, are so short and choppy that they sound as if they were written by a child:

Muhammad was born around 570. He was born in Mecca. He is the Prophet of Islam. He set out to make converts to his religion around 615. His enemies planned to murder him in Mecca. So he fled to Yathrib. There he established a model state. His ideas and teachings were inspirational. He died in 632. By then all of Arabia had accepted him as the true prophet.

With a little help from subordination and coordination, we can transform this piece into much more readable and mature prose:

Muhammad, the Prophet of Islam, was born in Mecca around 570. By 615 he set out to win converts to his religion, but his enemies planned to murder him in Mecca. Muhammad therefore fled to Yathrib, where he established a model state. His ideas and teachings were so inspirational that by the time he died in 632 all of Arabia had accepted him as the true prophet.

We can increase the density of the prose even further by combining the first three sentences into one sentence:

Muhammad, the Prophet of Islam, who was born in Mecca around 570, set out to win converts to his religion around 615, but because his enemies planned to murder him in Mecca, he fled to

Yathrib, where he established a model state. His ideas and teachings were so inspirational that by the time he died in 632 all of Arabia had accepted him as the true prophet.

How far we carry subordination and coordination depends on the complexity of our subject matter, the sophistication of our audience, and our own ability to construct lengthy but clear sentences. Obviously, if we construct sentences that are too complicated and intricate, we will lose readers; at the other extreme, we will also lose them if we write immature, choppy sentences.

APPLICATION

By practicing combining short, one-idea sentences into multi-clause sentences, you will become more aware of the stylistic options available to you, gain confidence in your ability to compose sophisticated sentences, and learn to assign relative emphasis among ideas. Your task, therefore, is to combine the following groups of basic sentences into a more fluid style. To increase your repertoire of sentence constructions, offer at least two ways of putting together each group of clauses.

Sample: Hermann Goering was a Nazi leader.
He headed the Gestapo.
He acted as air minister.
He committed war atrocities.
He was tried at Nuremberg.
He was sentenced to death.
He committed suicide shortly before he was to be hanged.

Hermann Goering, the Nazi leader who headed the Gestapo and acted as air minister, was sentenced to death at the Nuremberg trials for his war atrocities, but he committed suicide shortly before he was to be hanged.

"Commuting"
1. I ride a bus.
2. It is an express.
3. It goes downtown.
4. I ride it every weekday.
5. I ride it to work.

6. The bus is convenient.
7. I catch the bus two blocks from my house.
8. The trip is 11 miles.
9. The bus takes an hour.

10. The bus deposits me at my office building.
11. I get there at 7:50 A.M.

12. The bus is inexpensive.
13. The bus costs $1.60 round trip.
14. Parking would cost $4.00 a day downtown.

15. The same people ride the bus every day.
16. I have met some of these people.
17. I have talked to some of these people.

18. We catch up on each other's activities.
19. We talk about movies.
20. We talk about sports.
21. We talk about the weather.
22. We talk about our businesses.
23. We try not to talk about politics.

24. Many riders prefer to read the newspaper.
25. One guy reads only the sports section.
26. He gives the rest of the paper to whoever is sitting next to him.

27. One woman knits.
28. She is knitting a scarf.
29. The scarf is apparently for a giant.
30. It is already 6 feet long.
31. It continues to grow.

32. A friend usually sits beside me.
33. His name is Bill.
34. He is an engineer.
35. He works for a construction firm.
36. He does estimates for contract bids.

37. His real passion is flying.
38. He is a pilot.
39. He rents a small plane.
40. He flies every weekend.
41. He wants to retire.
42. Then he can fly all the time.

43. He also flies model airplanes.
44. He designs them.
45. He builds them.
46. They are radio controlled.
47. Some are large.
48. One has a 10-foot wingspan.

49. Bill reads *Aviation Weekly*.
50. He reads it from cover to cover.
51. He keeps me informed about aviation.
52. I don't care much about aviation.

53. Usually the buses are prompt.
54. Recently they haven't been prompt.

55. Tuesday morning my bus was late.
56. Wednesday afternoon it was late.
57. I got on the bus Wednesday afternoon.
58. It broke down on the freeway.
59. Thursday afternoon the bus didn't even show up.

60. I called the bus company.
61. I complained to the manager.
62. He listened.
63. He tried to calm me down.
64. He was unsuccessful.

65. I thanked him.
66. He had motivated me.
67. I decided to start a car pool.
68. Other former bus riders are in the car pool.
69. Bill joined.
70. The knitter joined.
71. The sports nut joined.

72. Carpooling is quicker than the bus.
73. We leave our neighborhood at 7:15 A.M.
74. We arrive downtown at 7:45 A.M.
75. Carpooling is cheaper than the bus.
76. We split the parking fee.

77. We haven't broken down yet.
78. The scarf is now 9 feet long.

"Esther Williams and the Olympics"
1. Esther Williams was born in 1923.
2. She was born in Los Angeles.
3. She was raised in Los Angeles.
4. Her family was very poor.

5. Esther became a champion swimmer.
6. The National Championship swimming meet was held in Des Moines.
7. Esther was 17 years old.

8. She won three gold medals.
9. She won in butterfly, freestyle, and medley swimming.

10. Esther Williams would have had a good chance for gold medals at the Olympics.
11. The 1940 Olympics were to be held in Helsinki.
12. In 1939 Russian troops invaded Finland.
13. By the summer of 1940 the Nazis had invaded most of Europe.
14. The Helsinki Olympics were cancelled.

15. Esther Williams took a job in Los Angeles.
16. The job was decorating windows for a clothing store.
17. The store was I. Magnin's on Wilshire Blvd.
18. She was making $78 a month.
19. She wanted to become a buyer for I. Magnin's.

20. MGM offered Williams a contract.
21. She wasn't sure whether to sign.
22. MGM gave her a screen test.
23. The screen test was with Clark Gable.
24. Clark Gable was her idol.
25. She signed.

26. Louis B. Mayer liked Esther.
27. Louis B. Mayer is the second "M" of MGM.
28. He thought she was too tall.
29. She thought he was too short.

30. Busby Berkeley was a Hollywood director.
31. He directed musicals.
32. He began to choreograph water ballets.
33. Esther was the star of the productions.

34. Esther's films made money.
35. They were popular.
36. Male audiences especially liked her movies.
37. Adolescent girls also liked them.
38. Critics hated her movies.

39. She starred in dozens of movies.
40. Her films included *Ziegfeld Follies, Million Dollar Mermaid, Bathing Beauty, Neptune's Daughter,* and *Pagan Love Song.*

41. The films were filled with pretty swimmers.
42. Esther popularized what is called synchronized swimming.
43. The swimmers performed acrobatics in the water.

44. The 1984 Olympics were held in Los Angeles.

45. Synchronized swimming was part of the 1984 Olympics.
46. Esther participated in the 1984 Olympics.
47. She did not compete in the Olympics.
48. She was a commentator for ABC-TV.
49. She announced a sports event.
50. The event was synchronized swimming.

Sentence Length

How long we make a given sentence depends on (1) the complexity of the thought, (2) the amount of emphasis we wish to give the idea, (3) the structure of the sentence, and (4) the length of the sentences around it.

Lengthy sentences—those over forty words long, for example—have the advantage of allowing us to put a great amount of related information together by inserting secondary material into phrases and subordinate clauses at the beginning, in the middle, or at the end of the sentence. When the idea we wish to communicate has many sides for readers to explore, a sentence with several clauses and phrases may best serve our needs. Just because a sentence is long doesn't mean that it is confusing or difficult to follow. Here, for instance, is a fairly long sentence that is perfectly clear:

> "And as though his life with all that were not sufficiently com-
> plicated, he tumbled head over heels into love the very next day
> with another woman almost his own age who was separated from
> a mountainous husband with a brutal temper and had four chil-
> dren: the eldest old and tall enough to beat Gold to a bloody pulp
> with his fists should that notion possess him, the next in age a girl
> worldly and pretty enough to seduce him should she choose to,
> and the youngest pair, twins of different sex, still tender enough in
> years for the tantrums, fever, and digestive upsets and messes of
> early childhood that turn parenthood into an uncivilized night-
> mare." (Joseph Heller)

If a sentence is constructed properly, it can be both long and clear; if it isn't constructed properly, clarity will decrease as the length of the sentence increases. In general, it is better to expand a sentence by adding clauses rather than prepositional phrases; that is, a sentence with two main clauses (compound sentence) or with one main clause and one or more subordinate clauses (complex sentence) can more easily accommodate several ideas than can a simple sentence (one main clause) that is expanded with phrases that start with *in, at, from, for, to,* and so on. Here is a simple sentence expanded beyond what its skeleton can carry.

> *With* the rise *in* wheat prices *in* the United States due *to* the drought last summer *in* the Midwest and the failure *of* the wheat crop *in* the Soviet Union *for* the second year *in* a row, the President *in* this election year is facing a difficult political decision *in* whether or not to sell wheat *to* the Russians and if so how many bushels and *at* what price or whether to store the grain *for* the time being, keeping the price stable *on* the world market if possible and try to get concessions or reciprocal agreements *on* agriculture and petroleum *from* the Russians.

At some point, we will cram so much material into a sentence that readers won't be able to sort out all the parts of the message, won't be able to retain all the qualifications and details, won't be able to see the relationships of the parts, and therefore won't be able to comprehend our meaning. Long sentences can be a strain on readers because they demand that readers store many bits of information in one breath. The longer the sentence, the greater the possibility of losing readers, and therefore the more careful we must be to ensure clarity. Don't be afraid to use long sentences, but be certain to expand them intelligently and clearly.

In addition to allowing us to consolidate a great amount of related information and to subordinate the secondary ideas, lengthy sentences have another, somewhat surprising, advantage: They are concise. Granted, it seems paradoxical that length can be concise. Usually people equate lengthy sentences with wordiness, but that's not necessarily the case. Consider these examples:

> Olga prefers to compose her first drafts on a word processor.
> She prefers composing on a word processor because it makes editing and revising easier and quicker.
> A word processor allows her to insert, delete, and rearrange material.

Individually, the three sentences appear to be succinct to the point of being terse. If we consider the whole message that they communicate, however, we realize that one longer sentence can incorporate it all more concisely and smoothly:

> Olga prefers to compose her first drafts on a word processor because when she wishes to revise or edit she can insert, delete, or rearrange material more quickly and easily.

Whereas the three short sentences require 38 words to communicate the message, the single longer sentence does the job in only 30 words. Obviously, then, the longer sentence is more concise.

Short sentences, of course, have their own advantages. They are emphatic. They are direct. They are clear. Because they aren't cluttered with numerous qualifications and secondary ideas, their message is unmistakable and striking. One short sentence amid longer sentences serves as an abrupt contrast to the textured layers of the other sentences, and it can be a powerful vehicle for summing up a paragraph or clinching an image or idea. But we should save these emphatic short sentences for emphatic material—that is, we should match the emphatic form with the emphatic content.

We should use short sentences sparingly because they lose their impact when they appear too frequently, and they make for choppy reading when several are used in succession. A diet of short sentences results in a halting style because of the abrupt stops and starts; the constant interruption of periods disrupts not only the flow of the prose, but also the continuity of thought.

A paragraph of all short sentences or all medium sentences or all long sentences becomes tedious, and therefore with sentences, as with most things, a mixture is best. By varying sentence length, we help to achieve rhythm and balance in a paragraph and help to keep our prose interesting, vigorous, and diverse. Sentences within paragraphs should be varied in length for the same reason that a speaker's voice should vary in volume and pitch: to avoid monotony, to help hold the readers' attention, and to give proper emphasis to ideas. If a person speaks in a monotone without occasionally varying the pitch or pattern, listeners' attention will drift and they will eventually nod off. Likewise, if our sentences are all the same length and type, a certain mental numbness will creep over our readers. Although every sentence doesn't have to be different from the one before it, writing four or five consecutive sentences of approximately the same length becomes monotonous, as the sample below illustrates.

A. Too Short

Spartacus was a slave who led a rebellion against ancient Rome. Little is known about his prerebellion years. Legend has it that he was either a deserter from the Roman army or a bandit chieftan. He was captured and made a slave. He became a gladiator and fought in the Coliseum to entertain the Roman citizens.

In 73 B.C. Spartacus escaped from a gladiator training school. He and seventy-five other gladiators escaped from Capua and went to Mt. Vesuvius. They established a stronghold there and killed the Roman soldiers sent to recapture them. Other slaves heard of their success and joined them. Soon their forces swelled to several thousand.

Roman citizens feared a slave insurrection more than an invasion by the barbarians. Spartacus declared all slaves free. Slaves outnumbered citizens by three to one. Of course, there had been previous attempted rebellions by slaves, but they had failed. Mainly they had lacked leadership.

B. Too Long

With Spartacus as its chieftan, though, this guerilla group, composed of many nationalities, including Germans, Gauls, Egyptians, Thracians, Greeks, and Celts, and growing increasingly strong with each day, had the type of leadership needed to continue to fight to its potential in their war of survival in the hills in the southern provinces of Italy. Although the gladiators controlled much of the south and raided at will, Spartacus' plan was to fight his way north, and once they were across the Alps the slaves would be free to return to their separate homelands, the only problem being that his followers didn't want to stop fighting—so the Gladiatorial War, as it came to be known, continued.

The Roman citizens were so outraged by the power of the slave army and the audacity of its leader, who was quickly becoming a hero to all slaves because he defeated several more Roman armies that were sent against his gladiators, that they demanded that the great commander in charge of the army of Rome, Marcus Licinius Crassus, go into the field with the most seasoned troops of the empire for the duration of the war.

C. Just Right

In 72 B.C., the Roman army surrounded the gladiators at their winter quarters, but Spartacus broke through the legions' lines and mounted a successful counteroffensive. Realizing that the Roman troops would eventually overtake him, however, he decided to divide his army and flee from Italy. While the Germans and Gauls headed north to escape across the Alps, Spartacus and the rest headed south, hoping to capture a port and sail to freedom across the Adriatic.

Disaster struck. Crassus' eight legions overwhelmed the northern army and took 6,000 prisoners. Wanting to make examples of the insurgents so that other slaves would not be tempted to rebel, Crassus ordered his troops to crucify all 6,000 prisoners along the highway to Rome. Their rotting flesh was to serve as a forceful lesson on rebellion.

Spartacus and his remaining troops were also trapped by a Roman army, this one under Lucullus. Although Spartacus knew that resistance was futile, he preferred to fight rather than to surrender. He assembled his troops, killed his war horse, and fought a desperate and gallant battle. Every slave was slain.

What we implicitly tell readers with such unvaried sentences as those in paragraphs A and B is that we don't care enough for the readers to interest them and we don't care enough for the content to put it into a form that will hold readers' attention.

APPLICATION

1. Revise paragraphs A and B above.

2. Analyze the prose on the first two pages of your last essay.
   A. How many words were in the longest sentence?
   B. How many in the shortest?
   C. What is the average length of the sentences in the entire essay?
   D. How many sentences are simple? Compound? Complex? Compound-complex?
   E. How many clauses per sentence did you write?
   F. What is the average length of the clauses within sentences?

Parallelism

Parallelism is a structural means of joining similar ideas and showing their equality. It is arranging similar ideas in similar grammatical structures:

"I came, I saw, I conquered." (Julius Caesar)
"One if by land, two if by sea." (Longfellow)
"To be, or not to be." (Shakespeare)
"Give me liberty, or give me death." (Patrick Henry)

In each of these examples, the striking effect results from the repetition of the same word forms (nouns, verbs, infinitives) in the same order. As in the following instance, the second idea in a parallel construction uses the pattern of the first idea:

VERB	ARTICLE	NOUN	/	VERB	ARTICLE	NOUN
Spare	the	rod	and	spoil	the	child.

The structure of one half intentionally mirrors that of the other half in order to achieve emphasis and to show the connection between the ideas in a memorable way. Such parallelism can occur between words, between phrases, or between clauses.

Words

The simplest form of parallelism is between two words:

I like *bacon* and *eggs.*

The two words are the same form (nouns), are of the same importance, and are in the same position. Point out the parallelism in this sentence:

"Politics offers yesterday's answers to today's problems." (Marshall McLuhan)

Parallelism can also occur in a series of words:

"I see one-third of a nation ill-housed, ill-clad, ill-nourished." (Franklin D. Roosevelt)

To achieve parallelism, we must be certain that we match verbs with verbs, nouns with nouns, adjectives with adjectives, and so forth. What is faulty about the following sentence?

The stranger was tall, dark, and had a handsome face.

The parallelism is broken because the sentence tries to match adjectives (tall and dark) with a verb (had). To make the elements parallel, we can eliminate the verb phrase "had a handsome face" and retain only the adjective:

The stranger was tall, dark, and handsome.

Phrases

The same principle applies when we want to make phrases parallel: The phrases must be in the same form, such as infinitive phrases with infinitive phrases, prepositional phrases with prepositional phrases, and so on.

"Government of the people,
      by the people, and
      for the people. . . ."

(Abraham Lincoln)

"Our duke was as calm at the mouth of a cannon
      as at the door of a drawing-room."

(William Makepeace Thackeray)

"This shows how much easier it is to be critical
                             than to be correct."
                                        (Benjamin Disraeli)
"Our task now is not to fix the blame for the past,
                       but to fix the course for the future."
                                        (John F. Kennedy)

Clauses

Even more elaborate parallelism can be established by using the same
pattern for entire clauses. By repeating the word order of a preceding
clause, a second clause links itself to the previous clause and suggests
that they are logically related. We can repeat either subordinate or main
clauses.

Subordinate Clauses

"But if I'd listened   when my grandmother begged me not to
                         make so many faces (Girls aren't *sup-
                         posed* to be funny),
    if I'd spent   fewer of girlhood's summers sprawled
                         comatose in the sun so I could strut my
                         hour later as Bronzed Goddess in White
                         Strapless Party Dress,
         if I'd only learned to get hysterical with a little *restraint*,
today I'd be able to risk looking in the mirror with my glasses on to
see where my lipstick should go."   (Judith Wax)

"The human race's prospects of survival were considerably better
    when we were defenceless against tigers than they are today
    when we have become defenceless against ourselves."
                                        (Arnold Toynbee)

Notice that the writers signal the parallelism by deliberately repeating
the introductory words each time: *if I'd* and *when we*. This draws readers'
attention to the parallelism and makes it more obvious.

Main Clauses

"He that will not   reason is a bigot;
 he that cannot   reason is a fool; and
 he that dares not   reason is a slave."
                                        (William Drummond)

```
"Homer        is not more decidedly the  first of heroic poets,
 Shakespeare  is not more decidedly the  first of dramatists,
 Demosthenes  is not more decidedly the  first of orators,
than  Boswell      is                    first of biographers."
```
                                          (Thomas Macaulay)

Elaborate parallelism is a characteristic of formal and lofty prose, and we should realize that when we use it extensively we are giving a formal cast to our thoughts. Where we wish to appear dignified and stately, elaborate parallelism is appropriate, and this is the effect in the following passages by Francis Bacon:

> "Studies serve for pastimes, for ornaments and for abilities. Their chief use for pastime is in privateness and retiring; for ornament is in discourse; and for ability is in judgment. For expert men can execute, but learned men are fittest to judge or censure. To spend too much time in them is sloth; to use them too much for ornament is affectation; to make judgment wholly by their rules is the humour of a scholar."

> "Some books are to be tasted, others to be swallowed, and some few to be chewed and digested. That is, some books are to be read only in parts, others to be read but cursorily, and some few to be read wholly and with diligence and attention. Reading maketh a full man, conference a ready man, and writing an exact man."

Because parallelism is clear and striking to the ear, speeches also rely on it heavily. Consider, for example, John F. Kennedy's Inaugural Address or this excerpt from Winston Churchill's address to the House of Commons in 1940 after the British defeat at Dunkirk:

> "I am myself full of confidence that if all do their duty, if nothing is neglected, and if the best arrangements are made, as they are being made, we shall prove ourselves once again able to defend our island home, to ride out the storm of war, and to outlive the menace of tyranny, if necessary for years, if necessary alone."

In less formal prose, however, excessive parallelism can appear artificial or merely decorative. As always, we want to suit our style to our content and audience. For most essays, a middlebrow style is appropriate, and a moderate amount of parallelism is appropriate.

Often instead of rigid and full parallelism between clauses—that is, following one pattern *exactly*—we can simply make the opening parts parallel. Parallelism does not have to be sustained indefinitely in a sentence; we can make the verbs in a sentence parallel and let the direct objects that follow them be structured independently. Exact repetition beyond the initial parallel construction is unnecessary and often is not even desirable because it can become mechanical.

Here is the difference between partial and full parallelism:

PARTIAL: We need to look at the various components, to consider alternatives to the current policy, and to write a proposal recommending the best option.

What elements are parallel, and where does the parallelism stop?

FULL: "If our predecessors were determined to test the maximum limits for the exercise of state power in order to correct imbalance, we are about to test the minimum limits for exercise of state power in order to enhance autonomy." (David J. Rothman)

The extent of parallelism will depend on how much similarity exists between the two situations, how much attention we wish to draw to that similarity, and how formal we want our style to be.

Purposes of Parallelism

Parallel constructions are handy devices not only for emphasis, but also for clarity and economy. They allow us to organize into one sentence related ideas that otherwise would take two or three sentences, and they allow us to keep the elements distinct. In one sense, then, parallelism is a packaging device. We can combine the following paired statements into a single sentence:

ORIGINAL: There is nothing so easy to learn as experience.
There is nothing so hard to apply as experience.

REVISION 1: There is nothing so easy to learn or so hard to apply as experience.

REVISION 2: Nothing is so easy to learn or so hard to apply as experience.

ORIGINAL: Your first task is to observe life.
Your second task is to read about life.
Your third task is to experience life.

REVISION 1: Your tasks are to observe life, then to read about it, and finally to experience it.

REVISION 2: Your first task is to observe life; the second, to read about it; and the third, to experience it.

In the process of knitting together similar ideas into one sentence, we usually can eliminate common words and thus achieve economy of expression. Repeating the whole thought is unnecessary in each member of a series, and therefore we can omit common words. In the first example above, we eliminated "there is" and "as experience" because there was no need to repeat them, and therefore the revisions are considerably shorter than the original. This process of omitting common words is known as *ellipsis*.

APPLICATION

What common words are omitted in these sentences:

"Government, even in its best state, is but a necessary evil; in its worst state, an intolerable one." (Thomas Paine)

" 'If I could have known Cicero, and been his friend, and talked with him in his retirement at Tusculum (beautiful Tusculum), I could have died contented.' " (Charles Dickens)

Advice, Warnings, Reminders

1. As a grammatical device, parallelism combines, equates, and clarifies ideas; as a rhetorical device, it strikes the ear with a deliberate rhythm and emphasizes the repeated elements. The symmetrical design, in which equal ideas are placed in equal structures, draws the readers' attention to the similarity between the ideas.

2. When listing nouns in a series, we can either use the article or preposition once at the beginning of the series and allow it to modify the whole list, or repeat the article or preposition before every member of the list.

either:	the students, the professors, and the administrators
or:	the students, professors, and administrators
not:	the students, professors, and the administrators

   | either: | by ship, by plane, and by train |
   | or: | by ship, plane, and train |

3. Another way to signal parallel ideas and structure is to use paired words called *correlative conjunctions: either . . . or; neither . . . nor; not only . . . but also; both . . . and.* We must be careful to position the correlative so that the word form following the second correlative conjunction is the same form as that following the first correlative conjunction.

ADVERB	PRONOUN

ORIGINAL: Judges are *either* too lenient *or* they are too strict.

REVISION 1: Judges are either *too* lenient or *too* strict.

REVISION 2: Judges either *are* too lenient or *are* too strict.

REVISION 3: Either *judges* are too lenient or *they* are too strict.

ORIGINAL: The reporter *not only* said that the bank had been robbed, *but also* that a teller had been wounded.

REVISION 1: The reporter said not only *that* the bank had been robbed, but also *that* a teller had been wounded.

REVISION 2: The reporter not only *said* that the bank had been robbed, but also *testified* that a teller had been wounded.

4. Whereas parallelism places *similar* ideas in similar structures, a related rhetorical device—antithesis—places sharply *contrasting* ideas in similar structures. By juxtaposing opposing ideas, antithesis emphasizes the contrast:

NOUN	VERB	ARTICLE	OBJECT	NOUN	VERB	ARTICLE	OBJECT
"Charms	strike	the	sight, but	merit	wins	the	soul."

(Alexander Pope)

The ideas are opposites, and the balanced structure sets up the opposition clearly.

" 'To lose one parent, Mr. Worthing, may be regarded as a misfortune; to lose both looks like carelessness.' " (Oscar Wilde)

"What interests us is not the good but the godly. Not living well but living forever." (John Updike)

"Ask not what your country can do for you—ask what you can do for your country." (John F. Kennedy)

APPLICATION

1. Here is an example that is set up to show the parallelism clearly:

"What moods,
 what passions,
 what nights   of despair and
         gathering storms of anger,
 what sudden cruelties and
         amazing tendernesses are buried and
                                   hidden and
                                   implied in every love story!"

(H. G. Wells)

Point out the parallelism in each of these sentences, and describe the purpose and effect of the parallelism.

A. "Freedom, and not servitude, is the cure of anarchy; as religion, and not atheism, is the true remedy for superstition." (Edmund Burke)

B. "A star is in balance. Its own gravitational field produces a tendency to contract, while the heat of the nuclear reactions at its core produces a tendency to expand." (Isacc Asimov)

C. "Principles, not policy; justice, not favor; men, their rights and nothing more; women, their rights and nothing less." (motto of *The Revolution*, a periodical published by Susan B. Anthony)

D. "Vigilantes found it hard to distinguish between taking the law into their hands when it could not function and taking the law into their hands when it did not function as they wanted it to." (Charles E. Silberman)

E. "Waterloo is a battle of the first class, gained by a captain of the second." (Victor Hugo)

F. "WE the PEOPLE of the United States, in order to form a more perfect Union, establish Justice, insure domestic Tranquillity, provide for the common Defense, promote the general Welfare, and secure the Blessings of Liberty to ourselves and our posterity, do ordain and establish this CONSTITUTION for the United States of America."

G. "The immense trees which encircled Boot Magna Hall, shaded its drives and rides, and stood (tastefully disposed at the whim of some forgotten, provincial predecessor of Repton) singly and in groups about the park, had suffered, some from ivy, some from lightning, some from the various malignant disorders that vegetation is heir to, but all, principally, from old age." (Evelyn Waugh)

2. Point out the economy of these parallel constructions. What common words are eliminated?

A. "Most Western religions long for a life after death; Eastern religions for relief from an extended cycle of deaths and rebirths." (Carl Sagan)

B. "Travel in the younger sort is a part of education, in the elder, a part of experience." (Francis Bacon)

C. "The race of men, while sheep in credulity, are wolves for conformity." (Carl Van Doren)

D. "The moment the very name of Ireland is mentioned, the English seem to bid adieu to common feeling, common prudence, and common sense, and to act with the barbarity of tyrants, and the fatuity of idiots." (Rev. Sydney Smith)

E. "His voice is very low as he speaks to Estraven, his posture faintly insolent, his smile frequent." (Ursula K. LeGuin)

F. "As the winter got colder, Doak got drunker, Julie less satisfied, and Buster bigger and meaner." (Geoffrey Wolff)

3. Find three striking examples of parallelism—from proverbs, from your reading, from graffiti, or from magazine ads.

4. Compose three sentences that have parallel phrases.

5. Compose three sentences that have parallel clauses.

6. Decide whether the elements in the following sentences are parallel. If some are not, make them parallel.
   A. She said that the amount of work to accomplish was unrealistic, having to meet the deadline was unrealistic, and where the staff was headquartered was too small.
   B. Pancho Villa was as much a bandit as a nationalist.
   C. A true Westerner has to know how to rope, spit, and to shoot.
   D. The water of White Oak Falls is drinkable, suitable for swimming, and also the home of some very large brown trout.
   E. The manager not only fired the secretary, but also the assistant manager.
   F. Because the rent was reasonable, and having enough money in his checking account for the deposit, Horatio took the apartment.
   G. Marriage, being a social contract as well as intended as an outlet for romantic love, has been encouraged by law for hundreds of years.
   H. Sexually molesting retarded women is perverted, heartless, and must be dealt with immediately.
   I. Hospitals should not use resident interns as a substitute for regular, full-time physicians but rather to supplement those staff physicians in providing medical care.
   J. Americans cannot decide whether they want to help the less fortunate countries in the world or the amount of money that should be sent to such countries.
   K. The investigation could determine neither how many recipients had falsified their applications, nor tell how many thousands of dollars the fraudulent grantees siphoned off.

Active and Passive Voice

   ACTIVE VOICE: Babe Ruth hit sixty home runs in 1927.
   PASSIVE VOICE: Sixty home runs were hit by Babe Ruth in 1927.

With active voice, the subject of the sentence acts: Babe Ruth *hit*. With passive voice, the subject is acted upon: Home runs *were hit*; instead of performing an action, they received the action. In a passive construction, someone does something to the subject.

As a general rule, active voice is preferable because it is more direct and forceful. We expect the subject of a sentence to be a doer and the verb to show the action that the subject initiates:

> Noah sailed the ark.
> Al Capone carried a gun.
> Virginia Woolf wrote novels.
> The accountant audited the books.
> Jim Shoulders rode bulls.

We could change any one of these sentences into passive voice, but doing so would shift the emphasis and would make the sentence more wordy. For example:

> Bulls were ridden by Jim Shoulders.

The emphasis of the sentence now falls on "bulls" because it has become the subject. Passive voice takes the direct object of a sentence (in the examples above, *ark, gun, novels, books, bulls*), elevates it to the position of subject, and downgrades what was once the subject into a prepositional phrase. In doing so, we add two additional words, *was* (or *were*) and *by*. Another problem with passive constructions is that often the doer isn't named at all, as in this sentence:

> Mortimer was given a good tongue-lashing for being late.

In this case, the passive construction omits vital information, and therefore readers don't know who reprimanded Mortimer. To include the necessary information, we have to insert the doer at the end of the sentence in a prepositional phrase:

> Mortimer was given a good tongue-lashing by Henrietta.

We can recognize passive voice not only by the fact that the subject is being acted upon, but also by its appearance. Passive voice uses some form of the verb *to be (am, is, are, was, were, been, being)* plus a past participle (a verb form similar to past tense).

> Mortimer *is surprised* by Henrietta when she comes home early from the office.
> He *was chased* out of the bedroom by his angry spouse.
> Mildred, the woman with Mortimer, *might have been killed* by the brick that *was thrown* by Henrietta, but Mortimer *was hit* instead.
> He *had to be carried* in an ambulance to the hospital, where he *is being cared* for by a slightly pudgy nurse named Matilda.
> They *were warned* to keep it platonic.

The problem with the passive voice is that it blurs the action in a sentence, robs the sentence of force, and makes our prose wordy as well as limp. Contrast the predominantly passive paragraph 1 below to paragraph 2, which is predominantly active, and point out all of the passive constructions in the first passage:

1. Saturday was a disastrous day for the Joneses. Stray dogs were watched by Mortimer as the garbage was overturned by them. Then the gas peddle was stepped on by Henrietta instead of the brake, and the car was driven through the garage wall. A roller skate had been left in the hallway by Mort, Jr., and it was stepped on by Mortimer and his back was landed on. Then $192 were charged by the TV repairman to fix the vertical hold, and Henrietta's antique punch bowl was broken by the maid, Michelle. A new racket was given to Mortimer by his friend Mike, and half a set of tennis was played by them before an ankle was sprained by Mortimer. Henrietta's wedding ring, which was taken off to wash dishes, was accidentally dropped down the drain. Mortimer was called at home by his chief client and his account was cancelled. And teenage daughter Mimi's new boyfriend, a 28-year-old parolee and freelance auto mechanic, was brought home. [167 words]

2. Saturday was a disastrous day for the Joneses. Mortimer watched as stray dogs overturned the garbage. Then Henrietta stepped on the gas peddle instead of the brake and drove the car through the garage wall. Mort, Jr. had left a roller skate in the hallway and Mortimer stepped on it and landed on his back. The TV repairman charged $192 to fix the vertical hold, and the maid, Michelle, broke Henrietta's antique punch bowl. Mortimer's friend Mike gave him a new racket, and they played half a set of tennis before Mortimer sprained an ankle. Henrietta took off her wedding ring to wash dishes and accidentally dropped it down the drain. Mortimer's chief client called him at home to cancel his account. Finally, teenage daughter Mimi brought home her new boyfriend, a 28-year-old parolee and freelance auto mechanic. [140 words]

Besides being more direct and readable, the second passage is 19 percent shorter.

Most writers who get in the habit of using passive voice aren't conscious of overusing it. As a general rule, we should use active voice unless we have a specific reason for using passive because, as demonstrated above, active voice is more emphatic, concise, and energetic.

Passive voice is certainly not incorrect, for it developed as a variation in the language to serve special functions. We should therefore learn what those special functions are and use passive constructions only for the following reasons:

1. *When the doer is unknown.* If we don't know who the agent of an action is, we must necessarily use passive voice. This is the value of passive voice—it allows us to present an action without presenting the doer.

> My suitcase was stolen at the airport.
> The hero was buried at Arlington National Cemetery.
> The city of Zimbabwe was built approximately 1,500 years ago in
> southern Africa.
> Billboards may be erected legally along most interstate highways.

2. *When we don't wish to name the doer.* We can use passive voice to avoid placing the blame on someone. Remember, for example, the ending of the famous Bogart movie *Casablanca?* The Nazi major is about to telephone the air tower to order that the plane carrying Ingrid Bergman to safety be stopped, so Bogie shoots him, and then the Nazi troops arrive. Because the French officer who witnessed the shooting doesn't want to tell the Nazis who shot the major, he tells them: "Major Strausser has been shot. Round up the usual suspects." By using passive voice—*has been shot*—he avoids turning in his friend Bogart. Had he used active voice, he would have had to say who shot the major.

3. *When the doer is insignificant or when the object is more important than the doer.*

> The television is fixed.

That the repairman is the person who fixed the television may be irrelevant, and therefore specifying the doer is neither necessary nor important; in fact, placing the emphasis on the doer may stress the wrong noun in the sentence.

Another case might be when a paragraph in general concerns the object instead of the doer; passive voice would be appropriate for the sake of emphasis and coherence.

> The Dean's Scholar Award serves to recognize superior work by
> students within the college. It gives $750 to each of three students
> whom the faculty selects on the basis of academic achievement.
> The award is presented at a ceremony during May and is applied
> to the tuition for the following year.

Because the general subject of the paragraph is *award*, the third sentence keeps *award* as its subject and uses passive voice: "Award is presented . . . and is applied." This way the emphasis stays on the topic of the paragraph, the award, and coherence is achieved by repeating the key term.

What we should keep in mind about active voice and passive voice is that they are stylistic options, and that we should use passive voice only for a specific reason. Otherwise, we should use active. In choosing one over the other, we exercise our critical judgment and decide which one is more appropriate in a given case.

Changing passive constructions into active ones is a relatively simple matter: Ask who or what does the action in the sentence, and make that person or thing the subject of the sentence. Often the doer is stated in a prepositional phrase following the passive verb, but sometimes the doer is not stated at all.

> The duty of checking the invoices has been assumed by the clerks. (12 words)

Who is assuming the duty? Clerks. Therefore, make *clerks* the subject of the sentence:

> Clerks have assumed the duty of checking the invoices. (9 words; 25 percent shorter)
>
> Clerks now check the invoices. (5 words; 58 percent shorter)
>
> The belief that more taxes could not be paid by property owners was expressed by several city council members. (19 words)

Who could not pay more? Property owners. Who expressed the belief? Several city council members. Make the subject of the main clause *council members* and the subject of the subordinate clause *property owners:*

> Several city council members believed [expressed the belief] that property owners could not pay more taxes. (13 words: 32 percent shorter)
>
> For years, military mules and horses were retired with full rations, but human employees were retired without benefits.

Who retired them? The sentence doesn't say, and perhaps the doer is unimportant. However, if we think that the doer should be made explicit, we can change the sentence to active voice by making the doer the subject:

> For years, the federal government retired mules and horses with full rations, but it retired human employees without benefits.

APPLICATION

Decide which clauses, if any, in the following sentences are passive. Of those that are passive, determine which ones would be more effective if changed to active, and change them into active.

1. My friends have left me.
2. Where you find the smell of horses and sweated leather, you find dry humor and friendly people.
3. Sunglasses are worn indoors only by pimps and dopeheads.
4. Scientists have found that the Spanish fly *Lytta vesicatoria*, which was once thought to be an aphrodisiac, is effective for curing warts.
5. My grandfather was somehow excused from senility.
6. People who avoid marriage usually are happier than those who discover divorce.
7. I don't care to live where land is sold by the square foot instead of by the acre.
8. Never hurt anyone unintentionally.
9. I am not loved by him the way you are not loved by him.
10. If you wish to outmaneuver an opponent, learn how the opponent does not think.
11. When a car was hit by a poultry truck, both drivers and forty-three chickens were killed.
12. If hatred was the great evil of past eras, indifference is that of ours.
13. Children are traditionally raised by mothers.
14. Burial is practiced only by human beings and by elephants, which sometimes cover the dead with branches.
15. No fire department is needed in La Paz, Bolivia, because, the city being 2½ miles above sea level, the air is too thin to support much of a fire.
16. Not seeing is believing for many people.
17. Two champion thoroughbreds and several stake winners were produced by Hildene, a blind "blue hen," which is a mediocre mare that produces champions.
18. Candles on a birthday cake should be lighted from the center to the outside rim of the cake.
19. A good cause is hurt by bad supporters.
20. They sell lottery tickets and lingerie there.
21. Someone stole $65 from my locker at the gym.
22. The Commodore 64 was bought by more people last year than was any other computer.
23. Arguments are carried in both pockets by most politicians.
24. His mind was thought to be not right.
25. Wars are fought over lines.
26. "On November 13, Felix Unger was asked to remove himself from his place of residence. That request came from his wife." *(The Odd Couple)*

Expletive Constructions

An expletive construction is a clause that opens with a space-filler such as *there are, there is, it is, it appears,* or *it seems* (where *it* doesn't refer to a specific noun).

> *There are* five people who know the secret code.
> *There is* a need within everyone to help others.
> *It is* impossible to get blood from a turnip.
> *It appears* that Congress will recess without having voted on the proposed mass transit subsidy.

Where is the subject located in these sentences? The true subject of the first example is *five people*, but that subject is postponed; the expletive suspends the meaning of the sentence because we read "There are" and still don't know what the sentence is about. In the second example, the true verb is forced into a noun—*need*—and in the last example, the expletive forces the real subject and verb—*Congress will recess*—into a subordinate clause in the middle of the sentence. The most emphatic position in a sentence is the beginning, but when we use an expletive construction, we waste that strategic position by inserting a false subject where the true subject should be.

We could improve the examples above, which have sacrificed all emphasis with their deadwood openings, by deleting the expletives and placing the true subjects at the beginning:

> Five people know the secret code.
> Everyone needs to help others.
> Getting blood out of a turnip is impossible.
> Congress apparently will recess without having voted on the proposed mass transit subsidy.

In each revision, we have achieved a more concise and emphatic sentence by omitting the expletive, which simply had usurped the important initial position and had added at least three unnecessary words to each sentence.

Expletive constructions devitalize prose by opening with a weak verb *(is, are, appears, seems)*, by substituting a meaningless filler for the real subject, and by delaying the true action. Such sentences are like trains that have the locomotive in the middle instead of at the front. A passage that relies heavily on expletive constructions will, like a misproportioned train, be sluggish and cumbersome, as the following paragraph illustrates:

> *There were* five people who knew the secret code. O'Neal had discovered that *it was* one of those five who was a traitor. *It appeared* that Killigrew was not the one because *it was* he who had first discovered that information was being leaked—and *there was* no reason for him to inform on himself. *It was* unlikely that it was Hargrove; after all, *there had been* times when she had had ample opportunity to sell the code but had not. Obviously, O'Neal did not suspect himself, so *there were* only Robertson and Jacobs left. *It was* probable that Robertson was the traitor, but *it would* take years for O'Neal to prove that. (113 words)

Notice how deleting the expletive constructions gives the paragraph more force and speed:

> Five people knew the secret code, and O'Neal had discovered that one was a traitor. Killigrew apparently was not the one because he had been first to discover that information was being leaked—and he had no reason to inform on himself. Hargrove was not likely the traitor; after all, she had had ample opportunity in the past to sell the code but had not. Obviously, O'Neal did not suspect himself, so only Robertson and Jacobs were left. Robertson was probably the traitor, but proving that would take O'Neal years. (90 words)

The revision is 20% leaner and equally more emphatic.

Expletive constructions arc not always inappropriate; like the passive voice, they developed in the language to serve a special purpose—mainly to give us a way of expressing a state of existence. To say: "More than one way exists to skin a cat" is not an improvement on "There is more than one way to skin a cat," and therefore the expletive construction is acceptable.

Occasionally we want to use an expletive because the construction simply works better than the alternative:

> "There are some politicians who, if their constituents were cannibals, would promise them missionaries for dinner." (H. L. Mencken)

The expletive construction allows the writer to suspend the "meat" of the sentence—missionaries for dinner—till the end, where it adds more punch. In the following sentence, the main idea—difficulty—is postponed until the end without reason:

ORIGINAL: Discovering all of the available options, comparing them with one another, and deciding which one is best are difficult tasks.

REVISION 1: It is difficult to discover all of the available options, to compare them with one another, and to decide which one is best.

REVISION 2: The difficulty lies in discovering all of the available options, comparing them with one another, and deciding which one is best.

Occasionally, therefore, expletive constructions are both appropriate and useful. If another verb occurs later in the sentence, though, we should delete the expletive, focus on the real verb, and place the real subject in the subject position.

APPLICATION

All of the sentences below are expletive constructions. Decide which ones would be improved by deleting the expletives, and rewrite those sentences. For those that you think should remain as they are, state your reasons.

1. There are times when I hear a train whistle that I would like to give in to my escape fantasies and to hop a freight, not caring where it is headed.
2. It might be expected that those people with fallout shelters will be attacked if there is a nuclear war.
3. There are a number of different ways that you can cook Cornish hens.
4. It seems that most science fiction deals not with fantasy but with projection of the present.
5. There are no requirements for entering the open university.
6. It was after there were no more fish in the pool that it was decided by Dave that there was a need to clean the pool.
7. There was a rattlesnake coiled around my boot when I woke; there was another rattler in my blanket.
8. There are two ways to do things: the wrong way, and his way.
9. There was enough dirt on the floor to plant a good corn crop.
10. It would be embarrassing to elect a person of such low ethical standards.
11. There are some people who maintain that political parties are too weak in the United States, and there are other people who maintain that political parties should be abolished.
12. There are numerous laws that should be deleted by the state legislature from the state constitution because they are obsolete.
13. The manager said that there are several deficiencies within the system that would hinder its effectiveness.
14. It has been 4 years since I saw Jenny.
15. There is laughter from her.
16. There are handshakes that crush instead of greet.
17. There may have been some decline in the quality of the cafeteria food, though it is doubtful that you have noticed because there was not much quality before.
18. There are eleven professors who serve on the Tenure and Promotion Committee.
19. There are two types of men.
20. There were no violent crimes in Whistleville, except one, a murder.
21. There were five coop programs on campus that failed because of mismanagement.
22. When the moon is full, there is a different texture to the night, for there is not the blind darkness that invites the imagination to create fiends.
23. Without thrift, there can be no savings.
24. It was only a temporary diversion.
25. It is unlikely that a woman will become president in this century.

Appendix II

PARAGRAPH DEVELOPMENT

A

Principles of
Paragraphing

If you travel all over the world and see every
brilliant and flying dance that human beings do, you
will maybe be surprised that it is only in our
traditional classic ballet dancing that the dancer can
leap through the air slowly. In other kinds of
dancing there are leaps that thrill you by their
impetuousness or accuracy; there are brilliant little
ones, savage long ones and powerful bouncing
ones. But among all dance techniques only classic
ballet has perfected leaps with that special
slow-motion grace, that soaring rise and floating
descent which looks weightless. It isn't that every
ballet leap looks that way. Some are a tough thrust
off the ground, some travel like a cat's, some quiver
like a fish's, some scintillate like jig steps; but these
ways of jumping you can find in other dancing too.
The particular expression ballet technique has
added to leaping is that of the dancer poised in
mid-flight, as easy in the air as if she were
suspended on wires. Describing the effect, people
say one dancer took flight like a bird, another was
not subject to the laws of gravity and a third paused
quietly in mid-air. And that is how it does look,
when it happens.

—From Edwin Denby, "Flight of the Dancer,"
Looking at the Dance

What makes this a paragraph instead of just a group of sentences? For one
thing, you might hesitatingly say, it is indented at the beginning. As
obvious and superficial as that answer sounds at first, it is important.
Paragraphs *are* visual units. We indent to give readers a break. Without
paragraphs—that is, without units of thought broken into units of
prose—readers would have a devilish time reading. Can you imagine
reading an entire book without paragraphs as visual breaks? The psychological relief provided by paragraphs is immeasurable.

A paragraph is more than a visual unit, though. If paragraphs were just visual units, we could indent every fifteen lines, disregarding the content and the progression of ideas. Paragraphs are mainly *cognitive* units—units of thought. A paragraph is a group of related sentences that develop a central idea, which is usually made explicit in the topic sentence. Together the sentences convey a developed thought and mark off one stage of thinking in a larger pattern.

Does the paragraph about ballet leaps develop a central idea? If so, what is that idea? Is there a topic sentence? Where is it located: at the beginning, in the middle, or at the end of the paragraph? Does the paragraph have unity—that is, does each sentence contribute to the central idea, or are there sentences that are irrelevant to the central idea? Does the paragraph have coherence—that is, are the sentences tied together in such a way that we can easily move from one sentence to the next? These are the questions we will be examining in this chapter as we analyze the characteristics of good paragraphing.

Topic Sentence

The topic sentence is the generalization that announces the subject and the controlling idea of the paragraph. The subject tells readers what topic we will discuss, and the controlling idea tells them the main point that we want to convey about that subject. For example, the subject of Edwin Denby's paragraph is dance leaps, and the controlling idea is suspension in midair—"leap through the air slowly."

APPLICATION

What are the subjects and the controlling ideas of the following topic sentences?

The future of private colleges in the United States is uncertain.
Robots, which are little more than computers with arms, have a variety of uses.
Many butterflies rely on camouflage for defense from birds.
Farmers are discovering the advantages of insuring their crops against natural disasters.

Topic sentences are of two types: assertions and summaries. The first type makes a controversial statement and implicitly pledges that we will prove that assertion in the rest of the paragraph. The second type encapsulates the information in the paragraph and gives readers an overview or a summary. Whereas the first is basically argumentative because it asserts an opinion, the second is basically expository because it sums up an explanation.

In either case, the characteristic of a good topic sentence is that it invites development. The difference between a topic sentence and a support sentence is that a topic sentence (1) is more general and (2) allows for development. A topic sentence leads readers to expect details that will support the controlling idea.

APPLICATION

According to the above criteria, which of the following sentences would make good topic sentences, and why or why not?

> White wines do not benefit from aging as do red wines.
> Many home remedies have been found to be medically effective.
> Children in day-care centers are ill more often than children who remain at home.
> 1939 was an outstanding year for Hollywood films.
> Flowers appeared about the time the dinosaurs disappeared, approximately 100 million years ago.
> "Urban pioneers" are middle-class whites who buy and renovate slum townhouses in downtown areas.
> Some medical expenses are not covered in group health insurance plans.
> Biographers should be more than fact-finders.
> First times are exciting.
> France still owes the United States over $7 billion from the two world wars.
> The Friday night television fights in the 1950s ruined many young boxers.
> Connoisseurs of decadence would appreciate my Aunt Ellen.
> One advantage of polygamy is that the strongest male's genes are distributed disproportionately.
> Only a few games are truly American.

Which of the sentences are assertions, which summaries, and which merely statements of fact?

Consider this topic sentence: "According to some scientists, the big bang theory of the origin of the universe is built on unacceptable assumptions." What is the subject of the paragraph? What is the controlling idea? What would readers expect to read about in this paragraph? Probably they would expect us to list the assumptions and tell why they are unacceptable to some scientists. The subject that is specified in a topic sentence is important because it tells readers that we will discuss that subject and not some other subject. Many beginning writers fail to realize that the controlling idea is even more important because it tells *how* we will treat the subject. One function of the controlling idea is to limit what we can say about the subject. In the topic sentence above, we may discuss *only* the unacceptable assumptions underlying the big bang theory, not other ideas about the theory, such as its development by Georges Lemaître or the reasons for believing that the assumptions are acceptable. Another function of the controlling idea is to express an opinion about the subject. By limiting the subject and by expressing an attitude about it, the controlling idea gives focus to the paragraph and serves as a point of reference for supporting sentences, each of which must in some way contribute to the controlling idea.

A controlling idea in a topic sentence should be precise and focused. An unfocused controlling idea allows such a variety of details that a resulting paragraph can be disunified because the details are not tightly related. A vague controlling idea invites rambling by allowing the writer to go into several areas at once. Here are several topic sentences with controlling ideas so broad and vague that they do not provide a proper focus for the paragraph; at the right are revisions that provide better focus:

ORIGINAL	REVISION
Mexico is changing. ("Changing" is too broad. Ask yourself what you mean by changing: Changing how?)	Because of its increasing financial and political importance as an oil producer, Mexico is asserting its independence from the United States.
I don't like country music. (The opinion lacks focus. Be more specific: what about country music don't you like?)	My main objection to country music is its sentimentality.
John Irving is a great novelist.	John Irving's novels abound in the comic grotesque.
The federal government is too big. (There is nothing wrong with broad generalizations like this one; it is simply that the broader the generalization, the more space we need to prove it. This generalization would make a good thesis statement, but a topic sentence must be limited sufficiently for us to develop the controlling idea within the space of one paragraph.)	The federal government is so big that agencies within the government are often at cross-purposes.

APPLICATION

1. Focus the following topic sentences in this same manner:

   Video games are more fun than other games.
   Ethnic cooking is becoming popular.
   Politicians are charlatans.
   The preppie look is silly.
   Contrary to general opinion, hawks are wonderful birds.
   Coed gyms are different.
   Prizzi's Honor was an unusual movie.

2. Discuss the merits and weaknesses of the following statements as topic
   sentences:
   A. Baxter is a cunning man.
   B. Breaking into a bank vault requires four tools and great skill.
   C. Everyone should jog.
   D. Proteins serve three basic functions in the human body.
   E. Disharmony in a community can be a healthy quality.
   F. People often love and detest friends for the same qualities.
   G. Belief in astrology is ridiculous.
   H. Pollution is destroying the oyster beds in Chesapeake Bay.
   I. Colleges are torn between the dual goals of expertise and wisdom.

3. What details could you offer to support these topic sentences?
   A. Public schools are not adequately educating our youth.
   B. The 1970s was the decade that America was knocked off its pedestal in
      world politics.
   C. Americans have a preoccupation with cleanliness.
   D. Each generation must undergo a type of rebellion.
   E. Television has had a profound effect on American presidential elections.

4. Write a topic sentence for five of these subjects, limiting the subjects and
   providing an interesting controlling idea.
   A. self-introductions at singles bars   H. pouting
   B. cacti   I. horror movies
   C. specialty shops   J. get-well cards
   D. unathletic people   K. laughing
   E. taxi drivers   L. breakfast
   F. friends' friends   M. birthdays
   G. beards

5. The following paragraph was written without a topic sentence. Read through
   the paragraph, decide what the subject and the controlling idea are, and
   compose your own topic sentence.

When I was 12, my father took me to his hunting lodge with a group of his cronies, who sat around the fireplace drinking whiskey from tin cups and telling lies about women and hunting. They invited me to join them, and although I had no lies to contribute, I drank enough of their whiskey to make me sick for the whole weekend. If this is a requisite for manhood, I thought, I might not make it. The first day of hunting, I killed a buck, and to signify my initiation into the masculine tribe, my father anointed my forehead with the deer's blood. Two years later my brother took me to a Memphis brothel and waited downstairs while I was initiated into another facet of manhood by a blonde twice my age. To make my instatement complete, when I was 18 Uncle Sam invited me to join other initiates in rigorous training in preparation for human killing and then sent me to defend my homeland 8,000 miles away.

Placement of the Topic Sentence

Whether we place the topic sentence at the beginning, in the middle, or at the end of the paragraph depends on the effect we want the paragraph to have on readers. Consider these two paragraphs, and try to articulate the different effects they have:

I. Remember for a moment what it is like to have the flu. You have no energy or strength, and any activity such as taking a bath or walking up a flight of stairs exhausts you. Certainly you don't feel like jogging or going to a party, and sometimes even reading requires more energy than you can muster. All that you want to do is rest, and so you watch television and doze off every few hours. But you can't sleep for long because congestion interrupts slumber. You wake up aching all over, pain in every joint and muscle. You don't feel like talking with visitors because even listening is tiring. At times you feel as though you'd rather die than put up with it any longer, but you take your medicine in hopes of making life tolerable. These are also the characteristics of advanced old age. Being old is like having the flu all the time.

Where is the topic sentence? Why is it positioned there instead of else-where? What would be the effect of placing the topic sentence at the front of the paragraph?

II. It's the little things about my roommate that make living with her an ordeal. For example, she never refills the ice trays; she puts the half-empty trays back into the freezer or, even worse, leaves them out on the drainboard. She refuses to discard ancient food, so our refrigerator is filled with molded cheese, curdled milk, withered carrots, and some green, unidentifiable thing that might once have belonged on a chicken. Another annoying habit is that when she peels carrots she slings the skins all over the kitchen—and leaves them drying on the walls and appliances. In the living room she positions her cola-stained chair directly in front of the TV (blocking my view), watches soap operas for hours, and scatters candy wrappers around the chair in an imperfect semicircular arrangement. With the TV on, she disarranges the morning newspaper so completely that I am daily unable to find one complete section. When she's not watching TV, she plays my records and puts them into the wrong album covers; yesterday after a half-hour search, I found Tchaikovsky in a Kiss cover. When she borrows a textbook— without asking—she turns down the corners of pages, writes in the margins, and bends the covers back until the binding breaks, though I seldom care because she then lends the book to one of her boyfriends and I never see it again. And finally, she leaves little black stubs of hair in the bathtub and has the gall to complain that the cleanser I use leaves gritty particles in the bottom of the tub.

How does the topic sentence situated at the beginning of the paragraph facilitate reading this paragraph? Does the topic sentence help to unify the support sentences? What effect would shifting the topic sentence to the end of the paragraph have?

Topic Sentence First

The typical paragraph opens with the topic sentence and then presents details to support the controlling idea in the topic sentence. We call this a general-to-specific paragraph because the most general statement comes first, followed by specific substantiation. Structurally, this type of paragraph looks like a *T*:

topic sentence
(subject and controlling idea)

support
sentences:
examples
reasons
statistics
details

The advantages of the general-to-specific paragraph are:

1. The most important information is placed in the most emphatic position of the paragraph—the first line. Because the main idea is highlighted, readers cannot miss the point of the paragraph.
2. By appearing first, the topic sentence gives readers an overview of the paragraph before they read the individual facts in the support sentences. This overview gives them a general context and a sense of perspective. When readers know the subject and controlling idea of the paragraph, they are better able to understand the significance of the support material and its relation to the main idea.
3. The topic sentence acts as a guide for writers as well as for readers. We can use the topic sentence to keep us focused on the main idea and to refer to in subsequent sentences.

By emphasizing the main idea, giving readers a sense of perspective, and helping to unify support material, the general-to-specific paragraph serves both readers and writers.

Does the following paragraph illustrate these three advantages?

The Cultural Revolution has hypocritically masked some of the most obvious forms of class divisions, without changing their substance. In trains, for instance, first, second, and third classes have disappeared *in name,* but you have now "sitting hard" *(ying tso),* "sleeping hard" *(ying wo),* and "sleeping soft" *(juan wo),* which are exactly the same classes as before and with the fares, as before, ranging from single to triple prices. External insignia have nearly completely disappeared in the army; they have been replaced by a loose jacket with four pockets for officers, two pockets for privates. In this way, a colonel traveling first-class on the railway is now merely a four-pocket military man "sleeping soft"—with a two-pocket man respectfully carrying his suitcase. In cities one can still distinguish between four-pocket men in jeeps, four-pocket men in black limousines with curtains, and four-pocket men who have black limousines with curtains and a jeep in front.

—From Simon Leys, *Chinese Shadows* (translation of *Ombres chinoises*)

Topic Sentence Last

The opposite structure of the general-to-specific paragraph is the inductive or specific-to-general paragraph, where the individual facts are presented first and the topic sentence comes at the end. This inductive paragraph resembles an inverted *T:*

```
                      ┌─────────────────┐
                      │     support     │
                      │   sentences:    │
                      │    examples     │
                      │     reasons     │
                      │    statistics   │
                      │     details     │
              ┌───────┤                 ├───────┐
              │        topic sentence           │
              │  (subject and controlling idea)  │
              └─────────────────────────────────┘
```

In inductive paragraphs, the facts themselves become the focus instead of simply being evidence; the support sentences assume disproportionate importance because they are not dominated by an initial topic sentence. Furthermore, inductive paragraphs require readers to interpret the evidence in support sentences without knowing what that evidence adds up to until they read the last sentence. Viewed this way, inductive paragraphs present something of a demand on readers.

Nevertheless, inductive paragraphs are appropriate in several situations. For example, an inductive structure is effective for building suspense in a narrative paragraph; because telling readers the outcome of a story at the beginning of a paragraph would spoil the narrative, we use chronological order and withhold the resolution of the action until the end. Other chronological sequences, such as tracing cause-effect relationships, also can be structured inductively. In addition, inductive paragraphs are appropriate when the topic sentence serves as a logical conclusion that we want readers to draw from the preceding material. They read the facts we present and then reach a conclusion, which is spelled out for them in the topic sentence. In short, inductive paragraphs allow readers to *discover* the main idea as they read instead of being told the main idea in advance.

APPLICATION

Why has the writer structured the following paragraph inductively?

In the autumn of 1773 seven bluff-bowed vessels beat their way across the stormy North Atlantic Ocean toward the American coastline. Stowed away in their holds were cargoes of tea—600,000 pounds in all—consigned by the famous East India Company of London to small groups of merchants in the ports of Boston, New York, Philadelphia, and Charleston. Although subject to the Townshend duty of threepence per pound, this tea was to be sold at a price low enough to compete with tea smuggled into the colonies from Holland and elsewhere. When the vessels arrived, however, the colonists were determined that none of the tea should be landed and that the Townshend duties should remain unpaid. At Charleston the tea was seized and stored by the customs officials; at Philadelphia and New York the ships were turned back; but on the night of 16 December 1773 the patriots of Boston dumped 340 chests of the dutied tea into the harbor.

—From Benjamin Woods Labaree, Preface to *The Boston Tea Party*

Other Placement Options

In addition to strictly general-to-specific and inductive paragraphs, other structures are possible. For example, the topic sentence in some paragraphs is split. A paragraph can open with a partial statement of the controlling idea, develop the idea in the body of the paragraph, and end with a fuller statement. In a long paragraph, we may wish to reiterate the topic sentence to reinforce the main idea; in this case the last sentence restates the controlling idea as a reminder to readers. A dual topic sentence also occurs in a paragraph where the opening sentence is a broad generalization and the closing sentence is a qualification of that statement.

Occasionally paragraphs have a topic sentence in the middle of the paragraph. An internal topic sentence may be appropriate in a paragraph that shifts direction midstream—such as first giving one side of an issue, then the other side. We should realize, though, that placing the topic sentence in the midst of support sentences in essence buries the main point, and readers can easily skim right over it and not know that they have just read the main point. The middle of a paragraph—or the middle of a sentence or of an essay—is not an emphatic position.

An even more dangerous practice is to omit the topic sentence altogether. A paragraph that lacks a topic sentence requires readers to struggle for the controlling idea and, even worse, allows for misinterpreting the evidence and reaching the wrong controlling idea. Although we sometimes read professional writing, especially narratives, in which topic sentences are implied rather than directly stated, apprentice writers should make a conscious effort to write topic sentences, particularly in expository and argumentative prose. The topic sentence aids readers by interpreting the evidence for them, and it aids writers by highlighting the main idea.

APPLICATION

Does each of the following paragraphs have a topic sentence? If so, which is the topic sentence? What is the effect of placing it where it is? Would placing it elsewhere in the paragraph improve the paragraph?

1.

On week days the street was very lively. It woke to its work about seven o'clock, at the time when the newsboys made their appearance together with the day laborers. The labors went trudging past in a straggling file—plumber's apprentices, their pockets stuffed with sections of lead pipe, tweezers, and pliers; carpenters, carrying nothing but their little pasteboard lunch baskets painted to imitate leather; gangs of street workers, their overalls soiled with yellow clay, their picks and long-handled shovels over their shoulders; plasterers, spotted with lime from head to foot. This little army of workers, tramping steadily in one direction, met and mingled with other toilers of a different description—conductors and "swing men" of the cable company going on duty; heavy-eyed night clerks from the drug stores on their way home to sleep; roundsmen returning to the precinct police station to make their night report; the Chinese market gardeners teetering past under their heavy baskets. The cable cars began to fill up; all along the street could be seen the shop keepers taking down their shutters.

—From Frank Norris, *McTeague*

2.

The iron asteroids are interesting because geophysicists believe that the parent body of an object greatly enriched in iron must have been molten so as to differentiate, to separate out the iron from the silicates in the initial chaotic jumble of the elements in primordial times. On the other hand, for the organic molecules in carbonaceous meteorites to have survived at all they must never have been raised to temperatures hot enough to melt rock or iron. Thus, different histories are implied for different asteroids.

—From Carl Sagan, *Broca's Brain*

3.

Narcisse did not, in truth, much resemble the pictures in my *Backyard Hobby* book. Dark brown in color, he stood motionless with the resignation of his kind, his face a study in melancholy. His neck was short and thick. His chest merged with a stomach that was a drooping barrel. His tail was short and wispy, the light brown hairs of varying lengths, as if someone had plucked some of them out in a game of he-loves-me-he-loves-me-not. His mane had been hacked off, leaving short, unruly bristles. But all this was nothing compared to his legs and feet, which made an absolute virtue of almost every fault enumerated in my book. Narcisse was, in fact, a classic example of what to avoid when shopping for a donkey. Each hoof resembled a kitchen spatula, and all four feet seemed to turn in different directions.

—From Jeanette Bruce, "Further Travels with a Donkey," *Atlantic Monthly,* November 1978

4.

During World War II, penicillin was new and scarce. Given the choice of treating the possibly mortal infections of the critically injured and treating venereal disease in soldiers who could be returned to combat, the latter was given preference. When resources are at hand to save one patient and two patients need them, whose life is judged more valuable, and by what criteria? The very young, the mature, those in the prime of life, those with the best prospects for a satisfactory life, those judged to have more to contribute to society? And, of course, who makes the judgment?

—From Leonard C. Lwein, "Bioethical Questions," *Harper's,* August 1978

5.

As so often in life, so with names: the grass is generally just as brown on the other side. Many a person with a plain surname would seem to prefer a gaudier handle. Primitive doctrine held that a man's or woman's name was intended to express his or her personality, and this doctrine, primitive though its origins may be, still retains some of its hold. I have rarely met a Smith or Jones who did not feel that his or her name was a bit too plain, too common—too drained, if not of distinction, then of the distinctiveness sufficient to express his or her by no means plain or common or indistinct personality. Whether they would be ready to trade in that Smith or Jones for a Scheittauer or an Abjørnsen is another question. Hollywood has long subscribed to the theory that names express personality. The actress Dyan Cannon (née something else) has the name she now bears because a Hollywood producer thought her looks required a name that was "explosive." Who is to say that, in their commercial instincts at least, the fantasy moguls of the West Coast were wrong? Would you go to see a movie starring Archie Leach and Issur Demsky, with Betty Perske in the female lead, a Gelbfisch Production? (Translation: a movie starring Cary Grant, Kirk Douglas, and Lauren Bacall, a Goldwyn Production.)

—From Bonnie Menes, "Sherlock Holmes and Sociology," *American Scholar,* Winter 1980/81

6.

Kennedy has been compared to Franklin Delano Roosevelt and he liked to pose in front of an F.D.R. portrait. In fact, some of his qualities more nearly recall Theodore Roosevelt, the apostle of the big stick, the strenuous life and the bully pulpit. Like T. R., for instance, Kennedy had a perhaps undue regard for Harvard and a craving for its approval. The only election he ever lost was one of the ones he wanted most to win—his first try for a seat on the Harvard Board of Overseers. He grimly ran again and his election to the Board was a cherished triumph. Like T. R., too, Kennedy fancies himself in the role of national taste maker—Roosevelt picked up Edwin Arlington Robinson and Kennedy adopted Robert Frost. Roosevelt let his rather rigid literary ideas get about and the Kennedys thought they ought to provide White House examples—Casals, Shakespeare and opera in the East Room—for the cultural uplift of the nation.

—From Tom Wicker, *Kennedy Without Tears*

7.

As almost invariably happens after a big storm, the papers have been full of editorials bemoaning the apparent inability of our weather predictors to furnish us with precise forecasts. We don't bemoan it at all. One of the nicest things about weather is its unexpectedness. When bad weather arrives unpredicted, it is apt to create emergencies, and emergencies bring out some of the best qualities in people—resourcefulness, neighborliness, and fortitude, for instance—which as a rule these days have precious little chance to manifest themselves. Good weather—unheralded good weather, that is—makes everybody smile, and a pleasant sight that can be on Fifth Avenue on a sunny morning following a sullen eve. We think that weather should always come as a surprise. How charmless it would be if the onset of spring (not the first day of spring but the first springlike day) could be dependably foretold on an insurance agent's calendar!

—From "Notes and Comment," *The New Yorker*, March 1, 1958

Unity

Unity means "oneness," and when applied to paragraphing it means that each paragraph should discuss only *one idea*. When we set off a group of sentences by an initial indentation, we are telling readers that those sentences belong together because they develop and prove one idea.

Most students know about the concept of unity, but they mistakenly believe that unity means discussing only one *subject* in a paragraph. Of course, unity does refer to subject matter; to have a unified paragraph, we must stick to one subject. However, since even a single subject can be very broad and cover many points, we must also limit a paragraph to one *idea*. Paragraph unity, therefore, means not only discussing one subject, but also discussing one idea about that subject.

According to this definition, is the following paragraph unified?

[1] Although we complain about the amount of violence in America today, many of the spectator sports that Americans enthusiastically support are physically violent and nurture an atmosphere of violence. [2] Football, which has replaced the more peaceful baseball as our national sport, is little

more than tribal warfare, with each team defending its own territory and invading the enemy's home ground. [3] Although this ritual warfare has sophisticated strategies and strict rules that limit the degree of violence, its essence is force: hand-to-hand combat on the line of scrimmage, fullbacks trampling opposing warriors, and headhunters ruthlessly tackling vulnerable ends. [4] In every game, wounded players with broken limbs, concussions, and torn muscles are carried off the battlefield. [5] For this, football players earn million-dollar contracts. [6] Football offers sex as well as violence, the Dallas cheerleaders being as famous as the Dallas players. [7] Hockey is even more aggressive than football because the violence is totally unleashed in team brawls, much to the approval of fans, who scream with delight at the explosive attacks. [8] Hockey hasn't caught on in the United States as much as football only because, like soccer, it is considered to be a European game. [9] But the most barbaric of popular sports is professional boxing, where no pretense of civilization is attempted. [10] It is gladiatorial combat—brutal, frequently bloody, and occasionally fatal. [11] Where other than "Saturday Boxing" can one turn on TV and see real blood gushing from open cuts in living color? [12] Even though the sport boasts of boxers with the finesse of an Ali or a Sugar Ray Leonard, it is basically fist and force. [13] By providing a model of winning based on physical violence, sports encourage enthusiasts to believe that violence is an acceptable, even laudable, form of behavior.

Each sentence in this paragraph deals with one topic, right? Yes, the topic of contact sports. So the paragraph is unified, right? No. Although the topic in each sentence is a contact sport, what is being said in every sentence is not related to the main idea of the paragraph—physical violence. Every sentence in the paragraph must relate to the main idea as well as to the subject of the paragraph.

	Subject of each sentence	Controlling idea
[1]	spectator sports	physically violent
[2]	football	warfare
[3]	its essence	force
[4]	wounded players	battlefield casualties
[5]	football players	earn millions
[6]	football	offers sex
[7]	hockey	more aggressive
[8]	hockey	considered European
[9]	boxing	barbaric
[10]	it	is gladiatorial combat
[11]	Saturday boxing	blood
[12]	it	is fist and force
[13]	sports	encourage violence

What we notice after analyzing the paragraph is that the writer has included irrelevant ideas. Sentences 5, 6, and 8, unlike all of the other sentences, do not develop the controlling idea of physical violence. Although million-dollar contracts, sex, and national sport preference may relate to the general topic of sports, they do not develop the idea of physical violence and therefore should not be included in this paragraph. Unity, remember, means oneness of subject *and* oneness of idea. Most student paragraphs achieve unity of subject, but they don't always achieve unity of idea.

In a unified paragraph, each sentence elaborates on the topic sentence by developing the controlling idea of the topic sentence. In this way, the topic sentence helps to achieve unity, for if we are guided by the controlling idea and stay within its boundaries, we will include only material that is relevant to that controlling idea. Consider the following paragraph: Does it achieve unity? Is there a topic sentence? What is the controlling idea?

[1] Cars also became less safe. [2] Not only were increasingly less maneuverable cars traveling at faster speeds on the highway, but these cars were generally over-powered, undertired, and underbraked for their weights. [3] Far more emphasis was placed upon styling than upon sound engineering in design, and several major styling innovations, such as the hardtop and the wraparound windshield, were obvious safety hazards. [4] The emphasis upon comfort rather than upon safety dictated poorly designed seats, springing that was too soft, and an overall loss of "road feel." [5] Accidents caused by mechanical failures resulted from the poor design of basic components and poor quality control. [6] Until the 1968 model year, cars were also poorly designed to prevent occupants from "secondary collisions" when an accident occurred: doors tended to fly open, dashboards had too many needless protrusions, steering columns did not collapse, and cars lacked restraining devices to keep occupants from being thrown through windshields.

—From James J. Flink, *The Car Culture*

The paragraph is unified because all the parts relate to and contribute to one central idea, which is articulated in the topic sentence.

Subject		*Idea*
[1]	cars	became less safe
[2]	cars	less maneuverable, faster, over-powered, undertired
[3]	design emphasis (of cars) and styling innovations	style over engineering, safety hazards
[4]	design emphasis	comfort over safety
[5]	accidents	resulted from poor design
[6]	cars	were poorly designed

Every sentence in the paragraph substantiates the assertion of the topic sentence: "Cars became less safe."

APPLICATION

What is the controlling idea in each of the following paragraphs? Are the paragraphs unified? That is, do the support sentences all relate back not only to the subject, but also to the controlling idea of the topic sentence?

1.

America's postwar food relief always had a political component. Subsidized U.S. food supported Marshal Tito's drive for independence from Soviet influence after Yugoslavia refused to join the Cominform in 1948. And the lion's share of P.L. 480 food aid went to foreign countries in which the United States had a political, economic, or military interest. Military clients such as Pakistan, South Korea, Israel, and Turkey all received substantial amounts of this food assistance. So did Yugoslavia and Poland, the two most independent Communist countries in Eastern Europe. Brazil and Indonesia, the sources of enormous reserves of raw materials, were also beneficiaries of subsidized American wheat, rice, and cotton. A State Department official justified the cotton and rice shipments to Indonesia succinctly: "They have the oil, we have the food." And the P.L. 480 leverage could also be used in reverse. When Egypt went to war against Israel in 1967, P.L. 480 stopped.

—From Dan Morgan, *Merchants of Grain*

2.

After school or college, the creative young woman seriously concerned with work will have to realize that marriage with the wrong man can be worse than no marriage. While all her sisters are marching down the aisle at nineteen and twenty for the sake of being married, she must have the nerve to resist the stampede and give herself time to learn, to experience, to grow in the direction of her free dreams. Above all, she must not be afraid of singleness or even loneliness, for I know of no woman, let alone man, who has any stature or worth without knowledge of either. It is the insecure and the immature who can not bear the thought of their own singularity, who must hold on to another hand from puberty onward, who surround themselves with human buffers against the world.

—From Marya Mannes, "The Singular Woman," *But Will It Sell?*

3.

Whenever you leave Paris for a few months, you invariably find on your return that it has been brutally improved here and there, with the modernizing of some old façade or with an entire edifice replaced by a huge hole, indicating one more skyscraper to come or an altitudinous new apartment house of the type the French call *"de grand standing,"* meaning luxury flats. It is said that the useless old Gare d'Orsay, which apparently belongs to the City of Paris, is scheduled to come down. Increasingly, tree-filled squares of the city are being undermined by new public garages. Even though we don't see the automobiles, there is the knowledge that viscerally they are there, inside the body of the city as well as rushing or crawling on the asphalt skin of its streets above. Because of the frequent *chantiers,* or work sites, for the continuing suburban Métros, Paris has become so choked on its own traffic that seven new "toboggans," as the French call these temporary bridges, are reportedly being built this autumn over certain congested key Paris streets and intersections. These toboggans always look tempting and perilous. There is already one on top of the stone bridge at Saint-Cloud—a bridge on top of a bridge—to handle the weekend country-going traffic heading for the Autoroute.

—From Janet Flanner, *Paris Journal*

4.

The fog of despair hung over the land. One out of every four American workers lacked a job. Factories that had once darkened the skies with smoke stood ghostly and silent, like extinct volcanoes. Families slept in tarpaper shacks and tin-lined caves and scavenged like dogs for food in the city dump. In October the New York City Health Department had reported that over one-fifth of the pupils in public schools were suffering from malnutrition. Thousands of vagabond children were roaming the land, wild boys of the road. Hunger marchers, pinched and bitter, were parading cold streets in New York and Chicago. On the countryside unrest had already flared into violence. Farmers stopped milk trucks along Iowa roads and poured the milk into the ditch. Mobs halted mortgage sales, ran the men from the banks and insurance companies out of town, intimidated courts and judges, demanded a moratorium on debts. When a sales company in Nebraska invaded a farm and seized two trucks, the farmers in the Newman Grove district organized a posse, called it the "Red Army," and took the trucks back. In West Virginia, mining families, turned out of their homes, lived in tents along the road on pinto beans and black coffee.

—From Arthur M. Schlesinger, Jr., "Prologue: 1933," *The Crisis of the Old Order*

5.

The statistics that mark the Age of Television are not without their human side. In 1975, a college professor concluded a two-year study in which he asked children aged four to six, "Which do you like better, TV or Daddy?" Forty-four per cent, he announced, preferred television. That same year, a fifty-year-old British bricklayer literally laughed himself to death while watching his favorite television program. His widow told reporters she would write to the program's producers to thank them "for making Alex's last moments so happy." In Washington, D.C., in 1975, physicians announced that a mini baby boom had occurred nine months after the conclusion of the televised Watergate hearings.

—From Frank Mankiewicz and Joel Swerdlow, *Remote Control*

6.

Equal educational opportunity is, indeed, both a desirable and a feasible goal, but to equate this with obligatory schooling is to confuse salvation with the Church. School has become the world religion of a modernized proletariat, and makes futile promises of salvation to the poor of the technological age. The nation-state has adopted it, drafting all citizens into a graded curriculum leading to sequential diplomas not unlike the initiation rituals and hieratic promotions of former times. The modern state has assumed the duty of enforcing the judgment of its educators through well-meant truant officers and job requirements, much as did the Spanish kings who enforced the judgments of their theologians through the conquistadors and the Inquisition.

—From Ivan Illich, *Deschooling Society*

7.

Medicine has always been under pressure to provide public explanations for the diseases with which it deals, and the formulation of comprehensive, unifying theories has been the most ancient and willing preoccupation of the profession. In the earliest days, hostile spirits needing exorcism were the principal pathogens, and the shaman's duty was simply the development of improved techniques for incantation. Later on, especially in the Western world, the idea that the distribution of body fluids among various organs determined the course of all illnesses took hold, and we were in for centuries of bleeding, cupping, sweating, and purging in efforts to intervene. Early in this century the theory of autointoxication evolved, and a large part of therapy was directed at emptying the large intestine and keeping it empty. Then the global concept of focal infection became popular, accompanied by the linked notion of allergy to the presumed microbial pathogens, and no one knows the resulting toll of extracted teeth, tonsils, gallbladders, and appendixes: the idea of psychosomatic influences on disease emerged in the 1930s and, for a while, seemed to sweep the field.

—From Lewis Thomas, "On Magic in Medicine," *The Medusa and the Snail*

8.

Mars has some of the most striking relief and the largest volanoes known in the solar system. Three of them tower 27 km above the Mars datum level (corresponding to Earth's mean sea level) and 17 km above surrounding plains. An even larger volcano—Olympus Mons—rises 25 km above the land. Diameters of these giants range from several hundred kilometers to well over 1,000 km. Earth's largest volcanoes, in Hawaii, are typically only nine km above the seabed and 120 km across. Vulcanism has played a major role on Mars and is thought to be still active, although there doesn't seem to be much plate tectonic action.

—From Robert C. Cowen, "Exploring the Planets," *Current*, February 1981

Types of Development

A topic sentence alone is too bare to communicate the total meaning of an idea. We need to explain an idea more fully, clarify it, elaborate on it, and substantiate it. In short, we need to develop it with other sentences that support the topic sentence and complete its thought.

If the topic sentence is an assertion, the remainder of the paragraph is the proof. Consider, for instance, this topic sentence: "Through research, universities are society's main source of new knowledge, and therefore universities contribute to society in utilitarian ways." Readers expect us to support that claim with evidence. How would we develop and prove such a statement? There are several options. We might divide "utilitarian ways" into categories: medical, engineering, business, and so forth. Then, under each classification we would have to provide examples of knowledge that is a direct result of university research, such as polio vaccine, birth control pills, the computer, and so on. Without the substantiation, the topic sentence is simply an opinion; with the substantiation, it becomes a proven statement.

The topic sentence gives the main idea of the paragraph; the supporting sentences explain or prove it.

Consider another topic sentence: "Doctors not only subject patients to medication which is sometimes addictive and has hurtful side effects; they also kill many patients outright." To substantiate this assertion, the writer must present facts, cite sources, and give examples. The writer has given an opinion and now must back it up. Here is the rest of the paragraph:

According to *U.S. News & World Report*, about 30,000 persons "die each year from adverse reactions to drugs." Sheer blundering on the part of medical practitioners takes the lives of many others. United States Senate hearings in 1975 revealed that fully 25 percent of all medical-laboratory tests conducted in the United States are "substandard or wrong." This means, according to *The Reader's Digest*, that "millions of Americans may be risking unnecessary hospitalization, unneeded surgery or inappropriate, and occasionally fatal treatment." Far from being a safe spot for recuperation, many hospitals are actually danger zones. In fact, as Illich points out, "the average frequency of reported accidents in hospitals was higher than in all industries but mines and high-rise construction." One of every twelve persons who enter a hospital as a patient incurs some injury or disease which he did not have when he came in the door. Research hospitals are even more dangerous, injuring one in every five patients, and killing one of every thirty. If you went to the hospital to live for two years, it would probably kill you—no matter what your health when you entered.

—From James Dale Davidson, *The Squeeze*

We can develop a paragraph in the same ways that we can develop an essay: by providing examples, narrating, giving facts and details, comparing and contrasting, defining, describing, making analogies, assigning causes and effects, tracing a process, or using a combination of these patterns. Usually the topic sentence will suggest to readers what kind of development they can expect in the paragraph. For example, the topic sentence "Robots have a variety of uses" will necessarily be developed by enumeration; the writer has made a commitment to enumerate the "variety of uses": automated civic tasks (garbage collection), tasks too dangerous for human beings (exploring and mining the ocean floor), and tasks that save human labor (assembly-line work).

What kind of development would readers expect from these topic sentences:

1. One way that organisms rearrange genes over thousands of years is known as mimicry.
2. Medical treatment is not the same as health care.
3. America has a long history of moral legislation.
4. Existing evidence suggests that early hominids were hunters rather than gatherers.

The following are examples of the different ways that paragraphs can be developed:

Examples

This association with, and imitation of, the wolf among American Indians was absolutely pervasive. The two great clan divisions of the northwest coast tribes were the wolf and the raven. One of the three divisions of the southern Arapaho were *Haqiba-na*, the wolves; one of the ten Caddo bands were *Tasba*, the wolf. A Cherokee setting out in winter on a long journey rubbed his feet with ashes and, singing a wolf song, moved a few steps in imitation of the wolf, whose feet he knew were protected from frostbite, as he wished his to be. Nez Perce warriors wore a wolf tooth pushed through the septum of their noses. Cheyenne medicine men wrapped wolf fur around the sacred arrows used to motion antelope into a trap. Arikara men wove wolf hair and buffalo hair together in small sacred blankets. Bella Coola mothers painted a wolf's gallbladder on a young child's back so he would grow up to perform religious ceremonies without making mistakes as a hunter. An Hidatsa woman experiencing a difficult birth might call on the familial power of the wolf by rubbing her belly with a wolf skin cap.

—From Barry H. Lopez, *Of Wolves and Men*

Illustration

Sometimes there is such a mix-up about selfness that two creatures, each attracted by the molecular configuration of the other, incorporate the two selves to make a single organism. The best story I've ever heard about this is the tale told of the nudibranch and medusa living In the Bay of Naples. When first observed, the nudi-branch, a common sea slug, was found to have a tiny vestigial parasite, in the form of a jellyfish, permanently affixed to the ventral surface near the mouth. In curiosity to learn how the medusa got there, some marine biologists began searching the local waters for earlier developmental forms, and discovered something amazing. The attached parasite, although apparently so specialized as to have given up living for itself, can still produce offspring, for they are found in abundance at certain seasons of the year. They drift through the upper waters, grow up nicely and astonishingly, and finally become full-grown, handsome, normal jellyfish. Meanwhile, the snail produces snail larvae, and these too begin to grow normally, but not for long. While still extremely small, they become entrapped in the tentacles of the medusa and then engulfed within the umbrella-shaped body. At first glance, you'd believe the medusae are now the predators, paying back for earlier humiliations, and the snails the prey. But no. Soon the snails, undigested and insatiable, begin to eat, browsing away first at the radial canals, then the borders of the rim, finally the tentacles, until the jellyfish becomes reduced in substance by being eaten while the snail grows correspondingly in size. At the end, the arrangement is back to the first scene, with the full-grown nudibranch basking, and nothing left of the jellyfish except the round, successfully edited parasite, safely affixed to the skin near the mouth.

—From Lewis Thomas, *The Medusa and the Snail*

Narration

One bright frosty morning I was out of doors collecting stones to make a vivarium for some captive frogs, stones that were small, mostly round and gray, the size and color of mice. I had not seen the owl that day and did not know he was near as I crouched on my heels, picking up the stones. At a moment when there were three in my hand, the owl struck. One instant I held the stones, the next instant the owl was perched on a branch of a bush about eight feet away, and he had the stones in his claws and I had a gash on my empty hand to prove he had taken them. A great gray owl is a huge bird. It has a wingspread of nearly five feet, and yet I had not seen him approach, or come down in front of my eyes, or take the stones, or fly to the bush with them. Human eyes and minds simply don't register motion this fast, and surely a mouse, whose life would have been squeezed out as the owl closed its claws, would never have known what happened.

—From Sally Carrighar, *Wild Heritage*

Analogy

Great writers are either husbands or lovers. Some writers supply the solid virtues of a husband: reliability, intelligibility, generosity, decency. There are other writers in whom one prizes the gifts of a lover, gifts of temperament rather than of moral goodness. Notoriously, women tolerate qualities in a lover—moodiness, selfishness, unreliability, brutality—that they would never countenance in a husband, in return for excitement, an infusion of intense feeling. In the same way, readers put up with unintelligibility, obsessiveness, painful truths, lies, bad grammar—if, in compensation, the writer allows them to savor rare emotions and dangerous sensations. And, as in life, so in art both are necessary, husbands and lovers. It's a great pity when one is forced to choose between them.

—From Susan Sontag, "Camus' Notebooks," *Against Interpretation*

Comparison/Contrast

Beyond these stylistic similarities, Switzerland and Nepal would at first appear to have little more in common than their mountain environments. The former is the epitome of modernization, while the latter is one of the world's least developed countries. Today, Nepal is struggling to establish a simple road system, while Switzerland's cantons are linked by modern highways and an extensive electric rail network. Most of Nepal is accessible only on foot; the Swiss, in contrast, can speed over 15,000 miles of track so rapidly that passengers complain of being unable to enjoy the mountain landscape. Nepal, where the per capita income is less than $120 per year, faces a vast development task, while Switzerland, with its industrial and commercial empires, is home to one of the world's greatest concentrations of wealth.

—From Robert E. Rhoades, "Cultural Echoes Across the Mountains," *Natural History*, Jan. 1979

Classification/Division

The reasoning, when you bring it to light, is something like this. There are two kinds of education in the world: the free, which develops the individual according to his nature, and the specialized, which turns out doctors, scientists, mechanics—useful servants of the state or of industry. In a democracy each individual has both types. In the Soviet he gets only the specialized—the whole plan is to make him a state slave.

—From Joyce Cary, "The Mass Mind"

Definition

What marks a generation? When the term categorizes a group of people unrelated by blood, the critical criteria defining a generation are endlessly variable, from the nearly meaningless numerical division by decades (the "sixties generation," for example) to the mutual participation in a specific event as profound as Vietnam or as trivial as drinking Pepsi-Cola. Age itself may mark a generation, with specific physical characteristics (gray beard and stooped posture) or behavioral patterns (as in Gibbon's "brisk intemperance of youth") providing the definitive signals. But our most secure standard for defining a generation rests on the Greek root of the word, *genos,* whose basic meaning is reflected in the verb *genesthai,* "to come into existence"; until 1961 the first definition of the word in Webster's unabridged dictionary was still "procreation." That moment when a child is born simultaneously produces a new generation separating parent and offspring—*gonos* ergo *genos*—and the very concept educes the paradox of an evershifting threshold in time.

—From Laura L. Nash, "Concepts of Existence: Greek Origins of Generational Thought," *Daedalus,* Fall 1978

Description

This was a full-grown timber rattler—a veritable serpent, six feet of ponderous, powerful snake. What shocked me more than its length was its muscularity, its solidity. Its neck was like a wrestler's wrist; its middle was round and bulging like a wrestler's forearm. Yet no wrestler (no matter how histrionic) ever entered a ring with that nympholeptic stare, that dragonlike, subhuman hate in its eye.

—From Alan B. Rothenberg, "Peaceful Coexistence with Rattlesnakes," *Harper's,* May 1962

Process

Positioning the lips is a problem that recurrently challenges the ingenuity of the embalmer. Closed too tightly, they tend to give a stern, even disapproving expression. Ideally, embalmers feel, the lips should give the impression of being ever so slightly parted, the upper lip protruding slightly for a more youthful appearance. This takes some engineering, however, as the lips tend to drift apart. Lip drift can sometimes be remedied by pushing one or two straight pins through the inner margin of the lower lip and then inserting them between the two front upper teeth. If Mr. Jones happens to have no teeth, the pins can just as easily be anchored in his Armstrong Face Former and Denture Replacer. Another method to maintain lip closure is to dislocate the lower jaw, which is then held in its new position by a wire run through holes which have been drilled through the upper and lower jaws at the midline. As the French are fond of saying, *il faut souffrir pour être belle* ["One must suffer in order to be beautiful"].

—From Jessica Mitford, *The American Way of Death*

Cause

What causes the thickening of the arterial walls is the deposit of cholesterol and other fatty substances (serum lipids) that float in the blood. Though diet is popularly associated with increases in cholesterol levels, stress has been demonstrated to increase cholesterol and other fat levels and contribute to the thickening of the arterial walls. Stress increases the secretion of adrenalin, and this in turn increases the amount of free fatty acids in the blood stream, an increase associated with an elevation of cholesterol. It has been demonstrated at the University of South Dakota that noise levels common to the environment of man raise cholesterol levels in rats and rabbits (and also cause heart enlargement in rats). Dr. Samuel Rosen of CQC has stated that loud noises cause adrenal hormone to be released into the blood stream to intensify tension and arousal. Stress itself has been implicated as a primary reason for cholesterol changes.

—From Robert Alex Baron, *The Tyranny of Noise*

Effect

The consequences of human cloning are almost impossible to imagine. Widespread human cloning would alter human society beyond recognition. The family would no longer exist, sexuality would have no connection with reproduction. The idea of parenthood would be completely changed. The diversity of human beings provided by sexual reproduction would vanish. One could imagine entire communities of people who looked exactly the same, whose range of potential was identical. Some scientists have suggested that "clones and clonishness" could replace our present patterns of nation and race.

—From Caryl Rivers, "Cloning: A Generation Made to Order," *Ms.,* June 1976

Enumeration of Facts

What is remarkable about the tomato from the grower's point of view is its rapid increase in popularity. In 1920, each American ate 18.1 pounds of tomato. These days we each eat 50.5 pounds of tomato. Half a million acres of cropland grow tomatoes, yielding nearly 9 million tons, worth over $900 million on the market. Today's California tomato acre yields 24 tons, while the same acre in 1960 yielded 17 tons and in 1940, 8 tons.

—From Mark Kramer, "The Ruination of the Tomato," *Atlantic Monthly*, January 1980

Achieving Coherence Within a Paragraph

Achieving coherence means linking sentences within a paragraph so that readers can move smoothly from one sentence to the next and can follow the logical progression of the controlling idea. A paragraph can have unity without having coherence—that is, all the sentences within a paragraph may relate to the controlling idea, but they might not be linked together. However, a paragraph cannot have coherence unless it already has unity; once we have achieved unity, we go back through the paragraphs and work on coherence.

To see how coherence is achieved, examine the following paragraph:

If we endeavour to form our conceptions upon history and life, we remark three classes of men. The first consists of those for whom the chief thing is the qualities of feelings. These men create art. The second consists of the practical men, who carry on the business of the world. They respect nothing but power, and respect power only so far as it [is] exercised. The third class consists of men to whom nothing seems great but reason. If force interests them, it is not in its exertion, but in that it has a reason and a law. For men of the first class, nature is a picture; for men of the second class, it is an opportunity; for men of the third class, it is a cosmos, so admirable, that to penetrate to its ways seems to them the only thing that makes life worth living. These are the men whom we see possessed by a passion to learn, just as other men have a passion to teach and to disseminate their influence. If they do not give themselves over completely to their passion to learn, it is because they exercise self-control. Those are the natural scientific men; and they are the only men that have any real success in scientific research.

—From Charles S. Peirce, "The Scientific Attitude and Fallibilism," *The Philosophy of Peirce*

We have no difficulty getting from one sentence to the next because the writer has structured the material logically and provided verbal ties to connect the ideas. We are able to follow the paragraph because of several coherence devices:

1. Order—The paragraph is structured climactically, listing the three types, the third being the one that the writer wishes to emphasize.

2. Repetition of key terms—The writer repeats words such as "class" and "men."
3. Use of pronouns—In sentence 2, *those* for men; in 3, *these*; in 5, *they* for practical men, and *it* for power; in 6, *it* for force, and so forth.
4. Transitional markers—First, second, third.
5. Parallelism—"The first consists of. . . . The second consists of. . . . The third class consists of. . . ." "For men of the first class, nature is a picture; for men of the second class, it is an opportunity; for men of the third class, it is a cosmos."

We work on coherence mainly during the revising stage of writing. After we have packaged our ideas into paragraphs, we read through those paragraphs to make certain that each sentence is connected to the sentence before it and the sentence after it. In essence, we consider the sentences of a paragraph in pairs, asking ourselves, "How do I get from sentence 1 to sentence 2, from sentence 2 to sentence 3," and so on. We must provide readers with subtle bridges that allow them to see the connection between sentence 4 and sentence 5, sentence 5 and sentence 6. If we fail to provide a logical link, the chain of thought is broken.

What follows is an examination of the five devices outlined above.

Arrange Sentences in Logical Order

A logical organization, which is simply a reflection of a logical pattern of thinking, is the backbone of a coherent paragraph. If our thinking is coherent, and if we organize our sentences to reflect that thinking, our paragraph will have a basic coherence. When a paragraph is organized in a clear and understandable way, readers can move through it easily because one thought leads to the next. For example, if we organize a paragraph chronologically, readers immediately (although perhaps unconsciously) recognize the structure and expect the sentences to be arranged according to a designated time sequence.

Paragraphs can be organized in as many different ways as essays, but there are six basic structures:

General-to-specific
Specific-to-general
Comparison/contrast
Chronological (time)
Order of importance
Spatial (physical space: up and down, left to right, etc.)

Naturally, the type of organizational pattern we use will be determined by the content of the paragraph.

Repeat Key Terms

A major way of tying sentences together and of keeping the focus directed on the main idea within a paragraph is to repeat key terms. By picking up on an important word from preceding sentences, a writer can form a bridge to the next sentence, though usually we try to repeat more than one key term. Sometimes, the emphasis may shift from one supporting idea to another within a paragraph, and the key terms will change accordingly.

What key terms are repeated in the following paragraph, how does the repetition help readers to follow the writer's ideas, and how does the repetition reinforce the focus of the paragraph?

After the Roman Empire went to pieces, wars were resumed; but, since civilization declined, they were the small and unimpressive affairs of people too barbarous to know how to wage war in the grand manner. With the revival of civilization, the art of war was gradually recovered, and with every advance in civilization it has become more efficient. Since 1618 there have been six periods of general war in Europe, and six intervening periods of general peace. The periods of war have lasted, on an average, about twenty-five years; the periods of peace, about thirty years. Generalizing roughly, the periods of peace have tended to become longer, the periods of war shorter—but also more destructive. In short, as Emile Lavisse tersely says, "War is a habit of civilization." If so, it is one of those habits which, even if known to be bad, are difficult to get rid of. For three centuries, to go no farther back, the will to war has not been curbed by the knowledge that war is evil. On the contrary, the more men know, the better, that is to say, the more destructively they fight, and the more destructively they fight, the more surely they know that to fight thus is futile in the long run.

—From Carl Becker, "Loving Peace and Waging War," *New Liberties for Old*

Notice two kinds of repetition within Becker's paragraph: One is repetition of the two main words from the topic sentence—*wars* and *civilization*—and the other is repetition in one support sentence of a term introduced in the preceding support sentence.

sentence 1: introduces *wars* and *civilization*
sentence 2: repeats both terms
sentence 3: introduces *periods of war* and *periods of peace*
sentence 4: repeats *periods of war* and *periods of peace*
sentence 5: repeats *periods of peace* and *periods of war*, and introduces *destructive*
sentence 6: repeats *War* and *civilization*
sentence 7: uses pronoun *it* for war, and introduces *known*
sentence 8: repeats *war* twice; uses *knowledge*, which connects to *known*

sentence 9:   uses *know,* which connects to *known* and *knowledge;*
repeats a form of *destructive (destructively);* and introduces *fight* and repeats it in the last two clauses

Even in the support sentences that introduce new key terms, those terms
reinforce the earlier terms from the topic sentence. For example,
although *periods of war* is a new phrase in the paragraph, it contains a key
word from the topic sentence; *destructive* and *fight* certainly reinforce
the central idea of war; likewise, *periods of war* prepares readers for its
opposite, *periods of peace,* and *knowledge, known,* and *know* all reinforce *civilization.* Introducing key terms within support sentences is
therefore acceptable so long as they are related to the key terms introduced in the topic sentence. Together, these main and secondary key
terms form a cluster that promotes one or two central ideas. Their
repetition helps to connect the sentences in the paragraph so that the
sentences form one chain, without any weak links.

Use Pronouns

Instead of repeating the exact term, we may also use pronouns and
synonyms for the same effect. Since coherence entails tying sentences
together, we can achieve this by using a similar term that is itself a type
of repetition or by using a pronoun that refers to a noun in the preceding
sentence. What pronouns and synonyms are used in the following paragraph, and how do they help tie the sentences together?

> Most students go to college for the wrong reasons. They attend, for example,
> because their parents expect them to or because their friends are going.
> Increasingly, another incentive for young people going to universities is
> money. They want to acquire professional skills so they can become en-
> gineers, lawyers, executives, computer programmers, and accountants.
> They want a certain standard of living and status. Other undergraduates
> frequent campuses simply because of indolence. Undecided about what
> they want and unmotivated to get a job, they swarm to school because it
> allows them time to continue a comfortable routine and to postpone de-
> cisions. What happened to young scholars' desire to appreciate design and
> language, to expand their perspective, to learn of new values and ideas, to
> exercise their imaginations, and to learn thinking instead of information?

Use Transitional Markers

Transitional markers are words such as *however, for example, first . . .
second . . . third,* and *similarly* that show readers how a sentence relates
to the one preceding it. The choice of transitional marker depends on the

kind of relationship we wish to show between two sentences, such as contrast, causation, or example. Here are some of the most common terms used to show various types of relationships:

Addition:	both, in addition, for the same reason, also, further, furthermore, moreover, besides, too
Example:	specifically, for example, first, second, third, last, namely, in fact, that is, in particular, to illustrate, for instance
Contrast:	but, however, on the other hand, in contrast, on the contrary, conversely
Comparison:	likewise, similarly, in the same way, coincidentally, correspondingly
Causation:	hence, therefore, thus, consequently, as a result
Time:	then, next, presently, suddenly, yesterday, today, tomorrow, not long after that, afterwards, since, up to that point, in 1986, last month, until
Place:	here, there, in Detroit, below, next to, alongside, in front of

These transitional markers serve two functions: They act as bridges from one idea to the next, and they act as pointers for readers. When readers come to a *however,* they expect a statement that is in contrast to the previous statement; when they read *for instance,* they expect an example. From the readers' point of view, these markers are like highway signs that tell them which direction our thoughts are going and that allow them to get smoothly from one point to another.

To get an idea of the usefulness of transitional markers, read the following paragraph in which all transitional markers have been deleted.

> Because of technology, meat producers are able to put weight on animals at a faster rate than ever before. Chicken ranchers mix high-potency vitamins and other supplements in chicken feed and raise a 2½-pound fryer in 7 weeks instead of the usual 3 months. The ratio of feed consumed to weight gained in chickens is increased; it takes less feed to raise a 7-week, 2½-pound fryer. Fish raisers profit from these technological advances. Beef feeders are able to increase a weaned steer's weight an average of 2½ pounds per day—75 pounds a month. The phenomenal increase is due to better control of animal illness as well as to dietary additives. Consumers usually believe that such dietary supplements should be banned. Most of the supplements not only have no harmful effects on human beings, they even benefit consumers because the lower cost to produce the meat is passed on to them.

Notice the seemingly abrupt changes in thought between sentences 3 and 4, 4 and 5, and 6 and 7. We are not prepared for those changes and are not given signals that indicate shifts from one idea to another. Here is the same paragraph with a few transitional markers inserted to make the relationships between sentences more understandable to readers and to smooth out the rough spots:

> Because of technology, meat producers *today* are able to put weight on animals at a faster rate than ever before. *For example,* chicken ranchers mix high-potency vitamins and other supplements in chicken feed and *thereby* raise a 2½-pound fryer in 7 weeks instead of the usual 3 months. The ratio of feed consumed to weight gained in chickens is increased; *hence,* it takes less feed to raise a 7-week, 2½-pound fryer. *Even* fish raisers profit from these technological advances. *Similarly,* beef feeders are able to increase a weaned steer's weight an average of 2½ pounds per day—75 pounds a month. The phenomenal increase is due to better control of animal illness as well as to dietary additives. *Although* consumers usually believe that such dietary supplements should be banned, most of the supplements not only have no harmful effects on human beings, they even benefit consumers because the lower cost to produce the meat is passed on to them.

This is a definite improvement because we immediately see how each sentence relates to the previous one, and the paragraph flows smoothly.

Most writers are already familiar with the advantages of transitional markers and use them, if anything, too frequently. The tendency is to load up a paragraph with them when there are problems within the paragraph, but plugging in transitional markers will not help a paragraph that is not well unified and structured. We should use transitional markers to show changes in direction and to emphasize relationships, not to try to make up for lack of unity in the subject matter.

Use Parallelism

Usually when we speak of parallelism we mean that elements *within* a sentence are structurally similar. For example:

> "A young man may well find quite as many enchantments in a first intrigue as in a first true love." (Honoré Balzac)

But parallelism also can function *between* two sentences, thereby calling attention to the relationship of those sentences and structurally linking them. For instance:

> "When a man with a gun threatens to shoot the passengers of an airplane unless some prisoners are released or a ransom is paid, we call that terrorism. When leaders threaten millions of deaths—and every nuclear weapon targeted on an enemy city is just such a threat—we call it strategy." (Richard Barnet)

If we think of coherence in terms of linking pairs of sentences, we can immediately see the value of parallelism between two sentences. Since coherence has to do with linking, and since parallelism links sentences structurally, parallelism can function as an effective device to achieve coherence. Here is another example in which partial parallelism ties two sentences together and allows readers to move smoothly from one to the next:

> "... Violence is the simple, ultimate solution for problems of status competition, just as gambling is the simple, ultimate solution for economic competition. The old pornography was the fantasy of easy sexual delights in a world where sex was kept unavailable. The new pornography is the fantasy of easy triumph in a world where status competition has become so complicated and frustrating." (Tom Wolfe)

APPLICATION

Are the following paragraphs coherent? To the extent that they are, how is the coherence achieved? Point out the logical order, instances of key terms repeated, use of pronouns or synonyms, transitional markers, and parallelism. Are there any places where the coherence breaks down and you have difficulty getting from one sentence to the next?

1.

Youth is imaginative, and if the imagination be strengthened by discipline this energy of imagination can in great measure be preserved through life. The tragedy of the world is that those who are imaginative have but slight experience, and those who are experienced have feeble imaginations. Fools act on imagination without knowledge; pedants act on knowledge without imagination. The task of a university is to weld together imagination and experience.

—From Alfred North Whitehead, "The Idea of a University"

2.

Marriages have always deviated widely from the model usually presented to boys and girls, but the partners involved have always been made to feel guilty about being different. Women who are dominant feel they must conceal their strength in the interest of public relations, or, worse yet, prove to themselves that they are not unnatural monsters. Men who are constitutionally unaggressive have compensated by unpleasant blustering. The first step is to render unto Caesar those things which belong to Caesar and unto love those things that belong to love. Husbands are not employers. Children are not jobs.

—From Caroline Bird, *Born Female*

3.

One recent morning in the country, we woke up to a rainstorm. We stood in a doorway and watched the high branches of the trees lurching under the assaults of the wind; the sky had become a gray, heaving sea. Water poured off the edge of the roof and pounded tall stalks of goldenrod that grew below; many by now were lying flat, crisscrossed in bubbling puddles. Except where the water fell from the eaves, and where it dripped slowly from a glistening power line, it was mostly invisible. What we saw was its impact: muddy pools responding to the drops, tossing small splashes upward from the bull's-eye; and, in the surrounding undergrowth of vines and weeds and wild flowers, a sporadic flashing of light—first here, now there—as one leaf and then another was struck, bent, and snapped back, shivering. A tremulousness swept across the landscape as the raindrops hit grape leaves, bull briar, swamp maple, bayberry, honeysuckle.

The next morning was clear—puddles on the steaming road, and, from the woods, what looked like smoke idling upward through shafts of sunlight—and the morning after that we were back in the city, having early breakfast at a corner window in the all-night restaurant. No leaves, no trees, no puddles, no wind; instead, sunlight streaming down the side street, and people. A family—father, mother, and small daughter—jumped out of a battered station wagon and carried bundles of newspapers to a newsstand. A young man on the street shouted abusively at someone out of sight, then walked away. When he reached the corner, he turned around and grinned: a joke between friends. A cop swaggered into the shop for a coffee to go. A one-eyed old man harangued him with grandiose gestures and followed him outside. A blond girl dressed in carefully selected yellows and tans and browns stood on the corner and looked at her watch. When the cop drove away, ignoring the old man's speech, the old man turned to her and continued. She smiled and nodded, watching the street. Presently, two men came by in a car; she greeted them, got in, drove off. A hunched elderly woman wearing an overcoat passed by, bright-eyed and mumbling. A very tall black man with cornrowed hair sat down in a booth behind us, ordered breakfast ("No fries," he said), and began to whistle a hymn. Looking out the window, we saw a tremulousness across the landscape.

—From "Notes and Comment," *The New Yorker*, Sept. 18, 1978

4.

One trouble [with America], it seems to me, is that the majority of the people who rule us, who have our money and power, are lawyers or military men. The lawyers want to talk our problems out of existence. The military men want us to find the bad guys and put bullets through their brains. These are not always the best solutions—particularly in the fields of sewage disposal and birth control.

—From Kurt Vonnegut, Jr., "Address to Graduating Class at Bennington College, 1970,"
Wampeters, Foma, & Granfalloons

5.

What lies behind my remarks is a distinction between two views of education. In one view, education is something externally added to a person, as his clothing and other accoutrements. We cajole him into standing there willingly while we fit him; and in doing this we must be guided by his likes and dislikes, by his own notion of what enhances his appearance. In the other view, education is an interior transformation of a person's mind and character. He is plastic material to be improved not according to his inclinations, but according to what is good for him. But because he is a living thing, and not dead clay, the transformation can be effected only through his own activity. Teachers of every sort can help, but they can only help in the process of learning that must be dominated at every moment by the activity of the learner. And the fundamental activity that is involved in every kind of genuine learning is intellectual activity, the activity generally known as thinking. Any learning which takes place without thinking is necessarily of the sort I have called external and additive—learning passively acquired, for which the common name is "information." Without thinking, the kind of learning which transforms a mind, gives it new insights, enlightens it, deepens understanding, elevates the spirit simply cannot occur.

—From Mortimer J. Adler, *Reforming Education*

Coherence Between Paragraphs

The principle of coherence is applicable not only within paragraphs, but also between paragraphs. Just as readers should be able to move smoothly from one sentence to another in a paragraph, they should be able to glide from one paragraph to the next and see the logical relationships between paragraphs. We need to provide connections between paragraphs to show readers that a new paragraph is in some way a continuation of the previous thought.

We achieve coherence between paragraphs by using the same devices as within paragraphs: transitional markers, parallelism, repetition of key terms, and, most important, logical order.

Just as transitional markers make explicit the relationship between two sentences, they can serve the same function between two paragraphs. Notice how the second of these two paragraphs uses a transitional marker to signal readers to expect an opposing idea.

What advantage do the incest taboos confer? A favored explanation among anthropologists is that the taboos preserve the integrity of the family by avoiding the confusion in roles that would result from incestuous sex. Another . . . is that it facilitates the exchange of women during bargaining between social groups. Sisters and daughters, in this view, are not used for mating but to gain power.

In contrast, the prevailing sociobiological explanation regards family integration and bridal bargaining as by-products or at most as secondary contributing factors. It identifies a deeper, more urgent cause, the heavy physiological penalty imposed by inbreeding. Several studies by human geneticists have demonstrated. . . .

—From Edward O. Wilson, *On Human Nature*

In addition to transitional markers, we can use parallelism between paragraphs as well as within paragraphs. By opening a series of paragraphs with topic sentences that are similar in grammatical structure, we call attention to the similarity in content or thought. Here, for example, are the opening sentences of three consecutive paragraphs dealing with the federal government's benign intrusion into private lives when it provides social services to the needy:

For people who needed shelter, the government provided public housing.

For people who needed money, the government provided welfare.

For children in trouble and whose families did not have the resources to help, the government provided "services" through a system of family courts.

—From Ira Glasser, "Prisoners of Benevolence," *Doing Good*

Another way to link paragraphs is to use a key term from one paragraph in the topic sentence of the next paragraph or to end one paragraph with a statement that prepares readers for the following paragraph. What key terms are carried over from one paragraph to the next in this excerpt, and where does the author include a transitional sentence to prepare readers for a new paragraph?

One of the least-considered effects of food is its influence on the relationships between species. In Africa there is a badgerlike animal called ratel. It has a tough skin and powerful claws and wanders around in bush country, living on beetles, snakes and small mammals—and all the time looking for honey to which it is particularly partial. In the same area lives a small brown bird which eats insects and grubs but, like the ratel, has a passion for honey. The local source of honey is a wild bee which builds nests in tree trunks and crevices. The bird finds these easily enough but cannot get inside them. The ratel has claws strong enough to rip the nests open but has difficulty finding them. So they join forces. The bird looks for a ratel and when it finds one, begins to chatter loudly and persistently. The ratel moves toward the bird, making chuckling and hissing sounds in reply. The honey guide, for that is its name, leads the ratel directly to the nest, waits while it breaks it open and eats its fill, and

716 Paragraph Development

then joins in the feast. Lately, the honey guide has discovered that man can usually be relied upon to provide the same cooperative service, and it often tries to entice him to a hive in the same way.

In southwest New Guinea there is a tribe of fishermen who have a similar working arrangement with the local dolphins. The men go out each morning to a particular cove and slap their oars on the water. Dolphins suddenly arrive and swim in front of the boats until they find a shoal of fish, which they herd into a compact mass. The men run a net around the fish and haul them into the boats, pausing every now and then to throw a particularly tasty one to the dolphins, who gather around with their heads out of the water to watch the whole performance. The interaction seems to be every bit as rewarding to them as the fish they receive.

In both of these examples, the common factor forming the bond between the species is food. Most associations between widely different animal species are based on a better feeding deal for one or both of the associates. All the close relationships between our species and the animals which we have domesticated began with our offering them food. The connection between food and friendship in our minds is so close that it has already caused one misunderstanding.

Opportunist animals in dull zoos are forced to create their own variety. They find the best potential source of interest in the people who pass by, and they perform all sorts of outlandish behavior patterns to attract our attention. With our often surprisingly limited imagination, we assume that they must be begging for food, so we ply them with buns and sticky sweets. To keep us there responding, they have to reward us by eating at least part of the rubbish we throw their way. And so every day animals in zoos die of overeating when all they really lack is attention.

—From Lyall Watson, *The Omnivorous Ape*

Even more important than transitional markers, parallelism, and repetition of key terms is the order of paragraphs; if we have arranged our paragraphs in a logical pattern, readers will conceptually be able to move from one unit of thought (i.e., one paragraph) to the next step in that train of thought (i.e., the following paragraph) without difficulty. A consideration of the arrangement of paragraphs leads us to another concern: the paragraph as part of an essay.

Paragraph as Part of a Larger Structure

Thus far, we have examined the paragraph largely as a self-contained unit, complete in itself, having all the elements needed for self-survival— an idea, evidence, unity, and coherence. In this view, the paragraph is a miniature essay and can be examined as an independent piece of writing. The topic sentence is to the paragraph what the thesis statement is to the essay, and the support sentences develop the topic sentence just as the paragraphs within an essay develop the thesis statement.

But one paragraph is not written in isolation. Although it must make sense by itself, it is incomplete alone and must rely on its fellow paragraphs to prove a thesis fully. To understand a paragraph completely, therefore, we must examine how it relates to the surrounding paragraphs, where it is situated within the essay, and what its purpose is. In short, we must view it in the context of the other paragraphs. Its tone, length, function, and structure are determined in part by factors outside of itself. Instead of an independent piece of writing, it is one stage of a larger structure, and it takes some of its shape and meaning from the totality. Each paragraph is partially formed by the tone and purpose of the entire essay, and in turn each paragraph contributes to the fulfillment of that tone and purpose. The movement from the first paragraph to the last in an essay should create a logical flow so that readers can discern a definite arrangement of ideas and see the interrelationships of ideas. The paragraphs will be tied together because our ideas are tied together; our paragraphs will be arranged logically because our ideas are logical; and our essay will be coherent because our ideas are coherent.

Advice, Warnings, Reminders

1. Writing would be considerably easier if paragraphs were uniform things that fit one prescribed shape. The fact is, however, they aren't mechanical, predictable, unvarying things at all, and try as we might we can't force them into one or two patterns. Because paragraphs are organic, they develop in various ways and take various shapes, and attempting to limit them to a basic pattern represents an oversimplification. We should recognize that there are two basic characteristics of good paragraphs—unity and coherence—but that there are many possibilities for composing paragraphs.

2. Another reason that paragraphing is difficult is that most of us don't think in paragraphs, and certainly not in unified paragraphs. Rather, our ideas tend to be associative or random and our brains flit from idea to idea, seldom developing one idea. When we offer our ideas to others, however, we must develop them, explain them, and prove them. Paragraphing for most of us must be a conscious activity that we work on constantly.

3. The most typical weaknesses in paragraphs are inadequate development, unrestricted subject, unfocused controlling idea, and weak coherence.

4. As with most rules, there are times when exceptions are appropriate to the paragraphing rules that (a) one should never write a one-sentence paragraph, (b) that every paragraph must have a topic sentence, and (c) that the topic sentence should be the first sentence. Unless we can justify breaking the rules, though, we should adhere to them.

5. Whether to use an inductive or general-to-specific paragraph depends on whether we are moving toward an abstraction in a paragraph or trying to substantiate an abstraction. Are we leading to a generalization or clarifying one? We find more general-to-specific than inductive paragraphs not only because they are reader-oriented, but also because writers usually start with generalizations—their opinions—and have to follow with facts to sub-stantiate those opinions.

6. One of the dangers of not writing topic sentences is that readers draw their own generalization from the facts. Instead of being readers, the become interpreters.

7. The controlling idea is the part of the topic sentence that we tend to neglect. Typically, our paragraphs fail to articulate the controlling idea, which is the focal point of the paragraph and the unifying element. A topic sentence should announce an idea that can be developed within the confines of a single paragraph.

8. Topic sentences serve as guides for writers as well as for readers. They focus what we will say in the body of the paragraph, tie the other sentences together, and keep us from straying in thought. In the prewriting stage, if we compose a topic sentence outline we will have divided our discourse into paragraphs and set up the logical flow of the entire essay. Then in the revising stage, we can use the controlling idea to check the unity of each paragraph.

9. The length of paragraphs should be varied in order to avoid monotony and to achieve balance and proper emphasis. We should try to mix the lengths so that we don't have all long, bulky paragraphs or all short, choppy ones. Although a long paragraph (over 150 words) is sometimes necessary to develop a complex idea, several consecutive long paragraphs bog down a discourse and make it seem ponderous. Similarly, although a short para-graph is a relief to readers, a series of short paragraphs (three to four sentences) doesn't establish the relative importance among sentences. When we break material into brief paragraphs, none of the sentences receive proper emphasis because they are all given equal emphasis, and therefore readers have difficulty distinguishing important matter from secondary information. A series of short paragraphs usually indicates that we need to combine them or to develop them more fully.

Examine the following multiparagraph example in terms of topic sent-ences, unity, coherence within paragraphs, and coherence between para-graphs.

HOW FLOWERS CHANGED THE WORLD

Loren Eiseley

When the first simple flower bloomed on some raw upland late in the Dinosaur Age, it   1
was wind pollinated, just like its early pine-cone relatives. It was a very inconspicuous
flower because it had not yet evolved the idea of using the surer attraction of birds and
insects to achieve the transportation of pollen. It sowed its own pollen and received
the pollen of other flowers by the simple vagaries of the wind. Many plants in regions
where insect life is scant still follow this principle today. Nevertheless, the true
flower—and the seed that it produced—was a profound innovation in the world of life.

In a way, this event parallels, in the plant world, what happened among animals.   2
Consider the relative chance for survival of the exteriorly deposited egg of a fish in
contrast with the fertilized egg of a mammal, carefully retained for months in the
mother's body until the young animal (or human being) is developed to a point where
it may survive. The biological wastage is less—and so it is with the flowering plants.
The primitive spore, a single cell fertilized in the beginning by a swimming sperm, did
not promote rapid distribution, and the young plant, moreover, had to struggle up from
nothing. No one had left it any food except what it could get by its own unaided efforts.

By contrast, the true flowering plants (angiosperm itself means "encased seed")   3
grew a seed in the heart of a flower, a seed whose development was initiated by a
fertilizing pollen grain independent of outside moisture. But the seed, unlike the
developing spore, is already a fully equipped *embryonic plant* packed in a little
enclosed box stuffed full of nutritious food. Moreover, by featherdown attachments, as
in dandelion or milkweed seed, it can be wafted upward on gusts and ride the wind for
miles; or with hooks it can cling to a bear's or a rabbit's hide; or like some of the
berries, it can be covered with a juicy, attractive fruit to lure birds, pass undigested
through their intestinal tracts and be voided miles away.

The ramifications of this biological invention were endless. Plants traveled as   4
they had never traveled before. They got into strange environments heretofore never
entered by the old spore plants or stiff pine-cone-seed plants. The well-fed, carefully
cherished little embryos raised their heads everywhere. Many of the older plants with
more primitive reproductive mechanisms began to fade away under this unequal
contest. They contracted their range into secluded environments. Some, like the giant
redwoods, lingered on as relics; many vanished entirely.

The world of the giants was a dying world. These fantastic little seeds skipping   5
and hopping and flying about the woods and valleys brought with them an amazing
adaptability. If our whole lives had not been spent in the midst of it, it would astound
us. The old, stiff, sky-reaching wooden world had changed into something that glowed
here and there with strange colors, put out queer, unheard-of fruits and little intricately
carved seed cases, and, most important of all, produced concentrated foods in a way
that the land had never seen before, or dreamed of back in the fish-eating, leaf-
crunching days of the dinosaurs.

That food came from three sources, all produced by the reproductive system of   6
the flowering plants. There were the tantalizing nectars and pollens intended to draw

insects for pollenizing purposes, and which are responsible also for that wonderful jeweled creation, the hummingbird. There were the juicy and enticing fruits to attract larger animals, and in which tough-coated seeds were concealed, as in the tomato, for example. Then, as if this were not enough, there was the food in the actual seed itself, the food intended to nourish the embryo. All over the world, like hot corn in a popper, these incredible elaborations of the flowering plants kept exploding. In a movement that was almost instantaneous, geologically speaking, the angiosperms had taken over the world. Grass was beginning to cover the bare earth until, today, there are over six thousand species. All kinds of vines and bushes squirmed and writhed under new trees with flying seeds.

The explosion was having its effect on animal life also. Specialized groups of   7
insects were arising to feed on the new sources of food and, incidentally and unknowingly, to pollinate the plant. The flowers bloomed and bloomed in ever larger and more spectacular varieties. Some were pale unearthly night flowers intended to lure moths in the evening twilight, some among the orchids even took the shape of female spiders in order to attract wandering males, some flamed redly in the light of noon or twinkled modestly in the meadow grasses. Intricate mechanisms splashed pollen on the breasts of hummingbirds, or stamped it on the bellies of black, grumbling bees droning assiduously from blossom to blossom. Honey ran, insects multiplied, and even the descendants of that toothed and ancient lizard-bird had become strangely altered. Equipped with prodding beaks instead of biting teeth they pecked the seeds and gobbled the insects that were really converted nectar.

Across the planet grasslands were now spreading. A slow continental upthrust   8
which had been a part of the early Age of Flowers had cooled the world's climates. The stalking reptiles and the leather-winged black imps of the seashore cliffs had vanished. Only birds roamed the air now, hot-blooded and high-speed metabolic machines.

The mammals, too, had survived and were venturing into new domains, staring   9
about perhaps a bit bewildered at their sudden eminence now that the thunder lizards were gone. Many of them, beginning as small browsers upon leaves in the forest, began to venture out upon this new sunlit world of the grass. Grass has a high silica content and demands a new type of very tough and resistant tooth enamel, but the seeds taken incidentally in the cropping of the grass are highly nutritious. A new world had opened out for the warm-blooded mammals. Great herbivores like the mammoths, horses and bisons appeared. Skulking about them had arisen savage flesh-feeding carnivores like the now extinct dire wolves and the saber-toothed tiger.

Flesh eaters though these creatures were, they were being sustained on   10
nutritious grasses one step removed. Their fierce energy was being maintained on a high, effective level, through hot days and frosty nights, by the concentrated energy of the angiosperms. That energy, thirty per cent or more of the weight of the entire plant among some of the cereal grasses, was being accumulated and concentrated in the rich proteins and fats of the enormous game herds of the grasslands.

On the edge of the forest, a strange, old-fashioned animal still hesitated. His   11 body was the body of a tree dweller, and though tough and knotty by human standards, he was, in terms of that world into which he gazed, a weakling. His teeth, though strong for chewing on the tough fruits of the forest, or for crunching an occasional unwary bird caught with his prehensile hands, were not the tearing sabers of the great cats. He had a passion for lifting himself up to see about, in his restless, roving curiosity. He would run a little stiffly and uncertainly, perhaps, on his hind legs, but only in those rare moments when he ventured out upon the ground. All this was the legacy of his climbing days; he had a hand with flexible fingers and no fine specialized hoofs upon which to gallop like the wind.

If he had any idea of competing in that new world, he had better forget it; teeth or hooves, he was much too late for either. He was a ne'er-do-well, an in-betweener. Nature had not done well by him. It was as if she had hesitated and never quite made up her mind. Perhaps as a consequence he had a malicious gleam in his eye, the gleam of an outcast who has been left nothing and knows he is going to have to take what he gets. One day a little band of these odd apes—for apes they were—shambled out upon the grass; the human story had begun. 12

Apes were to become men, in the inscrutable wisdom of nature, because flowers had produced seeds and fruits in such tremendous quantities that a new and totally different store of energy had become available in concentrated form. Impressive as the slow-moving, dim-brained dinosaurs had been, it is doubtful if their age had supported anything like the diversity of life that now rioted across the planet or flashed in and out among the trees. Down on the grass by a streamside, one of those apes with inquisitive fingers turned over a stone and hefted it vaguely. The group clucked together in a throaty tongue and moved off through the tall grass foraging for seeds and insects. The one still held, sniffed, and hefted the stone he had found. He liked the feel of it in his fingers. The attack on the animal world was about to begin. 13

If one could run the story of that first human group like a speeded-up motion picture through a million years of time, one might see the stone in the hand change to the flint ax and the torch. All that swarming grassland world with its giant bison and trumpeting mammoths would go down in ruin to feed the insatiable and growing numbers of a carnivore who, like the great cats before him, was taking his energy indirectly from the grass. Later he found fire and it altered the tough meats and drained their energy even faster into a stomach ill adapted for the ferocious turn man's habits had taken. 14

His limbs grew longer, he strode more purposefully over the grass. The stolen energy that would take man across the continents would fail him at last. The great Ice Age herds were destined to vanish. When they did so, another hand like the hand that grasped the stone by the river long ago would pluck a handful of grass seed and hold it contemplatively. 15

In that moment, the golden towers of man, his swarming millions, his turning wheels, the vast learning of his packed libraries, would glimmer dimly there in the ancestor of wheat, a few seeds held in a muddy hand. Without the gift of flowers and 16 the infinite diversity of their fruits, man and bird, if they had continued to exist at all, would be today unrecognizable. Archaeopteryx, the lizard-bird, might still be snapping at beetles on a sequoia limb; man might still be a nocturnal insectivore gnawing a roach in the dark. The weight of a petal has changed the face of the world and made it ours.

—From *The Immense Journey*

B

Introductions and Conclusions

Introductions and conclusions are of supreme importance because, coming first and last, they are the doors to and from our ideas. We invite readers into the front door by making our initial paragraph alluring, and when they exit from the back door of the essay, we want them to leave with a clear understanding of our ideas and our reasons. We place great demands on these special units that frame our writing: Introductions must entice, and conclusions must accentuate.

No formula exists for writing effective introductions and conclusions, and the types outlined below are merely a few of the more common possibilities. As with all writing, the choice among varied approaches depends on audience and purpose, and you should feel free to compose any type that will achieve your purpose.

Types of Introductions

The main purpose of an introductory paragraph is to capture readers' attention. Because readers are for the most part impatient folks, prone to instant judgments and short attention spans, they will not read anything that doesn't seem interesting from the beginning, so we have only a few sentences to attract their attention and to engage their curiosity.

Put yourself in their position: You're browsing through a magazine, scanning the titles and the opening paragraphs; if they don't engage you, you turn the page and try the next article. Likewise, if our readers yawn, we've lost them. "You can't expect to communicate with anyone," John Cheever reminds us, "if you're a bore." The opening paragraph, which journalists call a "hook," is crucial because it is our only chance to get someone to read the rest of our letter or report or proposal. The body of a paper may contain insightful and persuasive comments, but readers assume that the opening is representative of the whole and that an uninteresting introduction signals an uninteresting essay.

Perhaps the best way to engage readers is to challenge them intellectually, and the best way to challenge them intellectually is to have a provocative thesis. Ultimately, keeping readers' attention depends on the originality and soundness of our ideas: Once we engage their intellects, we have them for the duration. We should open with something that starts readers thinking—for example, a challenge to traditional wisdom or a startling insight into a situation. A good introduction makes readers ask "Why?" or "How?" even though the introduction itself is not in the form of a question. For instance, an opening such as "The Supreme Court is in immediate need of revision" causes readers to ask "Why is that so?" and "What should be changed?" The introduction whets the readers' curiosity and thereby ensures that they will continue to read. They are "hooked."

Besides gaining readers' attention, the opening also serves other important functions. Naturally, it should announce the specific subject that we plan to discuss, and usually it presents the thesis, or at least gives some indication of the central point. It also should establish the significance of the issue being discussed, for that in turn justifies our writing about it. Sometimes the introduction may even suggest the kind of development and organization that will follow. We should keep in mind that the first paragraph introduces not only the subject, but also the writer; we are introducing ourselves through our style, tone, and ideas. Whether readers accept our message depends partly on whether they accept us as intelligent and judicious human beings. If the essay is argumentative, the introduction has the additional function of gaining readers' consent to a point of view they may already oppose. In many ways, then, the introduction is the most important paragraph of the entire discourse.

When considering openers, we might ask ourselves these questions:

What do I want to accomplish with this introduction?
How can I legitimately gain the readers' attention?
How can I establish the importance of my topic?
Should I open with the thesis, or hold it until later?
What tone should I use?

As with any segment of writing, we have numerous options available in composing openers, and, as always, effectiveness lies in knowing which type to use with a given audience and purpose.

APPLICATION

Below are five different newspaper introductions on the same editorial topic: the Federal Trade Commission's order for the American Medical Association to lift its restrictions against physicians' advertising, the reason being to encourage competition among doctors and to lower doctors' fees. Which paragraphs entice you to read the rest of the editorial, and why? What implicit questions does each introduction arouse?

We usually think of large corporations when we think of antitrust cases, but lately antitrust officials have been focusing on antitrust abuses by professionals— optometrists, druggists, engineers, lawyers and now doctors.

—From *The Times-Picayune,* Oct. 26, 1979 (New Orleans)

Arguments by the Federal Trade Commission that advertising by physicians will lower doctor bills are not very persuasive. But neither are the physicians' claims that their profession will be harmed.

—From *The State,* Oct. 29, 1979 (Columbia, S.C.)

The Federal Trade Commission's ruling on medical advertising is a victory for competition in a field where competition traditionally has been limited.

—From *The Idaho Statesman,* Oct. 26, 1979 (Boise)

Throughout the 20th century virtually all American physicians have abided by a code of professional ethics that prohibits advertising beyond simple announcements of a new practice or change of address. That code, strictly enforced by the 200,000-member American Medical Association, was declared to be in restraint of trade last week by the Federal Trade Commission, and few outside the profession will regret that finding.

—From *Providence Journal,* Oct. 31, 1979 (Providence, R.I.)

For most people, shopping for doctors is like choosing a telephone company. There's no competition.

—From *St. Petersburg Times,* Oct. 26, 1979 (St. Petersburg, Fla.)

Although there are many ways to begin an essay, the following ten options are the most commonly used and might serve as models.

Direct Statement

The direct approach works well in two instances: (1) in standard reports when the busy reader wants a quick summary, much in the way that a newspaper story opens with a lead paragraph that encapsulates the main points; and (2) with controversial or dissenting theses. In the one, directness is expected; in the other, it is unexpected and intriguing.

Summary

Being the first black woman elected to Congress has made me some kind of phenomenon. There are nine other blacks in Congress; there are ten other women. I was the first to overcome both handicaps at once. Of the two handicaps, being black is much less of a drawback than being female.

—From Shirley Chisholm, *McCall's*, Aug. 1970

Controversy

THESIS: The hero is dangerous because he or she ignores majority wishes and ignores the democratic machinery, which is slow.

If the hero is defined as an event-making individual who redetermines the course of history, it follows at once that a democratic community must be eternally on guard against him.

—From Sidney Hook, "Hero and Democracy," *Hero in History*

Principle and Application

This is the famous "V-shaped" introduction; it begins very generally—citing an encompassing principle of some sort—and then applies that principle to the current situation. Such a structure, by conveniently focusing down at the end of the paragraph, leads immediately into the discussion.

An idea whose time has come arrives with explosive immediacy, creating the illusion of instant birth. But, of course, behind such an idea lies a process of maturing that has been taking place, subterraneanly, over a very great period of time—one that spans decades if not centuries. What is remarkable about this process is that up until the very moment of birth the maturing takes place individually, in a great many separate people. Then—seemingly overnight—the isolated perception of separate persons has become the focused understanding of a people; the idea is no longer simply an idea but has become a shared imperative.

Contemporary feminism, which seemed to burst suddenly upon America ten years ago, embodies just such a process.

—From Vivian Gornick, "The Conflict Between Love and Work," *Essays in Feminism*

Specifics

These are statistics, vivid details, current events, and examples. Whereas the previous type of introduction moved from the general to the specific, this type moves from the specific to the general. Opening an essay with concrete facts has an immediacy that abstract discussions lack, especially when the details are surprising or shocking.

Statistics

At the beginning of 1971, 38 per cent of the world's people lived in countries where legal abortion was liberally available. By early 1976, this figure had increased to 64 per cent, nearly two-thirds of the world. Few social changes have swept the world so rapidly.

—From Lester R. Brown and Kathleen Newland, "Abortion: A Worldwide Trend Toward Liberalization," *Washington Post,* March 6, 1976

Since 1972 there have been more bureaucrats drawing salaries in America than all the people at work in "all the durable goods manufacturing industries, including such giants as autos, electronics, steel, and heavy machinery." Each business day, the number of bureaucrats increases by about 1,300. And each new bureaucrat contributes an additional overhead cost to everything you buy: he makes your groceries more expensive—by imposing 4,100 regulations on a pound of plain hamburger; when you buy a new car you are paying more for the accumulated efforts of the bureaucrats than you are for all four wheels—General Motors alone must employ 23,000 persons simply to fill out government forms. If the estimates of experts are correct, then the total effect of all regulatory exactions is to impose an annual cost of more than $130 billion upon the economy. That is about $2,500 per family.

—From James Dale Davidson, *The Squeeze*

Examples

Ben Jonson, son of a poor preacher and stepson of a bricklayer, wrote some of the purest and most beautiful classic poetry in English; Bossuet, the supreme master of French classic eloquence, came of peasant stock; Keats, son of a livery stable man, became Keats; Proust, son of a distinguished physician who was the son of a small-town grocer and candlemaker, became one of the finest literary sensibilities and one of the greatest novelists who ever lived. In all these and in all such cases, education was the key that unlocked the prison of mere potentiality.

—From J. Mitchell Morse, " 'Keepum Ignunt,' " *The Chronicle of Higher Education,* Jan. 22, 1979

Narrative

The narative approach can be (1) historical or (2) anecdotal. Historical narration provides necessary background and orients readers to the present situation; it gives readers a broad perspective of the current issue.

Anecdotes, on the other hand, entertain and sometimes draw a moral. Because anecdotes are usually personal, they have the advantage of adding human interest and of introducing the writer's personality.

Historical

America is teetering on the brink of an energy revolution. Our first great step forward, from wood to coal, ushered in the Industrial Revolution and built our cities. Our second, the harnessing of electricity, provided the dramatic innovations of lighting, air conditioning, and automation. The third, the use of petroleum to power the automobile, created unprecedented individual mobility, spreading our population across the continent. And now our fourth—solar energy—"could perhaps do more to improve the material well-being of mankind, without increasing his tensions, than any other good available," says leading alternative-energy authority William Heronemus.

> —From Steven Ferrey, "Solar Eclipse: Our Bungled Energy Policy,"
> *Saturday Review*, March 3, 1979

Anecdotal

In 1967, when Gov. Ronald Reagan joined the Board of Regents of the University of California, the first order of business was the dismissal of Clark Kerr, the university's president. Outside, reporters were poised for Dr. Kerr's angry comments, which, characteristically, never came. Instead, he told the press calmly: "I leave this job the same way as I started it: Fired with enthusiasm."

> —From Fred M. Hechinger, "About Education: An Assessment of Clark Kerr,
> A Strong Moderate," *The New York Times*, Feb. 12, 1980

Question

Interrogative introductions have become less effective through overuse, but if we can pose the question in an alluring way and if we have an acceptable answer to follow, this is one means of introducing a topic. It is most useful when, instead of announcing our point of view on an issue, we wish to appear merely to be investigating the issue. Usually the question is the opening sentence or the final sentence of the introduction.

Should a doctor always tell his patients the truth?

> —From Dr. Mack Lipkin, "On Lying to Patients," *Newsweek*, June 4, 1979

Why does the Soviet Union, with its inferior economic system and technological base, now rate as the military equal of the West—or perhaps even its superior?

> —From Bruno Koeppl, "Tricks of the Arms Trade," *Newsweek*, April 21, 1980

I have a problem about being nearly sixty: I keep waking up in the morning and thinking I'm thirty-one. It makes me feel like the woman in the laxative ads on TV: "You're as young as you feel!" I do not find her an acceptable role-model, but here I am, missing my real age by a generation. It's not that I want to be thirty-one, nor that I think anyone else imagines me to be thirty-one, for the first is untrue and the second is impossible. In fact, for someone who likes to think she's reality-oriented, it's a mighty silly feeling. So why do I have it?

—From Elizabeth Janeway, "Breaking the Age Barrier,"
Ms., April 1973

Quotation

An introductory quotation or paraphrase has the advantage of lending the authority of the person cited and it borrows that person's wit or eloquence.

"The law, in its majestic equality," Anatole France observed, "forbids the rich as well as the poor to sleep under bridges, to steal bread, and to beg in the streets."

The French satirist would have appreciated the majestic equality of Monday's ruling by the U.S. Supreme Court.

—From an editorial, *San Jose Mercury,* July 4, 1980

"Human history," wrote H. G. Wells, "becomes more and more a race between education and catastrophe." Each new headline these days makes him sound less hyperbolic and more prophetic. The threads of our once well-knit societal fabric appear to be unraveling—in deteriorating international relationships, in disappearing energy supplies, in the incongruous and seemingly insoluble twin economic problems of waxing inflation and waning employment.

—From Frank E. Vandiver, "Washington Should Assess the Capabilities of Our Campuses,"
The Chronicle of Higher Education, Feb. 9, 1981

Definition

(See Chapter 5.)

Similarity, Analogy

Comparing a current situation to another can be either informative or witty, depending on our purpose. In both of the following examples, the introductions are two paragraphs long instead of the traditional one paragraph; sometimes an introduction may be even longer.

Why is it that National Geographic Specials share the proverbial fault of Chinese food? No matter how exotic the fare, or how elaborate the preparations, the dish is seldom filling. I have seen about a dozen Geographic specials on public television, and what I remember best is the basso profundo voice of host E. G. Marshall, the theme music, and pictures of hairy beasts and hairy explorers. Little meat sticks to the ribs.

Granted, the National Geographic Society by tradition stays on the sunny side of the street, and the formula of its hugely successful magazine features narrow escapes, preferably on foaming white water. Recently, the *National Geographic* surprised everybody, possibly including its editors, by carrying an article on South Africa that contained fairly critical words on apartheid. But such lapses are infrequent.

—From Karl E. Meyer, "The Limits of Gee-Whiz," *Saturday Review*, March 3, 1979

Paradox

Beginning with an apparent contradiction delights readers with its wit and causes them to question how the paradoxical ideas can be reconciled. They read further to find out. In such introductory paragraphs, the paradox is usually the first sentence so that it instantly engages the readers. Consider your own reaction to these opening sentences:

I do not believe in Belief.

—E. M. Forster

We were never more free than during the Nazi occupation.

—Jean Paul Sartre

I respect time too much to waste it on punctuality.

—From William A. Emerson, Jr., "Punctuality is the Thief of Time," *Newsweek*, Dec. 16, 1974

The more the United States is at peace, the more it spends for war.

—From Clayton Fritchey, *Washington Post*, April 3, 1976

Nonalignment

Occasionally in an argumentative paper we don't want to open with our thesis because readers who oppose it may stop reading. In such cases, an effective strategy is to present both sides of the issue without aligning ourselves with one side or the other, even though we in fact favor one. In effect, we postpone the thesis in order to appear to explore the issue objectively. Here is an example of a noncommittal introduction:

During most of this century, solar energy seemed to interest only dreamers, tinkerers, and radicals. But because of the oil embargo, the sun has become a serious alternative source of energy. The issue has now become how much solar energy, what kind—and when. According to the organizer of International Sun Day, "Forty percent of our energy could come from solar energy by the year two thousand if we make some dramatic moves *now.*" The editor of *World Oil* disagrees, saying that the source will have the impact over the next quarter-century of "a mosquito bite on an elephant's fanny."

The two estimates lay out the range of the debate on solar's near- and middle-term potential contribution to America's energy needs.

—From Modesto A. Maidique, "Solar America," *Energy Future: Report of the Energy Project at the Harvard Business School*

Last Words on First Paragraphs

1. A good introduction
   A. engages readers' attention,
   B. usually announces the subject,
   C. establishes the significance of the issue,
   D. often prepares the readers for what is to follow, and
   E. sets the tone.
2. The very first sentence should grab readers.
   A. "Human genes are an embarrassment." The irreverence of Adrian Desmond's opening sentence in his book *The Ape's Reflexion* is effective because it surprises readers.
   B. "All autobiographies are lies. I do not mean unconscious, unintentional lies; I mean deliberate lies." This is the way George Bernard Shaw opens his autobiographical essay "In the Days of My Youth."
   C. "I don't trust people who are busy making sense." (John Ciardi, "On Making Sense")
3. Avoid the "In this essay I will discuss" approach unless your intent is to bore readers.
4. Although we want an introduction that grabs readers by their lapels and says "Read me!" we shouldn't be deceptive. For example, we shouldn't begin with a piece of sensationalism that isn't relevant to the essential issue; readers will feel deceived and will stop reading when they realize it.
5. Don't feel obligated to write your introduction before writing the essay; in fact, some professional writers feel that the introduction should be written last because the focus of the essay often shifts during the writing process.

APPLICATION

1. Improve the following two introductions by making them striking and interesting. Both deal with potentially interesting topics.

   A. It is my belief that the Congressional filibuster rule is a bad idea. One senator can halt the entire legislative process by rambling on and on for hours and prevent action on an issue. It allows a small group to talk indefinitely, and the practice is increasing. It is an antiquated, abusive, time-consuming device. It's not a debate; it's a prolonged monologue.

   B. Chemical weapons are inhumane, and the United States should not produce them. For years there was a production moratorium on chemical weapons, but now funds are being allocated to produce an aerial bomb that contains lethal chemicals. It is called the Big Eye.

2. Take a topic of your choosing—for instance, the trend toward casting retired athletes as sports announcers, and write four different types of introductions on that topic.

3. Reread the introduction of your last essay. If someone else had written it, would you read the essay based on that introduction? If you think it can be improved, rewrite the introduction.

4. Write an introduction for each of these thesis statements:

   A. The American political system ensures that we end up with mediocre presidents.

   B. Prostitution should be legalized.

   C. Ethnic jokes almost always have a serious side.

   D. The space program should be cancelled.

5. Find three examples of excellent introductions from magazine articles, photocopy them, and identify the type of introduction.

6. For your next essay, turn in two introductions.

7. Based on their introductory paragraphs, which of these essays would you continue to read? Explain your reasons. What type of introduction is each?

   A.

At some point in life, a major daydream of any authentic Texan is to quit the job and become a rancher. Honest fatigue, . . . herding the dogies on the range, . . . sitting out on the porch listening to coyotes howl under a full moon, . . . wearing those great clothes. The only thing wrong with ranching is cattle: they are oafish creatures whose only roles on earth are to thicken themselves and to thin your savings. The going price is never right, the rainfall is always short, and there is always some new exotic disease. So forget cattle. The thing to do is ranch bees.

—From Richard West, "Honey, You're Still Driving Me Crazy," *Texas Monthly*, Sept. 1979

B.

What used to be called the War between Science and Religion was a hot war. That now in progress between Science and the Humanities is a cold one. It is being fought somewhat more chivalrously and with many protestations of respect on both sides. The scientist doesn't want to exterminate literature, and the humanist certainly doesn't want to abolish science. "Coexistence" is the catchword. But as in the case of the other cold war, the real question is, "On whose terms?" From both sides one gets something rather like the attitude of the Catholic priest who is said to have remarked to his Protestant opposite number: "After all, we are both trying to do God's work; you in your way and I—in His." There seems to be a good deal of question-begging and so many polite concessions that the terms are not usually clearly defined and the issues not squarely met.

—From Joseph Wood Krutch, *If You Don't Mind My Saying So . . .*

C.

I, Arthur David Seidenbaum, being of cluttered mind and middle-aged body, would like to be a number.

—From Arthur David Seidenbaum, "By the Numbers," *Newsweek,* Jan. 20, 1975

D.

Footsteps, and a man bursts into the Baker Street flat. "Have a seat," Sherlock Holmes might say. "I know not who you are, but that you are a bachelor, a clerk of some kind, and that you have not spoken to anyone in several days." Inevitably, Holmes's first deductions are sociological—marital status, occupation, social in-teractions. His methods and thought are the tools of the social scientist as much as of the "consulting detective," as Holmes calls himself. He says that he studies the criminal mind, but he really studies the criminal's social position. Sociology is crucial to Arthur Conan Doyle's stories, and Sherlock Holmes, in some ways the sociologist par excellence, is at their center.

—From Bonnie Menes, "Sherlock Holmes and Sociology," *American Scholar,* Winter 1980/81

E.

Fifteen years ago last month, the late Rep. Howard W. Smith, a Virginia Democrat, added the word "sex" to the equal-employment clause of the then pending civil-rights bill. He didn't really mean it. The Southern strategy was to make the bill so radical—by covering *even women*—that Congress to a man would vote it down. But the amended bill became law, making Smith, to his surprise, the father of this generation's most promising piece of feminist legislation.

—From Jane Bryant Quinn, "A Woman's Place," *Newsweek,* Feb. 26, 1979

F.

It is fashionable to say that economic growth will slow down from now on. I think it is much more likely to accelerate. The world's economic history is that, after a big surge when Man stopped being a mainly migratory animal in about 8000 B.C., real gross world product per capita stood practically still for 10,000 years to about 1776. Then it exploded. Real incomes have increased in 19 of the 20 decades since 1776 because of an increase in every decade in our knowledge and control over energy and matter. To this has been added, in the last two decades, a breakthrough in the processing of information, plus a nascent breakthrough in the distribution of information.

—From Norman Macrae, "United States Can Keep Growing—and Can Lead—If It Wishes," *Smithsonian,* July 1976

G.

When a lion comes to kill you, he does not bound or leap or make a great show of terrible rage. Such theatrics are for television lions and fatted cats trained to frighten children at the circus. A killing lion makes quick darting movements, running close to the ground and angling back and forth in deadly feints. His eyes are always on you, and you know that he knows exactly how he's going to kill you. Sharp snarls hiss at you like high-charged static, and when he is really close, the world switches into slow motion. Clawing, ripping death becomes a slowly danced pantomime.

Only it isn't happening slowly at all, the charge is lightning quick. It only seems that way because your senses and reflexes are elevated to a keenness never felt before. Every nerve in your body focuses on the source of immediate destruction, but there is also a soaring awareness of the world around you—the trees, the grass, the sun, the sky are there in vibrating detail. A tiny wildflower or a shy wren are minutely seen in your new awareness. I believe man experiences this sensation only when he is hunting—or being hunted.

—From Jim Carmichael, "When a Lion Comes to Kill," *Outdoor Life,* Aug. 1979

H.

In the middle of the nineteenth century, the largely self-educated British physicist Michael Faraday was visited by his monarch, Queen Victoria. Among Faraday's many celebrated discoveries, some of obvious and immediate practical benefit, were more arcane findings in electricity and magnetism, then little more than laboratory curiosities. In the traditional dialogue between heads of state and heads of laboratories, the Queen asked Faraday of what use such studies were, to which he is said to have replied, "Madam, of what use is a baby?" Faraday had an idea that there might someday be something practical in electricity and magnetism.

—From Carl Sagan, *Broca's Brain*

I.

Imagine watching a chess game without knowing any of the rules of chess. Complicated moves are being made; players are being captured; games are being won. Without being able to ask questions, how long would it take you to deduce the complete rules of chess from simply watching chess games? How many times would you make mistakes and postulate rules that later observations would disprove?

Now imagine a more complicated game in which some of the moves are random events not determined by the explicit rules of the game. Accidents occur. The game is also being played by players who do not always act in accordance with the rules. They make mistakes. In such a game, constructing the rule book would be a monumental task. Yet it is just such a game that economists are trying to dissect. What are the rules of the economic game? How are economic prizes distributed? What determines the actions of individual players?

—From Lester Thurow, *Generating Inequality*

Types of Conclusions

Just as we need a provocative opening paragraph to make potential readers interested in and receptive to our ideas, we need a strong concluding paragraph to leave readers with a favorable impression and a clear retention of our ideas. Because the conclusion is our last chance to drive home our main ideas, we want to make it emphatic and memorable. These final statements are often the ones left in readers' minds.

Most events end in a big way—football games, tragic plays, wars, boxing matches, pregnancies—and essays should be no different. Most beginning writers don't conclude essays, though; they just abandon them. The end of an essay shouldn't just be a stopping place where the essay dissolves or expires. Instead, it should be an act of fulfillment and completion. It is the culmination, the climax, the knockout blow. Think of books you've read that simply stop without a sense of closure or finality; the experience is unsatisfying, even irritating, and spoils the fine effort up to that point. We ought to end an essay as we do a fine dinner, with a memorable dessert—chocolate mousse or crêpes marcelle or cherries jubilee. Most beginning writers ruin their essay by ending with something comparable to an oatmeal cookie.

Granted, conclusions are even more difficult than introductions. One reason they are troublesome is that we use our best material and thoughts in the body of the paper and then discover at the end that we have said all that needs to be said and have nothing worthwhile with which to conclude. The solution: Look for good concluding material in the prewriting stage and save it until the end. Some writers, such as John Irving, write their conclusions before anything else.

The material that we put into a conclusion can be as varied as that in our introduction, and in fact the same types of devices are appropriate—quotations, statistics, anecdotes, and so on, as the following examples illustrate.

Statistics

You need not be a very sharp mathematician to see that the money stolen by such hefty taxation adds up. If you could take what is being lost at current tax rates and bank it with compound interest, you would be a millionaire in forty years. In fact, you would have almost $1,350,000. The figures are staggering, preposterous. The burden is so far out of proportion to what the average family has the ability to bear that things clearly cannot go on at this rate for another forty years. Between 1967 and 1978, while America's population was rising only by 10 percent, the cost of government increased by 212 percent. This is a major reason why the American standard of life is declining. John Marshall was not kidding when he wrote, "The power to tax is the power to destroy." Excessive taxation is playing a major role in the destruction of America's progressive way of life.

—From James Dale Davidson, *The Squeeze*

Anecdotal

The most spectacular tribute to Italian design was reported by the Bertone people in Turin. "There was this New York banker . . . very rich . . . loved automobiles . . . came to our factory and said he wanted the most beautiful Miura we could build. Took it to New York, hired a helicopter and lifted the car right up to the garden of his penthouse overlooking Park Avenue. There he keeps it for his guests to see. Once a week he revs up the motor and his neighbors think that enemy rockets are landing. We asked him why he did this, and he said, 'A car like this is too beautiful for the streets. It's a work of art.' "

—From James Michener, "Italian Designers," *A Michener Miscellany: 1950–1970*

Quotation

A good deal of my own perception of [Jackie] Robinson's character and historic uniqueness I gleaned from Roger Kahn's wonderful book, *The Boys of Summer.* When Robinson died, October 24, 1972, Kahn was quoted in the papers. Someone asked him what Jackie Robinson had done for his race. Kahn, a white man, beautifully replied, "His race was humanity, and he did a great deal for us."

—From Mark Harris, "Each Game Was a Crusade," *TV Guide*, Aug. 6, 1977

The type of conclusion we use will depend on the material that precedes it, each essay having its natural ending, just as Western movies naturally end in a shoot-out, romances end in a wedding, and horror stories end in the destruction of the monster. Regardless of whether we use quotes, questions, paradoxes, or examples, the intention of a conclusion is usually to summarize, to suggest a solution and to call for action on that solution, to outline the implications of a situation, or to evoke an emotion.

Summary

Summaries are especially appropriate for long papers with complex material. Restating the thesis and its major support has the advantage of reinforcing the most important material and of helping readers to retain those main points. By summing up all the separate ideas of an essay into one paragraph, we condense, focus, and reiterate, and such condensation and conciseness result in clarity.

The difficulty with summaries is that in reemphasizing the important parts of a paper we are repeating what we've already said—and repetition can bore readers. To avoid being repetitive and boring, we can (1) blend summary material with other material, such as an interesting quotation, (2) be as brief as possible, and (3) phrase our ideas differently from the body so that we are repeating only the ideas, not the exact language.

Thus, a realistic program to implement solar energy would consist of three phases: First, short-term incentives for a rapid commercialization of existing technologies. Second, a ten-year search to identify the best of the new alternatives. And finally, commercialization of the alternatives identified in the second phase, leading toward a gradual transition to an increasingly Solar America in the twenty-first century, when hydrocarbons would be reserved for premium uses.

Admittedly, what has been described here is a vision—but an eminently practical one. It deserves a fair chance.

—From Robert Stobaugh and Daniel Yergin, "Solar America," *Energy Future: Report of the Energy Project at the Harvard Business School*

Recommendations

These are calls for action, reform, or reconsideration. Recommendatory conclusions are most appropriate for problem-solving essays. The conclusion may ask readers to endorse or act on a solution that the essay has outlined, and usually the conclusion asserts that the proposed solution is practical and achievable.

The values leading to an environmental ethic will become increasingly important in the decade of the 80s. The presence of an environmental ethic in our everyday decisions could be more important than we realize. Our decisions as individuals—at home and at work, as citizens, workers, professionals, or corporate or public officials—taken together, determine the hopes and quality of life for everyone.

With the predominant values in society weighted toward narrow self-interest, the role of those who seek the environmentally ethical route is difficult and often unpopular. Yet if we do not make our choices on the side of the environment now, our options will narrow rapidly as the pressures of population growth, resource depletion and pollution irreversibly alter the quality of living on the planet. Each of us, individually, can look for ways of making fewer demands on natural resources. We can seek to live in harmony with the natural order. We can replace a self-only, short-range outlook with universal, long-term values. And we can bring environmental considerations into our decisions, from the smallest to the greatest.

That is the hope. And therein lies the conservation challenge of the coming decade.

—From Robert Cahn, "The State of the Parks," *Sierra,* May/June 1980

Warning

Often with problem-solving essays an effective ending is to predict the dire consequences that will ensue if our solution is not implemented. We project into the future and describe what the situation will be like if society doesn't correct the problem at hand.

Marshall McLuhan says we are in a period in which it will become harder and harder to stimulate lust through words and pictures—i.e., the old pornography. In the latest round of pornographic movies the producers have found it necessary to introduce violence, bondage, torture, and aggressive physical destruction to an extraordinary degree. The same sort of bloody escalation may very well happen in the pure pornography of violence. Even such able craftsmen as Truman Capote, Ian Fleming, NBC, and CBS may not suffice. Fortunately, there are historical models to rescue us from this frustration. In the latter days of the Roman Empire, the Emperor Commodus became jealous of the celebrity of the great gladiators. He took to the arena himself, with his sword, and began dispatching suitably screened cripples and hobbled fighters. Audience participation became so popular that soon various *illuminati* of the Commodus set, various boys and girls of the year, were out there, suited up, gaily cutting a sequence of dwarf and feebles down to short ribs. Ah, swinging generations, what new delights await?

—From Tom Wolfe, "Pornoviolence," *Mauve Gloves & Madmen, Clutter & Vine*

Emotion

In order to stir up readers' feelings about an issue and to move them to act on an idea, we occasionally may find emotional conclusions highly effective in argumentative essays. When the body of the argument appeals to readers' intellect with facts and logic, and the conclusion appeals to their emotions, the essay makes a comprehensively persuasive appeal. (See Chapter 12 for a more elaborate explanation and for examples.) In such conclusions, we should rise to the occasion with the fervor of a trial lawyer and deliver a forceful peroration that evokes an appropriate emotion in readers—pity, fear, anger, or love (of country, family).

Last Words on Last Paragraphs

1. Curtain lines are important. The last sentence of an essay, like the first sentence, should be remarkable.
2. Conclusions rely on the principle of recency: What comes last is most recent in readers' memory and therefore is most readily recalled.
3. Conclusions should answer the readers' question "So what?"
4. The tone of a conclusion should be one of confidence and assurance.
5. In general, conclusions should be succinct. Long goodbyes are tiresome, and clarity comes with brevity:

   We are on the horns of a dilemma. Censorship is a very treacherous path to tread, while permissiveness is a road to disaster.

   —From an editorial, *St. Louis Review*, July 3, 1981 [on the permissiveness of TV and the attempts by the Coalition for Better Television to boycott advertisers of permissive shows]

6. Don't end with a cliché such as "All's well that ends well" or "C'est la vie."
7. Usually there is no need to end a short essay with a summary.
8. In an argumentative essay, the conclusion should touch readers where their deepest conviction lies. Because it is our last chance to win readers over to our side, we must place the most forceful material in the final position.
9. Using set expressions such as "finally," "in conclusion," and "in summary" to signal the conclusion should be avoided if possible. If we properly design a discourse, we should not need such phrases to announce that the essay is closing. An essay should logically progress to a conclusion so that readers realize

the conclusion is approaching, just as in movies we know when the end is upon us before "The End" appears on the screen.

10. A feeble conclusion can ruin a strong paper, in the same way that a goodnight handshake at the front door can ruin an otherwise good date. Go ahead and kiss the reader goodnight.

APPLICATION

1. Read several essays in current magazines such as *Saturday Review, The New Yorker, Atlantic Monthly,* and *Nation* until you find three conclusions that are especially effective. Photocopy these and bring them to class to share.
2. Write two different concluding paragraphs for your next essay. Decide which is more effective and why.
3. Rewrite and hand in both the original conclusion and a revision of your last essay.
4. Which of the following conclusions strike you as being effective? What is the writer attempting to accomplish with each conclusion?

A. [On the nonsense of nuclear war]

By way of lending grim point to the consequences of invested nonsense we read a report from the U.S. Department of Agriculture which says that the nematode, a species of plant worm or parasite, carries within itself a mysterious ability to resist harm from radiation. Man, puny creature, gets into trouble when he is exposed to doses of 300 roentgens or more. But the nematode can take up to 600,000 units of radiation. Man need not therefore fear that his nonsense will empty life from this earth. If man doesn't want the world the nematode is perfectly willing to take it.

—From Norman Cousins, "Of Nonsense and Nematodes," *Saturday Review,* Nov. 29, 1958

B. [Endorsing use of federal funds to help railroads improve equipment and lines]

Fifteen billion dollars is a lot of money, but it's only about one-tenth of this year's defense budget. And track maintenance is a labor-intensive job that could absorb thousands of youths who are now unemployed and virtually unemployable in the private sector. We can't think of a better investment in the nation's future than a firm congressional commitment to restoring the rails.

—From an editorial, *Newsday,* March 1, 1978 (Garden City, N.Y.)

C.

We are at a crossroads in human history. Never before has there been a moment so simultaneously perilous and promising. We are the first species to have taken our evolution into our own hands. For the first time we possess the means for intentional or inadvertent self-destruction. We also have, I believe, the means for passing through this stage of technological adolescence into a long-lived, rich and fulfilling maturity for all the members of our species. But there is not much time to determine to which fork of the road we are committing our children and our future.

—From Carl Sagan, *Broca's Brain*

D.

Schools have a role to play—teachers have a role to play—in the struggle of individual freedom against institutional authority; in the struggle of the human spirit against the formulas; in the struggle of life against materialism. No one, indeed, has a more important role to play than the teacher. But his role—his role in this republic at least—is not to commit his students to belief. His role is to commit them to the human experience—to the experience of the human mind and the human soul—in the profound and never questioning confidence that if they truly taste of that experience, if they truly see the choices of their lives, they—they themselves—will choose. In that confidence political freedom was conceived. In that confidence the institutions of human freedom was established. In that confidence the faith of those who teach the free is founded.

—From Archibald MacLeish, "The Teacher's Faith," *A Continuing Journey*

E.

The writers who can find some rhythmic way of advancing and retreating—into the wide world, into their studies for work—might open the windows and let the novel breathe. The writer becomes a specialist only at a heavy price. To be a "man of letters" is to perform too narrowly. Work in the world brings in a bit of cash, and it also brings in the world. Perhaps the young writer should not seek independence and freedom "so that I can have time to write." His project for the future might be the reverse—to find a significant job—if he means to distill the largest significance from his lonely and committed fantastic journey.

—From Herbert Gold, "The Life Contained in Novels and the Novelist's Life," *The Magic Will*

Appendix III

MECHANICS

A

Usage and Punctuation Index

Whereas rhetoric concerns effectiveness of strategy and style, usage and punctuation are matters of correctness—rules rather than options. Such rules ensure that all of us are using words or punctuation in the same way, and they are standardized so that when a writer uses a semicolon, for instance, readers will know how to interpret the sign and how to follow the structure of a sentence. The rules are intended to clarify meaning and to make reading easier.

Knowing the rules also is important because correctness affects ethos in writing. If we use nonstandard English and incorrect punctuation, our ethos will suffer because readers will assume that we are illiterate. Rightly or not, readers equate grammatical correctness and intelligence. If we write "Irregardless of the risks, we must not loose site of our principals" instead of "Regardless of the risks, we must not lose sight of our principles," readers will be suspicious of our knowledge in all areas.

To say, however, that there is good usage and bad usage is not to suggest that language is fixed and unchanging. On the contrary, languages grow and change, but more through speech than through writing. Speech is the forerunner of new expressions, and it shifts in meaning because most of us are more tolerant about speech usage than about writing usage. We would accept "Who are they kidding?" in speech more quickly than in writing. Once an expression becomes acceptable in speech, it begins to earn respectability in writing; the tongue tries out usages that the pen will later use. Some expressions prove to be fads and disappear, but some persist and become respectable.

Words and usage have degrees of respectability or social status. Some words, such as *ain't*, are unacceptable regardless of the occasion; slang and colloquial words, such as *bummer* and *trashed out*, are acceptable in informal speech but not in general or formal writing; and certain distinctions—for example, the distinction between *which* and *that*—are made in formal writing but not in general writing. What constitutes "good usage," therefore, depends to some extent on the occasion and the audience. Even experts disagree as to whether certain expressions and usages are acceptable, and their disagreement demonstrates that usage reflects values and is dictated by judgment.

The alphabetical index that follows contains explanations of punctuation rules and of frequently misused expressions. Misusing a term usually results from confusion with a similar term (who/whom, proved/proven, stationary/stationery).

accept, except

Accept is a verb that means to receive something that is offered, such as an invitation, advice, or responsibility.

Except means exclusion of something.

adapt, adopt

To *adapt* is to adjust or modify for a particular situation.

> We adapted to the climate. We adapted the plan to our needs.

To *adopt* is to take as one's own without change, such as adopting a child.

advice, advise

Advice is the noun, *advise* the verb.

> J.R. advised Sue Ellen not to leave South Fork. Sue Ellen ignored the advice.

affect, effect

Affect, which is almost always a verb, means to influence.

> The drought affected the price of corn.

Effect, usually a noun, is synonymous with *result*.

> The biggest effect of a large national debt is high interest rates.

Confusion occurs because *effect* can also be a verb, and it means to bring about something, or to implement.

> She effected several administrative changes when she took office.

all right

Not *alright*.

allusion, illusion

An *allusion* is a reference to a literary or historical event or figure to clarify a point. For instance, "He was her Romeo and she his Juliet" is an allusion to Shakespeare's play.

An *illusion* is a false perception, as in "optical illusion."

a lot

Not *alot*.

altogether, all together

Altogether means wholly or completely.

> Eleanor was altogether surprised when her cousin Franklin proposed to her.

All together means as a group.

> The family then went all together into the parlor to make the announcement.

among, between

Use *between* when referring to only two things; use *among* for three or more.

as

Because *as* can be used to designate either time or causation, its usage can be confusing:

> As the Russian ambassador began to speak, the Polish delegation left the room.

Two interpretations are possible: *At the time that* the Russian ambassador began to speak; or, *Because* the Russian ambassador began to speak. To avoid confusion, substitute a less ambiguous term for *as*—for instance, *while, because,* or *when.*

as, like

See *like, as.*

assure, ensure, insure

Assure means to promise or to set a person's mind at ease, and it is followed by a reference to some person.

> Batman assured the mayor that the Penguin would not bomb Gotham.

Ensure and *insure* both mean make certain or make secure from harm, but *insure* has become associated with financial protection.

> The Batmobile is insured against collision.

> Bruce Wayne's butler ensures that the Batmobile is filled with gasoline.

bad, badly

Usually *bad* is an adjective and *badly* an adverb.

He's a bad influence.

He throws badly.

Note the crucial difference between these two statements:

I need someone bad.

I need someone badly.

beside, besides

Beside means next to or at the side of; *besides* means in addition to.

blond, blonde

When used as a noun, *blond* refers to males ("He's a blond"), *blonde* to females ("She's a blonde"). As an adjective, though, *blond* is generally used to designate either male or female ("He has blond hair; she has blond hair also").

burglar, thief, robber

All are persons who steal, obviously. A *burglar* breaks in with the intention of stealing. A *thief* steals without breaking and entering and without holding up a victim. A *robber* threatens or forces a victim to give up property.

can, may

The formal distinction between *can* and *may* is worth retaining, though in informal speech it seldom is. *Can* expresses ability: "I can bench press 270 pounds." *May* is reserved for permission: "May I accompany you to the Bahamas?"

can't help but

The preferable form is *can't help + -ing*.

NOT: Othello can't help but suspect Desdemona.

BETTER: Othello can't help suspecting Desdemona.

canvas, canvass

Canvas is the coarse fabric.

Canvass, a verb, means to solicit or to examine; *canvass*, a noun, means a survey.

capital, capitol

Capital refers to money or to the official seat of government.

Capitol is the building where Congress assembles.

The capital of the United States is Washington, D.C., where the Capitol is located.

censor, censure

To *censor* is to suppress or to delete objectionable passages from a performance or publication.

To *censure* is to criticize severely.

A *censor* is someone who either censors or censures.

colon

Colons announce and call attention to material that is to follow: a list, a description, an elaboration, a quotation. They follow introductory material and lead readers to expect related material; usually the material following a colon is equivalent to the material preceding a colon. The introductory half of the sentence builds anticipation, and the other half delivers the corresponding material.

A colon is used to introduce a list (often preceded by *the following* or *including*):

> Certain qualities are needed to be a good assassin: technical expertise in weaponry and explosives, nerves of steel, amorality, psychological insight, and silence.

> She mentioned many places, including: on the subway late at night, in glass elevators, in the men's room of Lord & Taylor's, in the park, in the gym closet, in airplanes, and on top of her desk.

The material following a colon usually is more specific than the preceding introduction, and it therefore clarifies that introductory statement by describing, defining, or elaborating on it. For example:

> "His grandfather the baronet had fallen into the second of the two great categories of English squires: claret-swilling fox hunters and scholarly collectors of everything under the sun." (John Fowles)

> "The other room was the dormitory: six beds, a lot of dust, a little mildew." (Ursula Le Guin)

> "The eagle . . . stood on Deke's shoulder as if in flight: body parallel to the wind and neck extended, angular white head aimed like an arrowhead into the blast, the three-foot white tail fan and seven-foot wings fully stretched." (Dirck Van Sickle)

> "Everyone watched silently, aware that they were witnessing the real thing: a crime of passion, naked woman, dying man." (Larry McMurtry)

A colon can be used to separate two clauses if the second somehow fulfills the first. This is the only instance in which either a colon or a semicolon may be used, and the choice between the two is stylistic. In such compound sentences, the second clause is a restatement or an effect of the first.

> "The words of a living language are like creatures: they are alive." (Morris Bishop)

> "There is only one thing that can be said for Hitler's vicious life: it refutes the theory that only vast, impersonal forces, and not individuals, can shake the world." (George F. Will)

A colon can also be used to introduce a quotation if the quotation is placed at the end of a sentence.

> "The English are mentioned in the Bible: Blessed are the meek, for they shall inherit the earth." (Mark Twain)

If, however, a quotation occurs in the middle of the sentence or is introduced by *that*, a colon is not used.

> Evelyn Waugh said that "Punctuality is the virtue of the bored," and I'm always punctual.

> Paul Valéry claimed that "Poems are never finished, only abandoned."

If long quotations (those 100 words or longer and set apart from the text by indenting and single-spacing) are introduced by a sentence in our text, that sentence should end in a colon.

There are also standardized uses for colons:

a. In formal letters, saluations are followed by a colon.

> Dear Madam or Sir:

b. In footnotes and bibliographies, a colon separates place of publication from the publisher.

> (Boston: Little, Brown & Co.)

c. In book titles, a colon separates the main title from the subtitle.

d. Between numbers a colon can clarify, as with time (5:30 P.M.), ratios (4:3), and chapter and verse (John 3:13).

comma

Commas separate words, phrases, and clauses from other words, phrases, and clauses. Specifically, we use commas:

a. between coordinate clauses in compound sentences

b. after introductory words, phrases, and subordinate clauses

c. after words in a series

d. with parenthetical and nonrestrictive material.

Some commas are mandatory, others are optional, and sometimes comma usage depends on sentence rhythm.

   a. Compound sentences require a comma before the coordinate conjunction *(and, but, yet, or, nor, for)* in order to signal readers that a new clause is beginning.

> "I think everyone fails, but there are so many kinds of failure." (E. M. Forster)

> "The Church says the earth is flat, but I know that it is round, for I have seen the shadow of the moon, and I have more faith in a shadow than in the Church." (Magellan)

> "A little sincerity is a dangerous thing, and a great deal of it is absolutely fatal." (Oscar Wilde)

In long compound sentences, the comma aids readers by providing a break and by marking the end of one clause and the start of another. In short compound sentences, however, the comma is occasionally omitted (unless the conjunction is *but* or *yet*, in which case the comma emphasizes the contrast).

> She shot and he fell.

Be certain, though, that the omission does not cause confusion, as it does here:

> The committee identified the major problems and the recommendations, which are being implemented at present, should improve the situation.

Without a comma after *problems*, readers think that the committee identified both the major problems and the recommendations.

   b. Preliminary words and phrases and introductory subordinate clauses are set off from the main clause by a comma.

Introductory word:

> Furthermore, no one cares if Marriott is a Mormon.

> Baffled, the cop stood aside and let the minister walk out with the money.

Introductory phrase:

> "Like the American Legion and the American Medical Association, I am pleased to report that my mind has not been violated by an original thought since the end of World War II." (Edward Abbey)

"Begun by Madero, interrupted by Huerta's brief reign, renewed by "First Chief" Carranz and his furiously battling rivals, the revolution had in the past year reduced Mexico to a bleeding ruin roamed by the pistol-happy private armies of General Villa, Zapata, Obergón, and other competing chieftans, while General Felix Díaz and Orozco, adherents of Huerta, marshaled their forces for the counter-revolution." (Barbara Tuchman)

Introductory subordinate clause:

Whenever I hear anyone arguing for slavery, I feel a strong impulse to see it tried on him personally. (Abraham Lincoln)

If I had my life to live over again, I would have made a rule to read some poetry and listen to some music at least once a week. (Charles Darwin)

c. Commas also separate items in a series, whether those items are words, phrases, subordinate clauses, or independent clauses.
Words:

The Seven Deadly Sins are pride, lust, envy, gluttony, sloth, anger, and covetousness.

Phrases:

"I fought migraine then, ignored the warnings it sent, went to school and later to work in spite of it, sat through lectures in Middle English and presentations to advertisers with involuntary tears running down the right side of my face, threw up in washrooms, stumbled home by instinct, emptied ice trays onto my bed and tried to freeze the pain in my right temple, wished only for a neurosurgeon who would do a lobotomy on house call, and cursed my imagination." (Joan Didion)

German troops tried to take Leningrad, but they could not carry on the battle without food, without ammunition, without proper clothing, and without the promise of an early spring.

Subordinate clauses:

Jesse told Frank that they would return to their Missouri farm after they had robbed two more banks, after they had shot the Pinkerton men who killed their brother, and after the governor gave them amnesty.

Independent clauses:

> They robbed two more banks, Jesse was killed, and Frank went to prison.

Although the comma before the last item is optional, including it is the safer practice. If every item in a series is followed by *and*, the commas are omitted.

> Jenny liked chocolate mousse and all-night parties and teddy bears and her job as assistant district attorney.

d. Parenthetical and nonrestrictive elements, whether they are embedded in the middle of the sentence or occur at the end, are set off by commas. (See *restrictive, nonrestrictive.*)

> Bill, my older brother, lives in Houston.

> Elephants, for instance, have four knees.

> "Everyone there, including his father, had at least one child who was a source of headache." (Joseph Heller)

> "Water, taken in moderation, cannot hurt anybody." (Mark Twain)

> "A cynic is a man who, when he smells flowers, looks around for a coffin." (H. L. Mencken)

> "Our piano lessons, taught by Sister Mary Patronella, a large woman who dosed with Listerine so that she might breathe freely over her pupils, cost fifty cents an hour and were not worth the price." (Maureen Howard)

> "Happiness in this world, when it comes, comes incidentally." (Nathaniel Hawthorne)

> "Late at night by the glow of torches they began to bring out the dead hunky miners, some so impregnated by coal dust they looked like ancient archaeological finds of considerable significance." (E. L. Doctorow)

complement, compliment

A *complement* is something that supplements or completes.

A *compliment* is praise or flattery.

Both can also be used as verbs: to *complement* is to complete; to *compliment* is to praise.

contemptible, contemptuous

Someone who is *contemptible* deserves contempt and is despicable.

Someone who is *contemptuous* shows contempt and is scornful.

continual, continuous

Continual refers to an event that recurs at intervals over a long period.

> The *continual* revolutions in the Southern Hemisphere threaten world peace.

Continuous applies to prolonged action without interruption.

> The Stuarts ruled Scotland *continuously* for more than three centuries.

council, counsel, consul

A *consul* is an official in the foreign service.

A *council* is an assembly or board, such as the student council or city council.

A *counsel* is an advisor, for example, a lawyer. *Counsel* is also a verb, meaning "to advise."

credible, credulous

Credible means believable.
Credulous means gullible.

criteria, criterion

Criteria is the plural form of *criterion.*

> The main criterion for personal success is self-confidence.

> The criteria for financial success are self-confidence, investment capital, and shrewdness.

dangling modifier

See *modifiers.*

dash

Dashes, which are typed as two hyphens, are used mainly for emphasis because the stylistic effect of dashes is abruptness. They interrupt a sentence and break its flow more so than commas and parentheses do, and therefore they call more attention to the material they mark off. We can use dashes to perform these functions:

a. To set off a parenthetical statement (parentheses or commas could be used in these situations, but dashes are more forceful):

> "Though his naval training and the practice of his vocation rested securely on the dogma that disobedience to his superior officer equaled disobedience to God—and was considerably more dangerous—still, in the farthest, deepest, darkest, most suppressed reaches of his being, there lay vast quicksands of reservations." (Katherine Anne Porter)

b. To present an unexpected or amusing concluding remark:

> "When the blind lead the blind, they both fall into—matrimony." (George Farquhar)
> "Man is the only animal that blushes—or needs to." (Mark Twain)

c. To introduce a summarizing statement after a series of examples:

> "Especially in India and Pakistan, the [wild] hoofed animals are rapidly disappearing, due to destruction of habitat by subsistence agriculture, overcutting of the forest, overgrazing by the scraggy hordes of domestic animals, erosion, flood—the whole dismal cycle of events that accompanies overcrowding by human beings." (Peter Mathiessen)

d. To perform the function of the more formal colon. Like a colon, a dash can introduce a list, an illustration, or a complementary clause:

> "Their quarrel was no more surprising than are most quarrels—inevitable at the time, incredible afterwards." (E. M. Forster)

> "The man who has not anything to boast of but his illustrious ancestors is like a potato—the only good belonging to him is underground." (Sir Thomas Overbury)

> "He brought a quality to uncleship that only certain childless men can bring—adult, and yet not domestic." (Larry McMurtry)

data

Whether *data* is singular or plural is a matter of controversy. Technically, *data* is the plural of *datum,* and therefore *data* should take a plural verb and pronoun.

These data do not support the conclusion.

However, many writers use *data* as a collective noun that takes a singular verb.

This data warrants further study.

desert, dessert

A *desert* is an arid region.
A *dessert* is what you eat.

device, devise

A *device* (noun) is a tool.
To *devise* (verb) is to plan or invent.

different from, different than
> *Different from* is preferred.

discreet, discrete
> *Discreet* means judiciously cautious or prudent.
> *Discrete* means separate.

disinterested, uninterested
> *Disinterested* means impartial.
> *Uninterested* means indifferent or not interested.
> The first indicates lack of self-interest; the second, lack of any
interest.

due to
> *Due to* is acceptable as a predicate adjective following a linking
verb.

> > Most highway fatalities are due to speeding.

But opening a sentence with *due to* or following a nonlinking verb with
due to is less acceptable.

> > UNACCEPTABLE: Due to the weather, the concert was can-
> > celled.

> > UNACCEPTABLE: The referee ended the fight due to the
> > challenger's broken nose.

Use *because of* or *owing to* instead.

due to the fact that
> Use *because* for conciseness.

effect
> See *affect, effect.*

e.g.
> This is the abbreviation of "for example." Many persons confuse *e.g.*
and *i.e.,* which stands for "that is." These abbreviations should be used
only in appendixes, footnotes, and parenthetical expressions.

either, neither
> As pronouns, *either* and *neither* take singular verbs.

> > Either refuses to burn.

> > Neither is flammable.

When *either* or *neither* is followed by a prepositional phrase containing a
plural pronoun, the tendency is to use a plural verb, but the tendency
should be guarded against.

> > UNACCEPTABLE: Neither of them are capable of parachuting.

> > ACCEPTABLE: I wonder if either of them is flying today.

The verb in *either . . . or* and *neither . . . nor* correlative conjunction constructions depends on the elements within the constructions. If both elements are singular, the verb is singular.

> Neither Gertrude nor Claudius sees the ghost.

If both elements are plural, the verb is plural.

> Either the Capulets or the Montagues are at fault.

If one element is singular and the other is plural, the verb agrees with the element closer to it.

> Neither the guards nor Hamlet is certain of the ghost's intentions.

> Either the President or his aides are lying.

elicit, illicit
Elicit is a verb meaning to evoke.
Illicit is an adjective meaning illegal.

eminent, imminent
Eminent means noteworthy or prominent.
Imminent means impending, about to occur.

> The eminent scientist knew that the volcanic eruption was imminent.

enthused
Use *enthusiastic* instead.

everyday, every day
Everyday is an adjective that means commonplace or routine, as in "everyday hassles" or "an everyday suit."
Every day means each day: "Every day that we are angry we lose a day."

everyone, everybody
Both *everyone* and *everybody* take a singular verb, and the subsequent pronoun must be singular.

> Everyone thinks he or she sees most clearly.

> Not: Everybody thinks they see most clearly.

except
See *accept*.

fact
Avoid *true fact*, which is redundant. Where possible, avoid also using *the fact that* because it is usually unnecessary and always wordy.

WORDY: She was amazed by the fact that she won the lottery.

IMPROVED: She was amazed that she won the lottery.

WORDY: He decided that he would leave the party due to the fact that all the liquor was consumed.

IMPROVED: He decided that he would leave the party since the liquor was consumed.

farther, further

Farther applies to physical distance.

Cheyenne is 5 miles farther from Dallas than Atlanta is.

Further applies to time, degree, and figurative distance.

After further consideration, the Haitians decided to risk the journey.

faze

See *phase.*

fewer, less

Fewer applies to things that are counted; *less* applies to amounts.

UNACCEPTABLE: This express line is for persons with ten items or less.

PREFERABLE: This express line is for persons with ten items or fewer.

fiancé, fiancée

Fiancé is masculine; *fiancée* is feminine.

financial, fiscal, monetary

Financial, the broadest term, refers to transactions of large sums of money.
Fiscal refers to governmental policies concerning money.
Monetary refers to the coinage, printing, or circulation of money.

good, well

Good is an adjective: "good food, good company, good wine."
Well is an adverb: "They fought well and lived long."

hanged, hung

People are *hanged* (meaning executed); objects are *hung.*

hardly

See *can't hardly.*

he or she

Many people rightly object to the use of *man* and *he* to designate both sexes because the generic terms are sexist and exclusive. The phrase *he or she* gives equal status, but it is stylistically awkward. A better solution is to make the pronouns plural since the plural is the same for both sexes, whether it is first person plural (we), second person plural (you), or third person plural (they).

SEXIST: A student who wants to attend the game must bring his activity card.

REPHRASED: A student who wants to attend the game must bring his or her activity card.

IMPROVED: Students wanting to attend the game must bring their activity cards.

See *sexist language.*

help but . . .

See *can't help but.*

hyphen

Use a hyphen:

a. To divide a word at the end of a line of type:

ser·geant   cross·bow   vin·di·cate
ev·o·lu·tion   gram·mar   par·a·dise
in·com·mu·ni·ca·tive throm·bo·sis   he·red·i·ty

Always divide between syllables. (Hence, never divide a monosyllabic word, such as *dance.*)

Never divide a word so that one letter is left dangling by itself: *i·dol, a·buse, e·quate, par·a·noi·a, o·gress.*

Always divide hyphenated words (e.g., *court-martial*) at the hyphen. Don't divide contractions: *they'll, couldn't.*

When in doubt, consult a dictionary to see where you should divide a word.

b. To join compound modifiers. When noun phrases act as adjectives, they are hyphenated.

Seneca lived in the first century. He was a first-century philosopher and dramatist.

She likes punk rock. Her sister sings in a punk-rock band.

Cinderella is a fairy tale. Farah leads a fairy-tale existence.

c. To separate certain prefixes and suffixes from the words they join:

Hyphens are used to separate prefixes from proper nouns: *post-Vietnam era, un-American, pro-Reagan, pre-Raphaelite.*

Hyphens are used with the prefixes *all-, ex-,* and *self-: all-absorbing, all-knowing, ex-husband, ex-convict, self-indulgent, self-confidence.*

Hyphens are used between single capital letters and suffixes: *A-frame, G-string, H-bomb, T-shirt, U-turn.*

    d. To divide compound numbers from twenty-one to ninety-nine

> "England has fifty-two religions and only two sauces." (Voltaire)

Fractions are hyphenated when used as modifiers.

> The pool is one-eighth full.

> One eighth of the delegates had hangovers.

    e. To join compound expressions:

so-called	go-getter	life-size	happy-go-lucky
hand-knit	gold-filled	drive-in	touch-and-go
well-spoken	one-sided	first-rate	holier-than-thou

There is little logic behind hyphenation of compound words. Sometimes words are hyphenated when they are one part of speech, but not hyphenated as another:

ice-skate (verb)	ice skate (noun)
free-lance (verb and adjective)	free lance (noun)
low-down (adjective)	lowdown (noun, meaning the whole truth)
middle-class (adjective)	middle class (noun)

The best advice is to consult a dictionary.

    f. To avoid confusion between words:

re-creation	recreation
re-sort	resort

i.e.

    See *e.g.*

if, whether

    In general practice, *if* and *whether* are used interchangeably to introduce questions or statements of uncertainty.

> It is difficult to say if living together before marriage decreases the chance of divorce for a couple.

> Diplomats could not predict whether sending military aid to Somalia would cause the Russians to send aid to Ethiopia.

When an alternative is explicitly stated, *whether* should be used.

> "What difference does it make to the dead, the orphans and the homeless, whether the mad destruction is wrought under

the name of totalitarianism or the holy name of liberty or democracy?" (Mahatma Gandhi)

imminent

See *eminent*.

illusion

See *allusion*.

imply, infer

To imply is to suggest or state indirectly; *to infer* is to draw a conclusion.

> The detective implied that it was not suicide.

> The wealthy young widow inferred that she was the prime suspect.

in, into

In indicates location or condition.

> Migrant workers in California are in a predicament because of the crop failure.

Into indicates movement to an inside.

> Illegal aliens from Mexico cross into California to find work on farms.

The distinction between the two prepositions is illustrated by these examples:

> He jumped into the pool.

> She jumped in the pool.

The first example means to jump from the deck or diving board into the water; the second means to be in the water already and to jump up and down in the pool.

irregardless

Incorrect. Use *regardless*.

italics

Writers indicate italics in their manuscripts by underlining the words that they want italicized. Italics are used for several purposes:

a. To indicate foreign words that have not become part of English.

> Power, not justice, was Ferdinand Marcos' *raison d'être*.

> After his overthrow, the Shah became *persona non grata* wherever he went.

Many borrowed words have become integrated into English: debutante, chauffeur, bourgeois, avant-garde, genre, hubris, cliché. Such naturalized words should not be italicized.

b. To indicate titles of books, newspapers, magazines, movies, plays, pamphlets, operas, symphonies, long poems, ships, and aircraft.

c. To indicate that a word is being considered as a linguistic example.

> Cheever uses the word *lugubrious* with great frequency.

d. To show emphasis.

> You *look*, but you do not *see*.

Most writers use emphatic italics too much; as with any device, it loses its power if used too frequently.

its, it's

> *Its* is a possessive pronoun, like *his*, or *her*.
>
> > Every action has its consequence.
>
> *It's* is a contraction, like *can't*, and means *it is* or *it has*.
>
> > It's not easy to predict consequences.

If you can substitute *it is* for the word, the word is *it's*.

lay, lie

> *Lay* means "to place or put."
> *Lie* means "to recline."

Confusion occurs because the past tense of *lie* is *lay*.

present:	lie	lay
past:	lay	laid
past participle:	lain	laid

lead, led

> The past tense of *lead*, meaning to escort, is *led*. Confusion occurs because *led* is pronounced as is the noun *lead* (a metal), which is spelled as is the verb *lead*.

less

> See *fewer*.

lighted, lit

> Either form is acceptable as the past tense of the verb *light*.

like, as

> Although the distinction between *like* and *as* is fading, formal

writing insists that *like* remain a preposition and *as* a conjunction; *like* introduces a word or phrase, while *as* introduces an adverbial clause.

> UNACCEPTABLE: The wine tasted like it had been uncorked for days.

> UNACCEPTABLE: Winston tastes good, like a cigarette should.

> UNACCEPTABLE: Visitors to Machu Picchu feel like Balboa did when he first gazed on the Pacific Ocean.

In all three of these constructions, what follows *like* is a clause, and therefore *as* or *as if* would be preferable. But when the clause is elliptical—that is, when the verb is not expressed—*like* is usually acceptable:

> The band sounded like [it was] country and western.

> A few presidents have acted like [they were] kings.

> It looks like [it is going to] rain.

Like is correct when it is used prepositionally:

> Like his brother, Michael Spinks is a boxer.

To avoid the issue altogether, some writers use *the way*:

> The band sounds the way a country-and-western band sounds.

loose, lose

   Loose (adjective) means unfastened or unrestrained; *lose* (verb) means to mislay or to be defeated.

media

   Media, meaning mass communications, is plural (*medium* is singular) and takes a plural verb.

> UNACCEPTABLE: The media seldom has anything cheerful to report.

> UNACCEPTABLE: The medias report destruction, murder, and failure because those are the things we like to hear about.

> ACCEPTABLE: Television is a passive medium.

> ACCEPTABLE: The media have certain obligations to the public.

modifiers

   A modifier is a word or group of words that describes or qualifies the meaning of another word or group of words. For example, adjectives modify nouns or pronouns, and adverbs modify verbs or other adverbs.

ADJECTIVE	ADVERB

Green houses   *always* make me homesick.

Other elements can also act as modifiers: infinitive phrases, prepositional phrases, participial phrases, and so forth.

The main thing to remember about modifiers is to place them as near as possible to the words they qualify. When modifiers are misplaced, the meaning is distorted, and confusion ensues:

> She looked at the horsemen with hatred.

Did the person look with hatred, or did the horsemen have hatred?

> "One morning I shot an elephant in my pajamas. How he got in my pajamas I'll never know." (Groucho Marx)

One particular kind of misplaced modifier is called a *dangling modifier,* and it occurs when a modifying phrase seemingly refers to a word other than the one intended. It is attached to the wrong noun or pronoun. Usually the intended meaning is eventually discernible, but the dangling modifier causes momentary confusion and often sounds absurd.

> To phone home, a communication system had to be built.

An introductory phrase modifies the first noun or pronoun after the phrase. According to the sentence above, the communication system itself is the agent wanting to phone home. The true agent is not even given.

> REVISION: To phone home, E.T. had to build his own communication system.

Here, the agent of the infinitive *to phone* is E.T., and the phrase no longer dangles.

> DANGLING INFINITIVE: To perform on stage, adrenalin is as necessary as talent.

Adrenalin is doing the performing? Of course not.

> REVISION: To perform on stage, one must have adrenalin as well as talent.

> DANGLING PARTICIPLE: Stranded on a desert island, a ship didn't rescue Alexander Selkirk for five years.

The ship wasn't stranded on a desert island.

> REVISION: Stranded on a desert island, Alexander Selkirk wasn't rescued for five years.

DANGLING GERUND: Running down the street, my nose felt cold.

Although noses have been known to run, they do not run in the sense expressed here; the person is running.

REVISION: Running down the street, I felt that my nose was cold.

ALTERNATIVE: As I ran down the street, my nose was cold.

DANGLING PREPOSITIONAL PHRASE: By debating the issue at length, a compromise was reached.

REVISION: By debating the issue at length, the committee reached a compromise.

DANGLING PREPOSITIONAL PHRASE: On his sixty-fifth birthday, the boss asked Lutwack to retire.

Not on the boss' birthday—rather, on Lutwack's birthday.

REVISION: On his sixty-fifth birthday, Lutwack was asked to retire by his boss.

ALTERNATIVE: The boss asked Lutwack to retire on Lutwack's sixty-fifth birthday.

DANGLING CLAUSE: When he was 12, Jim's father gave him a canoe.

REVISION: When Jim was 12, his father gave him a canoe.

(Certain idiomatic expressions have become acceptable even though their attachment to the sentence is loose: *strictly speaking, judging by, considering, granted, generally speaking, providing, to tell the truth,* and so on.)

Squinting, another form of misplaced modifier, occurs when a modifier—usually an adverb—is placed between two words, either of which might be the term being modified.

The FBI agents decided *when the hijackers landed* to storm the plane.

The sentence is ambiguous since the placement of the modifying clause allows for two interpretations:

a. After the hijackers landed, the FBI decided to storm the plane.

b. The FBI decided to storm the plane as soon as the hijackers landed.

SQUINTING: At the present time *only* the Seattle area is experiencing a power shortage.

Readers should not have to guess what our meaning is; our grammatical construction should clearly reflect our intended meaning.

most, almost

Most means the greatest in number or quantity.

Aunt Lil's pickled squash was judged the most tasty in the competition.

Most is also acceptable in the sense of *very* where no direct comparison is intended.

Faye Dunaway has a most enchanting face.

Almost means very nearly but not quite.

She weighs almost 200 pounds.

Almost everyone says her weight complements her personality.

Don't use *most* when you mean *almost.*

UNACCEPTABLE: Most everyone agrees on that point, including her husband.

nauseated, nauseous

Nauseated means suffering from nausea; *nauseous* means causing nausea.

I was nauseated from my own cooking; the boiled okra was particularly nauseous.

neither

See *either.*

none

None may take either a singular or plural verb. Use a singular verb when you can substitute *no one* for *none.*

None of the band members wants to play without pay.

Use a plural verb when you can substitute *no persons* or *no things.*

None are so pathetic as those who survive third-degree facial burns.

Regardless of whether the verb is singular or plural, the related pronouns must agree with the verb:

> None have their . . .
>
> None has his or her . . .

nonrestrictive
See *restrictive.*

number
The traditional rule for deciding whether *number* takes a singular or plural verb is that when preceded by *the* it takes a singular verb, but when preceded by *a* it takes a plural verb.

> A number of men are going alligator hunting.
>
> The number of alligators left is small.

old adage
Redundant because an adage is an old saying. Use *adage.*

one of those who
Takes a plural verb.

> She is one of those people who believe that they were born to rule.

only
Only should be placed next to the word it modifies. Precise placement prevents ambiguity. Notice the differences in meaning among these statements:

> My father gave my sister only $5.
>
> My father gave only my sister $5.
>
> My father only gave [he didn't loan] my sister $5.
>
> My father gave my only sister $5.
>
> Only my father gave my sister $5.

The tendency is to place *only* in front of the verb instead of the actual word it modifies. The song "I Only Have Eyes For You" implies that the rest of the person belongs to someone else; what is intended is "I have eyes only for you."

parentheses
Parentheses are used to mark off qualifying or amplifying remarks within a sentence. Parenthetical phrases are subdued interruptions;

unlike dashes, which emphasize an interpolation, parentheses subordinate digressive or incidental material.

> "There always seemed to be shoes to put on and shoes to take off, snowsuits to be zipped and unzipped, bottoms to be wiped, tears to be dried, and when the sun went down (she saw it set from the kitchen window) there was the supper to be cooked, the baths, the bedtime story, and the Lord's Prayer." (John Cheever)

> "She kept complaining that the hotel had no beauty parlor (untrue) and that she looked a mess (incontestable)." (S. J. Perelman)

> "American politicians from Thomas Jefferson through Franklin Roosevelt to Ronald Reagan (to list them in declining order) have spoken of the family farm as the backbone of the nation. Jefferson even meant it." (Edward Abbey)

> "One summer his parents brought a woman from the city to help with the housework; the first day the woman finished off the gin (filling the bottle with water, his father later discovered), and the next day she was sent back to the city." (Charles Simmons)

Notice that no punctuation mark ever precedes an opening parenthesis; punctuation marks (colon, semicolon, comma) follow the closing parenthesis.

phase, faze

A *phase* is one stage in a development.

> The second phase of the President's economic recovery plan isn't working.

Faze, a verb, means to disturb or to disrupt one's composure.

> The news that his economic recovery plan isn't working didn't faze the President.

phenomena, phenomenon

Many persons incorrectly believe that *phenomena* is singular; it is plural and takes a plural verb.

> UNACCEPTABLE: This is an interesting phenomena.

> REVISED: These are interesting phenomena.

> REVISED: This is an interesting phenomenon.

Phenomenon is the singular form.

presently

Presently does not mean "at the present time." It means "soon."

principal, principle

Principal is usually an adjective meaning foremost in importance; as a noun, it refers either to finance (the sum of money owed) or the person of highest position (such as a school principal).

> The principal reason for denying the request is your character.

> The principal of my junior high school was a firm believer in corporal punishment.

A *principle* (always a noun) is a basic assumption, a truth, or an ethical standard.

> The principle of equality demands that women be given the same pay that men receive.

proceed, precede

To *proceed* is to continue after an interruption.

> After a 15-minute recess, the judge asked the witness to proceed with her testimony.

To *precede* is to come before in time or rank.

> The court reporter preceded the judge into the courtroom.

proved, proven

Both are mistakenly thought to be acceptable as the past participle of *prove*; only *proved* is acceptable.

> UNACCEPTABLE: He has proven that he can fly.

> ACCEPTABLE: She has proved that she can fly farther.

Proven is an adjective meaning "tested by time"; as an adjective, it always modifies a noun or pronoun: "a proven record, a proven cure."

quotation marks

See page 575.

real, really

Don't use the adjective *real* to substitute for the adverb *really*.

> ACCEPTABLE: Her coat was real leopard.

> ACCEPTABLE: The killing of rare animals for their hides really ought to be prohibited.

UNACCEPTABLE: People who buy leopard and cheetah coats make me real angry.

reason is because, reason why
Both usages are redundant.

UNACCEPTABLE: The main reason why career persons become dissatisfied with their careers is because they reach their peak early.

IMPROVED: The main reason career persons become dissatisfied with their careers is that they reach their peak early.

IMPROVED: Career persons become dissatisfied with their careers mainly because they reach their peak early.

restrictive, nonrestrictive
A restrictive clause is essential to the meaning of a sentence, is not set off by commas, and is introduced by *that* or *who*.

Cowboys *who wear red chaps* are pretentious.

If we were to omit the restrictive clause, the meaning of the sentence would be different: "Cowboys are pretentious." The restrictive clause limits the modified term, cowboys, to a certain subcategory: cowboys who wear red chaps.

A nonrestrictive clause contains information that is not essential to the meaning of the sentence. A nonrestrictive clause provides description or detail that can be omitted without altering the meaning of the sentence, and the clause begins with *which* or *who*.

Joseph Conrad, who was Polish, didn't speak English until he was grown.

Notice that a nonrestrictive clause is set off by commas.

The Edsel, which was taken off the market after a couple of years, was a financial fiasco for Ford.

semicolon
The most frequent use of the semicolon is to connect two independent clauses. A semicolon substitutes for a period when we wish to show that two statements are closely related.

"Before I got married I had six theories about bringing up children; now I have six children, and no theories." (John Wilmot, Earl of Rochester)

> "In composing, as a general rule, run your pen through every other word you have written; you have no idea what vigor it will give your style." (Rev. Sydney Smith)

> "The brain is a wonderful organ; it starts working the moment you get up in the morning, and does not stop until you get into the office." (Robert Frost)

> "[Although] the adults usually left me alone, I had to watch out for the village boys. They were great hunters; I was their game." (Jerzy Kosinski)

In each example, a period might have been used because the statements on both sides of the semicolon can act as complete sentences. However, to emphasize the close relationship of the two statements, the writers used semicolons to create one compound sentence. The choice between period and semicolon in such instances is one of style as well as logic.

When the clauses use the same verb, we may omit the verb in the second clause for compression.

> The British excel at understatement; Americans, at overstatement.

The semicolon is necessary before transitional phrases (e.g., *as a result, in other words, on the contrary*) and conjunctive adverbs (*however, therefore, consequently, furthermore*) to separate independent clauses.

> The oil-producing countries in the Middle East realize that once their only natural resource is depleted they will again become politically powerless; therefore, they are buying Western companies, gold, land, and banks while they have excessive sums of money.

Semicolons are also useful for separating items in a list when the items have internal punctuation. In such cases, they replace commas. For example, the many commas in the following sentence cause confusion because readers can't tell where the units should be divided:

> Parisians accuse Americans of being loud, though no louder than the Italians, crass, particularly in matters of food and art, inarticulate, in English as well as in French, cultureless, prudish, especially the ones from the center of America, militaristic to the point of paranoia and dangerousness, politically naive, and, to a degree that offends the whole world, materialistic.

By substituting semicolons for the commas to indicate divisions, we achieve greater clarity:

> Parisians accuse Americans of being loud, though no louder than the Italians; crass, particularly in matters of food and art; inarticulate, in English as well as in French; cultureless; prudish, especially the ones from the center of America; militaristic to the point of paranoia and dangerousness; politically naive; and, to a degree that offends the whole world, materialistic.

Occasionally we use a semicolon to separate parts of a long sentence, especially if there are internal commas and if there is a logical place to make divisions, such as parallel elements:

> "One visualizes [London] as a tract of quivering grey, intelligent without purpose, and excitable without love; as a spirit that has altered before it can be chronicled; as a heart that certainly beats, but with no pulsation of humanity." (E. M. Forster)

sensual, sensuous

Sensual connotes sexuality or voluptuousness, as with Warren Beatty or Raquel Welch.

Sensuous is a broader term that refers to gratification of or appeal to any of the senses; the landscape of Normandy or the music of Ravel can be considered *sensuous.*

sexist language

Because our perception of reality is formed to some extent by our language, sexist language can perpetuate sexual stereotyping, which is why the women's movement has objected to sexist bias in language. *Sexist language* refers to masculine nouns and pronouns that are used to refer to both men and women. For example:

> *Man* is the only thinking animal.

> Every student must pay *his* tuition by October 1.

> All *mailmen* are required to wear official uniforms.

Each sentence deprives women of their identity by classifying them in male categories, although the categories are intended to be generic. Tired of this anonymity, women object to the exclusion and demand equal recognition in language.

Nouns. Avoid using masculine titles for jobs that either sex can perform. Almost always we can find a neutral term to express the same idea; such words as *operator, worker,* and *supervisor* are common gender nouns, meaning that they can refer to either sex.

> fireman—firefighter
> mailman—mail carrier, postal worker
> longshoreman—shipyard worker
> shine boy—shoe shiner
> bell boy—bell hop
> water boy—water carrier
> weather man—meterologist, weather forecaster
> policeman—police officer
> cattleman—rancher, cattle breeder
> salesman—sales representative, sales person

The practice of changing compound words from *-man* to *-person* sometimes sounds unnatural, and therefore substitutes should be sought:

> camera man—camera person—camera operator
> warehouseman—warehouse person—warehouse worker
> manpower—person power—personnel

Occasionally sexist language takes a different form: feminine nouns that have slightly derogatory connotations or that are used to designate duties traditionally assigned to women:

> girl Friday—assistant
> stewardess—flight attendant (to include men who work in this
>   position)
> housewife—homemaker
> wash woman—laundry worker

Pronouns. Try to avoid using masculine pronouns when referring to both sexes.

> Often Unsatisfactory: Everyone wonders about *his* future.

Usually we can avoid such constructions in one of the following ways:
   a. *his or her*:

> Everyone wonders about his or her future.

This alternative is wordy and awkward; when possible, rephrase.
   b. *they or we* (personal pronouns that can refer to both sexes):

> We all wonder about our future.

> All persons wonder about their future.

   c. *you*:

> You wonder about your future.

d. eliminate gender designation altogether:

> The future worries everyone.

> Everyone's future is a source of concern.

Writers should use their own judgment in these situations to eliminate sexist language.

sit, set

To *sit* is to rest *(sit, sat, sat)*; to *set* is to place *(set, set, set)*.

> Mr. Rick sits at a sidewalk café and sips Turkish coffee. He sets down his cup and fumbles for a cigarette.

Confusion occurs because occasionally *set* is intransitive: the sun sets, hens set, jello and cement set, people set out on a journey. And occasionally *sit* is transitive: a judge sits a jury, and Clint Eastwood sits a horse well.

site, sight

A *site* is a location or plot of land; a *sight* is a view or a spectacle.

> The site of the new high-rise building has been chosen.

> We visited the major sights of Paris: the Tower, the Louvre, Notre Dame, the Rive Gauche, and Montmartre.

split infinitive

When an adverb or adverbial phrase is inserted between the *to* and the verb form of an infinitive, the result is called a *split infinitive*; for example: "to continually interrupt." Split infinitives are unworthy of the controversy surrounding them. Just as there are good reasons not to split infinitives, there are good reasons to split them occasionally. The rule is that you shouldn't split infinitives unless you can't avoid splitting.

> The editor's job was *to periodically review* rejected reports.

If *periodically* was placed before or after the infinitive, the meaning would be ambiguous. Split infinitives are acceptable to avoid awkwardness or ambiguity; otherwise, the adverb should be positioned on either side of the infinitive, especially when several words separate the two parts of the infinitive (as in "*to* even a further degree *impede*").

To avoid split infinitives, we can sometimes restructure the sentence, delete the adverb (particularly if it is deadwood such as *actually, really, totally, further*), or change the adverb to an adjective.

Unnecessary split	Improvement
To really show improvement, a patient must have daily therapy.	To improve, a patient must have daily therapy.

We need to precisely analyze the market.

We must precisely analyze the market.
We need a precise analysis.

squinting modifier

See *modifier.*

stationary, stationery

Stationary (*a* for adjective) means not moving.
Stationery, a noun, is writing paper.

sure, surely

Sure is an adjective; *surely* is an adverb. In colloquial speech one frequently hears *sure* used as an adverb:

> The photographer sure had a difficult time getting the twins to pose.

In writing, though, *sure* is unacceptable as an adverb. If *surely* sounds too formal or pretentious, use *certainly.*

> If given half a chance, Mike and Ike could surely destroy a studio.

than

Is it *than me* (*her, him, them*—objective case) or *than I* (*she, he, they*—nominative case)? Consider the difference in meaning between these two statements:

> I hate to wash dishes more than her.

> I hate to wash dishes more than she.

The first means, "I hate to wash dishes more than I hate her"; or, "I hate to wash dishes more than I hate to wash her." The second means, "I hate to wash dishes more than she hates to wash dishes."

Problems arise in elliptical clauses—that is, where words are omitted, especially the verb:

> Joe Louis hit harder than he [hit], and Ali jabbed faster than he [jabbed], but the fans like him more than [they liked] them.

till, until

Both forms are acceptable and are interchangeable. *Until* is slightly more formal. *'Til* is a needless variant of *until.*

toward, towards

Toward is the preferred American form, though both are acceptable.

try and

Use *try to.*

UNACCEPTABLE:	Let's try and win this game.
IMPROVED:	Let's try to win this game.
UNACCEPTABLE:	Try and make me.

Similar misuses occur with *come and, see and,* and *be sure and.*

unique

Because *unique* means the only one of its kind, it should not be modified by adverbs of comparison or degree.

> UNACCEPTABLE: more unique, most unique, rather unique, very unique, somewhat unique

Instead of *unique* in situations of comparison, substitute *rare, remarkable, exceptional,* or *unusual.*

> ACCEPTABLE: more rare, most remarkable, rather exceptional, very unusual

waive, wave, waver, waiver

To *waive* is to relinquish a claim or to refrain from enforcing a rule; a *waiver* is a relinquishment or a document signifying relinquishment.

> The dean agreed to waive the foreign language requirement because the student stuttered. He gave the student a waiver.

To *wave* is to motion back and forth (like waving good-bye).
To *waver* is to vacillate or to show irresolution.

> The President wavers on the issue of aid to Nicaragua.

whether

See *if.*

which, that

The rule for formal writing is that *which* is used to introduce nonrestrictive clauses and *that* is used to introduce restrictive clauses. Often, however, *which* is also used in restrictive clauses.

One may frequently omit *that* in restrictive clauses:

> Ahab said [that] he would not turn back.

But if omitting the *that* causes confusion, keep it:

> Other policies presuppose the storage of and accountability for governmental supplies would be the responsibility of a central warehouse.

Without a *that* after *presuppose*, readers do not realize that a subordinate clause is starting.

> CLEARER: Other policies presuppose that the storage of. . . .

who, whom, whoever, whomever

Who or *whoever* acts as a subject of a clause.

> "I hate all sports as rabidly as a person who likes sports hates common sense." (H. L. Mencken)

> Golda was the kind of politician who the Israelis believed could keep the peace by keeping her opponents in a state of confusion.

> Who shot an apple off his son's head?

> The king declared that whoever refused to pay taxes would be imprisoned.

Whom or *whomever* is used as objects of infinitives or of prepositions, or as direct objects or as subjects of infinitives.

> Whom was the message addressed to?

> Whom would you like to see?

> Please apologize to whomever you spilled coffee on.

> Whom is the FBI wiretapping now?

whose, who's

Whose is the possessive form of who or which.

> Stalin, whose regime murdered thousands of political prisoners, is considered a tyrant even by the Soviet government.

Who's is a contraction of *who is* that appears in questions.

> Who's on first?

-wise

The practice in business and government of adding *-wise* at the end of nouns to mean "with respect to" should be avoided: saleswise, aviationwise, diseasewise, energywise, capitalwise, opportunitywise, costwise, and so forth. The same idea always can be expressed more gracefully another way.

> AWKWARD: Facilitywise, the new gym is superior, but staffwise, it is worse.

IMPROVED: The facilities of the new gym are superior, but the staff is inferior.

Attaching -*wise* to nouns is acceptable to indicate position or "in the manner of," and there are standardized words formed this way: clockwise, edgewise, lengthwise, likewise.

(continued from page iv)
of Pittsburgh Press. © 1979 by University of Pittsburgh Press.

Page 110 From *In Cold Blood*, by Truman Capote. Copyright © 1965 by Truman Capote. Reprinted by permission of Random House, Inc.

Page 119 Reprinted by permission; © 1960 John Updike. Originally in *The New Yorker.*

Page 120 Reprinted by permission of the author.

Page 121 Reprinted by permission of the author.

Page 123 Reprinted by permission of the author.

Pages 129 and 618 Reprinted by permission of Louisiana State University Press ¹from *A Confederacy of Dunces* by John Kennedy Toole. Copyright © 1980 by Thelma D. Toole.

Pages 130 and 769 Copyright 1951 by John Cheever. Reprinted from *The Stories of John Cheever*, by permission of Alfred A. Knopf, Inc.

Page 132 Reprinted by permission of the author.

Page 134 From *One Man's America*, by Alistair Cooke. Copyright 1952 by Alistair Cooke. Reprinted by permission of Alfred A. Knopf, Inc., and the author.

Pages 135 and 349 From *Nobody Ever Died of Old Age* by Sharon R. Curtin. Copyright © 1972 by Sharon R. Curtin. By permission of Little, Brown and Company in association with The Atlantic Monthly Press.

Pages 145, 692, 735, and 742 From *Broca's Brain*, by Carl Sagan. Copyright © 1979 by Carl Sagan. Reprinted by permission of Random House, Inc.

Pages 148 and 703 With permission from *Natural History*, Vol. 88, No. 1; Copyright the American Museum of Natural History, 1978.

Pages 148, 609, and 701 Barry Lopez, excerpted from *Of Wolves and Men*. Copyright © 1978 Barry Holstun Lopez. Reprinted with the permission of Charles Scribner's Sons.

Page 152 From *Keep the Last Bullet for Yourself* by Thomas B. Marquis. Reprinted by permission of Reference Publications, Inc., Algonac, Michigan.

Page 155 From "Introduction" in *Roget's Pocket Thesaurus*. Reprinted by permission of Pocket Books, a division of Simon & Schuster, Inc.

Page 157 Copyright 1969 Time, Inc. All Rights Reserved. Reprinted by permission from *Time.*

Page 158 Reprinted by permission of the author.

Page 164 Reprinted by permission of Farrar, Straus & Giroux Inc.: Excerpts from *The Amnesty International Report on Torture.* Copyright © 1975 by Amnesty International.

Page 166 Copyright 1986, by Newsweek, Inc. All Rights Reserved. Reprinted by permission.

Page 169 Reprinted by permission of International Creative Management. First published in *The New Yorker* magazine. Copyright © 1977 by Jane Kramer.

Page 174 From *The Common Sense of Science* by Jacob Bronowski. Reprinted by permission of Harvard University Press and Heinemann Educational Books.

Page 177 Copyright 1986, by Newsweek, Inc. All Rights Reserved. Reprinted by permission.

Page 183 Pages 52–54 of "Education" from *One Man's Meat* by E. B. White. Copyright 1939, 1967 by E. B. White. Reprinted by permission of Harper & Row, Publishers, Inc.

Page 186 From Donald Dike and David H. Zucker, eds., *Selected Essays of Delmore Schwartz* (Chicago: University of Chicago Press, 1970). Reprinted by permission of The University of Chicago Press.

Page 190 From *The New York Times Magazine*, May 20, 1956. Copyright © 1956 by The New York Times Company. Reprinted by permission.

Page 194 Reprinted by permission of the author.

Page 197 From *The World in a Frame* by Leo Braudy. Reprinted by permission of Doubleday & Company, Inc.

Page 200 From *The Nation*, July 7, 1979. Reprinted by permission of the Nation Associates Inc..

Page 204 From *The Stars in Their Courses,*

by Sir James Jeans. Copyrighted by and reprinted by permission of the publisher, Cambridge University Press.

Page 208 © 1973 by *Esquire* magazine. © 1973, 1985 by Peter Bogdanovich. Reprinted by permission of Arbor House Publishing Company.

Page 210 Reprinted by permission of Farrar, Straus & Giroux Inc.: Excerpt from "O Rotten Gotham—Sliding Down into the Behavioral Sink" from *The Pump House Gang.* Copyright © 1968 by Tom Wolfe. Copyright © 1966 by The World Journal Tribune Corporation. Copyright © 1964, 1965, 1966 by The New York Herald Tribune.

Page 216 Abridged from pages 118–126 of "Pilgrims, Saints and Spacemen" in *Disturbing the Universe* by Freeman Dyson. Copyright © 1979 by Freeman J. Dyson. Reprinted by permission of Harper & Row, Publishers, Inc.

Page 232 Excerpt "A psychologist friend . . . on the Samurai Scale." (pp. 97–99) from *The Genesis Factor* by Robert A. Wallace. Copyright © 1979 by Robert A. Wallace. By permission of William Morrow & Company.

Page 234 From *Essays of Five Decades* by J. B. Priestley. Reprinted by permission of A D Peters & Co., Ltd.

Page 239 Copyright 1986, by Newsweek, Inc. All Rights Reserved. Excerpted by permission.

Page 247 Reprinted by permission of the author.

Pages 248 and 630 From *Metropolitan Life* by Fran Lebowitz. Copyright © 1974, 1975, 1976, 1977, 1978 by Fran Lebowitz. Reprinted by permission of the publisher, E. P. Dutton, a division of New American Library.

Page 254 From *The Way Things Work*, Vol. II. Copyright © 1971 by George Allen & Unwin, Ltd. Reprinted by permission of Simon & Schuster, Inc.

Page 256 "Steps in the Survey Q3R Method" (pp. 32–33) from *Effective Study*, 4th edition, by Francis P. Robinson. Copyright 1941, 1946 by Harper & Row, Publishers, Inc. Copyright

© 1961, 1970 by Francis P. Robinson. Reprinted by permission of Harper & Row, Publishers, Inc.

Page 259 From *The New York Times Guide to Home Repairs Without a Man* by Bernard Gladstone. Reprinted by permission of the author.

Page 261 From *Esquire*, August 1983. Reprinted by permission of the author.

Page 264 From "How Dictionaries Are Made" in *Language in Thought and Action*, Fourth Edition, by S. I. Hayakawa, copyright © 1978 by Harcourt Brace Jovanovich, Inc. Reprinted by permission of the publisher.

Page 267 From *Red Giants and White Dwarfs* by Robert Jastrow. Reprinted by permission of the author.

Page 270 From p. 183 of "Stalking" in *A Pilgrim at Tinker Creek* by Annie Dillard. Copyright © 1974 by Annie Dillard. Reprinted by permission of Harper & Row, Publishers, Inc.

Page 275 Abridged from pp. 251–263 in *Brain Surgeon: An Intimate View of His World* by Lawrence Shainberg (J. B. Lippincott). Copyright © 1979 by Lawrence Shainberg. Reprinted by permission of Harper & Row, Publishers, Inc.

Page 295 From *Plagues and Peoples* by William McNeill. Reprinted by permission of Doubleday & Company, Inc.; reprinted by permission of the author (Alsop).

Page 297 Copyright 1946 by Sonia Brownell Orwell; renewed 1974 by Sonia Orwell. Reprinted from "Politics and the English Language" in *Shooting an Elephant and Other Essays* by George Orwell, by permission of Harcourt Brace Jovanovich, Inc., and Martin Secker and Warburg, Ltd.

Page 298 From *The American Experience*, by Henry B. Parkes. Copyright 1947, © 1955, 1959 by Henry Bamford Parkes. Reprinted by permission of Alfred A. Knopf, Inc.

Page 300 From *The Age of Uncertainty* by John Kenneth Galbraith. Copyright © 1977 by John Kenneth Galbraith. Reprinted by permission of Houghton Mifflin Company.

Page 304 From *The Sea Around Us*, revised edition by Rachel L. Carson. Copyright © 1950, 1951, 1961 by Rachel L. Carson; renewed 1979 by Roger Christie. Reprinted by permission of Oxford University Press, Inc.

Page 307   Excerpt from *People of the Lake* by Richard Leakey and Roger Lewin. Copyright © 1978 by Richard Leakey and Roger Lewin. Reprinted by permission of Doubleday & Company, Inc.

Pages 310, 402, and 668   From *Criminal Violence, Criminal Justice*, by Charles E. Silberman. Copyright © 1978 by Charles E. Silberman. Reprinted by permission of Random House, Inc.

Page 310   © 1966 The Atlantic Monthly Co. Reprinted with permission.

Page 311   Reprinted with permission of The Free Press, a division of Macmillan, Inc., from *The Facts About "Drug Abuse"* by The Drug Abuse Council. Copyright © 1980 by The Free Press, p. 84.

Page 313   © 1962 by *Saturday Review* magazine. Reprinted by permission.

Pages 315 and 464   From *At Large* by Ellen Goodman. Copyright © 1981 by The Washington Post Company. Reprinted by permission of Summit Books, a division of Simon & Schuster, Inc.

Page 317   From *A Choice of Catastrophes* by Isaac Asimov. Copyright © 1979 by Isaac Asimov. Reprinted by permission of Simon & Schuster, Inc.

Page 330   With permission from *Natural History*, Vol. 88, No. 3; Copyright the American Museum of Natural History, 1979.

Page 336   Reprinted by permission of *The New Republic*, © 1979, The New Republic, Inc.

Page 340   From *The Los Angeles Times*, April 29, 1980. Copyright, 1980, Los Angeles Times. Reprinted by permission.

Page 342   Reprinted by permission.

Page 347   From *National Geographic*, July 1976, p. 74. Reprinted by permission of the publisher.

Page 350   © 1978, Washington Post Writers Group, reprinted with permission.

Pages 373 and 391   Excerpted by permission of *The New Republic*, © 1980, The New Republic, Inc.

Page 374   © 1975 *Saturday Review* magazine. Reprinted by permission.

Page 374   From *Machiavelli: The Prince and Other Works*, translated and edited by Allan H. Gilbert. Reprinted by permission of Hendricks House, Inc.

Page 384   Reprinted by permission of the publisher and author.

Page 388   From *The Adventures of Sherlock Holmes* by Sir Arthur Conan Doyle. Reprinted by permission of André Milos.

Page 392   © 1980 *Saturday Review* magazine. Reprinted by permission.

Pages 396 and 510   Reprinted by permission of Current History, Inc.

Page 396   "Growing Old," by Robert Epstein in *Harvard Magazine*, July–August 1981, copyright © 1981 Harvard Magazine. Reprinted with permission.

Page 401   With permission from *Natural History*, Vol. 81, No. 2; Copyright the American Museum of Natural History, 1972.

Page 407   Used by permission of the producer.

Page 412   Reprinted by permission of the publisher.

Page 420   Copyright 1986, by Newsweek, Inc. All Rights Reserved. Reprinted by permission.

Page 422   Excerpt from pp. 4–9, "Ptolemy said—and the Church accepted . . . points of view, then, there would seem . . ." in *Many Mansions* by Gina Cerminara. Copyright © 1950 by Gina Cerminara. By permission of William Morrow & Company.

Page 425   Reprinted from *The Saturday Evening Post*, © 1964 The Curtis Publishing Co.

Page 432   From "On Natural Death" from *The Medusa and the Snail* by Lewis Thomas. Copyright © 1979 by Lewis Thomas. Reprinted by permission of Viking Penguin, Inc.

Pages 439 and 663   From *Starting in the Middle* by Judith Wax. Reprinted by permission of Henry Holt Co.

Pages 440 and 719   Copyright 1950, © 1957 by Loren Eiseley. Reprinted from *The Immense Journey*, by Loren Eiseley, by permission of Random House, Inc.

Page 445 Copyright © 1981 by The New York Times Company. Reprinted by permission.

Page 453 Copyright 1965 by John Ciardi. Reprinted by permission of estate of the poet.

Page 453 From pp. 18–19 of "Clear Days" in *One Man's Meat* by E. B. White. Copyright 1938, 1966 by E. B. White. Reprinted by permission of Harper & Row, Publishers, Inc.

Page 457 Excerpt totalling approximately 350 words from pp. 6–7 of *The Autobiography of Mark Twain* edited by Charles Neider. Copyright © 1959 by the Mark Twain Company. Copyright © 1959 by Charles Neider. Reprinted by permission of Harper & Row, Publishers, Inc.

Page 467 Reprinted by permission of the National Women's Political Caucus, 1275 K Street, NW, Suite 750, Washington, DC 20005.

Page 488 Reprinted by permission of the publisher (The Ann Arbor News).

Pages 491 and 697 From *Merchants of Grain* by Dan Morgan. Copyright © 1979 by Dan Morgan. Reprinted by permission of Viking Penguin, Inc.

Page 495 Copyright © 1977 by The New York Times Company. Reprinted by permission.

Page 496 Copyright © 1978 by *Harper's Magazine*. All rights reserved. Reprinted from the September issue by special permission.

Page 499 Reprinted by permission from Hansard, *The Official Report of Proceedings in Parliament of June 4, 1940*, Vol. 361, pp. 795–796.

Page 500 Reprinted by permission of the publisher (Pickering).

Page 505 Reprinted by permission of the publisher.

Page 507 Reprinted by permission of the publisher.

Page 509 Reprinted from *The American Scholar*, Volume 31, Number 2, Spring 1962. Copyright © 1962 by the United Chapters of Phi Beta Kappa. By permission of the publishers.

Page 533 From *Growing Old in America: The Bland-Lee Lectures Delivered at Clark University*, Expanded Edition by David Hackett Fischer. Copyright © 1977, 1978 by David Hackett Fischer. Reprinted by permission of Oxford University Press, Inc.

Page 544 "Sticking Up for Marsupials" is reprinted from *The Panda's Thumb, More Reflections in Natural History*, by Stephen Jay Gould, by permission of W. W. Norton & Company, Inc. Copyright © 1980 by Stephen Jay Gould.

Page 549 Reprinted by permission of *The New England Journal of Medicine*. Vol. 294, pp. 1189–1190, 1974. Copyright 1974 Massachusetts Medical Society.

Page 552 Reprinted by permission of Farrar, Straus & Giroux Inc.: "Notes from a Free-Speech Junkie" from *The Possible She* by Susan Jacoby. Copyright © 1973, 1974, 1976, 1977, 1978, 1979 by Susan Jacoby.

Page 576 Reprinted by permission of the author.

Page 588 From *All Things to All Men* by Godfrey Hodgson. Copyright © 1980 by Godfrey Hodgson. Reprinted by permission of Simon & Schuster, Inc.

Page 589 From *The Chief Executive* by Louis W. Koenig, copyright © 1964 by Harcourt Brace Jovanovich, Inc. Reprinted by permission of the publisher.

Page 624 Reprinted by permission of The Putnam Publishing Group, Inc. from *Laid Back in Washington* by Art Buchwald. Copyright © 1981 by Art Buchwald.

Page 628 From *Highly Irregular* by Carl Bode. Reprinted by permission of the author.

Page 629 From "On Transcendental Metaworry" from *The Medusa and the Snail* by Lewis Thomas. Copyright © 1979 by Lewis Thomas. Reprinted by permission of Viking Penguin, Inc.

Page 630 Reprinted by permission of The Curtis Publishing Co.

Pages 632 and 713 Excerpted from "Address to the Graduating Class" from the book *Wampeters, Foma & Granfalloons* by Kurt Vonnegut, Jr. Copyright © 1970 by Kurt Vonnegut, Jr. Originally published in *Vogue* under the title "Up Is Better Than Down." Reprinted by permission of Delacorte Press/Seymour Lawrence.

Page 633   From pp. 222–223 of "The Horns of the Altar" in *A Pilgrim at Tinker Creek* by Annie Dillard. Copyright © 1974 by Annie Dillard. Reprinted by permission of Harper & Row, Publishers, Inc.

Pages 693 and 734   Reprinted from *The American Scholar*, Volume 50, Number 1, Winter 1980/81. Copyright © 1980 by the author. By permission of the publisher.

Page 694   Reprinted by permission; © 1958, 1986 The New Yorker Magazine, Inc.

Page 699   From "On Magic in Medicine" from *The Medusa and the Snail* by Lewis Thomas. Copyright © 1978 by Lewis Thomas. Originally published in *The New England Journal of Medicine*. Reprinted by permission of Viking Penguin, Inc.

Pages 700, 728 and 737   From *The Squeeze* by James Dale Davidson. Copyright © 1980 by James Dale Davidson. Reprinted by permission of Summit Books, a division of Simon & Schuster, Inc.

Page 702   From "The Medusa and the Snail" from *The Medusa and the Snail* by Lewis Thomas. Copyright © 1977 by Lewis Thomas. Originally published in *The New England Journal of Medicine*. Reprinted by permission of Viking Penguin, Inc.

Page 705   Reprinted by permission of the author.

Pages 712 and 739   Reprinted by permission of Farrar, Straus & Giroux Inc.: Excerpts from "Pornoviolence" from *Mauve Gloves & Madmen, Clutter & Vine* by Tom Wolfe. Copyright © 1967, 1976 by Tom Wolfe.

Page 713   Reprinted by permission; © 1978 The New Yorker Magazine, Inc.

Page 714   From *Reforming Education* by Mortimer Jerome Adler. Reprinted by permission of Westview Press, Inc.

Page 715   From *The Omnivorous Ape* by Lyall Watson, published by Coward, McCann & Geoghegan, Inc. and Souvenir Press. Copyright © by Lyall Watson. Reprinted by permission.

Page 726   Reprinted by permission of the publisher (The Times-Picayune); reprinted by permission of the publisher (The State); reprinted with permission of *The Idaho Statesman*; reprinted by permission of The Providence Journal Company; reprinted by permission of the publisher (St. Petersburg).

Page 727   Reprinted with permission from the August 1970 issue of *McCall's*.

Page 728   Reprinted by permission of the publisher and author.

Page 729   © 1979 *Saturday Review* magazine. Reprinted by permission; copyright © 1980 by The New York Times Company. Reprinted by permission (Hechinger).

Page 730   Reprinted by permission of the publisher (San Jose); reprinted by permission of the publisher and author (Vandiver).

Page 731   © 1979 *Saturday Review* magazine. Reprinted by permission.

Page 733   Reprinted with permission from the September issue of *Texas Monthly*. Copyright 1979 by *Texas Monthly*.

Page 735   Reprinted by permission of the publisher.

Page 739   Reprinted by permission of the publisher.

Page 740   Reprinted by permission of the publisher.

Page 741   © 1958 *Saturday Review* magazine. Reprinted by permission.

Page 741   Copyright 1978, Newsday, Inc. Reprinted by permission.

Index